Qualifikationsphase
Sekundarstufe II
Ausgabe N

Pathway
Advanced

Lese- und Arbeitsbuch
für die gymnasiale Oberstufe

Herausgegeben und erarbeitet von:
Iris Edelbrock

Sprachliche Betreuung:
Elin Arbin

Schöningh
westermann

Begleitmaterialien zum Lehrwerk für Schülerinnen und Schüler

Pathway Advanced Audio-CDs
3 CDs mit Hörtexten und Songs, Transkripte im Booklet
Best.-Nr. 062651-4

Pathway Advanced Abi *kompakt*
Thematic Vocabulary – Important Facts – Relevant Skills
Best.-Nr. 040237-8

Das vollständige Programm finden Sie unter www.westermann.de.

westermann GRUPPE

© 2019 Bildungshaus Schulbuchverlage
Westermann Schroedel Diesterweg Schöningh Winklers GmbH, Braunschweig
www.westermann.de

Druck A[1]/ Jahr 2019
Alle Drucke der Serie A sind im Unterricht parallel verwendbar.

Umschlaggestaltung: Nora Krull, Bielefeld; Fotos: © John R. Rogers Photography (vorn);
Susanne Baumann (hinten)

Druck und Bindung: Westermann Druck GmbH, Braunschweig

ISBN 978-3-14-**040235**-4

Contents

M Mediation between German and English

☒ Comprehension tasks available (copies)

🎧 Listening comprehension

🎧 Listening comprehension (text supported)

Level of difficulty:

●○○ basic
●●○ intermediate
●●● advanced

The Individual and Society

Tradition and Change: The U.K. in the 21st Century

Postcolonial and Neo-Colonial Experiences: India and Britain

The American Dream – Dreams, Struggles and Nightmares

Science (Fiction) & Technology – Towards a Better World?!

Modern Media – Social, Smart and Spying?!

Shakespeare: Such Stuff As Dreams Are Made On …

How to Work with the Book

Symbols & Skills

🎧 Listening to a text/song/speech, etc.; listening comprehension tasks
The material can be found on the *Pathway Advanced* Audio CDs.
→ listening skills, intercultural competences

👥 Group work, work in a team, work with a partner
→ communication skills

💬 Communication training, e. g. discussion, debate, role play, hot seat, etc.
→ communication skills

M Mediation between English and German
→ mediation skills

✏ Creative writing task
→ writing skills

📝 Presentation of projects, results of group work or research
→ speaking skills

🎓 Tasks for advanced students

@ Internet research
→ intercultural competences

Webcode SNG-40235-001 @ Webcodes refer to additional material on the Internet. In order to use the webcodes, visit the following website: www.westermann.de/webcode
Enter the code to access the respective material.

drama* This * sign indicates that the word/term can be found in the Literary Terms section (pp. 433 ff.).

Task Markers

START-UP ACTIVITIES ⟫⟫⟫ Reactivating knowledge, preparing the new topic, introducing the new unit

AWARENESS ⟫⟫⟫ Introducing a new text, giving an impetus

COMPREHENSION ⟫⟫⟫ Tasks for the understanding, comprehension and reproduction of texts

ANALYSIS ⟫⟫⟫ Tasks for the analysis, examination and interpretation of texts

ACTIVITIES ⟫⟫⟫ Tasks for further discussion, creative writing, presentation, etc.

GRAMMAR/LANGUAGE ⟫⟫⟫ Reactivating grammar and language skills, grammar exercises in context. All solutions for grammar/language tasks can be found on the webcode SNG-40235-043 under www.westermann.de/webcode.

Abbreviations

		e. g.	for example	joc.	jocular (meant as a joke)
		esp.	especially	lit.	literary English
abbr.	abbreviation	euph.	euphemistic *(beschönigend)*	poet.	poetic
arch.	archaic (not used anymore)	fig.	figurative meaning *(metaphorisch)*	phr. v.	phrasal verb (multi-word verb)
BE	British English	fml.	formal English	sb.	somebody
cf.	compare (confer)	here:	special meaning in this context	sl.	slang
coll.	colloquial	idm.	idiomatic expression	sth.	something
derog.	derogative (offensive)	infml.	informal English	US	American English

Standardized Terminology for Tasks

In order to enable you to better understand and deal with the tasks in this coursebook, the following list gives you a survey of the key words and standardized formulations for tasks (*Operatoren*) used in the German *Zentralabitur*. Each key word is connected with a definition that not only explains the term itself but also shows you what you are expected to do in order to fulfil this task.

Kompetenzbereich: Schreiben

Key word/terminology	Example	Definition	What you are expected to do
Level I: Orientation/comprehension/understanding/reproduction of texts			
define *bestimmen/umreißen/ definieren*	Define the meaning of the term multi-cultural.	give a clear, precise meaning/explanation of a term/idea	● before writing, highlight/underline specific details in the text ● you should refer to details but do not write wordy explanations – be as precise and specific as possible ● make references to lines in the text but do not quote – paraphrase instead
describe *beschreiben*	Describe the woman's appearance.	give/present an accurate/a detailed account of sth./sb.	
state *angeben/sagen/ Gründe angeben*	State briefly the main development of the ecology movement.	specify clearly	
outline *darstellen*	Outline the author's stance on immigration.	work out the main features, structure or general principles of a topic – but omit minor details	● focus on the structure of the text, e. g. how the author develops his/her line of argument or how a story develops, etc. ● divide the text into paragraphs ● make references to lines/arguments etc. in the text but do not quote – paraphrase instead
present *darstellen*	Present the situation of Asians in London.	(re-)structure and write down	
point out *beschreiben/erläutern*	Point out the author's main ideas on …	find and explain certain aspects	● focus on the most relevant aspects/ideas/arguments of the text and avoid details ● make references to lines/aspects in the text but do not quote – paraphrase instead

sum up, summarize, write a summary
zusammenfassen
	Summarize the information given in the text about the American Dream.	give a concise account of the main points (→ no details, no direct speech)	● before writing a summary, underline the most relevant aspects in the text – avoid details
			● use your own words to paraphrase main aspects:
			  – do not quote from the text/do not use direct speech (!)
			  – do not refer to certain lines etc. in the text
			● be factual and precise
			→ FoS, Writing a Summary, p. 429

Key word/terminology	Example	Definition	What you are expected to do
Level II: Analysis and re-structuring of texts			
analyse/examine *analysieren/untersuchen*	Analyse the opposing views on immigration presented in the text. Examine the author's use of language.	describe and explain in detail certain aspects and/or features of a text	• focus on the structure of the text and pay attention to details • formulate a connecting sentence (contents → analysis) at the beginning • be as precise as possible by using the correct terms and expressions • use quotations/direct references to lines in the text to prove the accuracy of your analysis → FoS, Analysis of a (Non-)Fictional Text, pp. 402, 405 → FoL, Vocabulary and Phrases for Text Analysis, p. 440 → FoL, Connectives and Adverbs, p. 432
characterize/write a characterization *charakterisieren/im Detail beschreiben und erklären*	Characterize/Write a characterization of the main character in the play.	analyse the typical features of sb., then describe, explain and interpret the way in which the character(s) is/are presented	• highlight/underline important details about the character and take notes in the margin, using different colours for specific devices • pay attention to details: do not cover everything but focus on the most striking devices/details • use quotations/direct references to lines in the text to prove the accuracy of your analysis → FoS, Characterization of a Figure in Literature, p. 411
contrast *gegenüberstellen*	Contrast the main characters' opposing views on the USA.	emphasize the difference between two or more things	• before writing your text, make a table in two columns and juxtapose views/arguments/evidence that refers to the argument <u>and</u> the counterargument of the matter • refer directly to certain lines/arguments etc. and use quotations and/or refer to lines in the text • collect ideas/arguments and structure them before writing your text
explain *erklären*	Explain the protagonist's obsession with money.	describe and define in detail	• highlight/underline important details in the text and take notes in the margin, using different colours for specific devices • pay attention to details: do not cover everything but focus on the most striking devices/details • refer directly to certain lines/arguments etc. and use quotations and/or refer to lines in the text • be as precise as possible by using the correct terms and expressions → FoS, Analysis of a (Non-)Fictional Text, pp. 402, 405
illustrate *veranschaulichen*	Illustrate the author's use of metaphorical language.	use examples to explain or make clear	• pay attention to details: do not cover everything but focus on the most striking devices/details • choose the most relevant/significant examples from the text for your explanation • use quotations/direct references to lines in the text to prove the accuracy of your analysis
interpret *interpretieren*	Interpret the message the author wishes to convey.	make clear the meaning of sth.	• try to read "between the lines" and use your background knowledge • do not give wordy explanations and opinions but be as specific and precise as possible • refer directly to certain lines/arguments etc. and use quotations and/or refer to lines in the text

Key word/terminology	Example	Definition	What you are expected to do
compare *vergleichen*	Compare the view of the two writers on recycling. Compare the behaviour of the women.	point out similarities and/or differences of things/characters/situations	• before writing your comparison, underline the most relevant differences/similarities in the text using different colours • make a table in two columns and compare/juxtapose the different aspects and details • refer directly to certain lines/arguments etc. and use quotations and/or refer to lines in the text

Level III: Discussion/evaluation/text production

Key word/terminology	Example	Definition	What you are expected to do
comment (on) *Stellung nehmen*	Comment on the statement that the American Dream is over.	state clearly your opinions/views on a topic and support your views with evidence/arguments/reference to the text(s)	• before writing your text, make a table in two columns and juxtapose views/arguments/evidence that refer to the argument <u>and</u> the counterargument of the matter • give your opinion on the topic/matter but do not be personal – your judgment should be based on evidence and facts
evaluate *einschätzen/einordnen/bewerten*	Evaluate the author's view on the impact of global migration.	form an opinion after carefully considering a topic/question and presenting advantages and disadvantages	• connect aspects/arguments given in the text with your background knowledge and further references • be careful not to just reproduce something that you have learned by heart but paraphrase and refer to the most specific/exemplary aspects • finish your text with a concluding sentence → FoS, Basic Types of Non-Fictional Texts, p. 396 → FoL, Conversation and Discussion, p. 413
assess *beurteilen*	Assess the importance of standards in education.	make a judgement after thinking carefully about the points for and against sth.	
discuss* *erörtern*	Discuss the consequences of consumerism as referred to in the text.	investigate or examine by argument; give reasons/examples for and against	• weigh different aspects/arguments and counter-arguments of a matter • try to take different positions/views on an issue • collect ideas/arguments first and structure them before writing your text • finish your text with a conclusion that summarizes most important aspects • do not express your own opinion but refer to aspects dealt with in the text at hand → FoL, Conversation and Discussion, p. 413
justify *rechtfertigen/begründen*	You are a CEO of a company. Justify your decision to give a micro credit loan to a village in Nigeria.	show adequate grounds for decisions and conclusions	• before writing your text, collect reasons and examples that support your decision • consider the importance/weight of your arguments/reasons and structure them • finish your text with a concluding and summarizing sentence and/or statement → FoL, Conversation and Discussion, p. 413
prove *am Text belegen*	Prove the effects of Western values on developing countries.	give evidence to provide a clear and convincing argumentation	• before writing your text, collect ideas about the respective matter and structure them • give examples and refer to background information but focus on relevant aspects/arguments • do not give wordy explanations and opinions but be as specific and precise as possible • refer directly to certain lines/arguments etc. and use quotations and/or refer to lines in the text → FoS, Basic Types of Non-Fictional Texts, p. 396

Key word/terminology	Example	Definition	What you are expected to do
reflect on *reflektieren/bedenken*	Reflect on how the author deals with the problem of exploiting workers in sweat-shops.	express your thoughts in a carefully considered and balanced way	• before writing, underline/highlight keywords and relevant aspects in the text that you want to • collect ideas on how you want to respond to the matter • weigh up different aspects/arguments by juxtaposing them in a table • you may state your opinion on the issue but avoid being personal – be factual and precise • finish your text with a concluding and summarizing sentence and/or statement → FoL, Conversation and Discussion, p. 413
write (+ text type) *schreiben, verfassen, formulieren*	Write an ending of the story. Write an interior monologue that reflects the character's view of the situation and his/her feelings. Write a letter to the editor in which you discuss the assumption that the American Dream is dead.	produce a text with specific features	• be aware of the specific features of the literary genre and/or type of text you are working with • employ the formal characteristics of the respective text type or genre • put your analysis results and findings in a wider context that also includes aspects you have dealt with in class • make sure that your text is related to the input text and is based on your analysis results → FoS, Continuation of a Fictional Text, p. 420 → FoS, Writing a Comment and a Review, p. 421 → FoS, Writing an Interview, p. 426 → FoS, Writing a Newspaper Article, p. 427 → FoS, Writing a Letter to the Editor, p. 431

* The task "Discuss (in class)" focuses on an oral activity together with a group rather than a written evaluation of a topic.

Kompetenzbereich: Sprachmittlung

Key word/terminology	Example	Definition	What you are expected to do
explain *erklären/* *verdeutlichen*	Explain the principle of waste separation in Germany.	give a clear, precise definition/explanation of a term/idea	• mediating (parts of) a text into another language in general requires you to consider the addressee(s), the meaning of the input text, as well as cultural and situational aspects • before writing, highlight/underline specific details in the text • you should refer to details but do not write wordy explanations – be as specific as possible • make references to lines in the text but do not quote – paraphrase instead → FoS, Mediation, p. 412
outline *darstellen* present *darstellen*	For an international school project in the EU, present the relevant information on the image of migrants in the German media in a formal email.	give a concise account of the main points or ideas of a text (clarifying culture-related aspects if necessary)	• focus on the structure of the text, e.g. how the author develops his/her line of argument, how a story develops, etc. • divide the text into paragraphs • reference lines/arguments etc. in the text but do not quote – paraphrase instead → FoS, Mediation, p. 412

summarize, sum up
zusammenfassen
			• before writing a summary, underline the most relevant aspects in the text – leave out details
			• use your own words to paraphrase main aspects:
			  – do note quote from the text/do not use direct speech (!)
			  – do not refer to certain lines, etc. in the text
			• be factual and precise
			→ FoS, Writing a Summary, p. 429
			→ FoS, Mediation, p. 412

write (+ text type) *schreiben, verfassen,* *formulieren*	Using the information in the input article, write an article in English for your project website in which you inform your Polish partners how to get a sports scholarship at a German university.	produce a text with specific features	• be aware of the specific features of the literary genre and/or type of text you are working with • employ the formal characteristics of the text type or genre → FoS, Mediation, p. 412

Kompetenzbereich: Sprechen/an Gesprächen teilnehmen

Key word/terminology	Example	Definition	What you are expected to do
(try to) agree on, (try to) come to an agreement *sich einigen auf, eine Einigung/ einen Kompromiss finden*	Discuss which methods are best to prevent … Try to agree on two aspects …	to come to one opinion or one understanding; try to reach a compromise	**Oral examinations/presentations:** ● read the tasks carefully ● underline/highlight relevant keywords and take notes on the most important aspects ● do not write down completely formulated answers and sentences – jot down the most relevant phrases and terms
comment (on) *Stellung nehmen*	Talk about photos in public media and their message. Comment on whether such photos are an effective way to make people aware of certain problems.	give one's opinion and support one's view with evidence or reasons	● do not simply read out your notes/answers – paraphrase and explain them; speak as freely as possible ● make eye contact with your examiner
compare *vergleichen*	Compare the … pictures and talk about the lives of the people you see.	show similarities and differences	**Discussions:** ● interact with your partner(s) and respond to his/her/their remarks
discuss *diskutieren, erörtern*	Discuss the advantages and risks of … Decide which aspects are most … Agree on two things that you think should be organized ….	give arguments or reasons for or against and (try to) come to a conclusion	● do not simply read out your notes on the topic – formulate your ideas as precisely and possible and avoid wordy explanations and empty phrases ● listen carefully to the questions and remarks of your partner(s)
explain *erklären*	Explain the message of the cartoon/quote/ statement … and the means used to convey it.	make sth. clear	● make sure you understand what is being discussed – if you do not understand, ask your partner(s) to reformulate or repeat remarks or questions
give reasons/ justify *begründen*	Which photo/picture would you choose to make people aware of certain problems? Justify your choice.	present reasons for decisions, positions or conclusions	→ FoL, Conversation and Discussion, p. 413 → FoS, Oral Examinations, p. 416 → FoS, Giving a Speech, p. 418 → FoS, Presentations, p. 419
talk about (the …) *sich äußern zu etw.*	Talk about the photos. What do the photos suggest about …?	produce a text referring to certain aspects	

Kompetenzbereich: Hör-/Hörsehverstehen

Key word/terminology	Example	What you are expected to do
answer *beantworten*	Answer the question in about 5 …/10 …/100 words.	• usually this kind of task requires you to fill in a prepared sheet of paper with different types of standardized tasks, e.g. multiple choice, matching, true-false, sentence completion, note-taking, etc. • before the first listening, read the tasks and explanations carefully • make sure you understand exactly what to do (e.g. tick <u>one</u> or more possible answers; tick only the answer that does not fit; use the exact number of words for your answer, etc.) • if you are not sure about the correct answer, take notes on a piece of scratch paper and fill in or tick the answers after the second listening • while listening or viewing the first time, jot down notes and keywords and try to get a general understanding of the recording or scene • in a second listening, pay attention to details and complete your notes
complete *vervollständigen,* *komplettieren*	Complete the sentences below using 1 to 5 words. Complete the notes on the points listed below. Complete the table below.	
fill in *ausfüllen, ergänzen*	Fill in the missing information using 1 to 5 words.	
list/name *benennen, auflisten*	List/Name the most relevant aspects mentioned in the discussion.	
match *verknüpfen,* *etw. zuweisen,* *kombinieren*	Match each speaker with one of the statements.	
state *darstellen*	State the ideas supported by …	
tick *ankreuzen*	Tick the correct answer.	

The Individual and Society

Photo taken by Barry Boubacar in the New York City subway

Tips on vocab

to wear a (black) niqab [ˈnɪkæb] ▪ a thin slit for the eyes ▪ to be transgender ▪ dolled up (*aufgedonnert*) ▪ heavy make-up ▪ an orange wig; big/wavy hair ▪ silver earrings ▪ a shiny turquoise dress ▪ to be focused on/absorbed by sth.

Graffiti installation by British Artist Banksy and Brazilian street art and graffiti superstar Os Gêmeos, New York City, 2013

In a society that tries to standardize thinking, individuality is not highly prized.   *Alex Grey*

Do not ghettoize society by putting people into legal categories of gender, race, ethnicity, language, or other such characteristics.   *Preston Manning*

It is the individual who is timeless. Societies, cultures, and civilization – past and present – are often incomprehensible to outsiders, but the individual's hungers, dreams, and preoccupations have remained unchanged through the millennia.   *Eric Hoffer*

START-UP ACTIVITIES

1. Team up with a partner, with each partner picking one of the two photos – the snapshot taken on a commuter train or the installation (a work of art) by the artists Banksy and Os Gêmeos. Take a moment to get an understanding of the details and the possible message of your chosen picture.
   Then, describe the photos to each other and explain and discuss their messages.

2. Relate your findings to the title of this unit. What do the photos say about living in society?

3. Which of these phrases do you think is most fitting?
   - the individual *in* society
   - the individual *and* society
   - the individual *vs.* society

4. In class, read the statements above and choose the one that best matches the message of each photo. Explain and discuss your choices in class.

Identity: Individualism and Conformity

Samantha Raphelson

Getting Some 'Me' Time: Why Millennials Are So Individualistic

AWARENESS

First, look at the photo below. What image of the "young generation" does it convey?
Then, do research on these terms:
- Baby Boomers
- Generation X
- Millennials

What are the characteristics of each of these generations?

They are a class of self-centered, self-absorbed, selfie-snapping 20-somethings. This is how many critics have come to define the millennial generation.

But hold on, isn't this what was said about every gen-
5 eration when it was young? Minus the selfies of course. Some scholars argue that millennials aren't entitled[1] – they just have more time to be themselves.

Markers of Adulthood

The rise of individualism has been going on for centu-
10 ries, says Jean Twenge, a psychology professor at San Diego State University and author of *Generation Me: Why Today's Young Americans Are More Confident[2], Assertive[3], Entitled – and More Miserable Than Ever Before.* How we define adulthood has also changed, says Jef-
15 frey Jensen Arnett, a research professor at Clark University in Worcester, Mass., and the director of the Clark Poll of Emerging Adults. People used to feel like adults once they got married or had children, but that's not so much the case anymore.
20 The 2014 Clark Established Adult Poll found that the top three markers for adulthood were accepting responsibility for self, financial independence and making independent decisions.

Twenge first encountered this rise in individualism
25 when she was doing a project on gender roles in the 1990s. Both women and men scored[4] high on this masculine scale that includes highly individualistic traits, such as being independent, relying on yourself, being a leader, etc. Twenge began studying other traits such as

Millennials are often painted as the entitled, selfie-snapping generation. But many researchers say that "me" time will help young people make better decisions in the long run.

self-esteem[5] and extroversion[6] and recognized a pat-
30 tern that these traits were all increasing over time.
"You have emerging[7] adulthood – taking more time to find yourself in your 20s," Twenge says. "By definition that is an individualistic pursuit[8]. 'I want to have that time to myself before I settle down.' That is one that is
35 unknown in traditional collectivist[9] societies."

But Arnett wouldn't fully agree with Twenge's definition of emerging adulthood – a term he coined in his 2004 book, *Emerging Adulthood: The Winding Road from Late Teens through the Twenties.*
40

---

[1] **entitled** feeling that you have a right to the good things in life without necessarily having to work for them – [2] **confident** sure that you have the ability to do sth. well or deal with situations successfully – [3] **assertive** behaving in a confident way, so that people notice you – [4] **to score** *punkten* – [5] **self-esteem** the feeling of being satisfied with your own abilities, and that you deserve to be liked or respected – [6] **extroversion** the ability to be active and confident, and to enjoy spending time with other people – [7] **emerging** in an early state of development – [8] **pursuit** *Streben* – [9] **collectivist** societies in which the group is more important than the individual

"It's partly that, but it's more than that," Arnett says. "There's a space that's opened up in the 20s that is the most individualistic time of life. When you think about it, when are you freer from social rules than in your 20s?"

"I describe it as the self-focused time in life," he says. "I don't mean that they're selfish; I mean that they have fewer social rules and obligations[10] – the freedom to be self-directed."

Stable Jobs Aren't Easy to Come By

Emerging adults are ages 18 to the mid- to late 20s, so right now, the second wave of the millennial generation falls into this group.

But of course this phase of life wasn't always there. Fifty years ago, the median[11] age of marriage for women was 20. Today, it's 27, according to the Pew Research Center.

"I think it's hard for young women today to understand the kind of pressure their grandmothers were under to find a husband," Arnett says.

The stigma[12] around being single has evaporated[13], leaving more time for young people to explore and find themselves. Since 1970, there has been a dramatic shift in the average age Americans get married, Arnett says.

Pew's recent report said 25 percent of millennials will never marry.

There are economic pressures, Twenge says: "[It's] the idea of marrying only when you have stable jobs, and stable jobs aren't easy to come by."

The movements that took off in the 1960s and '70s – the sexual revolution and birth control, civil rights, the rise in college attendance[14] – caused this new life period to open up.

Young people still believe in the institution of marriage, Arnett says. They just want to wait longer. Nearly 69 percent of singles in this cohort[15] would like to marry eventually, according to the 2014 Clark Poll.

Less Politics, More Social Change

While increased individualism opened up new opportunities to people, some researchers suggest that democracy won't fare well in the long-run. Specifically, civic[16] engagement and social capital declined equally between the baby boomers and Generation X, and Generation X and the millennials, Twenge says.

"In Europe, their system ... also has very individualistic views which is usually accompanied by more civic involvement," she says. "We have this kind of empty individualism where we have the self-focus but not the engagement that we really need for an individualistic democracy."

Others say that young people recognize that the old institutions aren't working. It's not that they don't want to participate, but they lack trust that individual participation will make a difference.

"The reality is when you look at young people, all the data shows that young people are civic-minded in a very different way," says Erica Williams Simon, a social impact and communications strategist. "They are not as interested in politics, but are interested in social change and finding creative, innovative ways to make a difference that are in a way more effective than the systems of the past."

Neil Howe, who coined the term "millennial" in his 1990 book *Generations*, says unwanted backlash[17] arises when older generations jump to stereotype millennials.

Howe says when baby boomers view younger workers in a negative light it can lead to poorer productivity throughout the organization, and younger workers can have lower levels of engagement.

Arnett says while millennials are often criticized for being so individualistic, he thinks they will be better off in the long run.

"I've argued rather strenuously[18] that it's inaccurate to call them narcissists[19] because they have this temporary period that is self-focused," he says. "People do get used to making their own decisions. It's a challenge then to partner with somebody else and have to compromise about things. I think people will make much better choices[20] if they have their 20s to figure it out."

http://www.npr.org/2014/10/14/352979540/getting-some-me-time-why-millennials-are-so-individualistic, 14 October 2014 [04.07.2017]

---

[10] **obligation** *Verpflichtung* – [11] **median** middle value – [12] **stigma** a strong feeling in society that being in a particular situation is sth. to be ashamed of – [13] **to evaporate** *verdampfen, sich verflüchtigen* – [14] **attendance** *Anwesenheit, Zulauf* – [15] **cohort** a group of people who have the same age, class, etc., esp. when they are being studied – [16] **civic** *bürgerlich, gesellschaftlich* – [17] **backlash** a strong negative reaction by a number of people against recent events, esp. political or social development – [18] **strenuously** with great energy and determination – [19] **narcissist** a person who admires himself or herself too much – [20] **to make a choice** to choose sth., to make a decision

COMPREHENSION

1. In a **first reading**, try to get a general understanding of the text.

2. While reading the text a second time, find quotes from the text that help you to complete the following sentences:
   a) Individualism is not an invention of the millennials but …
   b) The basic markers of adulthood are …
   c) Highly individualistic character traits which are considered masculine include …
   d) Emerging adulthood is defined by …
   e) The most individualistic time of life is …
   f) Being self-focused means …
   g) Young people's attitude toward being single or getting married has changed because …
   h) Increased individualism threatens democracy because …
   i) Young people's view of societal institutions is …
   j) Young people are civic-minded, but …
   k) Baby boomers and millennials have a difficult relationship because …
   l) Being individualistic helps young people to …

ANALYSIS

3. Juxtapose the positive and negative effects the author connects with the increasing individualism of young people.

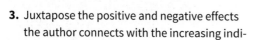

positive effects	negative effects
● being more confident, assertive …	● being self-centered, self-absorbed …
● …	● …

4. Examine the structure of the text and the author's line of argument* and explain how they emphasize her view of millennials.
   → Focus on Skills, Analysis of a Non-Fictional Text, p. 405
   → Focus on Facts, Basic Types of Non-Fictional Texts, p. 396

5. What means does the author employ to underline her credibility?
   Give examples from the text and explain their function.

ACTIVITIES

6. Is the young generation "self-centered" (l. 1) and a bunch of "narcissists" (l. 115) or do they want to find "innovative ways to make a difference" (ll. 100 f.)?
   Write a letter to the editor in which you explain your point of view.
   → Focus on Skills, Writing a Letter to the Editor, p. 431

GRAMMAR / LANGUAGE

7. In her article the author uses many different adjectives to characterize the millennial generation. Have a look at the various expressions below and find out their precise meaning. Use a dictionary for help.

self-centered ■ self-absorbed ■ entitled ■ confident ■ assertive ■ responsible ■ masculine ■ self-focused ■ extroverted ■ selfish ■ narcissistic ■ self-directed ■ opportunistic ■ civic-minded ■ innovative

Erich Fromm

The Illusion of Individuality

AWARENESS

The word "individuality" is derived from the Latin word "individuum" which literally translates as "the indivisible". Team up with a partner and try to find your own definition of the word "individuality" – and what being individual means to you.

1 The particular difficulty in recognizing to what extent our wishes – and our thoughts and feelings as well – are not really our own but put into us from the outside, is closely linked up with the problem of authority and freedom. In the course of modern history the authority of the Church has been replaced by that of the State, that of the State by that of conscience[1], and in our era, the latter has been replaced by the anonymous[2] authority of common sense and public opinion as instruments of conformity[3]. Because we have freed ourselves of the older forms of authority, we do not see that we have become the prey[4] of a new kind of authority. We have become automatons[5] who live under the illusion of being self-willing individuals. This illusion helps the individual to remain unaware of his insecurity, but this is all the help such an illusion can give. Basically the self of the individual is weakened, so that he feels powerless and extremely insecure. He lives in a world to which he has lost genuine[6] relatedness and in which everybody and everything has become instrumentalized, where he has become a part of the machine that his hands have built. He thinks, feels, and wills what he believes he is supposed to think, feel and will; in this very process he loses his self upon which all genuine security of a free individual must be built.

2 The loss of the self has increased the necessity[7] to conform, for it results in a profound[8] doubt of one's own identity. If I am nothing but what I believe I am supposed to be – who am "I"? We have seen how the doubt about one's own self started with the breakdown of the medieval[9] order in which the individual has been a major problem of modern philosophy since Descartes[10]. Today we take for granted that we are. Yet the doubt about ourselves still exists, or has even grown. [...]

The loss of identity [...] makes it still more imperative[11] to conform: it means that one can be sure of oneself if one lives up to the expectations of others. If we do not live up to this picture we not only risk disapproval[12] and increased isolation, but we risk losing the identity of our personality, which means jeopardizing[13] sanity[14].

3 By conforming with the expectations of others, by not being different, these doubts about one's own identity are silenced and a certain security is gained. However, the price is high. Giving up spontaneity and individuality results in a thwarting[15] of life. Psychologically, the automaton, while being alive biologically, is dead emotionally and mentally. While he goes through the motions of living, his life runs through his hands like sand. Behind a front of satisfaction and optimism modern man is deeply unhappy; as a matter of fact, he is on the verge of[16] desperation. He desperately clings to[17] the notion[18] of individuality; he wants to be "different", and he has no greater recommendation of anything than that "it is different". We are informed of the individual name of the railroad clerk we buy our tickets from; handbag, playing cards, and portable radios are "personalized", by having the initials of the owner put on them. All this indicates the hunger for "difference" and yet these are almost the last vestiges[19] of individuality that are left. Modern man is starved for life. But since, being an automaton, he cannot experience life in the sense of spontaneous activity he takes as surrogate[20] any kind of excitement and thrill: the thrill of drinking, of sports, of vicariously[21] living the excitements of fictitious persons on the screen.

---

[1] **conscience** [ˈkɒnʃəns] *Gewissen* – [2] **anonymous** [əˈnɒnɪməs] – [3] **conformity** behaviour or actions that follow the accepted rules of society – [4] **prey** *Beute* – [5] **automaton** [ɔːˈtɒmətən] – [6] **genuine** real – [7] **necessity** [nəˈsesəti] the need for sth.; *Notwendigkeit* – [8] **profound** *tiefgründig* – [9] **medieval** [ˌmediˈiːvəl] related to the Middle Ages – [10] **René Descartes** French philosopher, mathematician and scientist (1596–1650); considered to be the father of modern Western philosophy – [11] **imperative** [ɪmˈperətɪv] extremely important – [12] **disapproval** the feeling of having a negative opinion of sb./sth. – [13] **to jeopardize** [ˈdʒepədaɪz] *gefährden* – [14] **sanity** having a healthy mind – [15] **to thwart** *etw. durchkreuzen, vereiteln* – [16] **to be on the verge of sth.** to be very close to sth. – [17] **to cling to sth.** *sich an etw. festklammern* – [18] **notion** belief, idea – [19] **vestige** [ˈvestɪdʒ] *Überbleibsel* – [20] **surrogate** *Ersatz* – [21] **vicariously** [vɪˈkeəriəsli] *stellvertretend*

4 What then is the meaning of freedom for modern man?

He has become free from the external bonds[22] that would prevent him from doing and thinking as he sees fit[23]. He would be free to act according to his own will, if he knew what he wanted, thought, and felt. But he does not know. He conforms to anonymous authorities and adopts a self which is not his. The more he does this, the more powerless he feels, the more is he forced to conform. In spite of a veneer[24] of optimism and initiative, modern man is overcome by a profound feeling of powerlessness which makes him gaze[25] toward approaching catastrophes[26] as though he were paralyzed[27].

from *Readings for Rhetoric* by Erich Fromm. Wadsworth Publ., Belmont 1969, pp. 162–167

COMPREHENSION

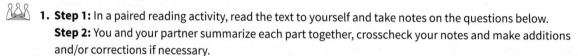

1. **Step 1:** In a paired reading activity, read the text to yourself and take notes on the questions below.
   Step 2: You and your partner summarize each part together, crosscheck your notes and make additions and/or corrections if necessary.

   1
   - Which core problems of being influenced from the outside does Fromm name?
   - Point out which different authorities have been replaced.
   - What are the consequences of man being turned into an "automaton"?
   - What kind of "illusion" does man believe in?

   2
   - Which problems does "the loss of the self" bring about?
   - What does "the loss of identity" mean for man specifically?

   3
   - Point out what has made modern man deeply unhappy.
   - How does modern man try to keep up the impression of being "different"?
   - What does modern man do to "experience life"?

   4
   - Point out what hinders modern man from "doing and thinking" like an individual.
   - What are the consequences of man's "feeling of powerlessness"?

   → Focus on Skills, Understanding Complex Texts, p. 399

2. In Fromm's depiction of man gradually becoming an automaton that lives under the false illusion that he is an "individual", one step seems to lead naturally to the other.
   Together with a partner, draw a concept map which visualizes Fromm's train of thought*.
   Display the concept maps in class and discuss your results.

   Example:

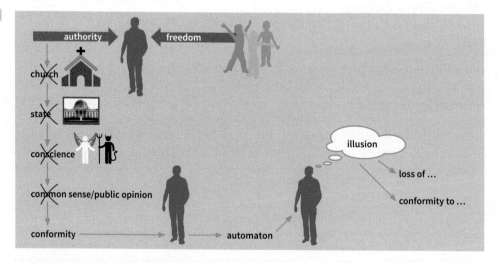

---

[22] **bond** a close connection between people – [23] **to do as one sees fit** *nach Gutdünken handeln* – [24] **veneer** [vəˈnɪər] *dünne Fassade* – [25] **to gaze** *etw. anstarren* – [26] **catastrophe** [kəˈtæstrəfi] – [27] **paralyzed** *gelähmt*

3. Describe the cartoon and relate its message to Fromm's ideas, e.g. concerning the influence of the media or surrogate excitement and entertainment.
   → Focus on Skills, Analysis of Visuals, p. 409

4. Analyse Fromm's depiction of modern man's striving to be an individual on the one hand and having to conform on the other.
   → Analysis of a Non-Fictional Text, p. 405

5. Explain Fromm's concluding statement (ll. 67 – 80) and relate it to the "approaching catastrophes" of our time, e. g. the European migrant crisis, climate change, the war in Syria, etc.

6. In 2011, the International Labour Organization (ILO) commissioned a study on volunteer work in 37 countries. Data revealed that ca. 140 million people in these countries are engaged in volunteer work, or about 12 % of the adult population. This is the equivalent of 20.8 million full-time paid workers – which means that volunteers make a $400 billion contribution to the global economy each year.
   Contrast this data to Erich Fromm's bleak conclusion that man seems to be "paralyzed".

Oliver R. Phillips

Individualist Culture vs. Collectivist Culture ☒

In today's globalised world, it is becoming increasingly important to be "culturally intelligent" and have so-called "intercultural competences".

In class, collect examples of intercultural competences and give reasons why you consider them to be important. Finally, make a ranking and discuss which competences are more or less important for getting along with people privately or professionally.

Webcode
SNG-40235-001 @

1. Use the link provided on the webcode and watch Oliver R. Phillips talk.

   Step 1: In a **first viewing**, try to understand **the gist** of what is said.

   Step 2: Exchange your first viewing impressions with a partner and clarify any questions.

   Step 3: In a **second viewing**, pay attention to details and take notes on the aspects listed below.

1
- the difference between individualist and collectivist approaches in general
- the prevailing attitude as symbolized by the American Dream
- characteristics of and values shared by individualist cultures

Tips on vocab »»»

adjustment when you change the way you behave or think ■ **fraught with peril** (*fml.*) filled with great danger ■ **approach** a way of doing sth. ■ **to take precedence over sth.** to be more important than sth. else ■ **to score** *punkten* ■ **to saturate** to fill a thing or place completely ■ **prevailing** existing/most common ■ **fabric of sth.** (*fml.*) basic foundations of sth. ■ **to nudge sb.** to push sb./sth. gently ■ **commitment** a willingness to give your energy and time to sth. you believe in ■ **to pursue** *etw. verfolgen* ■ **conceivable** possible to imagine or to believe ■ **avenue** (*fig.*) a method or way of doing sth. ■ **to infringe** to limit sb. else's rights ■ **affiliation** a connection with a political party, religion or organization ■ **accomplishment** *Leistung* ■ **self-actualization** *Selbstverwirklichung*

2
- characteristics of collectivist cultures
- personal and social values
- the position of the individual

Tips on vocab »»»

communal belonging to or used by a group of people ■ **to take primacy over sth.** to be more important than sth. else ■ **intrinsic** part of the real nature of sth./sb. ■ **mastery** complete control of sth. ■ **to maintain face** *das Gesicht wahren*

3
- McDonald's in India
- problems in motivating employees

Tips on vocab »»»

polarity poles on opposite ends of a spectrum ■ **franchise** a right to sell a company's products in a particular area using the company's name

4
- questions arising from the different systems
- suggestions on how to achieve mutual understanding

Tips on vocab »»»

to excel to be extremely good at sth. ■ **to ponder** (*fml.*) to think carefully about sth. ■ **to minister** to work in a leadership position in the church

ANALYSIS »»»»»»»»

2. Watch the lecture a third time and complete the grid below, juxtaposing the differences between individualist and collectivist cultures/societies.

individualist		collectivist	
• the individual is the focus • United States, Australia, etc. • …		• the group takes precedence • Singapore, China, India, etc. • …	

 3. Examine Phillips' explanations in the context of the American Dream and relate it to the Focus on pages *American Beliefs and Values* (FoF, p. 176) and *The American Dream* (FoD, p. 192).

4. Phillips chooses the example of the McDonald's franchise in India to illustrate various cultural clashes. View part 4 of Phillips' lecture again and relate his "thoughts to ponder" and tips on how to tackle inter-cultural problems to the magazine article *Manufacturing in India: The Masala Mittelstand* (pp. 126 ff.) in your Students' Book.
What similarities and differences can you detect?
→ Focus on Skills, Analysis of a Non-Fictional Text, p. 405

ACTIVITIES

5. You are the Indian manager of a McDonald's franchise in Mumbai, India and you think that your team is doing very well. However, the McDonald's company has criticized you and your team because they expect you to increase your sales figures and want you to run the restaurant more efficiently, e. g. by having competitions like "employee of the month".

In a group, prepare and act out role plays which present the different views and try to find solutions to the problems mentioned.
→ Focus on Language, Conversation and Discussion, p. 413

6. You are the Indian manager of a McDonald's franchise in Mumbai. Together with your team, you give an interview to the local newspaper to promote your restaurant and to underline the quality of your work and your achievements so far.
Prepare role cards and act out this interview in a role play.
→ Focus on Skills, Writing an Interview, p. 426

Martin Schwickert
Der bunte Widerstand einer Familie

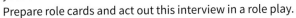
AWARENESS

Henry David Thoreau (1817 – 1862) was an American essayist, poet, philosopher, abolitionist, naturalist and historian. He was deeply interested in nature and discovering life's essential needs. From 1845 – 1847 Thoreau lived alone in a small wooden cabin on Walden Pond in the state of Massachusetts. During this time, Thoreau wrote two of his most famous and influential works: his book *Walden* (reflections on simple living) and his essay *Civil Disobedience* (an argument for not following the laws of an unjust state). In the 20th century, Thoreau became a role model to hippies and environmentalists, and also deeply influenced civil rights activists like Gandhi and Martin Luther King Jr.

Form groups of four students each and discuss Thoreau's thoughts:

(1) I learned this, at least, by my experiment: that if one advances confidently in the direction of his dreams, and endeavors[1] to live the life which he has imagined, he will meet with a success unexpected in common hours.

(2) I went to the woods because I wished to live deliberately[2], to front only the essential facts of life, and see
5 if I could not learn what it had to teach, and not, when I came to die, discover that I had not lived. I did not

---
[1] **to endeavor** [ɪnˈdevər] to try to do sth. – [2] **deliberately** intentionally; *mit Vorbedacht*

wish to live what was not life, living is so dear; nor did I wish to practise resignation, unless it was quite necessary. I wanted to live deep and suck out all the marrow[3] of life, to live so sturdily[4] and Spartan-like[5] as to put to rout[6] all that was not life, to cut a broad swath and shave close[7], to drive life into a corner, and reduce it to its lowest terms …

10 **(3)** The mass of men lead lives of quiet desperation. What is called resignation is confirmed[8] desperation. From the desperate city you go into the desperate country, and have to console[9] yourself with the bravery of minks[10] and muskrats[11]. A stereotyped but unconscious despair is concealed even under what are called the games and amusements of mankind. There is no play in them, for this comes after work. But it is a characteristic of wisdom not to do desperate things …

15 **(4)** You must live in the present, launch yourself[12] on every wave, find your eternity in each moment. Fools stand on their island of opportunities and look toward another land. There is no other land; there is no other life but this.

(5) All good things are wild and free.

Walden and Other Writings by Henry David Thoreau. Barnes & Noble Classics, New York 1993, pp. 267, 75, 7, 120, 272

Step 1: First, read the quotations to yourself and make sure you understand everything.

Step 2: Take notes on the questions below individually first, then discuss your findings with your group.

Tip: Make sure to use your own words for your notes. Use a dictionary if necessary.

- What observations does Thoreau make concerning people's lives?
- What was his motivation for living "in the woods" for some time?
- Which lessons did "life in the woods" teach Thoreau?
- What are Thoreau's recommendations to people for living a fulfilled life?
- What precisely does Thoreau want to express with statement no. 5?

COMPREHENSION

1. Before reading:

Captain Fantastic, a 2016 American comedy-drama film, deals with the Cash family who live isolated in the wilderness of Washington (state) for a decade but are forced to reintegrate into society after their mother Leslie commits suicide.

Both Ben and his wife are disillusioned with capitalism and the American way of life and therefore choose to teach their children survival skills, left-wing politics and philosophy. They teach them to think critically, be self-reliant and athletic as well as experience the beauty of coexisting with nature without technology. The film still below depicts the scene where Ben and his children – after leaving the wilderness – attend their mother's funeral, organized by Leslie's parents.

Work together in groups of four and take a close look at the film still below.
a) Describe the members of the Cash family in detail, paying attention to their outward appearance but also their body language and facial expressions.
b) Based on the film still, do you think the members of the Cash family are "free-thinking" and extraordinary individuals – or are they freaks and pitiful outsiders? Give reasons for your opinion.

---

[3] **marrow** *das Mark* – [4] **sturdily** physically strong and solid or thick – [5] **Spartan-like** simple and severe with no comfort – [6] **to put to rout** [raʊt] to defeat sb./sth. – [7] **to cut a broad swath and shave close** here: to live in an essential and very basic way – [8] **confirmed** here: *chronisch* – [9] **to console** *trösten* – [10] **mink** *der Nerz (das Tier)* – [11] **muskrats** *Bisamratte* – [12] **to launch yourself** to jump forwards with a lot of force

Ben and his six children in church, attending Leslie's funeral

Tips on vocab ⟫

to look defiant (*trotzig*) ■ to have one's arms hanging down ■ to look directly into the viewer's eyes ■ blue overalls ■ gas mask ■ a tomato red jacket ■ to wear a boutonnière on the lapel ■ a red and white patterned shirt ■ a purple jumper ■ striped shorts ■ hair ribbon ■ black pants ■ dark purple jacket ■ light green long-sleeved dress with a striped edging (*Bordüre*) ■ a multi-coloured vest ■ a whale costume with a hood

Webcode
SNG-40235-002

2. Watch the film trailer provided on the webcode and get futher background information about the social and cultural clashes the family has to deal with.

M **3.** Your American pen pal is thinking about seeing the film. He thinks the plot looks interesting, but he has heard mixed reviews. Therefore he asks you how the film was received in Germany.

Mediate the German review into English. Leave out less relevant details and write an e-mail to your friend that includes the following aspects:
- the Cash family's background
- the parents' educational goals for their children
- Ben's relationship with his children
- the author's evaluation of the film's plot and message
→ Focus on Skills, Mediation, p. 412

Tip: Keep in mind that your friend wants to know about Germans' reactions to the film – therefore do not forget to include the author's comments.

ANALYSIS ⟫⟫⟫⟫⟫

4. Compare what you have learned about the film *Captain Fantastic* to Thoreau's ideas introduced in the Awareness task (p. 27). Which similarities and differences can you detect in these philosophies of life?

5. Both the 2016 film *Captain Fantastic* and Thoreau's ideas and writings can be considered hymns of praise to individualism. In contrast, in his lecture, Erich Fromm states that individuality is an illusion (pp. 23 f.). Compare these two different views.

ACTIVITIES

6. Despite being a highly acclaimed writer, Thoreau's ideas were criticized as well.

Scottish author Robert Louis Stevenson (1850 – 1894; *Treasure Island*) said that Thoreau's *Walden* experiment was a "mark of unmanly effeminacy" (*Weiberkram*) and "womanish solitude" and considered Thoreau to be a "self-indulgent skulker" (*maßloser Schleicher*). American Quaker poet John Greenleaf Whittier (1807 – 1892) claimed that Thoreau wanted "man to lower himself to the level of a woodchuck (*Waldmurmeltier*) and walk on four legs".

 Now, almost two hundred years later, in times of climate change and the green movement, discuss and asses Thoreau's ideas as well as the film *Captain Fantastic*. Are these ideas merely freakish and escapistic or does humankind need to go back to nature to find itself?

→ Focus on Language, Conversation and Discussion, p. 413

Weihnachten wird bei den Cashs nicht gefeiert. Die Geburt Jesu ist den bekennenden[1] Atheisten[2] vollkommen egal, aber der Jahrestag des linken Intellektuellen[3] Noam Chomsky wird begangen. „Happy
5 Chomsky Day" sagt der Vater Ben (Viggo Mortensen) zu seinen Kindern und verteilt die Geschenke: Angel[4], Pfeil und Bogen und für die jüngste Tochter ein Jagdmesser[5], über das sich die Siebenjährige freut, wie andere Kinder über ein iPhone 6.
10 Ben und seine Frau Leslie (Trin Miller) haben vor vielen Jahren der amerikanischen Konsumgesellschaft[6] den Rücken zugekehrt und sich in die Wälder des pazifischen Nordwestens zurückgezogen, um ihre Kinder in der freien Natur nach ihren eige-
15 nen Werten zu erziehen. Die sechs Mädchen und Jungen sind nicht nur athletische Survival-Spezialisten, die es gewohnt sind, das Wild[7] für ihr Mittagessen selbst zu jagen. Sie sind auch philosophisch und literarisch hochgebildet. Die Jüngste
20 kann den Inhalt der „Bill of Rights" wiedergeben und die Zusatzartikel[8] der amerikanischen Verfassung[9] einem kritischen Diskurs[10] unterziehen. Auf die Frage, was eine Vergewaltigung sei, bekommt sie von ihrem Vater eine genaue und schonungslo-
25 se[11] Erklärung. Genauso klar, wahrhaftig und ohne Umschweife[12] berichtet Ben seinen Kindern, dass sich die depressive Mutter im Krankenhaus das Leben genommen hat.

Es ist eine herzzerreißende[13] Szene und gleichzeitig eine Begebenheit voller Würde[14], weil der Vater sei-
30 ne Töchter und Söhne als vollwertige[15] Menschen Ernst nimmt. Der Tod der Mutter ist der Ausgangspunkt[16] in Matt Ross' intelligentem Familienporträt „Captain Fantastic". Denn obwohl der Schwiegervater Ben verbietet, zur Beerdigung[17] zu kommen,
35 macht er sich mit seinen Kindern auf nach New Mexico, um der Mutter die letzte Ehre zu erweisen[18]. Auf dem Weg in den Süden werden die Kinder mit jener kapitalistischen[19] Gesellschaft konfrontiert, über die sie viel theoretisches Wissen angehäuft[20]
40 haben, ohne wirklich eine Vorstellung davon zu haben. Und die Welt jenseits der Wälder hält viele Überraschungen für sie bereit.

„Captain Fantastic" spiegelt die Konsumgesellschaft, indem der Film im Familienkreis eine radikale Ge-
45 genutopie[21] entwirft[22]. Aber Ross idealisiert den isolierten Antikapitalismus der Cashs nicht, sondern unterzieht das skurrile Lebensmodell[23] einer dialektischen Prüfung[24].

Rheinische Post, 10 February 2017, p. C8

---

[1] avowed – [2] atheist – [3] left-wing intellectual – [4] fishing rod – [5] hunting knife – [6] consumer society – [7] game – [8] ammendment –
[9] Constitution – [10] critical/reasoned discourse – [11] brutally honest / blunt – [12] direct and straightforward – [13] hearbreaking – [14] dignity –
[15] fully accepted – [16] starting point – [17] funeral – [18] to pay one's last respects to sb. – [19] capitalist – [20] to accumulate / to amass –
[21] anti-utopia – [22] to create – [23] way of life – [24] dialectical examination

Gender Diversity:
Professional Perspectives of Men and Women

Fiona Smith

Gender Diversity at Work:
Using Education to Tackle the Backlash[1]

AWARENESS

In a 4-corners activity, reflect on and collect examples of what you consider to be "typically male or female" jobs or professions. The four corners are jobs that …

- … are typically female
- … are not gender-specific
- … are typically male
- … used to be gender-specific but have changed over time.

Step 1: Write the names of the jobs/professions on slips of paper and place them in the respective corners.

 Step 2: Discuss in class whether or not you agree with the placement of the jobs/professions.

COMPREHENSION

1. Before reading:
   Describe the cartoons below using the vocabulary in the vocab box and/or a dictionary for help. Pay attention to the textual and pictorial elements. What do the cartoons say about gender diversity at work?
   → Focus on Skills, Analysis of Visuals, p. 409

"I need one Pepsi, one Coke, one 7-Up, one large coffee, one small coffee, one mint tea, one green tea, one iced tea, one orange juice, one bottled water, and one nonalcoholic Fuzzy Navel. They're for our Diversity Committee."

"Oh, you'll love working here. Nobody treats you any differently just because of your age, race, or gender."

Tips on vocab

(1) to have bulging eyes ■ permanent wave (*Dauerwelle*) ■ pleated skirt (*Faltenrock*) ■ pearl necklace ■ sweater ■ to give orders to sb. ■ secretary/assistant ■ to wear a dotted necktie ■ bald-headed (*glatzköpfig*) ■ to wear a moustache (*Schnurrbart*)

(2) grey business suits ■ a uniform outfit ■ to look identical ■ to resemble each other ■ male-dominated

[1] **backlash** *Gegenreaktion*

Conversations about the advancement[1] of women at work are now so commonplace that it can seem like a foregone conclusion[2] that, someday soon, women will have equal opportunities and pay.

5 But then you start wading through the comments under news articles on gender diversity and you realise there is a very angry, resentful[3] undertow[4] from some (mostly men) who demonstrate a fear that when women win, men and families will lose.

10 Women's empowerment advocate Julie McKay acknowledges the diversity movement hasn't always argued its case well – especially when it comes to that section of the community that fears it is being victimised and left behind.

15 "We say things like 'diversity is good for business' and we, accidentally, move on and talk about other things – having mistakenly thought everyone in the room agrees with us," says McKay, the former executive director of UN Women Australia, who starts a new job as 20 lead partner for diversity and inclusion at PwC[5] when she finishes her parental leave[6] in February 2017.

McKay says the people who actively resist diversity probably don't have all the information. "They have either been shut out of the conversation or told their 25 views are stupid or not valued. And so they haven't been part of an education process on what diversity is all about and why."

The data on the business case for diversity is widely available and so anyone with career ambitions should 30 know they will be more successful if they surround themselves with teams that represent a cross section[7] of society, says McKay.

"There is no evidence that maintaining the status quo of having a male-dominated, un-diverse team is better." 35 It is a failure of many businesses that they have underinvested[8] in preparing their staff for the massive societal and workplace changes that come with sharing jobs and power with women, she says.

If they were overhauling[9] an IT system or relocating an 40 office, teams of change management experts would be consulted to smooth the way.

Yet those same organisations implement[10] diversity policies[11] with no support system or training in place for the people who fear they may be displaced. And, when those people resist, some of those leaders get a 45 little gun-shy[12].

"What I see from a lot of leaders is that they come out with these bold[13] statements around diversity and inclusion and announce programs and they get a huge backlash," she says. 50

When they hear from staff they don't want it, or get pushback from those worried about being seen as "token" appointments[14], the leaders start to falter[15].

"What I tell leaders is: actually, if you are not getting any resistance, you are not doing anything effective. 55

"In Australia, we have seen a bit of the bold splash[16] … and then the retreat," McKay says.

Another misstep by employers is to focus on "fixing" the people who have formerly been excluded, rather than the incumbents[17], says McKay. This would include 60 offering things such as assertiveness[18] training for women in a male-dominated environment without offering inclusiveness training for the men around them.

"There was a fantastic example in the Swedish armed forces, where they got their whole budget that they 65 used to spend on women and other diverse groups and they cut all the programs," she says, referring to her Churchill Fellowship Report, 'Exploring effective strategies to engage women in leadership roles in non-traditional sectors'. 70

"They were not going to do any mentoring[19] or fixing-women conferences. They invested it in a major cultural change program for their men about how they would need to behave and lead and operate with a diverse workforce. 75

"And they saw a huge change in the way men felt about diversity and inclusion."

McKay has spent the past three years as gender advisor to the chief of the Australian Defence Force and says she has witnessed diversity-resisters change their 80 views when they have the right information and feedback from their teams.

---

[1] **advancement** progress in a job, social class, etc. – [2] **foregone conclusion** *ausgemachte Sache* – [3] **resentful** *grollend* – [4] **undertow** *Gegenströmung* – [5] **PwC** (*abbr.*) PricewaterhouseCoopers, a global audit and assurance, tax and consulting services company – [6] **parental leave** *Elternzeit* – [7] **cross section** *Querschnitt* – [8] **to underinvest** to fail to invest sufficient money or resources in a project or enterprise – [9] **to overhaul** to repair or improve sth. – [10] **to implement** to start using a plan or system – [11] **diversity policy** a plan of action to make sth., e. g. a workplace, more diverse – [12] **gun-shy** (*infml.*) frightened – [13] **bold** not afraid of taking risks – [14] **token appointment** sb. who is hired only because they are a member of a minority group – [15] **to falter** *stocken* – [16] **splash** sth. very noticeable – [17] **incumbent** *Amtsinhaber* – [18] **assertiveness** *Durchsetzungsvermögen* – [19] **to mentor** to help and give advice to a younger or less experienced person

She says she's had tough conversations with those who disagreed with her view of the role of women in combat[20] or in operational[21] leadership, but has had success shifting their mindsets.

"Some of the biggest supporters now of the [gender inclusion] work Defence is doing are people who openly say that three or five years ago, they weren't even aware that there was a problem.

"It wasn't that they were particularly negative, they just had no idea that [gender discrimination] was even an issue. They might have been resistant initially, but are now proponents[22] and actively supporting people and mentoring [women] to rise up through the ranks."

In her new role at PwC, she will be in charge of the firm's diversity and inclusion advisory business. McKay says she will be helping employers to convert their diversity sceptics.

"We have to spend a lot more time talking to men about what it actually means in practice and what the society that we are actually imagining looks like and what will that mean for them, personally, and for their families and daughters," she says.

In the commonly "binary" arguments[23] about women and work, it is rare to hear about what men gain when the financial future of their family no longer rests solely on their shoulders and they can spend more time caring for the people they love.

McKay says that should change. "When we talk about what the benefits are, it is more than just work. It is actually life. Diversity does enable men and women to live differently and that is good for both," says McKay. "It is not a win-lose situation."

https://www.theguardian.com/sustainable-business/2016/oct/10/gender-diversity-at-work-using-education-to-tackle-the-backlash, 10 October 2016 [30.06.2017]

COMPREHENSION

1. In a **first reading**, try to get a general understanding of the newspaper article.

2. **While reading** the article a **second time**, find evidence in the text that matches the following statements.

   Be careful: Some aspects listed are not found in the text.

   a) In the future, women will be treated equally at work.
   b) The media write about gender diversity at work rather one-sidedly.
   c) Julie McKay says that gender diversity is only being discussed half-heartedly.
   d) People resist diversity because they are not informed about its benefits.
   e) (Gender) diverse teams are more successful than non-diverse teams.
   f) Men in particular are critical and fearful of gender-diverse workplaces.
   g) Men need to be better informed and trained to help them accept diversity in the workplace.
   h) The biggest mistake is to implement diversity policies and not include people in the process.
   i) There is a wide gap between bold announcements and reality in companies.
   j) Leaders have to learn that resistance is unavoidable when making changes.
   k) Men <u>and</u> women have to be trained alike to learn to accept each other at work.
   l) The Swedish armed forces have successfully implemented gender diversity and shifted their mindset about women in combat leadership.
   m) At PwC, McKay wants to convince skeptics.
   n) In order to make people change their minds, society has to change as well.
   o) Men and women have to learn about the burden of work and caring for their families.

---

[20] **combat** fight, esp. during a war – [21] **operational** betrieblich – [22] **proponent** Befürworter – [23] **binary argument** when an issue is treated as having two opposing sides

ANALYSIS

3. Team up with a partner and relate the problems described in the article to the solutions offered by Julie McKay.

problems	solutions
● men fear that they and families will lose when women have equal opportunities and payment ● men have been shut out of the discussion … ● …	→ men need to learn that women add value, experience, etc. and thus benefit the whole team ● companies should provide diversity support and training for men in particular … ● …

Step 1: In groups, examine the statistical data given on
a) women's earnings in comparison to men's
b) the development of the gender pay gap.

Step 2: Explain whether the statistical data matches the observations made in the newspaper article.

4. International Women's Day commemorates the movement for women's rights and is celebrated on 6 March every year. It has been internationally celebrated since the early 20th century, first in the United States and later in European countries as well.

Step 1: Describe the photo of the "Fearless Girl" statue on p. 35 and explain its symbolism and message.

@ **Step 2:** Do further research on the statue, its background and public reception.
→ Focus on Skills, Analysis of Visuals, p. 409

ACTIVITIES

5. International Women's Day is a means of informing the public and raising awareness of women's rights. Based on the information given in the article about men's resentment and fears of being "victimised and left behind" (ll. 13 f.), discuss whether there should be a celebration of "gender diversity" that includes men and women.
→ Focus on Language, Conversation and Discussion, p. 413

6. In her conclusive statement, McKay says that "[d]iversity does enable men and women to live differently and that is good for both".
Comment on this view and state whether or not you agree.

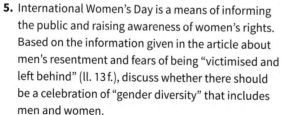

The gender pay gap

The gap in median hourly pay* has shrunk

1997   Men   2010

17.4%   10.2%

Women

How much men and women get paid for selected jobs — Gaps in full-time median hourly pay*

Men £11.29	Metal making and treating process operatives **48.6% gap**	Women £5.80
£28.75	Brokers **42.4%**	£16.55
£35.45	Doctors **28.5%**	£25.35
£28.45	Lawyers **23.6%**	£21.75
£49.70	Director of major organisation **21.6%**	£38.95
£13.01	All full-time jobs **10.2%**	£11.68
£22.94	Secondary school teachers **6.9%**	£21.36
£15.59	Physiotherapists **0%**	£15.59
£15.71	Journalists and editors **-0.7%**	£15.60
£16.78	Social workers **-1.4%**	£16.55
£13.83	Company secretaries **-41.8%**	£9.75

SOURCE: ONS   *EXCLUDING OVERTIME

7. In order to underline her credibility and professionality, the author of the article employs many technical terms and expert language.
Try to find everyday language substitutes for these terms to make them easier to understand.

- the advancement of women
- women's empowerment
- to be victimized
- to maintain the status quo
- to cut a program
- to shift one's mindset
- binary arguments

- gender diversity
- parental leave
- a cross section of society
- inclusiveness training
- leadership roles in non-traditional sectors
- inclusion advisory

The "Fearless Girl" statue in Manhattan's Financial District

From the pages of **TIME**

A statue of a young girl standing her ground before Wall Street's iconic *Charging Bull* was unveiled in New York City on March 7. Asset manager State Street Global Advisors commissioned the temporary installation for International Women's Day to address the lack of gender diversity on corporate boards and the gender pay gap. Women in the U.S. earn about 79¢ for every dollar men make at work.

From *New Travel Ban Helps U.S. – Iraq Relations but Still Stings Elsewhere* by Jared Malsin and Rebecca Collard.
In: TIME, 20 March 2017, p. 9
TIME and the TIME logo are registered trademarks of Time Inc. used under license.

Emily Bobrow

The Man Trap[1]

AWARENESS

Take a look at the cartoons below. How do the cartoonists portray the roles and situations of men and women at work? Discuss your ideas and findings in class.

→ Focus on Skills, Analysis of Visuals, p. 409

"You'll go far in this firm, Ms. Hobart. You think like a man."

"I used to lose my secretaries because they were getting married – now they leave to start their own companies."

COMPREHENSION

1. **While reading** the article, finish the following statements using evidence and information from the text.
   a) Couples' partnerships are often not egalitarian because …
   b) Marriage is still more beneficial to men because …
   c) Attributes associated with femininity are …
   d) Attributes associated with masculinity are …
   e) There are more incentives for women to act masculine than for men to act feminine because …
   f) Many professional workplaces demand that men …
   g) Pulling back from work for child-care reasons means
      - for women that …   - for men that …
   h) The consequences of more demanding jobs and increasing expectations are …
   i) Men and women are equally frustrated because …
   j) Maternity and paternity leave often results in …
   k) Egalitarian marriages work better because …

Nathan, a successful lawyer in Manhattan, hardly seems like a candidate for sympathy. His midtown office is smart, his suit is natty[2] and he earns a decent living negotiating contracts and intellectual-property rights for players in the city's dynamic entertainment industry. Divorced and in his late 40s, he speaks fondly[3] of his teenage children and is delighted with his fiancée, whom he will marry in a few weeks' time. His life is good, he assures me, and he is thriving in his career. So it is only with some hesitation that he admits something he has never discussed before, not even with his closest friends: "In the society that I live in, as a professional in New York City, I think it is easier being a woman than being a man." […]

"For the last 20-plus years I've been chained to a desk," he says. "I'm in a profession that I'm happy to be in, but

---

[1] **trap** *Falle* – [2] **natty** (*infml.*) stylish and tidy in every detail – [3] **fondly** in a happy and loving way

if I were a 20-year-old and told I could do anything I wanted with my life, I'm not sure I'd be doing this." Nathan speaks enviously of female friends who decided to leave their professional careers when they became mothers. [...] Nathan is not alone in his misgivings[4]. Between 1977 and 2008 the percentage of American fathers in dual-earner couples who suffered from work-family conflicts jumped from 35% to 60%. The percentage of similarly vexed[5] mothers grew only slightly, from 41% to 47%. Young men who get stuck supporting a family often report high levels of stress and sadness that they aren't spending more time with their kids. [...]

Women around the world may be graduating from college at higher rates than men, but they have yet to achieve similar rates of success in their careers. The uneven burdens of parenthood appear to be to blame. Although men in rich countries spend far more time cooking, cleaning and child-rearing[6] than ever before, their efforts continue to be dwarfed[7] by those of women. In America, for example, mothers devote nearly twice as much time to child care and housework as their male partners. Even couples with grand[8] plans for an egalitarian[9] partnership typically revert[10] to more traditional roles after the birth of a child. A new study of the time-diaries of highly educated dual-earning American couples found that the new fathers enjoyed up to three-and-a-half times as much leisure[11] as their female partners, as mothers who worked full time were still stuck with the lion's share of unpaid labour.

Feminists have long argued that men see little need to help out more at home because they already enjoy all the benefits of marriage and fatherhood without having to put in the extra work. "Even though it is shifting drastically, marriage is still a pretty good deal for men in terms of the actual labour they capture from[12] their wives," says Scott Coltrane, a sociologist at the University of Oregon. Coltrane has found that after controlling for variables like age and education, married American men earn significantly more than their unmarried or divorced peers, and their earnings go up with every child they have. Marriage seems to make men more productive at work because it allows them to outsource much of the housekeeping to their wives. Women, however, see no such "marriage premium[13]," and their earnings tend to go down with every new child. These parenthood effects can be seen across a variety of Western countries; they are greater in gender-conservative countries such as Austria and Germany, and weaker in more progressive countries, such as Sweden. This imbalance at home would seem to explain why the rate of female employment, after rising like gangbusters[14] from the 1960s through the 1980s, slowed through the 1990s and has levelled off[15] since the 2000s.

In order for more mothers to flourish in paid employment, more fathers need to pick up some of the slack[16] at home. But, as Nathan's frustration makes plain, this is not as simple as it sounds.

Women may not be moving as fast into male-dominated worlds as feminists would like, but they have moved much faster than men have into female-dominated ones. To understand better this asymmetry, we need to look more closely at the relative value we place on masculinity and femininity.

Most people assume that gender is simply a scheme for classifying differences or a template[17] for guiding the behaviour of children. The reality is more pernicious[18]. We typically prize the attributes we associate with men, such as competence, strength, virility[19] and stoicism[20], and underestimate the qualities we associate with women, like warmth, tenderness[21] and compassion[22]. We usually see masculinity in terms of power and dominance and femininity in terms of softness and subservience[23].

We defer[24] to men and indulge[25] women. In other words, gender is not merely a bunch of traits embodied by individuals, but a subtle[26] stratification system[27] that often advantages men and disadvantages women.

All of this means that there are far more incentives for women to act masculine than there are for men to act feminine. Women who behave like their male colleagues may be disliked for being "pushy"[28] or "bitchy," but these penalties[29] are offset[30] by the fact that they are also likely to enjoy more power and greater financial rewards. When men adopt the jobs and behaviours as-

---

[4] **misgiving** a feeling of doubt and worry about sth. – [5] **vexed** upset or annoyed – [6] **child-rearing** Kindererziehung – [7] **to dwarf** etw. klein erscheinen lassen – [8] **grand** impressive – [9] **egalitarian** gleichmacherisch – [10] **to revert to sth.** in etw. zurückfallen – [11] **leisure** ['leʒər] Freizeit – [12] **to capture from** to take sth. from another person – [13] **premium** bonus – [14] **like gangbusters** (sl.) with a lot of energy – [15] **to level off** sich stabilisieren – [16] **to pick up the slack** (infml.) to work harder – [17] **template** Schablone, Vorlage – [18] **pernicious** [pə'nɪʃəs] (fml.) having a very harmful effect – [19] **virility** male sexual power – [20] **stoicism** (fml.) Gleichmut – [21] **tenderness** Zärtlichkeit – [22] **compassion** Mitgefühl – [23] **subservience** Unterwürfigkeit – [24] **to defer to sb./sth.** (phr. v.) jdm./etw. den Vortritt lassen – [25] **to indulge** verhätscheln – [26] **subtle** ['sʌtəl] here: complex – [27] **stratification system** Schichten-system – [28] **pushy** aufdringlich – [29] **penalty** Strafe – [30] **to offset** etw. ausgleichen

sociated with women, however, they typically experience a loss of status with fewer perks[31] and more social sanctions, especially from other men. [...]

"It's seen as an unknowable crisis if men want to step
105 down," explains Barbara Risman, head of the department of sociology at the University of Illinois in Chicago. "It's not just being more like women, it's seen as being less than men. Because women are seen as less than men."

110 Once we see masculinity as an elite fraternity[32] that confers[33] special privileges, it becomes clearer why its membership is so strictly policed. Not every man qualifies. The hazing[34] begins early. We teach girls that they can be whatever they want to be, and wipe their tears
115 away when they struggle. But we teach boys that they need to toughen up, shake it off and take things "like a man". Parents are often charmed when their young girls eschew[35] dolls and dresses to play sport and build things, as if their daughters are already learning how to
120 "lean in"[36] at the playground. But many find it unsettling when their young boys want to trade a football for a tutu[37].

For many men, the workplace is merely the latest proving ground[38] for waging[39] a zero-sum[40] defence[41] of their
125 alpha-status. "Many professional workplaces involve a constant negotiation among men to establish a pecking order[42]," says Joan Williams, a feminist legal scholar and the founding director of the Centre for WorkLife Law at the University of California Hastings College of the Law.
130 "If working long hours is the way to prove that yours is the longest – we're talking schedules here – then most men are going to feel pressure to do that." [...]

Basically, when mothers pull back from work for childcare reasons, they may earn less money but they are still
135 seen as good women. When fathers do the same, they are often seen as lesser men. "The masculine mystique[43] has receded[44] less than the female mystique," observes Stephanie Coontz, a historian of marriage and the family at Evergreen State College. "Men are still dealing with
140 tremendous pressure to be a man." And, in the workplace, the pressure has been increasing. [...]

Many jobs have grown more demanding[45] in recent decades. Low earners often juggle[46] just-in-time schedules that change weekly and with little notice. High-earning professionals are expected to put in longer hours than
145 ever before, toiling[47] in offices long into the night. In 1979 16% of salaried American workers punched in[48] at least 50 hours a week. By 2014 that number was 21%. [...]

Increasingly punishing expectations at work reinforce a
150 more gendered division of labour at home. They encourage women to shift into part-time employment, and men to rely on women to look after the children. Many employers also presume from the outset[49] that mothers will – and should – put their families first, and that sprogs[50]
155 invariably[51] deter[52] women from climbing the corporate ladder[53]. [...]

Women rightly complain that they are often shunted[54] onto a mommy track with lower wages, fewer promotions and less prestige, whether they like it or not. But
160 many men are just as frustrated by the elusiveness[55] of a daddy track. [...]

Research shows that parents who take family leave or request a flexible schedule to tend to[56] young children often face harsh penalties, like lower long-term earn-
165 ings, fewer promotions and poorer performance reviews[57]. Mothers suffer from this too, but fathers often get an extra hit for defying[58] cultural expectations. Studies show that both men and women tend to see fathers who ask for paternity leave as weak and inadequate.
170 [...]

More egalitarian marriages seem to work better. A recent study of data gathered in 2006 found that couples with a more equitable approach to housework were happier with their marriages and reported having more and
175 better sex than those who divided things along more traditional lines. Fathers who take on more caregiving responsibilities not only tend to be more content and feel closer to their partners and children, but also appear to live longer.
180

The Economist 1843, A new magazine of ideas, lifestyle and culture, June & July 2017, pp. 90ff.

---

[31] **perks** Vergünstigung – [32] **fraternity** a social organization for male students at a college or university, Studentenverbindung – [33] **to confer** here: to give sb. sth. – [34] **hazing** Aufnahmeritual – [35] **to eschew** (fml.) to avoid sth. intentionally – [36] **lean in** reference to the 2013 book Lean In: Women, Work, and the Will to Lead by Sheryl Sandberg – [37] **tutu** ['tuːtuː] Ballettröckchen – [38] **proving ground** Erprobungsgelände – [39] **to wage** um etw. kämpfen – [40] **zero-sum** Nullsumme – [41] **defence** Verteidigung, Abwehr – [42] **pecking order** Hackordnung – [43] **mystique** (fml.) being special in a mysterious way – [44] **to recede** zurückweichen – [45] **demanding** anspruchsvoll – [46] **to juggle** jonglieren – [47] **to toil** to work hard – [48] **to punch in** die Stechuhr drücken – [49] **outset** beginning – [50] **sprog** (sl.) baby or child – [51] **invariably** always – [52] **to deter sb. from sth.** jdn. von etw. abschrecken – [53] **to climb the corporate ladder** die Karriereleiter emporklettern – [54] **to shunt** jdn. abschieben – [55] **elusiveness** Unerreichbarkeit – [56] **to tend to sb./sth.** (phr. v.) to deal with the problems or needs of a person/thing – [57] **performance review** Leistungsbewertung – [58] **to defy** sich jdm./etw. widersetzen

2. **After a second reading**, subdivide the magazine article according to the topics discussed. Find a suitable headline for each section using your own words.

ANALYSIS

3. In lines 136–137 the author refers to the "masculine and female mystique" which men and women are suffering from alike.

    Explain this statement using the excerpt from Betty Friedan's 1963 book *The Feminine Mystique*.
   → Focus on Skills, Analysis of a Non-Fictional Text, p. 405

4. In groups, examine the info graphic *Berufstätige Frauen in Deutschland* and the bar charts (p. 40) depicting the share of working women in Germany and Europe and their salaries. What does the data reveal about
   a) the share of women in certain professions?
   b) the share of women in leading positions?
   c) men's and women's salaries?
   d) the share of women working full time or part time?
   → Focus on Skills, Analysis of Statistical Data, p. 408

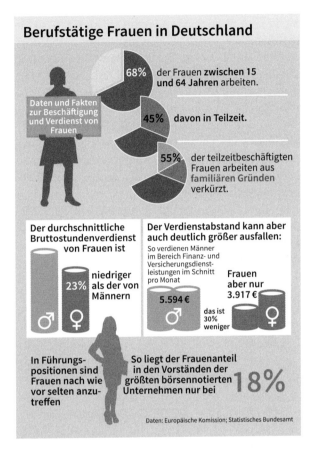

Berufstätige Frauen in Deutschland

Daten und Fakten zur Beschäftigung und Verdienst von Frauen

68% der Frauen **zwischen 15 und 64 Jahren** arbeiten.

45% davon in Teilzeit.

55% der teilzeitbeschäftigten Frauen arbeiten aus familiären Gründen verkürzt.

Der durchschnittliche Bruttostundenverdienst von Frauen ist **23%** niedriger als der von Männern

Der Verdienstabstand kann aber auch deutlich größer ausfallen: So verdienen Männer im Bereich Finanz- und Versicherungsdienstleistungen im Schnitt pro Monat **5.594 €**, Frauen aber nur **3.917 €**, das ist 30% weniger

In Führungspositionen sind Frauen nach wie vor selten anzutreffen

So liegt der Frauenanteil in den Vorständen der größten börsennotierten Unternehmen nur bei **18%**

Daten: Europäische Kommission; Statistisches Bundesamt

ACTIVITIES

5. Evaluate Emily Bobrow's claims that
   a) "… men see little need to help out more at home because they already enjoy all the benefits of marriage and fatherhood without having to put in the extra work." (ll. 46 ff.)
   b) "Women may not be moving as fast into male-dominated worlds as feminists would like, but they have moved much faster than men have into female-dominated ones." (ll. 74 ff.)
   c) "… gender is not merely a bunch of traits embodied by individuals, but a subtle stratification system that often advantages men and disadvantages women." (ll. 91 ff.)
   d) "Men are still dealing with tremendous pressure to be a man." (ll. 139 f.)

Betty Friedan

The Feminine Mystique

Betty Friedan (1921–2006) was an American writer, activist and feminist. She was a leading figure in the women's movement in the United States, and her 1963 book *The Feminine Mystique*, which describes the roles of women in industrial states, has gained cult status.

The feminine mystique says that the highest value and the only commitment[1] for women is the fulfillment of her own femininity. It says that the great mistake of Western culture, through most of its history, has been
5 the undervaluation of this femininity. It says this femininity is so mysterious and intuitive[2] and close to the creation and origin of life that man-made science may never be able to understand it. But however special and different, it is in no way inferior to the nature of man;
10 it may even in certain respects be superior. The mistake, says the mystique, the root of women's troubles in the past is that women envied men, women tried to be like men, instead of accepting their own nature, which can find fulfillment only in sexual passivity, male dom-
15 ination, and nurturing[3] maternal love.
But the new image this mystique gives to American women is the old image: "Occupation: housewife." The new mystique makes the housewife-mothers, who never had a chance to be anything else, the model for all
20 women; it presupposes[4] that history has reached a final and glorious end in the here and now, as far as women are concerned. Beneath the sophisticated trappings[5], it simply makes certain concrete, finite, domestic aspects of feminine existence – as it was lived by women whose lives were confined[6], by necessity, to cooking, cleaning, 25 washing, bearing children – into a religion, a pattern by which all women must now live or deny[7] their femininity.

from *The Feminine Mystique* by Betty Friedan. W. W. Norton, New York 1963

Frauenanteile bei Absolventen und Absolventinnen
in %

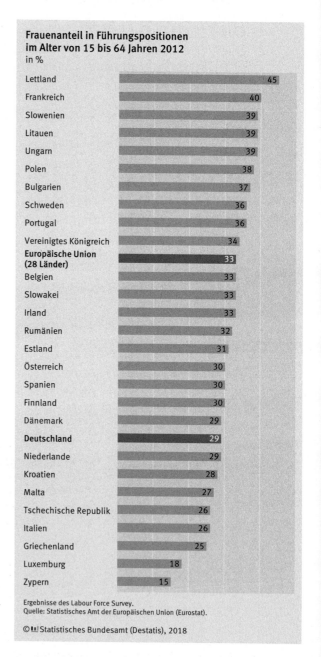

Frauenanteil in Führungspositionen im Alter von 15 bis 64 Jahren 2012
in %

Land	%
Lettland	45
Frankreich	40
Slowenien	39
Litauen	39
Ungarn	39
Polen	38
Bulgarien	37
Schweden	36
Portugal	36
Vereinigtes Königreich	34
Europäische Union (28 Länder)	33
Belgien	33
Slowakei	33
Irland	33
Rumänien	32
Estland	31
Österreich	30
Spanien	30
Finnland	30
Dänemark	29
Deutschland	29
Niederlande	29
Kroatien	28
Malta	27
Tschechische Republik	26
Italien	26
Griechenland	25
Luxemburg	18
Zypern	15

Ergebnisse des Labour Force Survey.
Quelle: Statistisches Amt der Europäischen Union (Eurostat).

© Statistisches Bundesamt (Destatis), 2018

[Absolventen chart data:]
2012 / 2002 — Insgesamt 2002 2012
Veterinärmedizin: 84 / 77
Sprach- und Kulturwissenschaften: 76 / 72
Kunst, Kunstwissenschaft: 66 / 64
Humanmedizin: 65 / 49
Agrar-, Forst- und Ernährungswissenschaften: 60 / 52
Rechts-, Wirtschafts- und Sozialwissenschaften: 53 / 47
Sport: 42 / 52
Mathematik, Naturwissenschaften: 41 / 37
Ingenieurwissenschaften: 23 / 21

© Statistisches Bundesamt (Destatis), 2018

---

[1] **commitment** *Verpflichtung* – [2] **intuitive** [ɪnˈtjuːɪtɪv] based on feelings – [3] **nurturing** *fürsorglich* – [4] **to presuppose** to accept that sth. is true before it has been proved – [5] **trappings** *Drumherum* – [6] **to confine** to limit a person in some way – [7] **to deny** *leugnen*

Into the Future: Counterculture vs. Establishment

Jim O'Neill

Hip Conservative Counter-Culture vs. Repressive[1] Liberal Establishment

American singer and song-writer Joy Villa

AWARENESS

Looking at the headline of the article – what do you associate with the terms
- conservatism
- counter-culture
- liberal
- left-wing
- establishment?

Discuss your ideas in class.

COMPREHENSION

1. **Before reading:**
   In the wake of the populist and nationalist movements, Donald Trump's election and Brexit, a new conservative culture emerged. Conservatism was suddenly considered by many as hip, whereas liberalism in connection with the "Establishment" was seen as oppressive and intolerant.
   Pair up with a partner and read the quotations below.
   a) Which qualities and attitudes are associated with the "new counter-culture"?
   b) What made people turn against liberalism and support conservatism?
   c) What was Joy Villa's motivation for promoting Trump's slogan *Make America Great Again*?

For at least a year now, I've been telling everyone who will listen that being right-wing is the new counter-culture, the new punk, an act of rebellion in an era of political correctness, safe spaces, multiculturalism and globalism.
Milo Yiannopoulos

Conservatism is the new counter-culture.
Paul J. Watson

The "long march through the institutions[2]" created not [a] collectivist utopia, but privileged elites in media, academe, and government whose stock portfolios[3], bank accounts, affluent[4] zip-codes[5], and tony[6] life-styles [are] indistinguishable from those of the robber-baron capitalists they demonized.
Bruce Thornton

I was tired of the bullying. I was tired of being pushed down so that I couldn't say my beliefs. And being fearful of losing sales. Losing fans. And a lot of my friends have the same thing. And we live in Hollywood, which is supposed to be the most open viewpoint city. But the truth is there was a lot of hate and a lot of negativity and I wanted to change the storyline to love and support and unity as an American.
Joy Villa on why she wore a Trump MAGA[7] dress to the Grammys

---

[1] **repressive** controlling what people do, esp. by using force – [2] **the long march through the institutions** a slogan coined by German student activist Rudi Dutschke in 1968 to describe his strategy of subverting society by infiltrating the institutions in order to establish the conditions for a revolution – [3] **stock portfolio** *Aktienbestände* – [4] **affluent** wealthy – [5] **zip-code** *Postleitzahl* – [6] **tony** stylish and expensive – [7] **MAGA** (*acronym*) Make America Great Again

James Delingpole[8] recently observed that Ted Malloch[9] believes that "the Brexit and Trump shocks of 2016 [...] are the counter-reaction to the global takeover by the liberal-left in 1968." This long-overdue[10] counter-reac-
5 tion is, in fact, [...] the vanguard[11] of a new counter-culture – *conservatism*.

Let me be quick to point out that I am not referring to "conservatism" as it has been understood in the past – and the new conservatism should by no means be con-
10 fused with the so-called "neo-conservatives" (neocons), who are, of course, *left* wing big government globalists posing as *right*-wing conservative Republicans.

Although the new counter-cultural brand of conservatism that I am talking about carries with it many key ele-
15 ments of traditional conservatism – such as passion for freedom, patriotism, capitalism, religious freedom, and tolerance – it tends to be more pragmatic[12] and less ideologically obsessed, more open-minded and less dogmatic[13] than traditional conservatism. Sort of libertarian-
20 ism[14] on a leash[15], with a dash[16] of brash[17] impertinence[18]. The core word in the new conservative counter-culture is *freedom*. As is free-spirited, free-thinking, free enterprise, free market, free speech – free, freer, freest.

By and large[19] our campuses are currently anti-freedom,
25 and promote and preach fear, intolerance, divisiveness, and scorn[20] – muzzling[21] free speech and indoctrinating students to be passionately and self-righteously fearful and contemptuous[22] of anyone perceived as being outside the officially sanctioned leftist thought box. Aca-
30 demia[23] has become, in a word, *repressive*. Much more repressive than they ever thought of being back in 1968. American academia has morphed[24] into a purveyor[25] of Draconian[26] thought policing that is diametrically opposed to what the counter-culture of the late 60s pur-
35 portedly[27] fought for. Perhaps the strangest of the leftist campus reversals is from a "If it feels good do it" hedonism[28] to a type of hysterical pearl-clutching[29] puritanism[30]. In any event, it is way past time for a radical shift in direction. I believe that with a cutting edge[31] conserv-
40 ative counter-culture leading the way, we won't get fooled again.

The days when the Left held a lock on "cool" counter-culture are *long* gone. Anymore the words that spring to mind when I think of the Left are: arrogant, dogmatic,
45 intolerant, bullying, and nasty.

The Democrats have doubled down[32] on their racist, intolerant, divisive, duplicitous[33] globalist agenda – while the Republicans (at least President Trump and his supporters) promote an agenda of unity, inclusiveness, hon-
50 esty, integrity, and patriotic pride of place.

I must say, it is refreshingly pleasant to be right and hip at the same time.

http://canadafreepress.com/article/hip-conservative-counter-culture-vs.-repressive-liberal-establishment, 18 February 2017 [29.06.2017]

COMPREHENSION

2. Define Jim O'Neill's understanding of the "new conservatism".

3. Present O'Neill's contrastive depiction of conservative and liberal culture.

conservative culture	liberal culture
• counter-reaction to liberal-left	• repressive
• passion for freedom	• establishment
• …	• …

4. Point out the reasons the author gives for the development of a new conservative counter-culture.

[8] **James Delingpole** (*1965) an English novelist and right-wing columnist – [9] **Ted Malloch** (*1952) American author, consultant and TV producer – [10] **overdue** *überfällig* – [11] **vanguard** the forefront – [12] **pragmatic** solving problems in a sensible way – [13] **dogmatic** *rechthaberisch* – [14] **libertarianism** belief that people should be free to think and behave as they want and not be restricted by government – [15] **leash** [liːʃ] *(Hunde-)Leine* – [16] **dash** a small amount of sth. – [17] **brash** confident in an aggressive way – [18] **impertinence** *Unverschämtheit* – [19] **by and large** *im Großen und Ganzen* – [20] **scorn** *Verachtung* – [21] **to muzzle** to stop a person from expressing independent opinions; *jdm. einen Maulkorb anlegen* – [22] **contemptuous** *verächtlich* – [23] **academia** the world of universities, learning, teaching and research – [24] **to morph** to change – [25] **purveyor** *(fml.)* a business that provides goods and services – [26] **Draconian** *(fml.)* laws, government actions, etc. that are extremely severe, or go further than what is right or necessary – [27] **purportedly** *angeblich* – [28] **hedonism** *Genusssucht* – [29] **pearl-clutching** *geheuchelte Empörung* – [30] **puritanism** the belief that it is important to work hard and control yourself, and that pleasure is wrong or unnecessary – [31] **cutting edge** *topaktuell* – [32] **to double down on sth.** *(phr. v.)* to do sth. in an even more determined way than before – [33] **duplicitous** *(fml.)* *heuchlerisch*

ANALYSIS

5. Categorize the article by examining its style and line of argument*.
→ Focus on Facts, Basic Types of Non-Fictional Texts, p. 396

6. Analyse the author's use of rhetorical devices and what they reveal about his point of view* and the message of the article.
→ Focus on Skills, Analysis of a Non-Fictional Text, p. 405

ACTIVITIES

7. Jim O'Neill claims that the "core word[s] in the new conservative counter-culture [are] freedom … free-spirited, free-thinking, free enterprise, free market, free speech – free, freer, freest" (ll. 21 ff.). Comment on this statement, taking into consideration the political and social developments and events since Donald Trump became president.
→ Focus on Skills, Writing a Comment and a Review, p. 421

8. The text says that "the Brexit and Trump shocks of 2016 … are the counter-reaction to the global takeover by the liberal-left in 1968" (ll. 2 ff.).

Webcode
SNG-40235-003

Step 1: Do research on what happened in 1968 politically, socially and culturally using the links provided on the webcode.

Step 2: Compile posters that illustrate your research results and display them in class.

Step 3: Discuss whether the author is right in claiming that the new conservatism is the "long-overdue counter-reaction" and that – as asserted in quotation no. 3 – "the long march through the institutions" did not create a "collectivist utopia, but privileged elites …".
→ Focus on Language, Conversation and Discussion, p. 413

Christopher Attard

Counterculture Is Here

AWARENESS

 Take a close look at the info graphic on p. 46 which gives a short overview of "Generation Z". Collect information about what is most characteristic of Generation Z.

The days of total liberal hegemonic[1] rule are fast coming to an end, as it seems like the dissident, mischievous[2], fresh youths will be the ones to spearhead[3] the battle against the continually faltering[4] leftist estab-
5 lishment. Indeed, Generation Z will continue driving the revolt against the liberal elitism that dominates academia, civic society, pop culture, entertainment and certain corners of politics.

But what is Generation Z or iGen (internet generation)? It is the demographic cohort[5] that follows mil- 10 lennials and represents those people born between the mid-1990s and 2010. This means that for better or worse, this will be the first generation in history whose majority does not know of life without the internet. Their being constantly surrounded by electronic de- 15 vices and smartphones earns them the badge of "digi-

---

[1] **hegemonic** *vorherrschend* – [2] **mischievous** ['mɪstʃɪvəs] *frech, spitzbübisch* – [3] **to spearhead** ['spɪəhed] *etw. anführen* – [4] **to falter** *stocken* – [5] **cohort** *Altersgruppe*

tal natives", a title that will undoubtedly have consequences.

Being in an environment of constant interconnectivity and online access, iGeners have never needed to ask another human being for instructions and have no interest in relying on one form of media, since the world of limitless information is completely open to them. However, one can see how this is a double-edged sword[6], as they may be the least prepared when disaster strikes and the lights go out.

They are driven thinkers, attracted to fast-paced data, and willing to sift through the clutter[7] to find evidence backing their own claims and beliefs – which could be construed[8] as both negative, in that they may have a high susceptibility[9] to confirmation bias[10] (as do we all), or positive, due to their evidence-based approach. Most likely, it's some combination of both.

Another noteworthy point is that iGen's early years were forged[11] right in the middle of the September 11 attacks and the ensuing[12] political landscape, and have therefore never known life without the constant threat posed by radical Islamic terrorism.

According to recent research, published by The Gild (UK), a global brand consultancy, Generation Z will be even more conservative than post-war baby-boomers. The study reveals that on same-sex marriage, transgender rights and marijuana legalisation, 59 per cent of Gen Z respondents described their attitudes as being between 'conservative' and 'moderate', in sharp contrast from the 80 per cent plus of millennials and Generation X-ers, who instead responded as 'quite' or 'very liberal'. Having grown up post-financial crisis, iGen seems to be a generation of savers, with 25 per cent saying they would rather save for the future than spend money they don't have, and 22 per cent saying they never spend on "unnecessary, frivolous things" because saving is a top priority. Such attitudes were shared with the silent generation (1920s – 40s), with 43 per cent and 25 per cent respectively.

At a glance, it appears that Generation Z is the most conservative generation in 70 years, with data compiled by Goldman Sachs detailing the figures that "will make the millennials shudder[13]".

iGeners are financially conservative, staunchly[14] supportive of personal freedoms, and strong on national security, including counterterrorism and cyber-security, with a hint of isolationism. They are issue-based[15], meritocratic[16] and trending towards individualism vs collectivism, while still motivated to affect social change.

What's certainly clear is that Gen Z does not fit the typical mould[17] offered by traditional media and politics, which is perhaps the reason behind their strong support for Donald Trump. Polling data collected by the Hispanic Heritage Foundation (US) just before the election found that students aged 14 to 18 showed a 46 per cent-31 per cent split in favour of the Republican candidate. [...]

That said, there is no question that Generation Z will bring with them a great amount of social and economic upheaval[18] in the coming years – with their desire for smaller government, border controls, sensible fiscal[19] policies and nationalism being central values. One could say that this next cohort is a product of prior generation's liberal extremism, and a reactionary response to today's 'anything goes' cultural and moral decadence[20]. [...]

Since political correctness and social justice are no longer seen as cool and trendy social movements, and their influence becoming more tyrannical and authoritarian over the years, Generation Z sees them as the establishmentarians[21] to rebel against.

This is the generation that grew up in a society rife with liberalism and a left-wing dominated political landscape, with conservative voices being silenced and pushed to the sidelines.

In truth, the current perceptual[22] shift comes as no surprise, as there is a natural cyclical[23] tendency for new generations to swing back towards a conventional mindset following a warped[24] era of liberal oversaturation[25], whose peak and subsequent decline became overtly apparent in 2016.

In tandem with this generational shift in attitudes is the change in mediums of conversation. Indeed, there is no denying that the internet has become the main platform for political discourse [...].

---

[6] **double-edged sword** [sɔːd] *zweischneidiges Schwert* – [7] **clutter** a lot of things in an untidy state – [8] **to construe sth. as** (*fml.*) *etw. als etw. deuten/auslegen* – [9] **susceptibility** [səˌseptəˈbɪləti] *Anfälligkeit* – [10] **confirmation bias** [ˈbaɪəs] when you only pay attention to evidence that supports your own beliefs – [11] **to forge sb.** *jdn. prägen* – [12] **to ensue** [ɪnˈsjuː] (*fml.*) *folgen, sich ergeben* – [13] **to shudder** *schaudern* – [14] **staunchly** strong and loyal – [15] **issue-based** *sachorientiert* – [16] **meritocratic** *leistungsorientiert* – [17] **mould** *Form, Vorgabe* – [18] **upheaval** *Aufruhr, Umbruch* – [19] **fiscal** connected with public money – [20] **decadence** *Niedergang, Verfall* – [21] **establishmentarians** people belonging to or supporting the establishment – [22] **perceptual** *Wahrnehmungs-* – [23] **cyclical** happening again and again – [24] **warped** radical – [25] **oversaturation** *Übersättigung*

Despite the fact that conservatives are now winning the culture war [...], the problem of having to deal with the repercussions[26] of leftist indoctrination for several more years to come is a boring reality – one that reasonable people must face soberly[27].

On the bright side, leftist hellspawns[28] like feminism and social justice are dying faster than the residual[29] cells of a decaying carcass[30]. But their latent effects in politics, academia and the media, which seem like the only sectors still insufficiently[31] red-pilled[32], can still be felt and must be dealt with head on[33].

The question that I leave you with is, if this new conservative renaissance continues, does this not at the very least suggest that the powers that be[34] have overstayed, and overstepped their welcome and provisional authority? We can only change the negatives if we highlight the negatives, and the left-wing establishment has made it clear that it will not allow this to happen while it holds the reins. Perhaps it is time for it to let go, and allow others to venture[35] where it has failed.

In the end, all we have is conversation, and anything that preserves it must be defended, while that which threatens it – replaced. All things considered, hope for a balanced, rational, sensible and pragmatic political transition is kindled[36], and one can only assist this inevitable changing of the guard through public discourse and debate.

https://www.timesofmalta.com/articles/view/20170314/opinion/
Counterculture-is-here.642348, 14 March 2017 [29.06.2017]

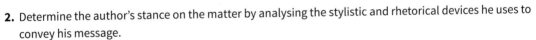

COMPREHENSION

1. In his article, the author predicts that Generation Z will be the leading force against today's liberal establishment and elites.

   Step 1: In a **first reading**, **scan** the article and get a general understanding of Generation Z and its background.

    Step 2: Pair up with a partner and summarize what the article says about
   - Generation Z's digital and technological competence (the media),
   - the influence of 9/11 on Generation Z,
   - Generation Z's political attitudes,
   - Generation Z's attitude towards money,
   - differences between Generation Z and previous generations (e. g. Baby Boomers),
   - future political transitions.
   → Focus on Skills, Writing a Summary, p. 429

ANALYSIS

2. Determine the author's stance on the matter by analysing the stylistic and rhetorical devices he uses to convey his message.
   → Focus on Skills, Analysis of a Non-Fictional Text, p. 405

 3. Taking the infographics on p. 46 as an example, use the information given in the article to create a diagram or infographic yourself.
   Use different colours, icons, images and/or snippets from newspapers/magazines to illustrate the various aspects of Generation Z.

---

[26] **repercussion** the effect that an action, event, or decision has on something, especially a bad effect – [27] **soberly** seriously and reasonably – [28] **hellspawn** Höllenbrut – [29] **residual** remaining after most of sth. has gone – [30] **decaying carcass** ein zerfallender Kadaver – [31] **insufficiently** not enough – [32] **red-pilled** enlightened – [33] **head on** directly – [34] **the powers that be** people who control the government – [35] **to venture** sich wagen, etw. riskieren – [36] **to kindle** [ˈkɪndəl] etw. anfachen, anzünden

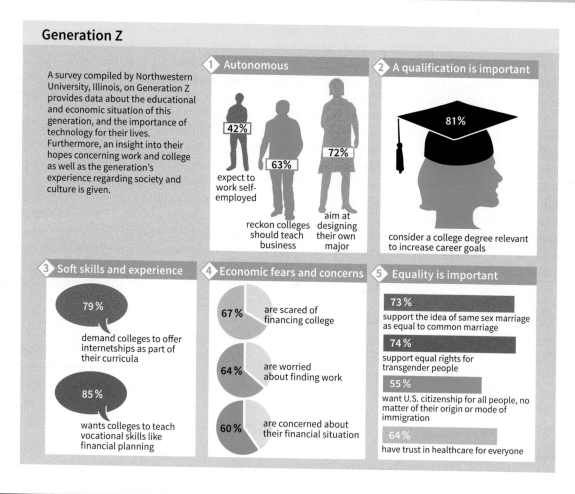

Generation Z

A survey compiled by Northwestern University, Illinois, on Generation Z provides data about the educational and economic situation of this generation, and the importance of technology for their lives. Furthermore, an insight into their hopes concerning work and college as well as the generation's experience regarding society and culture is given.

1 Autonomous

42% expect to work self-employed

63% reckon colleges should teach business

72% aim at designing their own major

2 A qualification is important

81% consider a college degree relevant to increase career goals

3 Soft skills and experience

79% demand colleges to offer internetships as part of their curricula

85% wants colleges to teach vocational skills like financial planning

4 Economic fears and concerns

67% are scared of financing college

64% are worried about finding work

60% are concerned about their financial situation

5 Equality is important

73% support the idea of same sex marriage as equal to common marriage

74% support equal rights for transgender people

55% want U.S. citizenship for all people, no matter of their origin or mode of immigration

64% have trust in healthcare for everyone

ACTIVITIES ⟫⟫⟫⟫

4. The author says that iGeners strongly supported Donald Trump in the 2016 election and that they are "the most conservative generation in 70 years" (ll. 56 f.).
Comment on this statement and give reasons why you (dis-)agree with it.
→ Focus on Skills, Writing a Comment and a Review, p. 421

Michael Seemann

Von der Wucht¹ der globalen Klasse

AWARENESS ⟫⟫⟫⟫

The 2010s as a decade seems to be dominated by demonstrations, riots and movements of infuriated citizens worldwide. The so-called German *Wutbürger* protests of 2010, the international Occupy movement of 2011, Brexit, the unexpected election of Donald Trump in 2016 and the French yellow vests movement of 2018 all reflect people's deep frustration with being dominated by elites and losing control over their lives.

a) In class, talk about whether or not you understand the frustration of so many people.

b) Do you think that recent trends like nationalism, isolationism and rejecting globalisation and international openness are promising tools for solving the world's problems?

 Discuss in class.

Es gibt heute eine globale Klasse der Informations-arbeiter, der die meisten von uns angehören und die viel homogener[2] und mächtiger ist, als sie denkt. Es sind gut gebildete, tendenziell eher junge Menschen, die sich kulturell zunehmend global orientieren, die die New York Times lesen statt die Tagesschau zu sehen, die viele ausländische Freunde und Freunde im Ausland haben, die viel reisen, nicht unbedingt, um in den Urlaub zu fahren. Es ist eine Klasse, die fast ausschließlich in Großstädten lebt, die so flüssig Englisch spricht, als sei es ihre Muttersprache, für die Europa kein abstraktes Etwas ist, sondern eine gelebte Realität, wenn sie zum Jobwechsel von Madrid nach Stockholm zieht. Europa und Nordamerika mögen Schwerpunkte sein, doch die Klasse ist tatsächlich global. Eine wachsende Gruppe global orientierter Menschen gibt es in jedem Land dieser Erde und sie ist gut vernetzt[3].

Diese neue globalisierte Klasse sitzt in[4] den Medien, in den Start-ups und NGOs, in den Parteien, und weil sie die Informationen kontrolliert („liberal media", „Lügenpresse"[5]), gibt sie überall kulturell und politisch den Takt vor[6]. Das heißt gar nicht, dass sie politisch homogen im eigentlichen Sinne ist – zumindest empfindet sie sich nicht so – sie ist zum Beispiel in Deutschland fast im gesamten Parteienspektrum[7] zu finden. Diese Klasse entspringt dem Bürgertum[8], aber hat sich von ihm emanzipiert.

Die Machtverschiebung ging im Stillen vor sich. Irgendwann begann sich der progressivere Teil des Bürgertums sozial enger mit seinesgleichen über Ländergrenzen hinweg zu vernetzen und kulturell zu orientieren. Die globale Klasse entstand und hat den kulturellen Wandel der Globalisierung beschleunigt. Globale Standards nicht nur in der Wirtschaft, sondern auch in Politik, Kultur und Moral. Die progressiven, zunehmend global Orientierten haben die anderen einfach abgehängt[9]. Aber weil sie anders herrscht, und weil sie sich dabei mit der Gesellschaft selbst verwechselt, merkt sie es nicht einmal. Sie hat keine Gewalt auf ihrer Seite, die meisten haben noch nicht einmal wahnsinnig viel Geld. Die globale Klasse hat zwar sehr reiche Individuen hervorgebracht – vor allem im Silicon Valley –, aber interessanterweise nutzen sie diesen Reichtum vor allem wieder, um es in diskursives Kapital[10] zurückzuverwandeln[11]; in andere Start-ups oder in ambitionierte Weltrettungsprogramme[12]. Denn insgeheim weiß sie längst, was die eigentliche Quelle ihrer Macht ist: Sie kontrolliert den Diskurs, sie kontrolliert die Moral. [...]

Und das merken die anderen, die kulturell Abgehängten[13]. Sie merken, dass uns ihre Welt zu klein geworden ist, dass wir uns moralisch überlegen[14] fühlen und dass wir nach Größerem streben. Vor allem merken sie, dass wir dabei erfolgreich sind, dass wir auf diesem Weg die Standards definieren, die nach und nach auch an sie selbst angelegt werden[15]. Ökologische, antirassistische, antisexistische Standards. Politisch korrekte Standards eben. Und die Standards, die dabei entwertet[16] und verdrängt[17] werden, kamen mal aus dem Bürgertum, aus einer Zeit, als sie noch das Sagen hatten. Es ist eine kulturelle Gentrifizierung[18].

Auf magische Weise hat das Bürgertum trotz Grundbesitz[19], privater Krankenvorsorge[20] und leitenden Angestelltenfunktion[21] die Deutungshoheit[22] verloren. „Take Back Control", der Slogan der Brexiter, ist der eigentliche Schlachtruf all der neurechten[23] Bewegungen. Es gibt gerade im Bürgertum das Gefühl des Kontrollverlusts. [...] Englische Standards wurden in England bestimmt, Deutsche in Deutschland, amerikanische in den USA. Die globale Klasse bringt alles durcheinander!

Und genau das ängstigt die Arbeiter genauso wie die Bürger selbst. Es ist nicht so, dass die Arbeiter Eliten ablehnen, im Gegenteil. Aber viele wollen ihre alten Eliten zurück, die noch in derselben Welt gelebt haben wie sie. Deswegen schafft Trump, was Mitt Romney[24] nicht schaffen konnte: Identifikationsfigur und positiver Entwurf[25] einer Elite zu sein, zu dem sich die Arbeiter verbinden können. Trumps Erfolg kommt ohne Bildung und ohne Political Correctness aus, deswegen wirkt er erreichbar[26]. Er repräsentiert eine entmachtete[27] Elite der guten alten Zeit, die sich die Leute zurückwünschen. Eine Elite, die zwar egoistisch und brutal kapitalistisch war, die aber kulturell anschlussfähig[28] und national bezogen[29] blieb.

Westdeutsche Zeitung, 28. Oktober 2016, p. 4

---

[1] impact/force – [2] homogenous – [3] to have a network/to be well connected – [4] to be based in – [5] fake media – [6] to set the pace/to set the tone – [7] political spectrum – [8] bourgeoisie/the middle class – [9] to leave sb. behind – [10] discursive capital – [11] to retransform – [12] world rescue programmes – [13] people who are culturally left behind – [14] morally superior – [15] to apply sth. to sth. – [16] to devalue sb./sth. – [17] to push sb./sth. aside – [18] gentrification (here: *Verdrängung*) – [19] property ownership – [20] private health care – [21] having an executive position/high-ranking job – [22] sovereignty of interpretation – [23] alt-right (alternative right) – [24] Mitt Romney, American businessman and politician; 2012 Republican presidential nominee – [25] sketch/model – [26] approachable – [27] deprived of power – [28] culturally connected – [29] nationally oriented

COMPREHENSION

1. Describe the cartoon. What image of the "enraged crowd" does the cartoon convey?
→ Focus on Skills, Analysis of Visuals, p. 409

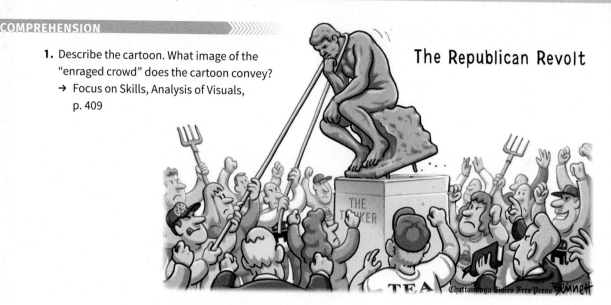

The Republican Revolt

THE THINKER

TEA

Chattanooga Times Free Press BENNETT

2. Your American friend Matthew is learning about the global trend of rising nationalism and people's frustration with globalisation in his social studies class. In an email, he asks you what the German media are reporting about this topic. You have found this article from the *Westdeutsche Zeitung* that talks about recent developments.

Mediate the article into English, focusing on the reasons why people are demanding to "take back control" and "make America great again".
→ Focus on Skills, Mediation, p. 412

3. Find information in the German newspaper article that matches the message of the cartoon and mediate it into English.

ANALYSIS

4. „Die globale Klasse entstand und hat den kulturellen Wandel der Globalisierung beschleunigt. Globale Standards nicht nur in der Wirtschaft, sondern auch in Politik, Kultur und Moral. Die progressiven, zunehmend global Orientierten haben die anderen einfach abgehängt." (ll. 32 ff.)

Explain this description of a "global class" and give examples of the "global standards" they shaped.
→ Focus on Skills, Analysis of a Non-Fictional Text, p. 405

5. Compare the explanations given by Michael Seemann to Joseph Stiglitz' lecture on the failure of globalization (pp. 261 f.). What similarities can you detect?

ACTIVITIES

6. Not only the so-called Brexiteers, but many people in various European countries are frustrated with the EU bureaucracy and EU standards they feel are being imposed on them. The German newspaper article says, "englische Standards wurden in England bestimmt, deutsche in Deutschland, amerikanische in den USA. Die globale Klasse bringt alles durcheinander!"(ll. 68 ff.)

Discuss whether "standards" should be defined regionally, nationally or internationally.
→ Focus on Language, Conversation and Discussion, p. 413

individualism and conformity		
affiliation	connection with a political party, religion, or organization	*Zugehörigkeit*
civic duties	sth. you have to do as a citizen for your community or city	*Bürgerpflicht*
civil disobedience	the act of refusing to obey laws to express disapproval	*ziviler Ungehorsam*
collectivist, collectivism	a political system that focuses on groups	*kollektivistisch, Kollektivismus*
conformity	behaviour that follows the standards that are expected	*Angepasstheit, Konformität*
emerging adulthood	the early stage of adulthood	*junges Erwachsensein*
individual, individualist	a single person; sb. who is different or original	*Individuum; Individualist*
millennials	people born around 2000	*die Millenniumsgeneration*
(social) obligation	sth. that you must do	*(soziale) Verpflichtung*
peer pressure	the strong influence of a group on its members	*Gruppenzwang*
self-actualization	a person's desire to use all their abilities to achieve what they can	*Selbstverwirklichung*
societal authorities	a group of people or organizations with a lot of responsibility and influence (church, police, etc.)	*gesellschaftliche Autoritäten*
social change	the result of new trends/developments in society/politics	*gesellschaftlicher Wandel*
stereotype, stereotypical	a set idea that people have about sb./sth.	*Stereotyp, Klischee*
gender diversity at work		
advancement	the development or improving of sth.	*Förderung*
assertiveness	behaving confidently and not frightened	*Durchsetzungsvermögen*
biological sex	the physical condition of being male or female	*biologisches Geschlecht*
child-rearing	the work of taking care of children	*Kindererziehung*
diversity	the fact of many different types of people being included	*Vielfalt*
egalitarian	believing that all people are equally important and should have the same rights	*gleichmacherisch*
familial	affecting several members of the same family	*familiär*
feminism	the belief that women should be allowed the same rights, power, and opportunities as men and be treated in the same way	*Feminismus*
gender	being male or female (especially socially learned traits)	*Gender, Geschlechtsidentität*
gender-specific	relating to one particular gender	*geschlechtsspezifisch*
to implement a policy	to start a new system that involves a set of ideas or plan	*eine (Firmen-)Politik einführen*
inclusiveness	the quality of including many different kinds of people	*verschiedene Menschen einbeziehen*
parental leave	time parents are allowed to spend away from work to take care of their baby	*Erziehungsurlaub (Eltern)*
payment gap	difference of payment between men and women	*Lohnlücke*
promotion	the act of appointing sb. to a higher position	*Beförderung*
social sanction	action taken in order to make people obey a law or rule	*Sanktion*
counterculture vs. establishment		
bias	the fact of preferring a particular subject or thing	*Voreingenommenheit*
conservative	not usually liking change; being more traditional	*konservativ*
counterculture	a way of life that is completely different from those accepted by most of society	*Gegenkultur*
establishment	the important and powerful people who control a country	*Führungsschicht*
left-wing, right-wing	politically left/right	*politisch links/rechts orientiert*
liberal, liberalism	respecting/allowing different beliefs or behaviour	*liberal, Liberalismus*
nationalism	the belief that your country is better than all others	*Nationalismus*
repressive	controlling what people do, esp. by using force	*unterdrückend*
social status	sb.'s position in relation to other members of society	*gesellschaftliche Stellung*

Tradition and Change: The U.K. in the 21ˢᵗ Century

The Queen's performance as a Bond girl with actor Daniel Craig during the opening ceremonies of the 2012 Summer Olympics in London

> "You have become, to many of us, a kaleidoscope Queen, of a kaleidoscope country, in a kaleidoscope Commonwealth."

John Bercow, Speaker of the House of Commons, in his address to HM the Queen, on occasion of her Diamond Jubilee in June 2012

Tips on vocab

- a parachute ■ Union flag/Jack design
- ■ Welsh Corgi ■ solar-powered collectible/
souvenir

"Solar-powered Queen and Corgi": solar panels on top of the Queen's bag and the pedestal of the Corgi power the Queen's royal hand wave and the movement of the Corgi's head

Tips on vocab »»

warm/earthy colours ■ symmetrical arrangement of ornaments ■ graphic design ■ native people ■ feathered headdress ■ pineapple ■ wooden club ■ protective shield ■ muscular physique ■ golden/silver bracelets

START-UP ACTIVITIES

1. The opening ceremony of the Olympic Games is commonly used to present the host country's culture and tradition.
   a) What does the Queen's performance as a Bond girl convey about Great Britain – and the Queen – in general?
   b) Watch the video of the Queen's performance using the webcode, and exchange your impressions in a group. What elements do you consider to be most appealing and convincing?
   c) The "Solar Queen" and her "Solar Corgi" are highly popular collectibles in the U. K. and elsewhere. Do you think these are funny and witty promotional items or kitschy "junk"?

   Webcode
   SNG-40235-004

2. What does John Bercow's remark reflect about the self-image of the British nation and its Queen?

3. What is the first thing that comes to your mind when you think about Britain? In a group, compile a website (e. g. "www.kaleidoscope-britain.co.uk") based on John Bercow's remark. Your websites can be funny, provocative or critical.

4. Look at the historical British advert dating back to the time of the Empire. Which function did the African colonies have – and what does the advert indirectly reveal about Britain as an imperial power?

5. Compare John Bercow's perception of Britain's position today with the view taken in the historical advert. Which similarities and differences can you detect? Discuss in class.

Britishness? Englishness? – Being British Today

What Being British Means …

AWARENESS

Look at the cartoon portraying a (stereotypical) Briton. Which image and clichés of "Being British"/"Britishness" does it convey?

In a group, collect further ideas of what
a) you associate with Britishness,
b) *commonly* is presented as "typically British".

Discuss your ideas in class.

A Briton seen by French cartoonist Aurel

1

Being British is about loving this country, remembering the past and honouring the people who fought from the battlefields of France, to the deserts of North Africa, into the sands of Arabia and jungles of Asia, but also looking to the future, learn from history and build upon past mistakes, be proud to be British as we are a happy race of man, these islands a testament of Nature's Beauty, we have inhabited these islands for Thousands of Years, we built a culture and identity that is uniquely British, we built an Empire, stood defiantly[1] against the Evils of Hitler Nazi German and Stalin's Soviet Union. Today I think the only way to describe Britain is from a poem by Alfred Tennyson[2], "Though we are not that strength which on old days moved Earth and Heaven, that which we are, we are, one equal temper[3] of heroic hearts made weak by time but not in will, to strive[4] to seek, but not to yield[5]". Remember We Are, We Can & We Will, go forward like a breath exhaled[6] from the Earth …

Toby, Maidstone, England

2

Being British isn't about being a specific race or culture, Britain is made up of 4 different countries, England, Ireland, Scotland and Wales. Do Scottish people call themselves British? Or do they call themselves Scottish? I was born it Britain and educated in Britain, worked etc. … Does that make me British? Both my parents are British and the family I know of also British, but who am I to call myself British if I'm unsure myself? Ancestors and people I do not know about may or may not be British, which makes me reevaluate[7] whether I'm British or not. Biased[8] opinions of having to be white and speak the English language are where most of the problems are at. Just because somebody is black or Muslim[9] – does that give us the right to judge on what identity they are? Being British is simply about loving the country we live in, being proud to call yourself British and doing anything possible to be a good British citizen. If you truly believe that you are British, you are citizen and you help …

Loren, Salford, United Kingdom

[1] **defiant** [dɪˈfaɪənt] *trotzig* – [2] **Alfred Tennyson** (1809–1892) one of the most popular and famous British poets – [3] **temper** here: character – [4] **to strive** (strove, striven) to try very hard to achieve sth. – [5] **to yield** here: to surrender; *aufgeben, kapitulieren* – [6] **to exhale** *ausatmen* – [7] **to reevaluate sth.** to think about sth. again, esp. to form a new opinion about it – [8] **biased** [ˈbaɪəst] *voreingenommen sein* – [9] **Muslim** [ˈmʊzlɪm]

3   To be British is to be multicultural. The 4 nations that make up Britain, each with their own cultures, the many peoples that conquered us in our ancient history and the many we conquered in more recent times have all contributed to our multi-cultural culture and multi-lingual language.
James, United Kingdom

5   I was born in Afghanistan and came to Britain (legally) as a child with my parents – I am a British Afghan. I am proud to be British and proud to be an Afghan. I value the cultural and religious diversity of the British society. Being a citizen is about making positive contribution to society and living in harmony with others. We Brits moan[12] too much instead of appreciating the good things that we have!!
Safia, London, United Kingdom

4   British characteristics are contradictory[10] – eccentricity with privacy, pride with self-effacement[11], pragmatism with tradition. We're a people of innovation, on a permanent nostalgia trip.
Tim Staddon, United Kingdom

6   Red Post boxes. Red buses. Number 10[13]. The Queen. British Bull dogs. Sunday Roast. Black Cabs. The Beatles. Bowler hats[14]. Laurel and Hardy[15]. Stiff upper lip[16]. London. The Union Jack. Parliament. Guy Fawkes[17]. British Ale. Margaret Thatcher[18]. Charles Darwin. The internet. Britannia[19]. Fish and Chips. Seaside Holidays. Blackpool. The BBC. The Church of England. Churchill. Lord Sugar[20]. Sir Paul McCartney. Queen. The 80's. CHAVs[21]. Council Estates[22]. Patrony[23].
Mary, Colchester, UK

www.webritish.co.uk [17.12.2014]

COMPREHENSION

1. Divide the class into groups of 3 – 4 students each, with half of the groups dealing with the "red" statements (1, 3, 6) and the other half with the "blue" statements (2, 4, 5).

   Step 1: In a **first reading**, **skim** the statements and try to understand the **gist** of what is said. Pay attention to the most relevant information (who – where – when – what – why).

   Step 2: In your groups, prepare posters on which you finish these sentences, using key terms from the statements above:
   - "Being British is about …"
   - "Important British characteristics are …"
   - "British culture is based on …"

   Step 3: Now, the "blue" and "red" groups mix and exchange their findings, adding further statements on their respective poster.

   When reporting to each other what the respective letter writer said, **use indirect speech** and be careful to backshift the tenses if necessary.

   Step 4: Display your posters in class and discuss your results, making alterations and/or corrections if necessary.

---

[10] **contradictory** *widersprüchlich* – [11] **self-effacement** *Zurückhaltung* – [12] **to moan** *stöhnen; lamentieren* – [13] **Number 10** 10 Downing Street, the address of the British Prime Minister in London – [14] **Bowler hat** *die Melone* – [15] **Laurel and Hardy,** Stan Laurel (1890 – 1965), Oliver Hardy (1892 – 1957), *Dick und Doof,* a comedy double act during the early Hollywood era – [16] **a stiff upper lip** (*idm.*) to keep calm and hide your feelings when you are in pain or in a difficult situation – [17] **Guy Fawkes** (1570 – 1606) a member of a group of English Catholics who planned the Gunfire Plot of 1605 – [18] **Margaret Thatcher** (1925 – 2013) Prime Minister of the UK (1979 – 1990) and Leader of the Conservative Party – [19] **Britannia** personification of Great Britain – [20] **Lord Sugar** (*1947) an English business magnate – [21] **CHAV** [tʃæv](*sl., derogatory*) a young lower-class person who displays brash and loutish behaviour and wears real or imitation designer clothes – [22] **Council Estates** *Siedlung mit Sozialwohnungen* – [23] **patrony** here: the act of patronizing one's peers

ANALYSIS

2. After a **second reading**, examine and analyse the choice of words and the use of positive and/or negative emotive words. What do they reveal about each person's stance on Britain's culture and tradition?

→ Focus on Skills, Analysis of a Non-Fictional Text, p. 405

3. Compare your findings from tasks 1 and 2 to your results from the awareness task – which similarities and differences in explaining "Britishness/Being British" can you detect? Complete the grid below.

external view (*your* findings)	internal view
● …	● a happy race of man
● …	● …

4. Take a closer look at clichés or stereotypes that
   a) the letter writers use themselves and
   b) you associated with Britishness in the awareness task.
Discuss possible similarities and differences in class.

Info »

cliché
a phrase or an idea that has been used so often that it no longer has much meaning and is not interesting

stereotype
an idea that many people have of a particular person or thing, but which is often not true in reality

The terms are often used as synonyms.

ACTIVITIES

5. Do you think that people see their home country more clearly when they are abroad – or are they blinded by nostalgic feelings? Give a comment.

6. For a long time, Germans were unable to express their national identity – "waving the flag" in particular was associated with Nazism and right-wing politics.
This changed in 2006, when Germany hosted the world football championship during the so-called *Sommermärchen* and showed itself to be a hospitable, open-minded and modern nation. And again, in 2014, the Germans celebrated the football championship as a "festival of black, red and gold" and have obviously become a more "relaxed nation" when it comes to showing national pride and cheering for their team.
Looking at the matter of "national pride" and "national identity" from a German perspective, do you think there is a German equivalent to "Britishness" – something like "Germanness"? Where do you consider the border to be between "healthy national pride" and a fascist way of thinking?
Discuss in class.

Tips on vocab »

national pride ■ to be proud of one's nationality ■ national consciousness ■ national feeling/sentiment ■ national anthem (*Nationalhymne*) ■ nationality ■ patriot/patriotic/patriotism ■ patriotically-minded ■ to sound patriotic

Webcode
SNG-40235-005 @ **7.** Do a project on the various facets and aspects of "Being British" using the links provided on the webcode. You might focus on British contributions to science, culture, economy, famous British inventions, etc. You can either prepare a presentation or compile a "Being British" homepage on the topic.
→ Focus on Skills, Presentations, p. 419
→ Focus on Facts, Landmarks in British History, p. 102

8. Prepare a presentation on "British-ness" based on the two-part BBC documentary provided on the web-code. The documentary presents a variety of different people and perspectives on the disputed topic of Britishness and national pride. Additionally, compile a brief handout for your classmates in which you outline the most relevant information given in the documentary.

→ Focus on Skills, Presentations, p. 419
→ Focus on Skills, Writing a Handout, p. 425

Info »»

On 5 July 2005, four Islamist men detonated bombs in the London Underground and on a bus, killing 52 civilians and injuring more than 700 people, which reignited a heated national debate on the potential danger radical Muslims pose on British society.
Against that background, the Chancellor of the Exchequer (*Finanz-minister*), Gordon Brown, gave a speech in 2006 in which he pro-moted a "modern patriotism" and the integration of diverse cultures into British society. Thus, he intended to fight Islamophobia (*Anti-Islamismus*) and to diminish the growing influence of right-wing parties in the U.K.
He suggested that Britain have a national day to celebrate its national identity and Britons should embrace the Union Flag as a symbol of unity, liberty, fairness and responsibility. Brown hoped to reclaim the flag from the right-wing British National Party (BNP), which in contrast used the flag as a symbol of racial division.

Stephen Castle

Sadiq Khan Elected in London, Becoming Its First Muslim Mayor

AWARENESS »»»»»»»

 Step 1: Pair up with a partner and research on the Internet what a mayor's duties, responsibilities and tasks are.

Step 2: Collect and exchange your ideas about the characteristics, professional qualifications and personal skills a mayor should have in order to
- address the needs of various social groups in the community/city,
- be a good contact person for (local) businesses and companies,
- manage the many areas of administrative work.

In a Europe struggling with a rise in Islamophobia, riven[1] by debates about the flood of Syrian migrants and on edge[2] over religious, ethnic and cultural dis-putes, London has elected its first Muslim mayor.
5 Sadiq Khan – Labour Party leader, a former human rights lawyer and a son of a bus driver from Pakistan – was declared the winner after a protracted[3] count that extended into Saturday. He will be the first Muslim to lead Britain's capital.
10 The victory also makes him one of the most prominent Muslim politicians in the West.
London is hardly representative of Britain: About a quarter of its residents are foreign-born, and one-eighth are Muslim. And Mr. Khan is not the first Mus-
15 lim to hold prominent office in Europe: Rotterdam, in the Netherlands, has had a Muslim mayor since 2009,

and Sajid Javid is the British secretary of state for busi-ness.
Nonetheless, Mr. Khan, 45, won a striking victory after a campaign dominated by anxieties over religion and 20

---

[1] **riven** violently divided – [2] **to be on edge** to be nervous, excited or bad-tempered – [3] **protracted** lasting for a long time or made to last longer than necessary

ethnicity. Britain has not sustained[4] a large-scale terrorist attack since 2005, and its Muslim population, in contrast to France, is considered well integrated. But an estimated 800 people have left Britain to fight for or support the Islamic State. Dozens of assaults on British Muslims were reported after the Paris terrorist attacks in November.

The Conservative candidate, Zac Goldsmith, attacked Mr. Khan's past advocacy[5] for criminal defendants, including his opposition to the extradition[6] of a man who was later convicted in the United States of supporting terrorism. Mr. Goldsmith said Mr. Khan had given "oxygen and cover" to extremists. When the Conservative prime minister, David Cameron, repeated those assertions[7] in Parliament, he was accused of racism.

Mr. Khan defended his work as a human rights lawyer, and has said he hoped Donald J. Trump – the presumptive[8] Republican presidential candidate who has called for barring Muslims from entering the United States – "loses badly."

Mr. Khan's victory was also his party's biggest boost in a series of elections on Thursday in which Labour further lost its grip on Scotland, once a stronghold[9], and clung[10], in some cases just barely, to seats in England and Wales.

Mr. Khan won with 56.8 percent of the vote, versus 43.2 percent for Mr. Goldsmith, according to London's election body. The results were not final until Saturday morning because in London's electoral system voters are allowed a first and second preference, and Mr. Khan did not win an outright majority in the first round.

In his acceptance speech, Mr. Khan said that the mayoral election "was not without controversy" and added that he was "proud that London has today chosen hope over fear and unity over division."

"I hope that we will never be offered such a stark choice again. Fear does not make us safer, it only makes us weaker and the politics of fear is simply not welcome in our city."

Mr. Khan's campaign focused on bread-and-butter issues like the cost of housing and transportation. He drew strong support from labor unions and kept a careful distance from his party's leader, Jeremy Corbyn, a socialist who has an ardent[11] base among young voters but faces heavy resistance among fellow Labour lawmakers.

In the past week, the Labour Party was distracted[12] by a dispute over anti-Semitism that led to the suspension[13] of a lawmaker, Naseem Shah, and a former London mayor, Ken Livingstone.

Mr. Khan argued that, as an observant Muslim, he was well placed to tackle extremism. "I'm a Londoner, I'm European, I'm British, I'm English, I'm of Islamic faith, of Asian origin, of Pakistani heritage, a dad, a husband," he said in a recent interview with The New York Times. The fifth of eight children, Mr. Khan was born in Tooting, South London, to recent immigrants from Pakistan, and grew up in a public-housing project. His father drove a bus, and his mother was a seamstress[14].

Elected to Parliament in 2005, Mr. Khan was appointed a junior minister for communities in 2008, and minister for transport in 2009 under the last Labour prime minister, Gordon Brown. Although he was not one of the highest-ranking ministers, he became the first Muslim to attend cabinet meetings regularly and was admitted to the Privy Council[15], a largely ceremonial body in which induction normally requires taking an oath to the queen.

"The palace called me and said, 'What type of Bible do you want to swear on?'" Mr. Khan told the magazine The New Statesman. "When I said the Quran, they said, 'We haven't got one.' So I took one with me."

As London's mayor, he will have significant power over transportation and planning – as well as responsibilities for the police, civil defense and fire services – in a city with an acute shortage of affordable homes and a creaking[16], overcrowded mass transit network.

Mr. Khan will succeed Boris Johnson, a Conservative who has held the post since 2008 and is a leading figure in the campaign for Britain's departure from the European Union. That vote will take place on June 23 [2016]. Mr. Johnson is seen as a possible successor to Mr. Cameron as leader of the Conservatives, particularly if Britain votes to leave; Mr. Cameron is campaigning for Britain to remain.

Within Britain, the news of the collapse of the Labour Party in Scotland was almost as big as Mr. Khan's victory.

---

[4] **to sustain sth.** *(fml.)* to experience something bad – [5] **advocacy** the act of publicly supporting an idea, development or way of doing sth. – [6] **extradition** the return of sb. accused of a crime to the country where the crime was committed – [7] **assertion** a statement that you strongly believe is true – [8] **presumptive** *mutmaßlich* – [9] **stronghold** *Festung, Bollwerk* – [10] **cling** (clung, clung) *sich an jdn./etw. klammern* – [11] **ardent** *leidenschaftlich, inbrünstig* – [12] **distracted** *abgelenkt* – [13] **suspension** a punishment in which a person is temporarily not allowed to work; *Suspendierung* – [14] **seamstress** *Näherin, Schneiderin* – [15] **Privy Council** [ˌprɪvi ˈkaʊnsəl] in the U.K., a group of people of high ranks in politics who sometimes advise the king or queen but who have little power – [16] **to creak** *quietschen*

110 The Scottish National Party won its third straight victory in the Scottish Parliament – a triumph that its leader, Nicola Sturgeon, called historic, even though the party narrowly lost its majority. The Labour Party fell to a humiliating third place, behind the Conservatives, who won seats in part by appealing to Scots op- posed to independence. Scots rejected independence in 115 a 2014 referendum, but there is speculation that a new referendum could be called, particularly if Britain leaves the European Union.

http://www.nytimes.com/2016/05/07/world/europe/britain-election-results.html?_r=0, 6 May 2016 [07.07.2016]

COMPREHENSION

1. Complete the following sentence with evidence from the text:
   Sadiq Khan, London's new mayor, has been a controversial mayoral candidate because …

2. Give examples from the text that
   - describe London's special/exceptional status,
   - reveal London's and Britain's ongoing controversy about Islamophobia and Muslims,
   - prove Mr Khan's suitability for the job,
   - refer to the difficult political situation Britain finds itself in.

 3. Team up with a partner and, in a paired reading activity, do the assignments below. After each step, exchange and crosscheck your results and make corrections and additions if necessary.

Tips on vocab »»

> **to be humbled** here: to be honoured ■ **council estate** an area with low-income houses built by a local council ■ **to thrive** to grow, develop or be successful ■ **commute** a regular journey between work and home ■ **to afford sth.** to be able to buy or do sth. because you have enough money or time ■ **stark** here: unpleasant

 Step 1: In a **first listening**, specify Khan's words and phrases that underline the inaugural and honorary character of the speech.
→ Focus on Skills, Listening Comprehension, p. 394

 Tip: In order to get a better impression of Khan's performance, use the links provided on the webcode and watch the speech.

Webcode SNG-40235-006

Step 2: In a **second listening**, take notes on what Khan states about
- his personal/family background,
- his electorate/voters,
- the city of London,
- his understanding of politics,
- his future plans as Mayor of London.

ANALYSIS

4. Examine the style of the *New York Times* article and determine what kind of text it is.
   → Focus on Facts, Basic Types of Non-Fictional Texts, p. 396

5. **Listen** to Sadiq Khan's mayoral acceptance speech **again** and examine his abilities as a speaker. Which specific rhetorical devices does he use to appeal to his listeners?
   → Focus on Skills, Analysis of a Political Speech, p. 407

ACTIVITIES

6. Sadiq Khan made a promise throughout his campaign which he confirmed after his election: "I promise to always be a mayor for all Londoners".

Discuss whether or not this is a realistic promise, given the controversy during Khan's election campaign and the ongoing discussion about Islamophobia and religious and cultural conflict in connection with refugees.
→ Focus on Language, Conversation and Discussion, p. 413

Huge Survey[1] Reveals Seven Social Classes in UK

AWARENESS

Look at the cartoon below and describe the people's outward appearance and behaviour. What "social classes" do you think these people belong to? Give reasons for your assumptions.

Step 1: Previously, the traditional categories for distinguishing social groups were working, middle and upper class. Together with a partner, collect ideas about possible social, economic and cultural characteristics that go along with the three social classes.

Step 2: As the headline of the article suggests, in addition to the three previous social classes, four "new" social classes have been revealed in a recent survey conducted[2] by the BBC. Speculate about these "new" social classes and about social, economic and cultural markers that identify them.

Tips on vocab

first class: to wear a bowler (hat) ■ to look dolled up (*aufgedonnert*) ■ teased (*toupiert*) hair ■ fur collar (*Pelzkragen*) ■ to look snobby/snobbish/uppish (*hochnäsig*)

economy class: backpacker ■ (traveling) salesman ■ shirt-sleeved (*hemdsärmelig*)

no class: drops of sweat ■ to be petrified of sb./sth. (*panische Angst haben vor jdm./etw.*) ■ to pick one's nose ■ to fart (*furzen*) ■ (to suffer from) flatulence (*an Blähungen leiden*) ■ to belch/to burp (*rülpsen*) ■ in disgust (*angewidert*)

People in the UK now fit into seven social classes, a major survey conducted by the BBC suggests.

It says the traditional categories of working, middle and upper class are outdated[3], fitting 39 % of people.

5 It found a new model of seven social classes ranging from the elite at the top to a "precariat[4]" – the poor, precarious[5] proletariat – at the bottom.

More than 161,000 people took part in the Great British Class Survey, the largest study of class in the UK.

Class has traditionally been defined by occupation[6], 10 wealth and education. But this research argues that this is too simplistic[7], suggesting that class has three dimensions – economic, social and cultural.

---

[1] **survey** Umfrage, Erhebung – [2] **to conduct sth.** etw. durchführen – [3] **outdated** no longer useful because of being old-fashioned –
[4] **precariat** the poor – [5] **precarious** not safe or certain, dangerous – [6] **occupation** job or profession – [7] **simplistic** (*disapproving*) making a situation or problem seem less difficult or complicated than it really is

The BBC Lab UK study measured economic capital – income, savings, house value – and social capital – the number and status of people someone knows.

The study also measured cultural capital, defined as the extent and nature of cultural interests and activities. The new classes are defined as:

- **Elite**[8]: the most privileged group in the UK, distinct from[9] the other six classes through its wealth. This group has the highest levels of all three capitals.
- **Established middle class:** the second wealthiest, scoring[10] highly on all three capitals. The largest and most gregarious[11] group, scoring second highest for cultural capital.
- **Technical middle class:** a small, distinctive[12] new class group which is prosperous[13] but scores low for social and cultural capital. Distinguished[14] by its social isolation and cultural apathy[15].
- **New affluent[16] workers:** a young class group which is socially and culturally active, with middling levels of economic capital.
- **Traditional working class:** scores low on all forms of capital, but is not completely deprived[17]. Its members have reasonably high house values, explained by this group having the oldest average age at 66.
- **Emergent[18] service workers:** a new, young, urban group which is relatively poor but has high social and cultural capital.

- **Precariat, or precarious proletariat:** the poorest, most deprived class, scoring low for social and cultural capital.

The researchers said while the elite group had been identified before, this is the first time it had been placed within a wider analysis of the class structure, as it was normally put together with professionals and managers.

At the opposite extreme they said the precariat, the poorest and most deprived grouping, made up 15% of the population.

The sociologists[19] said these two groups at the extremes of the class system had been missed in conventional approaches[20] to class analysis, which have focused on the middle and working classes. [...]

The researchers also found the established middle class made up 25% of the population and was the largest of all the class groups, with the traditional working class now only making up 14% of the population.

They say the new affluent workers and emergent service workers appear to be the children of the "traditional working class," which they say has been fragmented by de-industrialisation, mass unemployment, immigration and the restructuring of urban space.

www.bbc.com/news/uk-22007058, 3 April 2013 [23.07.2014]

COMPREHENSION

1. In a **first reading**, **skim** the article and jot down five aspects that the researchers found that had changed over time.

2. **Scan** the text in a **second reading**, looking for information about
   - what has changed in the definition of a social class,
   - which social classes have been determined,
   - new elements in the ranking system of society,
   - possible reasons for these social changes.

ANALYSIS

3. Have a look at the diagrams on p. 61 and relate the markers and characteristics given there to the information revealed in the text. Which additional information is given?

[8] **elite** [eɪˈliːt] – [9] **distinct from** clearly different or of a different kind – [10] **to score** to get points – [11] **gregarious** [grɪˈɡeərɪəs] sociable; gesellig – [12] **distinctive** characteristic – [13] **prosperous** rich – [14] **distinguished** very successful and admired by other people – [15] **apathy** [ˈæpəθi] the feeling of not being interested in things in general – [16] **affluent** (fml.) wealthy – [17] **deprived** sozial benachteiligt – [18] **emergent** aufsteigend – [19] **sociologist** [ˌsəʊsiˈɒlədʒɪst] – [20] **approach** Vorgehensweise, Denkansatz

4. Do further research on the BBC survey using the *Daily Mail* link provided on the webcode and compile a pie chart that gives an overview of the social classes and includes the relevant statistical information. Present your diagrams in class and discuss your various results.

→ Focus on Skills, Analysis of Statistical Data, p. 408

 5. Examine the choice of words used to categorize each of the social classes and compare them to the older expressions. Explain the respective implications.

social group	choice of words	intended meaning
elite	● wealthiest, most privileged ● …	→ superlatives; top rank in society
established middle class	● …	→ …
technical middle class	● …	→ …
new affluent workers	● …	
traditional working class	● traditional ● low on capital ● …	→ stagnation → …
emergent service workers	● …	
precariat (precarious proletariat)	● …	

ACTIVITIES

6. The text indicates that the elite group has traditionally been associated with "professionals and managers" and that the "traditional working class" has declined to only 14 % of the population.

Against the background of the information given on the seven social classes and their characteristics, which professions or jobs would you assign to the respective classes? How much annual income do you think the different social classes have? Discuss in class.

Info ⟫⟫

- In Germany, somebody who earns less than 60 % of the average income (= less than 940 euros a month) is considered poor.
- About 15 % of the German population is close to being defined as poor.
- In Germany, about 5.5 % of the population is defined as "working poor", i. e. people who have an extremely low-paying job.
- Examples: 3 % of the German population earn more than 4,500 euros per month; 14 % earn 2,100 – 2,600 euros per month; 19 % earn 901 – 1,300 euros per month and 6 % earn less than 500 euros per month.
- In the US, being poor is defined as
  - single person: earning less than $11,490 per year,
  - a family of four: earning less than $23,550 per year.

GRAMMAR / LANGUAGE

7. Reactivate your knowledge and **vocabulary** and collect words, expressions and phrases in connection with the topics
- social class,
- income,
- work/profession,
- culture.

Collect relevant words from the text and use your dictionary for further help. Arrange your findings in clusters, then compare your results with a partner.

1

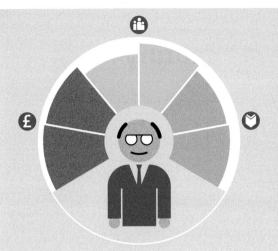

Elite

Percentage of population
6%

Average age
57

This is the wealthiest and most privileged group in the UK:

▶ They are the UK's biggest earners

▶ They score highest for social, cultural and economic factors

▶ Many went to private school and elite universities – 24% of people in this group were privately educated, far more than in any other class group

▶ This class is most likely to be found in London and the home counties

▶ This group is exclusive and very hard to join, most come from very privileged backgrounds

▶ 97% of people in this group own their own home

2

Technical middle class

Percentage of population
6%

Average age
52

This is a small, distinctive and prosperous new class group:

▶ People in this group tend to mix socially with people similar to themselves

▶ They prefer emerging culture such as using social media to highbrow culture such as listening to classical music

▶ Many people in this group work in research science and technical occupations

▶ They tend to live in suburban locations, often in the south east of England

▶ They come from largely middle class backgrounds

3

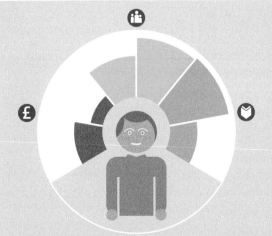

New affluent workers

Percentage of population
15%

Average age
44

This class group is sociable, has lots of cultural interests and sits in the middle of all the groups in terms of wealth:

▶ This youthful class group is economically secure without being well off

▶ These people have high scores for emerging culture, such as watching sport, going to gigs and using social media

▶ They do not tend to participate in highbrow culture, such as classical music and theatre

▶ People in this group are likely to come from a working class background

▶ Many people in this group live in old manufacturing centres of the UK in the Midlands and North West

Economic capital	Social capital	Cultural capital
The purple wedges show the economic "capital" score. The first wedge represents one's income and the second wedge shows the combination of one's savings and property value.	The orange wedges show the social "capital" score, based on the professions of the people one knows socially. The first wedge indicates the average social status of the people one socialises with, while the second shows the number of different occupations within one's social group.	The first green wedge shows the emerging cultural "capital" score and the second shows the "highbrow" cultural capital score. Emerging cultural activities include playing sport and going to gigs. Highbrow cultural activities include listening to classical music and going to the theatre.

Data: BBC

Splendid Isolation? – The U.K.'s Position in the 21st Century

Mark Mardell

Brexit: The Story of an Island Apart

AWARENESS

Look at the cartoon below, which was published in a German newspaper four days after the EU referendum, and describe it in detail.

What kind of "before and after" situation is depicted and what gruesome scenario does the cartoon hint at?

Tips on vocab

left side: to walk off a cliff ▪ blue skies ▪ to live/walk around in cloud cuckoo land ▪ to be a Johnny Head-in-the-Air *(Hans Guck-in-die-Luft)* ▪ to wear a grey business suit/a bowler hat/a moustache ▪ blindfold glasses ▪ a sign with the EU flag/logo

right side: to suddenly fall ▪ bulging eyes ▪ to fly off sb.'s head ▪ to tense up in fear ▪ to be torn apart ▪ to be torn in two ▪ the English flag (St George's Cross) ▪ the Scottish flag (St Andrew's Cross) ▪ flock of birds

COMPREHENSION

1. **Before reading:**

In the run-up to the EU referendum, the German media covered the possible Brexit scenario in detail, speculating about the outcome of the referendum and possible consequences.

The German political TV magazine *ARD Weltspiegel* visited and interviewed people from Cornwall *before* the referendum and people from Stoke-on-Trent *afterwards* and tried to capture the atmosphere and people's thoughts.

Webcode
SNG-40235-008 @

Step 1: In a group puzzle activity, divide the class into six groups. There are two documentaries provided on the webcode; three groups work with one documentary, three with the other.

Tip: Use the Tips on vocab boxes and/or your dictionary to mediate the statements and information into English. Keep your notes because you will need them later on (cf. task no. 7).

M **Step 2:** Watch the respective documentary and take notes in English on the aspects listed below.

Großbritannien: Das Referendum (19 June 2016)

- the social consequences of the Brexit campaign
- the position and problems of Cornwall's fishermen
- money and subsidization from Brussels
- people's stubbornness and (hurt) pride
- unforeseeable consequences for the younger generation

Tips on vocab »»»

cheesy romantic films ■ hedge ■ outer tip ■ sb.'s nerves are on edge ■ to go down the drain ■ xenophobia ■ core English ■ in the heat of the battle ■ fleet ■ to blame sb. ■ fishing quota ■ to the highest bidder ■ non-seafaring people ■ domestic market ■ cooling system ■ boardwalk ■ to hold sway ■ pension ■ vocational school ■ to leave sb. behind ■ to put sb. down as a scapegoat ■ stubbornness ■ tin mine ■ downhill ■ structural fund ■ to beat the drum for sb./sth. ■ stupid fool ■ to be subsidized ■ uncertainty ■ to snatch sth. away from sb. ■ nostalgia ■ to keep one's fingers crossed for sb. ■ to shoulder sth. ■ ballot box

Großbritannien: Katerstimmung auf der Insel (3 July 2016)

- the economic situation of the citizens of Stoke-on-Trent
- reasons for Stoke-on-Trent's economic decline
- Sajid Hashni's situation
- Islamophobia in Stoke-on-Trent
- reasons why Stoke-on-Trent voted for Brexit
- Stoke-on-Trent and the government in London

Tips on vocab »»»

hangover ■ pottery industry ■ decline ■ window cleaner ■ right-wing populist ■ to complain ■ to ruin sth. ■ barber ■ beauty salon ■ discrepancy ■ neglect ■ cross-off list ■ welfare organization ■ the necessity for saving money ■ public service ■ austerity ■ scapegoat ■ to serve as sth. ■ dilapidated ■ housing estate ■ mob, attackers ■ for sb.'s benefit ■ to rebel against sb./sth. ■ slogan ■ to become entangled ■ to teach sb. a lesson ■ to be based on lies ■ government leaders

Step 3: After completing your notes, remix the groups and exchange your results.

1 Our little archipelago[1] of isles on the outer edges of a huge land mass has often thought of itself as rather special, even before it was the centre of an empire that changed the world.

As so often, Shakespeare put it best: "This precious stone set in the silver sea/ Which serves it in the office of a wall/ Or as a moat[2] defensive to a house,/ Against the envy of less happier lands,/ This blessed plot, this earth, this realm, this England."

It is that silver sea that helps define our relationship with the rest of Europe.

These isles have very rarely been in isolation from it, whether splendid or otherwise. How could it be, as one historian recently argued, when the Magna Carta was signed by French nobles and the Bill of Rights designed for a Dutch prince?

But it has always kept a beady[3] eye on other powers across the water.

It has been often concerned with stopping other European powers dominating the continent, playing one off against another.

But from that physical separation flows a psychological distance too.

2 As the BBC's first Europe editor, I spent a lot of time thinking about our tricky relationship. After all, in my previous incarnation[4] as a political journalist based at Westminster I had seen how some politicians' pro-

---

[1] **archipelago** an extensive group of islands – [2] **moat** *Festungsgraben* – [3] **beady** bright and keenly observant; *wachsam* – [4] **incarnation** here: profession

found[5] distaste[6] for the evolving project of the European Union had blown back into British politics with profound and startling[7] consequences.

I had watched as Margaret Thatcher's[8] attitude towards the EU's nascent[9] plans for a single currency, summed up by "no, no, no", had her own side bringing her down. It was the defenestration[10] of a prime minister deeply beloved by most of her party.

I had reported for Newsnight as John Major's[11] government was harried[12] and hamstrung[13] by those who rebelled against the Maastricht treaty[14]. Europe meant it could do nothing. Blair's[15] government was much friendlier, with any tensions buried by his own project. Now Europe has claimed another scalp, that of a man who told his party to stop banging on about it. It will be the thing that David Cameron is remembered for – banging on about Europe, and losing the argument.

Now I know the European Union is not Europe. But those who stress that are missing the point. No, it is not the same as European culture. No it is not a geographically exact expression. But there are only a couple of European countries who are "out", and firmly intend to stay out. All the others, or at least their leaders, want a share in this deeply political expression of a dream.

3 By the end of my time based in Brussels I was convinced that I had understood the key difference. To many in the UK being part of the EU was a hard-headed[16] economic relationship, about free markets, selling and buying stuff. It was a sort of second best, a consolation prize[17] after the loss of empire, but not one that had a similar place in patriots' hearts.

But for nearly all the other countries it was a refuge. It was a home they were constructing as a bulwark[18] against history, against horror.

Germany was fleeing its role in spreading death and destruction to every corner of the continent, fleeing its own political ambitions. France was running away from defeat and occupation, from humiliation and powerlessness.

So were many other countries. Greece, Portugal and Spain found refuge – in an imagined future – from the real past of right-wing dictatorships. The countries of the East were replacing communist tyranny with a new attempt to create peace and democracy.

The thought that war could once again ravage[19] a continent, so risible[20] to David Cameron's detractors[21], do not seem so funny to many on the continent.

For many Britons, World War Two was our finest hour, standing alone, and putting those Europeans to shame, withstanding Hitler and beating him. Some realised the Russians and the Americans helped a little bit too. But we were still better than the rest of the Quislings[22] and dictators.

The European Union, for all its bureaucracy, is a deeply romantic project, a desire to forge[23] something new, something different. A new relationship binding nation states in a way that will exorcise forever the ghosts of the inglorious past.

4 I sat in a cafe next to some fairly senior people who work in the commission in Brussels. They were despairing of Brexit, making desperate, rather hysterical jokes about it and the future in Britain. But then one by one they confessed when they got up on Friday morning, switched on the news, checked their phones, they cried. Few in the UK would say that if another country left the EU.

But the irritations of these dozen or so people of different nationalities, with the UK – comments about British pride, warm beer and arrogant politicians – underlined a more fundamental frustration with British attitudes.

These Spanish, and Swedes, a Belgian and a Hungarian, were all emoting[24] and swearing and arguing in English. One said (in French) "maybe we can all go back to speaking French now". She was shouted down – in English – "that will never happen. English is the language of the European Union now."

I remember Neil Kinnock[25] joking that the EU changed forever when the Swedes arrived and started saying "good morning" in the lift.

One might think that is trivial. But maybe it highlights something we rarely realise in our desire for hard power

---

[5] **profound** intense, very great – [6] **distaste** dislike, aversion – [7] **startling** surprising, astonishing, remarkable – [8] **Margaret Thatcher** (1925–2013) British politician, leader of the Conservative Party and prime minister (1979–1990) – [9] **nascent** ['næsnt] *aufkeimend* – [10] **defenestration** *(infml.)* the act of dismissing sb. from a position of power – [11] **John Major** (*1943) British politician, leader of the Conservative Party and prime minister (1990–1997) – [12] **harried** *bedrängt* – [13] **hamstrung** *handlungsunfähig gemacht* – [14] **Maastricht Treaty** (1992) treaty that created the European Union – [15] **Tony Blair** (*1953) British politician, leader of the Labour Party and prime minister (1997–2007) – [16] **hard-headed** *stur* – [17] **consolation prize** *Trostpreis* – [18] **bulwark** *Bollwerk* – [19] **to ravage** ['rævɪdʒ] to cause severe and extensive damage – [20] **risible** *lächerlich* – [21] **detractor** opponent, critic – [22] **Quisling** a person who collaborates with an enemy occupying force – [23] **to forge** *schmieden* – [24] **to emote** *dramatisieren* – [25] **Neil Kinnock** (*1942) British Labour Party politician

110 – the extent of our soft power. It also underscores a real frustration with the British that has been growing. Many in Europe think we've won. While readers of some British newspapers have been treated to stories of little Britain being bullied by the big commission, that is
115 not how you see it if you are, say, Portuguese or Latvian. Then you would see, time after time, Britain being given a special deal, treated with kid gloves[26] and washed with buckets[27] of soft soap. [...]

They say we've won. We won and turned Europe on to
120 a free-market, anti-statist, liberal economic agenda.
We won on enlargement – the unlovely word for our insistence that the EU couldn't wait, and had to rapidly take in the countries of the former communist block. Then there are those deals.
125 We are outside the Euro. Outside home affairs and justice rules. Outside the passport-free Schengen zone. David Cameron won a concession that we would be outside "ever closer union".

Now we want to be outside the whole shebang[28]. Don't
130 be surprised if the instinct of some is to make sure that we feel some discomfort[29] on our way out.

5 I realised something else during my time based in Brussels. The old caricature of those who were opposed to the EU was less and less true. They didn't base their
135 arguments on dislike of foreigners. They professed to love Europe's variety and embraced its language and culture. It was the organisation they disliked.

Many of the political elites were snobby about these opponents, and felt the questions they were raising
140 were illegitimate[30]. They didn't engage with the argument but swept it under the carpet, turned a blind eye and hoped they wouldn't be heard.

The Dutch and French rejected the constitution in a referendum, but it was politicians from the UK who
145 voiced the discontent some European voters felt.

What was once as rare in Europe as a dodo[31] riding on a unicorn is now commonplace. All over Europe there is deep suspicion of the European Union.

It took the financial crisis to turn these new Eurosceptics
150 tics into an alternative to the mainstream. But the very heart of their objection will not go away for the European Union – and it is difficult to see how it is solved.

It is their old joke playing on the root of the word "democracy" – that the EU can't be a democracy as it has
155 a "cracy" [rule] but not a "demos" [people].

6 Now, there is nothing either sacred or immutable[32] about the nation state or people's fellow feeling towards others. Roman citizens felt Roman, even while not being what we would call Italian, let alone from the
160 Eternal City.

During the Depression, as recorded by John Steinbeck[33] in *The Grapes of Wrath*, people living in one US state, California, resented the poor from another American state, Oklahoma, moving there to work. Even though
165 they were all Americans.

But it is undoubtedly true the UK's immigration debate and the Greek crisis are so heated because people don't feel the same connection, the same (often limited) desire to help people from other European nations, as
170 they do those they define as their own.

That, not red tape[34] or some ill-defined responsiveness[35], is the EU's central problem. It will have to start recognising it and wrestling with it rather than resenting[36] it and ignoring it, if it wants to survive.
175

Indeed our exit leaves the European Union with multiple headaches. The threat of other countries following suit is perhaps the main one.

But it is what it does to Britain's old ambition that is perhaps more intriguing[37]. It changes the balance of
180 power.

Germany will almost certainly end up paying more. They will no longer be able to rely on the UK joining them and the Finns and the Swedes and the Dutch to join their side in an economic argument.
185

A hefty[38] weight will soon be withdrawn from the balance. A straight North-South fight will become sharper.

Economic liberals may not like the result. But there is an even more central problem.
190

I thought it odd when Boris Johnson during the campaign was picked up for claiming that the EU wanted to fulfil Hitler's ambitions by other means. He was lam-

---

[26] **kid gloves** *Samthandschuhe* – [27] **bucket** *Eimer* – [28] **shebang** matter, operation – [29] **discomfort** worry – [30] **illegitimate** [ˌɪləˈdʒɪtəmət] illegal, unlawful – [31] **dodo** an extinct bird; *Dodo* – [32] **immutable** unchanging or unable to be changed – [33] **John Steinbeck** (1902–1968) American author; winner of the 1962 Nobel Prize in Literature – [34] **red tape** bureaucracy – [35] **responsiveness** the quality of reacting quickly and positively – [36] **to resent** to feel bitterness – [37] **intriguing** [ɪnˈtriːgɪŋ] fascinating – [38] **hefty** large and heavy – [39] **to lambaste sb.** to criticize sb. harshly

195 basted[39] for the sin of mentioning Hitler, but not tack-led on the central point he was making.

You could argue the very purpose of the EU is not to achieve continent-wide dictatorship from some Brussels bunker, but to prevent the domination of Europe by one power, namely Germany. Now modern Germany is 200 sane and sober, cautious of military adventure and brutal power, to a degree rarely seen in other nations. There is perhaps little we need fear.

But the euro crisis and the refugee crisis shows that German political might is powerfully resented. As its 205 past recedes[40] it will inevitably[41] act more openly in its own interests, less cloaked in an apparently altruistic[42] care for the whole continent. Britain may have to watch from the sidelines, across the Channel, powerless to intervene, or offer guidance, unless by megaphone.

We see ourselves as separate, and so we shall soon be 210 cut out of councils and commission that are still shaping a continent. Some in Brussels may reflect smugly[43] on how John of Gaunt's[44] speech in Richard II[45] concludes: "That England that was wont[46] to conquer others/Hath made a shameful conquest of itself." 215

http://www.bbc.com/news/magazine-36620426, 25 June 2016 [14.09.2016]

COMPREHENSION

2. In the magazine article, the author reflects on Britain's complex, complicated and even contradictory relationship with the European continent.

In a **paired reading** activity, read the text on your own and take notes on the questions below. After each paragraph, you and your partner summarize the paragraph together, crosscheck the notes you have taken and make corrections and/or additions if necessary.

1
- Point out Britain's special place/position within Europe.
- What are the consequences of being an island nation?

2
- Present the different Prime Ministers' attitudes towards the EU.
- Describe the difference between the EU and Europe.

3
- What was the function of the EU to Britain?
- What did the EU mean to the other European nations?
- How did the Britons view themselves after WWII?

4
- Describe people's reactions to the British exit.
- Outline what makes Britain a soft power.
- What were the special deals that Britain enjoyed – much to the frustration of the other EU nations?

5
- Outline the process of more and more European nations becoming Eurosceptic.
- What did (most) European nations embrace and adopt from the EU as a whole?

6
- Point out the reasons that make people feel
  a) united,
  b) disconnected from others.
- Describe the consequences of the Brexit with regard to
  a) the (future) balance of power within the EU,
  b) Germany's position and power,
  c) Britain's exclusion from European politics.

[40] **to recede** to move further away – [41] **inevitable** [ɪnˈevɪtəb(ə)l] certain to happen; unavoidable – [42] **altruistic** unselfish – [43] **smugly** eingebildet, selbstgefällig – [44] **John of Gaunt** (1340 – 1399) 1st Duke of Lancaster; member of the House of Plantagenet; ancestor of the House of Lancaster, incl. King Henry VI; Richard II's uncle – [45] **Richard II King of England** (1377 – 1399); history play by William Shakespeare (ca. 1595) – [46] **wont** (lit.) in the habit of doing sth.; accustomed to sth.

ANALYSIS

3. Examine the author's observations and remarks on Britain's relationship with the EU and illustrate how he juxtaposes the contradictions and controversies that have existed throughout British-European relationship.
   → Focus on Skills, Analysis of a Non-Fictional Text, p. 405

4. Analyse the author's choice of words and explain how it emphasizes the ambivalent relationship Britain has to continental Europe and the EU.
   → Focus on Skills, Analysis of a Non-Fictional Text, p. 405

 5. **Step 1:** Take a look at the article from the German daily newspaper *Express* (p. 68) and extract further information on the negative consequences of the Brexit, in addition to the information given in the BBC article.
   → Focus on Skills, Mediation, p. 412

 Step 2: Explain to what extent the information in the article and the bar chart matches the impression conveyed in the German TV documentary *Großbritannien: Katerstimmung auf der Insel* (pp. 62 f.).
 Use your notes from the before-reading task (Step 2, p. 63) and discuss the similarities and differences in class.

ACTIVITIES

Webcode SNG-40235-008 @ 6. Do a project on the British referendum and subsequent Brexit using the weblinks provided on the webcode.

 7. Based on the information you have collected in the previous tasks, prepare and act out a panel discussion in which you reflect on the different positions taken on the matter, e.g.
   - Eurosceptic Britons who feel deprived of their right to independently decide on national matters
   - Euro-friendly Britons who primarily consider themselves to be European and who are concerned about being isolated economically and politically
   - young Britons who do not want to lose touch with continental Europe
   - old Britons who fear being overrun by immigrants and being economically disadvantaged by the EU
   - etc.
   → Focus on Language, Conversation and Discussion, p. 413

GRAMMAR / LANGUAGE

8. Against the different views taken on the Brexit, formulate different types of conditional sentences to express people's feelings and concerns.
   Example:
   - If older Britons had had less nationalistic views, the referendum would have had a different result. (type III)
   - If politicians do not listen to people's concerns and fears more carefully, the societal division of Britain will grow even more. (type I)

Zerrissenes Land: Die Alten stimmten für den Brexit, die Jungen sind entsetzt[1]

„Ich bin am Boden zerstört[2]", sagt die 51-jährige Londonerin Anne-Marie Williams angesichts[3] der Mehrheit für den Brexit. „Ich habe richtig Bauchschmerzen[4]."

Das Ergebnis der Volksabstimmung sei eine Katastophe. Abgesehen von den
5 wirtschaftlichen Folgen tut es ihr vor allem um ihre Kinder leid. „Meine Kinder haben weniger Möglichkeiten in der Zukunft. Sie werden weniger frei reisen und studieren können. Und wofür eigentlich? Da haben alte Leute über die Zukunft junger Menschen entschieden, das ist nicht fair", empört[5] sie sich.

10 In der Wählergruppe[6] er 65-Jährigen und Älteren stimmten 58 Prozent für den Austritt aus der EU, so viele wie in keiner anderen Altersgruppe. Bei den 18-24-Jährigen waren es dagegen nur 33 Prozent.

Pop-Sängerin Lily Allen (31) brachte die Stimmung in ihrer Generation drastisch auf den Punkt[7]: „Für uns ist die Sache richtig scheiße gelaufen[8]."
15 Es geht ein tiefer Riss[9] durch die britische Gesellschaft: Die jungen, gebildeten Menschen in den Städten hatten sich mit übergroßer[10] Mehrheit für die EU ausgesprochen.

Jetzt ist die Wut groß auf die Alten, eher Ungebildeten[11] auf dem Land, die für den Brexit waren. Schon 100,000 Menschen unterzeichneten gestern eine Pe-
20 tition. Darin wird angesichts des knappen[12] Siegs der Brexit-Befürworter[13] eine neue, zweite Volksabstimmung gefordert.

Express, 25 June 2016, p. 4

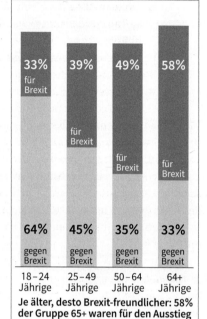

33% für Brexit	**39%** für Brexit	**49%** für Brexit	**58%** für Brexit
64% gegen Brexit	**45%** gegen Brexit	**35%** gegen Brexit	**33%** gegen Brexit
18–24 Jährige	25–49 Jährige	50–64 Jährige	64+ Jährige

Je älter, desto Brexit-freundlicher: 58% der Gruppe 65+ waren für den Ausstieg

Daten: YouGov

Boris Johnson

I Cannot Stress Too Much That Britain Is Part of Europe – And Always Will Be

AWARENESS

Boris Johnson (*1964), a British politician and member of the Conservative Party, was Mayor of London from 2008 until 2016 and has been Secretary of State for Foreign and Commonwealth Affairs since July 2016. He is a controversial figure in British politics. On the one hand, he has been praised for his wit and humour; on the other hand, he has been criticized for being elitist, cynical, lazy, dishonest, racist, and using xenophobic and homophobic language. In February 2016, Johnson endorsed the *VoteLeave* campaign for the U.K.'s EU membership referendum and became one of the most prominent figures in the Brexit discussion. After Britain's Brexit vote, Johnson was criticized for tearing apart the Conservative Party and for his role in the U.K.'s constitutional crisis.

Reflect and speculate on the headline of Johnson's article, published three days after the Brexit vote. What might have been Johnson's reason for writing the article?

---

[1] shocked – [2] devastated – [3] in view of – [4] makes me sick to my stomach – [5] to be up in arms against sb./sth. – [6] voting bloc – [7] to put sth. in a nutshell – [8] things went terribly wrong – [9] rift – [10] gigantic – [11] uneducated – [12] tight – [13] proponent, advocate

COMPREHENSION

1. While reading the article, finish the following statements using information from the text.
   a) The EU referendum was divisive for the U.K. because …
   b) People voted *Leave* because …
   c) The negative consequences are greatly overdone because …
   d) Despite the Brexit, Britain and British people will be able to …
   e) There is big cause for optimism because …

This EU referendum has been the most extraordinary political event of our lifetime. Never in our history have so many people been asked to decide a big question about the nation's future. Never have so many thought so deeply, or wrestled so hard with their consciences, in an effort to come up with the right answer.

It has been a grueling[1] campaign in which we have seen divisions between family and friends and colleagues – sometimes entirely amicable[2], sometimes, alas[3], less so. In the end, there was a clear result. More than 17 million people voted to leave the EU – more than have ever assented[4] to any proposition[5] in our democratic history. Some now cast doubt on their motives, or even on their understanding of what was at stake[6].

It is said that those who voted Leave were mainly driven by anxieties about immigration. I do not believe that is so. After meeting thousands of people in the course of the campaign, I can tell you that the number one issue was control – a sense that British democracy was being undermined by the EU system, and that we should restore to the people that vital power: to kick out their rulers at elections, and to choose new ones. I believe that millions of people who voted Leave were also inspired by the belief that Britain is a great country, and that outside the job-destroying coils[7] of EU bureaucracy we can survive and thrive[8] as never before. I think that they are right in their analysis, and right in their choice. And yet we who agreed with this majority verdict[9] must accept that it was not entirely overwhelming.

There were more than 16 million who wanted to remain. They are our neighbours, brothers and sisters who did what they passionately believe was right. In a democracy majorities may decide but everyone is of equal value. We who are part of this narrow majority must do everything we can to reassure the Remainers. We must reach out, we must heal, we must build bridges – because it is clear that some have feelings of dismay[10], and of loss, and confusion.

I believe that this climate of apprehension is understandable, given what people were told during the campaign, but based on a profound misunderstanding about what has really taken place. At home and abroad, the negative consequences are being wildly overdone, and the upside is being ignored. The stock market is way above its level of last autumn; the pound remains higher than it was in 2013 and 2014.

The economy is in good hands. Most sensible people can see that Bank of England governor Mark Carney has done a superb job – and now that the referendum is over, he will be able to continue his work without being in the political firing-line. Thanks in large part to the reforms put in place by David Cameron and George Osborne, the fundamentals of the UK economy are outstandingly strong – a dynamic and outward-looking economy with an ever-improving skills base, and with a big lead in some of the key growth sectors of the 21st century.

We should be incredibly proud and positive about the UK, and what it can now achieve. And we will achieve those things together, with all four nations united. We had one Scotland referendum in 2014, and I do not detect any real appetite to have another one soon; and it goes without saying that we are much better together in forging[11] a new and better relationship with the EU – based on free trade and partnership, rather than a federal system.

I cannot stress too much that Britain is part of Europe, and always will be. There will still be intense and intensifying European cooperation and partnership in a huge number of fields: the arts, the sciences, the universities, and on improving the environment. EU citizens living in this country will have their rights fully protected, and the same goes for British citizens living in the EU.

---

[1] **grueling** extremely tiring and difficult – [2] **amicable** [ˈæmɪkəbəl] *einvernehmlich* – [3] **alas** used to express sadness or feeling sorry about sth. – [4] **to assent to sth.** *(fml.)* to agree or give official approval to sth. – [5] **proposition** idea or opinion – [6] **to be at stake** *auf dem Spiel stehen* – [7] **coils** here: *Windungen; Hürden* – [8] **to thrive** to grow, develop or be successful – [9] **verdict** an opinion or decision made after judging the facts that are given – [10] **dismay** a feeling of unhappiness and disappointment – [11] **to forge** *schmieden*

75 British people will still be able to go and work in the EU; to live; to travel; to study; to buy homes and to settle down. As the German equivalent of the CBI[12] – the BDI[13] – has very sensibly reminded us, there will continue to be free trade, and access to the single market.

80 Britain is and always will be a great European power, offering top-table[14] opinions and giving leadership on everything from foreign policy to defence to counter-terrorism and intelligence-sharing[15] – all the things we need to do together to make our world safer.

85 The only change – and it will not come in any great rush – is that the UK will extricate[16] itself from the EU's extraordinary and opaque[17] system of legislation: the vast and growing corpus of law enacted by a European Court of Justice from which there can be no appeal.

90 This will bring not threats, but golden opportunities for this country – to pass laws and set taxes according to the needs of the UK.

Yes, the Government will be able to take back democratic control of immigration policy, with a balanced

95 and humane points-based system to suit the needs of business and industry. Yes, there will be a substantial sum of money which we will no longer send to Brussels, but which could be used on priorities such as the NHS[18]. Yes, we will be able to do free trade deals with the growth economies of the world in a way that is cur- 100 rently forbidden.

There is every cause for optimism; a Britain rebooted, reset, renewed and able to engage with the whole world. This was a seismic[19] campaign whose lessons must be learnt by politicians at home and abroad. We 105 heard the voices of millions of the forgotten people, who have seen no real increase in their incomes, while FTSE-100[20] chiefs now earn 150 times the average pay of their employees. We must pursue actively the one-nation policies that are among David Cameron's fine 110 legacy, such as his campaigns on the Living Wage and Life Chances. There is no doubt that many were speaking up for themselves.

But they were also speaking up for democracy, and the verdict of history will be that the British people got it 115 right.

http://www.telegraph.co.uk/news/2016/06/26/i-cannot-stress-too-much-that-britain-is-part-of-europe--and-alw/?utm_source=dlvr.it&utm_medium=twitter, 26 June 2016 [14.09.2016]

COMPREHENSION

2. After **reading** the article **a second time**, subdivide the text into paragraphs according to topic and find a suitable headline for each paragraph using your own words.

3. Step 1: Read the statements made by Britons who voted to leave the EU on pp. 72 ff.

Step 2: To find out more about people's motivation, sort the reasons given and complete the grid below.

political stability	social security	strong economy	suitable living standard	growth of production/ industry
			• … the housing situation … is abysmal … (l. 80)	
social equity	**employment of citizens**	**social unity**	**job security**	**freedom & independence**
	• The bosses love foreign workers (l. 75)			
cultural identity & acceptance	**political reform & renewal**	**lack of democracy**	**incompetent politicians**	
		• … feel my voice is heard and can influence change (ll. 47 f.)		

[12] **CBI** the UK's premier business organization, providing a voice for firms at a regional, national and international level to policymakers –
[13] **BDI** (abbr.) Bundesverband der Deutschen Industrie – [14] **top-table** the table at a formal meal where the most important people sit –
[15] **intelligence-sharing** Nutzen der selben Geheimdienste – [16] **to extricate** (fml.) to remove sth. or set sth. free with difficulty – [17] **opaque** [əʊˈpeɪk] sth. that is difficult to understand – [18] **NHS** [ˌeneɪtʃˈes] (abbr.) National Health Service; the U.K.'s publicly funded health care system – [19] **seismic** [ˈsaɪzmɪk] having very great and damaging effects – [20] **FTSE-100** (abbr.) Financial Times Stock Exchange 100 Index; a share index of the 100 companies listed on the London Stock Exchange with the highest market capitalization

ANALYSIS

 4. Analyse Boris Johnson's persuasive strategies by examining
a) his line of argument*,
b) his choice of words and
c) rhetorical devices and how they help to convey his message to the readers.
→ Focus on Skills, Analysis of a Non-Fictional Text, p. 405
→ Focus on Facts, Basic Types of Non-Fictional Texts, p. 396

𝓜 **5.** Describe the cartoon below in detail and relate its message to the statements made by the Britons on pp. 72 ff. Which similarities and differences can you detect?
→ Focus on Skills, Analysis of Visuals, p. 409

patriotische Europäer

Tips on vocab ≫

far left: the colours of the German flag ■ to carry a machete [məˈʃeti] ■ to have a grim facial expression ■ to carry a sign with an inscription ■ the German national anthem ('Germany, Germany, above all else')
left: the colours of the British flag (Union Jack) ■ to carry a rifle ■ Britain First: a far-right and British nationalist political party
centre: the colours of the French flag (the Tricolour) ■ to carry a club ■ bald-headed *(glatzköpfig)* ■ *Les Francais d'abord* ('the French first') slogan of Jean-Marie le Pen, a French far-right politician and founder of the Front National
right: a masked man ■ wearing a hood with a thin slit for the eyes ■ to carry a pack of dynamite ■ a sign with the inscription *Allahu akbar* ('Allah is the greatest'); title of the national anthem of Libya (1969 – 2011)

ACTIVITIES

6. You are one of the Britons who voted to *Remain* and are now extremely frustrated and concerned about the future. Write a letter to the editor in response to either Boris Johnson's article or one of the Britons' statements in which you express your view of the matter. If possible, also make suggestions about what should be done to improve the deplorable situation.
→ Focus on Skills, Writing a Letter to the Editor, p. 431

7. Even Boris Johnson admitted that the referendum was "grueling" and has caused a lot of "dismay". Obviously, people are deeply divided and mutual understanding and support seems hardly possible. In groups, collect ideas about what has to be done and compile a "Get Together" campaign to unite people again. Create posters and slogans that promote your ideas and appeal to the people.

Carmen Fishwick: Meet Britons Who Voted to Leave the EU

From wanting to hurt the government and banks to betrayal[1] of the working class, leavers explain what drove their decision

On 23 June, Britain voted to end its 43-year relationship
5 with the EU. We spoke to people around the country who responded to a Guardian callout[2] to find out why they voted to leave, and whether they're happy with the outcome.
Here's what they said.

10 **1 For a better standard of life**
I want a stable country where people from all counties across the UK are heard and not fed[3] scraps[4] from the south. I don't want to fear that when my daughter has children there's no room in schools due to overcrowd-
15 ing, or if she has health issues a medical appointment doesn't take longer than growing a baby.
We should feel safe in our jobs and not feel as though if we're not willing to work seven days a week, 10 hours a day then someone can quite easily be drafted in[5] from
20 abroad and subsequently thrown on the unemployment pile further straining[6] local economy.
When every Briton lives a suitable standard of life, then my tax money can be spent elsewhere. When the systems put into place – NHS[7], state schools, housing – are
25 well-equipped and capable of looking after each individual residing in the UK, then we can accept more and do right by others.
We, the little people, or even the big boys that apparently run the country haven't got full control over what
30 happens, and if suffering a downturn in wages due a weaker economy over trading deals is a price to pay to make the country and its people better educated and in a full bill of health[8] then so be it.

The image of racism is far from true and shouldn't be used as a smear[9] against the voiceless that live day-to-
35 day with the consequences of the decision makers that reside in a London borough away from real life and constantly roll the shit downhill.
What the writers in a swanky[10] London office or sat at home at a fine oak table with an Apple Mac drinking
40 espresso from Starbucks don't realise is that the leave voters from wherever they're from aren't afraid of rolling up their sleeves and putting in the graft[11] that will make the country great.
Danny Lancaster, 30, Barnsley
45

2 To feel like my voice is heard
I voted leave for empowerment, and to feel like my voice is heard and can influence change. The compromise to remain was too high a price. It's a reminder that democracy does exist here.
50
The present leaders have failed to address the have-nots, preferring to placate[12] the haves. Visiting London in 2014 there were no signs of a recession. The city has alienated itself from the rest of England. It felt obscene[13].
I have worked in mental health for 30 years. In that time
55 I have observed that society is reflected in the people who access our services. The biggest issues are feeling connected, or rather disconnected, in society. The majority are probably the people who have the smallest voice, but who rely on others to advocate for them. How
60 much energy and financial support is offered to EU nationals who are vulnerable, when our own are ignored? I haven't seen any EU benefits to mental health at all. I'm struggling to understand what they've done.
This is an opportunity. If people can see beyond the
65 loss, and see it as an opportunity, we can affect change

---

[1] **betrayal** *Verrrat, Vertrauensbruch* – [2] **callout** *Aufruf* – [3] **to feed** (fed, fed) to give food to sb. – [4] **scrap** *Abfall, Ausschuss* – [5] **to draft sb. in** *(phr. v.)* to bring sb. somewhere to do a particular job – [6] **to strain** to try to make sth. do more than it is able to do – [7] **NHS** *(abbr.)* National Health Service – [8] **bill of health** a report that says sb. is healthy – [9] **smear** *Verleumdung* – [10] **swanky** *(infml.)* very expensive and fashionable, attracting people's attention – [11] **graft** *(BE, infml.)* work – [12] **to placate** to stop sb. from feeling angry – [13] **obscene** morally wrong

for people and how they experience life. The people who are actually living the life made the choice. All these people who are aggrieved[14]. Why weren't they out campaigning? All these smug[15] people who thought it wouldn't happen … it shows a real sense of arrogance.
Fiona, mental health nurse, 52, Derby

3 The working classes have been betrayed, to be poor is now a sin

The bosses love foreign workers. They are non-union, cheap and pliable[16]. The British people who used to do those jobs have not gone on to university, they have gone on the dole[17] or worse. There is also an issue over the conditions that the foreign workers have to endure, and the housing situation in the UK is abysmal[18].
Elite media types and people like Bob Geldof have failed to understand the concerns of normal people. They look down on us and call us racist, but they are the ones guilty of bigotry[19].
Britain became a socialist country after the second world war through the sacrifices of ordinary people. A welfare state was their reward. Now to be poor is a sin and you are attacked from every direction, so there was an element of a "stuff you[20]" protest vote.
The EU sacrificed cohesion[21] for expansion that seems to be run by Germany. Angela Merkel decided to allow 1 million migrants into Germany, breaking EU law and not consulting the Bundestag. Germany broke Greece and is offering expedited[22] negotiations to allow Turkey into the EU. They do not consult and it is not a union.
Britain seemed stuck on the fringe[23] of the EU and our path to greater assimilation wasn't clear. There is no plan for creating a Europe with the same taxes and minimum wage, so the movement of people adversely[24] affects those countries with better conditions. The EU is monolithic[25] and so hard to understand. Where is it going? It failed to make itself clear, simple and accountable[26]. It just rumbles[27] on. […]
During the referendum campaign I was shocked by how much the establishment failed to provide balanced views. Reports were churned out[28] that predicted the worst case scenarios of Brexit but not the best. I am

happy, but concerned, that if Scotland gets a referendum to leave the UK then England and Wales will be stuck in Tory[29] hell for a century. I believe Scotland is its own country and maybe should become independent. They may be worse off financially, but freedom is worth a lot. […]
Angus, 52, Norwich

4 A way to hurt the government and banks

Politically, I would like to see Brussels and Westminster reformed, and arrogant politicians and public servants begin to serve public needs and not be bought like prostitutes by vested interests[30]. Eventually, under the right circumstances, I would like to see us return to the EU, with more visionary and ideologically driven representatives that are forced to make themselves accountable to both their home population and the wider European population. Europe could be a fantastic political structure that would promote the growth and needs of all its people, but not with the current political mentality.
The arrogance displayed by politicians here and all over Europe who suggest citizens are not "educated" enough to be left to decide is conceited[31] and undemocratic. Chief among these is Jean-Claude Juncker. I am very sad we are leaving the EU, but the administration of both the EU and the UK need fundamental reform that promotes the lives of its citizens rather than loading them up with debt to pay for a defunct political and economic system. The absolutely wrong people are being put in charge of an economic and political system that no longer allows people to rise through the ranks. Immigration would not be such a problem if the UK built homes and infrastructure and trained adequate doctors, nurses and essential workers, but politics is deliberately creating scarcity. […]
Kerry, 51, Essex

5 To support UK industry

I voted to support the UK fishing industry as UK fisherman are only allocated[32] 30 % of the quota for fishing in their own territorial waters. Hopefully all UK jobs, businesses and perhaps companies will now stop importing

---

[14] **aggrieved** unhappy and angry because of unfair treatment – [15] **smug** *selbstgefällig, blasiert* – [16] **pliable** [ˈplaɪəbəl] *gefügig, fügsam* – [17] **to go on the dole** *(BE, coll.) Arbeitslosengeld bekommen; „stempeln gehen"* – [18] **abysmal** *very bad* – [19] **bigotry** [ˈbɪgətri] *Engstirnigkeit* – [20] **stuff you** *(sl.) du kannst mich mal* – [21] **cohesion** [kəʊˈhiːʒən] *Zusammenhalt* – [22] **to expedite** *(fml.)* [ˈekspədaɪt] *to make sth. happen more quickly* – [23] **fringe** *the outer or less important part an area, a group, etc.* – [24] **adverse** *widrig, ungünstig* – [25] **monolithic** *monumental* – [26] **accountable** *haftbar, verantwortlich* – [27] **to rumble on** *weiterrumpeln* – [28] **to churn sth. out** *(infml., phr. v.) to produce large amounts of sth. quickly, usually of low quality* – [29] **Tory** *a member of the British Conservative Party* – [30] **vested interest** *a strong interest in sth. because you could get an advantage from it* – [31] **conceited** [kənˈsiːtɪd] *eingebildet* – [32] **to allocate** *jdm. etw. zuweisen*

goods and food that could be bought in the UK, in turn supporting UK industry and creating jobs. Perhaps we
150 will eventually start producing world class cars and machinery again, because all of that's gone tits up[33] since joining the EU with all the rules and regulations.

The EU is failing. The euro is collapsing, and the whole EU is going backwards while the rest of the world over-
155 takes.

I am not a Nazi racist and have no problem with immigration or free movement of people. I do, however, have a problem with immigrants being able to claim child support for children that don't live in the UK.
160 I don't agree with the remain campaign's false statistics, blocking fishermen's protests in the Thames, and shouting abuse at working class men just trying to provide for their families and general sneakily[34] hidden foul play.

Truthfully none of my friends or colleagues are having
165 second thoughts either, everyone here is happy. We knew the pound would temporarily fall, and knew the euro would too. I also know the pound will recover, more than recover in fact. Not sure if the euro will recover. Maybe we were never stronger in Europe, but
170 Europe was stronger with us.

I hope the media will start giving all the facts, not just the scaremongering[35] ones. I hope for the success of the working man and UK businesses, not just multinational businesses, millionaires or the upper class who make
175 all their money from investment banking.

Jay, 24, Devon

6 **To make politicians accountable**

I am a socialist and believe in democracy, and my main sticking point was the secret TTIP discussions and I was fearful for our NHS. I am an EU national as well as 180 a British citizen, and I also didn't like the lies from the remain camp telling us that our workers' rights exist only because of the EU. Trade unions fought for our rights as they have always done.

We need to hold our politicians accountable and vote 185 them out if necessary. We can now choose how we spend our own nation's money and not be given our pocket money like children. We can decide who we trade with. We shall decide the terms of that trade by negotiation. We shall set our own agenda. We shall be able to keep 190 our public services and not be forced to privatise them, and if we choose we can re-nationalise our industries which would not be allowed in the EU. [...]

I believe in every country determining its own fate and I have always supported nations claiming independ- 195 ence for its own people. Why are we considered bigots or racists for wanting to make our own decisions for our own country?

Whatever the long-term outcome for our country, I believe in freedom and self-determination. [...] 200

Jane, 19, north London

http://www.theguardian.com/politics/2016/jun/25/meet-10-britons-who-voted-to-leave-the-eu, 25 June 2016 [08.09.2016]

Reactions to Brexit …

The following pages provide you with different materials on different countries' reactions to the Brexit vote.

- a British popular newspaper article about the Scottish reaction
  1 Matt Dathan et al., *The Daily Mail*

- two statements from Scottish politicians
  2 Nicola Sturgeon, the Scottish First Minister (interview)
  3 Angus Robertson, a Scottish MP (political speech)

- two German newspaper/magazine articles that report and reflect on Brexit and its aftermath
  4 Christoph Scheuermann, *Der Spiegel*
  5 Jochen Wittmann, *Rheinische Post*

---

[33] **to go tits up** *(idm., infml.)* to go to ruin, to fall apart – [34] **sneakily** doing things in a secret and unfair way – [35] **scaremongering** [ˈskeəmʌŋgərɪŋ] the act of spreading stories that cause public fear

Before reading:

1. Together with a partner, take a look at the cartoon below and describe it to each other. Pay attention to details and the implications made concerning the English-Irish and English-Scottish relationship. What image is conveyed of England?

2. In a group puzzle activity, **divide the class the class into five groups**, with each group choosing **one** of the materials.

Tips on vocab ⟫⟫

left: a Queen's Guard/foot guard ■ a black bearskin cap (the Bearskin) ■ a scarlet tunic ■ white gloves ■ black pants ■ black boots ■ a grim facial expression ■ resemblance to a bull dog (→ reference to John Bull) ■ a white empty flag with stains of (black) dirt on a stick ■ a broken English flag/an English flag in pieces ■ to fall apart/to break into pieces ■ to point to the left ■ to order sb. to go a certain direction

centre: a signpost with the flag of the European Union pointing to the right ■ an Irishman ■ the flag of the Republic of Ireland ■ a Leprechaun ['leprəkɔːn] (a little, dwarf-like man from Irish folklore) ■ a green coat ■ stovepipe hat ■ green knee breeches *(Bundhose)* ■ a red full beard ■ a pipe in the corner of the mouth

right: a Scot in traditional Highland dress ■ a kilt in tartan pattern ■ a (red) kilt jacket ■ a Highland bonnet in tartan pattern with a red bobble ■ a sash *(Schärpe)* ■ white knee socks ■ black boots ■ the flag of Scotland (St Andrew's Cross)

---

1 Matt Dathan, Martin Robinson, Daniel Martin:
Scots React to Brexit Vote with Renewed Push for Scottish Independence

[...] Ms Sturgeon said the Scottish Government will begin to prepare the legislation required to enable a second independence referendum to take place and said it was 'inconceivable[1]' the UK Government could stop it.

She said: 'There is no doubt circumstances since 2014 have changed. The option of a second referendum must be on the table and it is on the table'.

---

[1] **inconceivable** impossible to imagine or think of

Her intervention has also led to calls by Sinn Fein[2] for
a vote on Irish unity because Northern Ireland also
backed *Remain*.

While the UK as a whole voted to leave the European
Union, Scots overwhelmingly opted to remain, with
Ms Sturgeon declaring the result meant there had
been a 'significant and material change in the circumstances in which Scotland voted against independence' in 2014.

Many Scots on social media who voted 'No' to the
country breaking away from the UK in 2014 say they
would change their vote if a new referendum was to be
held.

Ms Sturgeon said: 'As things stand, Scotland faces the
prospect of being taken out of the EU against our will.
I regard that as democratically unacceptable.'

Speaking at her official residence, Bute House in Edinburgh, she said: 'I intend to take all possible steps and
explore all possible options to give effect to how people
in Scotland voted – in other words to secure our continuing place in the EU, and in the single market in
particular.' [...]

Ms Sturgeon said: 'It is, therefore, a statement of the
obvious that a second referendum must be on the table,
and it is on the table.'

And last night, a key ally[3] of German chancellor Angela Merkel told Scots that they would be welcome to
remain in the EU if they left the United Kingdom.

Manfred Weber, leader of the biggest group in the European Parliament, said: 'On the Scottish level, to go the
other way, it is up to them. Europe is open to new member states, that is totally clear. Those who want to stay
are welcome in the European Union.'

The invitation is in stark[4] contrast to two years ago,
when senior Brussels figures said they would not accept Scotland as a member because they did not want
to reward secessionist[5] parts of member states.

All 32 local authority areas north of the border returned
a majority for Remain in the EU referendum, with the
country voting by 62% to 38% in favour of *Remain*.

Ms Sturgeon said: 'Unfortunately, of course, yesterday's result in Scotland was not echoed across the
whole of the United Kingdom. The UK-wide vote to
leave the EU is one that I deeply regret.

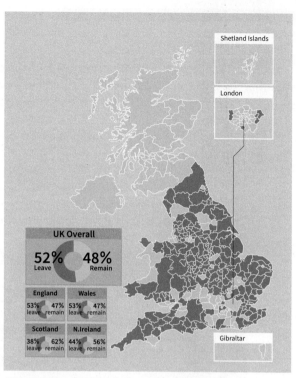

All 32 local authorities in Scotland delivered a vote for
Remain

'The vote across England and Wales was a rejection of
the EU and it was a sign of divergence[6] between Scotland and large parts of the rest of the UK and how we
see our place in the rest of the world.'

Furious Scottish nationalists had already pounced[7] on
today's historic vote to leave the EU by immediately demanding a second referendum on splitting from the UK.
The SNP said the UK faces a 'constitutional crisis' after
Scotland voted overwhelmingly in favour of staying in
the EU but is on course to cut ties[8] with Brussels after
the *Leave* won the overall UK vote.

All 32 authorities north of the border delivered majority wins for Remain and joined only London and
Northern Ireland as areas that did not vote for Brexit.

Irish republicans have already used the referendum
result to call for the reunification of Ireland. [...]

The passionate pro-union Harry Potter author JK
Rowling angrily hit out at David Cameron, accusing
him of putting the future of the UK in jeopardy[9] for
calling the referendum in the first place.

---

[2] **Sinn Fein** [ʃɪn ˈfeɪn] an Irish political party that wants Northern Ireland to become part of the Republic of Ireland – [3] **ally** [ˈælaɪ]
Verbündeter, Alliierter – [4] **stark** obvious – [5] **secessionist** *abtrünnig* – [6] **divergence** [ˌdaɪˈvɜːdʒəns] the situation in which two things
become different – [7] **to pounce** to jump or move quickly in order to catch or get hold of sth. – [8] **to cut ties** *die Verbindungen
abbrechen* – [9] **jeopardy** [ˈdʒepədi] in danger of being damaged or destroyed

She wrote: 'Scotland will seek independence now. Cameron's legacy[10] will be breaking up two unions. Neither needed to happen.'

This morning Ms Sturgeon's predecessor[11] as First Minister Alex Salmond said he was 'quite certain' Ms Sturgeon would 'implement the manifesto' because England is 'dragging us out the EU'.

He said a second referendum on splitting from the UK should be held within two years so Scotland is not forced out of the EU.

The process of withdrawing from Brussels will take up to two years from when the UK Government triggers Article 50 of the Lisbon treaty[12] – which sets out the formal arrangements for leaving.

'From when that starting gun is fired, it's a two-year period,' Mr Salmond said of the withdrawal process.

Insisting a second independence referendum was justified, he added: 'So whatever that period is – two years, two-and-a-half years, that would have to be the timescale of the next referendum because what you would want to do is remain in the European Union while the rest of the UK moved out.'

Holyrood[13] External Affairs Secretary Fiona Hylsop warned that a decision by the UK to quit Europe would have 'consequences'. [...]

To stage[14] a second vote on Scottish independence Nicola Sturgeon would have to secure agreement from the Westminster Government. This is because legislating for a referendum is a reserved power – not devolved to the Scottish Parliament. Without agreement from the UK Government, any vote held on Scottish independence would have no legal effect on the Union.

The Scottish Government could decide to hold an 'advisory[15] referendum on extending the powers of the Scottish Parliament' but the result could not be enforced. Lacking a majority, the SNP would need Green support to get a referendum through. But Ruth Davidson, the Scottish Tory leader, said a second vote would not be in Scotland's best interests.

If Mrs Sturgeon went ahead with an 'advisory' vote, she could use the results as proof of the overwhelming desire for independence and demand the UK Government grant her the right to hold a legally-binding second vote on Scottish independence.

In reality, despite Alex Salmond insisting the 2014 was a 'once in a lifetime' vote, Scottish voters will almost certainly be given another chance very soon in their lifetimes. The fact that all 32 authorities voted in favour of remaining in the EU means Scotland is being taken out of the EU against its will. This 'constitutional crisis' – as many have called it – is not going to go away anytime soon.

http://www.dailymail.co.uk/news/article-3657649/Now-Scotland-demands-independence-Nicola-Sturgeon-quite-certain-stage-second-referendum-raging-Scots-dragged-EU-against-says-furious-Alex-Salmond.html, 24 June 2016 [08.09.2016]

2 Nicola Sturgeon: Interview on the EU Referendum and Scotland's Position

Nicola Sturgeon (*1970) is a Scottish politician and current First Minister of Scotland and Leader of the Scotish National Party (SNP).

In a TV interview on 26 June 2016, she described the post-Brexit situation from the Scottish perspective and explained which political steps she planned to take.

Tips on vocab »»

to cast one's eyes to look at sb./sth. ■ **disarray** the state of being confused and having no organization ■ **shambolic** confused and badly organized ■ **to abdicate responsibility** to stop controlling or managing sth. that you are in charge of ■ **to let sb. down** (phr. v.) to disappoint sb. by failing to do what you agreed to or were expected to do ■ **to entail** to make sth. necessary, to involve sth. ■ **premise** an idea or theory on which a statement or action is based ■ **explicit** clear and exact ■ **uncharted** a situation that is completely new ■ **unprecedented** never having happened or existed before

---

[10] **legacy** ['legəsi] Erbe – [11] **predecessor** Vorgänger – [12] **Article 50** of the Lisbon treaty: the article that defines the procedure and timetable of the Brexit – [13] **Holyrood** seat of the Scottish Parliament – [14] **to stage** to arrange or organize sth. – [15] **advisory** [ədvaɪzəri] beratend

3 Angus Robertson: Scotland Is a European Country

Angus Robertson (*1969) is a Scottish National Party (SNP) politician and the SNP's Parliamentary Group Leader and spokesperson on the Constitution in the House of Commons of the U.K.

On 27 June 2016, he issued an insistent warning to the House of Commons, stating that taking Scotland out of the EU would be utterly undemocratic.

Tips on vocab »»

> **to cast one's vote** to vote ■ **Single European Market** the EU as one territory without any internal borders or other regulatory obstacles to the free movement of goods and services ■ **safeguard** a means to protect sb./sth. from harm ■ **diminished** reduced in size and importance ■ **farce** here: joke ■ **share prices** *Aktienpreise* ■ **volatile** *unberechenbar* ■ **to suspend** to stop from being active ■ **Sterling** Pound Sterling; British currency ■ **to repudiate** to refuse to accept sb./sth. as true, good or reasonable ■ **despicable** very unpleasant and bad ■ **prosecuting authorities** *Strafverfolgungsbehörden* ■ **interest rates** *Zinsraten* ■ **austerity** *Sparpolitik* ■ **unprecedented** never having happened or existed before ■ **drift** general development ■ **to exacerbate** to make worse ■ **to take a firm grip** to get/have control over sb./sth.

4 Christoph Scheuermann: Zorn[1] und Leere

Wer in diesen Tagen auf die britische Demokratie schaut, sieht ein bröckelndes[2] Gebäude. Das ist nicht nur metaphorisch gemeint. Teile des Palastes von Westminster, Sitz des Ober- und Unterhauses, sind von
5 Gerüsten[3] und Plastikplanen[4] umgeben. Die Fassade ist brüchig[5], durch das Dach dringt Wasser, Leitungen[6] und Abflüsse[7] sind undicht[8]. Die Renovierung wird Jahre dauern und Milliarden kosten. Am Montag musste die Sprecherin des Premierministers ihre wöchent-
10 liche Pressekonferenz immer wieder unterbrechen, weil das Gehämmer[9] der Arbeiter draußen zu laut war. Die Risse[10] zeigen sich im gesamten Königreich. Über dem Land liegt der Kater[11] einer Revolution, die niemand für möglich hielt. Seit dem Brexit-Votum wanken
15 viele Gewissheiten[12], das Parlament als Herzkammer[13] der Demokratie etwa. Oder die Bindungskraft[14] der großen Parteien. Bei den Konservativen wird er Krieg um die Nachfolge David Camerons vor den gierigen[15] Blicken der Öffentlichkeit ausgetragen, inklusive Ver-
20 rat[16] und Intrige[17]. Bei Labour kann die Abneigung zwischen der Fraktion und ihrem Vorsitzenden Jeremy Corbyn zu einer Spaltung der Partei führen.
Man verliert schnell den Überblick. Die Kurzfassung der vergangenen zwei Wochen: Der Premierminister
25 tritt ab, weil er die Krise nicht bewältigen möchte, die er verursacht hat. Sein wahrscheinlicher Nachfolger

wird vom Justizminister hintergangen[18], der selbst Premier werden will, damit aber kläglich scheitert. Während die Labour-Abgeordneten ihrem Chef die Schuld am Brexit geben, hoffen die Schotten auf eine zweite 30 Chance zur Abspaltung. Und der Mann, der die ganze Sache losgetreten hat – Nigel Farage – , schlendert in den Ruhestand[19], bevor der Austritt überhaupt vollzogen ist.
Am Ende bleibt nun eine Frau, die aufräumen muss, 35 was ihre Vorgänger angerichtet haben. Am Donnerstag wählten die Tory-Abgeordneten zwei Kandidatinnen für den Parteivorsitz; bis September können die Parteimitglieder zwischen den beiden entscheiden.
Theresa May, 59, bislang Innenministerin, hat die bes- 40 ten Chancen auf den Einzug in die Downing Street. Sie gilt als euroskeptische Technokratin, die hart gegen illegale Einwanderer vorging und kaum Verbündete in Westminster hat, eine Einzelgängerin. Nach der Jungsclique aus Eton und Oxford um Cameron herum wäre 45 sie die erfrischendere Wahl für turbulente Zeiten. [...]
Das EU-Referendum hat die Risse in der Gesellschaft nicht verursacht, sondern nur deutlicher hervortreten lassen. Die Kluft zwischen liberalen Großstädtern und Menschen auf dem Land, zwischen Jung und Alt, gebil- 50 det und weniger gebildet, zwischen Establishment und Unterschicht.

---

[1] anger – [2] to crumble – [3] scaffolding – [4] plastic tarpaulin – [5] crumbly, decayed – [6] plumbing – [7] drain – [8] to leak; leaky – [9] hammering – [10] crack – [11] a hangover – [12] certainty – [13] the heart – [14] cohesive power – [15] greedy – [16] betrayal – [17] intrigue – [18] to deceive sb. – [19] retirement

Das Referendum hat die Grundlagen der repräsentativen Demokratie erschüttert[20]. Die Abgeordneten im Unterhaus stehen nun vor der Aufgabe, in den kommenden Jahren eine Trennung zu begleiten, die sie nie wollten. Sie müssen sich die Frage stellen, ob sie ihre Wähler noch vertreten. [...]

Eine Folge des 23. Juni ist, dass Großbritannien bis auf Weiteres mit sich selbst beschäftigt sein wird. Große Teile der Regierung werden in den Austrittsgesprächen gebunden sein. Eine kohärente Außenpolitik[21] wird sich unter diesen Bedingungen kaum entwickeln, zumal Brexit-Kämpfer wie Michael Gove immer wieder versprochen haben, schnellstmöglich Handelsverträge[22] mit Indien, China, Australien und dem Rest der Welt auf den Weg zu bringen. Daran wird die neue Regierung gemessen werden. Außenpolitisch kann man die Briten für die nächsten Jahre abschreiben. [...]

Politisch war das EU-Referendum die teuerste Fehlspekulation[23] eines britischen Premierministers seit Jahrzehnten. Cameron wird in die Geschichte eingehen wie Lord North, der als Premier versehentlich die Kolonien in Amerika verlor, oder Blair, der seit dem Irakdesaster nur noch Tony „Bliar" heißt – Lügner. Traurige Figuren, alle drei.

Die Kunst für die nächste Regierung wird darin bestehen, das gespaltene Königreich wieder zu vereinen. In etliche Gegenden Englands stellen die Bürger schon lange keine Ansprüche[24] mehr an die Politik, nach all den Spesenskandalen[25] im Parlament, den Milliarden zur Rettung von Banken. Viele Briten haben nur das Bedürfnis, die Frage nach Aufstieg und Wohlstand beantwortet zu bekommen: Wird mein Leben morgen besser sein als heute, wenn ich mich anstrenge? Oder ist ohnehin alles verloren, egal, was ich tue?

Zynismus ist eine zersetzende[26] Kraft in einer Gesellschaft. Die Mehrheit der Briten vertraut ihren Eliten nicht mehr. Der ökonomische Pragmatismus der Briten, auf den immer Verlass war, kam irgendwann abhanden. Das Volk ist längst nicht mehr so staatsgläubig und konformistisch wie in den Nachkriegsjahren. Die EU-Gegner haben das gespürt. Der Brexit wurde aus Trotz[27] geboren.

Lässt sich der Brexit jetzt abwenden? Die einfache Antwort lautet: nein. [...]

Über 17 Millionen Briten haben für den Austritt aus der EU gestimmt, 1,3 Millionen mehr als für den Verbleib. Selbst wenn viele Briten zu dem Schluss kommen sollten, dass sie den Brexit doch nicht wünschen, lässt sich das Referendum nicht zurückdrehen[28]. Europa tut gut daran, diese Realität zu akzeptieren, auch wenn das Triumphgeheul eines Populisten wie Nigel Farage nur schwer erträglich ist.

Farage war kaum mehr als ein polternder Zwischenrufer im großen Pub der britischen Politik. Sein Abgang zeigt, dass er nie Verantwortung übernehmen wollte. Aus seiner Sicht war es konsequent zu verschwinden. Der Fehler war, die Leute, für die er sprach, nicht ernst zu nehmen.

Was bleibt, sind Zorn und Leere. „Ich kann mich an keine Zeit erinnern, in der so viel Wut so nah an der Oberfläche war", sagt der Historiker Garton Ash. [...] Europa muss einen Weg finden, die Briten in den kommenden Jahren nicht ganz zu verlieren. Denn was auch noch bleibt, sind jene 48 Prozent auf der Insel, die für die EU gestimmt haben. Fast ein halbes Land, das enttäuscht von seiner anderen Hälfte ist und nun auf Europa blickt. Der größte Fehler wäre es, diesen Teil Britanniens im Stich zu lassen[29].

DER SPIEGEL, 28/2016, 9 July 2016, pp. 80ff.

---

[20] to shatter sth. – [21] foreign policy – [22] trade agreement/treaty – [23] bad speculation – [24] claims – [25] public expenses scandal – [26] corrosive – [27] defiance – [28] to undo sth./to make sth. undone – [29] to let sb. down

5 Jochen Wittmann: Jetzt droht[1] Kleinbritannien

Das Brexit-Votum befeuert von Neuem das schottische Streben[2] nach Unabhängigkeit. In Nordirland fürchtet man noch ernstere Folgen.

Eine bittere Ironie der Entscheidung für den Austritt aus der Europäischen Union könnte sein, was stolze Brexit-Wähler sich gewiss nicht wünschen: dass nämlich aus dem angeblich bald wieder unabhängigen Groß- ein Kleinbritannien wird. Die Fliehkräfte[3], die das Referendum um den britischen EU-Austritt freigesetzt hat, befeuern[4] jetzt in Schottland ein zweites Unabhängigkeitsreferendum, und in Nordirland führen sie zumindest zum Nachdenken über ein Zusammengehen mit der Republik Irland im Süden.

Denn die Brexit-Entscheidung war in erster Linie eine der Engländer, also im bevölkerungsreichsten[5] Landesteil des Vereinigten Königreichs. [...]

In Schottland dagegen stimmten sämtliche 32 Bezirke[6] und insgesamt 62 Prozent der Bürger für den Verbleib, während es in Nordirland 55,8 Prozent waren. Jetzt ist die Situation eingetreten, dass Schottland gegen seinen Willen aus der Gemeinschaft mit der Europäischen Union gezerrt wird.

In Edinburgh, wo die EU-Abstimmung mit 74 Prozent am deutlichsten ausgefallen war, herrschte blankes Entsetzen[7]. [...]

Die Ministerpräsidentin der schottischen Regionalregierung, Nicola Sturgeon, unterstrich das deutliche schottische Votum: „Wir haben klar gesagt, dass wir nicht die EU verlassen wollen. Ich als Ministerpräsidentin werde alles tun, damit der Wählerwille respektiert wird." Das Brexit-Ergebnis, sagte sie, sei für Schottland „demokratisch inakzeptabel".

Sturgeon steuert ein zweites Referendum über die Unabhängigkeit an, nachdem 2014 eine solche Abstimmung für die Nationalisten verloren gegangen war. [...]

Die nordirische Ministerpräsidentin Arlene Foster begrüßte die Brexit-Entscheidung. Immerhin ist sie Chefin der rechten und pro-britischen Democratic Unionist Party, die für den EU-Austritt geworben hatte. Doch Foster stellt sich gegen die Volksmeinung. Die Nachfrage[8] unter Nordiren nach einem Pass der irischen Republik schnellte[9] nach dem Referendumsausgang steil nach oben. [...] Der stellvertretende Ministerpräsident in der nordirischen Regionalregierung, Martin McGuinness von der Sinn-Fein-Partei, sagte: „Uns aus Europa zu zerren, ist zum Nachteil für alle unsere Bürger und wird schlecht für Handel, Investment und die Gesellschaft sein." McGuinness sieht jetzt einen „demokratischen Imperativ" für ein nordirisches Referendum über das Zusammengehen mit Irland. Es ist aber unwahrscheinlich[10], dass die pro-britische und unionistische DUP diesem Ansinnen zustimmen würde.

In Nordirland könnte ein Brexit deshalb wirklich fatale Folgen haben – hier hatten sich pro-irische Katholiken und pro-britische Protestanten 30 Jahre lang einen Bürgerkrieg geliefert, der erst 1998 endete. Die beiden früheren britischen Premierminister Tony Blair und John Major haben erst kürzlich bei einem Besuch in der Provinz vor einem Wiederaufflammen[11] der Gewalt im Fall eines Brexit gewarnt.

Rheinische Post, 25 June 2016, p. A5

COMPREHENSION

1   Matt Dathan et al.

3. In a **first reading**, take notes on these aspects:
   * the Scottish vote in the EU referendum
   * the Scottish independence referendum of 2014
   * immediate reactions to the Brexit vote (Irish and Scottish)
   * political consequences and options resulting from Brexit
   * reactions from other EU member states
   * Nicola Sturgeon's plans for Scotland's future
   * the process of exiting the EU and Scotland's consequences in reaction to the U.K.'s withdrawal from the EU

---

[1] to threaten – [2] pursuit of/quest for sth. – [3] centrifugal force – [4] to incite sth. – [5] most-populated – [6] district [7] horror – [8] demand for sth. – [9] to skyrocket – [10] unlikely – [11] resurgence

4. After a second reading, summarize the article in about 200 words.
→ Focus on Skills, Writing a Summary, p. 429

5. Take a look at the map (p. 76) and give an overview of the voting results.

Tip: In order to get more detailed data, you can use the interactive maps provided on the webcode.

2 Nicola Sturgeon

6. Tip: To get a better impression of the interview, you can watch the video clip provided on the webcode.

Listen to/watch the interview with Nicola sturgeon **a first time** and take notes on what she states about:
- her view of the British government
- responsibility and political leadership with regard to Scotland
- protecting Scotland's interest
- possible options concerning another Scottish independence referendum and remaining in the EU
- the premises for Scotland's future
→ Focus on Skills, Listening Comprehension, p. 394

7. After a second listening/viewing, complete your notes.

3 Angus Robertson

8. Tip: To get a better impression of the interview, you can watch the video clip provided on the webcode.

Step 1: While listening to/watching Robertson's statement/speech **a first time**, extract information about:
- reasons for Scottish voters to vote for *Remain*
- EU citizenship vs. Little Britain
- Westminster's undemocratic demands
- the possibility of a new Scottish independence referendum
- the political and economic impact of Brexit
- demands on measures to be taken from Whitehall
→ Focus on Skills, Listening Comprehension, p. 394

Step 2: Now, **focus on David Cameron's response** to Robertson's statement and take notes on:
- his view of leaving the EU
- his comment concerning racist attacks on foreigners
- the economic dangers triggered by Brexit
- Scotland's specific economic position

Step 3: After listening to/watching the statement **a second time**, pay attention to the MPs' reactions to Robertson's statement and Cameron's response.
What is the overall atmosphere like at the House of Commons?

4 Christoph Scheuermann

9. The German media reported comprehensively about the British EU referendum and, after the *Leave* vote, reacted with concern and deep regret to Britain's tight decision to leave the EU.
The German magazine *Der Spiegel* even published a bilingual (German-English) edition entitled *Bitte geht nicht! – Please don't go! • Warum wir die Briten brauchen – Why Germany needs the British* (issue 24/2016, 11 June 2016). This article – published after Brexit – reflects the German view on the matter.

Step 1: Read the German magazine article, identify the key terms and put them in topical order.

Tip: Use the annotations to turn the relevant phrases into English. Be sure to use your own words whenever possible and do not translate word by word.

→ Focus on Skills, Mediation, p. 412

Step 2: Describe the *Spiegel* cover in detail and relate it to the statements made in the article.

→ Focus on Skills, Analysis of Visuals, p. 409

5 **Jochen Wittmann**

 10. The article taken from the daily newspaper *Rheinische Post* was published only two days after the Brexit vote. Find relevant passages concerning the aspects listed below and turn them into English.

- the Scottish and Northern Irish reaction to Brexit
- the Scottish vote
- consequences of the Brexit vote   – for Scotland   – for Northern Ireland
- the particularly complicated political situation in Northern Ireland

→ Focus on Skills, Mediation, p. 412

ANALYSIS

1 **Matt Dathan et al.**

11. By definition, the *Daily Mail* is a popular and rather sensationalist daily newspaper.

Step 1: Reactivate your knowledge of the characteristics of popular and quality newspapers and study the Focus on Facts page *The Press* (p. 398) in your Students' Book.

Step 2: Examine the article and determine its quality.

→ Focus on Skills, Analysis of a Non-Fictional Text, p. 405

12. Compare the article from the *Daily Mail* to Mark Mardell's article *Brexit: The Story of an Island Apart* published by the BBC (pp. 62 ff.). Which similarities and differences concerning journalistic quality can you detect?

2 **Nicola Sturgeon**

13. Examine Nicola Sturgeon's competence as a speaker in general and her persuasive strategies in particular. Which linguistic and rhetorical devices does she use to convey determination, responsible leadership and reliability to the viewer (and her electorate)?

→ Focus on Skills, Analysis of a Political Speech, p. 407

3 **Angus Robertson**

14. At first glance, Robertson does not appear to be a very skilled and charismatic speaker. However, the strong reaction of the other MPs reveals that his statements and views are shared and approved of. Analyse Robertson's line of argument and rhetorical strategy and explain how they convey his message.

→ Focus on Skills, Analysis of a Political Speech, p. 407

4 **Christoph Scheuermann**

15. Compare the *Spiegel* cover page *Jeder für sich* (p. 79) to the cartoon *Patriotische Europäer* by Gerhard Mester (p. 71). Explain

a) which visual you prefer and

b) which one you consider to be more effective.

→ Focus on Skills, Analysis of Visuals, p. 409

ACTIVITIES

16. In a role play, take on the positions of different politicians/citizens who are confronted with the post-Brexit situation, e.g. English, Scottish, Northern Irish, Republican Irish, members of the EU Parliament, etc. In groups:

a) compile a formal complaint/petition to Parliament that lists the problems, hardships and challenges and demand that action is taken to solve them.

or:

b) prepare short speeches which lay out the controversial topic/situation and call for immediate action.

→ Focus on Skills, Writing a Speech Script, p. 428 and Giving a Speech, p. 418

or:

c) prepare and act out a public hearing, presenting and discussing the various views on the matter with concerned citizens and politicians from different backgrounds. Prepare role cards and flesh out your line of argument with information and data from the articles and speeches.

→ Focus on Language, Conversation and Discussion, p. 413

17. Your English pen pal David is highly concerned about the situation of post-Brexit Britain. He and his friends have followed the political debates and British media reports. He wants to know how the German media have reported on Brexit and asks you to give him a short overview.

Use your results from tasks 9 and 10 and write a letter of about 300 words in which you inform your friend about the German perspective. Be prepared to add background information on the matter if necessary.

→ Focus on Skills, Mediation, p. 412

Theresa May

First Speech as Prime Minister

AWARENESS

Look at the cartoon below. How does it present Britain's situation after Brexit and what is the new Prime Minister, Theresa May, expected to do?

Tips on vocab »»»

the office of the Prime Minister / 10 Downing Street ■ cracked walls ■ a heap of rubble ■ files ■ to look like a cleaning lady ■ to carry a bucket/broom ■ to wear an apron ■ to roll up one's sleeves

Alles neu macht die May

COMPREHENSION

1. On 13 July 2016, Theresa May was appointed the new Prime Minister by the Queen. Shortly afterwards, she delivered her speech as PM. In **a first listening**, try to understand the gist of Theresa May's remarks. Exchange your first listening impressions with a partner and clarify any questions.
   → Focus on Skills, Listening Comprehension, p. 394

Tips on vocab

> **legacy** ['legəsi] *Erbe* ■ **mortgage** ['mɔːgɪdʒ] *Hypothek* ■ **just about** *gerade so, gerade eben* ■ **to take the big calls** here: to speak with people who have a lot of money or power ■ **prioritise** [praɪ'ɒrɪtaɪz] to decide which of a group of things are the most important so that you can deal with them first ■ **to entrench** to firmly establish something, especially an idea or a problem, so that it cannot be changed ■ **to forge** *schmieden* ■ **bold** brave and confident

2. After **listening a second time**, take notes on these questions:
   - What does May appreciate and praise about Cameron's work as PM?
   - What are the guiding principles for her work as the newly elected PM?
   - How does she want to tackle injustices?
   - Who does she particularly want to help and support?
   - How does she define the government's mission for the post-Brexit U.K.?

ANALYSIS

Webcode
SNG-40235-010 @

3. In order to get a deeper understanding of the speech, you can listen to and watch a video of the speech, which is provided on the webcode.

   Step 1: Divide the class into groups of four students each and **watch/listen** to the video clip. Each member of the group focuses on <u>one</u> of the devices listed below and takes notes on relevant aspects:
   - **language** (choice of words, phrases, etc.)
   - **grammar** (sentence structure, grammatical tenses, etc.)
   - **rhetoric** (key symbols, use of grammatical persons, metaphors, etc.)
   - **manner of speaking** (volume, tempo, stress, pauses, etc.)
   → Focus on Skills, Analysis of a Political Speech, p. 407

   Step 2: Inform each other about your findings and make sure that everything has been understood.

4. A few days before May was appointed PM by the Queen, she gave a speech to the members of the Conservative Party to position herself and announce her candidacy to become the Leader of the Conservative Party and Prime Minister. In your groups, take a close look at the following excerpt from her speech:

> [...] First, following last week's referendum, our country needs strong, proven leadership – to steer us through this period of economic and political uncertainty, and to negotiate the best possible terms as we leave the European Union.
>
> Second, we need leadership that can unite our Party and our country. With the Labour Party tearing itself to pieces, and divisive nationalists in Scotland and Wales, it is nothing less than the patriotic duty of our Party to unite and govern in the best interests of the whole country.
>
> And third, we need a bold, new, positive vision for the future of our country – a vision of a country that works not for a privileged few but for every one of us. [...]
>
> But beyond that, I want to use this opportunity to make several things clear.
>
> First, Brexit means Brexit. The campaign was fought, the vote was held, turnout was high, and the public gave their verdict. There must be no attempts to remain inside the EU, no attempts to rejoin it through the back door, and no second referendum. The country voted to

leave the European Union, and it is the duty of the Government and of Parliament to make sure we do just that.

Second, there should be no general election until 2020. There should be a normal Autumn Statement, held in the normal way at the normal time, and no emergency Budget. And there should be no decision to invoke Article Fifty until the British negotiating strategy is agreed and clear – which means Article Fifty should not be invoked before the end of this year.

Third, we should make clear that for the foreseeable future there is absolutely no change in Britain's trading relationships with the EU or other markets. And until a new legal agreement is reached with the EU, which will not happen for some time, the legal status of British nationals living or working in Europe will not change – and neither will the status of EU nationals in Britain.

And fourth, while it is absolutely vital that the Government continues with its intention to reduce public spending and cut the budget deficit, we should no longer seek to reach a budget surplus by the end of the Parliament. If before 2020 there is a choice between further spending cuts, more borrowing and tax rises, the priority must be to avoid tax increases since they would disrupt consumption, employment and investment.

These are all measures that will be taken by a Conservative Government I lead, and they offer stability and certainty to consumers, employers and investors for the foreseeable future. And I want to reassure foreign governments, international companies and foreign nationals living in Britain that we are the same outward-looking and globally-minded and big-thinking country we have always been – and we remain open for business and welcoming to foreign talent.

http://www.independent.co.uk/news/uk/politics/theresa-mays-tory-leadership-launch-statement-full-text-a7111026.html, 30 June 2016 [30.11.2016]

ACTIVITIES

5. Together with a partner, conduct an interview with Britain's new Prime Minister on her vision of Britain's post-Brexit future, with one of you playing Theresa May and the other playing the journalist.
Prepare role cards and act out your interview in class.
→ Focus on Skills, Writing an Interview, p. 426

Tip: As a **journalist**, you want to challenge the PM in order to get as much information as possible – but be careful not to be offensive. You want to make your interviewee talk, not insult him.
As **Prime Minister**, you want to show your commitment and responsibility – but you must be careful not make promises that you cannot keep.

Tips on vocab

Journalist
- Is leaving the EU a means that is justified by the end … so to speak?
- Do you think that threatening the EU commission might …?
- Against the background of the UK's impressive history, shouldn't it …?
- Can you talk more about …?
- Has the UK not always taken pride in …?
- Speaking about "a better deal for Europe" – what do you consider to be …?
- Regarding globalisation, what urgent measures need to be taken …?

Tips on vocab

Prime Minister
- It is unavoidable that …
- Compared to other European nations …
- If we do not … we will/will not …
- Economically/Socially, it is irresponsible …
- With regard to globalisation, the EU …
- The UK and the Continent share …
- The EU cannot afford … without the UK …
- It is part of our British tradition to …

The European Union

The European Union (EU) is an **economic and political union** of 28 member states (ca. 505 million citizens) that has developed a single market **ensuring free movement of people, goods, services and capital**. The EU operates through supranational and intergovernmental negotiations and treaties between the member states. Economically the EU generates ca. 25 % of the gross world product.

History

1957	**Rome Treaty** creates the European Economic Community (EEC) as a customs union. Members: Belgium, France, Italy, Luxembourg, the Netherlands, West Germany
1979	first direct democratic elections to the **European Parliament**
1985	**Schengen Agreement** creates open borders without passport control between most member states
1986	the European flag is first used
1990	after German reunification, (former) East Germany joins the community
1993	in the **Maastricht Treaty**, the European Union is formally established
2002	the **Euro** is introduced as European currency and replaces national currencies in twelve of the member states
2016	23 June: 51.9 % of Britons vote in favour of leaving the European Union (→ Brexit)

Fundamental rights

- In 2009, the **Lisbon Treaty** gave legal effect to the **Charter of Fundamental Rights of the European Union** which is a catalogue of fundamental (human) rights which were derived from the constitutional traditions of the member states (e. g. **Article 1:** Human dignity is inviolable. It must be respected and protected; **Article 2:** Everyone has the right to live. No one shall be condemned to the death penalty, or executed).

Important EU institutions

- the **European Council** is the EU's supreme political authority; it defines the EU's political agenda and strategies
- the **European Commision** is the EU's executive branch and responsible for its legislation
- the **European Parliament** (in Strasbourg) forms half of the EU's legislature; the members of the European Parliament are directly elected by the EU citizens every five years
- the **Council of the European Union** is the other half of the EU's legislature; in addition to legislative functions it also has executive functions, e. g. the Common Foreign and Security Policy
- the **Court of Justice of the European Union** interprets and applies the treaties and the law of the EU
- the **European Central Bank** administers the monetary policy of the 18 member states taking part in the **Eurozone**; it is one of the world's most important central banks

The 28 EU member states

10 countries became new members in 2004
2 countries became new members in 2007
Croatia became a new member in 2013
withdrawal exspected in March 2019

The Political System of the United Kingdom

The **United Kingdom** (of Great Britain and Northern Ireland) is **a constitutional monarchy**, in which the **monarch is the head of state** and **the Prime Minister is the head of government**. The UK has been a multi-party system since the 1920s, the two largest parties being the Conservative Party and the Labour Party.

Political parties

The Conservative Party	Labour Party
• centre-right • conservatism • British Unionism (against Scottish and Welsh independence) • opposition to the Euro, strong defense of Pound Sterling • Eurosceptic position • free-market policy • criticism of Labour's state multiculturalism	• left to centre-left • democratic socialist party • supports government intervention in the economy • for redistribution of wealth • advocates increased rights for workers • favours an extended welfare state • support of multiculturalism

The U. K. system of government (separation of powers)

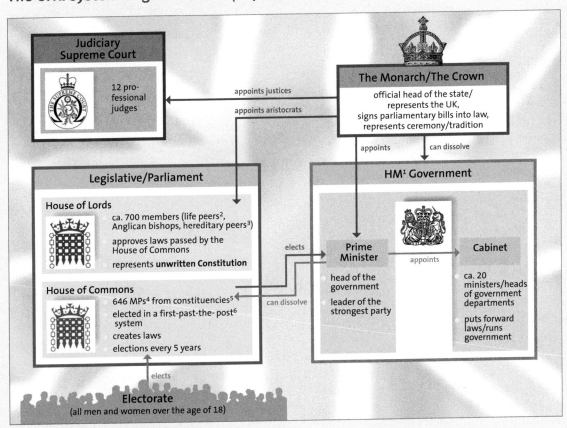

[1] **HM** (*abbr.*) Her/His Majesty's – [2] **peer** in Britain, a person who has a high social position and any of a range of titles, including baron, earl, and duke, or a life peer – [3] **hereditary peer** [həˈredɪtəri] someone who became a peer (= a high social rank) when a parent died, and who can pass it on to their oldest child; *Mitglied des Hochadels mit ererbtem Titel* – [4] **MP** (*abbr.*) Member of Parliament – [5] **constituency** [kənˈstɪtjuənsi] *Wahlbezirk* – [6] **first-past-the-post** system using a voting system in which a person is elected because they get more votes than anyone else in the area that they want to represent; *einfache Mehrheitswahl*

Focus on Facts

Dan Stewart

Britain Stumbles Toward Exit Talks with a Reinvigorated[1] Europe

AWARENESS

Pair up with a partner and describe the cover page of *The Economist*, paying attention to details.

- What does it reveal about the situation of post-Brexit Britain in general?
- How do the Britons react to the situation they are confronted with?
- In what way can the headline be interpreted?

→ Focus on Skills, Analysis of Visuals, p. 409

Tips on vocab

background:
coastline ■ the White Cliffs of Dover ■ to stretch along the coastline

centre:
an endless beach ■ countless people bending over ■ to bury one's head in the sand ■ ostrich effect (*Vogel-Strauß-Politik*) ■ to avoid sth.

foreground:
a pair of feet sticking out of the sand ■ to be buried head-long in the sand up to the feet ■ leopard print kitten-heel courts (*Pumps*) ■ a little toddler in shorts ■ to look puzzled (*verwirrt, beunruhigt*) ■ to carry a shovel and a bucket

textual element:
to face up to sth. (*phr. v.*) to accept that a difficult situation exists ■ wordplay/pun

From the pages of

TIME

It must have seemed like a good idea at the time. In April [2017], British Prime Minister Theresa ⁵May called for a snap election[2] in hopes of consolidating[3] her power. Polls[4] suggested that her Conservative Party would easily defeat the left-of-center Labour Party led by Jeremy Corbyn, an unreconstructed[5] socialist estranged[6] from ¹⁰many of his parliamentary colleagues. The vote, May said, would give the country the chance to unite behind her leadership as she guides the United Kingdom out of the European Union.

May's gamble now looks like a grave political miscalculation. Far from gaining a mandate, the Conservatives ¹⁵lost their parliamentary majority in the June 8 election, in part thanks to a resurgent[7] Corbyn's attracting younger voters to the polls. Now no party commands enough seats to push through legislation on its own. Instead, May's Tories must ally[8] with a socially con-²⁰servative party in Northern Ireland, the Democratic Unionist Party, to get anything passed. It's a highly fragile base on which to build a government, and May is vulnerable[9] to a leadership challenge if she falters[10]. What's more, only days after the result, the weakened ²⁵Prime Minister must begin the most daunting[11] task a

---

[1]**to reinvigorate** to make sb. feel healthier and more energetic again – [2]**snap election** an election called earlier than expected – [3]**to consolidate** to cause sth. to become stronger and more certain – [4]**poll** *Umfrage* – [5]**unreconstructed** having opinions or behaving in a way not considered to be modern or politically acceptable in modern times – [6]**estranged** *entfremdet* – [7]**resurgent** increasing or becoming popular again – [8]**to ally yourself with sb.** [ə'laɪ] (*phr. v.*) to start to support sb. – [9]**vulnerable** *verletzlich* – [10]**to falter** *stocken* – [11]**daunting** *entmutigend, einschüchternd*

U.K. leader has faced in generations: forging[12] a Brexit that will satisfy not only her fractured Parliament and divided country but also the 27 other E.U. member states. And she hasn't much time to do it. May triggered[13] the formal mechanism for leaving the E.U. in March [2017], setting in motion a rigid[14] two-year period of negotiations over the terms of withdrawal.

Those talks were due to begin on June 19, almost exactly a year after Britain voted to leave the E.U. Doing so will not be a simple task. Britain must first settle financial commitments already made to the bloc[15], worth perhaps as much as $112 billion, and clarify the future of 3 million E.U. citizens who currently reside in the U.K. as well as the 900,000 Britons living in the E.U. Once it has left, it can begin the knotty[16] renegotiations of at least 759 trade treaties with 132 separate entities[17]. The election was framed[18] as an opportunity to choose one of the two ways to move forward. May's Tories led the charge for a so-called hard Brexit, pulling Britain out of the E.U.'s single market completely so it could attempt to build new trade links with the world. The Labour Party and others advocated a soft Brexit, keeping trade and customs agreements intact. Crucially[19], a hard Brexit would allow the U.K. to control migration of E.U. citizens. Under a soft Brexit, those citizens might live and work freely in the U.K., much as they do now.

But voters had other things on their minds. An exit poll found that only 28 % considered Brexit the election's most important issue. Among Labour voters, the share was only 8 %. Instead, the national debate centered on the role of the state in providing public services and,

after the terrorist attacks in London and Manchester[20], national security.

Meanwhile, the E.U. looks only more focused and confident. Since the shock of Britain's exit vote a year ago, it has been buoyed[21] by the defeat of populist nationalists in the Netherlands and the election of the unabashedly[22] pro-E.U. Emmanuel Macron as President of France. Then there's the seeming indomitability[23] of German Chancellor Angela Merkel. Polls suggest that Europe's strongest champion will win a fourth term in September [2017]. The talk in Brussels is of closer integration over defense and security, not the threat of dissolution. Britain looks increasingly like an outlier[24] when it comes to pulling out.

Yet that process is bound to continue, whether or not talks begin on June 19 [2017] and even if May is chucked out[25] of Downing Street. The U.K. will leave the bloc in April 2019 even if negotiations collapse – which would be the hardest Brexit of all. At that point, Britain could face steep[26] tariffs[27] on monthly exports of more than $15 billion to E.U. nations, unleashing what the Confederation for British Industry called a "Pandora's Box[28] of economic consequences."

There was talk, in the aftermath[29] of the surprise 2016 referendum result, that E.U. negotiators might be especially hard on the U.K. as a warning to other member states that might be considering exits. But given the U.K.'s miserable experience even before talks begin, that might look like piling on[30].

TIME, 26 June 2017, pp. 5 f.
TIME and the TIME Logo are registered trademarks of TIME Inc. used under license.

COMPREHENSION

1. In a **first reading**, try to understand the **gist** of the article.

2. Exchange your first reading impressions with a partner, trying to get a **general understanding** of what the text is about and clarifying questions.

[12] **to forge** to produce sth., esp. with difficulty – [13] **to trigger** to start sth. – [14] **rigid** fixed – [15] **bloc** a group of countries that have similar political interests; here: the European Union – [16] **knotty** (*infml.*) complicated and difficult to solve – [17] **entity** (*fml.*) *Einheit, Gebilde* – [18] **to frame** *etw. entwerfen* – [19] **crucially** *ausschlaggebend* – [20] **terrorist attacks in London and Manchester** in 2017, there were three terrorist incidents in London; in May and June 2017 there were terrorist attacks in Manchester – [21] **to buoy** [bɔɪ] to make sb. feel cheerful or confident – [22] **unabashedly** without any worry about possible criticism or embarrassment – [23] **indomitability** *Unbezwinglichkeit* – [24] **outlier** [ˈaʊtˌlaɪər] *Ausreißer* – [25] **to chuck sb./sth. out** (*infml.*) to force sb. to leave a place – [26] **steep** (*infml.*) too much or more than is reasonable – [27] **tariffs** a charge; *Gebühren* – [28] **Pandora's Box** an artefact in Greek mythology; today: an action that seems to be small and innocent, but turns out to have far-reaching negative consequences – [29] **aftermath** the period that follows an unpleasant event or accident, and the effects that it causes – [30] **to pile on** here: to be too harsh on sb.

3. **While reading** the article **a second time**, pay attention to details and take notes on these aspects:
   - PM May's intention in calling for a snap election
   - the actual outcome/result of the June 2017 election
   - the challenges the Brexit negotiations pose to Britain, its population and the British economy
   - the consequences of
     a) a hard Brexit and
     b) a soft Brexit
   - the position of the European nations and their political leaders
   - the consequences of the worst scenario, a hard Brexit, for the U.K.

ANALYSIS

4. Dan Stuart's article has an ironic undertone with regard to May's and the U.K.'s situation. Find examples of this in the text and explain the effect and function of each rhetorical device.
   → Focus on Skills, Analysis of a Non-Fictional Text, p. 405

M 5. Examine the cartoon below and explain German cartoonist Nik Ebert's view on the Brexit negotiations.
   → Focus on Skills, Analysis of Visuals, p. 409

BREXIT

17.07.17

Tips on vocab 〉〉〉

hotel reception ■ receptionist

left: a board with room keys ■ to work at a computer ■ to type sth. in ■ to have a grim facial expression

centre: adding machine/calculator receipt paper roll ■ to present sb. a bill/receipt

right: customer ■ to sneer/smirk (*spotten*) ■ to be/look annoyed

6. Since the EU referendum and subsequent Brexit, the U.K. and its citizens have had to face a seemingly endless row of unexpected pitfalls and problems.
   The German media in particular have watched the various events with growing concern and headshaking.

Step 1:

Subdivide the German newspaper article on p. 91 into thematic units and find a suitable English headline for each of them.

Step 2:

M Omit less relevant information and mediate the article into English, following the thematic units and headlines. Write a text of about 250–300 words.
   → Focus on Skills, Mediation, p. 412

Tip: Do not forget to include relevant statistical data in your text.

7. First, describe the cartoon which presents PM Theresa May facing a heap of rubble. Pay attention to details as well as textual and pictorial elements.

Second, relate the cartoon's message to the information given in the English and German articles.

→ Focus on Skills, Analysis of Visuals, p. 409

Tips on vocab »»»

(to stand on) a giant heap of rubble ■ to lie in ruins ■ to be in shambles ■ a cracking rock ■ to try to fix/repair sth. with cello tape ■ buckets of cement ■ trowel (*Kelle*) ■ to bend over ■ to look down on sth. ■ to look helpless ■ to be at a loss ■ to frown/sneer

---

Jochen Wittmann

Zerrissenes[1] Königreich

Vier Terrorangriffe in nur drei Monaten hatten Großbritannien zugesetzt, dann löste der Brand im Grenfell Tower in London Entsetzen aus[2]. Nun legt der Brexit offen: Die britische Gesellschaft ist [5] **gespaltener[3] denn je.**

Irgendwann werden sie ihn abreißen[4] müssen, aber noch steht der Turm der Schande[5]. Es ist ein düsteres Mahnmal[6], das da in den Himmel über London ragt. In der nordwestlichen Ecke, der Armenecke des „Königli[10]chen Stadtbezirks von Kensington und Chelsea", steht die Ruine des Grenfell Tower: Ein 74 Meter hohes Grabmal, das bis zum obersten Stock ausgebrannt ist. Die schwarzberußte[7] Außenhaut[8]: zerfetzt[9], zerbeult[10]. Voller Löcher dort, wo die Fensterscheiben barsten.

[15] „Wenn ihr sehen wollt, wie die Armen sterben", beginnt ein Gedicht des Lyrikers Ben Okri, „kommt und seht Grenfell Tower." Mindestens 80 Menschen sind hier gestorben, das ist die offizielle Angabe[11]. Großbritannien erlebte in der Nacht zum 14. Juni [2017] die größte Feu[20]erkatastrophe der Nachkriegszeit[12], als ein Kühlschrank explodierte und einen Brand im Hochhaus auslöste.

Vier Terroranschläge in drei Monaten, drei davon im Zeitraum von nur drei Wochen, haben die Briten erschreckt und alarmiert. Das Grenfell-Inferno hat sie nun erschüttert[13]. [25]

Wenn es um Terror geht, haben die Briten ein dickes Fell[14]. Durch die Anschläge von Extremisten werden sie in ihrer stoischen Mentalität[15] geeint. Doch die Katastrophe in Nord-Kensington hatte den umgekehrten Effekt: Der Hochhausbrand steht für die Spaltung[16] der [30] Gesellschaft. Das Gefühl, das viele Briten mit Grenfell verbinden, sagt ihnen: Etwas ist zutiefst falsch, etwas ist ganz und gar aus dem Ruder gelaufen[17]. Grenfell war keine Katastrophe, die reinigend wirkt[18]. Stattdessen ist es eine Wunde, die schwärt[19]. „Es hat die Unterströ[35]mungen[20] unserer Zeit enthüllt", heißt es in Ben Okris Gedicht.

Es ist, als ob ein Schleier weggezogen[21] wurde, als ob sich jetzt etwas kristallisiert in einem Symbol, dem Turm der Schande. Das Unglück hat die soziale Spal[40]tung des Landes, die Konsequenzen von sieben Jahren Austeritätspolitik[22] unter der konservativen Regierung und den scheinbaren Vorrang der Interessen von begüterten Eliten[23] sinnfällig[24] gemacht. Und es fällt in eine Zeit, in der die wachsende gesellschaftliche Polarisie[45]rung immer deutlicher wird.

---

[1] divided – [2] to provoke/to unleash horror/fear – [3] more divided – [4] to tear sth. down – [5] tower of disgrace – [6] memorial – [7] black with soot – [8] the outer shell – [9] ragged – [10] battered – [11] official declaration – [12] post-war era – [13] shaken – [14] to have a thick skin – [15] stoic mentality – [16] divison – [17] to get out of control – [18] to have a clarifying effect – [19] to fester – [20] undercurrent – [21] to unveil – [22] austerity policy – [23] wealthy elites – [24] to make sth. obvious

Die vorgezogene Neuwahl[25] Anfang Juni [2017] hat dies eindrucksvoll demonstriert. Nachdem in den vergangenen Jahren der Trend zum Mehrparteiensystem[26] immer stärker geworden war, gab es bei dieser Wahl einen Umschwung: die Rückkehr zum Zweiparteiensystem[27]. Die Zeiten sind ernst, dachten die Leute, der Brexit steht bevor, da müssen die Erwachsenen ran: Wir haben nicht den Luxus, uns mit kleinen Parteien abzugeben. Zur Wahl standen somit vor allem die zwei großen Parteien, Labour und Konservative, die zusammen über 82 Prozent der Stimmen einsammelten.

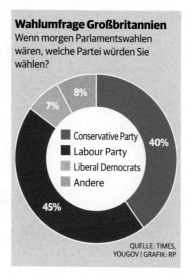

Wahlumfrage Großbritannien
Wenn morgen Parlamentswahlen wären, welche Partei würden Sie wählen?

- Conservative Party — 40%
- Labour Party — 45%
- Liberal Democrats — 7%
- Andere — 8%

QUELLE: TIMES, YOUGOV | GRAFIK: RP

„Eine starke und stabile Führung" strebe sie an, um gestärkt in die Brexit-Verhandlungen ziehen zu können, hatte Premierministerin Theresa May verkündet, als sie die vorgezogene Neuwahl für Juni ansetzte. Die Briten entschieden anders. Die überraschende Stärkung von Labour, die ihren Stimmenanteil um zehn Prozent anheben konnten, hat deutlich gemacht: May hat kein klares Mandat[28] mehr für ihren harten Brexit-Kurs. Stattdessen ist Großbritannien ein zerrissenes Land. Ein Land, gespalten in Jung und Alt, Brexit-Fans und EU-Freunde, englische und schottische Nationalisten sowie urbane Zentren, von Labour dominiert, und Rest-England, wo Konservative den Ton angeben. Statt für klare Verhältnisse hat May für Unübersichtlichkeit[29] gesorgt. Und das in Zeiten, in denen die Wirtschaft erste negative Konsequenzen des Brexit spürt.

Nun schwindet Mays Glaubwürdigkeit[30] auch noch, weil Finanzminister Philip Hammond weiter stichelt[31]. Der Schatzmeister[32] ist nicht nur zum größten internen Widersacher für May geworden. Hammond wird neben Oppositionsführer Jeremy Corbyn hinter vorgehaltener Hand sogar schon als ihr Nachfolger[33] gehandelt. Bereits bei der britischen Volksabstimmung[34] vor einem Jahr hatte sich Hammond gegen den Brexit ausgesprochen, obwohl er die EU in Teilen kritisch sieht. Der 61-Jährige sagt, was sich sonst keiner traut: dass der EU-Austritt schmerzhaft wird. Und er hat öffentlich gesagt, dass die Mehrheit des Parlaments nicht den harten Brexit wollte, den May anstrebt, sondern den sanften EU-Abschied befürworte.

„Es ist schwierig", hatte die Queen anlässlich ihrer offiziellen Geburtstagsfeierlichkeit verlauten lassen, „sich der sehr düsteren[35] nationalen Stimmung zu entziehen." Vordergründig[36] mag Elizabeth II. die Terrorattacken der vergangenen Monate gemeint haben, und natürlich hatte sie auch auf das Inferno von Grenfell angespielt. Die Queen, die laut der ungeschriebenen Verfassung[37] politisch strikt neutral bleiben muss, wird aber auch einerseits die desolate politische Lage und andererseits die beispiellose[38] politische Herausforderung[39] Brexit im Blick gehabt haben. Großbritannien, befand die britische Zeitung „Guardian", gehe in die Brexit-Gespräche, „ohne Regierung und ohne Plan, wie man die größte geopolitische Kursänderung[40] in die Tat umsetzt". Das ist nur ein klein wenig überspitzt[41]. Natürlich hat das Königreich zur Zeit eine Regierung. Aber sie ist eine Minderheitsregierung, steht auf tönernen Füßen[42], muss sich die Unterstützung durch die nordirische DUP mit einer Finanzspritze[43] von einer Milliarde Pfund erkaufen, wird durch innerparteiliche Querelen bei den Konservativen genauso bedroht wie durch eine wiedererstarkte Opposition und hat beste Aussichten, demnächst erneut Neuwahlen überstehen zu müssen. Und was den Brexit-Plan angeht: Auch der ist vorhanden, aber angesichts der innenpolitischen Unabwägbarkeiten[44] nicht mehr als eine Absichtserklärung[45].

Großbritannien geht schweren Zeiten entgegen[46] und ist sich über den zukünftigen Kurs unsicherer denn je.

Rheinische Post, 19 July 2017, p. A 2

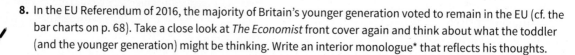

ACTIVITIES

8. In the EU Referendum of 2016, the majority of Britain's younger generation voted to remain in the EU (cf. the bar charts on p. 68). Take a close look at *The Economist* front cover again and think about what the toddler (and the younger generation) might be thinking. Write an interior monologue* that reflects his thoughts.

---

[25] snap election – [26] multi-party system – [27] two-party system – [28] mandate – [29] confusion – [30] credibility – [31] to taunt – [32] treasurer – [33] successor – [34] referendum – [35] bleak – [36] ostensibly – [37] unwritten constitution – [38] second to none – [39] challenge – [40] geopolitical shift – [41] exaggerated – [42] to be built on sand – [43] cash injection – [44] imponderability – [45] declaration of intent – [46] to face hard times

just emerged from a war of an intensity never seen before or since and had slipped into the shadow of the Korean conflict. Sixty years ago, a new "Elizabethan Era" was awaited with enthusiasm tinged[17] with uncertainty about the challenges ahead for the country.

If, as Gandhi asserted[18], "the best way to find yourself is to lose yourself in the service of others", then Your Majesty must have found Yourself countless times over the past six decades. You have dedicated Your life to others. The daily example that You set, mirrored by our courageous armed forces of which You are Commander-in-Chief, is extraordinary. Yet perhaps Your Majesty's most profound[19] contribution has been to the continuity that has made change manageable.

For transformation is inevitably[20] turbulent. It has been Your singular accomplishment[21], Your unique capacity, to hold together that which could have been torn asunder[22]. You have moved with the times and allowed the times to move around the rest of society.

This is a different Britain from 1952 but not one detached from[23] then. We are in so many ways a much bigger, brighter and better United Kingdom. This is a land where men and women today are equal under the law and where Your people are respected, regardless of how they live, how they look or how they love. This is a nation of many races, faiths and customs, now beginning to be reflected in Parliament. All this progress has occurred during Your reign. You have become, to many of us, a kaleidoscope Queen of a kaleidoscope country in a kaleidoscope Commonwealth.

This gathering is one of many diverse events across these islands in tribute to You and this great anniversary. Our affection as a nation will rightly embrace the Duke of Edinburgh and other members of Your family. These will be moments striking for the sincerity[24] expressed as much as for the scenery encountered. Sixty years of stability. Sixty years of security. Sixty years of certainty. Sixty years of sacrifice. Sixty years of service. Gandhi also observed that "in a gentle way, you can shake the world". Your Majesty, in a gentle way You have shaken this United Kingdom and the world for six decades. On behalf of all the members of the House of Commons, may I thank You wholeheartedly for all that You have done, are doing and will do for the good of our country.

www.parliament.uk/business/news/2012/march/speaker-addresses-hm-the-queen, 22 March 2012 [18.12.2014]

3 Queen Elizabeth II: Address to Both Houses of Parliament

My Lords and Members of the House of Commons, I am most grateful for your Loyal Addresses and the generous words of the Lord Speaker and Mr Speaker.

This great institution has been at the heart of the country and the lives of our people throughout its history. As Parliamentarians, you share with your forebears[25] a fundamental role in the laws and decisions of your own age. Parliament has survived as an unshakeable cornerstone of our constitution and our way of life. History links monarchs and Parliament, a connecting thread[26] from one period to the next. So, in an era when the regular, worthy[27] rhythm of life is less eye-catching than doing something extraordinary, I am reassured that I am merely the second Sovereign to celebrate a Diamond Jubilee.

As today, it was my privilege to address you during my Silver and Golden Jubilees. Many of you were present ten years ago and some of you will recall the occasion in 1977. Since my Accession[28], I have been a regular visitor to the Palace of Westminster and, at the last count, have had the pleasurable duty of treating with twelve Prime Ministers.

Over such a period, one can observe that the experience of venerable[29] old age can be a mighty guide but not a prerequisite[30] for success in public office. I am therefore very pleased to be addressing many younger Parliamentarians and also those bringing such a wide range of background and experience to your vital, national work.

During these years as your Queen, the support of my family has, across the generations, been beyond measure. Prince Philip is, I believe, well-known for declining compliments[31] of any kind. But throughout he has been a constant strength and guide. He and I are very proud and grateful that The Prince of Wales and other members of our family are travelling on my behalf in this Diamond Jubilee year to visit all the Commonwealth Realms and a number of other Commonwealth countries.

---

[17] **to tinge** [tɪndʒ] *leicht einfärben* – [18] **to assert** (*fml.*) to say sth. is certainly true – [19] **profound** *tiefgründig* – [20] **inevitably** [ɪˈnevɪtəbli] *unvermeidbar* – [21] **accomplishment** *Errungenschaft* – [22] **to tear sth. asunder** *etw. auseinanderreißen* – [23] **detached from** separated from – [24] **sincerity** *Aufrichtigkeit* – [25] **forebear** (*fml.*) *Vorgänger* – [26] **thread** [θred] here: link, connection – [27] **worthy** (*fml.*) deserving respect, admiration, support – [28] **accession** *Thronbesteigung* – [29] **venerable** [ˈvenərəbl] deserving respect because of its importance – [30] **prerequisite** [ˌpriːˈrekwɪzɪt] (*fml.*) *Voraussetzung* – [31] **to decline a compliment** *ein Kompliment zurückweisen*

These overseas tours are a reminder of our close affini-
40 ty[32] with the Commonwealth, encompassing about one-
third of the world's population. My own association
with the Commonwealth has taught me that the most
important contact between nations is usually contact between its peoples. An organisation dedicated to certain
45 values, the Commonwealth has flourished and grown by
successfully promoting and protecting that contact.
At home, Prince Philip and I will be visiting towns and
cities up and down the land. It is my sincere hope that
the Diamond Jubilee will be an opportunity for people
50 to come together in a spirit of neighbourliness and celebration of their own communities.
We also hope to celebrate the professional and voluntary service given by millions of people across the
country who are working for the public good. They are
55 a source of vital support to the welfare and well-being
of others, often unseen or overlooked.
And as we reflect upon public service, let us again be
mindful of the remarkable sacrifice and courage of our

Armed Forces. Much may indeed have changed these
past sixty years but the valour of those who risk their 60
lives for the defence and freedom of us all remains undimmed[33].
The happy relationship I have enjoyed with Parliament
has extended well beyond the more than three and a
half thousand Bills[34] I have signed into law. I am there- 65
fore very touched by the magnificent gift before me,
generously subscribed[35] by many of you. Should this
beautiful window cause just a little extra colour to
shine down upon this ancient place, I should gladly settle for[36] that. 70
We are reminded here of our past, of the continuity of
our national story and the virtues[37] of resilience[38], ingenuity[39] and tolerance which created it. I have been privileged to witness some of that history and, with the
support of my family, rededicate myself to the service 75
of our great country and its people now and in the
years to come.

www.bbc.com/news/uk-politics-17446804, 20 March 2012 [20.07.2014]

ANALYSIS

3. Although the overall tone of the speeches is highly official and rather "stiff", John Bercow and the Queen herself try to ease the atmosphere by employing some humorous remarks. Identify these remarks and explain what they hint at in particular.
→ Focus on Skills, Analysis of a Political Speech, p. 407

4. The three speeches are so-called "honorary speeches". Compare these speeches to political speeches that you know of (e.g. Sadiq Khan, Theresa May, pp. 55 ff., 83 ff.) and explain the differences in style and tone.

5. In 2013, the BBC commissioned an artwork called *The People's Monarch* that depicts the Queen at the time of her accession in 1952 and at her Diamond Jubilee in 2012 (see next page). It is a 38-square-metre canvas containing 5,000 photos of British people who contributed their private photos, snapshots, etc.

> ### The People's Monarch Stories
> Helen Marshall says: "Many people submitted family portraits, photos of their ancestors, snaps of im-
> portant occasions in their lives and of times that made them laugh. Some viewers also used the oppor-
> tunity to share precious memories of loved ones they had lost. Everyday family snapshots, scans of
> photos of ancestors or from an era gone by, times of celebration and ceremony or times of trouble and
> 5 loss, all remind us of our century old love affair with the camera. But more important, this project
> proves that we do not need to be professional photographers or artists to be recognised or represented
> in an artwork, and that the photograph has a unique and simple ability to speak directly to all of us, no
> matter of our differences."
>
> www.thepeoplespicture.com/helen-widget-test [20.07.2014]

---

[32] **affinity** a close relationship between two things – [33] **undimmed** here: *ungeschmälert* – [34] **bill** *Gesetzesvorlage* – [35] **to subscribe**
unterschreiben, abzeichnen – [36] **to settle for sth.** (*phr. v.*) to accept or agree to sth. – [37] **virtue** *Tugend* – [38] **resilience** [rɪˈzɪliəns] (*fml.*)
Ausdauer – [39] **ingenuity** [ˌɪndʒəˈnjuːɪti] *Genialität*

'The People's Monarch' by artist Helen Marshall was commissioned by BBC South East and depicts the Queen at the time of her coronation and at her Diamond Jubilee. It is 38 square metres containing 5.000 photos. It's current home after touring at Towner Gallery, Turner Contemporary and Rochester Cathedral is at Gatwick Airport.

a) Describe the artwork and state what effect it has on the viewer.

b) Watch the video clips and examine further photos provided on the webcode and relate the message of *The People's Monarch* to John Bercow's remarks that Queen Elizabeth II is a "kaleidoscope Queen …" (l. 39). Explain the implications and allusions employed in the speech as well as in the artwork. Can the Queen really be considered a "people's monarch"?

→ Focus on Skills, Analysis of Visuals, p. 409

ACTIVITIES

6. John Bercow focused on the Queen's adaptability to change and her ability to "move with the time" – he calls her a "kaleidoscope Queen of a kaleidoscope country in a kaleidoscope Commonwealth" (ll. 39 f.). Assess John Bercow's observations and remarks and state whether or not you can subscribe to this view of the Queen, the UK and the Commonwealth.

Tip: Refer to texts and material from this unit you have already dealt with to underpin your assessment.

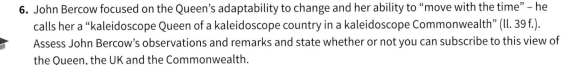

GRAMMAR / LANGUAGE

7. Choose one of the speeches and report it to a friend who has not watched the ceremony. Use **indirect speech** and be sure to use the correct **tenses** and to **backshift** if necessary. Do not forget to employ appropriate introductory verbs and sentences.

Examples:
- (ll. 11 f.)   Baroness D'Souza said that the Queen's role <u>had evolved</u> imperceptibly.
- (ll. 15 f.)   The Queen emphasized that it <u>had been</u> her privilege to address the Houses of Parliament during her Silver and Gold Jubilees.

Webcode
SNG-40235-011

Christina Patterson

A Pay Rise for the Queen? She's Worth Every Penny

M **Step 1:** Look at the photo of the Queen amidst construction workers, taken after the official dedication of the renovated station of Reading [rɛdɪŋ], London, by Her Majesty, then read the German text below the photograph. What image of the Queen and her "job" as monarch is conveyed?

 @ **Step 2:** Watch the video clip of the Queen's visit to Reading using the webcode and describe the overall atmosphere during the Queen's visit. State how the construction workers might have felt after the event.

Gut gelaunt im Job – Eine Queen unter Bauarbeitern

Kürzertreten sieht anders aus: Im Juni [2014] belegen die Eintragungen im offiziellen Hofkalender des britischen Königshauses an 26 Tagen Aktivitäten von Elizabeth II., 88; meistens absolvierte die älteste amtierende Königin der britischen Geschichte mehrere Termine an einem Tag. Auch im Juli sind bis jetzt viele Empfänge, Besichtigungen und Einweihungen dokumentiert, darunter die Eröffnung des erneuerten Bahn-
5 hofs von Reading, an dem jahrelang gebaut worden war. Die Queen erschien, taufte einen Zug, besichtigte das Gelände und traf „einige Mitarbeiter", wie es im Kalender auf der Website „The British Monarchy" heißt. Das Foto von der offenbar gut gelaunten Monarchin inmitten nicht minder gut gelaunter Bauarbeiter zeigt: Elizabeth genießt ihren Job königlich.

ks, in: DER SPIEGEL, 31/2014, 28 July 2014, p. 132

Monarchy may be a ridiculous system, but we should celebrate a lifetime of hand-shaking and plaque-unveiling[1]

1 This week, the Queen got a pay rise. One of the richest women in the country, with a "personal net worth" of £340m, is to get an increase in her "sovereign grant[2]" of 5%. That's five times higher than the pay rise given to most public sector workers. It's a rise, in fact, of over £2m. Or you could buy a nice big house in north London.

The Queen doesn't really need a house in north London. She's got Balmoral Castle, Buckingham Palace, Windsor Castle, Kensington Palace, the Royal Parks, the Royal art collection, Ascot racecourse … Oh, and she's got swans. In spite of all the stories about the slaughter of our most precious birdlife by migrants, she's still got a few swans. If she ever grew tired of grilled Dover sole[3], she could always barbecue a swan. Most of this, it's true, she couldn't flog off[4]. If, for example, she decided she wanted to swap[5] a Da Vinci cartoon for one of those Chapman Brothers[6] mannequins studded[7] with tiny penises, she couldn't. And if she wanted to downsize to a bungalow in Bexhill[8], she couldn't do that either. She couldn't do it because the rules say she can't. It isn't absolutely clear how the rules were made. They don't seem to come from Magna Carta, though since most of us haven't read it we can't be sure. But the rules are there, and the Queen seems to think that rules, like promises, are things you don't break.

2 On her 21st birthday she made a big promise. "I declare before you all," she said, in a broadcast to the Commonwealth, "that my whole life, whether it be long or short, shall be devoted to your service." You might have thought this was the kind of promise most of us make at least once a year, like saying you'll go to the gym or cut back[9] on the booze[10]. But, it turned out, it wasn't. Sixty-seven years after she made it, Elizabeth Windsor still tries to keep that promise every day.

If you were rich, very rich, and also technically in charge[11] of everyone, you might want to make sure that most of the things you did were quite good fun. You might, for example, want to spend the morning in bed, eating chocolate and reading novels, and then go and meet a friend or two for lunch. You might want to spend the afternoon going to see some art – or perhaps a matinee – and then host a reception for Barack Obama before collapsing on to the sofa with a box set of The West Wing[12].

You probably wouldn't choose to get up early, go to your desk, read a pile of letters from your subjects, then a pile of policy papers, then a pile of official documents and then a pile of briefing notes for the meetings you had coming up. You probably wouldn't think, after quite a modest lunch, that what you really wanted to do was go to a school, and then a hospital, and then a "visitor attraction," and give a speech or unveil a plaque. You certainly wouldn't think that the best way of passing your precious time was by asking an awful lot of polite questions and shaking an awful lot of hands in the knowledge that you'll probably have to carry on doing this until you die.

If the Queen is tempted to follow the example of the Spain's King Juan Carlos and hand her boring job to her eldest son, she hasn't shown much sign of it.

At 88, she still carries out about 430 engagements a year. Those, by the way, are on top of the paperwork that starts and ends her day. The light in her study, according to palace insiders, is often one of the last to go out.

3 Of course, it's ridiculous, in the 21st century, to have a constitutional system based on birth. You might as well pick a monarch through Russian roulette. But sometimes in life, you just get lucky.

And when a young king decided that he loved an American divorcee[13] more than his country, we as a nation got lucky. We could have a President Hollande[14], or Zuma[15], or even a President Miliband[16]. Instead, we have a head of state who is respected throughout the world.

There aren't all that many public figures who believe in public service. There aren't many who still think it's better to listen than to speak. There certainly don't seem to be many who think that what matters in life isn't what you say, or think, or feel, but how you behave.

---

[1] **plaque-unveiling** *die Enthüllung von Gedenktafeln* – [2] **sovereign grant** the amount of money given to the Queen by the government – [3] **Dover sole** *Seezunge* – [4] **to flog sth. off** (*phr. v.*) to sell a part of a business or industry – [5] **to swap sth.** *etw. tauschen* – [6] **Chapman Brothers** Jake and Dinos Chapman; British visual artists – [7] **studded with sth.** having a lot of sth. on or in it – [8] **Bexhill** a seaside town in the county of East Sussex – [9] **to cut back on sth.** (*phr. v.*) to do less of sth. – [10] **booze** (*infml.*) alcohol – [11] **to be in charge** being the person who is responsible for sb./sth. – [12] **The West Wing** US political drama TV series set primarily in the West Wing of the White House – [13] **American divorcee** reference to Wallis Simpson (1896–1986), an American socialite, for whom King Edward VIII abdicated his throne to marry her; Edward was her third husband – [14] **President Hollande** President of France since 2012–2017 – [15] **Zuma** (Jacob) President of South Africa since 2009 – [16] **Miliband** (Edward) Leader of the British Labour Party since 2010

The Queen makes it clear through her actions that she does. She thinks it's fine to have a boring job, and a boring day, if your boring day is a highlight of someone
85 else's life. She thinks, in other words, that it's a good idea to live your life as if it is not all about you.

The Queen's "sovereign grant" which will largely go on the cost of carrying out her duties and on maintaining royal palaces, comes from the profits of the crown estate[17]. It's set to rise to £40m a year. That's a bit more 90 than a penny a person a week. All that dignity, and all that wisdom, for a penny per person per week. Whoever next gets to shake the royal hand should tell her: "Ma'am, you're cheap."

The Guardian, 28 June 2014, p. 36

COMPREHENSION

1. According to the author, the Queen is always busy doing a rather boring job.

Step 1: In a **first reading**, **scan** the article and **get a general understanding** of the Queen's "job".

Step 2: Pair up with a partner and summarize what the article depicts about:
- the Queen's properties and income
- the rules and regulations that (seem to) determine the Queen's life
- the promise the Queen made on her 21st birthday and its far-reaching consequences for her private life and job
- the hard life of being Queen
- the benefits of having Queen Elizabeth II as head of state
- why the Queen is worth every penny she is paid

2. Großbritannien: Brexit – Charmeoffensive der Royals

Webcode
SNG-40235-012 @

M

Watch the German *ARD Weltspiegel TV* documentary using the link provided on the webcode and take notes on the following aspects:
- the strategy behind the royal visit
- the royals being forced to entertain and entice (*umgarnen*) important politicians
- limits to diplomacy
- William and Kate visiting European neighbours
- Prince Charles visiting Romania
- the true mission of royal diplomacy
- → Focus on Skills, Mediation, p. 412

Tips on vocab »»

charm offensive ■ His Royal Highness ■ Romania ■ folklore ■ royal correspondent ■ to do a huge amount of travelling ■ to soften/to polish ■ to create sharp/hard edges ■ to cancel ■ soft side of sth. ■ hard Brexit ■ a masterpiece of diplomacy ■ subtle/understated staging/enactment ■ to trace/look into ■ valuable ■ ultimate adjusting screws ■ tool kit ■ bearskin ■ coach ride ■ to put a good face on things ■ reason of state ■ state visit/ official visit ■ prostitution of the royals ■ to hit sb. over the head ■ sign of despair ■ creative high-performance sport ■ tone ■ brush stroke ■ important place ■ stuffed toys ■ masterfully orchestrated ■ to filter out ■ the William-and-Kate brand ■ travelling salesman ■ reconstruction/rebuilding ■ children's foundations/charities ■ dingy ['dɪndʒi] ■ trade agreements

ANALYSIS

3. Examine the ironic tone of the article and explain how the rhetorical and stylistic devices create the humorous and satirical effect.
→ Focus on Skills, Analysis of a Non-Fictional Text, p. 405

---

[17] **the crown estate** *Immobilienverwaltung der britischen Krone*

4. In lines 26 ff. the author jokingly refers to the Magna Carta in connection with rules and regulations that (supposedly) were imposed on British monarchs. Take a closer look at the Focus on Facts page *Domesday Book and Magna Carta* (p. 104) and find out about the restrictions that were put on King John by his subjects in 1215.
   → Focus on Skills, Analysis of a Non-Fictional Text, p. 405

5. Look at the cartoon and analyse the grim humour it conveys.

   Step 1: Describe the cartoon, paying attention to details and visual symbols and their function and effect.
   → Focus on Skills, Analysis of Visuals, p. 409

   Step 2: Compare the views taken in the text and the cartoon and identify similarities and differences.

£36.2m a year from us, 60 years and counting.

Tips on vocab >>>

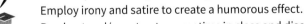

| call girl posture ■ sagging bosom ■ cellulite ■ protruding teeth ■ oversized mouth ■ to smirk ■ the royal swan ■ to heave sb. up ■ the Royal Guards ■ to buckle under a heavy weight/burden ■ Corgies ■ to hump sb.'s leg ■ to pee on sb./sth. |

ACTIVITIES >>>>>>>>>

6. In a group, turn the information you have gained about Queen Elizabeth II's life and job into a satirical text, for example "The Busy and Boring Life of a Queen".
   Employ irony and satire to create a humorous effect.
   Read out and/or act out your satires in class and discuss the various results.

7. Act out a panel discussion in which you discuss whether the monarchy is really "worth every penny" or too costly and should be reconsidered, especially in economically difficult times.
   → Focus on Language, Conversation and Discussion, p. 413

Landmarks in British History

Earliest times

Prehistory
2500 B.C. — construction of Neolithic monuments, e. g. Stonehenge

The Celts
700 – 55 B.C. — the technically advanced Celts arrive from central Europe; skilled metalwork with iron; agriculture; simple economic capitals and trade across tribal borders; Druids (priests) are very important

The Romans
55 B.C. – 430 A.D. — foundation of the province Britannia; introduction of reading and writing; foundation of many towns; construction of Hadrian's wall against attacks of Scottish tribes

Stonehenge

The Middle Ages

Anglo-Saxon invasion
430 A.D. – 800 A.D. — Germanic tribes, the Angles, Saxons and Jutes, invade Britain and raid cities; establishment of a number of kingdoms; division of the land into administrative areas called 'shires'

7th century — spread of Christianity

Vikings
800 – 1066 — Norway and Denmark invade Britain

Norman conquest
1066 — William the Conqueror defeats the Saxon King Harold in the battle of Hastings; William is crowned in Westminster Abbey; the Saxon land is given to Norman nobles; establishment of 'feudalism' (= land is given in return for service to a lord)

1086 — Domesday Book – economic survey of England is carried out

Magna Carta
1215 — agreement between King John and nobles grants subjects political freedom; collapse of English feudalism

The beginnings of parliament
— the word 'parliament' was used to describe meeting of the king and the barons: barons → House of Lords; people from the counties → House of Commons

Plague and disorder
1348 – 49 — ca. 1/3 of the British population dies because of the Plague; shortage and therefore increased value of labour leads to the end of serfdom; revolts against the king's taxes

Crises of kings and nobles – War of the Roses
1460 – 85 — fight between the house of Lancaster and the house of York for the crown (York's symbol is a white rose, Lancaster's a red rose); result: half of the lords and the noble families are killed in the wars → Tudors become powerful

The Stanwick horse mask, Iron Age, 50 B.C. – 100 A. D.

Sutton Hoo Anglo-Saxon gold helmet

Bayeux tapestry: the Norman conquest of England

The Tudors (1485 – 1603)

1509 – 47 **Henry VIII**
— breaks with the Roman Catholic Church; foundation of the Church of England; England becomes a Protestant country; has three children: Edward, Mary and Elizabeth; beginning of the Ulster plantation (Ireland)

Elizabeth I
1558 – 1603 — after the reign of Edward and Mary, Elizabeth has to deal with the struggle between Catholics and Protestants; trade rivalry between England and Spain

1588 — defeat of the Spanish Armada → England becomes Europe's leading sea power; establishment of East India Company, colonies

Culture
— literacy increases; Thomas More writes *Utopia*; William Shakespeare's works become famous and popular

The roses of York and Lancaster

Elizabeth I

The Stewarts

1642 – 45	**Civil War**
	• ongoing quarrels between the kings and Parliament about rising debts; disputes and fights between Protestants and Catholics; (religious) rebellions in Ireland and Scotland
1649 – 60	• Britain: a republic under leadership of Oliver Cromwell who dissolves Parliament; he calls himself 'Lord Protector of England'
	Revolution of thought
1688	• the 'Glorious Revolution' takes place; based on theories of thinkers like John Locke, Parliament has more power than the king; Britain becomes a constitutional monarchy; → Bill of Rights; Act of Settlement
1689/1701	• rising influence of Puritanism; revolution in scientific thinking, e. g. Francis Bacon, Isaac Newton and Christopher Wren

Oliver Cromwell

Isaac Newton

The 18th century

	Beginning of Imperialism
1759	• British control over Canada (defeat of the French in Quebec); defeat of the French in India → control of most of India; rise of transatlantic trade
	• growing radicalism leads to loss of the American colonies
1775 – 83	• war against the rebellious American colonies
	Industrial Revolution
1769	• James Watt invents the steam engine which revolutionizes the (industrial) production of steel, cotton, etc.; rising numbers of factories and increasing production of goods

Watt's steam engine

The 19th century

	The workshop of the world
	• British factories produce more than any other country in the world; control of world traffic and world markets
	• exploitation of workers and suffering farmers → rise of poverty and misery; Charles Dickens → descriptions of crime and poverty
1824/34	• first workers' unions are founded/workers' revolt in London
	British Empire/Victorian Age
1837 – 1901	• reign of Queen Victoria; she is very popular – connects monarchy with Britain's 'glorious history'

Queen Victoria

The 20th century

1914 – 18	**World War I**
	• after disastrous destruction and high number of casualties there is great hatred against Germany; Germany is severely punished
	• demand of home rule for Ireland; riots and fighting; civil war
1939 – 45	**World War II**
	• more than 360,000 Britons are killed; Britain, the USA, France and the Soviet Union become allies to fight Germany
1945	• the United Nations comes into existence
1945 – 65	• 500 million people in former colonies become self-governing
1973	• Britain joins the EU
1982	• in a war, Britain is able to recapture the Falkland Islands from Argentina
1980s	• black immigrants riot against bad housing and economic problems in London, Liverpool, Bristol

PM Winston Churchill

The 21st century

	Wars on Iraq
1990 – 91	• Gulf War; invasion led by USA and UK
2003 – 10	• Iraq War; UK ends combat in 2009
2014	• Scottish independence referendum: the majority of Scots vote against independence (55.3 % vs. 44.7 %)
2016	• 23 June: referendum to leave the European Union (Brexit): 51.9 % of Britons vote in favour of leaving the EU
	• 24 June: David Cameron announces resignation
	• 13 July: Theresa May becomes new Prime Minister

PM Theresa May

Domesday Book and Magna Carta

Domesday Book (1086)

In 1086, **William the Conqueror** commissioned a great land survey to assess the extent of land and resources in England, which served as a basis for raising taxes. Royal commissioners were sent around to collect and record the information – which was written in Latin.

5 It contained details about how many people occupied the land, the amounts of woodland, meadows, animals, livestock, fish and ploughs – as well as buildings on the land, e. g. churches, castles, mills, etc. In all, there are 13,418 towns and villages recorded in the Domesday Book. In 2006, a complete online version was made available (www.domesdaybook.co.uk).

The Magna Carta (1215)

The Magna Carta was the first document forced onto an English king by a group of his subjects in order to limit his powers and protect their privileges. In 1215, the Charter required **King John of England** to proclaim certain liberties. This constitutional document is considered **the foundation of the freedom of the individual against the arbitrary[1] authority of the despot**. It led to the constitutional law in the English-speaking world and was

5 the first of a series of constitutional documents such as the **Petition of Rights (1628)**, the **Habeas Corpus Act (1679)**, the **Bill of Rights (1689)** and the **Act of Settlement (1701)**. It greatly inspired the United States Constitution of 1789.

> **John, by the grace of God King of England, Lord of Ireland, Duke of Normandy and Aquitaine, and Count of Anjou, to his archbishops, abbots, earls, barons, justices, foresters, sheriffs, stewards, servants, and to all his officials and loyal subjects, Greeting.** [...]
>
> (1) First, that We have granted to God, and by this present charter have confirmed for us and our heirs[2] in
> 5 perpetuity, that the English Church shall be free, and shall have its rights undiminished, and its liberties unimpaired. That We wish this so to be observed, appears from the facts that of our own free will, before the outbreak of the present dispute between us and our barons, We granted and confirmed by charter the freedom of the Church's elections – a right reckoned to be of the greatest necessity and importance to it – and caused this to be confirmed by Pope Innocent III. [...] To all free men of our kingdom We have also granted, for us and
> 10 our heirs for ever, all the liberties written out below [...]: [...]
> (12) No 'scutage' (e. g. cash payment) or 'aid' of money paid instead of may be levied[3] in our kingdom without its general consent, unless it is for the ransom[4] of our person, to make our eldest son a knight, and (once) to marry our eldest daughter. [...]
> (13) The city of London shall enjoy all its ancient liberties and free customs, both by land and by water. We also
> 15 will and grant that all other cities, boroughs, towns, and ports shall enjoy their liberties and free customs. [...]
> (39) No free man shall be seized or imprisoned, or stripped of his rights or possessions, or outlawed or exiled, or deprived of his standing in any other way, nor will We proceed with force against him, or send others to do so, except by the lawful judgement of his equals or by the law of the land.
> (40) To no one We will sell, to no one deny or delay right or justice. [...]
> 20 (42) In future it shall be lawful for any man to leave and return to our kingdom unharmed and without fear, by land or water, preserving his allegiance[5] to us, except in time of war, for some short period, for the common benefit of the realm. People that have been imprisoned or outlawed in accordance with the law of the land [...] are excepted from this provision.

[1] **arbitrary** decided or arranged without any reason or plan, often unfairly – [2] **heir** [eə(r)] *Erbe, Erbberechtigter* – [3] **to levy** ['levi] to officially say that people must pay a tax or charge – [4] **ransom** *Kaution* – [5] **allegiance** [ə'li:dʒəns] loyalty

constitution/independence/treaties/politics		
act	a law that has been officially accepted	*Gesetz*
Article 50	Article 50 of the Lisbon treaty: the article that defines the procedure and timetable of the Brexit	*Artikel 50 des Vertrags über die europäische Union regelt den Austritt eines Mitgliedsstaates der EU*
to appoint sb.	to choose sb. for a job or position of responsibility	*jdn. berufen, ernennen*
bill	a written proposal for a new law that is brought to parliament to be discussed	*Gesetzesentwurf*
charter/carta	a statement of the principles, duties and purposes of an organization	*Charta, Satzung*
constitutional document	an officially/legally accepted document	*Verfassungsurkunde*
constitutional monarchy parliamentary monarchy	a country ruled by a king or queen whose power is limited by a constitution/parliament	*konstitutionelle Monarchie*
despot [ˈdespɒt]	tyrant	*Despot, Tyrann*
diplomacy	the activity of managing relations between different countries	*Diplomatie*
electorate	all the people who are allowed to vote	*Wählerschaft*
empire	a group of countries that are ruled or controlled by one ruler or government	*Empire*
establishment	the important and powerful people who control a country	*Führungsschicht; Establishment*
foreign policy	a government's policy on dealing with other countries	*Auslandspolitik*
head of government	the official leader of a government	*der Kopf (die Leitung) der Regierung*
House of Commons	one of the two parts of parliament in the UK and Canada, whose members are each elected to represent a particular official area of the country, or its members	*das britische Unterhaus*
House of Lords	one of the two parts of the UK parliament, whose members are not elected but have a high social position, or its members	*das britische Oberhaus*
judiciary [dʒuːˈdɪʃəri]	the part of a country's government that is responsible for its legal system, including all the judges in the country's courts	*die Justiz*
mayor	a person who is elected or chosen to lead the group who governs a town or city	*Bürgermeister*
MP (Member of Parliament)	a member of a parliament	*britische(r) Parlamentsabgeordnete(r)*
multi-party system	a system in which multiple political parties across the political spectrum run for national election	*Mehrparteiensystem*
to negotiate, negotiation	to discuss sth. in order to reach an agreement, esp. in business or politics	*verhandeln; Verhandlung*
Parliament; Parliamentarian	the group of (usually) elected politicians or other people who make the laws for their country	*das Parlament*
poll	a study in which people are asked for their opinions about a subject or person	*Umfrage*
red tape	bureaucracy	*Bürokratie*
referendum (on sth.)	when people vote to make a decision about a particular subject, rather than voting for a person	*Referendum; Volksentscheid*
Secretary of State	in the UK, a Member of Parliament who is in charge of a government department	*Kabinettsminister*

sovereign, sovereignty ['sɒvərɪn]	having the highest power or being completely independent; the power of a country to control its own government	souverän; unabhängig; Souveränität
Tory	a member of the British Conservative Party	der Tory; Mitglied der konservativen Party
treaty	a written agreement between two or more countries, formally approved and signed by their leaders	Vertrag; Abkommen
to trigger sth.	to start sth.	etw. in Gang setzen

Britishness/class system/royals		
to abdicate	if a king or queen abdicates, he or she makes a formal statement that he or she no longer wants to be king or queen	abdanken
affluent	wealthy	reich, wohlhabend
Britain/British Isles	England, Scotland, and Wales	Großbritannien, die britischen Inseln
coronation (ceremony)	a ceremony in which a person is made king or queen	Krönung(szeremonie)
council estate	an area with low-income houses built by a local council	sozialer Wohnungsbau
to (officially) dedicate sth.	when a building, especially a religious building, is dedicated, there is a ceremony at which it is formally opened for use and its particular purpose is stated	etw. offiziell einweihen
elite [i'li:t]	wealthiest most privileged class	die gesellschaftliche Elite
emergent	starting to emerge or become known	aufsteigend
HRH; His/Her Royal Highness	a title of some members of the royal family	Ihre/Seine königliche Hoheit
legacy ['legəsi]	sth. that is part of your history	Erbe
precariat	the poor	gesellschaftliche Unterschicht
the Queen's Guard	infantry and cavalry soldiers charged with guarding the official royal residences in the United Kingdom	die königliche Garde
realm [relm]	a country ruled by a king or queen	Reich
reign	the period of time when a king or queen rules a country	Herrschaftszeit
social class	a particular group of people in a society	soziale Schicht
sovereign	a king or queen	Herrscher/in
sovereign grant	the payment which is paid annually to the monarch by the government	jährlicher Etat, den ein Herrscher vom Staat bekommt
to sustain sth.	to experience sth. bad	etw. ertragen
the Union Flag; the British flag	the red, white and blue flag of the UK	der Union Jack; die britische Flagge
the United Kingdom/the U.K.	the country that consists of England, Scotland, Wales, and Northern Ireland	das Vereinigte Königreich
working class	a social group that consists of people who earn little money, often being paid only for the hours or days that they work, and who usually do physical work	die Arbeiterklasse

economy		
austerity (policy)	a difficult economic situation caused by a government reducing the amount of money it spends	Sparpolitik
to be economically worse off	to have less money/income than before	wirtschaftlich schlechter dran sein
to force sb. out of business	to make sb. lose their job/business	jdn. aus dem Markt drängen
to generate sth.	to produce sth.	etw. herstellen
to liberalize trade	to make trade laws less severe; to open trade barriers	den Handel liberalisieren
living standard/standard of living	the amount of money and comfort people have in a particular society	Lebensstandard

(to take) measures	a way of dealing with a situation and improving it	*Maßnahmen ergreifen*
NHS; National Health Service	the service in the UK that provides free or cheap medical treatment for everyone and is paid for through taxes	*staatliches Gesundheitssystem*
prosperity	the state of being successful and having a lot of money	*Wohlstand, Reichtum*
protectionist barriers against imports	to prevent foreign goods from being imported into your country, e. g. by imposing high taxes on them	*Importschranken zum Schutz der heimischen Wirtschaft*
public expenses	money that is spent by the state, e.g. for public services	*öffentliche Gelder/Ausgaben*
social equity	the situation of people of a state of being treated fairly and equally	*soziale Gleichheit*
to subsidize; subsidy	to pay a part of the cost of sth.	*etw./jdn. subventionieren*
regionalism/nationalism/Islamophobia		
British Overseas Territories	territories under the jurisdiction and sovereignty of the United Kingdom	*britisches Hoheitsgebiet/ Staatsgebiet*
ethnic minority	minority belonging to a particular race of people	*völkische Minderheit*
Islamophobia	unreasonable dislike or fear of, and prejudice against, Muslims or Islam	*der Islamhass*
Muslim [ˈmʊzlɪm]	a person who follows the religion of Islam	*Muslim(a)*
national consciousness	strongly identifying with a particular state/nation	*Nationalbewusstsein*
national pride	being proud of belonging to a particular nation and what it represents	*Nationalstolz*
prejudice; to be prejudiced	an unfair and unreasonable opinion or feeling, especially when formed without enough thought or knowledge	*Vorurteil; Vorurteile haben*
xenophobia	a strong feeling of dislike or fear of people from other countries	*Fremdenfeindlichkeit*
European Union		
bloc	a group of countries that have similar political interests	*Staatenblock/-verbund*
to compile a formal complaint	to officially express that you do not want/like sth.	*eine formelle Beschwerde einreichen*
continental Europe; the Continent	the continuous continent of Europe excluding its surrounding islands; Europe, especially western Europe, but not including the British Isles	*das europäische Festland*
economically disadvantaged	being in an economically worse situation than other people; being poor	*wirtschaftlich benachteiligt*
EU benefits	the advantages a country has from being a member of the EU	*EU-Vorteile*
euro crisis	a multi-year debt crisis that has been taking place in the European Union since the end of 2009	*Eurokrise*
euro-friendly	a person, country or government that supports the EU and likes being a member of it	*EU-freundlich*
Eurosceptic, Euroscepticism	sb. who is critical of the EU and its policy	*kritisch gegenüber der EU eingestellt sein*
intergovernmental	between two or more governments	*zwischenstaatlich*
Single European Market	a single market which seeks to guarantee the free movement of goods, capital, services, and labour – the "four freedoms" – within the European Union	*der europäische Binnenmarkt*
trade agreement	a formal agreement between two or more countries to facilitate trade with each other, for example by removing import taxes	*Handelsabkommen*
trade barrier	something such as an import tax or a limit on the amount of goods that can be imported that makes international trade more difficult or expensive	*Handelsschranke*

Focus on Vocab

Postcolonial and Neo-Colonial Experiences: India and Britain

Indian students celebrating Holi, the Hindu festival of colours, which is celebrated across India. The festival takes place at the end of the winter season and marks the beginning of spring

START-UP ACTIVITIES

1. Listen to the music taken from the soundtrack of the film *The Best Exotic Marigold Hotel* and imagine the atmosphere. In a round robin activity, exchange your listening impressions. What pictures, colours, smells, etc. does the music evoke in you?

2. First, describe the photo above and the atmosphere and mood it conveys. Then state whether your listening impressions match the photo. Does the photo match your ideas about India?

 3. In groups, read the excerpt from the screenplay of *The Best Exotic Marigold Hotel* and take notes on what is said about a) the hotel itself, b) its manager and CEO Sonny and c) India in general.

 4. In groups, work creatively with the film script and choose between these tasks:
   a) Based on the description of the hotel as well as Sonny's comments, design a homepage in which you promote the hotel to (British) pensioners.
   b) As there is almost no dialogue in the excerpt, you are asked to add either interior monologues* depicting the thoughts of the pensioners or dialogues* in which they talk to each other or to Sonny about the situation. In order to get further ideas, you can watch the film trailer provided on the webcode.

> **Tips on vocab**
>
> blotch of paint ■ multi-coloured ■ bright ■ flower garland ■ to grin ■ to smirk (*schmunzeln*) ■ to exchange telling (*vielsagend*)/meaningful looks ■ to scream with laughter ■ horselaugh (*wieherndes Lachen/laute Lache*)

Ol Parker

The Best Exotic Marigold Hotel ✖

Seven British pensioners have decided to spend their old age at a retirement hotel called "The Best Exotic Marigold Hotel" in Jaipur, India. Based on pictures on the hotel's website the Britons expect to find a picturesque hotel, dating back to the time of the Raj[1], which offers luxurious accommodation[2] and services at affordable rates. The following excerpt from the screenplay depicts the last part of their long and exciting journey to the hotel.

32 EXT. BUS – DAWN 32

The sun rises. A beautiful, pearly dawn. The bus drives through the great gates of Jaipur. Below, the city shimmers in the heat. It's a magnificent sight.

5 EVELYN (O.S.)   What exactly is a tuk-tuk[3]?

33 EXT. JAIPUR STREET – DAWN 33

Our heroes are squashed[4] into a pair of them, facing forwards and backwards, attempting not to swallow too much dust as they wheel crazily through the teeming[5] morning streets of the city.
10 They stare in amazement at the world racing past them.
A scooter overtakes. A young man is driving, his girl-friend riding side-saddle on the back. Her sari billows out behind her. Douglas and Evelyn both watch her, struck by this image of beauty, youth and vitality.

15 34 EXT. STREET/GARDEN PATH. MARIGOLD HOTEL – MORNING 34
The tuk-tuks have pulled up, and our travelers emerge[6], exhausted and dirty, staring through some garden gates at the Marigold Hotel. Once a beautiful building, once possibly even luxurious, it
20 is clearly in the process of being given at least half the face-lift it badly needs. Parts of the building are freshly painted, some of the ornate[7] balconies are crumbling[8], and one wall is clad[9] with crazily skewed[10] bamboo scaffolding[11]. A huge old tree towers over an untended[12] garden, its branches poking[13] into the win-
25 dows of the building.

34A EXT. ROOFTOP. MARIGOLD HOTEL – MORNING 34A
A young man leans out from an upper balcony to see the arrival below: SONNY KAPOOR (early 20s). He deposits a paint pot and brush on a parapet[14], and races off across the rooftop.

30 34B EXT. GARDEN/PATH/COURTYARD. MARIGOLD HOTEL – MORNING 34B
Dazed[15] and horrified, the travelers wander up the pathway. A cow standing in front of them is pushed into the garden by a couple of young houseboys who then run to the tuk-tuks to col-
35 lect their luggage.

www.imsdb.com/scripts/Best-Exotic-Marigold-Hotel.-The.html [10.08.2014]

23.
34C EXT. STAIRWAY/COURTYARD. MARIGOLD HOTEL – MORNING 34C
Sonny clatters[16] down the steep[17] steps, and comes tearing[18] out onto a verandah, as the travelers arrive in the courtyard below. 40
He spreads his arms wide.

SONNY   Welcome to India!!!
They stare up at him.

35 EXT/INT. COURTYARD/HALLWAY. BEDROOM. MARIGOLD HOTEL – DAY 35   45
The courtyard is not without charm, although somewhat dilapidated[19]. A fountain at the centre does not look as if it has seen water in years, and faded awnings are strung up haphazardly[20]. Sonny is leading Madge into the darkness of the building, towards her room.   50

SONNY   This is a building of the utmost[21] character, which means that perhaps not everything will function in the way you expect it to. But as the manager and chief executive supervising officer of the Marigold Hotel, I can tell you with great pride that the building has stood for centuries, and will stand for many 55 more, in 100 % shipshape[22] condition. Please follow me, carefully avoiding that naughty stone there round this corner, leading us most successfully all the way to – your bedroom!
The room is very small, comfortable, and tastefully decorated. But there's no door.   60

MADGE   Where?

SONNY   Here. In here.

MADGE   My dear man. Rooms have doors. What you're showing me here is an alcove[23].

SONNY   The door is coming soon, most definitely.   65

MADGE   How soon?

24.
SONNY   Let us not concern ourselves with details, Mrs Hardcastle. Rather than speaking of doors, we should instead take pleasure in the freedom to roam[24].   70

[1] **Raj** [rɑːdʒ] British rule in India – [2] **accommodation** Unterbringung – [3] **tuk-tuk** a motorized three-wheeled rickshaw – [4] **to squash sb./sth.** quetschen – [5] **teeming** von Menschen wimmelnd – [6] **to emerge** heraustreten – [7] **ornate** verschnörkelt – [8] **to crumble** zerbröckeln – [9] **clad** here: covered – [10] **skewed** schräg – [11] **scaffolding** Gerüst – [12] **untended** ungepflegt – [13] **to poke** ausstrecken – [14] **parapet** Brüstung – [15] **dazed** benommen – [16] **to clatter** klappern – [17] **steep** steil – [18] **to tear** to move somewhere very quickly or in an excited way – [19] **dilapidated** baufällig – [20] **haphazard** [ˈhæpˈhæzəd] willkürlich – [21] **utmost** greatest – [22] **shipshape** clean and neat – [23] **alcove** Wandnische – [24] **to roam** to wander freely

The Raj – Britain's Dreams and India's Nightmares

Mahatma Gandhi

There Is No Salvation[1] for India (1916)

> "Be the change that you want to see in the world."
> "First they ignore you, then they laugh at you, then they fight you, then you win." *Mahatma Gandhi*

Discuss these Gandhi quotations in class.

The following speech from which this excerpt is taken was given on the occasion of the opening of the Banares Hindu University on 4 February 1916. The Viceroy, Lord Hardinge, as well as eminent persons from all over India attended.

Our language is the reflection of ourselves, and if you tell me that our languages are too poor to express the best thought, then I say that the sooner we are wiped out of existence the better for us. Is there a man who
5 dreams that English can ever become the national language of India? (Cries of 'Never') Why this handicap on the nation? Just consider for one moment what an unequal race our lads have to run with every English lad. I had the privilege of
10 a close conversation with some Poona[2] professors. They assured me that every Indian youth, because he reached his knowledge through the English language, lost at least six precious years of
15 life. Multiply that by the number of students turned out by our schools and colleges, and find out for yourselves how many thousand years have been lost to the nation. The charge[3] against
20 us is that we have no initiative. How can we have any if we are to devote the precious years of our life to the mastery of a foreign tongue? ...
The only education we receive is Eng-
25 lish education. Surely we must show something for it. But suppose that we had been receiving during the past fifty years education through our vernaculars[4], what should we have today? We

should have today a free India, we should have our edu- 30 cated men, not as if they were foreigners in their own land but speaking to the heart of the nation; they would be working amongst the poorest of the poor, and whatever they would have gained during the past fifty years would be a heritage for the nation. (Applause) 35
His Highness the Maharajah who presided[5] yesterday over our deliberations[6] spoke about the poverty of India ... But what did we witness in the great pandal[7] in which the foundation ceremony was per- 40 formed by the Viceroy? Certainly a most gorgeous[8] show, an exhibition of jewellery which made a splendid feast for the eyes of the greatest jeweler who chose to come from Paris. I compare 45 with the richly bedecked[9] noblemen the millions of the poor. And I feel like saying to these noblemen, 'There is no salvation for India unless you strip[10] yourselves of this jewellery and hold it 50 in trust for your countrymen in India.' ('Hear, hear' and applause) [...]
Look at the history of the British Empire and the British nation; freedom-loving as it is, it will not be a party to 55 give freedom to a people who will not take it themselves.

Gandhi at 10 Downing Street in 1931

www.mkgandhi.org/speeches/bhu.htm [17.12.2014]

---

[1] **salvation** *Erlösung, Errettung* – [2] **Poona** an important centre in the religious and social movements of the late 19th century in India – [3] **charge** *Anschuldigung* – [4] **vernacular** [vəˈnækjələ(r)] local language – [5] **to preside** [prɪˈzaɪd] *den Vorsitz haben* – [6] **deliberation** careful consideration or discussion – [7] **pandal** *provisorische Plattform* – [8] **gorgeous** extremely attractive – [9] **bedecked** decorated – [10] **to strip** to remove sth.

British Perspectives on the Raj

George Orwell: Reflections on Gandhi

At about the time when the [Gandhi's] autobiography first appeared I remember reading its opening chapters in the ill-printed[1] pages of some Indian newspaper. They made a good impression on me, which Gandhi himself, at that time, did not. The things that I associated with him – homespun cloth, 'soul forces' and vegetarianism – were unappealing, and his medieval[2] programme was obviously not viable[3] in a backward, starving, overpopulated country. It was also apparent that the British were making use of him, or thought they were making use of him. Strictly speaking, as a Nationalist, he was an enemy, but since in every crisis he would exert[4] himself to prevent violence – which, from the British point of view, meant preventing any effective action whatever – he could be regarded as 'our man'. In private this was sometimes cynically admitted. The attitude of the Indian millionaires was similar. Gandhi called upon them to repent[5], and naturally they preferred him to the Socialists and Communists who, given the chance, would actually have taken their money away. How reliable such calculations are in the long run is doubtful; as Gandhi himself says 'in the end deceivers deceive only themselves'; but at any rate the gentleness with which he was nearly always handled was due partly to the feeling that he was useful. The British Conservatives only became really angry with him when, as in 1942, he was in effect turning his non-violence against a different conqueror.

But I could see even then that the British officials who spoke of him with a mixture of amusement and disapproval also genuinely liked and admired him, after fashion.

from *Essays* by George Orwell. Penguin, London, 1984, pp. 459 f.

Viscount Rothermere (1861–1949), highly successful newspaper publisher (*Daily Mail, Daily Mirror*)

British rule in India is irreplaceable. It has been bought by British lives and built up by British capital. If we had not gone to India, she would still be in a state of semi-barbaric[6] anarchy[7]. Our duty there is not to argue with base agitators[8], but to govern.

India, 1930s

transcription from the DVD *The British Empire*, narrated by Art Malik, Lingua Video, Bonn

Marjorie Usher, an officer's wife

Entertaining in this country is very simple. You just tell the servants how many are coming and they see to[9] everything.

We have nine servants, including the ayah, the head servant, who acts as valet[10] to Colonel Sterling, the kitmugar, who waits at table and looks after the silver and the dhobi, or washerman, who does our clothes very well indeed.

Chakrata, 1930s

transcription from the DVD *The British Empire*, narrated by Art Malik, Lingua Video, Bonn

A sahib being pedicured and fanned by servants, early 1900s

[1] **ill-printed** of bad quality – [2] **medieval** [ˌmediˈiːvl] *mittelalterlich* – [3] **viable** [ˈvaɪəbl] realistic – [4] **to exert oneself** [ɪɡˈzɜːt] to work very hard and use a lot of physical or mental energy – [5] **to repent** [rɪˈpent] (*fml.*) to be sorry for sth. and wish you had not done it – [6] **semi-barbaric** [ˌsemibɑˈbærɪk] half uncivilized – [7] **anarchy** [ˈænəki] a situation in which there is no effective government and no order – [8] **agitator** [ˈædʒɪteɪtə(r)] sb. who encourages people to change sth. in society – [9] **to see to sth.** to make sure or check that sth. is done, to take care of sth. – [10] **valet** [ˈvæleɪ] a male servant who looks after a man's clothes, serves his meals, etc.

COMPREHENSION

1. In a paired reading activity,
   a) subdivide the excerpt from Gandhi's speech into thematic units,
   b) summarize these units to each other and
   c) find an appropriate headline for each thematic unit.

2. State why Gandhi thinks that education is so important for the identity of the people.

3. Specify who in particular Gandhi is criticizing.

4. Looking at George Orwell's reflections on Gandhi and Gandhi's second quote at the top of p. 110, say who the players and the winner were and give reasons for your answer.

5. Listen to the statements of Viscount Rothermere and Marjorie Usher: How do they see their role in colonial India?

Info

Mahatma Gandhi (1869 – 1948) was the most important political, ideological and spiritual leader of India during the Indian independence movement. His idea and strategy was to resist British rule through mass civil disobedience and total non-violence. He inspired movements for civil rights and freedom across the world. In 1930, he and his followers protested the British-imposed salt tax with the non-cooperation movement and the famous salt march. In 1942, he launched the "Quit India" civil disobedience movement. On 30 January 1948 he was assassinated by a Hindu extremist.

Info

George Orwell (1903 – 1950) was an English author and journalist, known for his awareness of social justice and opposition to totalitarianism. His grandmother lived in Moulmein, and Orwell spent several years in Burma and Moulmein (1922 – 1927), where he first served as an Imperial Police Officer. Later he was promoted to Assistant District Superintendent. Based on these experiences he wrote numerous essays on politics, literature and culture. He is best known for the dystopian novel *Nineteen Eighty-Four* and the satirical novella *Animal Farm*.

ANALYSIS

6. Gandhi could not end his speech in 1916 because his audience was very upset. Analyse his arguments and his choice of words and try to find out what upset them most.
   → Focus on Skills, Analysis of a Political Speech, p. 407

7. Compare the photo showing Gandhi in front of 10 Downing Street in London to Orwell's impression and assessment of Gandhi. How does he interpret people's reaction to Gandhi?

8. Take a close look at Gandhi's concluding remarks (ll. 53 – 57): Which events in British history might Gandhi have had in mind?

@ Study the Focus on Facts page *Landmarks in British History* (p. 102) and/or do research on the Internet and find examples that match Gandhi's assumption.

ACTIVITIES

 9. Look at the photo below taken of a tea party. Choose one of the people in the picture and imagine what they might have been thinking. Write an interior monologue*.
In a role play, stage the photo and read out your monologues.

Sahibs being waited on by their Indian servants, early 1900s

GRAMMAR / LANGUAGE

10. Imagine you are a journalist who listened to Gandhi's speech. Write an editorial in which you outline the main aspects of his speech as well as the audience's reaction to it. Use **indirect speech** and think about appropriate **introductory verbs and phrases** to report what Gandhi said. Be careful to use the correct grammatical tenses.

Example: Mr Gandhi recalled a close conversation he had had with some Poona professors. They had assured him that ...

Tips on vocab ≫

to emphasize sth. ■ to criticize sb./sth. ■ to imply ■ to refer to sth. ■ to allude to ■ to mention ■ to state ■ to express (clearly) ■ to blame sb. for sth. ■ to address sb./sth. ■ to call sth. into question/to doubt sth.

Alice Perrin

The Rise of Ram Din

AWARENESS

The following excerpt is taken from a short story that was written during British rule in India. The daughter of a general serving in the Bengal Cavalry, Perrin wrote many novels and short stories based on her experiences. Do you think that the phrase "I was just following orders …" is an excuse for doing something bad or criminal? Discuss in class.

COMPREHENSION

1. **Before reading/listening:**
   Take a close look at the historical photo on page 115.
   a) What do you assume to be each servant's job/chore [tʃɔːr] (*Hausarbeit*) in the household?
   b) What do you consider to be the servants' hierarchy? Make a ranking and give reasons for your answer.
   c) Relate the historical photo to the title of the short story and speculate: How can a servant "rise", i.e. get promoted and reach a higher position in the household?
   → Focus on Skills, Analysis of Visuals, p. 409

1 It was in the year of the famine[1], when my father, Ram Bux of Kansrao in the Mathura district, bade me make ready to go with him to the city of Kings – which is two days' journey by road from the village – that I
5 might there obtain[2] employment as dish-washer in the service of a sahib[3]; for there were many of us in my father's house, and his crops had failed for want[4] of rain, so that there was not enough food to fill our stomachs. In his youth my father, Ram Bux, had himself served
10 the *Feringhees*[5], and having heard him speak much of those days I felt that I should learn my duties with the greater ease[6]; and as we journeyed through the dry, empty fields in the early morning time, he also told me many more things concerning the ways of the sahibs,
15 which are not the ways of the dark people. I was but a stripling[7], and knew little of what happened beyond the village of my birth where I worked in the fields and tended the cattle until the day came of which I now speak; and I learned from my father that it is well to
20 obey the orders of the master without thought or question, even when it might be hard to understand the reason of his wishes.
[…]

'And what if the sahib beats me for no fault, as thou[8] sayest[9] will happen on occasions?'
25 'Take thy[10] beating and say nothing. Above all things, do not run away. The *Feringhees* themselves are brave, though they are dogs and sons of dogs, and when they behold[11] courage in others do they respect it. A beating does little harm. I lived once with a colonel-sahib who
30 gave medicine as a punishment, and that was bad. There are certain sahibs who neither drink, nor beat, nor swear, but it is hard for a newcomer without recommendations or experience to obtain service with such, and the sahibs whom I served in the old days have now
35 all died or gone back across the black water many years since. Thou must be content at first with what thou canst[12] get; only remember this – obey orders without question, quarrel not with thy fellow-servants, and squander[13] not thy wages in the bazaar.' […]
40

2 My father told me that, though the native city was wide and full of people, there were now but few sahibs, and no regiments at all; whereas he remembered that before the Mutiny[14] there had been a large cantonment[15] and many sepoys[16].
45

---

[1] **famine** ['fæmɪn] *Hungersnot* – [2] **to obtain sth.** to get sth. – [3] **sahib** used when talking to a man in authority – [4] **for want of sth.** for lack of sth. – [5] **feringhee** European, lit. foreigner – [6] **with ease** easily – [7] **stripling** (*old-fashioned*) youth – [8] **thou** [ðaʊ] (*old use*) you – [9] **thou sayest** (*old use*) you say – [10] **thy** [ðaɪ] (old use) your – [11] **to behold** (*lit.*) to look at sth. – [12] **thou canst** (*old use*) you can – [13] **to squander sth.** ['skwɒndə(r)] here: to waste – [14] **Mutiny** Indian Mutiny against the British in 1857 – [15] **cantonment** a camp where soldiers live – [16] **sepoy** Indian soldier in the British army

There was no service to be had at the house of the mag-
istrate-sahib, or with the colonel – sahib of police, nor
with the doctor-sahib, so we went to the bungalow of
the engineer-sahib who looked after the roads and
50 buildings of the district. There we heard that a dish-
washer was needed, and the *khansamah-jee*[17] said that
if my father gave him a *backsheesh*[18], and I promised
him a percentage of my pay, he could get me the place
without any recommendation. He also said that the
55 engineer-sahib was a good sahib, and the service to be
desired, and that I should be well treated. So after some
argument my father paid the *khansamah*, who was
named Kullan, and I gave the promise. My father told
me again to obey orders and answer not[19] to abuse, and
60 then he left me and went back to his village. […]

3 Two days later, when the sahib was sitting at breakfast eating but little and drinking whisky, the *khansamah* spilt some sauce on the tablecloth, and my knees
shook as the sahib rose slowly from his seat, and, look-
65 ing at Kullan with eyes like those of a tiger, walked towards him just as the striped-one[20] approaches its victim. Kullan knelt and prayed for mercy, but the sahib
dragged him over the floor till his coat came off in the
sahib's hand, and he kicked the man along the ground
70 like a game ball, driving him into the verandah. Kullan
rose quickly, looking like a beast that is hunted, but
before he could flee the sahib caught him and pushed
him into the lamp-closet[21] that led from the verandah,
and locked the door. He laughed as he put the padlock[22]
75 key in his pocket, and heard Kullan crying and smit-
ing[23] at the door from the darkness within the godown[24]. When he turned and saw me looking, he shook
his fist at me, and told me to go to my work. Then the
sahib went to his room and lay on the bed and slept,
80 and I cleared away the breakfast and washed up everything; afterwards I went to the kitchen and found it
empty, and none answered to my call. They had all fled
in fear, having doubtless heard the noise of the sahib's
rage, and there was no one left save I, Ram Din the
85 dish-washer, and Kullan the *khansamah*, who was crying and calling in the lamp godown.
Towards sundown a telegram came for the sahib, and
not without misgiving[25] in my heart I took it to his

Domestic servants at Madras in 1870

room. He awoke and read the telegram, and then arose
in haste, speaking of trouble concerning a bridge in the 90
district, and bidding me pack his bag with clothes sufficient for a day and night, and order his trap[26] to be got
ready, and bring him whisky.
I packed the bag and brought the whisky, and I said,
'Your highness, there is no syce[27] in the stables, they 95
have all run away. But thy slave can harness[28] the horse.'
I went straightaway, and with trouble and patience I put
the horse to the cart and brought it to the door. The sahib
did not beat me, though from want[29] of knowledge I had
done it badly, and when I told him there were no serv- 100
ants left at all he cursed[30] their souls to hell, and bade me
stay and take care of everything till he should return.
I asked him, 'What are the orders concerning Kullan
khansamah who is imprisoned with the lamp godown?'
He laughed, and the sound was like the cry of a hyena[31] 105
round the walls of the village at dusk[32]. 'The order is
that he stay there till I return. Dost thou understand?'
I *salaamed*[33], and he drove away.

4 Then did my heart glow within me, for now had my
time come, and the sahib should see that I was of use, 110
and could obey. All that evening was I alone in the

---

[17] **khansamah-jee** cook, -jee: a term of respect – [18] **backsheesh** tip, present – [19] **to answer to sth.** (*phr. v.*) here: to object to sth. –
[20] **striped-one** tiger – [21] **closet** *Vorratskammer, Abstellkammer* – [22] **padlock** a strong lock – [23] **to smite** [smaɪt] (smote, smitten) (*old use*)
to hit sb./sth. very hard – [24] **godown** here: closet – [25] **misgiving** doubt – [26] **trap** here: a vehicle with two wheels, pulled by a horse –
[27] **syce** [saɪs] a stable groom – [28] **to harness** *einem Pferd Zaumzeug anlegen* – [29] **want of sth.** (*idm.*) because of a lack of sth. –
[30] **to curse sb.** *jdn. verfluchen* – [31] **hyena** [haɪˈiːnə] *Hyäne* – [32] **dusk** *Abenddämmerung* – [33] **to salaam** to greet sb. with a bow of the
head and right palm raised to forehead

kitchen, and Kullan cried in the godown. I fed the horses and the fowls[34], and after locking up the house at night I took my bed and placed it in the verandah that I

115 might guard against thieves. But I could not sleep by reason of the noise made by the *khansamah*, and I answered him not, for I feared he might persuade me to disobey orders and break open the padlock, and I remembered my father's words. Also did I rejoice[35] that

120 Kullan was in trouble, for had he not deceived my father and taken money under false pretences[36], and did he not get exact percentage from my miserable pay as dish-washer? So I smiled when I heard him beating on the door and calling, and I only feared that when the

125 sahib returned and let him out Kullan might kill me for heeding[37] not his entreaties[38].

But the sahib did not return the next evening nor the next, and I was forced to move my bed from the front verandah to back of the house on account of the howl-

130 ing of Kullan in the godown. I slept on the other side of the house, and I kept away from the front verandah, but still could I hear him wailing[39] and calling, and I refrained[40] from bursting open the padlock on the door because of the orders of the sahib.

135 On the fourth day the sahib had not returned; and the voice of Kullan was hoarse[41] and faint[42]. By the sixth day it was altogether silent, and I thought, 'Now shall I rise to be chief servant; also now will the household accounts be in my hands, and I shall amass[43] wealth.'

140 **5** When the sahib came back on the morning of the seventh day he looked weary[44], and as though he had suffered much care and anxiety[45]; he took no notice of me nor did he ask me any questions. I led his horse and trap to the stables, I got his bath and laid out his clean

145 clothes, and brought his breakfast. All the time he was deep in thought and was making figures with a pencil on a piece of paper. I wished to speak, and remind him about Kullan, but it was hard to attract his attention. I coughed[46] and walked about the room, and moved the

150 plates on the breakfast-table, and I took a fly-trap[47] and killed flies with some noise.

At last, when the sahib began to light a big cheerot[48], I carved[49] permission to speak, and he told me to say what I had to say quickly and not to disturb him.

'Sahib,' I said, with humility[50], 'concerning the matter 155 of Kullan *khansamah* who is in the godown, it is necessary to get out the lamp oil.'

He stared at me maybe for one minute, and then he dropped his cheerot, and his red face became white as my clean muslin[51] coat. He rose and pushed me aside, 160 saying no word, and strode[52] into the verandah, I following him. He searched for the key of the padlock in his pockets, but found it not: so he wrenched[53] the chain from the woodwork of the door with great force, and the dead body of Kullan *khansamah* fell out of the 165 godown face downwards on the verandah floor.

Then the sahib caught me by the shoulder and shook me backwards and forwards, shouting in mine[54] ear and calling me names, and his voice sounded as though his throat were filled with dust. He cried out that he 170 had meant to return in a day and a night, but that the damage to the bridge had delayed him, and he had forgotten all about Kullan the *khansamah*. He cursed[55] me for a fool because I had not broken open the padlock.

'Sahib,' I said, and bowed my head before him, 'the or- 175 der was that Kullan should stay in the godown until the day of thine honour's return. This slave did but[56] obey thy commands.'

Then the face of the sahib grew purple, and he choked[57] and gasped[58], and fell at my feet with foam on his lips; 180 and with much effort I got him into the house, and laid him on his bed.

Afterwards he was ill for many days; but no one, not even the doctor-sahib, or the nurse-*mem*[59] who came to take care of him ever knew what had happened, for 185 before I fetched the doctor-sahib I pushed the body of Kullan *khansamah* back into the godown and left it there till the night-time, when I buried it in a corner of the compound[60] with all precaution[61].

There were none to witness the burial or to ask any 190 question, for he was a down-country man, and I said in the bazaar that he had departed to his home.

---

[34] **fowl** [faʊl] *Geflügel* – [35] **to rejoice** (*lit.*) to feel very happy – [36] **pretence** [prɪˈtens] *Vortäuschung* – [37] **to heed** (*fml.*) to pay attention to sb. – [38] **entreaty** [ɪnˈtriːti] (*fml.*) a serious request in which you ask sb. to do sth. for you – [39] **to wail** to cry – [40] **to refrain** (*fml.*) to not do sth. – [41] **hoarse** *heiser* – [42] **faint** here: difficult to hear – [43] **to amass sth.** to gradually collect a large amount of sth., e. g. money – [44] **weary** [ˈwɪəri] tired and exhausted – [45] **anxiety** [æŋˈzaɪəti] fear – [46] **to cough** [kɒf] *husten* – [47] **fly-trap** *Fliegenklatsche* – [48] **cheerot** a Burmese cigar – [49] **to carve** here: to ask for sth. very politely – [50] **humility** *Bescheidenheit* – [51] **muslin** [ˈmʌzlɪn] *Musselin (ein Gewebe)* – [52] **to stride** (strode, stridden) *durchschreiten* – [53] **to wrench sth.** to twist and pull sth. roughly from a place – [54] **mine** (*old use*) my – [55] **to curse sb.** *jdn. verfluchen* – [56] **but** here: only – [57] **to choke** to be unable to breathe properly – [58] **to gasp** *nach Luft schnappen* – [59] **(nurse-)mem** used when talking to a woman in authority; here: a white/British nurse – [60] **compound** an area that contains a group of buildings, *Anwesen* – [61] **precaution** *Vorsichtsmaßnahme*

6 While the sahib lay sick I made for him jelly, soup and custard[62], for I had learned from Kullan how to cook. I took my turn in watching by his bedside, and when his health returned I told him privately of what I had done.

For many years after this was I the sahib's head-servant on thirty rupees a month, and he was as wax in the hands of his slave, Ram Din. I it was who had charge of the sahib's keys and kept his money. It was I who appointed the other servants and exacted percentage from their wages. It was I who made payments and gave the orders, and the sahib ever settled my accounts[63] without argument. I had authority in the compound. I grew prosperous, and had a large stomach, and a watch and chain.

Now has the sahib retired from the service of the Government and has gone to England, and I, Ram Din, have bought land in mine own district and have married four wives and am a person of importance in the village.

So is it true what my father had told me: that by obeying orders and being fearless may a man rise in the service of the sahib-people, and gain wealth and honour.

from *The Oxford Anthology of Raj Stories* by Saros Cowasjee (ed.). Oxford University Press, Oxford 1998, pp. 161 ff.

COMPREHENSION

2. The material at hand can be dealt with in different ways:
- You can improve your **listening skills** and listen to the **audio version** of the short story.
- Alternatively, you can **read the print version**.
- Finally, you can **combine both text versions** and listen to the audio version while reading the short story in order to get a deeper understanding of details.

While reading or listening to the text, focus and take notes on these points:

(12 CD1) **1**
- Ram Din's familial situation
- Ram Din's father's pieces of advice and orders

(13 CD1) **2**
- the situation in the city
- the process of finding work for Ram Din

(14 CD1) **3**
- the incident at breakfast and its consequences
- the sahib's orders and Ram Din's new tasks

(15 CD1) **4**
- Ram Din's way of following the sahib's orders
- Ram Din's plans for making a career

(16 CD1) **5**
- the sahib's return
- the sahib's reaction to Kullan's death

(17 CD1) **6**
- Ram Din's new position in the sahib's household
- Ram Din's "rise" after the sahib's return to England

→ Focus on Skills, Listening Comprehension, p. 394

 3. After completing the listening/reading tasks, team up with a partner and summarize the short story to each other.

4. Based on your results from the awareness task: What "lesson" does the story teach the reader?

---

[62] **custard** a sweet yellow sauce that is made with milk, sugar, eggs and flour – [63] **to settle sb.'s accounts** to pay money that is owed; to pay bills

ANALYSIS

5. Characterize the narrator, Ram Din, and his master and their relationship.
   Pay attention to means of direct and indirect characterization* employed in the excerpt.

   Examples:
   - the sahib was sitting at breakfast … drinking whisky
     → the sahib is an alcoholic/addicted to alcohol (→ indirect characterization)
   - the sahib … looking … with eyes like those of a tiger
     → unpredictable, dangerous (→ direct characterization)
   - → Focus on Skills, Characterization of a Figure in Literature, p. 411

6. Analyse the kind of language the father uses to prepare his son for his future life in the sahib's household.

   Example:
   It was in the year of the famine … to the city of Kings (ll. 1 ff.) → fairy tale-like, long-ago past …

7. Examine how the narrative devices* create the unique atmosphere of the short story.

 8. Can the short story be interpreted as an allegory*? Give examples from the text that support your thesis.

   Info »»

   > An **allegory** is a fictional text in which the characters are usually personifications of abstract ideas or qualities and the plot is sometimes related to e.g. a historical or political event.
   > A rather simple storyline conveys a great deal of meaning, thus allowing the reader to understand general concepts.

ACTIVITIES

 9. Imagine: Ram Din does not bury the khansamah's body and the corpse is found. As the engineer's commanding officer you have to investigate the case of the dead servant.
   a) Describe the scene of the crime.
   b) Take notes on the statements of the Indian servant and the British engineer.
   c) Write a closing statement and come to a conclusion about who is to blame and what should be done.

 10. Imagine the investigations of the police finally lead to a trial at court.
   Choose *one* of the following persons and write a statement. Be prepared to read it out loud in class:
   a) a British prosecutor (*Ankläger*) accusing Ram Din of murdering Kullan
   b) an Indian prosecutor accusing the British engineer of murdering Kullan
   c) a British counsel for the defence (of the engineer)
   d) an Indian counsel for the defence (of Ram Din)
   e) the British engineer defending himself at court
   f) Ram Din defending himself at court
   In a role play, act out the trial and present the respective statements in class. Finally, the class should consider the evidence and announce a verdict.

The British Empire

The system of triangle trading

British involvement with the **triangular trade began with the colonization of America in 1607 and the West Indies in 1623**. The chief British ports were London, Liverpool, Bristol and Glasgow.

Triangular trade is a historical term that refers to trade among three ports or regions and countries. The best-known triangular trading system is the **transatlantic trade** that operated from the seventeenth until the early
5 nineteenth century, carrying manufactured goods, raw materials, cash crops – and slaves – between West Africa, the Caribbean and American colonies and the European colonial powers.

The **use of African slaves was fundamental** to growing crops such as cotton and tobacco, which were then exported to Europe. In turn, European goods were used to buy slaves from traders in Africa or the Caribbean.

The slaves were trans-
10 ported to the Americas on the sea lane, the so-called middle passage, which was a horrible journey during which many slaves
15 died of diseases and mal-treatment. **Slave trade was started in 1501** by Portuguese and Spanish traders; in 1807, the UK
20 Parliament passed a bill that officially abolished the trading of slaves, but illegal slave trade across the Atlantic Ocean was
25 still practiced until the second half of the nine-teenth century. There are an estimated 27 million victims of slavery world-
30 wide today.

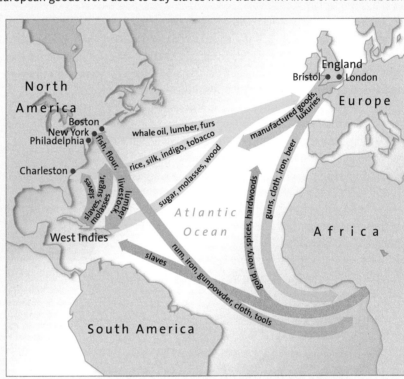

The British Empire in 1750

The British Empire in the 1750s (the blue shaded areas) traded goods worth £17 million – £8.7 million in exports and £8.3 million in imports. Britain's trade grew enormously as it gained control over many different parts of the world. The wish for expansion and the need for raw materials during the **Industrial Revolution** caused a series of overseas wars among several European countries such as France, Spain and Holland. However, one of the first
5 British trading companies, the **East India Company**, founded in 1600 during the reign of Elizabeth I, and the **Virginia Company**, founded by her successor James I, which was the basis for the first North American colony, the **Jamestown Colony in 1607**, formed the foundations of the growth and rise of the British Empire. Many colonies began as trading centres or were founded to protect a trade route, and were run for the profit of the mother country. The wealthiest area in the early days of the Empire was the **West Indies** thanks to large profits from sugar
10 cane and tobacco. Slaves were brought to the West Indies to work on the plantations.

The map shows the variety of goods that Britain imported from all over the world that greatly influenced the British economy and people's lives in the **mother country**.

The British Empire in 1900

Starting in 1801 the expanding empire was managed from London by the **Colonial Office**. District officers and civil servants were sent out to administer the colonies on behalf of Britain. Regular **imperial conferences** were held in Britain to discuss matters of general concern, such as trade, defence and foreign policy.

India was controlled for many years by the wealthy **East India Company**, roads and railroads were built to make
5 trade easier, a **Governor-General** was put in charge, and British troops and civil servants were sent to the region. In 1858, following the Indian Mutiny, India was placed under the direct control of the British government and a **viceroy** replaced the Governor-General. British influence in India had expanded from a few trading stations into the **Raj** (= British rule). In 1876, **Queen Victoria** was proclaimed **Empress of India**. India brought Britain great wealth and strategic advantage, and was called the 'jewel in the crown of the Empire'. Local Indian rulers were
10 allowed to remain in power provided they were loyal to the viceroy. Many British people spent years working in India as civil servants, engineers, police officers, etc. and took their families with them. The second period of empire-building took place in the late nineteenth century. The British Empire was at its largest and most powerful around 1920, when about 25 % of the world's population lived under British rule and over a quarter of the land in the world belonged to Britain. It was said that it was an empire **'on which the sun never sets'**, and the value of
15 exports and imports was £970 million. At that time Britain was **one of the greatest economic and political powers in the world**. It was also thought by some people to be a moral obligation and destiny to govern poorer, less advanced countries and to pass on European culture to the native inhabitants. This was what Rudyard Kipling called
20 the 'white man's burden'.

Britain did not only import foreign goods; there was also a great influence of foreign ideas, especially from India.

In the eighteenth century curry recipes and the famous 'mulligatawny soup' (the Tamil word for 'pepper-water')
25 appeared in England. Indian designs influenced art and architecture, and polo, snooker and billiards, games which were played by British soldiers in India, were 'exported' to Britain.

The Brighton Pavillion was built in 'Hindoo' style in the early nineteenth century.

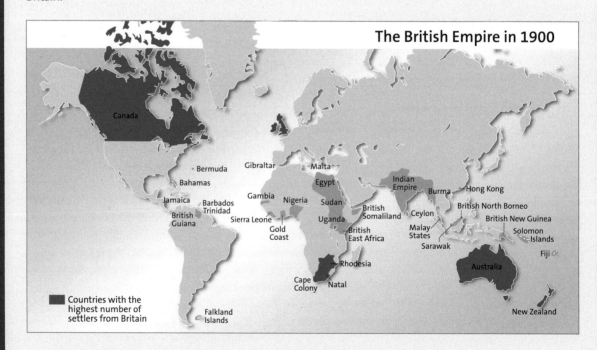

The British Empire in 1900

Canada · Bermuda · Bahamas · Jamaica · Barbados · Trinidad · British Guiana · Gibraltar · Malta · Egypt · Gambia · Nigeria · Sudan · Sierra Leone · Gold Coast · Uganda · British Somaliland · British East Africa · Indian Empire · Burma · Hong Kong · Ceylon · British North Borneo · Malay States · Sarawak · British New Guinea · Solomon Islands · Fiji · Rhodesia · Cape Colony · Natal · Australia · New Zealand · Falkland Islands

Countries with the highest number of settlers from Britain

Jawaharlal Nehru

A Tryst[1] with Destiny – Independence Day Speech of 1947

AWARENESS

The following speech was given by India's first prime minister, Jawaharlal Nehru, after India gained its independence in 1947. It was held before the Constituent Assembly of India in New Delhi shortly before midnight on 14 August 1947. It is considered to be a masterpiece of oratory, and marks the triumph of the 100-year Indian struggle against the Raj, the British Empire in India.

Put yourself into Nehru's shoes: Finally, after decades of suffering, struggle and fighting, India's independence is about to become reality. Being the Prime Minister, what would you tell the people of India? In groups, collect ideas and sketch out short speeches. Afterwards, perform them in class.

Long years ago we made a tryst with destiny, and now the time comes when we shall redeem[2] our pledge, not wholly or in full measure, but very substantially.

At the stroke of the midnight hour, when the world
5 sleeps, India will awake to life and freedom. A moment comes, which comes but rarely in history, when we step out from the old to the new, when an age ends, and when the soul of a nation, long suppressed, finds utterance[3].

It is fitting that at this solemn[4] moment we take the
10 pledge of dedication to the service of India and her people and to the still larger cause of humanity.

At the dawn of history India started on her unending quest[5], and trackless[6] centuries are filled with her striving and the grandeur[7] of her success and failures.
15 Through good and ill fortune alike she has never lost sight of that quest or forgotten the ideals which gave her strength. We end today a period of ill fortune[8] and India discovers herself again. […]

Freedom and power bring responsibility. The responsi-
20 bility rests upon this assembly, a sovereign body representing the sovereign people of India. Before the birth of freedom we have endured[9] all the pains of labour and our hearts are heavy with the memory of this sorrow. Some of those pains continue even now. Nevertheless,
25 the past is over and it is the future that beckons[10] to us now.

That future is not one of ease or resting but of incessant[11] striving so that we may fulfill the pledges we have so often taken and the one we shall take today.
30 The service of India means the service of the millions

Prime Minister Jawaharlal Nehru (left) discussing matters with Mahatma Gandhi

who suffer. It means the ending of poverty and ignorance and disease and inequality of opportunity.

The ambition of the greatest man of our generation [Gandhi] has been to wipe every tear from every eye. That may be beyond us, but as long as there are tears 35 and suffering, so long our work will not be over.

And so we have to labour and to work, and work hard, to give reality to our dreams. Those dreams are for India, but they are also for the world, for all the nations and the peoples are too closely knit together today for 40 anyone of them to imagine that it can live apart.

---

[1] **tryst** [trɪst] (*lit., joc.*) a meeting between lovers in a secret place or at a secret time – [2] **to redeem** (*fml.*) to do what you promised to do – [3] **utterance** ['ʌtərəns] here: a voice – [4] **solemn** *feierlich* – [5] **quest** (*fml.*) a long search for sth. – [6] **trackless** here: uncountable, very many – [7] **grandeur** ['grændʒə(r)] impressive beauty, power or size – [8] **ill fortune** misery, hardship, suffering – [9] **to endure** to be in a difficult or painful situation for a long time without complaining – [10] **to beckon to sb.** *jdn. heranwinken* – [11] **incessant** [ɪnˈsesnt] constant

Peace has been said to be indivisible[12]; so is freedom, so is prosperity now, and so also is disaster in this one world that can no longer be split into isolated frag-[45]ments.

To the people of India, whose representatives we are, we make an appeal to join us with faith and confidence in this great adventure. This is no time for petty[13] and destructive criticism, no time for ill will or blaming [50]others. We have to build the noble mansion[14] of free India where all her children may dwell[15]. [...]

The future beckons to us. Whither[16] do we go and what shall be our endeavour[17]? To bring freedom and opportunity to the common man, to the peasants[18] and work-ers of India; to fight and end poverty and ignorance and [55] disease; to build up a prosperous, democratic and progressive nation, and to create social, economic and political institutions which will ensure justice and fullness of life to every man and woman.

[...] To all the nations and peoples of the world we send [60] greetings and pledge ourselves to cooperate with them in furthering[19] peace, freedom and democracy.

And to India, our much-loved motherland, the ancient, the eternal and the ever-new, we pay our reverent[20] homage[21] and we bind ourselves afresh to her service. [65] Jai Hind[22].

www.indianembassy.org/inews/aug15 [26.09.2010]

COMPREHENSION

1. **Step 1:** Listen to the historical audio document of Nehru's speech to get an impression of his voice and intonation.
   → Focus on Skills, Listening Comprehension, p. 394

   Step 2: Read the excerpt from the speech.
   a) Point out what Nehru states about the difficulties in the making of India.
   b) State what he wants India to be like in the future.

2. Point out what Nehru says about India's relevance in the world.

ANALYSIS

3. Examine the images as well as rhetorical and stylistic devices that are employed in the speech.
   → Focus on Skills, Analysis of a Political Speech, p. 407

4. Show how euphemistic language is used instead of naming problems directly.

   Example: ll. 12 ff.: ... her unending quest → India's never-ending struggle, fight, etc.

---

[12] **indivisible** that cannot be divided – [13] **petty** ['peti] small and unimportant, trivial – [14] **mansion** a very large house – [15] **to dwell** to live in a particular place – [16] **whither** ['wɪðə(r)] where – [17] **endeavour** [ɪn'devə(r)] (*fml.*) an attempt to do sth. new or difficult – [18] **peasant** ['peznt] a poor farmer who owns a small piece of land – [19] **to further** to help sth. progress or to be successful – [20] **reverent** (*fml.*) respectful – [21] **homage** ['hɑmɪdʒ] (*fml.*) showing respect – [22] **Jai Hind** salutation used in speeches, "Hail India" or "Long live India"

Indian Independence Act (1947)

After months of negotiations, the Indian Independence Act was formulated by the British government when representatives of the Indian National Congress (led by Jawaharlal Nehru), the Muslim League (led by Muhammad Ali Jinnah), and the Sikh community came to an agreement with the Viceroy of India, Lord Mountbatten. It was signed on 18 July 1947, and its result **was the independence of the dominions India (Hindu) and Pakistan (Muslim) beginning on 15 August 1947.**

Be it enacted by the King's most Excellent Majesty, by and with the advice and consent of the Lords Spiritual and temporal[1], and Commons[2], in this present Parliament assembled, and by the authority of the same as follows:

1. (1) As from the fifteenth day of August, nineteen hundred and forty-seven, two independent Dominions[3]
5 shall be set up in India, to be known respectively as India and Pakistan. [...]

6. (1) The Legislature[4] of each of the new Dominions shall have full power to make laws for that Dominion, including laws having extra-territorial operation. [...]
(3) The Governor-General of each of the new Dominions shall have full power to assent in His Majesty's name to any law of the Legislature of the Dominion ... [...]

10 **7.** (1) As from that appointed day –
(a) His Majesty's Government in the United Kingdom have no responsibility as respects the government of any of the territories which, immediately before that day, were included in British India;
(b) the suzerainty[5] of His Majesty over the Indian States lapses[6], and with it, all treaties and agreements in force at the date of the passing of this Act between His Majesty and the rulers of Indian States, all functions
15 exercisable by His Majesty at that date with respect to Indian States, all obligations[7] of His majesty existing at that date towards Indian States or the rulers thereof, and all powers, rights, authority or jurisdiction to Indian States by treaty, grant[8], usage, sufferance[9] or otherwise; and
(c) there lapse also any treaties or agreements in force at the date of the passing of this Act between His Majesty and any persons having authority in the tribal areas, any obligations of His Majesty existing at that date
20 to any such persons or with respect to the tribal areas, and all powers, rights authority or jurisdiction exercisable at that date by His Majesty in or in relation to the tribal areas by treaty, grant usage, sufferance or otherwise: [...]
(2) The assent[10] of the parliament of the United Kingdom is hereby given to the omission[11] from the Royal Style and Titles of the words "Indiae Imperator" and the words "Emperor of India" and to the issue by His Majesty
25 for that Purpose of His Royal Proclamation under the Great Seal of the Realm[12].

---

[1] **Lord Spiritual and temporal** members of the House of Lords; spiritual refers to members who are bishops in the Church of England; temporal refers to life peers and members of the nobility – [2] **Commons** the House of Commons – [3] **Dominions** autonomous polities under British sovereignty – [4] **legislature** [ˈledʒɪsleɪtʃə(r)] (fml.) Legislative – [5] **suzerainty** [ˈsuːzərənti] the fight of a country to rule over another country – [6] **to lapse** to gradually come to an end or stop – [7] **obligation** Verpflichtung – [8] **grant** guarantee – [9] **sufferance** Duldung – [10] **assent** (fml.) approval or agreement from sb. who has authority – [11] **omission from sth.** (fml.) the act of not including sb./sth.; Ausschluss von – [12] **realm** [relm] empire; Reich

21st Century India: Booms, Boons and Burdens

Andrea Glaubacker

Gesellschaft im Wandel – Tata und Cola

AWARENESS

The German author and graphic designer Sebastian Löschner has documented his impressions of a journey to India in a sketch book from which the illustrations below are taken. Ruha, a 20-year-old Indian student he met in Bangalore, gives him a ride on her moped.

What do the sketches below tell you about "modern India" and "modern Indian women"?

Tips on vocab

neon signs ■ billboards ■ advertising ■ international companies ■ heavy traffic ■ traffic junction (*Verkehrsknotenpunkt*) ■ crowded streets ■ to speed forward/through sth. (*vorwärtsschießen/rasen*) ■ passenger seat ■ to hold on to sb. ■ rear view mirror (*Rückspiegel*) ■ (to have a) topknot (*Haarknoten*)

The German text below is taken from a travel journal which portrays India in 151 essays and photos.

"Tata", the name mentioned in the headline, is an Indian multinational conglomerate headquartered in Mumbai. It includes seven major business sectors: communications and information technology, engineering, materials, services, energy, consumer products and chemicals. More than 550,000 people work for the company worldwide. Speculate: How do Tata and Coca Cola change Indian society – as indicated in the headline?

Das *Monsoon* ist angesagt bei den Jugendlichen. Kareena und ihre Freundinnen haben es geschafft, einen Tisch zu ergattern, packen ihre Smartphones auf den Tisch und plaudern über die gestrige Party und harm-
5 lose[1] Jungsgeschichten.

Hier gibt's die beste Pizza und mit einer Cola dazu fühlen sich die Jugendlichen in ihren Jeans und engen Shirts vor allem eines: angesagt[2] und hip. Sie sind es vergleichsweise[3] auch. Das Mädchen vor der Türe, das
10 Nüsse verkauft, hat allerdings mit Sicherheit anderes im Kopf, als angesagt zu sein.

Kareenas Eltern sind beide berufstätig. Der Vater programmiert Software, die Mutter ist Ärztin. Sie will in die USA, wie ihr Cousin, der in Los Angeles studiert.
15 Die USA stehen hoch im Kurs[4]. Wessen Eltern es finanzieren können, der geht ins Land der unbegrenzten Möglichkeiten und will dort auch am liebsten bleiben.

Ein Drittel der Bevölkerung, um die 300 Millionen
20 Menschen, wird der indischen Mittelschicht zugerechnet. Zusammen mit der sehr reichen Oberschicht verfügt diese über die Kaufkraft[5] der US-amerikanischen Mittelschicht. Das rief US-Konzerne auf den Plan[6], die in der großen Hoffnung auf Milliardengewinne[7] den
25 indischen Markt enterten. Aber ganz entgegen der Einschätzung[8] der Konzerne blieben die meisten kaufkräftigen Inder bei indischen Produkten. Bata-Schuhe statt Nike, Idlis statt Kellogg's, Tata statt Mercedes Benz.

Bei einer Reise durchs Land fällt ins Auge, wie viele Häuser heutzutage massiv[9] statt aus Lehm[10] gebaut
30 werden, wie viele Fernsehantennen und Satellitenschüsseln[11] aus den Dächern wachsen, wie viele Autos und Motorräder vor den Häusern stehen.

Doch wie sieht es im Innenleben aus? Werden Traditionen mit zunehmender Kaufkraft verworfen[12]? Ja und
35 Nein. Die Gesellschaft ist zwar in einem Wandel begriffen, aber der geht langsam voran und ist momentan hauptsächlich in den Städten zu beobachten. Moderne Mädchen wie Kareena haben im Dorf keinen Platz. Und Traditionen spielen noch immer eine große
40 Rolle. Ehen werden noch immer arrangiert, Kastengrenzen heben sich nur in den Städten auf, Frauen sind weit von der Gleichberechtigung entfernt. Jahrhunderte alte Traditionen sind einfach langlebiger[13] als ein Paar Nike-Schuhe.
45 Und auch Kareena weiß, dass sie sich ihren Zukünftigen nicht ganz alleine aussuchen[14] kann, aber sie hätte Mitspracherecht[15], sagt sie nicht ohne Stolz und nimmt erst mal einen Schluck Cola.

from *Indien 151, Porträt eines Landes mit vielen Gesichtern in 151 Momentaufnahmen* by Andrea Glaubacker. Conbook Medien, Meerbusch 2013, pp. 98 f.

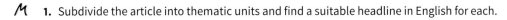

COMPREHENSION

M **1.** Subdivide the article into thematic units and find a suitable headline in English for each.

M **2.** Your American pen pal is planning a gap year in India and collecting information on "modern India". Summarize each of the paragraphs in English, being sure to
- focus on the most relevant information,
- leave out irrelevant data and facts,
- use predominantly the present tense.
→ Focus on Skills, Mediation, p. 412

---

[1] harmless, naive – [2] hip, hot – [3] comparatively – [4] to be of great importance – [5] purchasing power – [6] to bring sb. to the scene –
[7] profits in billions – [8] estimation – [9] solid – [10] mud – [11] satelite dish – [12] to neglect, to abandon – [13] durable, long-lasting – [14] to choose –
[15] to have a say in sth.

ANALYSIS

3. Examine the cartoon on page 124 and pay attention to details. What do the neon signs, billboards and the advertising in general convey about
- India's economy,
- India's global role,
- the influence of Western culture?

→ Focus on Skills, Analysis of Visuals, p. 409
→ Focus on Facts, India: From Raj to Modern Democracy, p. 131

ACTIVITIES

4. Step 1: Use the information given in the text and turn it into an interview (in English) with
a) the German journalist Andrea Glaubacker about her travelling experiences or
b) Kareena and her friends.
Think up suitable questions that match the answers and information given in the text.
- Ms Glaubacker, after having visited India – which of your encounters there do you remember best?
- Kareena, your cousin is already studying in the US – what are your plans?

 Step 2: Together with a partner, think about further questions you would like to ask either of them about "modern India" and think up possible answers.

Tip: Be careful not to ask questions that can simply be answered with "yes" or "no"; instead, ask open questions that make people talk.

 Act out your interviews in class and discuss the various results.
→ Focus on Skills, Writing an Interview, p. 426

GRAMMAR / LANGUAGE

 5. After doing the interview (cf. no. 4), report the interview to each other using **indirect speech**, the right **tenses** and the appropriate **introductory verbs**.

Example: Asked which of her encounters she remembered best, Ms Glaubacker said …

Manufacturing in India: The Masala[1] Mittelstand

AWARENESS

 Together with a partner, take a close look at the visual on the following page and describe it in detail, using the words provided in the vocab box.
Tip: Pay particular attention to the dichotomy (*Zweiteilung, Gegensätzlichkeit*) of the different people, their body language and environments.

"traditional India"	"manufacturing India"
<ul><li>elephant</li><li>jungle</li><li>…</li></ul>	<ul><li>robots</li><li>modern building</li><li>…</li></ul>

[1] **masala** [məˈsɑːlə] (*Indian English*) a traditional South-Asian dish made with a sauce containing a mixture of spices

Tips on vocab »»

background: manufacturing robots ■ manufacturing belt/assembly line ■ to assemble sth. ■ to operate a dashboard ■ square building ■ German flag ■ company logo ■ blue/steely-grey colours ■ safety helmet ■ to wear (orange) overalls

foreground: jungle ■ palm trees ■ to watch sth. with interest ■ to wear traditional clothes (turban, sari, loincloth (*Lendenschurz*)) ■ to applaud sb./to clap one's hands ■ to sit in a semicircle ■ to rest on one's elbows ■ brown/sepia coloured

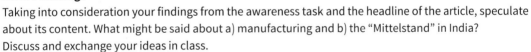

COMPREHENSION

1. **Before reading:**
   Taking into consideration your findings from the awareness task and the headline of the article, speculate about its content. What might be said about a) manufacturing and b) the "Mittelstand" in India?
   Discuss and exchange your ideas in class.

Manufacturing is taking off[1] in India. But not in the way many hoped

If India is to become "the next China" – a manufacturing powerhouse – it is taking its time about it. "We have to industrialise India, and as rapidly as possible," said the country's first prime minister, Jawaharlal Nehru, in 1951. Politicians have tried everything since, including Soviet-style planning. But India seems to prefer growing crops and selling services to making things you can drop on your foot.

Manufacturing is still just 15% of output (see chart), far below Asian norms. India needs a big manufacturing base. No major country has grown rich without one and nothing else is likely to absorb the labour of the 250m youngsters set to reach working age in the next 15 years. But it can seem a remote[2] prospect[3]. In July power cuts[4] plunged[5] an area in which over 600m people live into darkness, reminding investors that India's infrastructure is not wholly[6] reliable. And workers boiled over[7] at a car factory run by Maruti Suzuki. Almost 100 people were injured and the plant was torched[8]. The charred[9] body of a human-resources chief was found in the ashes. Yet not all is farce[10] and tragedy. Take Pune in west India, a booming industrial hub[11] that has won the steely

---

[1] **to take off** to become successful or popular very quickly or suddenly – [2] **remote** here: *abwegig* – [3] **prospect** *Aussicht* – [4] **power cut** an interruption in the supply of electricity – [5] **to plunge into sth.** to experience sth. unpleasant – [6] **wholly** completely – [7] **to boil over** to become very angry – [8] **to torch sth.** to burn a building intentionally – [9] **charred** burned and black – [10] **farce** [fɑːs] a situation that is badly organized and/or unfair – [11] **hub** the central and main part of sth. which has the most activity

25 hearts of Germany's car firms. Inside a $700m Volkswagen plant on the city's outskirts[12], laser-wielding[13] robots test car frames' dimensions and a giant conveyor belt slips by, with sprung-wood[14] surfaces to protect workers' knees. It is "probably the cheapest factory we
30 have worldwide," says John Chacko, VW's boss in India. In time it could become an export hub. Nearby, in the distance it takes a Polo to get to 60 mph, is a plant owned by Mercedes-Benz.

Both German firms were attracted by (fairly) reliable
35 power and access to land but also Pune's engineering colleges and tradition of manufacturing. "It is a hub for auto-suppliers," says Peter Honegg, Mercedes's boss. Smaller firms are arriving too. Zubin Kabraji, of the Indo-German chamber of commerce, says Pune hosts[15]
40 262 German companies, up from 130-odd in 2008.

The foreign influx is not limited to Germans; and local suppliers benefit regardless. Three-quarters of VW's parts are bought locally. Some foreigners are not really manufacturing but rather assembling[16] imported parts
45 to get around Indian customs duties. Still they use some Indian suppliers too – 30–40% of Mercedes's components are local. Indian champions are also prospering. Tata, a conglomerate[17], has been in Pune for decades and has a new plant assembling Land Rover cars. Bharat
50 Forge, with $1.3 billion of sales, makes car parts, with 70% going abroad. Its boss, B. N. Kalyani, says local entrepreneurs are "doing a damn good job".

Industrial hotspots such as Pune, Chennai and the state of Gujarat are not the only evi-
55 dence that manufacturing has momentum[18]. India's share of global merchandise exports has doubled to 1.5% since 2000 (but is still far below China's 11%).

60 **The next China, or more of the same?**

Exports have shifted towards engineering products, which now make up a fifth of the total.
65 Indian firms have become good at flogging[19] everything from motorbikes to spare parts[20], particularly to Africa and the Middle East. And most have got fighting fit. Anil Gupta, the boss of Havells, a Noida-headquartered firm which makes electrical equipment, recalls visiting a vast
70 Chinese factory in 2002: "It was a shock." But now his firm has invested heavily and, he says, can hold its own. Indian labour may even have grown relatively cheaper. A 2010 study by America's Bureau of Labour Statistics found that, at just under a dollar an hour, labour costs
75 (including social-security costs and taxes) were similar to China's and just 3% of American levels. Since the data were collected the rupee has fallen by a third against the renminbi[21] and a fifth against the dollar, making things even cheaper. And those data only in-
80 cluded elite workers in the "official" sector – an unskilled labourer might get four dollars a day. Unadjusted for productivity, Indian labour is dirt cheap.

Of course scarce land, red tape[22], poor education and infrastructure, and onerous[23] labour laws partly offset
85 this. But optimists can point to a government policy, in place since late 2011, to create giant new special economic zones (SEZs) that deal with these problems.

Japan, then South Korea, then China. Will India become the next workshop of the world? It is far too soon to
90 crack open the champagne[24]. For one thing, the state seems incapable[25] of resolving[26] bottlenecks[27], even through SEZs. Some 300 km north-west of Pune lies Silvassa, part of an enclave[28] governed by Portugal until 1954. It has long been lavished[29] with tax breaks to attract
95 industry and is controlled by the central government. Yet today it is notable for derelict[30] factories and its trade selling grog[31] to Gujarat, a dry state next door.
100 What is happening in Pune is more sophisticated than epic feats[32] of metal-bashing[33]. While VW's plant is more labour-intensive than its German equiva-
105 lent, it still relies more on computers than humans. Local firms, such as Bharat Forge, have been shedding[34] unskilled labour, in-

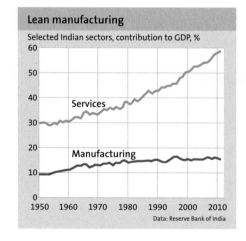

Lean manufacturing

Selected Indian sectors, contribution to GDP, %

Services

Manufacturing

1950 1960 1970 1980 1990 2000 2010

Data: Reserve Bank of India

---

[12] **outskirt** *Außenbezirk* – [13] **to wield** *handhaben* – [14] **sprung-wood** *Sperrholz* – [15] **to host sb.** *jdns. Gastgeber sein* – [16] **to assemble** *zusammenbauen* – [17] **conglomerate** *Großkonzern* – [18] **momentum** *Schwung* – [19] **to flog sb./sth.** (*BE, infml.*) to sell sth., esp. very quickly and cheaply – [20] **spare part** *Ersatzteil* – [21] **renminbi** the currency of the People's Republic of China – [22] **red tape** *Bürokratie* – [23] **onerous** difficult to do – [24] **to crack open the champagne** (*infml.*) *die Korken knallen lassen* – [25] **incapable** unable to do sth. – [26] **to resolve** to find an acceptable solution to a problem or difficulty – [27] **bottleneck** *Engpass* – [28] **enclave** ['eŋkleɪv] *Enklave; fremdstaatliches Gebiet im eigenen Staatsgebiet* – [29] **to lavish sb. with sth.** *jdn. mit etw. überhäufen* – [30] **derelict** *verfallen* – [31] **grog** *Grog* – [32] **feat** *Kunststück, Meisterleistung* – [33] **metal-bashing** *Metallverarbeitung* – [34] **to shed** to get rid of sth. you do not need or want

vesting in technology and building brands and distribution overseas. "Indian firms that are technology-focused are extremely successful," says Mr Kalyani. But "commodity[35] manufacturing is unsuccessful. It is the opposite of China ... We have archaic labour laws. Nobody in their right mind is going to set up a plant employing 10,000 people." His ambition is to make his firm another Siemens or General Electric.

This fits a pattern. Even as high-end engineering boomed, manufacturing jobs dropped slightly between 2004 and 2010, to 50 m. Basic industries that soak up[36] labour, such as textiles and leathers, are in relative decline. India is at last getting good at making things – but not in quite the way its founding fathers envisioned. Visitors to the country's industrial centres, such as Pune, can only marvel[37] at the great leaps[38] Indian firms and entrepreneurs are making. And worry about the consequences of another decade in which the country struggles to create jobs.

www.economist.com/node/21560263, 11 August 2012 [20.09.2014]

COMPREHENSION

2. In a **first reading**, try to get a general understanding of what is written.

3. While reading the magazine article **a second time**, find sentences that match the following statements. **Be careful:** There are more aspects listed than can be found in the text.

a) India has the potential to become a manufacturing powerhouse.

b) The only option India has in order to catch up to the rich countries is to develop major manufacturing industries.

c) India will face major unemployment of young people in the future.

d) India's infrastructure and technical development are backward and underdeveloped.

e) In contrast to other areas in India, Pune offers reliable infrastructure to VW and Mercedes.

f) Pune has a tradition of manufacturing and therefore is a reliable partner for foreign investors.

g) Germany is particularly interested in Pune.

h) Foreign investment supports the local industry and suppliers.

i) India's global exports have significantly risen in recent years.

j) Chinese companies are technologically far more advanced than Indian ones.

k) India's low wages attract foreign manufacturing investors.

l) India's ongoing problems with corruption are major obstacles to attracting foreign investors.

m) India is very successful at high-end engineering and IT but is struggling to manage its manufacturing capacities.

ANALYSIS

4. Together with a partner, compile a diagram that visualizes the various statistical data given in the article on
a) successes and failures in manufacturing,   b) foreign investment,
c) India's economic position compared to Africa, China and the Middle East.

5. Step 1: Juxtapose the information given in the article about the opportunities India offers to the problems it is still struggling with.

possible opportunities/advantages	problems/disadvantages
• 250 m young people	• bad infrastructure
• low wages	• ...
• ...	

---

[35] **commodity** *Massenware, Verbrauchsartikel* – [36] **to soak up** here: to require a great number of people – [37] **to marvel** to show great surprise or admiration – [38] **leap** a big increase or improvement

Step 2: Analyse whether there are more advantages or disadvantages for foreign investors.
→ Focus on Skills, Analysis of a Non-Fictional Text, p. 405

6. Examine the author's choice of words* and explain how it emphasizes his/her line of argument* as well as the overall message of the text.

7. Compare the data given in the line graphs on p. 128 and below to the statements made in the text.
→ Focus on Skills, Analysis of Statistical Data, p. 408

ACTIVITIES

8. You are a local Indian businessman who thinks that he is "doing a damn good job" (l. 52) and you are upset and concerned about the negative image that the world and potential foreign investors might get of India. Write a critical letter to the editor in response to the many problems mentioned in the article and present India and its potential in a better light.

   Tip: Use your previous results (cf. task no. 5) for your argumentation as well as the data given on the Focus on Facts page *India* (p. 131).
   → Focus on Skills, Writing a Letter to the Editor, p. 431

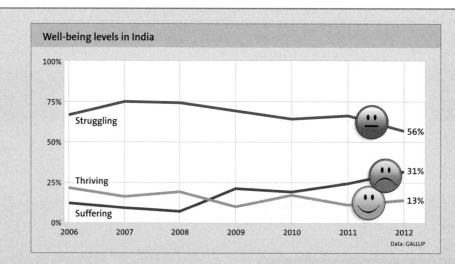

Well-being levels in India

Struggling — 56%
Thriving — 31%
Suffering — 13%

2006 2007 2008 2009 2010 2011 2012

Data: GALLUP

From the pages of

TIME

More than 3 out of every 10 Indians consider themselves to be "suffering", a worrying sign that long-standing social inequities[1] in the world's largest democracy are getting worse. Although the nation boasts[2] a booming, dynamic economy, Gallup[3] data –
5 drawn from 5,000 people spread over 90% of the country – suggest that success hasn't trickled down[4] to many of its citizens. Exacerbating[5] the misery is a lack of access to decent education, a problem India's sclerotic[6] government is struggling to address amid a host[7] of corruption scandals and political infighting[8].

From *World* by Megan Gibson, Joe Jackson, Ishaan Tharoor. In: TIME, 14 May 2012, p. 9
TIME and the TIME logo are registered trademarks of Time Inc. used under license.

---

[1] **inequity** [ɪˈnekwɪti] *Ungerechtigkeit* – [2] **to boast** to have sth. that is impressive and that you can be proud of – [3] **Gallup** American research-based global consulting company – [4] **to trickle down** *heruntertröpfeln* – [5] **to exacerbate** [ɪgˈzæsəbeɪt] *etw. verschlimmern, verschärfen* – [6] **sclerotic** *erstarrt, verhärtet* – [7] **a host of sb./sth.** a large number of people or things – [8] **infighting** competition between people within a group

India: From Raj to Modern Democracy

With its 1.237 billion people (2012) **the Republic of India** is the second-most populous country in the world and the world's largest democracy.

Today India is a federal constitutional republic with a parliamentary democracy and consists of 28 states and 7 union territories. Head of State is the President of India, but the most executive power is exercised by the Prime Minister, who is also the head of government.

India is considered to be one of the fastest-growing economies in the world and is well known for its pluralistic, multilingual and multi-ethnic society and for its commercial and cultural wealth and diversity.

India's flag, the Tricolour, with the navy blue wheel with 24 spokes (= Ashoka's Dharma Chakra). Each spoke depicts one hour of the day and portrays the prevalence of righteousness all 24 hours.

India's national emblem, the Lion of Sarnath, third century B. C.

History

Third cent. B. C.	**Ashoka the Great** unites most of South Asia
320 – 550 A. D.	the **Gupta dynasty** is considered to be the **Golden Age of India**; extensive inventions and discoveries in science, technology, art, literature, religion and philosophy were the foundation of the **Hindu culture**
1526 – 1857	age of the **Mughal Empire**; Mughal Emperors control most of the Indian subcontinent by means of a highly centralized administration
16th cent.	European powers establish trading posts
1616	the **British East India Company** is founded
1856	the British East India Company controls most of India
1857	**Indian Mutiny:** native soldiers employed by the British Army rebel against racial injustice and inequities; as a consequence civilian rebellions follow → the East India Company is dissolved and India is directly governed by the Crown → **British Rule/Raj**
1885	the **Indian National Congress** is founded and developed into one of the largest democratic political parties in the world; it is a major force in the struggle against British rule in India
1920s	the Indian National Congress adopts **Gandhi's ideas of non-violent civil disobedience and resistance**, which later leads to the **Quit India Movement** which is also led by Gandhi
1947	the **Indian Independence Act** leads to the dissolution of the British Indian Empire
15 Aug. 1947	India gains independence; **Partition of India** into two independent states: the **Dominion of Pakistan** (later Islamic Republic of Pakistan and People's Republic of Bangladesh) and the **Union of India** (later Republic of India)
1948	**Mahatma Gandhi is assassinated** by a Hindu fanatic
1948/1965/ 1971/1999	**Indo-Pakistan wars** over disputed territory in Kashmir and Jammu
1974	first **nuclear test explosion** under the codename "Smiling Buddha" (five further tests in 1998)
1991	economic liberalization and major reforms initiated by Prime Minister Rajiv Gandhi
2005	the **Right to Information Act** ensures the right to information for citizens
2009	the **Right to Education Bill** provides free and compulsory education for children between 6 and 14; it requires all private schools to reserve 25 % of seats for children from poor families
2013	the **National Food Security Act** aims at providing subsidized food grains to ca. two thirds of India's population; beneficiaries can buy 5 kg per eligible person per month of cereals like rice, wheat or millet (*Hirse*); pregnant women, lactating (breastfeeding) mothers and certain categories of children are eligible for daily free meals

Facts and figures: Modern India

Name	Republic of India
Capital	New Delhi
Area	3,287,590 square km
Population	1.237 billion (2012)
Growth of population	1.58 % p. a. (2014) (Germany: -2.7 %; 2011)
Life expectancy	68.89 years (Germany: 80.89; 2012)
Child mortality	44 deaths (per 1,000) (Germany: 3.8)
Official languages	17 major languages (e. g. Hindi, English, Telugu, Assamese, Urdu, Santali, Punjabi, Bengali, Tamil, etc.) and 844 dialects
Literacy rate	74.04 % (men: 82.14 %; women: 65.46 %) (Germany: 99 %)
Religions	Hinduism 80.5 %, Islam 13.4 %, Christianity 2.3 %, Sikhism 1.9 %, Buddhism 0.7 %, Jainism 0.5 %
Government type	Sovereign Socialist Democratic Republic with a Parliamentary system of Government
National days	**26 January – Republic Day** 15 August – Independence Day 2 October – Mahatma Gandhi's birthday
GDP[1] by sector	service: 64.8 % agriculture: 13.7 % industry: 21.5 % (2013) Germany: service: 69.0 % agriculture: 0.8 % industry: 25.5 % (2013)
GDP per capita	$1,504 (2013) (Germany: $45,097; 2013)
GDP growth	4.7 % (2013) (Germany: 3.2 %; 2013)
Population below poverty line	22 % (data: Reserve Bank of India, 2012) 14.3 % (data: World Bank, 2014) (Germany: 15 %; OECD, 2014)
Main industries	telecommunications, information technology, textiles, chemicals, pharmaceuticals, food processing, steel, transportation equipment, cement, mining, petroleum, machinery
Natural resources	oil, natural gas, coal (ca. 10 % of world's coal reserve), iron, bauxite, titanium, chromite, etc.

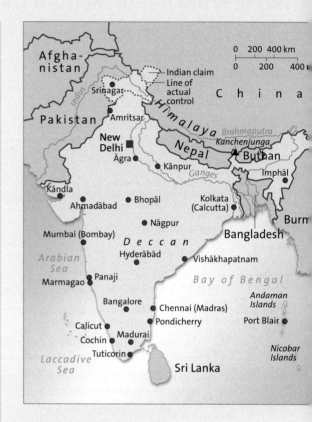

Share of top eight investing countries in FDI[2] inflows in 2014

Rank	Country	Inflows (Million USD)	Inflows (%)
1	Mauritius	78,527	36 %
2	Singapore	25,445	12 %
3	U.K.	20,764	10 %
4	Japan	16,268	8 %
5	USA	11,927	6 %
6	Netherlands	11,236	5 %
7	Cyprus	7,446	3 %
8	Germany	6,519	3 %

dipp.nic.in/English/Publications/FDI_Statistics/2014/india_FDI_March2014.pdf

[1] **GDP** (abbr.) Gross Domestic Product; *Bruttoinlandsprodukt* – [2] **FDI** (abbr.) Foreign Direct Investment

Laxman Khumbi

Living in Dharavi, Mumbai (India)

In 2008, for the first time in history, more people lived in cities than rural areas worldwide. One third of these urban dwellers[1] – more than one billion people – live in slums. Their number will double in the next twenty-five years, according to a United Nations forecast. Although the common perception of slums is that they are locations of poverty, danger and neglect[2], their people are ambitious and hard workers. Mumbai is one of India's richest and most densely populated cities with its approximately 18 million people, two-thirds of whom live in slums called "zopadpattis". Dharavi is Mumbai's best-known slum which is situated in its center, and is home to ca. one million people.
What do you think are the daily challenges that people living in slums have to deal with?

They will demolish this area, but we don't know when they'll give us notice. Some say it will be demolished within one month, some say within two, some say within three months. There are no guarantees. Whose
5 house will be taken down first?
They say they'll give people new places to live after the demolitions, near Mankhurd. But over there, there's no water. It's also very far away, and there are no work or business opportunities. We'd had to come back here for
10 work, and the transportation fares are expensive. But when they give us a room, we'll have to go. As the government solves this for everyone, it has to be good for everyone.
I have been living in this area since my childhood. We
15 used to stay in a chawl building with my parents where we had our own room. But after I got married and my father and mother died, we had to sell that place and move here. We've been staying in this place for the last four years; no one lived here before that. This place was just a creek before; there was muck all around. This
20 area is very fast, there are thousands of shanties here. For toilet purposes, we have to go outside – it's a problem – we have to go on the road.
The electricity is on for two days, then off two days, or not on at all. We don't have much space for the children
25 to play in. They use the road to play, and accidents take place, again and again.
I've not studied at all and am illiterate.
For work, I stitch government jeans and pants. It's fine, but the workday ends late. I want to educate my kids.
30 Until I die, I'll educate them – as long as I'm around, that's guaranteed.

from *The Places We Live* by Jonas Bendiksen. aperture foundation, New York 2008

1 Laxman Khumbi and his son

Tips on vocab ⟫

Laxman Khumbi and his son
tarpaulin (*Zeltplane*) ■ sackcloth ■ dampness (*Feuchtigkeit*) ■ windowless ■ dark ■ dismal (*trostlos*) ■ stone floor ■ camp bed/cot (*Feldbett*) ■ broken-down/skinny people ■ tinware (*Blechgeschirr*) ■ shabby ■ flimsy sheets (*fadenscheinige Laken*) ■ barefoot

[1] **dweller** inhabitant – [2] **neglect** *Verwahrlosung*

Walking on a
water main   **2**

Tips on vocab »»»

Water main
corrugated iron shacks
(*Wellblechhütten*) ■
sewage water (*Abwasser*)
■ waste water ■ cess-
pool (*Jauchegrube*) ■
rags (*Lumpen*) ■ dilapi-
dated (*verfallen*) huts/
shacks ■ narrow street/
lane ■ rusty sheet
metal ■ cramped (*be-
engt, überfüllt*) ■ card-
board roofs ■ unsani-
tary ■ sandbags to keep
out water ■ plastic bags

COMPREHENSION   »»»»»»

1. Describe the photos, paying attention to details, and say
what they reveal about the living conditions of the people.
  → Focus on Skills, Analysis of Visuals, p. 409

2. Summarize what Laxman Khumbi says about Mumbai's
largest slum area.

ANALYSIS   »»»»»»

3. Explain the hierarchy of the Indian caste system and relate
it to Laxman Khumbi's situation and his ambitions. Looking at his situation, what opportunities and perspectives
do you realistically see for him and his children?

ACTIVITIES   »»»»»»

   4. Compare the seemingly archaic Indian caste system to
modern social (class) barriers – what differences and similarities do you perceive? Discuss in class.

Webcode
SNG-40235-014
@   **5.** Watch the video clips provided on the webcode and collect information about
  ● the history and development of Dharavi,
  ● the living conditions of the people,
  ● opportunities and risks the inhabitants of Dharavi face (e. g. crime, health conditions, poverty,
    (un-)employment, etc.).

   Afterwards, prepare and give a short presentation (ca. 5 minutes) in class that depicts the most relevant
information.
  → Focus on Skills, Presentations, p. 419

Info »»»

The Indian Caste [kast] **System**
The Indian caste system involves four castes
(= varnas) and one outcast social group:
1. Brahmins (teachers, scholars, priests)
2. Kshatriyas (kings, warriors)
3. Vaishyas (farmers, traders)
4. Shudras (service providers, laborers)
All those who do not match these norms, e. g.
foreigners, tribals or nomads, were considered
contagious (*ansteckend*) and untouchables
(= Harijans). These people were segregated
and had unpleasant or toxic jobs, often lived in
extreme poverty and suffered from social discrimination. These barriers have mostly broken down in large cities, but still exist in rural
areas. Since the Constitution of India (1950)
outlawed the practice of untouchability, it has
declined significantly – even allowing former
untouchables to take up high political offices.

Sanjeev Bhaskar

Bangalore – India's Silicon Valley

In 2007, British actor and comedian Sanjeev Bahskar took a tour through India on occasion of India's 60th Independence Day. During his tour, he visited the city of Bangalore, which is considered to be India's Silicon Valley.
In class, reactivate your knowledge of Silicon Valley, USA, and what it stands for.

Tips on vocab

a hub *Drehscheibe* ■ **surreal** very strange ■ **to recede** to become gradually less ■ **lawn** *Rasenfläche* ■ **nestled in** *eingebettet in* ■ **scale** level ■ **parcel** *Parzelle* ■ **heritage** *Erbe, Hinterlassenschaft* ■ **precarious** not safe or certain ■ **remains** *Überreste* ■ **cutting** unpleasant ■ **to run in tandem** *parallel laufen* ■ **Orwellian** George Orwell (1903 – 1950), British author, journalist and critic; famous for his dystopian novels "Nineteen Eighty-Four" and "Animal Farm" ■ **ancestral** *Ahnen-*

Infosys Pyramid in Bangalore which houses the CDG (= Corporate Design Group) of Infosys

Before listening:

1. Look at the photo showing the Infosys campus in Electronic City, Bangalore.
   - Describe the overall impression that is evoked.
   - Specify what the design of the building alludes to and implies.
   → Focus on Skills, Analysis of Visuals, p. 409

2. **Step 1:** Team up with a partner and, while **listening a first time**, take notes on these questions:
   - What specifically does Bangalore specialize in?
   - Who studies at Bangalore University?
   - What does the so-called "heritage building" represent?
   - Why did the builders of the campus have to chase away ancient spirits?
   - What is the significance of the "map room"?
   → Focus on Skills, Listening Comprehension, p. 394

   Step 2: Compare your findings with your partner's results and make additions and corrections if necessary.

   Step 3: Listen to the audio text **a second time** and complete your notes.

3. In order to emphasize Bangalore's uniqueness, Sanjeev Bhaskar uses a certain choice of words. **Listen** to Bhaskar's observations and remarks **a third time** and explain the meaning and function of the words and terms on the following page in the context of his description and comments.

- surreal
- relatively heritage
- futuristic dreamscape
- 21st-century vision of India
- a spiritual super highway
- a utopian oasis of calm
- the normal Indian madness
- in tandem with the information superhighway
- Orwellian landscape of Infosys
- technological reinvention without limits

→ Focus on Skills, Analysis of a Non-Fictional Text, p. 405

4. **Step 1:** Analyse the statistical data below and explain India's position compared to other emerging economies worldwide.
   → Focus on Skills, Analysis of Statistical Data, p. 408

Step 2: Compare the statistical data at hand to Sanjeev Bhaskar's description of the city of Bangalore and its economic potential.

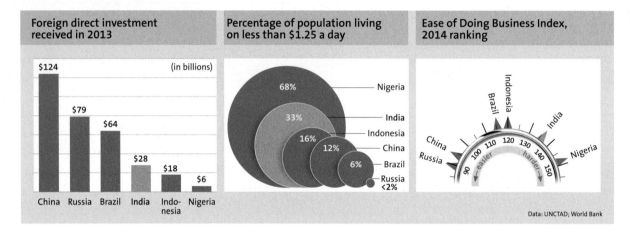

Foreign direct investment received in 2013

Percentage of population living on less than $1.25 a day

Ease of Doing Business Index, 2014 ranking

Data: UNCTAD; World Bank

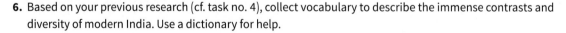

ACTIVITIES

5. Do research on Bangalore and the Infosys corporation and the businesses and services it includes. Contrast this seemingly utopian oasis of science and innovation to the dystopian and nightmarish slums like Dharavi (cf. pp. 133 f.).
   What do the contrasts reveal about "modern India"?

GRAMMAR / LANGUAGE

6. Based on your previous research (cf. task no. 4), collect vocabulary to describe the immense contrasts and diversity of modern India. Use a dictionary for help.

☺	☹
futuristic, future-oriented, innovative, safeguarding the future, …	appalling, poverty-stricken, under-privileged, dystopian, …

Next, use the vocabulary you have collected and compile either
a) a brochure or website that promotes Bangalore and its futuristic university campus to foreign investors and scientists or
b) a brochure or website for a human rights organization that wants to make people aware of the appalling situation millions of Indian people live in.

Employ as much of the collected vocabulary as possible to provide vivid descriptions.

Aravind Adiga
Between the Assassinations[1]

In a 4-corners activity, reflect on and discuss whether you think that corruption
- damages the economy of a country,
- fosters the economy of a country,
- has little or no influence at all,
- is a serious crime that should be punished severely.

Choose a "corner" and collect arguments that support your view.

1. **Before reading:**
   Describe the cartoon below using the vocabulary in the vocab box and/or a dictionary for help.
   Pay attention to details and specify the meaning of certain visual symbols.
   → Focus on Skills, Analysis of Visuals, p. 409

Tips on vocab »

a large bill ■ a pudgy (*dicklich*) hand ■ a pretentious (*protzig*) golden watch ■ bracelet ■ to bribe sb. (*bestechen*) ■ bribery ■ the Lion of Sarnath (national emblem) ■ Mahatma Gandhi ■ to look horrified ■ to peer at sb./sth. (*auf jdn./etw. schielen*)

The setting of the excerpt on the following pages is the fictitious Indian city of Kittur, whose inhabitants are a representative cross section of Indian society. In the following, the difficult life of small-time businessmen in general and of the textile sweatshop owner Abbasi, who struggles with corrupt officials, is presented.

[1] **assassination** the murder of sb. famous or important; *Attentat*

1 The Bunder, or the area around the port, is now mostly Muslim. The major landmark here is the Dargah, or tomb-shrine[2], of Yusuf Ali, a domed[3] white structure to which thousands of Muslims from across
5 Southern India make pilgrimage[4] each year. [...] If you walk to the other end of the Bunder, you will find the industrial area, where dozens of textile sweatshops operate in dingy[5] old buildings. The Bunder has the highest crime rate in Kittur, and is the scene of frequent
10 stabbings[6], police raids[7], and arrests. [...]
Abbasi uncorked the bottle – Johnnie Walker Red Label blended, the second-finest whisky known to God or man – and poured a small peg[8] each into two glasses embossed[9] with the Air India *maharajah* logo. He
15 opened the old fridge, took out a bucket of ice, and dropped three cubes by hand into each glass. He poured cold water into the glasses, found a spoon and stirred. He bent[10] his head low and prepared to spit into one of the glasses.
20 Oh, too simple, Abbasi. Too simple.
He swallowed spittle[11]. Unzipping his cotton trousers, he let them slide down. Pressing the middle and index finger of his right hand together, he stuck them deep into his rectum[12]; then he dipped them into one of the
25 glasses of whisky and stirred.
He pulled his trousers and zipped them. He frowned[13] at the tainted[14] whisky; now came the tricky part – things had to be arranged so that the right man took the right glass.

30 **2** He left the pantry[15] carrying the tray.
The official from the State Electricity Board, sitting at Abbasi's table, grinned. He was a fat, dark man in a blue safari suit, a steel ballpoint pen in his jacket pocket. Abbasi carefully placed the tray on the table in front
35 of the gentleman.
'Please,' Abbasi said, with redundant[16] hospitality[17]; the official had taken the glass closer to him, and was sipping and licking his lips. He finished the whisky in slow gulps[18], and put the glass down.
40 'A man's drink.'
Abbasi smiled ironically.

The official placed his hands on his tummy.
'Five hundred,' he said. 'Five hundred rupees.'
Abbasi was a small man, with a streak of grey in his beard which he did not attempt to disguise with dye[19], 45 as many middle-aged men in Kittur did; he thought the white streak gave him a look of ingenuity[20], which he felt he needed, because he knew that his reputation among his friends was that of a simple-minded creature prone[21] to regular outbreaks of idealism. 50
His ancestors, who had served in the royal darbars[22] of Hyderabad[23], had bequeathed[24] him an elaborate sense of courtesy and good manners, which he had adapted for the realities of the twentieth century with touches of sarcasm and self-parody. 55
He folded his palms[25] into a Hindu's namaste[26] and bowed low before the official. 'Sahib, you know we have just reopened the factory. There have been many costs. If you could show some –'
'Five hundred. Five hundred rupees.' 60
The official twirled his glass around and gazed at the Air India logo with one eye, as if some small part of him were embarrassed by what he was doing. He gestured at his mouth with his fingers: 'A man has to eat these days, Mr Abbasi. Prices are rising so fast.' [...] 65
Abbasi closed his eyes. He reached towards his desk, pulled out a drawer[27], took out a wad[28] of notes, counted them, and placed the money in front of the official. The fat man, moistening[29] his finger for each note, counted them one by one; producing a blue rubber 70 band from a pocket of his trousers, he strapped it around the notes twice.

3 But Abbasi knew the ordeal[30] was not over yet. 'Sahib, we have a tradition in this factory that we never let a guest depart without a gift.' 75
He rang the bell for Ummar, his manager, who entered almost at once with a shirt in his hands. He had been waiting outside the whole time.
The official took the white shirt out of its cardboard box: he looked at the design: a golden dragon whose 80 tail spread round onto the back of the shirt.
'It's gorgeous.'

---

[2] **tomb** [tu:m] grave – [3] **domed** kuppelförmig – [4] **pilgrimage** ['pɪlgrɪmɪdʒ] Pilgerreise – [5] **dingy** schäbig – [6] **stabbing** Messerstecherei – [7] **raid** Überfall – [8] **peg** a unit of alcohol, ca. one shot – [9] **to emboss** gravieren – [10] **to bend** beugen, bücken – [11] **spittle** Speichel – [12] **rectum** Mastdarm – [13] **to frown** die Stirn runzeln – [14] **tainted** spoiled – [15] **pantry** a room for storing food – [16] **redundant** überflüssig – [17] **hospitality** a friendly welcome for guests or strangers – [18] **gulp** Schluck – [19] **dye** Färbemittel – [20] **ingenuity** [ɪndʒəˈnjuəti] Erfindungsgabe – [21] **prone** likely to experience; zu etw. neigend – [22] **darbar** ceremonial gatherings in India during the Raj, held as demonstrations of loyalty to the crown – [23] **Hyderabad** [ˈhaɪdrəˌbæd] metropolis in southern India – [24] **to bequeath** [bɪˈkwiːð] vererben – [25] **palm** the inner part of one's hand – [26] **Namaste** a customary greeting or farewell – [27] **drawer** Schublade – [28] **wad** Bündel – [29] **to moisten** befeuchten – [30] **ordeal** Geduldsprobe, Quälerei

'We ship them to the United States. They are worn by men who dance professionally. They call it "ballroom dancing." They put on this shirt and swirl under red disco lights.' [...]

'That dragon is the reason I closed,' Abbasi said. 'To stitch the dragon takes very fine embroidery[31] work. The eyes of the women doing this work get damaged. One day this was brought to my attention; I thought, I don't want to answer to Allah for the damage done to the eyes of my workers. So I said to them, go home, and I closed the factory.'

The official smiled ironically. Another of those Muslims who drink whisky and mention Allah in every other sentence. [...]

4 Corruption. There is no end to it in this country. In the past four months, since he had decided to reopen his shirt factory, he had had to pay off:

The electricity man; the water board man; half the income tax department of Kittur; half the excise[32] department of Kittur; six different officials of the telephone board; a land tax official of the Kittur City Corporation; a sanitary[33] inspector from the Karnataka State Health Board; a health inspector from the Karnataka State Sanitation Board; a delegation of the All India Small Factory Workers' Union; delegations of the Kittur Congress Party, the Kittur BJP[34], the Kittur Communist Party, and the Kittur Muslim League. [...]

5 The next day, he turned up to work at ten-forty, his head throbbing[35] with pain.

Ummar opened the door for him. Abbasi nodded and took the mail from him. With his head down to the floor, he moved to the stairs that led up to his office; then he stopped. At the threshold[36] of the door that led to the factory door, one of the stitching women was standing staring at him.

'I'm not paying you to waste time,' he snapped.

She turned and fled. [...]

In the six weeks since his factory had reopened, he had not once gone through this doorway; Ummar had handled the affairs of the factory floor. But now the doorway to his right, black and yawning[37], had become inescapable.

He felt he had no option but to go in. [...]

The women were sitting on the floor of the dimly[38] lit room, pale fluorescent[39] lights flickering overhead, each at a work station indicated by a numeral in red letters painted on the wall. They held the white shirts close to their eyes and stitched gold thread[40] into them; they stopped when he came in. He flicked his wrist[41], indicating that they should keep working. He didn't want their eyes looking at him: those eyes that were being damaged as their fingers created golden shirts that he could sell to American ballroom dancers.

Damaged? No, that was not the right word. That was not the reason he had shunted[42] them into a side room. Everyone in that room was going blind.

He sat down on a chair in the centre of the room.

The optometrist[43] had been clear about that; the kind of detailed stitchwork needed for the shirts scarred[44] the women's retinas[45]. He had used his fingers to show Abbasi how thick the scars[46] were. No amount of improved lighting would reduce the impact on the retinas. Human eyes were not meant to stare for hours at designs this intricate[47]. Two women had already gone blind; that was why he had shut down the factory. When he reopened, all his old workers came back at once. They knew their fate; but there was no other work to be had.

Abbasi closed his eyes. He wanted nothing more than for Ummar to shout that he was urgently needed upstairs.

But no one came to release him and he sat in the chair, while the women around him stitched, and their stitching fingers kept talking to him: we are going blind; look at us! [...]

6 He kneaded[48] the cloth between his fingers. He could feel, between his fingers, the finespun fabric[49] of corruption. 'The factory is closed,' he wanted to shout out to the dragon.

'There – you happy with me? The factory is closed.'

And after that? Who would send his son to school? Would he sit by the docks with a knife and smuggle cars like Mehmood? The women would go elsewhere, and do the same work.

He slapped his hand against his thigh[50].

---

[31] **embroidery** *Stickerei* – [32] **excise** *Verbrauchssteuer* – [33] **sanitary** *Gesundheits-* – [34] **BJP** (*abbr.*) Bharatiya Janata Party; second largest party in India – [35] **to throb** *pochen* – [36] **threshold** *Türschwelle* – [37] **yawning** wide open – [38] **dimly** not bright – [39] **fluorescent** [fluəˈresnt] *fluoreszierend* – [40] **thread** [θred] *Faden* – [41] **wrist** *Handgelenk* – [42] **to shunt** *abschieben* – [43] **optometrist** [ɒpˈtɒmətrɪst] *Augenoptiker* – [44] **to scar** *vernarben* – [45] **retina** *Netzhaut* – [46] **scar** *Narbe* – [47] **intricate** complicated – [48] **to knead** [niːd] *kneten* – [49] **fabric** *Gewebe* – [50] **thigh** [θaɪ] *Oberschenkel*

Thousands, sitting in the teashops and universities and workplaces every day and every night, were cursing[51] corruption. Yet not one fellow had found a way to slay[52] the demon without giving up his share of the loot[53] of corruption. So why did he – an ordinary businessman given to whisky and snooker and listening to gossip[54] from thugs[55] – have to come up with an answer?

But just a moment later, he realized he already had an answer.

He offered Allah a compromise. He would be taken to jail, but his factory would go on with its work: he closed his eyes and prayed to God to accept this deal.

from *Between the Assassinations* by Aravind Adiga. Atlantic Books, London 2010, pp. 23 ff.

COMPREHENSION

2. **Step 1: Skim the first part** of the text and try to understand the **gist** of what is said. Take notes on the w-questions (who – what – where – when – why).

 Step 2: Pair up with a partner and summarize the most relevant information to each other. Correct and/or add information that you consider to be important.

 Step 3: Together with a partner, speculate on how the story might go on. Work out a storyline that follows the narrative style of the first part and is based on the clues given about what might happen next.

Tip: Pay attention to clues/hints given about the setting or plot, e.g. "the highest crime rate" (ll. 8 f.), "textile sweatshops" (l. 7) or "that the right man took the right glass" (ll. 28 f.). <u>Do not</u> read the subsequent parts of the story yet – make up ideas of your own and use your imagination!

 Write your storyline on posters and display them in class.

Example:

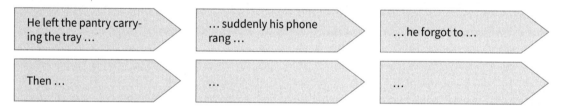

→ Focus on Skills, Continuation of a Fictional Text, p. 420

Step 4: Present your storylines and discuss whether they follow the style and clues given in part 1 and whether the continuation is convincing and plausible.

3. Now, **read parts 2 – 4** of the text and take notes on
   - the State Electricity Board official's behaviour,
   - Abbasi's opinion of corruption.
   - Abbasi's strategy of bribing (*bestechen*) the official,

4. After **reading parts 5 and 6**, point out
   - the impact of the embroidery work,
   - Abbasi's "deal with God".
   - Abbasi's pangs of conscience (*Gewissensbisse*),

ANALYSIS

5. Examine the view taken on corruption and sweatshop work in the story. Refer to specific lines in the text that reveal the author's critical and even sarcastic way of looking at "small-time business" in India.

---

[51] **to curse** *verfluchen* – [52] **to slay** to kill – [53] **loot** *Beute* – [54] **gossip** *Klatsch* – [55] **thug** a violent brutal person

6. Analyse the mode of presentation* and explain how it emphasizes the message of the text.
→ Focus on Skills, Analysis of a Fictional Text, p. 402

ACTIVITIES

7. Taking into consideration your previous results, speculate on the novel's title. Which "assassinations" might the author have had in mind – and what happens "in between"?

8. Comment on Abbasi's "deal with God".
Imagine you are "God" – how would you respond to Abbasi's attempt to get "a clean bill of health" (*Persilschein*) and to kill two birds with one stone (*zwei Fliegen mit einer Klappe schlagen*)?
→ Focus on Skills, Writing a Comment and a Review, p. 421

GRAMMAR / LANGUAGE

9. Talking or writing about the economy usually requires a lot of technical terms and abstract formulations. Turn the expressions below into everyday English to get a better understanding of what is really meant. Use a dictionary for help.

Tip: Do not simply copy the annotations or explanations given in a dictionary. Try to use your own words.

• graft	• private sector	• real-estate business	• commodity	• petty corruption
• corruption	• investigator	• unprecedented growth	• malfeasance	• insider-trading
• profit	• state-run	• investigative agency	• privatization	• malpractice
• red tape	• financier	• good governance		

Suketu Mehta

India's War on Its Women

AWARENESS

The media has frequently reported violence against women in India. Whether it is beatings, (gang) rape, human trafficking (*Menschenhandel*), murder or female foeticide – Indian women are faced with an unimaginable amount of aggression and crime against them.
In a placemat activity, reflect on possible reasons for this appalling situation as well as possible solutions to it.

From the pages of

Every Indian media outlet has a name for her: Amanat (Treasure). Nirbhaya (Fearless). Brave-
5 heart. India's Girl. She can't be named, but she bears the name of every woman in India.
If she had been allowed to live, she would have been a paragon[1] of the progress Indian women are making. She was studying to be a physiotherapist. She was the only 10 person supporting her rural family. She was going to marry a software engineer in February. She was 23. She was, for God's sake, only 23. But she lived – and has now been cremated[2] – in Delhi.
Every one of my female friends who's visited or lived in 15 New Delhi has a story about the men there. Christine from Paris was walking in Connaught Place, the heart of the city, with her mother. Christine is an anthropologist[3]

---

[1] **paragon** a perfect example of a good quality – [2] **to cremate** to burn dead (human) bodies – [3] **anthropologist** [ˈænθrəˈpɑlədʒɪst] a person who studies human society, customs, beliefs

who wanted to show her mother, who was in India for
20 the first time, what a wonderful country it was. A man
came up to them and thrust[4] his hand between Christine's legs, grabbing her crotch[5]. He laughed and sauntered off[6]. "My mother had to watch this," Christine said,
weeping. But she knows that Indian women – especially
25 the poor and the low caste – suffer worse.

New Delhi isn't the only Indian city where bad things
happen to women, but it has a special reputation. Perhaps it's the political corruption that transforms into
moral corruption; perhaps it's North Indian machismo[7];
30 perhaps it's the skewed[8] sex ratio – 866 females for every 1,000 males, because many girls are killed at birth by
parents who'd rather have a son. The numbers bear it
out: New Delhi has more rapes than Mumbai, Kolkata,
Chennai, Bangalore and Hyderabad put together.

35 All over the country, the gang rape has galvanized[9] Indians into an agonized[10] national discussion about how
badly we treat our women. But some of the proposed[11]
solutions are wildly off the mark[12]. Internet forums
seethe[13] with demands for the death penalty for rapists.
40 Given the promptness with which Indian police round
up the usual suspects in any high-profile case, this
would result in many innocent men being hanged. "Enforcement[14] is more important than a new law," pointed
out the victim's fiancé, who was attacked with her.

45 The way the country deals with sexual assault[15] has to
change at the most basic level: at the police stations
where rape is reported, in the doctors' clinics where the
victim is examined and in the courts where the victim
is cross-examined. [...]
50 Most women in that part of the world stay clear of police stations for their own safety. A friend, an influential filmmaker, told me about what happened when he

reported the embezzlement[16] of a large sum by his accountant[17]. The accountant had fled town, so the police
arrested the accountant's sister – who had not been 55
involved in the crime – to put pressure on her brother
to surrender. When my friend went to the station, the
officer in charge told him that the sister was in the
lockup[18] and invited him to "do what you want with
her." Fearing for her safety, my friend had a man from 60
his office sit at the station day and night, guarding her
from the police.

The rot begins at the top[19]. Six sitting members of state
legislatures have been charged with rape; two members
of Parliament and 36 state legislators have been charged 65
with crimes against women. In the 2009 national elections, political parties fielded[20] no fewer than 40 candidates who were charged with rape or other crimes
against women.

The country seems to have had enough. There are si- 70
lent marches, candlelit vigils[21]. There is outrage in the
papers, on television. Thus did people gather after the
2008 terrorist attacks here to demand better security;
thus did people gather in 2011 to protest corruption.
This is the third massive wave of protest, and this time 75
it's to demand the most elementary respect for India's
591 million females. But can it be sustained[22]?

"Here's the bottom line," said Barack Obama about gun
control. "We're not going to get this done unless the
American people decide it's important." About fighting 80
rape in India, here's the bottom line. We're not going to
get this done unless the Indian people decide it's important.

TIME, 14 January 2013, p. 47

TIME and the TIME logo are registered trademarks of Time Inc. used under
license.

COMPREHENSION

1. Present the different forms of violence that women face in New Delhi and other Indian cities.

2. Outline how India's doctors and police deal with sexual assault on women.

3. Find examples in the article that support the thesis that "the rot begins at the top" (l. 63).

[4] **to thrust** to push suddenly and violently – [5] **crotch** *Schritt* – [6] **to saunter off** to walk about without much hurry – [7] **machismo**
[məˈtʃɪzməʊ] *Männlichkeitswahn* – [8] **skewed** unfair – [9] **to galvanize** *jdn. plötzlich aktiv werden lassen* – [10] **agonized** showing great pain
and suffering – [11] **to propose** to suggest – [12] **off the mark** (*infml.*) *daneben* – [13] **to seethe** *brodeln* – [14] **enforcement** *Durchsetzung, Erzwingung* – [15] **assault** attack – [16] **embezzlement** *Veruntreuung* – [17] **accountant** *Buchhalter* – [18] **lockup** here: jail cell – [19] **the rot begins at
the top** (*proverb*) *der Fisch stinkt immer vom Kopf* – [20] **to field** to be represented by – [21] **vigil** *Nachtwache* – [22] **to sustain sth.** to make
sth. continue for some time without becoming less

4. Describe the photo – what demands do the demonstrators have?

Public anger over the poor state of women's safety in Delhi was one reason that the ruling Congress Party was wiped out in local elections in the city last month

ANALYSIS

5. Analyse the author's stance on violence against (Indian) women and the involvement of (state) authorities in sexual assaults. In order to do so, examine the author's
  - line of argument*,
  - use of rhetorical devices* (e. g. the choice of words, metaphors, positive and negative emotive words, etc.).
  → Focus on Skills, Analysis of a Non-Fictional Text, p. 405

6. Examine the reasons given in the article for the appalling situation. Who – according to the author – is to blame for the rising violence against women and who/what has to be changed to improve the situation?

ACTIVITIES

7. Use the links provided on the webcode and read the *Telegraph* article in which "a woman's clothes" are considered to be the reason for rape. Relate the allegations (*Behauptungen*) made here to the article at hand.
  Which different views on Indian society and gender roles are taken in the articles?
  Give a critical comment and evaluation of the plausibility of the different perspectives.

8. In groups, study the Focus on Documents page *The Universal Declaration of Human Rights* (p. 304).

  Step 1: Extract the most relevant articles in connection with "violence against women".

  Step 2: As member of an activist group, compile a pamphlet in which you
  a) inform the public about the different forms of violence against Indian women,
  b) refer to the Universal Declaration of Human Rights,
  c) demand necessary changes and reforms.

  Present and discuss your pamphlets in class.
  → Focus on Skills, Presentations, p. 419

Ethnic Communities in the U. K. – A Multicultural Kaleidoscope?!

Emily Dugan

Living in Mixed Communities 'Makes People Feel British'

AWARENESS

Imagine you were born somewhere outside of Europe and are thinking about leaving your mother country – which country/countries would you want to immigrate to? Make a ranking and give reasons for your choice(s).

People from ethnic minorities are more likely to feel British if they live in mixed communities rather than being surrounded by neighbours of their own background.

5 The most comprehensive study of community cohesion[1] in the UK ever conducted has found clear evidence of the positive impact of integration.

Researchers from Essex University and the University of Oxford analysed data from two surveys of 4,391
10 British people. Of these, 3,582 came from ethnic minorities.

When people from these minority groups live in very mixed areas, where there were few people from their own ethnicity, they are five percentage points more
15 likely to identify with Britain as a whole than those who live amongst people from their own background, researchers found.

"Diversity is really good for minority members in Britain," the report's co-author, Neli Demireva, said. "If
20 they live in diverse scenarios they identify more with Britain. Contact is good because they don't create reactive identities[2]."

In addition, the study established that living as a minority amongst other ethnicities does not lessen[3] trust
25 in neighbours, willingness to help neighbours, or how often a person takes part in community activities.

The research, published in the journal *Sociology*, also found that white Britons living in deprivation[4] with little education are less likely to trust their neighbours
30 than their richer, better educated peers.

These factors make more difference to levels of trust for white Britons than how ethnically diverse their neighbourhood is. Previous[5] studies in America and Europe had been more negative about the effects of ethnic mixing on trust and civic spirit[6]. But this study 35 found that "if anything, diversity should be encouraged to cement the integration progress of migrants."

Sunder Katwala, director of the integration think-tank British Future, welcomed the study. "The everyday story of integration working well in Manchester and Shef- 40 field or Birmingham and Leicester often doesn't get reported. The overall story of Britain is of being a bit better at this than we thought we would be."

Mr Katwala believes better integration of the kind found by the researchers could be promoted by more commu- 45 nity activities. "We can make this work and we have a history of making it work well," he said. "We should promote more contact with people who wouldn't otherwise meet."

Although white Britons living in areas with concen- 50 trated numbers of people from different ethnic backgrounds were five percentage points less likely to trust others than white people living in low diversity areas, this was closely linked to deprivation and fears of crime. The single most dramatic impact on whether 55 white Britons trust others is education. Overall, white Britons with degrees[7] were 27 percentage points more likely to trust others than those with no education.

www.independent.co.uk/news/uk/home-news/living-in-mixed-communi ties-makes-people-feel-british-9100347.html, 31 January 2014 [23.07.2014]

---

[1] **cohesion** [kəʊˈhiːʒən] (*fml.*) a situation where the members of group or society are united – [2] **reactive identity** an identity based on other people's prejudices rather than one's own self-expression – [3] **to lessen** to become less strong – [4] **deprivation** *Entbehrung, Mangel* – [5] **previous** *früher* – [6] **civic spirit** showing that you are an active member of your community and feel responsible – [7] **degree** *Schul- oder Universitätsabschluss*

1. Describe the effect of diverse neighbourhoods on minority groups.

2. Point out the connection made between higher education and the ability/willingness to trust multiethnic neighbours.

3. Illustrate the difference between white Britons and ethnic communities concerning the aspect of trusting people in their neighbourhood.

4. Visualize the information given in the article and the implied correlations in a diagram.
   → Focus on Skills, Analysis of Statistical Data, p. 408

5. In groups, compile a collage that depicts *your* understanding of "multiculturalism".
   Use snippets from newspapers or magazines, headlines, short texts, statistical data, cooking recipes, etc. and arrange them on a poster.

   Organize a little exhibition in your class or school in which you present and discuss your ideas.

Ethnic Minorities – Into the Melting Pot

Take a look at the visual below and, in a Think! Pair! Share! activity, reflect on what it might express concerning the topics "multiethnic society" or "ethnic minorities".

The rapid rise of mixed-race Britain is changing neighbourhoods – and perplexing the authorities
Zadie Smith, a novelist born to a black Jamaican mother and a white British father, recently recalled that when
5 she was growing up in Willesden Green, a London district with a large immigrant population, "nothing could be more normal than a mixed-race girl". The surprise, she said, was entering publishing and finding that people thought it unusual. Nobody could get that impres-
10 sion now: Britons are mixing at extraordinary speed. The 2011 census revealed a country that is decreasingly white and British: England's ethnic-minority population grew from 9% of the total in 2001 to 14%. But the biggest single increase was in the number of people
15 claiming a mixed-ethnic background. This almost doubled, to around 1.2 m. Among children under the age of five, 6% had a mixed background – more than belonged to any other minority group. Mixed-race children are now about as common in Britain as in America – a country with many more non-whites and a longer his- 20 tory of mass immigration.

As Britain's mixed-race population swells, another group appears destined to shrink. The Labour Force Survey reveals that 48% of black Caribbean men and 34% of black Caribbean women in couples are with partners of a different ethnic group – with higher proportions still among younger cohorts[1]. Black Caribbean children under ten years old are outnumbered[2] two-to-one by children who are a mixture of white and black Caribbean.

Rob Ford of Manchester University points out that Caribbean folk are following an Irish pattern of integration, in that their partners are often working-class. The Irish parallel also suggests they will eventually be fully absorbed into the British population. Polls[3] show that adults who are a mixture of white and black Caribbean tend to see themselves not so much as black, Caribbean or even as British, but rather as English – the identity of the comfortably assimilated.

Indians, who began arriving in large numbers in the 1960s, were slower to mix. They are now doing so – but along Jewish, rather than Irish, lines. For them, assimilation follows education: according to research by Raya Muttarak and Anthony Heath, Indians with degrees are far more likely to marry whites. Indians are not so much marrying into the white majority as into its suburban middle class, says Shamit Saggar at the University of Essex.

Their children are quietly transforming Britain's suburbs and commuter towns[4]. Whereas Asians are still concentrated in cities such as Leicester and in London boroughs like Tower Hamlets and Harrow, mixed Asian and white children are widespread. In Chiltern, an affluent commuter district in Buckinghamshire, 5% of children under five years old were mixed Asian and white in 2011 – more than in most of London. Their parents may have met at university or while working in the capital. Within Birmingham, too, mixed Asian and white children are especially common in the largely middle-class white suburbs of Edgbaston, Moseley and Harborne.

Still warming up

Pakistanis and Bangladeshis mostly remain in cities, and are mixing more slowly. Just 8% of Pakistani men and 7% of Bangladeshi men in couples are with people of a different ethnic group, and the proportions for women are smaller. Oddly, older Pakistani men are more likely to have partners of another ethnicity, perhaps because many early migrants were single men. But even these groups are assimilating: another study finds that Pakistanis and Bangladeshis born in Britain are far likelier to socialise with whites than their parents were.

Britain's newer minorities are blending into[5] the larger population, too, but in ways that defy[6] easy categorisation. Mixed black-African and white children are particularly common in working-class suburbs and commuter towns such as Croydon and Southend-on-Sea, possibly because black Africans are rarely tied to city centres through social-housing tenancies[7]. They are also mixing with new immigrants from continental Europe. Most of the 21,000 children born to Polish mothers in 2012 had Polish fathers; but of the rest, 23% had African or Asian fathers.

Such esoteric[8] partnerships can confuse the authorities. Last November the Home Office invited journalists to accompany officers on a raid[9] of an apparent sham wedding[10] between an Italian man and a Chinese woman in north London. After interrogating the bride, groom[11] and guests, the officers emerged[12] sheepishly to admit that the union was probably real.

As race becomes less clear-cut, schools, hospitals and police forces, which record people's ethnic identity at almost every opportunity, will have to deal with more fragmented definitions. So too will researchers trying to measure racial injustices. Confusingly, police officers now record the ethnicity of the people they stop and search according to two separate systems: observed ethnic appearance (which does not include a mixed-race category) and self-identified ethnicity (which does).

Politicians in the habit of treating Britain's ethnic groups as distinct[13] "communities" will also have to adapt. The shrewder[14] black and Asian politicians have already built power bases that do not depend on ethnic block votes. Speeches such as the one made by Tony Blair in 2007 about the culture of black youth violence will look silly when so many black teenagers have

---

[1] **cohort** a group of people who share a characteristic – [2] **to outnumber** to be greater in number than sb. else – [3] **poll** *Umfrage* – [4] **commuter town** a town with many inhabitants who regularly travel between work and home – [5] **to blend into** (*phr. v.*) to look the same as surrounding people and therefore not easily noticeable – [6] **to defy** to refuse to obey a person, decision – [7] **social-housing tenancy** *Sozialwohnungsmietverhältnis* – [8] **esoteric** here: very unusual – [9] **raid** *Überfall* – [10] **sham wedding** *vorgetäuschte Heirat* – [11] **groom** *Bräutigam* – [12] **to emerge** *heraustreten* [13] **distinct** *eigen* – [14] **shrewd** *gewitzt*

white parents too. Crude[15] racist politics, thankfully now rare in Britain, ought to become almost impossible as more white families acquire[16] non-white members. Englishness, which has remained distinctly a white identity for many, may become less exclusive.

Most of all, the rise of mixed-race Britain shows that Britain is capable of absorbing even large numbers of newcomers. For the young, who are used to having people of all backgrounds in their midst, race already matters far less than it did for their parents. In a generation or two more of the melting pot, it may not matter at all.

www.economist.com/news/britain/21595908-rapid-rise-mixed-race-britain-changing-neighbourhoodsand-perplexing, 8 February 2014 [23.07.2014]

COMPREHENSION

1. Give an outline of what the 2011 census revealed about Britain's changing ethnicities.

2. Present Britain's mixed-raced population trends and people's assimilation and socializing habits focusing on:
   - Caribbeans
   - Indians
   - Asians
   - Pakistanis
   - Bangladeshis

ANALYSIS

3. Explain which "problems" multi-ethnicity poses on politicians and social researchers.
   → Focus on Skills, Analysis of a Non-Fictional Text, p. 405

4. Specify the positive "side effects" that growing numbers of mixed-race British newcomers have.

5. Examine and analyse the information and data given on the Focus on Facts pages (pp. 149 f.).
   Explain:
   a) What made people move to Britain throughout history, and what changes have taken place concerning the motivation and need to migrate?
   b) What facts support the thesis that Britain is a multicultural society?
   c) What measure is Britain taking in order not to lose control of migrant flows?
      Do you consider the PBS system to be a promising tool to control and filter the flow of migrants?
   → Focus on Skills, Analysis of Statistical Data, p. 408
   → Focus on Facts, Great Britain – Immigration and Minorities, p. 149

 6. Originally, the term "melting pot" was used in connection with US-American beliefs of how to integrate immigrants (→ Focus on Facts, American Beliefs and Values, p. 176). This concept has been replaced over time by different new concepts like the "pizza" or "salad bowl" models, both focusing rather on keeping the immigrants' cultural and ethnic identity than on giving up one's cultural heritage and identity.

Against this background, explain the term "melting pot" in the context of the article at hand.

---

[15] **crude** *roh, ungehobelt* – [16] **to acquire** to get sth.

ACTIVITIES

7. "For the young … race already matters far less than it did for their parents. In a generation or two more of the melting pot, it may not matter at all" (ll. 117 ff.).
   Comment on this statement and give reasons why you (dis-)agree with this thesis.
   → Focus on Skills, Writing a Comment and a Review, p. 421

@ 8. Do research on the Internet and find examples of multiracial celebrities ("ethnicelebs") and/or politicians who have a multi-ethnic identity (e. g. Halle Berry, Naomi Campbell, Barack Obama, Thandie Newton, etc.). Discuss how they serve as "modern role models".

GRAMMAR / LANGUAGE

9. When you talk or write about ethnicity, migration and/or multiculturalism you have to be careful with your choice of words in order not to offend anybody should be as politically correct as possible.
   Have a look at the various terms and phrases below and find out about their precise meaning. Use your dictionary for help. Which of these terms/phrases are politically incorrect and thus should not be used or at least be handled carefully?

• migrant	• race	• black(s)	• refugee	• ethnicity
• immigrate	• emigrate	• brown	• coloured	• first-generation immigrant
• asylum seeker	• ethnic	• mixed	• racial	• second-generation immigrant

Great Britain – Immigration and Minorities

Immigration, minorities and ethnic groups

After World War II, Britain needed more workers and admitted citizens of Commonwealth countries without restriction. Many came from the Caribbean and from India, Pakistan and Bangladesh. They found work in hospitals, the textile industry and the public transport system, for example. **Nearly 500,000 Commonwealth citizens came to Britain before 1962**, many of whom were later joined by their families. When there were no longer enough jobs, the **Commonwealth Immigrants Act (1962)** was passed to restrict the number of immigrants entering Britain. In the following years, several more acts were passed. **Immigration is now strictly controlled.** Normally, only people from the European Union and certain Commonwealth citizens can get permission to live in Britain. Until the Brexit of 2016, Britain accepted about 50,000 immigrants every year.

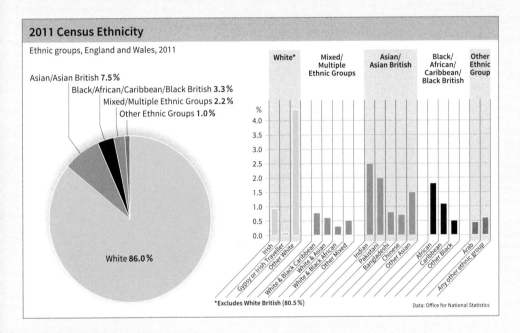

2011 Census Ethnicity

Ethnic groups, England and Wales, 2011

Asian/Asian British **7.5 %**
Black/African/Caribbean/Black British **3.3 %**
Mixed/Multiple Ethnic Groups **2.2 %**
Other Ethnic Groups **1.0 %**
White **86.0 %**

*Excludes White British (80.5 %)

Data: Office for National Statistics

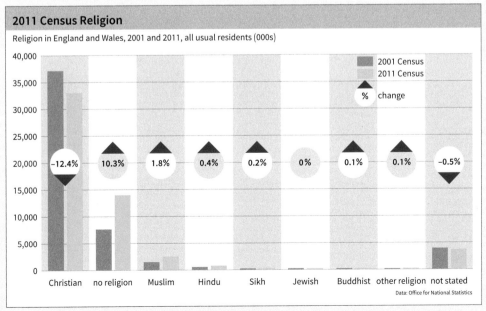

2011 Census Religion

Religion in England and Wales, 2001 and 2011, all usual residents (000s)

2001 Census / 2011 Census / % change

Christian −12.4%, no religion 10.3%, Muslim 1.8%, Hindu 0.4%, Sikh 0.2%, Jewish 0%, Buddhist 0.1%, other religion 0.1%, not stated −0.5%

Data: Office for National Statistics

Focus on Facts

In order to control and systematize immigration, Britain introduced a **Points Based System (PBS)** in 2008, which categorizes non-EU citizens into five tiers according to their professional qualifications and background.

Skilled work visa applications by industry sector

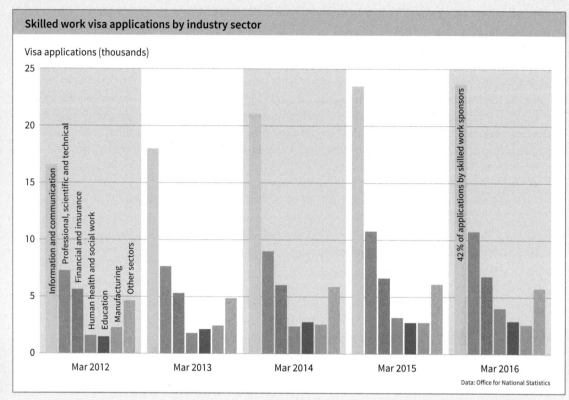

Visa applications (thousands)

Information and communication
Professional, scientific and technical
Financial and insurance
Human health and social work
Education
Manufacturing
Other sectors

42 % of applications by skilled work sponsors

Mar 2012 — Mar 2013 — Mar 2014 — Mar 2015 — Mar 2016

Data: Office for National Statistics

Entry clearance visas granted to the UK, top 10 nationalities, March 2016

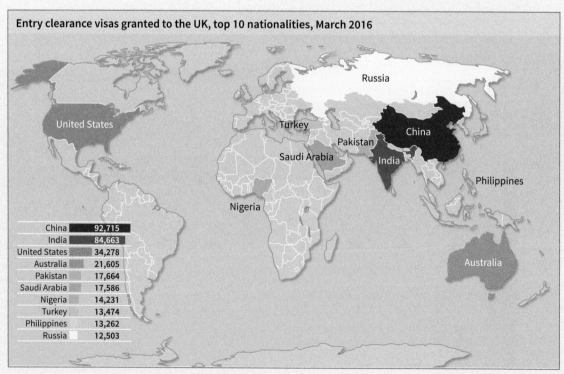

China	92,715
India	84,663
United States	34,278
Australia	21,605
Pakistan	17,664
Saudi Arabia	17,586
Nigeria	14,231
Turkey	13,474
Philippines	13,262
Russia	12,503

Monica Ali

Brick Lane

The novel *Brick Lane* is set in London's multicultural East End, where the protagonist Nazneen lives with her husband Chanu. At the age of seventeen she was married off to the older man and left her Bangladeshi home to begin her new life in England as a devoted wife and mother in a block of flats. In the following excerpt, Nazneen, her husband Chanu and their baby son Raqib are visiting Dr. Azad and his wife, who are well-to-do immigrants and can afford a rather luxurious and more westernized lifestyle.

What do you think are the most striking differences Nazneen experiences in her new life in England compared to her former life in India?

1 She showed them into the sitting room, where a pair of snarling[1] tigers guarded a gas fire. Nazneen sank inside a large gold sofa. Chanu placed his box of kalojam[2] on a gilded[3], claw-footed[4] table and stood with his arms
5 behind his back, as if afraid he might break something. Raqib clapped his fat hands to summon[5] the servants who were surely lurking in the kitchen.

Mrs. Azad stubbed out her cigarette in an ivory dish. She adjusted her underwear with a thumb and wiggle[6]
10 of her opulent backside. "One minute", she said, and strode to the hallway. "Azad!" she screeched. "You've got visitors".

Nazneen exchanged a glance with her husband. He raised his eyebrows and smiled. She smothered[7] a gig-
15 gle on Raqib's cheek.

Mrs. Azad climbed inside an armchair. She tucked[8] her feet up and her skirt rode up her large brown thighs. Chanu swayed[9] a little. Nazneen eyed the curtains: miles of velvet swagged[10] with gold braid, enough ma-
20 terial to wrap up a tower block. Chanu cleared his throat. Mrs. Azad sighed. She tucked her fingers in her armpits and squeezed her breasts. The baby wriggled[11] and Nazneen put him down on the thick cream carpet, where he coughed up some of his supper. Nazneen put
25 her foot over the spot.

Gradually, Nazneen became aware that Chanu was staring at something over her shoulder. When she turned her head she saw that Dr. Azad was standing in the doorway. The two men appeared to be frozen. The
30 doctor was as neat as a tailor's dummy[12]. He held his arms smartly to his sides. White cuffs[13] peeped out of his dark suit. His collar and tie held up his precise chin and his hair was brushed to an ebony sheen[14]. He looked as if he had seen a ghost. Nazneen looked at Chanu. He made a poor ghost, in his broken-down 35 shoes and oversize green anorak.

"For the love of God!" said Mrs. Azad. "Get your friends some drinks. I'm the one who's been on my feet all day". She pushed her breasts higher up her chest. "I'll have a beer". 40

That stirred them. "We're just passing", Chanu explained, in a rush, as if he had just remembered his line. Dr. Azad rubbed his hands. "I'm delighted to welcome you. I'm, ah, afraid we have already had our meal, otherwise –" 45

"You'll stay for dinner", his wife cut in. She challenged Nazneen with her battle-hard eyes. "We've not eaten yet".

Dr. Azad rocked on his toes. "Not eaten as such. We've had some snacks and so forth". 50

2 They ate dinner on trays balanced on their laps. An unidentified meat in tepid[15] gravy, with boiled potatoes. It was like eating cardboard soaked[16] in water. Mrs. Azad switched on the television and turned the volume up high. She scowled[17] at Chanu and her husband when 55 they talked and held up her hand when she wished to silence them altogether. She drank a second glass of beer and belched[18] with quiet satisfaction. Her husband had brought orange juice at first, and she jumped up in

---

[1] **to snarl** to show the teeth as a sign of aggression – [2] **kalojam** a sweet Bengali delicacy – [3] **gilded** golden – [4] **claw-footed** *Tischbein mit einer Tierpranke* – [5] **to summon** (*fml.*) to order sb. to come to a place – [6] **wiggle** small movements from side to side or up and down – [7] **to smother** to hold back – [8] **to tuck one's feet up** (*phr. v.*) to sit comfortably – [9] **to sway** to move slowly from one side to another – [10] **swag** *Girlande* – [11] **to wriggle** to twist your body from side to side with small quick movements – [12] **a tailor's dummy** *Schneiderpuppe* – [13] **cuffs** *Manschetten* – [14] **sheen** a soft smooth shiny appearance – [15] **tepid** slightly warm, often unpleasant – [16] **soaked** very wet – [17] **to scowl** [skaʊl] to look at sb. in an angry way – [18] **to belch** to burp, *rülpsen*

60 her chair as if she would strike him. Dr. Azad drank two glasses of water in his exact manner. He used his knife and fork like surgical[19] instruments. Nazneen chased[20] the soggy[21] mess around her plate and clenched[22] her stomach to try to stop it growling.

65 "I'll join you", said Chanu to Mrs. Azad, "in a beer". He made the offer as if he were proposing to lend her a kidney[23]. She shrugged and kept her eyes fixed on the screen.

My husband does not say his prayers, thought Nazneen, 70 and now he is drinking alcohol. Tomorrow he may be eating pigs.

"Of course, all the Saudis drink", said Chanu. "Even the royal family. All hypocrites[24]. Myself, I believe that a glass every now and then is not a bad thing".

75 "As a medical man, I cannot recommend it. As for the religious aspect, I hold no opinion".

"You see", said Chanu, in the voice of a man who has deliberated long and hard, "it's part of the culture here. It's so ingrained[25] in the fabric of society. Back home, if 80 you drink you risk being an outcast. In London, if you don't drink you risk being the same thing. That's when it becomes dangerous, and when they start so young they can easily end up alcoholic. For myself, and for your wife, there's no harm done". He looked over at his 85 hostess[26] but she was engrossed[27] in a scene of frantic and violent kissing. Chanu still had his coat on. He perched[28] on a chair with his knees wide and his ankles crossed. He looked like the gardener who had come in to collect his wages.

90 Not for the first time, Nazneen wondered what it was that kept bringing Dr. Azad to see Chanu. They were an ill-matched pair. Perhaps he came for the food.

[...]

Mrs. Azad switched off the television. Let's go, thought 95 Nazneen. She tried to signal with her eyes to Chanu, but he smiled vaguely back at her. "This is the tragedy of our lives. To be an immigrant is to live out a tragedy". The hostess cocked her head. She rubbed her bulbous[29] nose. "What are you talking about?"

100 "The clash of cultures".

"I beg your pardon?"

"And of generations", added Chanu.

"What is the tragedy?"

"It's not only immigrants. Shakespeare wrote about it". He cleared his throat and prepared to cite his quotation. 105 "Take your coat off. It's getting on my nerves. What are you? A professor?"

Chanu spread his hands. "I have a degree in English literature from Dhaka University. I have studied at a British university – philosophy, sociology, history, econom- 110 ics. I do not claim to be a learned gentleman. But I can tell you truthfully, madam, that I am always learning".

"So what are you then? A student?" She did not sound impressed. Her small, deep-plugged eyes looked as hard and dirty as coal. 115

"Your husband and I are both students, in a sense. That's how we came to know each other, through a shared love of books, a love of learning".

Mrs. Azad yawned[30]. "Oh yes, my husband is a very refined man. He puts his nose inside a book because the 120 smell of real life offends him. But he has come a long way. Haven't you, my sweet?"

He comes to our flat to get away from her, thought Nazneen.

"Yes", said the doctor. His shirt collar had swallowed his 125 neck.

"When we first came – tell them, you tell them – we lived in a one-room hovel[31]. We dined on rice and dal[32], rice and dal. For breakfast we had rice and dal. For lunch we drank water to bloat out[33] our stomachs. This 130 is how he finished medical school. And now – look! Of course, the doctor is very refined. Sometimes he forgets that without my family's help he would not have all those letters[34] after his name".

"It's a success story", said Chanu, exercising his shoul- 135 ders. "But behind every story of immigrant success there lies a deeper tragedy".

"Kindly explain this tragedy".

"I'm talking about the clash of Western values and our own. I'm talking about the struggle to assimilate and 140 the need to preserve one's identity and heritage. I'm talking about children who don't know what their identity is. I'm talking about the feelings of alienation engendered[35] by a society where racism is prevalent. I'm talking about the terrific struggle to preserve one's 145 sanity while striving to achieve the best for one's family. I'm talking –"

---

[19] **surgical** relating to medical operations – [20] **to chase around** here: to push the food back and forth on the dish – [21] **soggy** unpleasantly wet and soft – [22] **to clench** to hold sth. tightly – [23] **kidney** *Niere* – [24] **hypocrite** ['hɪpəkrɪt] *Heuchler* – [25] **ingrained** firmly established and difficult to change – [26] **hostess** *Gastgeberin* – [27] **engrossed** being interested in sth. so much that you do not notice anything else – [28] **to perch on sth.** to sit on top of sth. or on the edge of sth. – [29] **bulbous** fat, round and unattractive – [30] **to yawn** *gähnen* – [31] **hovel** a small dirty place where sb. lives, especially a very poor person – [32] **rice and dal** classic/traditional Indian dishes – [33] **to bloat out** *aufblähen* – [34] **all those letters** here: PhD (doctor's degree) – [35] **to engender** (*fml.*) to represent

"Crap[36]!"

Chanu looked at Dr. Azad, but his friend studied the backs of his hands.

"Why do you make it so complicated?" said the doctor's wife. "Assimilation this, alienation that! Let me tell you a few simple facts. Fact: we live in a Western society. Fact: our children will act more and more like Westerners. Fact: that's no bad thing. My daughter is free to come and go. Do I wish I had enjoyed myself like her when I was young? Yes!"

Mrs. Azad struggled out of her chair. Nazneen thought – and it made her feel a little giddy[37] – *She's going to the pub as well.* But their hostess walked over to the gas fire and bent, from her waist, to light it. Nazneen averted[38] her eyes.

Mrs. Azad continued. "Listen, when I'm in Bangladesh I put on a sari and cover my head and all that. But here I go out to work. I work with the white girls and I'm just one of them. If I want to come home and eat curry, that's my business. Some women spend ten, twenty years here and they sit in the kitchen grinding[39] spices all day and learn only two words of English". She looked at Nazneen, who focused on Raqib. "They go around covered from head to toe, in their little walking prisons, and when someone calls to them in the street they are upset. The society is racist. The society is all wrong. Everything should change for them. They don't have to change one thing. That", she said, stabbing the air, "is the tragedy". The room was quiet. The air was too bright, and the hard light hid nothing. The moments came and went, with nothing to ease their passing.

"Each one of us has his own tragedy", said Chanu at last.

from *Brick Lane* by Monica Ali. Doubleday, London 2003, pp. 110 ff.

COMPREHENSION

1. Describe the situation and atmosphere in the Azads' sitting room as depicted in the **first part** of the text.

2. Give an outline of the course of the conversation carried out in the **second part** of the text.

3. Detect the different views on Asian and Western culture expressed here, and complete the grid:

Mrs. Azad	Dr. Azad	Chanu	Nazneen
• Mrs. Azad stubbed out her cigarette …	• drank two glasses of water … • …	• … I'll join you in a beer • … • …	• my husband doesn't say his prayers … • …
conclusions about the person's attitude/view			
→ she violates Hindu/Muslim religious laws → …	→ …	→ …	→ …

4. Point out what the text reveals about the characters' social status and background.

5. Collect examples from the text that serve as a marker of social and cultural identity.

ANALYSIS

6. Explain how the different modes of presentation* contribute to the effect of the text.
→ Focus on Language, Literary Terms, p. 433

7. Examine the use of direct and indirect characterization* and their function.
→ Focus on Skills, Characterization of a Figure in Literature, p. 411

---

[36] **crap** (*sl.*) sth. that is completely wrong or not true; rubbish – [37] **giddy** feeling overwhelmingly happy or excited – [38] **to avert** abwenden – [39] **to grind** (ground/ground) *mahlen*

8. Interpret the setting* (e. g. the sitting room) and its symbolic meaning.

9. Analyse the rhetorical devices* and determine how they emphasize "the clash of cultures".
   → Focus on Skills, Analysis of a Fictional Text, p. 402

10. Give examples of the narrator's* ironic* view of the situation.
    Explain how this relates to the intention of the text.

ACTIVITIES

11. Imagine that Nazneen and Chanu are back home from their visit. Write a dialogue in which they reflect on the conversation with the Azads.
    Present your dialogues in class.

12. Now put yourself in Mrs. Azad's position: What might she say to her husband about the evening with Chanu and Nazneen?

13. Imagine that you are volunteering in a self-help group for (Asian) women who only recently immigrated. What advice would you give them to help them assimilate and overcome alienation? In a group, compile short guides for women/girls/boys/men in which you give tips and recommendations that help them "fit in".

14. For some reason, the given excerpt from the novel has been omitted in the film version. First, compile a storyboard based on the scene. Next, act out an audition (= *Sprechprobe*) in class.
    → Focus on Facts, Screenplays and Storyboards, p. 397

15. The pictures of the family were taken during a sightseeing tour through London in front of Buckingham Palace. State what the facial expressions as well as body language reveal about how the characters feel about their situation.
    → Focus on Skills, Analysis of Visuals, p. 409

0:50:21

0:49:30

Harriet Sherwood

Muslim Leaders in UK Warn of "Worrying" Levels of Islamophobia

AWARENESS

 Team up with a partner and do the following tasks:

M a) Describe the pictorial elements of the cartoon in detail and mediate the textual elements into English.

@ b) Get informed about the plot of the opera/music drama composed by Wolfgang Amadeus Mozart in 1782.

c) Specify the implied message of the cartoon with regard to Islamophobia.

Tips on vocab

The Abduction from the Seraglio
background: scenery ■ an Eastern town ■ minaret ■ palm trees ■ a dark sky
centre: centre stage ■ curtains ■ actors dressed as Muslims ■ the manager ■ a grey suit ■ to have a defensive demeanor *(Abwehrhaltung)*
speech bubble: stage direction ■ bearded actors/ performers ■ production ■ hipsters
foreground: seats for the spectators/audience ■ to boo sb. ■ to make a cuckoo/screw loose gesture ■ to be up in arms against sb./sth. ■ to revolt against sb./sth. ■ to berate sb. *(jdn. ausschimpfen)*

COMPREHENSION

1. **Before reading:**

Webcode SNG-40235-016 @

M Watch the German news documentary from the ARD Weltspiegel provided on the webcode, and take notes on the tasks and questions below.

Tip: Watch the complete video clip before taking notes – and be prepared to watch the video clip at least two times. Use the vocabulary and phrases in the Tips on vocab box on the following page for your notes.

Tips on vocab »»»

> **Malediven** Maldives ■ **zäh** tough, hard-bitten ■ **Gefeilsche** haggling ■ **besänftigen** to appease sb. ■ **Fremden-feindlichkeit** xenophobia ■ **sich zu seinem Glauben bekennen** to confess one's faith ■ **S-Bahn** transit system/suburban railway ■ **Selbstmordattentäter/in** suicide attacker ■ **jdn. diffamieren** to villify sb. ■ **Kopftuch** head-scarf ■ **Zielscheibe** target ■ **körperlicher Angriff** physical attack ■ **Übergriff** assault/attack ■ **Schlampe** slut/bitch (*sl.*) ■ **Steigerung** increase ■ **jdn. anpöbeln** to harass/verbally abuse sb. ■ **Boulevardpresse** popular press ■ **Stimmung machen gegen jdn./etw.** to stir up hatred/resentment against sb./sth. ■ **etw. zuspitzen** to acuminate ■ **Studie** survey ■ **den Verdacht nahelegen** to raise suspicion against ■ **etw. schüren** to fuel sth. ■ **zuständig sein für etw.** to be in charge of sth. ■ **Maßnahmen** measures ■ **unter Polizeischutz** under police protection ■ **Zivil-courage** civil courage ■ **Mitfahrer** fellow passenger ■ **jdn. überwältigen** to subdue sb. ■ **Schutzengel** guardian angel ■ **sich nicht unterkriegen lassen** to not let sth. get one down/to keep one's chin up

- Which Islamophobic tendencies and trends have become obvious in the U.K.?
- What were Ruhi's experiences when riding on a suburban railway from Newcastle?
- How does the organization Tell MAMA try to help victims?
- What overall trend does Iman Aboutta see concerning violence against foreigners?
- Which traumatizing experience did Joynoor and his girlfriend have?
- What is the image of Muslims created by the media and politicians?
- What is Ruhi's strategy to cope with her shocking experiences?

1 The Muslim Council of Britain has warned of increasing levels of Islamophobia in the UK after recent videos showing anti-Muslim abuse on public transport were posted online and police forces in England and Wales were ordered to treat such attacks in the same vein[1] as antisemitism.

Miqdaad Versi of the Muslim Council of Britain said: "As a whole, we have to understand that the UK is a very tolerant society, with London one of the most cosmopolitan cities in the world, and thankfully these kinds of attacks are relatively rare. But they are on the rise.

"The growth in Islamophobia has reached levels which are very worrying. Most Muslims know someone who's suffered some form of abuse, whether online, physical or verbal. We're now in a very serious situation and have been for the past year."

The furore[2] surrounding the videos has also underlined the difficulties of compiling[3] reliable data on religiously motivated attacks, particularly when such abuse takes place online. In one attack, a woman was filmed shouting abuse at two Muslim women, one of whom was pregnant, and calling them "Isis bitches." A 36-year-old woman from north-west London was subsequently arrested and pleaded guilty[4] to causing racially aggravated[5] distress[6].

In the same week, a 25-year-old man handed himself in to police after video footage emerged that purportedly[7] showed a man screaming Islamophobic abuse at a pensioner in Tottenham, north London, and then apparently throwing his walking frame[8] out on to the pavement.

2 The videos, which were widely shared on social media, emerged shortly after the Metropolitan police released figures indicating that anti-Muslim attacks in London had increased by 70% in the 12 months to July, from 478 incidents the previous year to 816.

Yet the underlying picture is that religiously motivated crime is extremely rare in the UK, affecting 0.1% of adults, according to Home Office figures.

In total, 52,528 hate crimes were recorded by police in England and Wales in 2014–15, an increase of 18% on the previous year. Of those, 3,254 were religiously motivated. That is only 6% of the total number of hate crimes – but the figure was a 43% increase on the previous year. The recording of data by police, while still patchy[9], has improved, which could help explain the increase. But the reluctance of victims to report attacks may also underestimate the true figures. Figures from the Crime Survey for England and Wales (CSEW), a face-to-face[10] victimization[11] poll[12], estimated that there were 222,000

---

[1] **vein** a particular style or manner – [2] **furore** [fjʊˈrɔːri] a sudden excited or angry reaction to sth. by a lot of people – [3] **to compile** to collect information and arrange it – [4] **to plead guilty** [pliːd] *sich schuldig bekennen* – [5] **aggravated** serious, violent – [6] **distress** a feeling of extreme worry, sadness or pain – [7] **purportedly** *angeblich* – [8] **walking frame** *Rollator* – [9] **patchy** only existing in some parts – [10] **face-to-face** *von Angesicht zu Angesicht* – [11] **victimization** *Schikane* – [12] **poll** a study in which people are asked for their opinions

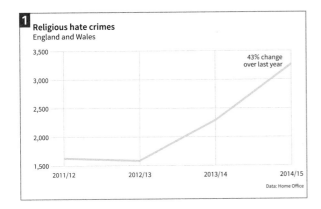

1 Religious hate crimes
England and Wales

43% change over last year

Data: Home Office

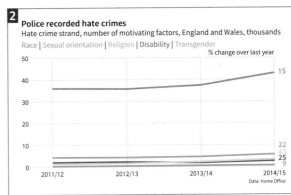

2 Police recorded hate crimes
Hate crime strand, number of motivating factors, England and Wales, thousands
Race | Sexual orientation | Religion | Disability | Transgender

% change over last year

15

22
43
25
9

Data: Home Office

hate crimes per year between 2012 and 2015. About a sixth (38,000 a year) of this estimate related to religiously motivated hate crimes. Among groups who are the
55 targets of religiously motivated attacks, Muslims are by far the biggest group – although the chances of being a victim are still very small. According to the CSEW figures, 0.8% of Muslims are the victims of hate crimes, compared to 0.3% of Hindus, 0.1% of Christians and
60 0.5% of other religious groups.

3 Last year, the College of Policing defined hate crime as offences motivated by hostility[13] or prejudice on the grounds of race, religion, sexual orientation, transgender status or disability.
65 According to Tell MAMA, an organisation that monitors anti-Muslim attacks through self-referrals[14], women are much more likely to be targeted because their dress makes them more vulnerable. "Women wearing the headscarf are more likely to experience name call-
70 ing, have things thrown at them, general abuse," Fiyaz Mughal of Tell MAMA said. "Women wearing the full-face veil will suffer both more incidents and more aggressive incidents, such as people pulling off their veils." He added that Muslim women also faced high
75 levels of abuse online, with their faith and gender targeted for humiliation. "It's the intersectionality[15] of prejudice."

4 A recent report for Tell MAMA, We Fear For Our Lives, based on in-depth interviews with the targets of
80 Islamophobic attacks, found a spike[16] in the number of

incidents following "trigger[17]" events such as the Charlie Hebdo shootings in Paris in January and the Tunisia terrorist attack in June.
The report gives examples of online threats relating to the Charlie Hebdo killings. One read: "Fill your car 85 with Calor gas canisters, park it next to a mosque, light the fuse then leave. #JeSuisCharlie #KillAllMuslims #ParisShooting." Others urged driving a car into a crowd of Muslims leaving a mosque and compiling a "hitlist" of Muslim homes and schools. 90
While Home Office data shows an increase following the murder of Lee Rigby in July 2013, there was no clear increase following the Charlie Hebdo shootings.
According to Mughal, there has also been in increase in anti-Muslim attacks directly relating to the refugee cri- 95 sis, which has seen hundreds of thousands of people fleeing persecution and conflict in the Middle East and Africa trying to reach safe haven in Europe.
"People see women in hijabs[18] coming into Europe, so the poor British woman just going to work or to the 100 shops gets it[19]," he said.

5 Earlier this month, David Cameron ordered police forces to record data on anti-Muslim hate crimes and to treat them as seriously as antisemitic attacks, a move welcomed by the MCB and Tell MAMA. 105
The move means police forces across the UK will adopt uniform recording mechanisms that will help build a more comprehensive picture of Islamophobic crime, Mughal said. "But it will take up to five years to properly implement that", he added. 110

---

[13] **hostility** *Feindseligkeit* – [14] **self-referral** *Selbstbezogenheit* – [15] **intersectionality** the complex, cumulative manner in which the effects of different forms of discrimination combine, overlap, or intersect – [16] **spike** here: a sharp increase in sth. – [17] **trigger** an event that is the cause of a particular action, process or situation – [18] **hijab** [hɪˈdʒɑːb] the head covering that some Muslim women wear when they are outside – [19] **to get it** *(infml.)* to be punished (here: harassed)

Versi said better recording was the first step in the long process of reducing the occurrences of Islamophobic crimes. "Islamophobia and antisemitism are both serious crimes, but work to tackle antisemitism is well developed. Now we need to replicate[20] that fantastic work with Islamophobia. All forms of bigotry[21] need to be treated equally." Many Muslims were wary[22] of reporting attacks to the police, he said, believing they would be viewed "through the lens of counter-terrorism. We need a situation where the police are seen as allies against hate crimes".

http://www.theguardian.com/world/2015/oct/26/muslim-leaders-in-uk-warn-of-worrying-levels-of-islamophobia, 26 October 2015 [19.05.2016]

COMPREHENSION

2. In a **paired reading activity**, read the article from *The Guardian* and find a suitable headline for each of the thematic units 1–5.

3. After **reading** the article **a second time**, say whether the statements below are true or false or not mentioned in the text. Take notes on necessary corrections in your notebook.
   - The British government has ordered police to treat crimes in connection with Islamophobia like antisemitism.
   - Because London is very cosmopolitan, racially motivated crimes are rare.
   - Most British Muslims have suffered from online, physical or verbal abuse.
   - Videos showing anti-Muslim abuse have led to a significant rise in arrests and self-accusations.
   - Statistics reveal that religiously motivated crime is very low in Britain.
   - Muslims are by far the biggest group of victims of religiously motivated attacks.
   - Muslim women are often victims of gender-motivated abuse and attacks.
   - Online threats have been increasing after the Charlie Hebdo shootings in Paris in January 2015.
   - David Cameron ordered police forces to record data on anti-Muslim hate crimes.
   - Muslims all over the U.K. welcome the new anti-Islamophobia policy.

ANALYSIS

4. Examine the style of the newspaper article and explain how the author shows credibility and reliability. Pay particular attention to
   - the choice of words,
   - examples and references,
   - citations,
   - statistical data.
   → Focus on Skills, Analysis of a Non-Fictional Text, p. 405
   → Focus on Facts, The Press, p. 398

5. Compare the article from the renowned British quality newspaper *The Guardian* and the German TV documentary from *ARD Weltspiegel*. Which similarities and differences can you detect between the formats?
   → Focus on Facts, The Press, p. 398
   → Focus on Facts, The Media, p. 351

6. Analyse the line graphs on page 157 and explain the recent trends of hate crimes in England and Wales.
   → Focus on Skills, Analysis of Statistical Data, p. 408

---

[20] **to replicate** *(fml.)* to make or do sth. in exactly the same way – [21] **bigotry** ['bɪgətri] *Borniertheit, Fanatismus* – [22] **wary** feeling or showing caution about possible dangers or problems

ACTIVITIES

7. Based on the information given in the German news documentary and the article from *The Guardian*, discuss the cartoon below. Is there some truth in the women's remarks or are they both wrong?
→ Focus on Skills, Analysis of Visuals, p. 409
→ Focus on Language, Conversation and Discussion, p. 413

Cruel Culture

Tips on vocab

left side: to wear a pony tail ▪ sunglasses ▪ bikini ▪ high heels ▪ to be dolled up ▪ to strut (stolzieren)
right side: to wear a (black) Niqab [nɪˈkɑb] (that covers the entire body, with a thin slit for the eyes)

8. Examine the statistical data on immigration and ethnic groups on the Focus on Facts page (pp. 149 f.) and relate them to the information in the article.
Do the statistical data justify the described Islamophobic fears and anxieties?

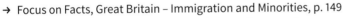

Discuss in class.
→ Focus on Facts, Great Britain – Immigration and Minorities, p. 149
→ Focus on Language, Conversation and Discussion, p. 413

The Commonwealth – Common Sense? – Post-Colonial Tasks & Challenges

The Commonwealth – What Is It For?

What does the name "Commonwealth" suggest about its function? Collect ideas in class.

Opening ceremony of the Commonwealth heads of government meeting (CHOGM) at the Mediterranean conference center in Valletta, 2005

The biggest achievement of the Commonwealth, its admirers say, is the fact of its unlikely[1] existence. That so many former British colonies and dominions should be content to co-exist in a club which has the queen as its head is remarkable. However, this is a low bar[2] to set for the success of an organisation nominally[3] committed to promoting democracy, human rights and the rule of law. Quite how nominally will be evident in Colombo[4] this weekend – at a gathering of Commonwealth leaders hosted by a nasty[5] and abusive[6] regime.

Be in no doubt of that. The most heinous[7] allegation[8] against Mahinda Rajapaksa's[9] family-based government – a battlefield slaughter of some 40,000 Tamil civilians –

is complicated by the exigencies[10] of the appalling[11] civil war it helped end. It took ruthlessness[12] to defeat the Tamil Tigers, and Sri Lanka is better off as a result. Yet the war was also marked by reprisals[13] against journalists, human-rights activists and opposition politicians, and intimidation[14] continues today. Mr Rajapaksa has meanwhile dug in[15] for the long haul[16] – having used his popularity as a war victor to scrap[17] presidential-term limits. This amounts to a textbook transgression[18] of the Commonwealth Charter, which includes a commitment to freedom of expression, the separation of powers and the like[19], promulgated[20] by the queen in March. The meeting should never have been held in Sri Lanka.

---

[1] **unlikely** unwahrscheinlich – [2] **low bar** niedrige Messlatte – [3] **nominally** dem Namen nach – [4] **Colombo** capital of Sri Lanka – [5] **nasty** bad, very unpleasant – [6] **abusive** misshandelnd – [7] **heinous** ['heɪnəs] abscheulich – [8] **allegation** Anschuldigung – [9] **Mahinda Rajapaksa** President of Sri Lanka since 2005 – [10] **exigency** ['eksɪdʒənsi] (fml.) demand that you must deal with – [11] **appalling** abstoßend – [12] **ruthlessness** Unbarmherzigkeit – [13] **reprisal** Vergeltungsmaßnahme – [14] **intimidation** Einschüchterung – [15] **to dig in sth.** (infml.) über etw. herfallen – [16] **for the long haul** for a long period of time – [17] **to scrap** to get rid of sth. – [18] **transgression** Überschreitung – [19] **the like** desgleichen – [20] **to promulgate** to announce sth. publicly

The Commonwealth has too often failed to enforce its values. Nigeria was partially suspended[21] from the club after it hanged Ken Saro-Wiwa in 1995, as was Pakistan after its 1999 coup. But the club's overall record is timid[22]. With many more coups and killings left unsanctioned, membership is as likely to dignify[23] rights-abusers as to correct them.

What, then, is the point of the Commonwealth? Hardly any of its members' citizens can say; asked to name its head, a quarter of Jamaicans cited Barack Obama. Officials in the secretariat, housed in a splendid London mansion, toil away[24]. It is an open secret that many Commonwealth leaders attend the biennial[25] shindig[26] mainly for an opportunity to be photographed with the queen. Even that pleasure has been denied them in Colombo: for the first time in 40 years, perhaps because of her age, she is giving it a miss.

Despite these conspicuous[27] frailties[28], the Commonwealth has a few things going for it. It is cheap, costing only around £16m ($26m) a year. It runs a fine quadrennial[29] games, a respected annual literary prize and a decent scholarship programme. It could also help boost prosperity among a third of the world's population. Colonial ties, including a common law and language, boost trade; by one estimate, the cost of doing business within the Commonwealth is 20% lower than the cost outside. By reforming its tangled[30] and ineffective bureaucracy, and using it to strengthen these advantages, the club could make more of them. That would make membership more valuable, and expulsion[31] more costly.

Come on, India

Yet bringing reform and toughness to the Commonwealth requires leadership, which it lacks. Britain, Australia and Canada would like to provide this, but cannot. Whenever they seek to improve the club – which they largely pay for – they mainly succeed in uniting its poorer members in resentful[32] opposition to their perceived post-colonial condescension[33]. The decision of Canada's prime minister, Stephen Harper, to boycott Mr Rajapaksa's fest has caused the regime little concern. His absence supports Sri Lanka's claim – with which many of its visitors sympathise – to be a victim of rich-world bullying.

The direction needs to come from the club's poor but powerful members: South Africa, Nigeria and, above all, India. Manmohan Singh, India's prime minister [until 2014], also refused to show up in Colombo – a decision he reached, ridiculously, this week. It looked like politics, not principle. A shrewder[34] India would have insisted earlier that the gathering not be held in Sri Lanka. Together with Nigeria and South Africa, Mr Singh should use the farce in Colombo as a pretext for change. Hold the members to high standards, deepen business ties – and this peculiar organisation could be a serious one.

www.economist.com/news/leaders/21589887-unreformed-commonwealth-deserves-die-improved-it-could-be-rather-useful-what-it, 16 November 2013 [23.07.2014]

COMPREHENSION

1. **Step 1:** Study the Focus on Facts (p. 163) and Focus on Documents (p. 164) pages.

   Step 2: Watch the video clip about the Commonwealth provided on the webcode.

   Step 3: After gaining an overview of the Commonwealth, its member states and its goals, take notes on the questions below:
   - What is the status of the Commonwealth member states?
   - What are the basic criteria the member states have to meet?
   - Which aims and goals are promoted, and which principles are pursued by the Commonwealth?
   - What are the essential benefits for the member states?

2. Now read the magazine article and point out what information is given regarding the questions above.

3. What further aspects does the article refer to?

---

[21] **to suspend** *jdn. ausschließen* – [22] **timid** *zurückhaltend* – [23] **to dignify** *würdigen* – [24] **to toil away** to work hard – [25] **biennial** [baɪˈeniəl] every second year – [26] **shindig** (*infml.*) a noisy event; *Budenzauber* – [27] **conspicuous** very noticeable and attracting attention; *auffallend* – [28] **frailty** *Schwäche* – [29] **quadrennial** every fourth year – [30] **tangled** complicated, and not easy to understand – [31] **expulsion** *Ausschließung* – [32] **resentful** *aufgebracht* – [33] **condescension** *herablassende Haltung* – [34] **shrewd** *gewandt*

ANALYSIS

4. Examine the structural devices* employed in the article in order to express the author's critical view of the Commonwealth.
   → Focus on Skills, Analysis of a Non-Fictional Text, p. 405

5. Analyse the rhetorical devices* and explain how they create the overall tone of the article.

6. Now take another close look at the documents and examine the devices that are used to emphasize
   a) aims and principles,
   b) behaviour that should be opposed.

7. Interpret the cartoon and relate its message to the criticism expressed in the newspaper article.
   → Focus on Skills, Analysis of Visuals, p. 409

ACTIVITIES

 8. Considering the author's harsh criticism, discuss whether it really makes sense to be a member of this organization.

The Commonwealth of Nations

The Commonwealth of Nations is an **intergovernmental organization** of 54 independent member states. All but three of these states were formerly part of the British Empire. **The cooperation of these states follows a set of values and goals outlined in the Singapore Declaration of 1971 and the Harare Declaration of 1991.** The Head of the Commonwealth is a ceremonial and representative position held by the English king or queen, currently Queen Elizabeth II.

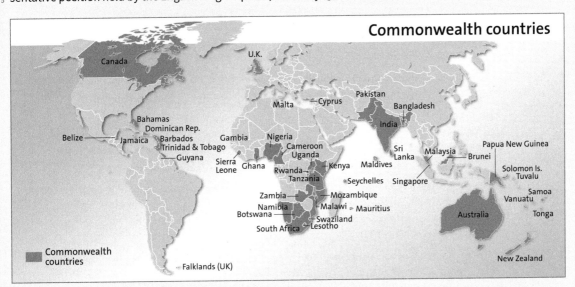

Commonwealth countries

Canada, U.K., Malta, Cyprus, Pakistan, Bangladesh, India, Bahamas, Dominican Rep., Belize, Jamaica, Barbados, Trinidad & Tobago, Gambia, Nigeria, Cameroon, Uganda, Sri Lanka, Malaysia, Papua New Guinea, Brunei, Guyana, Sierra Leone, Ghana, Rwanda, Kenya, Maldives, Solomon Is., Tuvalu, Tanzania, Seychelles, Singapore, Samoa, Vanuatu, Zambia, Mozambique, Namibia, Malawi, Mauritius, Tonga, Botswana, Swaziland, Australia, South Africa, Lesotho, New Zealand

Commonwealth countries

Falklands (UK)

History

1926	in the **Balfour Declaration** at the Imperial Conference, Britain and its dominions agree they are equal in status, united by the common allegiance to the Crown and freely associated members of the **British Commonwealth of Nations**
1949	following the **London Declaration**, the word "British" is dropped from the title to reflect its changing nature (mostly politically independent member states)
1971	**Singapore Declaration**
1991	**Harare Declaration**
2003	**Aso Rock Declaration** states: "We are committed to democracy, good governance, gender equality, and a more equitable sharing of the benefits of globalisation."

Headquarters

The **Secretariat** was established in 1965 and is based in London; **headquarters** are in Marlborough House.

Members

The **54 current members** comprise all six inhabited continents, a population of 2.1 billion (= 1/3 of the world's population) and ca. 20 % of the world's trade. The three largest Commonwealth members are Canada, Australia and India.

Membership criteria include the promotion of (racial) equality, world peace, liberty, human rights and free trade.

Since 1939, every four years the **Commonwealth Games** are held, featuring the usual athletic disciplines as well as sports popular in the Commonwealth such as netball and rugby (2018: Gold Coast City, Queensland, Australia).

Singapore Declaration of Commonwealth Principles (1971)

This declaration was issued in Singapore on **22 January 1971** and set out the core political values that would form the main part of the Commonwealth's membership criteria. Along with the **Harare Declaration**, issued in 1991, it is considered one of the two most famous and important Commonwealth documents.

1. The Commonwealth of Nations is a voluntary association of independent sovereign states, each responsible for its own policies, consulting and co-operating in the common interests of their peoples and in the promotion of international understanding and world peace. [...]

4. Within this diversity, all members of the Commonwealth hold certain principles in common. It is by pursu-
5 ing these principles that the Commonwealth can continue to influence international society for the benefit of mankind.

5. We believe that international peace and order are essential to the security and prosperity of mankind; we therefore support the United Nations and seek to strengthen its influence for peace in the world, and its efforts to remove the causes of tension between nations.

10 **6.** We believe in the liberty of the individual, in equal rights for all citizens regardless of race, colour, creed or political belief, and in their inalienable right to participate by means of free and democratic political processes in framing the society in which they live. We therefore strive to promote in each of our countries those representative institutions and guarantees for personal freedom under the law that are our common heritage.

7. We recognise racial prejudice as a dangerous sickness threatening the healthy development of the human
15 race and racial discrimination as an unmitigated[1] evil of society. Each of us will vigorously[2] combat this evil within our own nation. No country will afford to regimes which practice racial discrimination assistance which in its own judgment directly contributes to the pursuit or consolidation of this evil policy.

8. We oppose all forms of colonial domination and racial oppression and are committed to the principles of human dignity and equality. We will therefore use all our efforts to foster human equality and dignity every-
20 where, and to further the principles of self-determination and non-racialism.

9. We believe that the wide disparities in wealth now existing between different sections of mankind are too great to be tolerated. They also create world tensions. Our aim is their progressive removal. We therefore seek to use our efforts to overcome poverty, ignorance and disease, in raising standards of life and achieving a more equitable international society.

25 **10.** To this end, our aim is to achieve the freest possible flow of international trade on terms fair and equitable to all, taking into account the special requirements of the developing countries, and to encourage the flow of adequate resources, including governmental and private resources, to the developing countries, bearing in mind the importance of doing this in a true spirit of partnership and of establishing for this purpose in the developing countries conditions which are conducive to sustained investment and growth.

30 **11.** We believe that international co-operation is essential to remove the causes of war, promote tolerance, combat injustice, and secure development among the peoples of the world. We are convinced that the Commonwealth is one of the most fruitful associations for these purposes. [...]

Note: In **1991, the Harare Commonwealth Declaration** reaffirmed and reinforced the Commonwealth's core principles and values, but additionally emphasized the equality of men and women, reducing debt burdens for developing countries as well as fighting environmental destruction.

[1] **unmitigated** *vollkommen* – [2] **vigorously** [ˈvɪgərəsli] using a lot of energy and determination

historical development		
to gain independence (from)	to win political freedom from control by the government of another country	*Unabhängigkeit (von ...) erlangen*
(historical) landmark	one of the most important events or discoveries	*wichtiges Datum*
to occupy; occupation of sth.	to enter a place and keep control of it (especially by military force)	*belagern; Belagerung*
prehistory	time in history before everything was written down	*Prähistorie, Vorgeschichte*
to rebel [rɪˈbel] **rebellion** [rɪˈbeljən] **rebel** [ˈrebəl]	to oppose/fight against people in authority or against an idea which you do not agree with	*sich auflehnen, rebellieren; Rebellion, Widerstand; der Rebell*
to recapture sth. from sb.	to win back sth. that you already had in the past	*zurückerobern*
to revolt against sb./sth.; revolt [rɪˈvəʊlt]	to rebel; rebellion	*gegen etw./jdn. rebellieren; Aufstand*
tribe; tribal [ˈtraɪbl]	a social group whose members have the same customs, etc. and live in one particular area ruled by their leader; relating to a tribe or tribes	*(Volks-)Stamm; Stammes-*
challenges for a modern India		
caste [kɑːst] **system**	a hierarchical system of fixed social classes into which people are born	*Kastensystem, Kastenwesen*
challenge	sth. that tests strength, skill or ability	*Herausforderung*
to cope with	to succeed in dealing with a difficult problem	*mit etwas zurechtkommen*
crowded	too full of people or things	*überfüllt, beengt*
culture shock	the feeling of being confused or anxious that sb. gets when they visit a foreign country or a place very different from the one they are used to	*Kulturschock*
to face (a problem)	having to deal with a difficult situation	*vor einem Problem stehen*
foeticide [ˈfiːtɪˌsaɪd]	an act that causes the death of a (female) foetus	*absichtliches Töten eines (weiblichen) Fötus*
infrastructure	the basic systems and structures that a country needs in order to work properly, e. g. roads, railways, banks, hospitals, etc.	*(öffentliche) Einrichtungen, die für das Funktionieren einer Volkswirtschaft notwendig sind*
mobility	the ability to move easily from one job, area, or social class to another (also: social mobility)	*Mobilität, Bewegungsfreiheit, Freizügigkeit*
pollution	the process of making air, water, soil, etc. dangerously dirty and not suitable for people to use; the state of being dangerously dirty	*Verschmutzung*
population density	the degree to which an area is filled with people	*Bevölkerungsdichte*
to rape; rape	to force sb. to have sex	*vergewaltigen; Vergewaltigung*
rural	happening in or relating to the countryside	*ländlich, Land-*
sanitation	the protection of public health by removing and treating waste, dirty water, etc.	*Abwassersystem, Entsorgung; Hygiene*
slum	an area of a city that is in very bad condition, where very poor people live	*Elendsquartier, Armenviertel*
social inequality	an unfair situation in which some groups in society have more opportunities etc. than others	*soziale Ungleichheit*
(human) trafficking	the activity of taking people to another country and forcing them to work	*Menschenhandel*
traditional	following ideas and methods that have existed for a long time	*traditionell, althergebracht, überliefert*
urban growth	the expansion of cities	*Städtewachstum*

economy and trade		
to benefit from sth.; benefit	to get an advantage from sth.; advantage	*von etwas profitieren; Profit, Vorteil*
commerce ['kɒmɜːs]	trade	*Handel*
corruption	dishonest, illegal or immoral behaviour, especially from someone in power, often involving money	*Korruption, Bestechung*
demand	the need or desire people have for particular goods and services	*Nachfrage*
developing country	a poor country that is trying to increase its industry and trade and improve life for its people	*Entwicklungsland*
(the) digital age	a period in history that is characterized by the shift from traditional industry to an economy based on information technology	*das digitale Zeitalter, Computer-, Internet-Zeitalter*
economic growth	relating to a positive development of a country's economy	*Wirtschaftswachstum*
economic power	a country that is economically strong and important and can influence events	*Wirtschaftskraft, Wirtschafts-macht*
economy	the system by which a country's money and goods are produced and used, or a country considered in this way	*Wirtschaft*
emerging market	a country/an economy in an early stage of development, a country that does not (yet) meet the standards of a developed market	*Schwellenland, Wachstums-markt*
to export sth. [ɪk'spɔːt] **export**	to sell goods to another country	*etwas exportieren; Waren-export, Warenausfuhr*
foreign investment	business and investments of money involving other countries	*Auslandsinvestitionen*
goods (*pl.*)	things that are produced in order to be sold	*Waren*
living standard	the level of comfort and the amount of money people have; standard of living	*Lebensstandard*
low-wage country	a country where workers only earn very little money	*Niedriglohnland*
to import sth.; import of goods	to bring a product from one country into another so that it can be sold there	*etwas importieren; Waren-import, Wareneinfuhr*
to manufacture sth.; manufacturing	to produce sth.; the process or business of producing goods in factories; production	*etwas herstellen; Produktion, Fertigung*
(natural) resources [rɪ'sɔːsəz]	soil, minerals, forests, water and energy sources	*natürliche Ressourcen*
outsourcing	when a company uses workers from outside the company to do a job	*Ausgliederung von Produktion oder Dienstleistungen an Externe*
to provide sth.	to make sth. available	*zur Verfügung stellen*
raw [rɔː] **materials**	natural substances that are used in manufacturing goods	*Rohstoffe*
supply and demand	the relationship between the quantity of goods for sale and the quantity of goods that people want to buy, especially the way it influences prices	*Angebot und Nachfrage*
sweatshop	a small business, factory, etc. where people work hard in bad conditions for very little money	*ausbeuterischer Betrieb*
to trade	to buy and sell goods	*handeln; Handel treiben*
trade route [treid ruːt]	a way across land or sea used by traders	*Handelsweg*
trading company	business that buys and sells goods, esp. internationally	*Handelsgesellschaft*
waste imports	litter/rubbish that is brought from one country to another so that it can be sold to businesses that specialize in treating, dumping or burning it	*Einfuhr von Abfällen*

the Commonwealth		
allegiance to sb./sth. [əˈliːdʒəns]	loyalty to a leader	*Loyalität/Ergebenheit gegenüber jmd.*
ceremonial position	a position that gives no real power	*zeremonielle/ förmliche Position*
declaration	an official statement	*(öffentliche) Erklärung, Bekanntgabe*
geopolitics	ideas and activities relating to the way that a country's position, population, etc. affect its political development and its relationship with other countries	*politische Geografie*
head of state	a leader or a person in charge of a state	*Staatsoberhaupt*
to share a common heritage	to have the same traditional beliefs, values, customs, etc.	*ein gemeinsames Erbe/ Kultur haben*
intergovernmental	between different governments	*zwischenstaatlich, international*
legacy [ˈlegəsi]	sth. that exists as a result of sth. that happened at an earlier time	*Erbe*
representative position	a position in which sb. represents a state, a community, an interest, etc.	*repräsentative Position*
self-determination	the right of the people to govern themselves	*Selbstbestimmung*
sovereign [ˈsɒvrɪn] **sovereignty** [ˈsɑvrənti]	independent; complete freedom and power to govern	*uneingeschränkt, unabhängig, souverän; Eigenstaatlichkeit*
multicultural Britain		
alien	foreigner; foreign	*Fremder; fremd*
asylum seeker [əˈsaɪləm ˈsiːkə(r)]	sb. who leaves their own country because they are in danger and who asks the government of another country to allow them to live there	*Asylbewerber*
citizen; citizenship	a member of a state, subject; the legal right of belonging to a particular country	*Staatsbürger; Staatsbürgerschaft*
culture clash	a conflict arising from the interaction of people with different cultural values	*Zusammenprall der Kulturen*
(racial) discrimination	the practice of treating people in an unfair way because of their ethnicity	*(rassistische) Diskriminierung*
diversity [daɪˈvɜːsəti]	the fact of including many different types of people or things	*Vielfalt*
emigrant	sb. who leaves their own country to live in another	*Aussiedler, Emigrant*
to emigrate; emigration	to leave one's own country in order to live in another	*auswandern, emigrieren; Auswanderung, Emigration*
hospitable [hɒˈspɪtəbl] **hospitality**	friendly and welcoming to visitors	*gastfreundlich; Gastfreundschaft*
identity crisis, crisis of identity	a feeling of uncertainty of who you really are and what your purpose is	*Identitätskrise*
immigrant	sb. who enters another country to live there permanently	*Einwanderer, Immigrant*
to immigrate; immigration	to come into a country in order to live there permanently	*einwandern, immigrieren; Einwanderung*
immigration control, border control	the place at an airport, sea port, etc. where officials check the documents of everyone entering the country	*Grenzkontrolle*
to integrate (sb. into/with) integration	to become part of a group or society and be accepted by them, or to help someone do this	*integrieren; Integration*
interracial marriage	marriage between people of different races	*Ehe zwischen Angehörigen verschiedener Ethnien*
labour shortage	a situation in which there are not enough workers	*Mangel an Arbeitskräften*

the middle class	the social class that includes people who are educated and work in professional jobs, e. g. teachers or managers	*die Mittelklasse/Mittelschicht*
minority	a small group of people or things within a much larger group (= majority)	*Minderheit*
race relations	the relationship that exists between people from different countries, religions, etc. who are now living in the same place	*Beziehungen zwischen ethnischen Gruppen*
refugee [ˌrefjuˈdʒi]	sb. who has been forced to leave a country, especially during a war, or for political or religious reasons	*Flüchtling*
temporary stay	a stay continuing for a limited period of time	*befristeter Aufenthalt*
Western values	the beliefs, traditions, customs, etc. of the Western community	*westliche Werte*

British Empire		
diplomacy [dɪˈpləʊməsi]	the job or quality of managing the relationships between countries	*Diplomatie, Verhandlungsgeschick*
emperor/empress	the man/woman who rules an empire	*Kaiser(in)*
to expand; expansion	to become larger in size or number; growth	*expandieren, sich vergrößern; Expansion, Wachstum*
fall	loss of power, failure	*Sturz, Umsturz*
foreign policy	involving or dealing with other countries	*Außenpolitik*
to found sth.; foundation	to start sth., to establish sth.	*etwas beginnen/gründen; Gründung*
to gain independence	to become independent	*(an) Unabhängigkeit gewinnen*
to grant sb. independence	to allow sb. to act on their own	*jmd. Unabhängigkeit bewilligen*
(policy of) imperialism	a political system in which one country rules a lot of other countries	*Imperialismus; imperialistische Politik*
indigenous [ɪnˈdɪdʒənəs]	native people who have always lived in a place	*einheimisch*
to be loyal to sb.	to support sb.	*jdm. treu sein*
maharaja [ˌmɑːhəˈrɑːdʒə]	an Indian prince or king	*Maharadscha*
overseas	to or in a foreign country that is across the sea	*Übersee*
to possess sth.	to own sth.	*etwas besitzen*
Raj [rɑːdʒ]	British rule in India	*Britische Kolonialzeit in Indien*
to reign	to rule a nation as their king, queen or emperor	*regieren*
rule	to have the official power to control a country	*Herrschaft*
self-government	a country or organization that is controlled by its own members	*Selbstverwaltung*
superiority over sth.	the quality of being better, more skilful, powerful, etc. than other people or things	*Überlegenheit*
viceroy [ˈvaɪsrɔɪ]	a man who was sent by a king or queen in the past to rule another country	*Vizekönig*

colonization		
the acquisition of colonies	here: the act of getting land	*Aneignung von Land/Fläche*
to civilize sb.	to improve a society so that it is more organized and developed	*jdn. zivilisieren, jdm. Manieren beibringen*
to claim a territory	to conquer a territory	*ein Territorium erobern/ in Anspruch nehmen*
colonial power	when a powerful country rules many weaker ones, and establishes its own trade and society there	*Kolonialmacht*
to colonize; colonization [ˌkɒlənaɪˈzeɪʃn]	to establish political control over another country, and send your citizens there to settle	*kolonisieren, besiedeln; Kolonisierung, Besiedlung*

colony	a country/area that is under the political control of a more powerful country, usually one that is far away	*Kolonie*
colonist	sb. who settles in a new colony	*Kolonist, Siedler*
to conquer [ˈkɒŋkə(r)] **conquest**	to take control of a country by fighting	*erobern; Eroberung, Sieg*
conqueror	a person (often an army) who fights to take control of a country	*Eroberer*
to decolonize sb.	to make a former colony politically independent	*jdn. entkolonialisieren/in die Unabhängigkeit entlassen*
to discover; discovery	if sb. discovers a new place, they are the first person to find it	*entdecken; Entdeckung*
to divide sth. up	to separate sth. into parts and share them between people	*etwas aufteilen*
to establish	to start e. g. an organization, esp. one that exists for a long time; to set up	*etwas gründen*
to exploit; exploitation	to try to get as much as you can out of a situation, sometimes unfairly	*ausnutzen, ausbeuten; Ausbeutung*
to explore; exploration	to travel to or around a place in order to learn about it	*erforschen; Erforschung, Erkundung*
to gain control over sb.	to obtain or achieve control over sb. you want or need	*Kontrolle über jdn. erlangen*
to invade; invasion [ɪnˈveɪʒn]	to enter a country using military force in order to take control of it	*einmarschieren; Einmarsch*
mother country, motherland, fatherland	the country where someone was born (implies a strong emotional connection)	*Herkunftsland, Vaterland*
native	someone who lives in a place all the time or has lived there a long time	*Ureinwohner*
negotiations	diplomatic talks to reach an agreement	*Verhandlungen*
postcolonial	later than or after colonialism	*postkolonial*
to settle; settlement	to go to a place where no people have lived permanently before and start to live there	*(be-)siedeln; Besiedlung*

The American Dream – Dreams, Struggles and Nightmares

Banksy: *Child disguised as Liberty*, New York

Tips on vocab ⟫

to pick one's nose ■ shawl (*Umhängetuch*) ■ a long train (*Schleppe*) ■ a crown with 6 rays ■ to stand on a crate (*Kasten*) ■ a sack dress ■ rough shoes ■ to look defiant (*trotzig*) ■ peeling/flaking paint ■ cracks in the wall

START-UP ACTIVITIES

1. The Statue of Liberty: a defiant child "from the streets"?
   a) Team up with a partner and describe the mural to each other, paying attention to details such as the child's facial expression, body language, the condition of the wall, etc.
   b) Speculate about the child's social background and what she might be thinking.

2. In class, speculate on the artist's intention to personify one of America's core symbols in this way.
   → Focus on Skills, Analysis of Visuals, p. 409

Bruce Springsteen

American Land

What is this land of America, so many travel there
I'm going now while I'm still young, my darling meet me there
Wish me luck my lovely, I'll send for you when I can
And we'll make our home in the American Land

5 Over there all the women wear silk and satin to their knees
And children dear, the sweets, I hear, are growing on the trees
Gold comes rushing out the rivers straight into your hands
When you make your home in the American Land

There's diamonds in the sidewalks, there's gutters[1] lined in song[2]
10 Dear, I hear that beer flows through the faucets[3] all night long
There's treasure for the taking[4], for any hard working man
Who will make his home in the American Land

I docked[5] at Ellis Island in a city of light and spire[6]
I wandered to the valley of red-hot steel and fire
15 We made the steel that built the cities with the sweat of our two hands
And I made my home in the American Land

There's diamonds in the sidewalk, there's gutters lined in song
Dear I hear that beer flows through the faucets all night long
There's treasure for the taking, for any hard working man
20 Who will make his home in the American Land

The McNicholas, the Posalskis, the Smiths, Zerillis too
The Blacks, the Irish, Italians, the Germans and the Jews
Come across the water a thousand miles from home
With nothing in their bellies but the fire down below

25 They died building the railroads, worked to bones and skin
They died in the fields and factories, names scattered[7] in the wind
They died to get here a hundred years ago, they're still dyin' now
The hands that built the country we're always trying to keep down[8]

There's diamonds in the sidewalk, there's gutters lined in song
30 Dear I hear that beer flows through the faucets all night long
There's treasure for the taking, for any hard working man
Who will make his home in the American Land …

Text (OT): Bruce Springsteen
Copyright: Bruce Springsteen Music
Rondor Musikverlag GmbH, Berlin

 3. Listen to/read the song by Bruce Springsteen.
  a) What dreams and hopes of America are expressed by the speaker?
  b) Which ethnic groups try to "make a home" in the US?
  c) What has become of people's dreams?

[1] **gutter** Straßengraben; Gosse – [2] **to be lined in sth.** here: to be covered in sth. – [3] **faucet** (US) Wasserhahn, Fasshahn – [4] **for the taking** easily available – [5] **to dock at** andocken – [6] **spire** (Turm-)Spitze – [7] **scattered** dispersed; verteilt – [8] **to keep sb. down** (phr. v.) to oppress sb.

America and Americans – Insights and Outlooks

John Steinbeck

America and Americans

For centuries, America has fascinated and inspired people all over the world. Whether they love it or hate it, there is hardly anyone who doesn't have an opinion about the United States of America and its people. Prepare two slips of paper, the first titled "America is …", the second titled "Americans are …". Write down three thoughts that come to your mind on each slip, then attach them to the board. In a next step, sort your slips according to topic and discuss your findings in class.

COMPREHENSION

1. **Before reading:**
   Describe the cartoon and the clichés it conveys and compare it to your own thoughts about Americans.

1 This essay is not an attempt to answer or refute the sausage-like propaganda which is ground out[1] in our disfavor[2]. It cannot even pretend to be objective truth. Of course it is opinion, conjecture[3], and speculation.
5 What else could it be? But at least it is informed by America, and inspired by curiosity, impatience, some anger, and a passionate love of America and the Americans. For I believe that out of the whole body of our past, out of our differences, our quarrels, our many in-
10 terests and directions, something has emerged that is itself unique in the world: America – complicated, paradoxical, bullheaded, shy, cruel, boisterous[4], unspeakably dear, and very beautiful. […]

2 E Pluribus Unum[5]
15 Our land is of every kind geologically and climatically – and our people are of every kind also – of every race, of every ethnic category – and yet our land is one nation, and our people are Americans. Mottoes have a way of being compounded of wishes and dreams. The
20 motto of the United States, "*E Pluribus Unum,*" is a fact. This is the strange and almost unbelievable truth; and

even stranger is the fact that the unit America has come into being in slightly over four hundred years – almost exactly the same amount of time as that during which England was occupied by the Roman legions. 25 It is customary[6] (indeed, at high-school graduations it is a requirement) for speakers to refer to America as a "precious inheritance[7]" – our heritage[8], a gift proffered[9] like a sandwich wrapped in plastic on a plastic tray. Our ancestors, so it is implied, gathered to the invita- 30 tion of a golden land and accepted the sacrament of milk and honey. This is not so.
In the beginning, we crept, scuttled[10], escaped, were driven out of the safe and settled corners of the earth to the fringes[11] of a strange and hostile[12] wilderness, a 35 nameless and hostile continent. Some rulers granted large sections of unmapped territory, in places they did not own or even know, as cheap gifts to favorites or to potential enemies for the purpose of getting rid of them. Many others were sent here as a punishment for 40 penal[13] offenses. Far from welcoming us, this continent resisted us. The Indigenes[14] fought to the best of their ability to hold on to a land they thought was theirs. The

---

[1] **to grind sth. out** to produce information, writing etc. in such large amounts that it becomes boring – [2] **disfavor** (*US*) the feeling that you do not like sth. – [3] **conjecture** guess – [4] **boisterous** wild, ungestüm – [5] **E Pluribus Unum** (Latin for "out of many, one") motto found in 1776 on the Seal of the United States suggesting that out of many colonies, states or ancestries emerges a single people and nation [6] **customary** usual – [7] **inheritance** *Erbe* – [8] **heritage** *Kulturerbe* – [9] **to proffer sth.** *anbieten* – [10] **to scuttle** to run with quick short steps – [11] **fringes** the outer edge of an area, *Randbereich* – [12] **hostile** ['hɒstaɪl] very unfriendly and aggressive – [13] **penal** ['piːnl] connected with or used for punishment, esp. by law – [14] **Indigenes** ['ɪndəˌdʒinz] native people

rocky soils fought back, and the bewildering forests, and the deserts. Diseases, unknown and therefore incurable, decimated[15] the early comers, and in their energy of restlessness they fought one another. The land was no gift. The firstlings worked for it, fought for it, and died for it. They stole and cheated and double-crossed[16] for it, and when they had taken a little piece, the way a fierce-hearted man ropes a wild mustang, they had then to gentle it and smooth it and make it habitable at all. Once they had a foothold, they had to defend their holdings against new waves of the restless and ferocious[17] and hungry.

America did not exist. Four centuries of work, of bloodshed, of loneliness and fear created this land. We built America and the process made us Americans – a new breed, rooted in all races, stained and tinted[18] with all colors, a seeming ethnic anarchy. Then in a little, little time, we became more alike than we were different – a new society; not great, but fitted by our very faults for greatness, *E Pluribus Unum*. [...]

What happened is one of the strange quirks[19] of human nature – but perhaps it is a perfectly natural direction that was taken, since no child can long endure[20] his parents. It seemed to happen by instinct. In spite of all the pressure the old people could bring to bear, the children of each ethnic group denied their background and their ancestral language.

Despite the anger, the contempt, the jealousy, the self-imposed ghettos and segregation, something was loose[21] in this land called America. Its people were Americans. The new generations wanted to be Americans more than they wanted to be Poles or Germans or Hungarians or Italians or British. They wanted this and they did it. America was not planned; it became. [...]

3 Paradox and dream

One of the generalities[22] most often noted about Americans is that we are a restless, a dissatisfied, a searching people. We bridle and buck[23] under failure, and we go mad with dissatisfaction in the face of success. We spend our time searching for security, and hate it when we get it. For the most part we are intemperate[24] people: we eat too much when we can, drink too much, indulge[25] our senses too much. Even in our so-called virtues we are intemperate: a teetotaler[26] is not content not to drink – he must stop all the drinking in the world; a vegetarian among us would outlaw the eating of meat. We work too hard, and many die under the strain; and then to make up for that we play with a violence as suicidal.

The result is that we seem to be in a state of turmoil[27] all the time, both physically and mentally. We are able to believe that our government is weak, stupid, overbearing, dishonest, and inefficient, and at the same time we are deeply convinced that it is the best government in the world, and we would like to impose[28] it upon everyone else. We speak of the American Way of Life as though it involved the ground rules for the governance of heaven. A man hungry and unemployed through his own stupidity and that of others, a man beaten by a brutal policeman, a woman forced into prostitution by her own laziness, high prizes, availability, and despair – all bow[29] with reverence toward the American Way of Life, although each one would look puzzled and angry if he were asked to define it. We scramble[30] and scrabble[31] up the stony path toward the pot of gold we have taken to mean security. We trample friends, relatives, and strangers who get in the way of our achieving it; and once we get it we shower it on psychoanalysts to try to find out why we are unhappy, and finally – if we have enough of the gold – we contribute it back to the nation in the form of foundations and charities. [...]

4 Now there is a set of generalities for you, each one of them cancelled out by another generality. Americans seem to live and breathe and function by paradox; but in nothing are we so paradoxical as in our passionate belief in our own myths. We truly believe ourselves to be natural-born mechanics and do-it-yourself-ers. We spend our lives in motor cars, yet most of us – a great many of us at least – do not know enough about a car to look in the gas tank when the motor fails. Our lives as we live them would not function without electricity, but it is a rare man or woman who, when the power goes off, knows how to look for a burned-out fuse[32] and replace it. We believe implicitly[33] that we are the heirs[34] of the pioneers; that we have inherited self-sufficiency and the

---

[15] **to decimate** to kill large numbers of animals, plants or people in a particular area – [16] **to double-cross sb.** to cheat or trick sb. – [17] **ferocious** [fəˈrəʊʃəs] *wild, grausam* – [18] **tinted** [ˈtɪntəd] *sth. that has a small amount of colour to it* – [19] **quirk** *Eigenheit* – [20] **to endure** *here: to bear* – [21] **to be loose** *here: not strictly organized or controlled* – [22] **generality** *Verallgemeinerung* – [23] **to bridle and buck** (*lit.*) *to show that you are annoyed at sth.* – [24] **intemperate** (*fml.*) *unmäßig* – [25] **to indulge** *sich etw. hingeben* – [26] **teetotaler** *a person who does not drink alcohol* – [27] **turmoil** *a state of confusion or anxiety* – [28] **to impose sth. on/upon sb./sth.** *to force sb./sth. to accept your ideas* – [29] **to bow to sth.** *here: to agree unwillingly to do sth.* – [30] **to scramble** – *klettern* – [31] **to scrabble** *herumwühlen* – [32] **fuse** *(elektrische) Sicherung* – [33] **implicitly** [ɪmˈplɪsɪtli] *absolutely* – [34] **heir** [eə(r)] *Erbe, Erbin*

ability to take care of ourselves, particularly in relation to nature. There isn't a man among us in ten thousand who knows how to butcher a cow or a pig and cut it up for eating, let alone a wild animal. By natural endowment[35], we are great rifle shots and great hunters – but when hunting season opens there is a slaughter of farm animals and humans by men and women who couldn't hit a real target if they could see it. Americans treasure the knowledge that they live close to nature, but fewer and fewer farmers feed more and more people; and as soon as we can afford to we eat out of cans, buy frozen TV dinners, and haunt[36] the delicatessens[37]. Affluence[38] means moving to the suburbs, but the American suburbanite[39] sees, if anything, less of the country than the city apartment dweller with his window boxes and his African violets carefully tended under lights. In no country are more seeds and plants and equipment purchased, and less vegetables and flowers raised. […]

5 The pursuit of happiness

In nothing are the Americans so strange and set apart from the rest of the world as in their attitudes toward the treatment of their children. […]

The great change seems to have set in toward the end of the last [19th] century; perhaps it came with the large numbers of poor and bewildered immigrants suddenly faced with hope of plenty and liberty of development beyond their dreams. Our child sickness has developed very rapidly in the last sixty years and it runs parallel, it would seem, with increasing material plenty and the medical conquest of child-killing diseases. No longer was it even acceptable that the child should be like his parents and live as they did; he must be better, live better, know more, dress more richly, and if possible change from his father's trade to a profession. This dream became touchingly national. Since it was demanded of the child that he or she be better than his parents, he must be gaited[40], guided, pushed, admired, disciplined, flattered, and forced. But since the parents were and are no better than they are, the rules they propounded[41] were based not on their experience but on their wishes and hopes. […]

from *America and Americans* by John Steinbeck. Viking Press, New York 1966, pp. 7 ff.

from *America and Americans* by John Steinbeck. Viking Press, New York 1966, pp. 7 ff.

COMPREHENSION

2. The material at hand can be dealt with in various ways:
  a) as a **text-supported listening comprehension** exercise to improve listening skills with textual support if necessary
  b) as **text only** to improve your reading skills
  c) as **audio text only** for an advanced listening comprehension exercise

Tip: Be prepared to listen to/read the essay at least two times, as it contains a lot of elaborated and metaphorical language.

Here are some **methodological instructions** first:

Step 1: Divide the class into four groups, each group working with one paragraph:
However, **all** groups read the first introductory paragraph.

Step 2: First, **listen to/read the paragraph individually**, trying to get a general understanding of the text. Then, in your groups, ask each other questions about the paragraph to make sure you have understood everything correctly.

Step 3: While **listening to/reading the paragraph a second time**, take notes on the questions below. Crosscheck your findings with your group and make additions and/or corrections if necessary.

---

[35] **endowment** [ɪnˈdaʊmənt] (*fml.*) here: a quality or an ability that you are born with – [36] **to haunt** [hɔːnt] here: continuously visit a place – [37] **delicatessen** a shop that sells cooked meats and cheeses and special or unusual foods that come from other countries – [38] **affluence** wealth – [39] **suburbanite** [ˈsʌbɜːbənaɪt] a person who lives in the suburbs of a city – [40] **gaited** *gegängelt* – [41] **to propound** to suggest an idea for people to consider

1
- What is the author's reason for writing this essay?
- What – according to the author – makes America and the Americans unique?
- Which qualities define America?

 2
- Define America's motto, "E Pluribus Unum".
- What is said about America's diversity?
- Outline the reasons/examples given to prove that in the beginning America was not a "land of milk and honey".
- Present the different stages in the process of "becoming America/American".

 3
- What is depicted about the Americans' character?
- What is the result of the "American way of life"?
- Point out the manifold contradictions of the "American character" and behaviour.

 4
- Which "generalities" and "paradoxes" does the author exemplify?
- Which different areas of American life are presented?
- Which "myths" are mocked?

 5
- Which "child sickness" does the author refer to?
- Which "cures" or "remedies" does he mention to treat it?
- State the author's view of the Americans' capacity to cure their "child sickness".

Finally, after finishing the various tasks, the groups remix and exchange their results.

3. In order to highlight the line of argument* in Steinbeck's essay, find further sub-headlines for each of the aspects mentioned in the text.

ANALYSIS

 4. Show which stylistic devices* Steinbeck uses to juxtapose myth and reality.
→ Focus on Skills, Analysis of a Fictional Text, p. 402

Examples:
- Our ancestors … gathered … golden land (ll. 30 ff.) → myth (reference to Bible)
- This is not so. (l. 32) … we crept, scuttled … (l. 33) → reality

 5. Examine the means of irony* Steinbeck employs to sketch and mock the typical traits of Americans.

Example: Of course it is opinion … speculation. What else could it be? (ll. 4 ff.) → irony

6. Explain in detail what is meant by America's "precious inheritance … a gift proffered like a sandwich wrapped in plastic and on a plastic tray." (ll. 28 ff.)

 7. Compare what Steinbeck says about the Americans' "attitudes toward the treatment of [their] children" and "child sickness" (ll. 156 ff.) to the childlike Lady Liberty on p. 170.
What kind of "child sickness" does the author hint at?
→ Focus on Skills, Analysis of Visuals, p. 409
→ Focus on Skills, Analysis of a Fictional Text, p. 402

ACTIVITIES

 8. Reflect on why Steinbeck deems it necessary to emphasize his deep love of America in the introductory part before he starts to criticize it.

American Beliefs and Values

Although there have been significant shifts in societal concepts and traditions, the following ideals, beliefs and values continue to be some of the most important in American culture.

Fundamental, inalienable and God-given rights

- **Liberty:** personal and religious freedom
- **Pursuit of happiness:**
  - (personal and material) success and wealth
  - optimism and belief in "anticipated success"
  - individuality/individual ways of pursuing one's dreams and realizing one's goals
- **Equality:** equal rights for men and women/equal rights for people from different ethnicities and social backgrounds
- **Life:** leading a secure life protected by the law, government and military

Patriotism

- importance of **national symbols** (e.g. the Statue of Liberty, the Declaration of Independence, the Constitution, the U.S. flag, the National Anthem, etc.)
- strong identification with one's nationality and **pride in being American**

Puritanism/Protestant work ethic

- the **Puritan belief that hard work, thrift, discipline, self-improvement and responsibility** lead to worldly success and prosperity and that this is a sign of God's benevolence and grace
- continuous and active participation in society and entrepreneurial endeavors
- believing that one is exceptional, **a member of "God's chosen people"**, following a divine providence (→ **Manifest Destiny**)
- belief in authority as a means of protecting the personal rights of the people

The American Dream

- the phrase "American Dream" was first expressed by the American historian and writer **James Truslow Adams in 1931**, describing a set of complex beliefs, promises of religious and personal freedom and opportunities for prosperity and success, as well as political and social expectations
- its basic underlying concept has roots in the **Declaration of Independence of 1776** which refers to basic human rights such as **"Life, Liberty and the Pursuit of Happiness"** which are **"inalienable"** and God-given and based on the assumption that "all [people] are created equal"
- → Focus on Documents, The American Dream, p. 192

An Uncle Sam wind wheel toy for children

An open and dynamic society

- being generally open to new ideas and inventions (→ progress)
- being generally open to immigrants of any nationality, provided they contribute positively to the country
- different concepts of how to integrate immigrants:
  a) the **melting pot** image: people are "melted together", i.e. they are expected to give up their original culture and identity and are "transformed" into a homogeneous "American culture"
  b) the **salad bowl** image: national, ethnic and cultural patterns/habits are kept distinct by the immigrants while they are rather loosely integrated into the "American culture"
- → Focus on Facts, The United States: Immigration and Minorities, p. 219

J. Hector St. John de Crèvecœur

The American Is a New Man (1782)

AWARENESS

John Hector de Crèvecœur was a French-American writer who immigrated to America in 1755, where he wrote about life in the American colonies and the emergence of an American society. In 1782, his observations were published in London under the title *Letters of an American Farmer*. The book was immediately successful and helped create an American identity in the minds of Europeans. Imagine what life was like for the colonists in the "new world", and discuss what kind of personality and "pioneer spirit" a colonist might have had.

What attachment[1] can a poor European emigrant have for a country where he had nothing? The knowledge of the language, the love of a few kindred[2] as poor as himself, were the only cords[3] that tied him: his country is now that which gives him land, bread, protection and consequence[4]. *Ubi panis ibi patria*[5], is the motto of all emigrants. What then is the American, this new man? He is either a European or the descendant of a European; hence that strange mixture of blood which you will find in no other country. I could point out to you a family whose grandfather was an Englishman, whose wife was

Archibald M. Willard (1836 – 1918):
The Spirit of '76 (1875)

Dutch, whose son married a French woman, and whose present four sons have now four wives of different nations. *He* is an American, who, leaving behind him all his ancient prejudices and manners, receives new ones from the new mode of life he has embraced, the new government he obeys, and the new rank he holds. He becomes an American by being received in the broad lap of our great *Alma Mater*[6]. Here individuals of all nations are melted into a new race of men, whose labors and posterity[7] will one day cause great changes in the world. Americans are the western pilgrims who are carrying along with them the great mass of arts, sciences, vigor[8], and industry which began long since in the east; they will finish the great circle. The Americans were once scattered all over Europe; here they are incorporated into one of the finest systems of population which has ever appeared, and which hereafter become distinct by the power of the different climates they inhabit. The American ought therefore to love this country much better than that wherein either he or his forefathers were born. Here the rewards of his industry[9] follow with equal steps the progress of his labor; his labor is founded on the basis of nature, *self-interest*; can it want a stronger allurement[10]? Wives and children, who before in vain demanded of him a morsel[11] of bread, now, fat and frolicsome[12], gladly help their father to clear those fields whence exuberant[13] crops are to arise to feed and to clothe them all, without any part being claimed, either by a despotic prince, a rich abbot, or a mighty lord. Here religion demands but little of him; a small voluntary salary to the minister[14], and gratitude to God; can he refuse these? The American is a new man, who acts upon new principles; he must therefore entertain new ideas, and form new opinions. From involuntary idleness[15], servile[16] dependence, penury[17], and useless labor, he has passed to toils[18] of a very different nature, rewarded by ample[19] subsistence[20]. This is an American.

from *Letters of an American Farmer* by J. Hector St. John de Crèvecœur. Philadelphia, Matthew Carey, 1793, pp. 46 f.

---

[1] **attachment** belief in and loyalty towards a particular idea, organization, etc. – [2] **kindred** [ˈkɪndrəd] relative by birth – [3] **cord** bond, relation – [4] **consequence** social importance – [5] **Ubi panis ibi patria** (*Latin*) where there is bread (livelihood), there is (my) fatherland – [6] **Alma Mater** (*Latin*) bountiful mother; the school, college, etc. that sb. used to attend, used figuratively here – [7] **posterity** (*fml.*) all the people in the future who will be alive after you are dead – [8] **vigor** [ˈvɪgə(r)] energy – [9] **industry** here: (*fml.*) the act of working hard – [10] **allurement** attraction – [11] **morsel** a very small amount of sth., esp. food – [12] **frolicsome** lively – [13] **exuberant** [ɪgˈzjuːbərənt] plentiful – [14] **minister** priest – [15] **idleness** [ˈaɪdlnəs] laziness – [16] **servile** [ˈsɜːvaɪl] slave-like – [17] **penury** [ˈpenjəri] (*fml.*) severe poverty – [18] **toil** hard work – [19] **ample** more than enough – [20] **subsistence** money or food

COMPREHENSION

1. Point out the qualities of "old Europe" and the reasons why some Europeans emigrated.

2. Describe what America has to offer to the immigrants.

3. Define who the "new American" is and describe the process of becoming American.

ANALYSIS

4. Analyse the stylistic devices* Crèvecœur uses
a) to juxtapose the situation in Europe and in America,
b) to depict the opportunities America has to offer.
→ Focus on Skills, Analysis of a Non-Fictional Text, p. 405

line(s)	Europe vs. America	line(s)	opportunities
1	… poor European immigrant … land, bread, protection … → contrast	22 f.	… new mode of life … new government … → repetition
21	… ancient prejudices … new mode of life … → …		…

5. Give evidence from the text that reveals the author's view on America and its new inhabitants.

6. Explain how the cartoon views the immigrants' qualities and intentions and relate it to the concept of the "melting pot" that Crèvecœur depicts.
→ Focus on Skills, Analysis of Visuals, p. 409
→ Focus on Facts, American Beliefs and Values, p. 176

cagleecartoons.com

FLORIDA TODAY JEFF PARKER ©2006

PLYMOUTH ROCK

"THEY SAY THEY'RE BUILDING A WALL BECAUSE TOO MANY OF US ENTER ILLEGALLY AND WON'T LEARN THEIR LANGUAGE OR ASSIMILATE INTO THEIR CULTURE…"

7. Compare Crèvecœur's statement "his labor is founded on the basis of nature" (p. 177, ll. 43 f.) with Steinbeck's remarks on inheritance and reality (pp. 172 f., ll. 26 ff.).

ACTIVITIES

8. Crèvecœur's book was translated into several European languages. What do you think was so appealing about his views and descriptions to European readers at that time? Discuss in class.

9. Discuss in class whether the views expressed by Crèvecœur are still relevant. What would Crèvecœur write about America and the "American man" today?

10. Imagine it's the year 1800. Based on the information given in the text and your knowledge of history, design an advert in which you promote America and the benefits of becoming an American to Europeans.

Barack Obama

Let's Dream – Commencement Address at Knox College

AWARENESS

In 2005, then newly-elected Senator Barack Obama delivered a speech to the graduates of Knox College in Galesburg, Illinois, in which he talked about American ideals and the various challenges the US faces because of its involvement in wars and the impact of globalisation.

In class, collect ideas about what the Senator might say on the occasion of a college graduation. What would you expect or want him to say?

COMPREHENSION

1. **Before listening:**
   Here are some keywords and phrases taken from the excerpt:

   - Talent is the 21st century wealth.
   - the opportunity to upgrade
   - everybody's got a shot at opportunity
   - the winners in life's lottery
   - new skills and a world-class education
   - land of big dreams and big hopes
   - ownership society
   - collective responsibilities
   - Social Darwinism
   - life-long education
   - biotechnology research lab
   - national commitment
   - brainpower
   - individual initiative
   - reform
   - resources
   - talent

 Step 1: Together with a partner, get an overview of the keywords and phrases above and arrange them thematically.

Step 2: Speculate on the speech Barack Obama might have held and sketch out the potential structure of this speech using your previous notes.

 Step 3: Deliver 2–3 minute off-the-cuff speeches (*Stegreifrede*) on the topic "Let's Dream" in class using your previous notes and ideas.
→ Focus on Skills, Writing a Speech Script, p. 428
→ Focus on Skills, Giving a Speech, p. 418

Tips on vocab

Part 1:
commencement the ceremony at which students officially receive their degree ■ **to divvy sth. up** (*phr. v.*) to share sth. between a number of people ■ **tax break** *Steuererlass* ■ **tempting** *verlockend* ■ **ingenuity** *Geniaität* ■ **tuition** the money that you pay to be taught, especially in a college or university ■ **Maytag** an American home and commercial appliance company ■ **Donald Trump** American business magnate ■ **chump** a silly or stupid person ■ **decent** *anständig* ■ **to prosper** to be or become financially successful ■ **mutual** *gegenseitig*

Part 2:
to sustain to keep alive ■ **affordable** not expensive ■ **to cut budgets** *Budgets kürzen* ■ **to fuel sth.** to increase sth. or make it stronger ■ **refinery** *Raffinerie* ■ **cusp** the dividing line between two very different things; *Scheitelpunkt* ■ **to churn sth. out** (*phr. v., infml.*) to produce large amounts of sth. quickly; *etw. am laufenden Band produzieren* ■ **to hit the books** (*infml.*) to study hard

2. In a **first listening**, take notes on these questions:

 1
- Point out the importance of talent and education for the 21st century.
- Define the terms "ownership society" and "Social Darwinism".
- Present the reasons why "Social Darwinism" will not work in the US – according to Obama.
- What challenges does globalisation pose?

 2
- Which "dreams" of America's past does Obama refer to?
- What "dreams" does Obama have for the 21st century?
- Which skills and attitudes do these "21st century dreams" require?
- What are America's resources for making future dreams come true?
- → Focus on Skills, Listening Comprehension, p. 394

After listening, team up with a partner and compare your results. Make sure that you have understood everything correctly and make additions or corrections if necessary.

3. After a second listening, complete your notes.

ANALYSIS

 4. Before listening to the speech again, form groups of four students each, with each group focusing on one particular stylistic/rhetorical device*.
Examine and take notes on these aspects:
a) the use of **repetition** (e. g. anaphora, parallelism)
b) the use of **conditional sentences**
c) the use of **rhetorical questions**
d) the **choice of words** (e. g. keywords, key phrases, positive/negative emotive words)
In a group puzzle activity, compare and exchange your results with the other groups.

5. Explain how the use of various rhetorical devices affects the audience and motivates them to take action.
→ Focus on Skills, Analysis of a Political Speech, p. 407

6. Step 1: Describe Vik Muniz' collage *Obama* on the following page which he created after Obama's re-election in 2012, and explain its overall effect.
Does it convey elements of the "dream" that Barack Obama had as a young Senator back in 2005?

Step 2: Compare the collage *Obama* with the collage *The People's Monarch* depicting Queen Elizabeth II (p. 97). Which similarities and disparities concerning the intention and message of the artworks can you detect?
→ Focus on Skills, Analysis of Visuals, p. 409

7. Step 1: Examine Barack Obama's 2005 analysis and criticism (p. 181) of how businesspeople and politicians like Donald Trump want American society to be. What does he criticize about people like Donald Trump?

 Step 2: After becoming the President of the United States himself, Donald Trump also talked about the "dream" and how to improve the situation of the American people.
Compare his presidential announcement speech (pp. 224) to Barack Obama's speech.
- What does Trump criticize about Washington in general and politicians in particular?
- Which solutions does he offer?
- How do his choice of words and the overall tone of his speech differ from Barack Obama's 2005 speech?
- → Focus on Skills, Analysis of a Political Speech, p. 407

Once again, there are those who believe that there isn't much we can do about this as a nation. That the best idea is to give everyone a big refund on their government – divvy it up by individual portions, in the form of tax breaks, hand it out, and encourage everyone to use their share to go buy their own health care, their own retirement plan, their own child care, their own educa-
5 tion, and so on.

In Washington, they call this the Ownership Society. But in our past there has been another term for it –Social Darwinism – every man or woman for him or herself. It's a tempting idea, because it doesn't require much thought or ingenuity. [...] And it's especially tempting because each of us believes we will always be the winner in life's lottery, that we're the one who will be the next
10 Donald Trump, or at least we won't be the chump who Donald Trump says: "You're fired!"
But there's a problem. It won't work.

http://obamaspeeches.com/019-Knox-College-Commencement-Obama-Speech.htm, 4 June 2005 [08.05.2018]

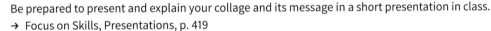

ACTIVITIES

8. Do research on Barack Obama's presidency and compile a collage yourself.
Collect snippets from newspapers, magazines or printouts from Obama's speeches and arrange them.
Be prepared to present and explain your collage and its message in a short presentation in class.
→ Focus on Skills, Presentations, p. 419

Vik Muniz, Obama (2012); photographs, digital print

Founding and Shaping a Nation: Political and Historical Visions and Challenges

Presidents' Views on Democracy

AWARENESS

What do you know about the presidents who delivered the following speeches? Collect your ideas in class – if necessary, do research in your history book or on the Internet.

Thomas Jefferson (1743–1826)

Let us, then, fellow-citizens, unite with one heart and one mind. Let us restore[1] to social intercourse that harmony and affection without which liberty and even life itself are but dreary[2] things. And let us reflect that, having banished from our land that religious intolerance under which mankind so long bled and suffered, we have yet gained little if we countenance[3] a political intolerance as despotic, as wicked[4], and capable of as bitter and bloody persecu-
5 tions[5]. [...] A wise and frugal[6] government, which shall restrain[7] men from injuring one another, shall leave them otherwise free to regulate their own pursuits of industry and improvement, and shall not take from the mouth of labour the bread it has earned. This is the sum of good government, and this is necessary to close the circle of our felicities[8]. [...] Equal and exact justice to all men, of whatever state or persuasion, religious or political; peace, commerce, and honest friendship with all nations, entangling[9] alliances with none; [...] encouragement of agriculture, and of commerce as its handmaid; the diffusion of information
10 and arraignment of all abuses at the bar of the public reason; freedom of religion; freedom of the press and freedom of person under the protection of the habeas corpus[10] [...].

Inaugural Address, 4 March 1801

Abraham Lincoln (1809–1865)

Plainly the central idea of secession[11] is the essence of anarchy. A majority held in restraint[12] by constitutional checks and limitations, and always changing easily with deliberate changes of popular opinions and sentiments, is the only true sovereign of a free people. Whoever rejects it does of necessity fly to anarchy or despotism. Unanimity[13] is impossible. The rule of a minority, as a permanent arrangement, is wholly inadmissible[14]; so that, rejecting
5 the majority principle, anarchy or despotism in some form is all that is left. [...] Physically speaking, we cannot separate. We cannot remove our respective sections from each other nor build an impassible[15] wall between them. A husband and wife may be divorced and go out of the presence and beyond the reach of each other, but the different parts of our country cannot do this.

First Inaugural Address, 4 March 1861

Franklin D. Roosevelt (1882–1945)

In the future days, which we seek to make secure, we look forward to a world founded upon four essential human freedoms. The first is the freedom of speech and expression – everywhere in the world. The second is freedom of every person to worship God in his own way – everywhere in the world. The third is freedom from want, which translated into world terms, means economic understandings which will secure to every nation a healthy peace-
5 time life for its inhabitants – everywhere in the world. The fourth is freedom from fear, which, translated into world terms, means a world-wide reduction of armaments to such a point and in such a thorough fashion that no nation will be in a position to commit an act of physical aggression against any neighbor – anywhere in the world. That is no vision of a distant millennium. It is a definite basis for a kind of world attainable[16] in our own time and generation. That kind of work is the very antithesis of the so-called "new order" of tyranny which the dictators seek to create with the crash of a bomb. To that new order we oppose the
10 greater conception – the moral order. A good society is able to face schemes of world domination and foreign revolutions alike without fear.

Franklin D. Roosevelt, The Four Freedoms, 6 January 1941

---

[1] **to restore** *wiederherstellen* – [2] **dreary** ['drɪəri] boring and making you feel unhappy – [3] **to countenance** ['kaʊntənəns] to permit sth. –
[4] **wicked** *böse* – [5] **persecution** *Verfolgung* – [6] **frugal** *sparsam* – [7] **to restrain sb.** to control sb.'s actions or behaviour – [8] **felicity** (*lit.*)
happiness – [9] **to entangle** *sich verfangen* – [10] **habeas corpus** ['heɪbiəs 'kɔːpəs] a law which says that a person can only be kept in
prison following a court's decision – [11] **secession** the act of withdrawing from a country to start one's own country – [12] **restraint**
Beherrschung – [13] **unanimity** [ˌjuːnəˈnɪmɪti] (*fml.*) *Einmütigkeit, Einstimmigkeit* – [14] **inadmissible** *unakzeptabel* – [15] **impassible** *unpassierbar* – [16] **attainable** (*fml.*) possible to achieve

John F. Kennedy (1917–1963)

But I tell you the New Frontier[17] is here, whether we seek it or not. Beyond that frontier are the uncharted[18] areas of science and space, unsolved problems of peace and war, unconquered pockets of ignorance and prejudice, unanswered questions of poverty and surplus[19]. It would be easier to shrink back from that frontier, to the safe mediocrity[20] of the past, to be lulled[21] by good intentions and high rhetoric – and those who prefer that course should not cast their votes
5   for me, regardless of party. […] But I believe the times demand new invention, innovation, imagination, decision. I am asking each of you to be pioneers on that New Frontier. […] All mankind waits upon our decision. A whole world looks to see what we will do. We cannot fail their trust, we cannot fail to try.   Address Accepting the Nomination for the Presidency of the United States, 15 July 1960

Bill Clinton (*1946)

The promise of America was born in the eighteenth century out of the bold conviction that we are all created equal. It was extended and preserved in the nineteenth century, when our nation spread across the continent, saved the Union, and abolished the awful scourge[22] of slavery. Then, in turmoil[23] and triumph, that promise exploded onto the world stage to make this the American century. What a century it has been! America has become the world's mighti-
5   est industrial power, saved the world from tyranny[24] in two world wars and a long cold war, and time and time again reached across the globe to millions who longed for the blessings of liberty.   Second Inaugural Address, 20 January 1997

COMPREHENSION

1. Divide the class into five groups, each group focusing on one president.
   - First, collect detailed background information on the respective president (biographical information, historical data).
   - In your group, devise a grid to collect and structure your findings and data.

President	biographical info	historical background	America's international position
Thomas Jefferson	• drafted the Declaration of Independence • third President	• fighting for independence • …	• isolationist policy • …
Abraham Lincoln	• …	• …	• …

2. Now listen to the excerpts from the speeches and pay attention to key terms and phrases that refer to
   a) responsibilities of the government,   b) the understanding of democracy,
   c) America's international/global position,   d) future duties and responsibilities of the US.
   → Focus on Skills, Listening Comprehension, p. 394

ANALYSIS

3. Examine and analyse the rhetorical devices* the speakers employ to emphasize their views and requests.
   → Focus on Skills, Analysis of a Political Speech, p. 407

ACTIVITIES

4. Finally, each group displays its completed grid, then presents and explains its findings and results to the class.
   → Focus on Skills, Presentations, p. 419

---

[17] **frontier** [ˈfrʌntɪə(r)] the limit of sth., esp. the limit of what is known of sth., e.g. of science – [18] **uncharted** (*lit.*) unerforscht – [19] **surplus** *Überfluss* – [20] **mediocrity** [ˌmiːdiˈɒkrəti] *Mittelmäßigkeit* – [21] **to lull sb.** [lʌl] *jdn. einlullen, einschläfern* – [22] **scourge** [skɜːdʒ] *Plage, Geißel* – [23] **turmoil** *Tumult, Aufruhr* – [24] **tyranny** [ˈtɪrəni]

Landmarks in United States History

The colonial period

1607	the **first English settlement: Jamestown, Virginia** is financed by the Virginia Company in London
1620	voyage of the **Pilgrim Fathers** with their ship **Mayflower**; founding of Plymouth Plantation at Cape Cod, Massachusetts; **Mayflower Compact** (cf. FoD, p. 122) is established; more and more **Puritans** leave England to escape religious persecution
May 1626	**Peter Minuit** (Dutch governor) "buys" Mannahatta from the Algonquin Indians for trade goods worth $24; settlement along the coast is called "**New Amsterdam**"; the colony is owned and run by the Dutch West India Company
June 1626	the **first eleven African slaves** arrive in New Amsterdam
1664	English warships take the harbour of New Amsterdam; the Dutch surrender and the colony is officially renamed "**New York**"
1681	**William Penn founds Pennsylvania**, a growing community of Quakers
1733	**the British own thirteen separate colonies** along the Atlantic coast of America, largest city: Philadelphia (28,000 inhabitants)

Advert of a voyage to America, 1609

Fighting for independence

1751 – 65	several **acts are passed by the British** government to control the economy of the American colonies (e. g. Navigation Act, **Stamp Act**); this leads to rising anger and opposition among the colonists
1770	the **Boston Massacre**: in a riot five civilians are killed by the British troops, which helps spark the rebellion against the British
1773	the **Boston Tea Party**: colonists object to the British Tea Act, board the ships of the British East India Company and destroy the tea by throwing it into the harbour; their slogan is "**No taxation without representation**" because the American colonists do not have a political voice in the British parliament
1774	a group of political leaders form the **First Continental Congress**, the first American national government
1775	begin of the **War of Independence**; leading American general is George Washington
4 July 1776	the Continental Congress issues the **Declaration of Independence**, drafted by Thomas Jefferson
1783	**Treaty of Paris**: Britain officially recognizes its former colonies as an independent nation, the **United States of America**

Etablishing a new nation

1789	the Constitutional Convention works out a completely new system of government, the **Constitution of the United States,** a federal system in which the power to rule is shared and representatives are elected; **a system of "checks and balances"** is established
1791	the **Bill of Rights** is issued; amendments ensure civil rights (e. g. freedom of religion, freedom of speech, a free press, the right to carry arms, the right to a fair trial by a jury)

Slave advert, South Carolina, 1787

The 19th century – westward expansion and politics of isolationism

1803	**Louisiana Purchase**: a huge area west of the Mississippi is sold to the USA by Napoleon for $15 million (under President Thomas Jefferson)
1823	**Monroe Doctrine**: President James Monroe warns European nations not to interfere with Latin American affairs; it is one of the most important ideas in American foreign policy
1830	**Indian Removal Act**: all Native Americans living east of the Mississippi River are moved west
until 1850s	**exploration of the West** – the frontier; the idea of "Manifest Destiny", making the US stretch from east to west coast, is born; Lewis and Clark explore the western plains
1848	Mexico is annexed; westward expansion is completed – the **Manifest Destiny has come true**

1862	**Homestead Act** is passed by Congress, offering free farms in the West to settlers
1861–65	**Civil War** between the Confederate States of America (South) and the Union (North)
1863	**Emancipation Proclamation**: official abolition of slavery
1890	massacre of Sioux Indians in the **Battle of Wounded Knee**

The 20ᵗʰ century – politics of interventionism – "The American Century"

1913	**Henry Ford** invents assembly-line production to produce his most famous car, the **Model T**
1900–20	**peak years of immigration** to the USA (ca. 16 million immigrants)
1917	US declares **war on Germany**; President Wilson wants to defeat Germany "**to make the world safe for democracy … and to end all wars**"
1918	"Wilson's Fourteen Points"; ideas for lasting peace and **a League of Nations**
1920s	**The Roaring Twenties**; first Immigration Acts are passed by Congress to reduce immigration
1929	**Wall Street Crash**
1930s	the **Great Depression** and **Roosevelt's New Deal** policy
1939–45	**World War II**; 1944 invasion of Normandy (D-Day, 6 June)
1945	6 August: American B29 bomber drops **atomic bomb on Hiroshima**; 9 August: second atomic bomb is dropped on the city of **Nagasaki**
1948–52	Marshall Plan: humanitarian aid for millions of suffering people in Europe; Berlin Airlift
1940s–89	**Cold War**; communist versus capitalist nations; 1950s: "Balance of Terror": politics of deterrence, nuclear armament
1961–63	**John F. Kennedy**: first Catholic president; assassinated in Nov. 1963
1955–68	**Civil Rights Movement: Martin Luther King** is its most famous leader; he is assassinated in 1968
1964	**Civil Rights Act** outlaws racial discrimination and segregation
1950–53	**Korean War**
1962	**Cuban Missile Crisis**
1965–73	**Vietnam War**
1969	**Moon landing**; US astronauts are the first human beings on the moon
1987–89	**Mikhail Gorbachev** and Ronald Reagan **end the era of the Cold War**; destruction of nuclear missiles; German reunification
1990/91	President George Bush begins the **Gulf War**

The 21ˢᵗ century

2001	**9/11 attacks** on World Trade Center and Pentagon; invasion of Afghanistan → President declares "War on Terror" and the so-called "Axis of Evil"
2002	**Department of Homeland Security** is created; US Naval base in **Guantánamo**, Cuba is turned into a detainment camp for prisoners charged with terrorism
2003	invasion of **Iraq, begin of Iraq War**
2007	the **US "housing bubble" collapses** causing the crash of the real estate market and damaging financial institutions worldwide
2008	the bankruptcy of Lehman Brothers Holdings Inc. causes drastic losses on the stock market which lead to one of the most serious **global economic crises** since 1929
2009	**Barack Obama** is the first African-American President, re-elected in 2012
2010	gradual **withdrawal of the troops in Iraq**
	the **Patient Protection and Affordable Care Act ("Obamacare")** is signed into law
	Don't Ask, Don't Tell Repeal Act allows gays, lesbians and bisexuals to serve openly in the US Armed Forces
2013	**US Federal Government Shutdown** (Oct 1–16) due to lack of funds in the state budget
2014	as the **crisis in Iraq** worsens and ISIS (Islamic State of Iraq and Syria) attacks become more violent, the US sends military personnel to Iraq to protect Iranian citizens and the US embassy
2016	**Donald Trump** is elected President

Historical advert, 1921

Apollo 11 moon landing

Attack on World Trade Center, 9/11

Obama election poster

Focus on Facts

America's Cornerstone Documents

The Mayflower Compact

The Mayflower Compact was **the first political agreement for self-government in America**. It was signed on 21 November **1620**, aboard the ship **Mayflower** anchored off Cape Cod, Massachusetts. This course of action was deemed necessary because the Pilgrims were about to settle in an area outside the jurisdiction of their patent issued by the Virginia Company of London, and because several passengers threatened to make their own rules once
5 ashore. The Pilgrim leaders persuaded forty-one of the male adults on board to sign the **Mayflower Compact** and set up a government in **Plymouth Colony**.

> In the name of God, Amen. We, whose names are underwritten, the Loyal Subjects of our dread[1] Sovereign Lord King James, by the Grace of God, of Great Britain, France and Ireland, King, Defender of the Faith, &c. Having undertaken for the Glory of God, and Advancement of the Christian Faith, and the Honour of our King and Country, a Voyage to plant the first colony in the northern Parts of Virginia; Do by these presents,
> 5 solemnly[2] and mutually[3] in the Presence of God and one another, covenant[4] and combine ourselves together into a civil Body Politick, for our better Ordering and Preservation, and Furtherance[5] of the Ends aforesaid; And by Virtue[6] hereof do enact[7], constitute, and frame, such just and equal Laws, Ordinances[8], Acts, Constitutions, and Offices, from time to time, as shall be thought most meet and convenient for the general Good of the Colony; unto which we promise all due Submission and Obedience. In WITNESS whereof we have here-
> 10 unto subscribed our names at Cape Cod the eleventh of November, in the Reign of our Sovereign Lord King James of England, France, and Ireland, the eighteenth and of Scotland, the fifty-fourth. Anno Domini 1620
>
> from *America's Freedom Documents*, Thomas Publications, Gettysburg, PA, USA, 1989

The Declaration of Independence

In the Declaration of Independence the thirteen American colonies announced their **freedom from British rule**. On 11 June 1776, Congress appointed a committee to draft a formal **Declaration of Independence**. **Thomas Jefferson**, one of the appointed members, was asked to write the draft, which he completed in about two weeks. The date of its adoption by the Second Continental Congress on **4 July 1776**, is celebrated as **the birthday of**
5 **the United States**.

> When, in the course of human events, it becomes necessary for one people to dissolve the political bands which have connected them with another, and to assume[9] among the powers of the earth, the separate and equal station[10] to which the Laws of Nature and of Nature's God entitle them, a decent respect to the opinions of mankind requires[11] that they should declare the causes which impel[12] them to the separation. –
> 5 We hold these thruths to be self-evident, that all men are created equal; that they are endowed[13] by their Creator with certain unalienable[14] rights; that among these, are life, liberty, and the pursuit[15] of happiness. – That, to secure these rights, governments are instituted among men, deriving[16] their just powers from the consent[17] of the governed; – that, whenever any form of government becomes destructive of these ends, it is the right of the people to alter or to abolish it, and to institute a new government, laying its foundation on such principles,
> 10 and organizing its powers in such form, as to them shall seem most likely to effect their Safety and Happiness.
>
> from *America's Freedom Documents*, Thomas Publications, Gettysburg, PA, USA, 1989

[1] **dread** (*lit.*) [dred] making you feel afraid – [2] **solemnly** *feierlich* – [3] **mutual** *gegenseitig* – [4] **to covenant** to promise – [5] **furtherance** (*fml.*) the act of helping sth. progress – [6] **virtue** an attractive or useful quality – [7] **to enact** (*fml.*) to make a proposal into a law – [8] **ordinance** *Verordnung* – [9] **to assume** *etwas übernehmen* – [10] **station** (*fml.*) position, status – [11] **to require** to demand – [12] **to impel** [ɪmˈpel] (*fml.*) here: to force – [13] **to endow sb. with sth.** [ɪnˈdaʊ] (*phr. v., fml.*) to give sb. a particular quality – [14] **unalienable** cannot be taken away – [15] **pursuit** the act of trying to achieve sth. – [16] **to derive** to get sth. from sth. – [17] **consent** [kənˈsent] agreement about sth.

The Bill of Rights

The original Constitution had few guaranties for the protection of individual liberties, and most Americans felt that a clear statement of these rights was necessary in order to make the document complete. The Bill of Rights describes **the basic rights of the people** and forbids the government from denying these liberties. Included are the **freedoms of speech, religion, the press and the right to assemble**. By 15 December **1791**, a majority of the
5 states had approved the ten amendments which became **a permanent addition to the Constitution** and are known as the Bill of Rights.

Amendment 1: Congress shall make no law respecting an establishment of religion, or prohibiting[18] the free exercise thereof; or abridging the freedom of speech, or the press; or the right of the people peacefully to assemble[19], and to petition the government for a redress[20] of grievances[21].

Amendment 2: A well-regulated militia, being necessary to the security of a free state, the right of the
5 people to keep and bear arms shall not be infringed[22]. [...]

Amendment 4: The right of the people to be secure in their persons, houses, papers, and effects, against unreasonable searches and seizures[23], shall not be violated, and no warrants[24] shall issue, but upon probable cause, supported by oath or affirmation, and particularly describing the place to be searched, and the persons or things to be seized.

10 **Amendment 5:** No person shall be held to answer for a capital, or otherwise infamous crime, unless on a presentment or indictment[25] of a grand jury, except in cases arising in the land or naval forces, or in the militia, when in actual service in time of war or public danger; nor shall any person be subject for the same offense to be twice put in jeopardy[26] of life or limb[27]; nor shall be compelled[28] in any criminal case to be a witness against himself, nor be deprived[29] of life, liberty, or property, without the process of law; nor shall
15 private property be taken for public use, without just compensation.

Amendment 6: In all criminal prosecutions[30], the accused shall enjoy the right to a speedy and public trial, by an impartial[31] jury of the state and district wherein the crime shall have been committed, which district shall have been previously ascertained[32] by law, and to be informed of the nature and cause of the accusation; to be confronted with the witnesses against him; to have compulsory process for obtaining[33]
20 witnesses in his favor, and to have the assistance of a counsel for his defense.

Amendment 7: In suits of common law, where the value in controversy shall exceed[34] twenty dollars, the right of trial by jury shall be preserved, and no fact tried by jury, shall be otherwise re-examined in any court of the United States, than according to the rules of the common law.

Amendment 8: Excessive bail[35] shall not be required, nor excessive fines[36] imposed, nor cruel and un-
25 usual punishments inflicted[37]. [...]

from *America's Freedom Documents*, Thomas Publications, Gettysburg, PA, USA, 1989

[18] **to prohibit** to stop – [19] **to assemble** to come together as a group – [20] **redress** [rɪˈdres] (*fml.*) money that sb. pays you because they have caused you harm or damaged your property – [21] **grievance** [ˈgriːvəns] *Missstand* – [22] **to infringe** to break a law – [23] **seizure** [ˈsiːʒə(r)] *Festnahme, Beschlagnahme* – [24] **warrant** *Haftbefehl* – [25] **indictment** (*US*) *Anklage* – [26] **jeopardy** [ˈdʒepədi] the danger of being harmed – [27] **limb** serious injury – [28] **to compel** [kəmˈpel] to force sb. to do sth. – [29] **to deprive sb. of sth.** [dɪˈpraɪv] (*phr. v.*) to prevent sb. from having sth. – [30] **prosecution** *(Straf-)Verfolgung* – [31] **impartial** *unparteiisch* – [32] **to ascertain** (*fml.*) to find out sth. – [33] **to obtain** to get – [34] **to exceed** (*fml.*) *überschreiten* – [35] **bail** *Kaution* – [36] **fine** *Geldstrafe* – [37] **to inflict** to make sb. suffer

The Exploration of the USA and the Frontier

The settlement of the American continent from the Atlantic to the Pacific Ocean

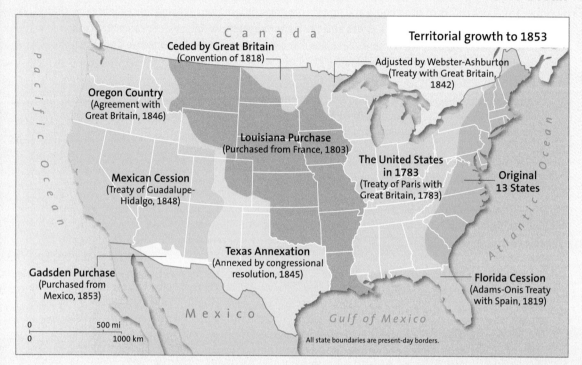

Territorial growth to 1853

Canada

Ceded by Great Britain
(Convention of 1818)

Adjusted by Webster-Ashburton
(Treaty with Great Britain,
1842)

Oregon Country
(Agreement with
Great Britain, 1846)

Louisiana Purchase
(Purchased from France, 1803)

The United States
in 1783
(Treaty of Paris with
Great Britain, 1783)

Original
13 States

Mexican Cession
(Treaty of Guadalupe-
Hidalgo, 1848)

Texas Annexation
(Annexed by congressional
resolution, 1845)

Gadsden Purchase
(Purchased from
Mexico, 1853)

Florida Cession
(Adams-Onis Treaty
with Spain, 1819)

Mexico

Gulf of Mexico

Pacific Ocean

Atlantic Ocean

0   500 mi
0   1000 km

All state boundaries are present-day borders.

In 1800, the western boundary of the USA was the Mississippi River. The land west of the river, Louisiana, belonged to France. In **1803**, **Thomas Jefferson** made a deal to buy the Louisiana Territory from the French for $15 million (**Louisiana Purchase**), as Napoleon needed money for the war against Britain. The land of the United States more than doubled and now almost reached to the Rocky Mountains. Jefferson hoped to find an
5 easy way across the continent to the Pacific Ocean, and in 1804 he hired seasoned army officers **Meriwether Lewis and William Clark** to explore the geography, the lands, the people and the animals in that unknown and uncivilized **frontier** area. After two years they returned with valuable information about the land they had crossed.

The lands beyond Louisiana were known as Oregon, an area which included today's Washington, Oregon, Idaho
10 and the Canadian province of British Columbia. Although the British still had trading posts and many settlements there, they were soon outnumbered by thousands of American settlers who had been "infected" by the "Oregon Fever". In **1832**, **the first Oregon Trail settlers** started in Independence, Missouri, packed their possessions on wagons and set off for the West.

American newspapers and politicians began to talk about an idea called "**Manifest Destiny**", meaning that it
15 was the clear intention of fate that the United States should reach from the east coast to the west coast, i. e. from the Atlantic to the Pacific Ocean. In **1848**, after two years of fighting and war, the **annexation of the Mexican territories** completed the "Manifest Destiny" of the USA, which had grown from a small area along the east coast to one of the largest countries in the world.

When the **Puritans** disembarked in **Massachusetts in 1620**, they believed they were "**God's Chosen People**"
20 who were being guided by God and divine Providence, and that **America was the "Promised Land"** in which they would establish the New Israel. Thomas Jefferson and Benjamin Franklin considered images of the Promised Land for the Nation's Great Seal. By the middle of the nineteenth century this promise seemed to have been delivered to the American people.

The American Dream: "Opportunity for Each"?

John Steinbeck

Cannery Row

AWARENESS

John Steinbeck (1902 – 1968) was an American writer who was awarded the Pulitzer Prize for his famous novel *The Grapes of Wrath* (1939), and the Nobel Prize for Literature in 1962. As Steinbeck was a native of Salinas, California, the area of Monterey and Salinas served as a background for several of his novels. In 1944, after returning from World War II, where he served as a correspondent, he became nostalgic for his Pacific Grove/Monterey life in the 1930s and wrote the novel *Cannery Row*. The novel revolves around the people living in the abandoned sardine fisheries in Monterey during the Great Depression.

Based on the novel's background – the economic crisis of the 1930s and the abandoned canning and fishing companies in Monterey – imagine what kind of people might have lived there and what the atmosphere might have been like.

1 Cannery Row in Monterey in California is a poem, a stink, a grating[1] noise, a quality of light, a tone, a habit, a nostalgia, a dream. Cannery Row is the gathered and the scattered[2], tin and iron and rust and splintered
5 wood, chipped pavement and weedy[3] lots and junk heaps, sardine canneries of corrugated iron[4], honky tonks[5], restaurants and whore houses, and little crowded groceries, and laboratories and flophouses[6]. Its inhabit-
10 ants are, as the man once said, "whores, pimps[7], gamblers, and sons of bitches," by which he meant Everybody. Had the man looked through another
15 peephole he might have said, "Saints and angels and martyrs[8] and holy men," and he would have meant the same thing.

20 **2** In the morning when the sardine fleet has made a catch, the purse-seiners[9] waddle[10] heavily into the bay blowing their whistles. The deep-laden
25 boats pull in against the coast where the canneries dip their tails into the bay. The figure is advisedly[11] chosen, for if the canneries dipped their mouths into the bay the canned sardines which emerge[12] from the other end would be metaphorically, at least, even more horrifying. Then cannery whistles 30 scream and all over the town men and women scramble[13] into their clothes and come running down to the

A film still of Cannery Row from the 1982 movie

[1] **grating** (of a sound or sb.'s voice) unpleasant to listen to – [2] **scattered** spread far apart over a wide area – [3] **weedy** here: full of or covered with weeds (*Unkraut*) – [4] **corrugated iron** *Wellblech* – [5] **honky tonk** here: a cheap, noisy bar or dance hall – [6] **flophouse** (*infml.*) a cheap place to stay for people who have no home – [7] **pimp** a man who employs prostitutes and who lives on the money they earn – [8] **martyr** [mɑːtə(r)] a person who suffers very much or is killed because of their religious or political beliefs – [9] **purse-seiner** a type of fishing boat – [10] **to waddle** to walk with very short steps, swinging from side to side like a duck – [11] **advisedly** (*fml.*) carefully – [12] **to emerge from sth.** to come out of a dark or hidden place – [13] **to scramble** here: to move quickly, esp. with difficulty

Row to go to work. Then shining cars bring the upper classes down: super-intendents, accountants[14], owners
35 who disappear into offices. Then from the town poor Wops[15] and Chinamen and Polaks, men and women in trousers and rubber coats and oilcloth aprons[16]. They come running to clean and cut and pack and cook and can the fish. The whole street rumbles and groans[17] and
40 screams and rattles while the silver rivers of fish pour in out of the boats and the boats rise higher and higher in the water until they are empty. The canneries rumble and rattle and squeak until the last fish is cleaned and cut and cooked and canned and then the whistles scream
45 again and the dripping, smelly, tired Wops and China-men and Polaks, men and women, straggle out and droop[18] their ways up the hill into the town and Cannery Row becomes itself again – quiet and magical. Its normal life returns. The bums[19] who retired in disgust under the
50 black cypress tree come out to sit on the rusty pipes in the vacant lot. The girls from Dora's emerge for a bit of sun if there is any. Doc strolls[20] from the Western Bio-logical Laboratory and crosses the street to Lee Chong's

grocery for two quarts[21] of beer. Henri the painter noses like an Airedale through the junk in the grass-grown lot 55 for some part or piece of wood or metal he needs for the boat he is building. Then the darkness edges in and the street light comes on in front of Dora's – the lamp which makes perpetual[22] moonlight in Cannery Row. Callers arrive at Western Biological to see Doc, and he crosses 60 the street to Lee Chong's for five quarts of beer.

3 How can the poem and the stink and the grating noise – the quality of light, the tone, the habit and the dream – be set down[23] alive? When you collect marine animals there are certain flat worms[24] so delicate that 65 they are almost impossible to capture whole, for they break and tatter[25] under the touch. You must let them ooze[26] and crawl of their own will onto a knife blade and then lift them gently into your bottle of sea water. And perhaps that may be the way to write this book – to 70 open the page and to let the stories crawl in by them-selves.

from *Cannery Row* by John Steinbeck. Viking Press, New York 1945, pp. 1f.

COMPREHENSION

1. What impression of the atmosphere on Cannery Row does the film still of the 1982 film version convey?

2. The text at hand has already been subdivided into three sections to give you some structural help.
Read the different paragraphs **individually** at first, and try to get a general understanding.
 Next, **team up with a partner** and compare and crosscheck your findings.
Finally, read the text **a second time and complete your notes** on the following tasks:

1
- Point out the overall atmosphere of Cannery Row.
- What kinds of buildings are there?
- Who are the inhabitants of Cannery Row and what kind of people work there?

The description here presents a kind of "before and after" situation:
2
- What happens in the morning when the sardine fleet has made a catch?
- What different kinds of men and women work in the factories/canneries and offices?
- How does the scenery change after the catch is taken care of?
- What kind of people "emerge" then?
- What is the atmosphere like in the evening?

---

[14] **accountant** *Buchhalter* – [15] **Wop** (*sl.*) a very offensive word for a person from southern Europe, esp. an Italian – [16] **oilcloth aprons** *Wachstucharbeitsschürzen* – [17] **to groan** to make a long, deep sound because you are annoyed or in pain – [18] **to droop** here: to sag downwards from being tired – [19] **bum** here: sb. who has no job or home – [20] **to stroll** to walk somewhere in a slow relaxed way – [21] **a quart (of sth.)** a unit for measuring liquids, equal to about one litre – [22] **perpetual** continuous – [23] **to set sth. down** to write sth. down on paper in order to record it – [24] **worm** [wɜːm] *Wurm* – [25] **to tatter** here: tear – [26] **to ooze** to move or flow very slowly (esp. a thick liquid)

3
- What "strategy" is used in order to catch a certain delicate kind of marine animal?
- Which similarities does the narrator see between delicate marine animals and the description of life in Cannery Row?

ANALYSIS

3. Steinbeck makes use of different kinds of enumeration*. Find examples and explain the effect they have.

4. In this excerpt Steinbeck juxtaposes metaphorical* and poetic language with colloquialisms and slang. In what way does this use of different language registers* reflect Cannery Row and its inhabitants?

5. Many of the verbs employed in the excerpt refer to the senses and motion. Find examples from the text and explain their effect.

6. "If we are to make the dream come true we must all work together, no longer to build bigger, but to build better. There is a time for quantity, and a time for quality" (cf. FoD, The American Dream, p. 192). Compare the situation described in the text at hand to the quotation from John Truslow Adams' book. How has "the dream come true"?
   → Focus on Skills, Analysis of a Fictional Text, p. 402

ACTIVITIES

7. Imagine you are a migrant and have ended up on Cannery Row. Write a letter home describing your life.

8. This excerpt is the expository part of the novel. Especially in the last paragraph Steinbeck reflects on how to make his characters come to life. Against the background of who and what is introduced here, what do you expect to happen in the novel and what will it focus on?

Focus on Documents

The American Dream

The phrase "American Dream" includes a wide range of hopes and beliefs that are commonly connected with the ideas expressed in the Declaration of Independence (1776), such as "Life, Liberty and the Pursuit of Happiness".
5 The Founding Fathers themselves, in fact, never used this term.

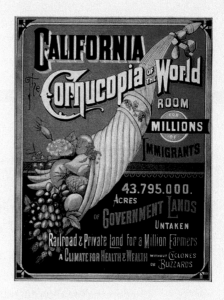

How "the dream" came into existence

In the middle of the Great Depression, in **1931**, the American writer and historian **James Truslow Adams** (1878 – 1949) coined the term "the American Dream" in his book *The Epic of America*.
In the preface to this book Adams expresses his attempts to paint a
5 picture of "the beginnings at their several points of entry of such American concepts as '**bigger and better**,' and of our attitude toward business, of many characteristics which are generally considered as being 'typically American,' and, in special, of that **American dream of a better, richer, and happier life for all our citizens of every rank** which is the greatest contribution we have as yet made to the thought
10 and welfare of the world. That dream or hope has been present from the start."

How the American settlers shaped "the dream"

"The settlers had come from a land with a strongly stratified social scale. They were not engaged in building a Utopia. Their hope was for a civilization which should be, as soon as might be, like that they had known, but in which they would each **be freer, richer, and more independent**."
"It was this **'land in the woods' as a possibility for almost every inhabitant** of America that was to prove one
5 of the most powerful of the forces which worked toward **a democracy of feeling and outlook**, toward the shaping of our American Dream."

The "dream" in the twentieth century

"… there has been also the *American dream*, that dream of a land in **which life should be better and richer and fuller for every man**, with **opportunity for each according** to his ability or achievement. It is a difficult dream for the European upper classes to interpret adequately, and too many of us ourselves have grown weary and mistrustful of it. It is not a dream of motor cars and high wages merely, but **a dream of a social order** in which
5 **each man and each woman shall be able to attain to the fullest stature** of which they are innately capable, and **be recognized by others for what they are**, regardless of the fortuitous circumstances of birth or position."
"… the American dream that has lured tens of millions of all nations to our shores in the past century has not been a dream of merely material plenty, though that has doubtless counted heavily. It has been much more than that. It has been **a dream of being able to grow to fullest development as man and woman**, unhampered
10 by the barriers which had slowly been erected in older civilizations, unrepressed by social orders which had developed for the benefit of classes rather than for the simple human being of any and every class. And that dream has been realized more fully in actual life here than anywhere else, though very imperfectly even among ourselves. It has been a great epic and a great dream."
"If the American dream is to come true and to abide with us, it will, at bottom, depend on the people themselves.
15 If we are to achieve a richer and fuller life for all, they have got to know what such an achievement implies. […] If we are to make the dream come true we must all work together, **no longer to build bigger, but to build better. There is a time for quantity and a time for quality.**"

from *The Epic of America* by James Truslow Adams. Little, Brown & Co., Boston 1931

Wanted: The Dream – Dead or Alive?

Before reading the article about the "American Dream" on the following page, complete the following activity: Together with a partner, take a look at the cartoons below depicting views on income inequality and social mobility in the US. Describe the cartoons to each other using the vocab boxes and paying attention to details.

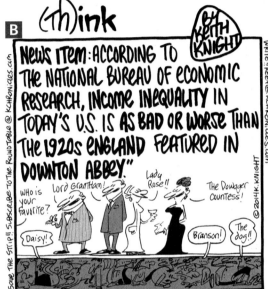

Tips on vocab »

bunk bed ■ rope ladder ■ to fall off

top: golden ornaments ■ to loll (*sich lümmeln*) ■ to lounge ■ to drink champagne ■ to be dolled up

middle: different ethnicities ■ to sit cross-legged ■ to lean against sth. ■ reading lamp ■ duvet (*Federbett*)

bottom: to be cramped ■ to look sleepy ■ ragged blankets ■ metal springs ■ naked bulb (*Glühlampe*) ■ to look stunned

Tips on vocab »

top: to wear evening dress ■ tuxedo/dinner jacket

bottom: to be crammed (*eingepfercht sein*) ■ squeezed (*gequetscht*) ■ to crawl (*herumkriechen*) ■ to squat (*hocken, kauern*) ■ to crouch down (*sich zusammenkauern*)

1. Now, what would happen if the American Dream did *not* go on?
   In a 4-corners activity, reflect on and discuss the introductory question of the first article: "Could America survive the end of the American Dream?"
   Before choosing "your" corner and collecting arguments, reactivate your knowledge of the American Dream and read the corresponding Focus on pages in your Students' Book (→ FoF American Beliefs and Values, p. 176; FoD The American Dream, p. 192).

1 The American Dream, RIP?

Could America survive the end of the American Dream? The idea is unthinkable, say political leaders of right and left. Yet it is predicted in "Average is Over", a bracing[1] new book by Tyler Cowen, an economist. Mr Cowen is no stranger to controversy. In 2011 he galvanized[2] Washington with "The Great Stagnation", in which he argued that America has used up[3] the low-hanging fruit of free land, abundant[4] labour and new technologies. His new book suggests that the disruptive[5] effects of automation and ever-cheaper computer power have only just begun to be felt.

It described a future largely stripped[6] of middling jobs and broad prosperity. An elite 10–15% of Americans will have the brains and self-discipline to master tomorrow's technology and extract profit from it, he speculates. They will enjoy great wealth and stimulating[7] lives. Others will endure[8] stagnant or even falling wages, as employers measure their output with "oppressive precision". Some will thrive as service-providers to the rich. A few will claw[9] their way into the elite (cheap online education will be a great leveler), bolstering[10] the idea of a "hyper-meritocracy[11]" at work: this "will make it easier to ignore those left behind".

Mr Cowen's vision is neither warm nor fuzzy[12]. In his future, mistakes and even mediocrity[13] will be hard to hide: e. g., an ever-expanding array[14] of ratings will expose so-so doctors and also patients who do not take their medicines or otherwise spell trouble. Young men will struggle in a labour market that rewards conscientiousness[15] over muscle. With incomes squeezed, many Americans will head to the sort of cheap, sun-baked sprawling[16] exurbs[17] that give the farmers'-market-and-bike-lanes set[18] heartburn[19]. [...] The left is sure that inequality is a recipe for riots. Mr Cowen doubts it. The have-nots will be too engrossed[20] in video games to light real petrol bombs. An ageing population will be rather conservative, he thinks. There will be lots of Tea-Party sorts[21] among the economically left-behind. Aid for the poor will be slashed[22] but benefits for the old preserved. He does not fear protectionism, as most jobs that can be sent overseas have already gone. He notes that the late 1960s, when society was in turmoil, was a golden age of income equality, while some highly unequal moments in history, including in medieval times, were rather stable. [...]

Inter-generational tensions fuelled 1960s unrest and would be back with a vengeance[23], this time in the form of economic competition for scarce resources. The Middle Ages were stable partly because peasants[24] could not vote; an unhappy modern electorate, by contrast, would be prey[25] to demagogues[26] peddling[27] simple solutions, from xenophobia[28] to soak-the-rich taxes[29], or harsh, self-defeating crime policies. Yet Mr Cowen's main point is plausible: gigantic shifts are under way, and they may be unstoppable. [...]

In short, both sides never tire of explaining how the other is destroying the American Dream. Alas, neither can explain, convincingly, how to revive it. [...]

Many voters remember a time when hard work was reliably rewarded with economic security. This was not really true in the 1950s and 60s if you were black or female, but the question still remains: what if Mr Cowen is right? What if the bottom 85% today are mostly doomed[30] to stay there? In a country founded on hope, that would require something like a new social contract. Politicians cannot duck[31] Mr Cowen's conundrum[32] forever.

The Economist, 21 September 2013, p. 41

---

[1] **bracing** here: thought-provoking – [2] **to galvanize** *wachrütteln* – [3] **to use sth. up** *etw. aufbrauchen* – [4] **abundant** more than enough – [5] **disruptive** *Unruhe stiftend* – [6] **to strip sth.** to remove sth. – [7] **stimulating** interesting – [8] **to endure** to suffer sth. difficult or painful – [9] **to claw your way** (*idm.*) *sich durchkämpfen* – [10] **to bolster** to support sth. or make it stronger – [11] **hyper-meritocracy** [haɪpər-ˈmerɪˈtɒkrəsi] *Über-Leistungsgesellschaft* – [12] **warm and fuzzy** making you feel happy and comforted – [13] **mediocrity** [ˈmiːdiˈɒkrəti] *Mittelmaß* – [14] **array** here: a large number – [15] **conscientiousness** [ˈkɒnʃiˈenʃəsnəs] *Pflichtbewusstsein* – [16] **sprawling** spreading in an untidy way– [17] **exurb** a commuter town that lies beyond the suburbs, usually wealthy – [18] **farmers'-market-and-bike-lanes set** wealthy, privileged people who lead an alternative, environmentally conscious lifestyle – [19] **heartburn** *Sodbrennen* – [20] **to engross** *sich vertiefen* – [21] **Tea-Party sorts** (*disapprov.*) supporters of the Tea Party – [22] **to slash** *etw. drastisch kürzen* – [23] **with a vengeance** [ˈvendʒəns] (*infml.*) to a greater degree than is expected or usual – [24] **peasant** [ˈpezənt] *Landarbeiter* – [25] **prey** victim – [26] **demagogue** [ˈdeməgɒg] *Populist* – [27] **to peddle** *hausieren* – [28] **xenophobia** *Fremdenfeindlichkeit* – [29] **soak-the-rich taxes** tax laws that favour the wealthy – [30] **doomed** *verdammt* – [31] **to duck sth.** to avoid sth. – [32] **conundrum** a problem that is difficult to deal with

2 Class in America: Mobility, Measured

America is no less socially mobile than it was a generation ago

Americans are deeply divided as to whether widening inequality is a problem, let alone what the government should do about it. Some are appalled[1] that Bill Gates has so much money; others say good luck to him: But nearly everyone agrees that declining[2] social mobility is a bad thing. Barack Obama's state-of-the union speech on January 28th [2014] dwelt on[3] how America's "ladders of opportunity" were failing [...].

Paul Ryan and Marco Rubio, two leading Republicans, recently gave speeches decrying[4] social immobility and demanding more effort to ensure poor people who work hard can better their lot. Just as the two sides have found something to agree on, however, a new study suggests the conventional wisdom may be wrong. Despite huge increases in inequality, America may be no less mobile a society than it was 40 years ago.

The study, by a clutch[5] of economists at Harvard University and the University of California, Berkeley, is far bigger than any previous effort to measure social mobility. The economists crunch numbers[6] from over 40 m tax returns of people born between 1971 and 1993 (with all identifying information removed). They focus on mobility between generations and use several ways to measure it, including the correlation of parents' and children's income, and the odds that a child born into the bottom fifth of the income distribution will climb all the way up to the top fifth.

They find that none of the measures has changed much. In 1971, a child from these poorest fifth had an 8.4% chance of making it to the top quintile[7]. For a child born in 1986 the odds[8] were 9%. The study confirms previous findings that America's social mobility is low compared with many European countries. (In Denmark, a poor child has twice as much chance of making it to the top quintile as in America.) But it challenges several smaller recent studies that concluded that America had become less socially mobile. [...]

The result has caused a huge stir[9], not least because it runs counter[10] to public perceptions. A recent Gallup[11] poll found that only 52% of Americans think there is plenty of opportunity for the average Joe[12] to get ahead, down from 81% in 1998. It also jars[13] with other circumstantial evidence. Several studies point to widening gaps between rich and poor in the factors you would expect to influence mobility, such as the quality of schools or parents' investment of time and money in their children. Cross-country analyses also suggest there is an inverse[14] relationship between income inequality and social mobility – a phenomenon that has become known as the "Great Gatsby" curve[15]. [...]

Most likely, the answer lies in the nature of America's inequality, whose main characteristic is the soaring[16] share of overall income going to the top 1% (from 10% in 1980 to 22% 8n 2012). The correlation between vast wealth accruing[17] to a tiny elite and the ability of people to move between the rest of the rungs[18] of the income ladder may be small – at least for now.

Whatever the explanation, it would be unwise to take much comfort from this study. For a start, since the gap between top and bottom has widened, the consequences of an accident of birth have become bigger. Second, if the gains of growth are going mostly to those at the top, that bodes ill[19] for those whose skills are less in demand. Many economists worry that living standards for the non-elite will stagnate for a long time. [...]

The economists found five factors that were correlated with differences in social mobility in different parts of America: residential segregation (whether by

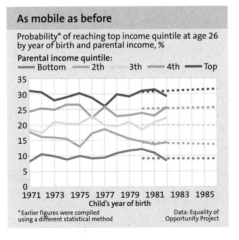

As mobile as before

Probability* of reaching top income quintile at age 26 by year of birth and parental income, %

Parental income quintile:
— Bottom — 2th — 3th — 4th — Top

Child's year of birth
1971 1973 1975 1977 1979 1981 1983 1985

* Earlier figures were compiled using a different statistical method

Data: Equality of Opportunity Project

---

[1] **appalled** *entsetzt* – [2] **to decline** to gradually become less, worse or lower – [3] **to dwell on sth.** (*phr. v.*) to keep thinking or talking about sth., esp. sth. unpleasant – [4] **to decry** (*fml.*) to criticize sth. as bad, without value or unnecessary – [5] **clutch** a small group of people – [6] **to crunch numbers** *rechnen* – [7] **quintile** a fifth – [8] **the odds** *Wahrscheinlichkeit* – [9] **stir** (*infml.*) a lot of interest or excitement – [10] **to run counter sth.** *etw. entgegenlaufen* – [11] **Gallup** an American research-based consulting company – [12] **the average Joe** sb. who is just like everyone else; a normal person – [13] **to jar** to disagree – [14] **inverse** opposite in relation to sth. else – [15] **the Great Gatsby curve** a chart illustrating the relationship between inequality and intergenerational social immobility in several countries around the world – [16] **to soar** to rise very quickly to a high level – [17] **to accrue** (*fml.*) to increase in number over a period of time – [18] **rung** one of the bars that forms a step in a ladder – [19] **to bode ill** to be a sign that sth. bad will happen in the future

income or race); the quality of schooling; family struc-ture (e. g. how many children live with only one par-ent); "social capital" (such as taking part in community groups); and inequality (particularly income gaps among those outside the top 1%). Social mobility is higher in integrated places with good schools, strong families, lots of community spirit and smaller income gaps within the broad middle class. Not a bad agenda[20], for politicians to push, if only they knew how.

The Economist, 1 February 2014, p. 35

③ Barack Obama: State of the Union Address, 28 January 2014

Tips on vocab »

to rebound *zurückschnellen, sich erholen* ▪ **grit** (*fig.*) *Entschlossenheit* ▪ **to hinder** to limit the development of sth. ▪ **rancorous** [ˈræŋkərəs] (*fml.*) having a feeling of hate and continued anger about sth. in the past; *verbittert* ▪ **stock price** *Aktienpreis* ▪ **scope** extent or range ▪ **CEO** (*abbr.*) chief executive officer; the person with the highest rank in a company ▪ **to insource** to do work within a company rather than employing another organization to do it ▪ **riddled with sth.** (*idm.*) full of sth., especially sth. bad ▪ **loophole** *Schlupfloch* ▪ **to flip sth.** to turn sth. over quickly ▪ **equation** a difficult problem or complex situation

COMPREHENSION »»»»»

2. The three texts above – two magazine articles and an excerpt from a political speech – take different views on the "well-being" of the American Dream and its promises. They were all published within four months, between September 2013 and February 2014.

Before reading/listening, divide the class into three groups, with each group working with one of the texts and doing the respective assignments.

Here are some **methodological tips** on how to work in your team:

Step 1:
- Read/listen to the text individually first.
- Take notes on words, phrases, references, etc. you do not understand.
- Take notes on information, facts, numbers, etc. you consider relevant.

Step 2:
- In your group, ask each other questions about anything you do not understand and clarify unknown vocabulary, etc.
- Use a dictionary for help.
- Correct and/or add relevant information to your notes if necessary.

Step 3: Read/listen to your text a second time and complete your notes.

While reading/listening, focus and take notes on these points:

1
- the effects of automation and cheap computer power
- the widening gap between the elite and "the rest"
- the effects of ratings on people and businesses
- the reaction of a growing group of have-nots
- the consequences of political and social instability

---

[20] **agenda** [əˈdʒendə] *Tagesordnung*

2
- the political disparity in America
- Harvard University's findings on social mobility
- the results of the Gallup poll and other studies
- America's income inequality
- the five factors of social mobility

3
- the positive results of the government's efforts
- the threat to the upward trend
- future opportunities
- current inequalities and stagnations
- factors affecting opportunity

→ Focus on Skills, Listening Comprehension, p. 394

Finally, the groups should present their results to the whole class in short presentations.
→ Focus on Skills, Presentations, p. 419

ANALYSIS

C

DAVE GRANLUND © www.davegranlund.com

All groups:

3. Examine the line of argument* and train of thought* in your text and explain how the given examples and factual information emphasize the message of the text.
→ Focus on Skills, Analysis of a Non-Fictional Text, p. 405

4. Against the background of Barack Obama's State of the Union Address, describe and analyse cartoon no. 3.
→ Focus on Skills, Analysis of Visuals, p. 409

ACTIVITIES

5. a) Contrast the social and economic realities of 2013/14 as presented in the texts to Obama's "wishlist" of 2005 (cf. pp. 179 ff.). Which of his dreams have come true?
   b) As a hard-working American citizen and long-standing supporter of Obama's politics, you are disappointed and annoyed about the social and economic state of the country. Write a letter to your president in which you express your frustration and demand the change that was promised.

Tip: Your letter should refer to the president's speech(es) as well as the information given in the articles.
→ Focus on Skills, Writing a Formal Letter, p. 424
→ Focus on Skills, Writing a Letter to the Editor, p. 431

GRAMMAR / LANGUAGE

6. Report the excerpt from Obama's State of the Union speech to a friend who has not had the opportunity of listening to it. Use **indirect speech** and pay attention to the **tenses** and **pronouns**. Do not forget to formulate an appropriate introductory sentence.
The vocab box provides you with some verbs to begin with.

Examples:
- The President <u>emphasized</u> the importance of the citizens to strengthen the state …
- He then <u>presented</u> the results of <u>their</u> efforts …

Tips on vocab »
> to highlight ■ to present ■ to focus on ■ to criticize ■ to doubt ■ to refer to ■ to ask for sth. ■ to accuse sb. of sth. ■ to demand ■ to question whether … ■ to underline

Broke[1] in the 'Burbs[2]

Years ago, people moved from the cities to the suburbs in order to find a better quality of life. Collect ideas why
a) living in the suburbs was attractive for many people and families in the past,
b) suburban areas have become increasingly problematic with regard to poverty, crime and municipal services like schools, hospitals, sanitation and transportation.

Kim, who is 35 years old and has two children, left high school to look after her mother, a cocaine addict[3]. When Kim's marriage began to fail and her husband fell ill, she developed addictions of her own – to alcohol and pills, from which she has been free for eight months. She now works at a fast-food restaurant, making, she guesses, around $14,000 a year.

Melissa once had an event-planning company. She says it was doing well, but "when the economy went down it took my company with it". She is now jobless. She and her 16-month-old son live in an apartment provided by the Centre for Family Resources (CFR), a charity. Kim and Melissa live in Cobb County, north-west of Atlanta. It ranks fifth out of Georgia's 159 counties in income per head, at $33,514 – well above the American median of $27,915 and nearly three times the poverty level of $11,484 for a single person. It is home to a big convention centre[4] and some smart malls[5] and hotels. But it is also home to many who are hard-up[6]. In 2000 6.5% of the people in Cobb County were poor; in 2011, 12.6% were. CFR saw requests for help with the rent rise from 207 in January 2010 to 577 in January this year. The number of people who came in asking for assistance of some kind rose from 754 in January 2009 to 1,326 in January 2013.

Americans tend to think of poverty as urban or rural – housing estates[7] or shacks[8] in the woods. And it is true that poverty rates tend to be higher in cities and the countryside. But the suburbs are where you will find America's biggest and fastest-growing poor population, as Elizabeth Kneebone and Alan Berube of the Brookings Institution explain in their book "Confronting Suburban Poverty in America". Between 2000 and 2010 the number of people living below the federal poverty line ($22,314 for a family of four in 2010) in the suburbs grew by 53%, compared with just 23% in cities. In 2010 roughly 15.3m poor people lived in the suburbs, compared with 12.8m in cities (see chart).

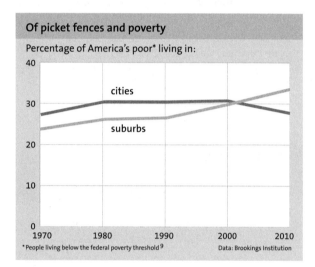

Of picket fences and poverty

Percentage of America's poor* living in:

*People living below the federal poverty threshold [9]   Data: Brookings Institution

Suburban poverty began to rise before the recession. As American cities have grown safer and richer, homes there have become less affordable. During the subprime[10] bubble, many people with bad credit scores[11] got mortgages[12] and moved to the suburbs. A shift towards housing vouchers[13] and away from massive urban projects encouraged people in subsidized[14] housing to make the same move. Immigrants, too, chased the American dream of neat lawns and picket fences[15]. Now 51% of immigrants (who are more likely than the native-born to be poor) live in suburbs, compared with just 33% in cities.

When the bubble burst, the suburbs suffered. Construction and manufacturing, two of the most suburban industries, lost more jobs between 2007 and 2010 than any other sector.

---

[1] **broke** bankrupt – [2] **burb** (*abbr., infml.*) suburb – [3] **addict** *Süchtige(r)* – [4] **convention centre** *Messezentrum* – [5] **smart mall** shopping centre, especially for wealthy people – [6] **hard-up** (*infml.*) having very little money – [7] **estate** a large area of land owned by a family or business – [8] **shack** *Baracke* – [9] **threshold** *Schwelle* – [10] **subprime** the practice of lending money to people who may not be able to pay it back – [11] **score** *Bewertung* – [12] **mortgage** [ˈmɔːɡɪdʒ] *Hypothek* – [13] **voucher** coupon – [14] **to subsidize** *subventionieren* – [15] **picket fence** *Lattenzaun*

Nowhere is it easy to be poor, but the suburbs present particular difficulties. Consider Cobb County, where Kim and Melissa live. Atlanta's commuter-rail system, MARTA, does not run to Cobb. That leaves the carless, such as Kim, or those who have a car but worry about the cost of petrol, like Melissa, dependent on the bus. But Cobb's bus network bypasses much of the county and does not run on Sundays. During non-rush hours, service is spotty[16]; during rush hours, the traffic is awful. So relying on buses can easily add two or three hours to an eight-hour day. Rents have been rising, says Kate Tettamant, a CFR case manager; some of her clients spend half their income on rent. Flexible child care – essential if you are working odd[17] hours – is also hard to find.

One might wonder why the suburban poor do not simply pack up and move back to the cities. Many remain in the suburbs for the same reasons others do: safety, better schools and cheaper homes. And increasingly, suburbia is where the jobs are: between 2000 and 2010 the number of jobs within three miles of central business districts in America's 100 biggest cities fell by 10.4 %, while the number of jobs 10 – 35 miles away rose by 1.2 %.

But while suburban jobs and suburban poverty are both growing, America's anti-poverty infrastructure lags[18]. Suburban safety nets can be thin and patchy[19]; grant-making[20] organisations are often used to focusing on urban rather than suburban poverty. Just as many of the suburban poor have never experienced poverty before, so many of the organisations that help the poor have been overwhelmed by the rapid rise in numbers, says Lesley Grady, a vice-president of the Community Foundation for Greater Atlanta, a charity. Unlike cities, too, suburbs are not politically cohesive[21] entities[22]: they shift, expand and cut across[23] boundaries. Metropolitan Atlanta, for instance, comprises[24] nearly 30 counties, each with its own government, laws and regulations. To be effective, aid organisations must find a way to co-ordinate across those political boundaries. Doing so will not be easy: governments do not easily cede[25] or share power. But for the sake of Kim, Melissa and millions like them, America will have to try.

www.economist.com/news/united-states/21582019-poverty-has-moved-suburbs-broke-burbs, 20 July 2013 [20.08.2014]

COMPREHENSION

1. Give quotes from the text that refer to these topics:
- Cobb County faces increasing poverty rates
- American cities and suburban areas have undergone dramatic changes
- well-to-do people move back to the cities
- suburbs pose problems for low-income families
- many Americans stay in the suburbs
- America's anti-poverty measures are insufficient
- charity and aid organizations fail to help in suburban areas

 2. Team up with a partner and summarize the main points of the text.

ANALYSIS

3. Categorize the magazine article after examining
- the topical order and structure of the text,
- the article's style (e. g. matter-of-fact, passionate, etc.),
- the use of rhetorical devices.
- → Focus on Skills, Analysis of a Non-Fictional Text, p. 405
- → Focus on Facts, Basic Types of Non-Fictional Texts, p. 396
- → Focus on Facts, The Press, p. 398

---

[16] **spotty** lückenhaft – [17] **odd** ungewohnt, seltsam – [18] **to lag** to move so slowly that you are behind other people or things – [19] **patchy** lückenhaft – [20] **grant-making** spendend – [21] **cohesive** [kəʊˈhiːsɪv] united and working together effectively – [22] **entity** Einheit – [23] **to cut across sth.** (phr. v.) überqueren, kreuzen – [24] **to comprise** (fml.) to have sb./sth. as parts and members – [25] **to cede** aufgeben

"Separate But Equal" ... The African-American Struggle for Civil Rights

African-American Encounters ...

While hundreds of thousands of people from all over the world immigrated to the USA to gain freedom and prosperity, a large section of the population involuntarily "immigrated" to the USA – the enslaved people who were caught by slave hunters in Africa and transported to the American colonies via the West Indies.

a) In class, exchange your first impressions of the painting and speculate about its message.

b) Then, reactivate your knowledge of slavery and triangular trade.
→ Focus on Facts, The British Empire, p. 119

c) Now take a closer look at the painting and relate your background knowledge to the crowned figure. What might the artist's intention be?

Jean-Michel Basquiat: Untitled (1982)

Phillis Wheatley: On Being Brought from Africa to America

'Twas mercy brought me from my *Pagan*[1] land,
Taught my benighted[2] soul to understand
That there's a God, that there's a *Saviour* too:
Once I redemption[3] neither sought nor knew.
5 Some view our sable[4] race with scornful[5] eye,
"Their colour is a diabolic die[6]."
Remember *Christians, Negroes*, black as *Cain*[7],
May be refin'd[8], and join th' angelic[9] train.

from *Poems and Letters* by Phillis Wheatley. Ed. C. F. Heartman, New York 1916

Tips on vocab »»

> Aztec god ▪ skull (*Schädel, Totenkopf*) ▪ crown ▪ skeleton ▪ skeletal hands ▪ bone ▪ demonic ▪ distorted/twisted limbs (*deformiert, verdreht*) ▪ archaic ▪ grimace ▪ grotesque face ▪ square contours ▪ colossal ▪ over-sized ▪ scepter ▪ graphic colour patches ▪ shadow ▪ (to) scrawl (*kritzeln*) ▪ strong contrasts

[1] **pagan** ['peɪgən] *heidnisch* – [2] **benighted** (*lit.*) having no knowledge or understanding – [3] **redemption** *Erlösung* – [4] **sable** (*lit.*) black or very dark in colour – [5] **scornful** *verächtlich* – [6] **diabolic die** devilish colour – [7] **Cain** [keɪn] in the Bible Cain is the son of Adam and Eve and the older brother and murderer of Abel – [8] **refined** polite and well-educated – [9] **angelic** [æn'dʒelɪk] heavenly

COMPREHENSION

1. Describe the highly symbolical painting by the American neo-expressionist artist Jean-Michel Basquiat, who was of mixed Haitian and Puerto Rican heritage, and try to find a suitable title for it.
   → Focus on Skills, Analysis of Visuals, p. 409

2. What was the speaker* of the poem taught on the journey to America?

3. State how "some" view the skin colour and race of the African people.

4. What thought does the speaker offer to the "Christians"?

ANALYSIS

5. Specify the topic of the poem.

6. Analyse the poet's use of contrast.

7. Explain the importance of "redemption" for the speaker. Why is this aspect emphasized throughout the poem?

 8. Compare Basquiat's painting and Wheatley's poem. What do the "Pagan" (l. 1) and the crowned figure in the painting have in common?
   → Focus on Skills, Analysis of Poetry and Lyrics, p. 406
   → Focus on Skills, Analysis of Visuals, p. 409

> **Info**
>
> **Phillis Wheatley (1753 – 1784)** was kidnapped from Senegal as a child and sold as a slave to John Wheatley in Boston who discovered her talent and made her take lessons at his home. In 1767, she wrote her first poems which immediately attracted enormous interest. After the death of Wheatley and his wife, who had enfranchised[1] her, she married a free African-American, who left her after a short marriage. Shortly afterwards, she died in humble[2] circumstances.

ACTIVITIES

 9. Do research on Jean-Michel Basquiat and his particular way of portraying the history of African-Americans and slavery, and prepare a presentation in class.
   → Focus on Skills, Presentations, p. 419

Historical African-American Views on Liberty and Slavery

AWARENESS

Reactivate your knowledge of slavery and the American Civil War and try to clarify the terms below in class
(→ FoF The British Empire, p. 119; FoF Landmarks in United States History, p. 184).

Triangular Trade	Civil War	the Union	Confederate States
Underground Railroad	Emancipation Proclamation		Fugitive[1] Slave Law

---

[1] **to enfranchise** to give sb./a group of people the right to vote – [2] **humble** here: of low social class or position

[1] **fugitive** ['fjuːdʒɪtɪv] *Flüchtling*

Before reading:

1. Together with a partner, write down what you associate with the "Fourth of July" (1776) and its importance for Americans.

2. Frederick Douglass (1818 – 1895) was an African-American social reformer, orator, writer and statesman who, after escaping slavery, became a leader of the abolitionist movement and fought for the emancipation of African-Americans in the U. S. In class, reflect on the title of Frederick Douglass' speech. What would a slave's answer have been to that question?
Collect possible answers and discuss them in class.

Frederick Douglass: What, to the Slave, Is the Fourth of July? (1852)

1 Fellow citizens, I am not wanting[2] in respect for the fathers of this republic. The signers of the Declaration of Independence were brave men. They were great men, too – great enough to give frame to a great age. [...] They loved their country better than their own private interests; and, though this is not the highest form of human excellence, all will concede[3] that it is a rare virtue, and that when it is exhibited, it ought to command respect. He who will intelligently lay down his life for his country is a man whom it is not in human nature to despise[4]. Your fathers staked[5] their lives, their fortunes and their sacred honor on the cause of their country. In their admiration of liberty, they lost sight of other interests.
They were peace men; but they preferred revolution to a peaceful submission[6] to bondage[7]. They were quiet men; but they did not shrink[8] from agitating[9] against oppression. They showed their forbearance[10], but that they knew its limits. They believed in order, but not in the order of tyranny[11]. With them, nothing was "settled" that was not right. With them, justice, liberty and humanity were "final", not slavery and oppression. You may well cherish[12] the memory of such men. They were great in their day and generation. Their solid manhood stands out the more as we contrast it with these degenerate times. [...]

2 Fellow citizens, pardon me, allow me to ask, why am I called upon to speak here today? What have I, or those I represent, to do with your national independence? [...] I am not included within the pale[13] of this glorious anniversary! Your high independence only reveals the immeasurable distance between us. The blessings in which you, this day, rejoice[14], are not enjoyed in common. The rich inheritance of justice, liberty, prosperity and independence, bequeathed[15] by your fathers, is shared by you, not by me. The sunlight that brought light and healing to you, has brought stripes[16] and death to me. This Fourth of July is *yours*, not *mine*. *You* may rejoice, *I* must mourn[17]. [...]
What, to the American slave, is your Fourth of July? I answer: a day that reveals to him more than all the other days in the year, the gross[18] injustice and cruelty to which he is a constant victim. To him, your celebration is a sham[19]; your boasted[20] liberty an unholy license; your national greatness swelling[21] vanity[22]; your sounds of rejoicing are empty and heartless; your denunciations of tyrants brass-fronted[23] impudence[24]; your shouts of liberty and equality hollow[25] mockery[26]; your prayers and hymns, your sermons and thanksgivings, with all your religious parade and solemnity[27], are to Him mere bombast, fraud[28], deception[29], impiety[30] and hypocrisy[31] – a thin veil[32] to cover up crimes which would dis-

---

[2] **to be wanting** *mangeln an* – [3] **to concede** to admit, often unwillingly, that sth. is true – [4] **to despise** *verachten* – [5] **to stake** here: to risk sth. – [6] **submission** *Unterwürfigkeit* – [7] **bondage** (*lit.*) the state of being another person's slave – [8] **to shrink** (shrank, shrunk) **from sth.** (*phr. v.*) to avoid doing sth. that is unpleasant or difficult – [9] **to agitate** *gegen etw. agitieren* – [10] **forbearance** (*fml.*) *Duldsamkeit* – [11] **tyranny** ['tɪrəni] – [12] **to cherish** *verehren* – [13] **within the pale** (*fig.*) *innerhalb der Genzen* – [14] **to rejoice** to feel great happiness about sth. – [15] **to bequeath** *vererben* – [16] **stripe** here: *Peitschenhieb* – [17] **to mourn** *trauern* – [18] **gross** unacceptable – [19] **sham** *Betrug, Augenwischerei* – [20] **to boast** *prahlen* – [21] **swelling** *aufgebläht* – [22] **vanity** *Eitelkeit* – [23] **brass-fronted** *mit einer Messingfront* – [24] **impudence** *Unverfrorenheit, Unverschämtheit* – [25] **hollow** *hohl* – [26] **mockery** *Verhöhnung* – [27] **solemnity** *Feierlichkeit* – [28] **fraud** *Betrug* – [29] **deception** *Betrug, Schwindel* – [30] **impiety** [ɪmˈpaɪəti] *Pietätlosigkeit* – [31] **hypocrisy** [hɪˈpɒkrɪsi] *Heuchelei* – [32] **veil** *Schleier*

grace[33] a nation of savages[34]. There is not a nation on the earth guilty of practices more shocking and bloody than the people of the United States at this very hour. Go where you may, search where you will, roam[35] through all the monarchies and despotisms of the Old World, travel through South America, search out every abuse, and when you have found the last, lay your facts by the side of the everyday practices of this nation, and you will say with me, that, for revolting[36] barbarity and shameless hypocrisy, America reigns without a rival.

from *Great Speeches by African Americans* by James Daley (ed.). Dover Publications Inc., New York 2006, pp. 17 ff.

Frank Bell: When I Was a Slave

I was owned by Johnson Bell and born in New Orleans, in Louisiana. Accordin' to the bill of sale, I'm eighty-six years old, and my master was a Frenchman and was real mean to me. He run a saloon and kept bad women. I don't know nothing about my folks, if I even had any, 'cept Mama. They done tell me that she was a bad woman and a French Creole. I worked round master's saloon, kept everything cleaned up after they'd have all night drinkin' parties, men and women. I earned nickels to tip off where to go, so's they could sow wild oats[37]. I buried the nickels under rocks. If Master done cotch[38] me with money, he'd take it and beat me nearly to death. All I had to eat was old stuff those people left, all scraps[39] that was left. [...]

When war[40] was over he won't free me, says I'm valuable to him in his trade. He say, "Nigger, you's supposed to be free but I'll pay you a dollar a week and if you runs off I'll kill you." [...] After long time I marries Feline Graham. Then I has a home and we has a white preacher marry us. We has one boy and he farms and I lives with him. I worked at sawmill and farms all my life, but never could make much money.

You know, the nigger was wild till the white man made what he has out of the nigger. He done educate them real smart.

from *When I Was a Slave, Memoirs*, ed. by Norman Yetman. Dover Publications Inc., New York 2002 (republication from *The Slave Narrative Collection*, 1936 – 1938); pp. 9 ff.

Andrew Goodman: When I Was a Slave

I was born in slavery and I think them days was better for the niggers than the days we see now. One thing was, I never was cold and hungry when my old master lived, and I has been plenty hungry and cold a lot of times since he has gone. But sometimes I think Marse[41] Goodman was the bestest man God made in a long time.

[...]

Marse Bob didn't put his little niggers in the fields till they's big 'nough to work, and the mammies[42] was give time off from the fields to come back to the nursin' home to suck the babies. He didn't never put the niggers out in bad weather. He give us somethin' to do, in out of the weather, like shellin' corn[43], and the women could spin and knit. They made us plenty of good clothes. In summer we wore long shirts, split up the sides, made out of lowerings[44] – that's same as cotton sacks was made out of. In winter we had good jeans and knitted sweaters and knitted socks. [...]

We didn't know what the War was about but Master was gone four years. [...] When Marse Bob come home, he sent for all the slaves. [...] Then he said, "I got something to tell you. You is just as free as I is. You don't belong to nobody but yourselves. We went to the War and fought, but the Yankees[45] done whip[46] us, and they say the niggers is free. You can go where you wants to go, or you can stay here, just as you likes." He couldn't help but cry. The niggers cry and don't know much what Marse Bob means. They is sorry about the freedom, 'cause they don't know where to go, and they's always 'pend on Old Marse to look after them.

from *When I Was a Slave, Memoirs*, ed. by Norman Yetman. Dover Publications Inc., New York 2002 (republication from *The Slave Narrative Collection*, 1936 – 1938); pp. 52 ff.

[33] **to disgrace** *Schande bringen* – [34] **savage** ['sævɪdʒ] (*old-fashioned, taboo*) an offensive word for somebody who belongs to a people that is simple and not developed – [35] **to roam** to move about or travel – [36] **revolting** appalling, *abscheulich* – [37] **to sow your wild oats** *sich die Hörner abstoßen* – [38] **cotch** catch – [39] **scraps** food left after a meal – [40] **war** here: Civil War (1861 – 65) – [41] **Marse** Master – [42] **mammy** (*US, old use*) a black woman whose job is to take care of white children – [43] **to shell corn** *Getreide schälen* – [44] **lowering** *Abfall* – [45] **Yankee** (*infml.*) an American who comes from the northern US – [46] **to whip sb.** here: to defeat sb.

COMPREHENSION

3. The orator uses the first part of the speech to praise the American Founding Fathers and their outstanding political achievements and selfless service to the nation.

In a paired reading activity, read **the first part** of the excerpt and find evidence in the text that matches the aspects mentioned in the statement above.

4. In the **second part**, the speaker's tone changes significantly.

Together with a partner, detect examples in the excerpt in which Douglass
   a) refuses to celebrate the "blessings" of the nation's independence in general,
   b) specifically criticizes the Americans'
   - injustice,   - arrogance/vanity,   - hypocrisy,   - savagery/brutality.

5. First, divide the class into **two groups**, each group working with one of the memoirs – **Frank Bell or Andrew Goodman**.
Then, present the respective person's remarks on
   - how he was treated by his master,
   - what happened to him after the Civil War,
   - what kind of person his master was,
   - how he observed the lives of slaves in general.

ANALYSIS

6. Examine Frederick Douglass' abilities as a speaker and analyse
   - the line of argument*,
   - the choice of words*,
   - the use of rhetorical devices*

he employs in his speech to bring across his message to the audience.
→ Focus on Skills, Analysis of a Political Speech, p. 407

7. Take a close look at the slave memoirs again and compare the language registers of Frederick Douglass and the other two former slaves and find out to what extent they differ.
What does it reveal about their respective education and social status?
→ Focus on Skills, Analysis of a Non-Fictional Text, p. 405

ACTIVITIES

8. Based on your results from task no. 5, imagine how Frank Bell or Andrew Goodman would have responded to Frederick Douglass' question in the title of his speech.

Work out short answers and statements and display and discuss them in class.

Martin Luther King

Letter from Birmingham Jail

AWARENESS

Martin Luther King wrote this open letter from the city jail in Birmingham, Alabama, on 16 April 1963, where he was confined for planning and taking part in the non-violent campaign against racial segregation by Birmingham's city government and downtown retailers.
In a group, explain and define the terms "extreme" and "extremism" and their implications.

But though I was initially disappointed at being categorized as an extremist, as I continued to think about the matter I gradually gained a measure of satisfaction from the label. Was not Jesus an extremist for love:
5 "Love your enemies, bless them that curse you, do good to them that hate you, and pray for them which despitefully[1] use you, and persecute you." Was not Amos[2] an extremist for justice: "Let justice roll down like waters and righteousness like an everflowing stream."
10 Was not Paul an extremist for the Christian gospel: "I bear in my body the marks of the Lord Jesus." Was not Martin Luther an extremist: "Here I stand; I cannot do otherwise, so help me God." And John Bunyan[3]: "I will stay in jail to the end of my days before I make a butch-
15 ery of my conscience." And Abraham Lincoln: "This nation cannot survive half slave and half free." And Thomas Jefferson: "We hold these truths to be self-evident, that all men are created equal ..." So the question is not whether we will be extremists, but what kind of
20 extremists we will be. Will we be extremists for hate or for love? Will we be extremists for the preservation of injustice or for the extension of justice? In that dramatic scene on Calvary's hill[4] three men were crucified for the same crime – the crime of extremism. Two were
25 extremists for immorality, and thus fell below their environment. The other, Jesus Christ, was an extremist

for love, truth, and goodness, and thereby rose above his environment. Perhaps the South, the nation, and the world are in dire[5] need of creative extremists.

from *A Documentary History of the United States* ed. by Richard D. Heffner. Mentor, New York, [5]1991, pp. 333

COMPREHENSION

1. Point out why King thinks that the world is in need of extremists.

2. What kind of extremism is he speaking of? Make a list.

---

[1] **despiteful** *boshaft, gemein* – [2] **Amos** 8th-century B. C. Hebrew prophet whose revolutionary ideas paved the way for cooperation among nations and the belief in one God – [3] **John Bunyan** 7th-century English preacher and author who was jailed for twelve years for preaching without a license – [4] **Calvary's hill** Golgotha, the hill on which Jesus was crucified – [5] **dire** [ˈdaɪə(r)] extremely serious or terrible

ANALYSIS

3. Analyse King's strategy of self-persuasion and pay special attention to the conjunction "but".
→ Focus on Skills, Analysis of a Non-Fictional Text, p. 405

4. Compare the photo taken of King in jail and the cover from *The Economist* and speculate why America locks up too many people.

Webcode SNG-40235-018 @ Do research using the links provided on the webcode and find statistical data about who is in jail and for what reasons/offenses.
→ Focus on Skills, Analysis of Visuals, p. 409

ACTIVITIES

5. Write a letter to Martin Luther King in answer to his letter. What could you tell him that might encourage him to continue to fight for human rights?

6. Fighting for civil rights took place on many different levels and African-American women in particular courageously participated in this struggle. The historical photographs below show two famous African-American women who were forerunners of their time.

a) In a first step, describe the photos and the impression the women make on you.

Webcode SNG-40235-018 @ b) Do further research using the links provided on the webcode and explain which social taboos of their time the women broke.
→ Focus on Skills, Analysis of Visuals, p. 409

Elizabeth Eckford, 15, bullied by a mob at Little Rock Central High School on the first day of the school year, 4 September 1957

Josephine Baker's "banana dance" in the Folies Bergère production "Un Vent de Folie", 1927

Chimamanda Ngozi Adichie
Americanah

The photos below show four famous female artists of African descent who have become either style icons or role models to millions of African-American women. In class, describe the impression the women make on you and speculate about possible reasons for their success. Compare their image and outward appearance to African-American VIPs like Michelle Obama or Oprah Winfrey. What similarities and differences can you detect? Discuss.

American actress, singer and novelist Marsha Hunt, 1969, star of the musical *Hair*

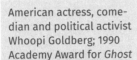

American actress, comedian and political activist Whoopi Goldberg; 1990 Academy Award for *Ghost*

American novelist and professor Toni Morrison; 1993 Nobel Prize in Literature

Mexican-Kenyan actress, film and music director Lupita Nyong'o; 2013 Academy Award for *12 Years a Slave*

The novel *Americanah* by Nigerian author Chimamanda Ngozi Adichie tells the story of Ifemelu, a young Nigerian woman who immigrates to the United States for a university education. In the U.S. she encounters an issue she never thought of in Nigeria: the importance of race.

1 Each heat wave reminded Ifemelu of her first, the summer she arrived. It was summer in America, she knew this, but all her life she had thought of "overseas" as a cold place of wool coats and snow, and because
5 America was "overseas," and her illusions so strong they could not be fended off[1] by reason[2], she bought the thickest sweater she could find in Tejuosho market for her trip. She wore it for the journey, zipping it all the way up in the humming interior of the airplane and
10 then unzipping it as she left the airport building with Aunt Uju. The sweltering heat alarmed her, as did Aunt Uju's old Toyota hatchback[3], with a patch of rust on its side and peeling fabric on the seats. She stared at buildings and cars and signboards, all of them matte[4], disap-
15 pointingly matte; in the landscape of her imagination, the mundane[5] things in America were covered in a high-shine gloss. She was startled[6], most of all, by the teenage boy in the baseball cap standing near a brick wall, face down, body leaning forward, hands between his legs. She turned to look again. 20
"See that boy!" she said. "I didn't know people do things like this in America."
"You didn't know people pee in America?" Aunt Uju asked, barely glancing at the boy before turning back to a traffic light. 25
"Ahn-ahn, Aunty! I mean that they do it outside. Like that."
"They don't. It's not like back home where everybody does it. He can get arrested for that, but it is not a good neighborhood anyway." [...] 30

2 The career services office, an airless space, piles of files[7] sitting forlornly on desks, was known to be full of counselors who viewed résumés and asked you to

[1] **to fend sth. off** (*phr. v.*) *jdn./etw. abwehren* – [2] **by reason** *mit dem Verstand* – [3] **hatchback** *Auto mit Fließheck* – [4] **matte** (*US*) *matt* –
[5] **mundane** [mʌnˈdeɪn] very ordinary; *banal* – [6] **startled** surprised, worried

change the font[8] of your format and gave you outdated contact information for people who never called you back. The first time Ifemelu went there, her counselor[9], Ruth, a caramel-skinned African-American woman, asked, "What do you really want to do?"

"I want a job." [...]

"Do you have a passion, a dream job?"

Ifemelu shook her head. She felt weak, for not having a passion, not being sure what she wanted to do. Her interests were vague[10] and varied, magazine publishing, fashion, politics, television; none of them had a firm shape. [...]

When she told Ruth about the interview in Baltimore, Ruth said, "My only advice? Lose the braids[11] and straighten your hair. Nobody says this kind of stuff but it matters. We want you to get that job." [...]

Since she had come to America, she had always braided her hair with long extensions[12], always alarmed at how much it cost. She wore each style for three months, even four months, until her scalp[13] itched[14] unbearably and the braids sprouted[15] fuzzily[16] from a bed of new growth.

American singer, songwriter and actress Beyoncé Knowles

And so it was a new adventure, relaxing her hair. She removed her braids, careful to leave her scalp unscratched[17], to leave undisturbed the dirt that would protect it. Relaxers[18] had grown in their range[19], boxes and boxes in the "ethnic hair" section of the drugstore, faces of smiling black women with impossibly straight and shiny hair, beside words like "botanical" and "aloe" that promised gentleness. [...] "Girl, you need a professional," the hairdresser said as she reapplied[20] another relaxer. "People think they're saving money by doing it at home, but they're really not."

Ifemelu felt a slight burning, at first, but as the hairdresser rinsed out[21] the relaxer needles of stinging pain shot up from different parts of her scalp, down to different parts of her body, back up to her head.

"Just a little burn," the hairdresser said. "But look how pretty it is. Wow, girl, you've got the white-girl swing[22]!" Her hair was hanging down rather than standing up, straight and sleek[23], parted[24] at the side and curving to a slight bob at her chin. The verve[25] was gone. She did not recognize herself. She left the salon almost mournfully[26]; while the hairdresser had flat-ironed the ends, the smell of burning, of something organic dying which should not have died, made her feel a sense of loss. [...]

At night, she struggled to find a comfortable position on her pillow. Two days later, there were scabs[27] on her scalp. Three days later, they oozed[28] pus[29]. Curt wanted her to see a doctor and she laughed at him. It would heal, she told him, and it did. Later, after she breezed through the job interview, and the woman shook her hand and she said she would be a "wonderful fit" in the company, she wondered if the woman would have felt the same way had she walked up into that office wearing her thick, kinky[30], God-given halo[31] of hair, the Afro. She did not tell her parents how she got the job; her father said, "I have no doubt that you will excel[32]. America creates opportunities for people to thrive. Nigeria can indeed learn a lot from them," while her mother began to sing when Ifemelu said that, in a few years, she could become an American citizen.

from *Americanah* by Chimamanda Ngozi Adichie. Alfred A. Knopf, New York 2014, pp. 104 ff.

---

[7] **file** *Akte* – [8] **font** *Schriftart* – [9] **counselor** *Berater* – [10] **vague** [veɪg] – [11] **braid** *Zopf* – [12] **extensions** *Haarverlängerung* – [13] **scalp** the skin on a person's head – [14] **to itch** *brennen* – [15] **to sprout** *sprießen* – [16] **fuzzy** in an untidy mass of tight curls – [17] **unscratched** without scratches (*Kratzer*) – [18] **relaxer** *Haarglättungsmittel* – [19] **range** *Auswahl* – [20] **to reapply sth.** *etw. erneut auftragen* – [21] **to rinse out** *ausspülen* – [22] **swing** swinging movement – [23] **sleek** *geschmeidig, glatt, glänzend* – [24] **parted** *mit einem Scheitel* – [25] **verve** *Schwung* – [26] **mournful** very sad – [27] **scab** *Schorf* – [28] **to ooze** *heraussickern* – [29] **pus** [pʌs] *Eiter* – [30] **kinky** (*infml.*) *verkorkst* – [31] **halo** [ˈheɪləʊ] *Heiligenschein* – [32] **to excel** [ɪkˈsel] to be extremely good at sth.

3 From Ifemelu's blog

A Michelle Obama Shout-Out Plus Hair as Race Metaphor

White Girlfriend and I are Michelle Obama groupies. So the other day I say to her – I wonder if Michelle Obama has a weave[1], her hair looks fuller today, and all that heat every day must damage it. And she says – you mean her hair doesn't grow like that? So is it me or is that the perfect metaphor for race in America right there? Hair.
5 Ever notice makeover shows on TV, how the black woman has natural hair (coarse[2], coily[3], kinky, or curly) in the ugly "before" picture, and in the pretty "after" picture, somebody's taken a hot piece of metal and singed her hair straight? [...] When you DO have natural negro hair, people think you "did" something to your hair. Actually, the folk with the Afros and dreads[4] are the ones who haven't "done" anything to their hair. You should be asking Beyoncé what she's done. [...] I have natural kinky hair. Worn in cornrows[5], Afros, braids. No, it's not
10 political. No, I'm not an artist or poet or singer. Not an earth mother either. I just don't want relaxers in my hair – there are enough sources of cancer in my life as it is. (By the way, can we ban Afro wigs[6] at Halloween? Afro is not a costume, for God's sake.) Imagine if Michelle Obama got tired of all the heat and decided to go natural and appeared on TV with lots of woolly hair, or tight spirally curls.

from *Americanah* by Chimamanda Ngozi Adichie. Alfred A. Knopf, New York 2014, p. 299

COMPREHENSION

Ifemelu, the novel's protagonist, is a young Nigerian woman who dreams of beginning a new life in the US. While studying and navigating the new country and its culture, she gradually realizes the importance of race in all areas of life in contemporary America.

The material offers different ways to improve your comprehension skills. You can choose between
a) **reading** the text and improving your reading skills,
b) **listening** to the audio version of the text and improving your listening skills,
c) **combining listening and reading** in order to get a better understanding of textual details.

 1. 1. Listen to/read **the first part** of the text and juxtapose Ifemelu's illusion of America with the reality she encounters when arriving in New York City.

illusion	reality
● a cold place	● heat wave
● a place of …	● sweltering heat
● …	● …

2. Sum up Ifemelu's impression of the "American way of life" presented in the first part of the text.
→ Focus on Skills, Writing a Summary, p. 429

 3. Divide the class into two groups, one group working with **part 2**, the other group working with Ifemelu's blog (**part 3**).

 Step 1: Listen to/read the respective part by yourself, taking notes on the questions and aspects mentioned below.

Step 2: In your group, clarify possible questions and crosscheck your listening/reading results.

Step 3: Listen to/read the text again and complete your notes.

[1] **weave** *Haarverlängerung* – [2] **coarse** rough and not smooth or soft – [3] **coily** *gewickelt* – [4] **dreads** (*abbr.*) dreadlocks; *Rastalocken* –
[5] **cornrows** *Flechtfrisur mit vielen eng am Kopf anliegenden Zöpfchen* – [6] **wig** *Perücke*

Step 4: In a group puzzle activity, the groups remix and inform each other about their results.

- Give a short description of the "career services office" and Ruth, the counselor.
- What kind of job does Ifemelu "dream of"?
- Outline Ifemelu's efforts to change her hairstyle.
- Point out the results of Ifemelu's new hairstyle on a) her career and b) her sense of identity.

- Outline Ifemelu's understanding of "hair as a race metaphor" in America.
- What does she criticize about the presentation of black women on TV?
- What reason does Ifemelu give for no longer wanting to have "relaxers in her hair"?
- What does Ifemelu think about Michelle Obama's hair(style)?

→ Focus on Skills, Listening Comprehension, p. 394

ANALYSIS

4. Take a look at the photographs on p. 207 and 208 and relate them to Ifemelu's blog and her understanding of "hair as a race metaphor".
   → Focus on Skills, Analysis of Visuals, p. 409

5. Examine the career services counselor's advice to Ifemelu to "lose the braids and straighten [her] hair" because "it matters" (ll. 47 ff.) in connection with Ifemelu's observations of Michelle Obama's hairstyle. Could Michelle Obama – in her position as First Lady – decide to "go natural" and appear with "lots of woolly hair, or tight spirally curls"?
   → Focus on Skills, Analysis of a Fictional Text, p. 402

6. Examine the reasons given in the text for Ifemelu's changing her outward appearance. Explain which forms of (indirect) racism are depicted by giving evidence from the text.

7. Examine how the mode of presentation* conveys the message of the text (parts 1 and 2).

8. Analyse the rhetorical devices* used in the blog and explain how they support the thesis that hair is a metaphor for race.

9. Explain the hairdresser's remark about Ifemelu's new look ("Wow, girl, you've got the white-girl swing", l. 71). What do you think she means by this?

ACTIVITIES

10. Imagine you work as a career services counselor: You want to strengthen black women's self-esteem and encourage them to "be themselves" but at the same time you need to make them aware of certain rules and requirements of the business world.
    Together with a partner, work out role cards and act out a counselling interview that takes both sides into account. Give Ifemelu tips and recommendations about how to be successful.

11. Ifemelu wonders whether she would have got the job if she had worn "her thick, kinky, God-given halo of hair, the Afro" (ll. 89 f.).

Together with a partner, work out this job interview, employing dialogue* and interior monologue*. What might the woman have said to and asked Ifemelu – what might she have thought about her Afro hairstyle?

Act out these interviews in class and discuss the implications made.

Tip: Your interview can be critical and tense, or humorous and satirical.
→ Focus on Skills, Job Interview, p. 415
→ Focus on Language, Literary Terms, p. 433

12. Comment on and evaluate Ifemelu's blog, and state whether or not you share her views on "hair".
→ Focus on Skills, Writing a Comment and a Review, p. 421

Chris Melzer

Afro – eine Frisur, die Wahlen gewinnt

AWARENESS 》》》》》》》》

"Hair" – whether the Afro hairstyle or growing different kinds of beards – has obviously become fashionable again.
a) In class, reflect on whether or not a certain hairstyle expresses a person's personality.
b) Do you think that having a trendy or exotic hairstyle should be strictly a private matter or should there be something like a "dress code" for hair as well? Discuss in class.

Bill de Blasio wird neuer Bürgermeister von New York. Seinen Sieg hat er wohl Sohn Dante zu verdanken und seinem Afro.

Als die New York Times ihren Lesern den neuen Bür-
5 germeister der Weltstadt vorstellt, ist Bill de Blasio nur das Zweitwichtigste auf der Titelseite. Viel prominenter ist auf der Titelseite sein Sohn Dante – oder besser dessen Frisur. Der gewaltige[1] Afrolook des 16-Jährigen dominiert das Bild, wie er vorher den Wahlkampf[2] do-
10 miniert hat. Hat eine Frisur über den neuen New Yorker Bürgermeister entschieden? Das fragen politische Medien in den USA. Die nicht ganz so politischen Medien fragen sich eher, ob nun ein Trend zurückkehrt. De Blasio lag im Rennen um die Nachfolge[3] von Bürger-
15 meister Michael Bloomberg lange weit hinten. Die Wende kam erst, als der 52-Jährige seine Familie mit in den Wahlkampf einbrachte: seine schwarze Frau Chirlane, seine Tochter Chiara und seinen Sohn Dante. Und dessen Afrofrisur, die wie eine dunkle Pusteblume[4] –

Eine Familie, die für das vielfältige, multikulturelle New York steht – der neue Bürgermeister Bill de Blasio (Mitte) mit seiner Frau Chirlane McCry (r.) und den Kindern Dante und Chiara

---

[1] enormous – [2] election campaign – [3] succession – [4] dandelion/blowball

20 oder auch wie ein Heiligenschein[5] – den Kopf des Teenagers umrahmt[6].

De Blasios Familie ist ein Symbol für das vielfältige, multikulturelle New York, und Dantes Frisur wurde ein Symbol für diese Familie. Anfangs ohne Chancen, 25 gewann letztlich diese Familie die Wahl mit 73,3 Prozent.

„Bill hat die Familie nach vorn gestellt mit einem Afro aus den Siebzigern", sagt Wahlkampfexperte[7] Henry Singleton. „Und das hat alles geändert".

„Dantes Frisur ist so cool", jubelte hollywoodlife.com. 30 Und selbst das Time-Magazine sprach von „Amerikas bekanntestem Afro".

„Kommt der Afro wieder?", fragen bereits einige Modemagazine. Dabei war er ja nie ganz weg. In Deutschland etwa sorgt der brasilianische Abwehrspieler Dante seit 35 Jahren auch mit seinen Haaren für Aufsehen[8]. Mit dem Bürgermeistersohn aus New York teilt er nicht nur den Namen, sondern auch die ungewöhnliche[9] Frisur.

wgr/© dpa

COMPREHENSION

1. Describe the photo of the de Blasio family taken shortly after the announcement of Bill de Blasio's victory. What image of the new mayor of New York City and his family is conveyed?
   → Focus on Skills, Analysis of Visuals, p. 409

_M_ 2. You are given the opportunity to attend an American high school as an exchange student.
   But after reading the German newspaper article you feel unsure about the rules of conduct (*Verhaltensregeln*) in general and the dress code in particular.
   Mediate the article into English and ask the counsellor at your exchange school about the Dos and Don'ts.

_M_ 3. Find information in the German newspaper article that matches the message of the photo and mediate it into English.
   → Focus on Skills, Mediation, p. 412

ANALYSIS

4. **Step 1:** Examine the reasons given in the article for the unexpected landslide victory of Bill de Blasio.

   Step 2: Compare your findings to John de Crèvecœur's text *The American Is a New Man* (pp. 177 f.) and his understanding of somebody who is truly American.
   What similarities and differences do you detect?
   → Focus on Skills, Analysis of a Non-Fictional Text, p. 405

ACTIVITIES

5. You are a journalist from *Ebony* or *Jet*, magazines for African-American readers, and are asked to write an editorial about the new mayor of New York City and his multiethnic family – and the son's hairstyle.

   Refer to political and cultural aspects using the links provided on the webcode.
   → Focus on Skills, Writing a Newspaper Article, p. 427

---

[5] halo – [6] to frame sb./sth. – [7] election campaign expert – [8] to cause a sensation/stir – [9] extraordinary/unusual

The Civil Rights Movement: Fighting for Freedom and Equality

The **peak years of the American civil rights movement** were the **1950s** and **1960s**, when African-Americans kept demonstrating and fighting for human and civil rights, thus forcing the U.S. government **to guarantee** them certain **constitutional rights**, e.g. the right to vote and to attend public facilities like schools, buses or restaurants together with white Americans.

However, African-Americans have been struggling to overcome slavery and racial injustice since the 1717th century and famous leaders and activists like **Sojourner Truth** (1798 – 1883), **Booker T. Washington** (1856 – 1915), **W. E. B. Du Bois** (1868 – 1963) and **Frederick Douglass** (1817 – 1895) paved the way for "modern" activists like **Martin Luther King Jr.** (1929 – 1968) and **Malcolm X** (1925 – 1965).

June 1623	the **first eleven slaves** arrive in New Amsterdam (New York)
1863	President Abraham Lincoln signs **Emancipation Proclamation** that officially abolishes slavery
1865	● 15 April: **President Lincoln is assassinated** by a fanatical Confederate ● the **Thirteenth Amendment** to the Constitution **abolishes slavery** by law; more than 4 mio slaves gain freedom *"Neither slavery nor involuntary servitude … shall exist within the United States, or any other place subject to their jurisdiction."*
1865/66	the **Black Codes**, a set of rules, are passed in the South to "restore all of slavery but its name"; southern blacks are ● denied the right to vote, ● restricted from moving freely, ● denied the right to own land, ● excluded from certain jobs, ● subject to a separate and much more severe penal code, ● prohibited from possessing firearms.
1866	the **Ku Klux Klan** is founded in Tennessee as a fraternal organization opposed to the emancipation of the blacks; white southern "aristocracy" fears "nigger domination" and aims at restoring white supremacy in the South; terrorist acts against blacks like lynching are carried out
1868	the **Fourteenth Amendment** affirms **black citizenship**
1870	the **Fifteenth Amendment** guarantees blacks **the right to vote**
1870s	**racial segregation** is gradually enforced in the **American South**
1890	Louisiana passes a law enforcing "**equal but separate**" access to colleges, trains, etc.
1880s–1920s	peak years of black **lynchings**
1910	**NAACP** (National Association for the Advancement of Colored People) is founded; the U. S.'s oldest civil rights organization
1920s	the **Black Muslims**, later the Nation of Islam, promotes the separation of blacks from white Americans
WWI	**segregated regiments** of white and African-Americans fight for the U. S.
WWII	ca. 1 mio African-American soldiers fight for the U. S.
1955/56	● **Rosa Parks** is arrested in Montgomery, Alabama ● **Montgomery bus boycott** ● 26-year-old Baptist Reverend **Martin Luther King Jr.** begins active participation in the civil rights movement
1957	the **SCLL** (Southern Christian Leadership Conference) is founded to support the protest movement; leader: Martin Luther King Jr.
1960s	● **Malcolm X** becomes famous leader of **Black Muslims**; promotion of a separate black state and acceptance of violence as a means of self-defense

1960s	• **Freedom Riders**: black and white civil rights activists travel through the segregated South to peacefully protest against racial segregation → Gandhian philosophy of non-violent resistance • **sit-ins** at segregated lunch counters in southern towns
1961	January: **John F. Kennedy** is elected **President** of the U.S.
1963–1965	• Martin Luther King Jr. leads **marches from Selma to Montgomery**; civil rights activists march peacefully for the African-Americans' right to vote • 28 August: **March on Washington**; 250,000 people listen to **Martin Luther King's famous speech "I have a dream"**, delivered in front of the Lincoln Memorial in Washington D.C. • 22 November: **assassination of John F. Kennedy** in Dallas, Texas
1964	• President Lyndon B. Johnson signs **Civil Rights Act**, ensuring voting rights to African-Americans • **Freedom Summer**: a campaign to register as many African-American voters in the state of Mississippi as possible • **revival of the Ku Klux Klan** in Mississippi
1965	• 21 February: **assassination of Malcolm X** • President Lyndon B. Johnson signs **Voting Rights Act**; literacy tests required to be allowed to vote are suspended in order to allow many illiterate southern blacks to vote
1965–1968	• **Black Power Movement**; stronger political focus; urban protests • **Black Panthers**: culminating frustration; radicalization; guns; urban protests
1967	Martin Luther King launches **Poor People's Campaign**: economic protest and civil disobedience of rural and urban poor of all races
1968	• 3 April: **Martin Luther King is assassinated** in Memphis, Tennessee • eruption of violence in 125 cities nationwide
1992	April: **riots in Los Angeles** following the beating of African-American Rodney King by white policemen
1995	October: **Million Man March** to Washington D.C. organized by the Nation of Islam to promote "unity, atonement, and brotherhood"; more than 250,000 participants
2008/2012	**Barack Obama** becomes **first African-American President**
2012/2014	• public protests following the killing of unarmed African-American teenagers • 26 February 2012: 17-year-old African-American teenager **Trayvon Martin** is shot by a Hispanic security officer in Sanford, Florida • 9 August 2014: 18-year-old African-American student **Michael Brown** is shot by a white police officer in Ferguson, Missouri
2016	• 5 July: Alton Sterling, a 37-year-old black man, is shot by white police officers in Baton Rouge, Louisiana • 6 July: Philando Castile is shot by a St. Anthony, Minnesota police officer; his girlfriend livestreams a video of the shooting on Facebook • 7 July: at the end of a peaceful *Black Lives Matter* protest, African-American Army Reserve Afghan War veteran Micah Xavier Johnson, 25, shoots five police officers in Dallas, Texas • in response to these shootings, civil unrest and protests are held in New York, St. Paul, Minnesota and Baton Rouge, Louisiana; at least 261 people are arrested

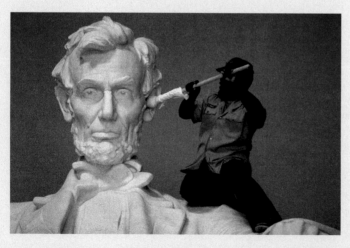

Lincoln Memorial in Washington D.C. being cleaned by an African-American worker

Minorities in the USA: Trying to Get Their Share of the Pie

Mark Helprin

Ellis Island

AWARENESS

The following audio text is an excerpt from a short story that takes place at a time when Ellis Island was still used as a US immigration port (1892 – 1954). It depicts the situation of the protagonist as he goes through the immigration procedure. Reactivate your knowledge about Ellis Island and gather information in class.

COMPREHENSION

1. Look at the photo taken in 1907. What impression do you have of the newly-arrived immigrants and what might their hopes and expectations be?

Fresh off the boat, immigrants wait with their possessions at Ellis Island, 1907

 2. Now, **listen to the first part** of the excerpt and describe the journey across the Atlantic Ocean. How do the passengers try to adapt to the situation on board?
   → Focus on Skills, Listening Comprehension, p. 394

 3. Outline the narrator's observations on Ellis Island as depicted in **the second part** of the excerpt.

4. State the course of the "conversations" between the narrator and the immigration inspectors. What abilities are required of the immigrants?

ANALYSIS

5. Which words does the narrator use to characterize the strenuous (*anstrengend*) journey across the ocean?

6. Examine the stylistic devices* the author employs to underline the challenging and exhausting procedure on Ellis Island.

7. Find allusions to "the dream" in the text.

8. Why do you think the inspector is "very suspicious"?
   → Focus on Skills, Analysis of a Fictional Text, p. 402

9. The immigration procedure has always been a difficult and frightening barrier for immigrants, and inspectors have been trained to critically examine the immigrants' eligibility (*Eignung*) of becoming a U. S. citizen. What impression of the U. S. is conveyed in the cartoon on the following page?
   Compare: How has "Miss Liberty" (and what she represents) changed?
   → Focus on Skills, Analysis of Visuals, p. 409

10. Imagine you work for the American immigration authority (today or in the past) and – in a group – compile a catalogue of questions that immigrants have to answer. You want to find out who is capable of becoming a "real American citizen". Act out this "interview" in class, one student playing the immigrant and one student playing the immigration inspector.

Pathway to U.S. Citizenship

AWARENESS

For an adult immigrant to become a U.S. citizen, he or she must go through the process of naturalization.
The following graphics explain the general requirements.
In a group, discuss what kinds of requirements you consider to be most important when somebody wants to obtain citizenship in their new country.

COMPREHENSION

1. Get an overview of the different steps leading to U.S. citizenship and categorize them according to the different fields they belong to.

residency	lawfulness	moral standards	knowledge	...
• ...	• lawfully admitted	• ...	• basic English skills	• ...
	• ...		• ...	

2. Do further research on the process of naturalization in the USA by using the links provided on the webcode. Gather the information in class.

ANALYSIS

3. Compare the infographic "Pathway to U. S. Citizenship" (p. 218) to the cartoon on page 216. What further qualities and qualifications that immigrants are required to have after 9/11 does the cartoon hint at?

ACTIVITIES

4. Together with a partner, first describe the cartoons and explain how the "path to US Citizenship" is interpreted and mocked.

Then read the Focus on Facts page *The United States: Immigration and Minorities* (p. 219) and inform yourself about recent US immigration reforms. How do the cartoons view the political efforts?

→ Focus on Skills, Analysis of Visuals, p. 409

Tips on vocab »»

to follow a serpentine path ▪ rows of plants ▪ agricultural worker ▪ to be stunned ▪ Hispanic worker ▪ to carry a bundle/bag ▪ to be fooled

Tips on vocab »»

construction site (*Baustelle*) ▪ concrete mixer/concrete lorry ▪ to pour concrete ▪ chute (*Schütte*) ▪ concrete paving slab (*Betonbodenplatte*) ▪ construction worker ▪ donkey (symbol of the Democratic Party) ▪ elephant (symbol of the Republican Party) ▪ to wear working clothes/ garment ▪ out of the corner of one's eye ▪ to steal a glance (*einen verstohlenen Blick werfen*) ▪ bashful (*verschämt*) ▪ to whistle (*pfeifen*) ▪ to be stuck in sth. ▪ to harden (*aushärten*) ▪ to look desperate

Webcode
SNG-40235-020 **5.** Do research on the requirements that immigrants to Germany have to meet by using the links provided on the webcode. Point out the differences and similarities to the U. S. system of naturalization and discuss the possible consequences for potential immigrants in class.

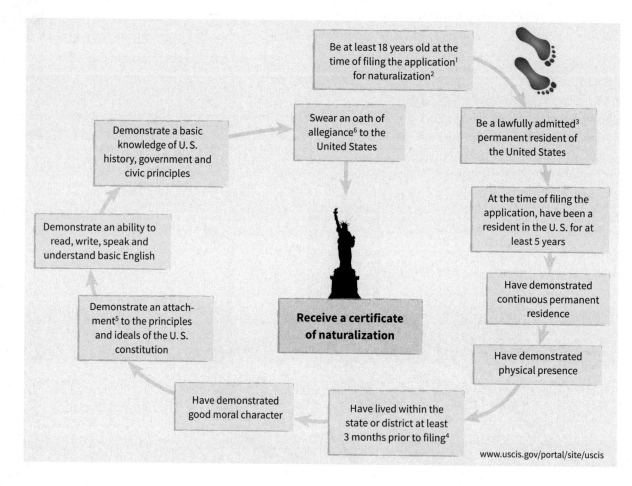

Be at least 18 years old at the time of filing the application[1] for naturalization[2]

Swear an oath of allegiance[6] to the United States

Be a lawfully admitted[3] permanent resident of the United States

Demonstrate a basic knowledge of U. S. history, government and civic principles

At the time of filing the application, have been a resident in the U. S. for at least 5 years

Demonstrate an ability to read, write, speak and understand basic English

Have demonstrated continuous permanent residence

Receive a certificate of naturalization

Demonstrate an attachment[5] to the principles and ideals of the U. S. constitution

Have demonstrated physical presence

Have demonstrated good moral character

Have lived within the state or district at least 3 months prior to filing[4]

www.uscis.gov/portal/site/uscis

[1] **to file an application** (*fml.*) *einen offiziellen Antrag stellen* – [2] **naturalization** *Einbürgerung* – [3] **lawfully admitted** *rechtmäßig/legal zugelassen* – [4] **filing** *Einreichung* – [5] **attachment** *a strong feeling for sb./sth.* – [6] **oath of allegiance** [əʊθ əv əˈliːdʒəns] *Treueeid*

The United States: Immigration and Minorities

The English have been going to North America from the late 16th century on; Spain sent people to the southern part of the region and many Dutch and Germans also went over. When the U.S. became independent, it was written into the **Constitution** that there could be no limits on immigration until 1808. The main period of immigration was between 1800 and 1917. Early in this period, many immigrants arrived from Britain and Germany, and many Chinese went to California. Later, the main groups were Italians, Irish, Eastern Europeans and Scandinavians. Many Jews came from Germany and Eastern Europe. Just before World War I, there were nearly a million immigrants a year. Most Americans have a clear idea of what life was like for the immigrants: they left home because they were poor and thought they would have better opportunities in the U.S. Many immigrants came to New York and Boston, and **Ellis Island**, near New York, became famous as a receiving station. The **Immigration Act of 1917**, and other laws that followed it, limited the number of immigrants and the countries that they could come from. Since then, immigration has been limited to a few people who are selected for an **immigrant visa**, commonly called a **green card**. Hispanics and Asians now make up the largest groups of immigrants. **The Immigration and Naturalization Service** (INS) is responsible for issuing visas. It also tries to prevent people from crossing the borders and entering the U.S. illegally.

In 2013, a bipartisan (*aus Mitgliedern beider Parteien bestehend*) group of eight Senators ("The Gang of Eight") announced four basic principles for a comprehensive immigration reform:
- a citizenship path for illegal immigrants already in the US
- business immigration system reforms
- an expanded and improved employment verification system
- improved work visa options for low-skill workers and an agricultural worker programme

On 27 June 2013, the U.S. Senate approved the "Border Security, Economic Opportunity, and Immigration Modernization Act of 2013" (short "S. 744"). However, so far the bill has ended in deadlock in the U.S. House of Representatives.

Ethnic minorities in the USA (US census of 2010)

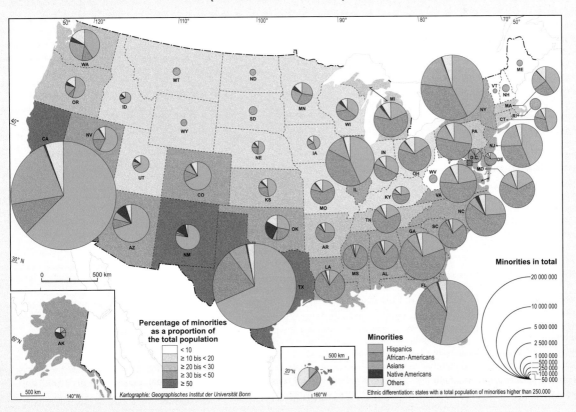

Jimmy Santiago Baca

So Mexicans Are Taking Jobs from Americans

AWARENESS

Look at the photos on p. 221 showing Mexican migrant workers on their way to work and pay attention to details.
What do these photos tell you about the migrants, their lives and their work?

1 O Yes? Do they come on horses
with rifles, and say,

        Ese[1], gringo[2], gimme your job?
And do you, gringo, take off your ring,
5 drop your wallet[3] into a blanket
spread over the ground, and walk away?

I hear Mexicans are taking your jobs away.
Do they sneak[4] into town at night,
and as you're walking home with a whore[5],
10 do they mug[6] you, a knife at your throat[7],
saying, I want your job?

Even on TV, an asthmatic leader
crawls[8] turtle heavy[9], leaning on an assistant,
and from a nest of wrinkles[10] on his face,
15 a tongue paddles through flashing waves
of lightbulbs, of cameramen, rasping[11],
"They're taking our jobs away."

Well, I've gone about trying to find them,
asking just where the hell are these fighters.

20 **2** The rifles I hear sound in the night
are white farmers shooting blacks and browns
whose ribs I see jutting out[12]
and starving[13] children,
I see the poor marching for a little work,
25 I see small white farmers selling out[14]

to clean-suited farmers living in New York,
who've never been on a farm,
don't know the look of a hoof[15] or the smell
of a woman's body bending[16] all day long in fields.

30 I see this, and I hear only a few people
got all the money in this world, the rest
count their pennies to buy bread and butter.

3 Below that cool green sea of money,
millions and millions of people fight to live,
35 search for pearls in the darkest depths
of their dreams, hold their breath for years
trying to cross poverty to just having something.

The children are dead already. We are killing them,
that is what America should be saying;
40 on TV, in the streets, in offices, should be saying,
    "We aren't giving the children a chance to live."

    Mexicans are taking our jobs, they say instead.
    What they really say is, let them die,
    and the children, too.

from *Immigrants in Our Own Land and Selected Early Poems* by
Jimmy Santiago Baca. New Directions Publishing, New York 1982

[1] **ese** (*Spanish*) that one, you – [2] **gringo** (*infml., disapproving*) used in Latin American countries to refer to a person from the US – [3] **wallet** (*US*) Brieftasche, Portemonnaie – [4] **to sneak into** *sich hineinschleichen* – [5] **whore** prostitute – [6] **to mug sb.** to attack sb. violently in order to steal their money – [7] **throat** Kehle – [8] **to crawl** *kriechen* – [9] **turtle heavy** (*infml.*) heavy and slow, like a turtle – [10] **wrinkle** *Falte (im Gesicht)* – [11] **to rasp** to say sth. in a rough unpleasant voice – [12] **to jut out** *hervorstehen* – [13] **to starve** to die of hunger – [14] **to sell out** to sell your business at a very low price – [15] **hoof** Pferde-, Rinderhuf – [16] **to bend** *sich vornüber beugen, bücken*

COMPREHENSION

 1. The poem can roughly be subdivided into three thematic units.

Step 1: While **listening** to (and reading) the poem for the **first time**, take notes and try to find suitable headlines for the three thematic units.

Step 2: Listen to and read the poem **a second time** and take notes on the following questions:

1
- How do Mexicans try to get jobs from the "gringos"?
- What kind of white people or "gringos" does the speaker describe?

2
- What observations does the speaker make about
  - white farmers,
  - poor "blacks and browns",
  - small white farmers,
  - rich farmers in New York?
- What is his conclusion from these observations?

3
- How do people try to forget poverty?
- What does America do to children?

→ Focus on Skills, Listening Comprehension, p. 394

ANALYSIS

2. Analyse the structure of the poem and the stylistic devices* that are used.
→ Focus on Skills, Analysis of Poetry and Lyrics, p. 406

3. Explain the influence and function of the media, particularly TV, in dealing with the situation.

4. Interestingly, the poet combines harsh sarcasm and rather offensive language with metaphorical and poetical phrases. Try to explain his intention and the effect of this unusual combination.

ACTIVITIES

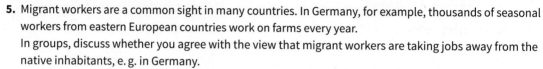

5. Migrant workers are a common sight in many countries. In Germany, for example, thousands of seasonal workers from eastern European countries work on farms every year.
In groups, discuss whether you agree with the view that migrant workers are taking jobs away from the native inhabitants, e. g. in Germany.
→ Focus on Language, Conversation and Discussion, p. 413

The Role of the USA in the 21ˢᵗ Century: New Beliefs, Norms and Values?

The 2016 Election Campaign

AWARENESS

In early 2015, Hillary Clinton and Donald Trump launched their presidential election campaigns. In July 2016, they became the official candidates of the Democratic and Republican Party, respectively.

In groups, look at their campaign slogans and collect ideas about what each campaign might have focused on. Stepping into the candidates' shoes, what would you do to "make America great again" and be "stronger together"?

COMPREHENSION

1. **While reading/listening:** You can choose between either **listening** to the audio version of the speeches or **reading** the texts provided here.

Webcode
SNG-40235-021 @

Tip: To get a better impression of the speakers' rhetorical abilities and the overall atmosphere, watch the video clips provided on the webcode.

20
CD 2

Step 1: While reading/listening to Donald Trump's announcement speech, finish the following statements using evidence and information given in the text.
   a) The U.S. has serious (economic) problems because …
   b) Many Americans are unemployed because …
   c) Politicians will *not* make America great again because …
   d) The American people can make their country great again because …
   e) The U.S. is like a third world country because …

Step 2: After **a second reading/listening**, subdivide the speech into thematic units and find a suitable headline for each unit that captures its message.
   → Focus on Skills, Listening Comprehension, p. 394

Donald Trump: Presidential Announcement Speech

Our country is in serious trouble. We don't have victories anymore. We used to have victories, but we don't have them. When was the last time anybody saw us beating, let's say, China in a trade deal? They kill us. I
5 beat China all the time. All the time.

When did we beat Japan at anything? They send their cars over by the millions, and what do we do? When was the last time you saw a Chevrolet in Tokyo? It doesn't exist, folks. They beat us all the time.

10 When do we beat Mexico at the border? They're laughing at us, at our stupidity. And now they are beating us economically. They are not our friend, believe me. But they're killing us economically.

The U.S. has become a dumping ground[1] for everybody
15 else's problems. [...]

And our real unemployment is anywhere from 18 to 20 percent. Don't believe the 5.6. Don't believe it.

That's right. A lot of people up there can't get jobs. They can't get jobs, because there are no jobs, because China
20 has our jobs and Mexico has our jobs. They all have jobs. But the real number, the real number is anywhere from 18 to 19 and maybe even 21 percent, and nobody talks about it, because it's a statistic that's full of nonsense.

Our enemies are getting stronger and stronger by the
25 day, and we as a country are getting weaker. Even our nuclear arsenal doesn't work. [...]

So I've watched the politicians. I've dealt with them all my life. If you can't make a good deal with a politician, then there's something wrong with you. You're cer-
30 tainly not very good. And that's what we have representing us. They will never make America great again. They don't even have a chance. They're controlled fully – they're controlled fully by the lobbyists[2], by the donors[3], and by the special interests, fully.

35 Yes, they control them. Hey, I have lobbyists. I have to tell you. I have lobbyists that can produce anything for me. They're great. But you know what? It won't happen. It won't happen. Because we have to stop doing things for some people, but for this country, it's destroy-
40 ing our country. We have to stop, and it has to stop now. Now, our country needs – our country needs a truly great leader, and we need a truly great leader now. We need a leader that wrote "The Art of the Deal[4]." [...]

So ladies and gentlemen ... I am officially running ... for president of the United States, and we are going to 45 make our country great again.

It can happen. Our country has tremendous potential. We have tremendous people.

We have people that aren't working. We have people that have no incentive to work. But they're going to have 50 incentive to work, because the greatest social program is a job. And they'll be proud, and they'll love it, and they'll make much more than they would've ever made, and they'll be – they'll be doing so well, and we're going to be thriving as a country, thriving. It can happen. 55

I will be the greatest jobs president that God ever created. I tell you that.

I'll bring back our jobs from China, from Mexico, from Japan, from so many places. I'll bring back our jobs, and I'll bring back our money. [...] 60

So the reporter said to me the other day, "But, Mr. Trump, you're not a nice person. How can you get people to vote for you?"

I said, "I don't know." I said, "I think that number one, I am a nice person. I give a lot of money away to charities 65 and other things. I think I'm actually a very nice person." But, I said, "This is going to be an election that's based on competence, because people are tired of these nice people. And they're tired of being ripped off[5] by everybody in the world. And they're tired of spending more 70 money on education than any nation in the world per capita, than any nation in the world, and we are 26th in the world, 25 countries are better than us in education. And some of them are like third world countries. But we're becoming a third world country, because of our 75 infrastructure, our airports, our roads, everything. So one of the things I did, and I said, you know what I'll do. I'll do it. Because a lot of people said, "He'll never run. Number one, he won't want to give up his lifestyle." They're right about that, but I'm doing it. [...] 80

Sadly, the American dream is dead.

But if I get elected president I will bring it back bigger and better and stronger than ever before, and we will make America great again.

Thank you. Thank you very much. 85

http://time.com/3923128/donald-trump-announcement-speech,
16 June 2016 [10.11.2016]

---

[1] **dumping ground** a place where sth. that is not wanted is left; *Müllhalde* – [2] **lobbyist** sb. who tries to persuade the government or an official group to do sth. – [3] **donor** sb. who gives money or goods to an organization; *Spender* – [4] **The Art of the Deal** a 1987 book written by Donald Trump and journalist Tony Schwartz; part memoir, part business advice book – [5] **to rip sb. off** (*infml.*) to cheat sb. by making them pay too much, by selling them something of poor quality, etc.

ANALYSIS

2. **Step 1:** Analyse the persuasive techniques employed in the speech, focusing on these aspects:
   - the line of argument*
   - the use of contrast/antithesis* with regard to
     a) personal and possessive pronouns and b) positive and negative emotive words.
   → Focus on Skills, Analysis of a Political Speech, p. 407

3. Identify and explain the speaker's references and allusions to American core beliefs and values.
   → Focus on Facts, American Beliefs and Values, p. 176
   → Focus on Documents, America's Cornerstone Documents, p. 186
   → Focus on Documents, The American Dream, p. 192

ACTIVITIES

4. Discuss the various aspects mentioned in Trump's announcement speech. What do you think convinced people to vote for him?
   → Focus on Language, Conversation and Discussion, p. 413

The Winner ...

AWARENESS

After winning or losing an election, it is customary for candidates to give a speech to their voters, campaign team, supporters and donors. What important aspects do you think should be mentioned in these speeches, especially after a hard-fought campaign like this one?

COMPREHENSION

 @ 1. **Before reading:** Use the link provided on the webcode and watch **Donald Trump's election night victory speech** which he delivered to his supporters at a hotel in New York City. Get an impression of the overall atmosphere.

2. **While reading/listening:** You can choose between either **listening** to the audio version of the speech or **reading** the text provided here.

 Step 1: Team up with a partner. In a paired reading/listening activity, complete the tasks below. After each step, exchange and crosscheck your findings and make corrections and additions if necessary.

 Step 2: In **a first reading/listening**, take notes on these aspects:
   - Trump's remarks on Hillary Clinton
   - Trump's pledge to every citizen of the United States
   - the "movement" that his campaign incited
   - the most urgent tasks for the future
   - Trump's plans for reviving the economy
   - foreign/international relationships
   - the American Dream
   → Focus on Skills, Listening Comprehension, p. 394

Step 3: In a second reading/listening, complete your notes.

1 Donald Trump: Presidential Acceptance Speech

Thank you. Thank you very much, everybody. Sorry to keep you waiting. Complicated business. Complicated. Thank you very much.

5 I've just received a call from Secretary Clinton. She congratulated us. It's about us. On our victory, and I congratulated her and her family on a very, very hard-fought campaign.

10 I mean, she fought very hard. Hillary has worked very long and very hard over a long period of time, and we owe her a major debt of gratitude[1] for her service to our country. I mean

15 that very sincerely.

Now it is time for America to bind the wounds of division, have to get together.

To all Republicans and Democrats

20 and independents across this nation,

I say it is time for us to come together as one united people. It is time. I pledge[2] to every citizen of our land that I will be President for all of Americans, and this is so important to me.

25 For those who have chosen not to support me in the past, of which there were a few people, I'm reaching out to you for your guidance[3] and your help so that we can work together and unify our great country.

As I've said from the beginning, ours was not a cam-

30 paign but rather an incredible and great movement, made up of millions of hard-working men and women who love their country and want a better, brighter future for themselves and for their family.

It is a movement comprised of[4] Americans from all

35 races, religions, backgrounds, and beliefs, who want and expect our government to serve the people – and serve the people it will.

Working together, we will begin the urgent[5] task of rebuilding our nation and renewing the American

40 dream. I've spent my entire life in business, looking at the untapped[6] potential in projects and in people all over the world.

That is now what I want to do for our country. Tremendous potential. I've gotten to know our country so well. Tremendous potential. It is going to be a beautiful 45 thing.

Every single American will have the opportunity to realize his or her fullest potential. The forgotten men and women of our country will be forgotten no longer.

We are going to fix our inner cities and rebuild our 50 highways, bridges, tunnels, airports, schools, hospitals. We're going to rebuild our infrastructure, which will become, by the way, second to none. And we will put millions of our people to work as we rebuild it.

We will also finally take care of our great veterans who 55 have been so loyal, and I've gotten to know so many over this 18-month journey. The time I've spent with them during this campaign has been among my greatest honors. Our veterans are incredible people.

We will embark upon[7] a project of national growth and 60 renewal. I will harness[8] the creative talents of our people, and we will call upon the best and brightest to leverage[9] their tremendous talent for the benefit of all. It is going to happen.

---

[1] **to owe sb. a debt of gratitude** *jdm. Dank schuldig sein* – [2] **to pledge** to formally promise to give or do sth. – [3] **guidance** ['gaɪdəns] help and advice – [4] **to comprise of sb./sth.** to have as members or parts – [5] **urgent** needing attention very soon; *dringend* – [6] **untapped** not yet used or taken advantage of – [7] **to embark upon sth.** to start sth. new or important – [8] **to harness sth.** to control and use the force or strength of sth. to produce power or to achieve sth. – [9] **to leverage sth.** *(US)* ['levərɪdʒ] to get as much advantage or profit as possible from sth.

65 We have a great economic plan. We will double our growth and have the strongest economy anywhere in the world. At the same time, we will get along with all other nations willing to get along with us. We will have great relationships.

70 We expect to have great, great relationships. No dream is too big, no challenge is too great. Nothing we want for our future is beyond our reach.

America will no longer settle for[10] anything less than the best. We must reclaim our country's destiny and dream big and bold[11] and daring[12]. We have to do that. 75 We're going to dream of things for our country, and beautiful things and successful things once again.

I want to tell the world community that while we will always put America's interests first, we will deal fairly with everyone, with everyone. All people and all other 80 nations. We will seek common ground, not hostility; partnership, not conflict.

http://www.telegraph.co.uk/news/2016/11/09/donald-trumps-victory-speech-in-full, 9 November 2016 [07.12.2016]

ANALYSIS ⟫⟫⟫⟫

4. Examine Trump's abilities as spaker:
   a) Examine the argumentative structure of his speech.
   b) Analyse the most relevant rhetorical devices that are used to convey the speaker's messages, e.g.:
   - references to the American Dream and the Declaration of Independence
   - metaphors*
   - words that create a feeling of common identity and solidarity
   → Focus on Skills, Analysis of a Political Speech, p. 407
   → Focus on Documents, The American Dream, p. 192
   → Focus on Documents, America's Cornerstone Documents, p. 186

5. Compare the issues mentioned in Trump's acceptance speech to his presidential announcement speech of June 2015. What similarities and differences can you detect? How has Trump's overall tone changed?

6. Immediately after Trump's victory, the cartoon below was published.
   a) Describe it in detail.
   b) Explain what the cartoonist is criticizing about Trump's campaign, his qualifications and personality.
   → Focus on Skills, Analysis of Visuals, p. 409

Tips on vocab ⟫⟫

the Statue of Liberty ■ the upper part of the body ■ to have one's eyes blindfolded (with a toupee) ■ to wear a baseball cap (with an inscription) ■ to wear a card-board nose

---

[10] **to settle for sth.** *(phr. v.)* to accept or agree to sth. – [11] **bold** brave – [12] **daring** brave and taking risks

Joe Klein

Donald Trump, the Astute[1] Salesman, Has Captured and Targeted America's Mood: Nostalgic[2]

Donald Trump's prevailing slogan since he started to run for president has been *Make America Great Again* – which can be interpreted as "Let's bring back the good old days".

Do you think that glorifying the past is a promising strategy for a president whose job is to take care of the country's future? Discuss in class.

From the pages of

TIME

1 Politicians are malleable[3]. They rarely stand on principle when there's a nice comfy pragmatic
5 seat to be had. So the Republican Party is learning to love Donald Trump. Even Paul Ryan, bastion[4] of conservative righteousness[5], seems ready to reconcile[6] – after a suitable[7] courtship[8] – with the policy-challenged[9] tycoon, and a good thing
10 too: the Republican electorate has demonstrated a distinct[10] indifference[11] this year to the party's stated philosophy. It seems opposed to free trade, to entitlement cuts[12], to tax breaks for the wealthy and to neoconservative adventurism overseas. It doesn't seem to care all
15 that much about unisex bathrooms, either. All of the above are positions – or "suggestions," in his most recent formulations – posited[13] by Trump. So the question: What remains of conservatism? I'm tempted to say: only the nasty bits – nativism[14], isola-
20 tionism[15], protectionism[16]. […]

2 First a bit of history: In the 1950s, C. Vann Woodward wrote an essay called "The Burden of Southern History". He believed that the South was different because it was the only part of the country to have lost a
25 war. Consequently, it was choked by nostalgia for its antebellum self, a chivalrous, courteous – and white – fantasy. Woodward wrote before Vietnam.

In the mid-1970s, as that disaster [the Vietnam War] ended, market testers began to pick up a new trend, which they called "natural/nostalgia." It was a wistful-
30 ness[17] for pre-Vietnam America – and not just for the country that "always" won wars, but also for the humming[18] factories, belching[19] smokestacks[20], intact families – and, of course, the place where blacks and women knew their respective places and homosexuality and
35 Latinos had yet to be invented. […]

Democrats are today nostalgic for the economy of the 1950s – concentrated, with Big Business and Big Labor synergistic[21] – and for the New Deal[22] notion[23] that massive government programs to alleviate[24] poverty
40 and regulate industry were an unalloyed[25] good. Republicans are nostalgic for the family values of that period, the homogeneity[26] of society and the fleeting[27] reality of transcendent[28] American power.

3 What has happened since is a fracturing[29]. It has af-
45 fected every aspect of our society. We have gone from three television networks to a thousand. A new immigrant wave, a tide that commenced in 1965, has made us polychromatic[30] and multicultural. Both parties became obsessed by the deregulation[31] of restraints[32] – on per-
50

[1] **astute** [əˈstʃuːt] *gerissen* – [2] **nostalgic** feeling happy and also slightly sad when you think about things that happened in the past – [3] **malleable** [ˈmæliəbəl] easily influenced, controlled – [4] **bastion** sth. that defends a belief or way of life that is fading; *Bollwerk* – [5] **righteousness** *Selbstgerechtigkeit* – [6] **to reconcile** to restore friendly relations – [7] **suitable** *angemessen* – [8] **courtship** *das Werben* – [9] **policy-challenged** not having strong principles when it comes to policy – [10] **distinct** clearly noticeable – [11] **indifference** *Gleichgültigkeit* – [12] **entitlement cut** *Anspruchskürzung* – [13] **to posit** *etw. postulieren; etw. unbewiesen als gegeben voraussetzen* – [14] **nativism** the political idea that people who were born in a country are more important than immigrants – [15] **isolationism** the political principle or practice of showing interest only in your own country and not being involved in international activities – [16] **protectionism** the actions of a government to help its country's trade or industry by taxing goods bought from other countries – [17] **wistfulness** *Wehmut* – [18] **to hum** *brummen* – [19] **to belch** *aufstoßen, rülpsen* – [20] **smokestack** *Schlot, Schornstein* – [21] **synergistic** *synergistisch* – [22] **New Deal** a series of federal programs in the U.S. in the 1930s in response to the Great Depression – [23] **notion** a belief or idea – [24] **to alleviate** *erleichtern, mildern* – [25] **unalloyed** *ungetrübt* – [26] **homogeneity** [ˌhɒmədʒəˈneɪəti] *Gleichartigkeit* – [27] **fleeting** short or quick – [28] **transcendent** greater, better, more important than others – [29] **to fracture** to break or divide sth. – [30] **polychromatic** having many colours; here: diverse – [31] **deregulation** removing government controls from a business – [32] **restraint** here: control

sonal behavior for the Democrats and economic behavior for the Republicans. This has been the golden age of marketing, an essentially fragmentary[33] phenomenon. America was founded on the principle that the things we have in common are more important than the things that divide us. The fundamental principle of marketing is the opposite: you sell to the things that make us different. We have become a nation of niches[34] – which is wonderfully liberating but lonelier and less easy to govern than, say, Dwight Eisenhower's[35] America. We have moved from the restrictive safety of conformity, Levin argues, to enervated[36] hyperindividualism[37]. […]

 It's amazing that it has taken so long for someone like Trump to appear. He is the ultimate hyperindividualist and – hilariously[38], brilliantly – he is selling nostalgia big-time: Make America Great … Again. Like it was before the Chinese and Mexicans stole our jobs and all those furriners[39] invaded our communities.

Trump is the first presidential candidate to truly understand the grammar of the Too-Much-Information Age, the new technologies that have made everything seem less private and personal, the false intimacy of reality TV. As I moved from primary to primary this year [2016], Trump supporters were likely to tell me two things: he'll bring back jobs and he talks the way we do.

In other words, he's done a stunning job of repurposing[40] the past as the future. In the end, though, nostalgia is a sepia-toned[41] refuge for those suffering a sense of diminished capacity – of wars, and manufacturing jobs lost, of father knows best, of racial privilege. It is a nursing home for those more comfortable looking back than looking forward.

TIME, 19 May 2016, p. 19
TIME and the TIME logo are registered trademarks of Time Inc. used under license.

---

 1. Pair up with a partner and
   a) read the magazine article to yourself,
   b) summarize the different parts to each other and make sure you have understood everything correctly,
   c) find an appropriate headline for each part.

2. Point out what – according to the author – (many) Americans are nostalgic about.

3. Outline the reasons that have led to the present "hyperindividualism".

ANALYSIS

4. Explain the following statements by referring to information given in the article.
   a) Donald Trump has focused the Republican party's philosophy of nativism, isolationism and protectionism.
   b) In the 1970s, nostalgia helped Americans to overcome the trauma of the Vietnam War.
   c) Republicans and Democrats alike are dreaming of the 1950s.
   d) 1965 changed the demographic and cultural landscape of the U.S.
   e) Marketing has fragmented American society.
   f) A political phenomenon like Donald Trump has been long overdue.
   g) Trump has been able to perfectly instrumentalize the (new) media and appeal to public sentiment.
   → Focus on Skills, Analysis of a Non-Fictional Text, p. 405

---

[33] **fragmentary** existing only in small parts and not complete – [34] **niche** [niːʃ] here: separate, independent person or community –
[35] **Dwight D. Eisenhower** 34th President of the United States (1953 – 1961) – [36] **to enervate** (fml.) to make sb. feel weak and tired –
[37] **hyperindividualism** [ˈhaɪpər ˌɪndɪˈvɪdʒuəlɪzəm] strong belief in the idea that freedom of thought and action for each person is the most important quality of a society, rather than shared effort and responsibility – [38] **hilarious** extremely funny – [39] **furriner** here: foreigner; it is implied that people who do not like foreigners are not well educated and cannot pronounce the word properly –
[40] **to repurpose** to find a new use for an idea, product or building – [41] **sepia-toned** [ˈsiːpiə] having the reddish-brown colour of old photos

Why Americans voted for Trump

Thomas, police officer, and Erica, a hairstylist, voted largely on economic issues.
"Go back 60, 70 years and this area had industry and people had good jobs," he says. "When Trump talked about getting rid of all this free-trade stuff, he brought to life the way this country should be going."
Thomas and Erica McTague, 38 and 33, Plymouth, Pennsylvania

After two decades as a car salesman, Wimbley hopes to fran-chise[1] his hot dog-stand business. This year was the first time he voted for a Republican President over a Democrat.
"America is a business. It is not a soup kitchen," he says. "I have made a lot of money for other people. It is time I make it for myself."
Darryl Wimbley, 48, Saginaw Michigan

A beauty-salon owner, Casey voted for Trump because he promised change, the same reason she voted for Barack Obama in 2008.
"I'm scared about every dollar that comes into my business. I'm scared about what that means in Obamacare, in taxes," she says. "Every single thing happening to me is out of my control."
Cassey Voss, 36, and daughter Sydney, 16, Owosso, Michigan

A student who works part-time in retail[2], Vasquez sees her grandfather as a role model. A migrant worker from Mexi-co, he died as a U.S. citizen who she says owned a million-dollar home.
"I'm all for immigration if it's done legally, and for people wanting to live the American Dream, like my grandfather did," she says.
Sara Vasquez, 27, Saginaw, Michigan

A first-time voter who doesn't consider herself a Democrat or a Republican, Goodin says Trump earned her support by being "a big poster child for change," adding, "Politicians don't appeal to us. Clinton would go out of her way to ap-peal to minorities, immigrants, but she didn't really for eve-ryday Americans."
Shannon Goodin, 24, Owosso, Michigan

A fourth-generation resident, Kalinowski says he foresaw Trump's victory early.
"I think people saw us as hicks[3] with pitchforks[4]," the local reporter says. "But the Trump supporters in this community are small-business owners, firefighters, correctional officers[5] – good people trying to take care of their families."
Bob Kalinowski, 35, Nanticoke, Pennsylvania

A lifelong Democrat and former mayor of his small town, Dougherty became a Republican to vote in the primary for Trump, who he says is more representative of "hardwork-ing, blue collar workers[6] looking for family-sustaining jobs." Says Dougherty: "we didn't leave the Democratic Party. The Democratic Party left us."
Joseph Dougherty, 49, Nanticoke, Pennsylvania

As the daughter of a Teamster[7] and a textile worker, Woodrosky always thought of her membership in the Dem-ocratic Party "as a birthright." But the real estate investor says Trump and his promise to bring back jobs changed her mind. "He's a champion for hardworking people like us," she says.
Kimberly Woodrosky, 53, Wilkes-Barre, Pennsylvania

From: TIME, 19 December 2016, pp. 37 ff.

5. Read the statements made by Trump voters and a) describe their demographic and political background
   b) explain the reasons they give for voting for Trump.

6. Relate the statements and the reasons people give for their voting decision to the magazine article. Explain whether their reasons match Joe Klein's explanations and analysis.

ACTIVITIES　》》》》》》

7. In the concluding paragraph (ll. 77 – 83), the author gives a rather harsh and cynical criticism of Trump's policy and people's longing for nostalgia. Give a comment on the author's view and state whether you agree with it.
   → Focus on Skills, Writing a Comment and a Review, p. 421

[1] **to franchise** to give the right to sb. to sell a company's products in a particular area using the company's name – [2] **retail** _Einzelhandel_ –
[3] **hick** (_infml., disapproving_) a person from the countryside who is considered to be stupid and without experience – [4] **pitchfork** _Heu-gabel_ – [5] **correctional officer** sb. who works in a correctional center (= prison) – [6] **blue collar worker** sb. who does manual/physical work rather than office work – [7] **teamster** sb. who drives a truck for a living

Trump's America – A Divided Country

AWARENESS

Look at the cartoon and the photo below and describe them in detail.
a) How does the cartoon depict the attitudes of right-wing and left-wing voters?
b) What are the people demonstrating for/against?
→ Focus on Skills, Analysis of Visuals, p. 409

Union members and citizens protest against new laws banning Muslims from immigrating to the U.S.

COMPREHENSION

1. **Before reading:** Reactivate your knowledge of the American Revolution/War of Independence and why (celebrating) the Fourth of July is so important to Americans.
   → Focus on Facts, Landmarks of United States History, p. 184
   → Focus on Documents, America's Cornerstone Documents, p. 186

Donald Trump was elected to shake Washington out of its paralysis[1]. He is adding to America's problems.

July 4th ought to bring Americans together. It is a day to
5 celebrate how 13 young colonies united against British rule to begin their great experiment in popular government. But this July 4th Americans are riven[2] by mutual[3] incomprehension[4]: between Republicans and Democrats, yes, also between factory workers and university
10 students, country folk and city-dwellers. And then there is President Donald Trump, not only a symptom of America's divisions but a cause of them, too.

Mr Trump won power partly because he spoke for voters who feel that the system is working against them, as our special report this week sets out. He promised 15 that, by dredging[5] Washington of the elites and lobbyists too stupid or self-serving to act for the whole nation, he would fix America's politics.

His approach is not working. Five months into his first term, Mr Trump presides over a political culture that is 20 even more poisonous than when he took office. His core voters are remarkably loyal. Many businesspeople still believe that he will bring tax cuts[6] and deregulation[7]. But their optimism stands on even shakier ground. The

[1] **paralysis** [pəˈræləsɪs] a situation in which you are unable to take action – [2] **riven** (*lit.*) violently divided – [3] **mutual** *gegenseitig* –
[4] **incomprehension** (*fml.*) a person's failure or inability to understand sth. – [5] **to dredge** to remover unwanted persons or things –
[6] **tax cuts** *Steuersenkung* – [7] **deregulation** the process of removing government controls or rules from a business or other activity

25 Trump presidency has been plagued[8] by poor judgement and missed opportunities. The federal government is already showing the strain[9]. Sooner or later, the harm will spread beyond the beltway[10] and into the economy.

From sea to shining sea[11]

30 America's loss of faith in politics did not start with Mr Trump. For decades, voters have complained about the gridlock[12] in Washington and the growing influence of lobbyists, often those with the deepest pockets. Francis Fukuyama, a political theorist, blamed the decay on the 35 "vetocracy[13]", a tangle[14] of competing interests and responsibilities that can block almost any ambitious reform. When the world changes and the federal government cannot rise to the challenge, voters' disillusion only grows.

40 Mr Trump has also fueled[15] the mistrust. He has correctly identified areas where America needs reform, and botched[16] his response – partly because of his own incontinent ego. Take tax. No one doubts that America's tax code is a mess, stuffed full of loopholes[17] and 45 complexity. But Mr Trump's reform plans show every sign of turning into a cut for the rich that leaves the code as baffling[18] as ever. So, too, health care. Instead of reforming Obamacare, Republicans are in knots[19] over a bill[20] that would leave millions of Mr Trump's voters 50 sicker and poorer. [...]

Mr Trump's hostility[21] has already undermined the courts, the intelligence services, the state department and America's environmental watchdog. He wants deep budget cuts and has failed to fill presidential ap- 55 pointments. Of 562 key positions identified by the *Washington Post*, 390 remain without a nominee.

As harmful as what Mr Trump does is the way he does it. In the campaign he vowed[22] to fight financial interests. But his solution – to employ businesspeople too 60 rich for lobbyists to buy – is no solution at all. Just look at Mr Trump himself: despite his half-hearted attempts to disentangle[23] the presidency and the family business, nobody knows where one ends and the other begins. He promised to be a dealmaker, but his impulse to belittle his opponents and miasma[24] of scandal and leaks sur- 65 rounding Russia's role in the campaign have made the chances of cross-party operation even more remote[25]. The lack of respect for expertise[26], such as the attacks on the Congressional Budget Office over its dismal[27] scoring of health-care reform, only makes Washington 70 more partisan. Most important, Mr Trump's disregard for the truth cuts into what remains of the basis for cross-party agreement. If you cannot agree on the facts, all you have left is a benighted[28] clash of rival tribes.

Til selfish gain no longer stain[29]

75

Optimists say that America, with its immense diversity, wealth and reserves of human ingenuity and resilience[30] can take all this in its stride. Mr Trump is hardly its first bad president. He may be around for only four years – if that. In a federal system, the states and big cities can be 80 islands of competence amid the dysfunction. America's economy is seemingly in rude health[31], with stockmarkets near their all-time high. The country dominates global tech and finance, and its oil and gas producers have more clout[32] than at any time since the 1970s. 85

Those are huge strengths. But they only mitigate[33] the damage being done in Washington. Health-care reform affects a sixth of the economy. Suspicion and mistrust corrode all they touch. If the ablest Americans shun[34] a career in public service, the bureaucracy[35] will bear the 90 scars. Besides, a bad president also imposes opportunity costs. The rising monopoly power of companies has gone unchallenged. Schools and training fall short[36] even as automation and artificial intelligence are about to transform the nature of work. If Mr Trump serves a 95 full eight years – which, despite attacks from his critics, is possible – the price of paralysis and incompetence could be huge.

The dangers are already clear in foreign policy. By pandering[37] to the belief that Washington elites sell 100 America short, Mr Trump is doing enduring harm to American leadership. The Trans-Pacific Partnership

---

[8] **to plague** [pleɪg] to cause worry, pain, or difficulty to sb. or sth. over a period of time – [9] **strain** a force that puts pressure on sth., sometimes causing damage – [10] **beltway** a main road that goes around the edge of a town, allowing traffic to avoid the town centre – [11] **from sea to shining sea** verse from *America the Beautiful*, an American patriotic song – [12] **gridlock** a situation in which no progress can be made – [13] **vetocracy** a dysfunctional system of governance in which no single part has enough power to bring about change or make decisions – [14] **tangle** a state of confusion or difficulty – [15] **to fuel sth.** *etw. schüren, anheizen* – [16] **to botch sth.** to spoil sth. by doing it badly – [17] **loophole** *Schlupfloch* – [18] **to baffle** *jdn. verblüffen* – [19] **to be in knots** (*infml.*) to be in a confused or chaotic state – [20] **bill** *Gesetzesvorlage* – [21] **hostility** *Feindseligkeit* – [22] **to vow** to make a determined decision or promise to do sth. – [23] **to disentangle** to separate things that have been joined or confused – [24] **miasma** [miˈæzmə] (*lit.*) an unpleasant fog that smells bad; *Gestank* – [25] **remote** far away – [26] **expertise** [ˌekspɜːˈtiːz] a high level of knowledge or skill – [27] **dismal** sad and without hope – [28] **benighted** (*lit.*) without knowledge or morals – [29] **til selfish gain no longer stain** verse from *America the Beautiful* – [30] **resilience** (*fml.*) *Ausdauer, Belastbarkeit* – [31] **in rude health** *kerngesund* – [32] **clout** power and influence – [33] **to mitigate** (*fml.*) *etw. abschwächen* – [34] **to shun** to avoid sth. – [35] **bureaucracy** [bjʊəˈrɒkrəsi] – [36] **to fall short** *etw. verfehlen* – [37] **to pander to sb./sth.** (*phr. v.*) *sich (bei) etw./jdm. anbiedern*

would have entrenched[38] America's concept of free markets in Asia and shored up its military alliances.
105 He walked away from it. His rejection of the Paris climate accord[39] showed that he sees the world not as a forum where countries work together to solve problems, but as an arena where they compete for advantage. His erratic[40] decision-making and his chummi-
110 ness[41] with autocrats lead his allies to wonder if they can depend on him in a crisis.

July 4th is a time to remember that America has renewed itself in the past; think of Theodore Roosevelt's[42] creation of a modern, professional state, FDR's New Deal[43], and the Reagan[44] revolution. In principle it is 115 not too late for Mr Trump to embrace bipartisanship[45] and address the real issues. In practice, it is ever clearer that he is incapable of bringing about such a renaissance. That will fall to his successor.

The Economist, 1 July 2017, p. 9

COMPREHENSION

2. In a first reading, **skim** the article and jot down at least five things that have gone wrong or that President Trump has failed to do since he took office in January 2017.

3. **Scan** the text in a second reading looking for information about
- the difficult situation in America, five months after Donald Trump was elected,
- reasons for the loss of faith in American politics,
- how Donald Trump has made the problems worse at home and abroad,
- the outcome of Donald Trump's attempts to tackle the problems and bring about change,
- the United States' ability to handle a bad president.

4. The German media covered the 2016 US election campaign in detail and, following the election, the German political TV programme *ARD Weltspiegel* visited people from all over the US and interviewed them about their hopes, concerns and political preferences.

Webcode
SNG-40235-023 **@**

Step 1: Divide the class into groups and work with the documentary provided on the webcode.

Tip: Use the Tips on vocab box and/or your dictionary to mediate the various statements and information given into English. Keep your notes because you will need them later on (cf. task no. 8).

M

Step 2: Watch the documentary and take notes in English on the aspects listed below.

USA: Euphorie oder Ernüchterung? – Unterwegs im Trump-Land
- Matt Seely's precarious economic situation and his hopes for Trump
- optimism in the Rust Belt
- cooperation with the Democrats
- the desolate situation in Johnston, Pennsylvania
- Trump, the US and climate change
- meeting Trump supporters

Tips on vocab »»

euphoria [juːˈfɔːriə] ▪ disillusion ▪ steel hook ▪ heavy industry/smokestack industries (U.S.) ▪ North American Free Trade Agreement (NAFTA) ▪ trade agreements ▪ to be beneficial for sb. ▪ commercial optimism ▪ way of getting down to business ▪ to pick up (speed) ▪ prosperous ▪ monstrosity ▪ half-truth ▪ pastor ▪ doer ▪ long-term ▪ achievement ▪ to achieve a bi-partisan policy ▪ to boost sales/the business volume ▪ chief financial officer/chief personnel manager ▪ steel roll ▪ museum piece ▪ to roll steel ▪ orders ▪ suppliers ▪ replenishment ▪ delivery times ▪ bumpy ▪ to abandon principles ▪ to be all for sth. ▪ to do one's bit ▪ to call sb. a hillbilly/redneck ▪ the local section of … ▪ to have a go at sb. ▪ to fight sb./sth. tooth and nail ▪ newspaper publisher ▪ cattle breeder ▪ threats and hate mail ▪ uneducated block-head/fool ▪ to talk rubbish (*infml.*) ▪ to urge ▪ the city limits ▪ despair/desperation

---

[38] **to entrench** *sich verschanzen* – [39] **accord** a formal agreement – [40] **erratic** *unberechenbar* – [41] **chumminess** (*old use, infml.*) friendship – [42] **Theodore Roosevelt** 26th President of the U.S. (1901–1909) – [43] **FDR's New Deal** Franklin Delano Roosevelt's (32nd President of the U.S., 1933–1945) government program in response to the Great Depression – [44] **Reagan** Ronald Reagan, 40th President of the U.S. (1981–1989) – [45] **bipartisanship** [ˌbaɪˈpɑːtɪzænʃɪp] *Überparteilichkeit, Unparteilichkeit*

ANALYSIS

5. The given text is an extract from the editorial of a special report on the "state of the nation". In order to convey and emphasize his view of the matter, the author has employed numerous rhetorical and stylistic devices in the article.

   Team up with a partner and examine the specific style of the text, paying particular attention to:
   - the author's line of argument*
   - language (e.g. choice of words, phrases, etc.)
   - grammar (e.g. sentence structure, grammatical tenses, etc.)
   - rhetoric (e.g. key symbols, metaphors, etc.)
   → Focus on Skills, Analysis of a Non-Fictional Text, p. 405

@ 6. Do research on the three presidents the article highlights: Theodore Roosevelt, Franklin Delano Roosevelt and Ronald Reagan. Compare their achievements to Trump's plans and achievements so far.

Info

An **editorial**, leading article (*US*) or leader (*BE*) is an important, often unsigned article in a newspaper or magazine written by the senior editorial staff or publisher expressing their opinion about an item of news or an issue. In the U.S. an editorial is also a comment broadcast on the radio or TV that expresses the opinion of the station or network. Illustrated editorials may appear in the form of editorial cartoons. Editorials are typically published on a dedicated page, called the editorial page; the page opposite this page is called op-ed page and sometimes directly presents opinion pieces by writers not affiliated (*zugehörig*) with the publication.

M 7. Describe the German cartoon and relate its message to the headline of the editorial.

   Tip: Pay particular attention to the symbolism of the Statue of Liberty.

TRUMPRESSIONEN

ACTIVITIES

8. Based on the information you have collected in the previous tasks and the various viewpoints presented, prepare and act out a panel discussion in which you depict the different positions on Trump's presidency, e.g.:
   - (former) factory owners from the Midwest (Rust Belt) who are desperate and frustrated with the Establishment and are calling for radical change
   - unemployed workers who feel left behind and ignored by politicians
   - former Obama supporters who feel they are not being taken seriously by politicians
   - supporters of the Democratic Party who are utterly shocked by "Trumpism" and who are concerned that the US will become an international outsider and the laughing stock (*Witzfigur*) of the economic and political world.
   - etc.
   → Focus on Language, Conversation and Discussion, p. 413

Joseph Stiglitz

How US Became a Rogue State

AWARENESS

The term "rogue state" is used by international theorists to describe states that are considered a threat to world peace. Characteristics of a rogue state include being ruled by an authoritarian regime that severely restricts human rights, sponsors terrorism and seeks to proliferate (*ausbreiten*) weapons of mass destruction. This term is used mostly by the United States, though the U.S. State department officially stopped using the term in 2000.

@ a) Do research on the Internet and find out which nations worldwide are considered to be rogue states and what makes them so dangerous.

b) Speculate about what might have induced Joseph Stiglitz, an internationally renowned U.S. economist and Nobel Prize winner, to use this term to characterize the United States.

COMPREHENSION

1. **While reading** the article, finish the following statements using information from the text.
   a) Trump's withdrawal from the Paris climate agreement attacked the core of American democracy because …
   b) The Enlightenment initiated …
   c) Trump's attitude and behaviour threatens the functioning of American society and economy because …
   d) Trump's true objectives are …
   e) Angela Merkel's reply to Trump was right because …
   f) The world must not fall back to cold war habits but …
   g) It's time to take action because …

Trump's rejection of the Paris climate agreement means the world's most powerful nation can no longer be relied upon

Donald Trump has thrown a hand grenade into the glob-
5 al economic architecture that was so painstakingly[1] con-
structed in the years after the second world war. The
attempted destruction of this rules-based system of
global governance – now manifested in Trump's withdrawal of the United States from the 2015 Paris climate
10 agreement – is just the latest aspect of the US president's
assault[2] on our basic system of values and institutions.
The world is slowly coming fully to terms[3] with the malevolence[4] of the Trump administration's agenda. He
and his cronies[5] have attacked the US press – a vital in-
15 stitution for preserving Americans' freedoms, rights and
democracy – as an "enemy of the people". They have

attempted to undermine the foundations of our knowledge and beliefs – our epistemology[6] – by labelling as
"fake" anything that challenges their aims and arguments, even rejecting science itself. Trump's sham* jus- 20
tifications[7] for spurning[8] the Paris climate agreement is
only the most recent evidence of this.
For millennia before the middle of the 18th century,
standards of living stagnated[9]. It was the Enlightenment[10], with its embrace of reasoned discourse[11] and 25
scientific inquiry, that underpinned the enormous increases in standards of living in the subsequent two-
and-a-half centuries.
With the Enlightenment also came a commitment to discover and address our prejudices. As the idea of human 30
equality – and its corollary[12], basic individual rights for
all – quickly spread, societies began struggling to elimi-

---

[1] **painstakingly** *sorgfältig, gewissenhaft* – [2] **assault** a violent attack – [3] **to come to terms with sth.** to gradually accept a sad situation –
[4] **malevolence** [məˈlevələns] (*lit.*) *Böswilligkeit* – [5] **crony** (*infml., disapproving*) *Kumpan* – [6] **epistemology** [ɪˌpɪstəˈmɒlədʒi] *die Erkennt-*
nistheorie – [7] **sham justification** *vorgetäuschte Rechtfertigung* – [8] **to spurn sb./sth.** *jdn./etw. verächtlich zurückweisen* – [9] **to stagnate**
to stay the same and not grow or develop – [10] **the Enlightenment** the period in the 18th century in Europe when many people began
to emphasize the importance of science and reason, rather than religion and tradition – [11] **reasoned discourse** clear and carefully considered communication in speech and writing – [12] **corollary** (*fml.*) sth. that results from sth. else; *Folgerung*

nate discrimination on the basis of race, gender, and, eventually, other aspects of human identity, including disability and sexual orientation.

Trump seeks to reverse that. His rejection of science, in particular climate science, threatens technological progress. And his bigotry[13] toward women, Hispanics, and Muslims (except those, like the rulers of the Gulf oil sheikdoms, from whom he and his family can profit), threatens the functioning of American society and its economy, by undermining trust that the system is fair to all. As a populist, Trump has exploited the justifiable[14] economic discontent[15] that has become so widespread in recent years, as many Americans have become downwardly mobile amid soaring[16] inequality.

But his true objective – to enrich himself and other gilded rent-seekers[17] at the expense of those who supported him – is revealed by his tax and health-care plans.

Trump's proposed tax reforms, so far as one can see, outdo[18] George W. Bush in their regressivity (the share of the benefits that go to those at the top of the income distribution). And, in a country where life expectancy is already declining, his health care overhaul[19] would leave 23 million more Americans without health insurance.

While Trump and his cabinet may know how to make business deals, they haven't the slightest idea how the economic system as a whole works. If the administration's macroeconomic policies are implemented, they will result in a larger trade deficit and a further decline in manufacturing.

America will suffer under Trump. Its global leadership role was being destroyed, even before Trump broke faith[20] with over 190 countries by withdrawing from the Paris accord. At this point, rebuilding that leadership will demand a truly heroic effort. We share a common planet, and the world has learned the hard way that we have to get along and work together. We have learned, too, that cooperation can benefit all.

So what should the world do with a babyish bully in the sandbox, who wants everything for himself and won't be reasoned with[21]? How can the world manage a "rogue" US?

Germany's Chancellor Angela Merkel gave the right answer when, after meeting with Trump and other G7 leaders last month, she said that Europe could no longer "fully count on others", and would have to "fight for our own future ourselves". This is the time for Europe to pull together, recommit[22] itself to the values of the Enlightenment, and stand up to[23] the US, as France's new president, Emmanuel Macron, did so eloquently with a handshake that stymied[24] Trump's puerile[25] alpha-male approach to asserting power[26].

Europe can't rely on a Trump-led US for its defence. But at the same time, it should recognize that the cold war is over – however unwilling to acknowledge it America's industrial-military complex may be. While fighting terrorism is important and costly, building aircraft carriers and super fighter planes is not the answer. Europe needs to decide for itself how much to spend, rather than to submit to[27] the dictates[28] of military interests that demand 2% of GDP[29]. Political stability may be more surely gained by Europe's recommitment to its social-democratic economic model.

We now also know that the world cannot count on the US in addressing the existentialist threat posed by climate change. China did the right thing in deepening their commitment to a green future – right for the planet, and right for the economy. Just as investment in technology and education gave Germany a distinct advantage over a US hamstrung[30] by Republican ideology, so, too, Europe and Asia will achieve an almost insurmountable[31] advantage over the US in the green technologies of the future.

But the rest of the world cannot let a rogue US destroy the planet. Nor can it let a rogue US take advantage of it with unenlightened – indeed anti-Enlightenment – "America first" policies. If Trump wants to withdraw the US from the Paris climate agreement, the rest of the world should impose a carbon-adjustment tax[32] on US exports that do not comply with[33] global standards.

---

[13] **bigotry** [ˈbɪɡətri] *Borniertheit* – [14] **justifiable** [ˈdʒʌstɪfaɪəbəl] *gerechtfertigt* – [15] **discontent** the feeling of wanting better treatment or an improved situation – [16] **to soar** to rise very quickly to a high level – [17] **rent-seeker** sb. who tries to change or control public policy or economic conditions in order to increase their own profits – [18] **to outdo** to do more or better than sb. else – [19] **to overhaul** to repair or improve sth. – [20] **to break faith** *das Vertrauen brechen* – [21] **to reason with sb.** (*phr. v.*) *mit jdm. vernünftig reden* – [22] **to recommit oneself** *sich neu verpflichten* – [23] **to stand up to** (*phr. v.*) *sich zur Wehr setzen gegen* – [24] **to stymie** [ˈstaɪmi] *hindern* – [25] **puerile** [ˈpjʊəraɪl] (*disapproving*) behaving in a silly way, not like an adult – [26] **to assert power** *Macht ausüben* – [27] **to submit to sth.** *sich etw. unterwerfen* – [28] **dictate** an order that should be obeyed – [29] **GDP** (*abbr.*) Gross Domestic Product; the total value of goods and services produced by a country in a year – [30] **to hamstring** (hamstrung, hamstrung) *jdn. handlungsunfähig machen* – [31] **insurmountable** [ˌɪnsəˈmaʊntəbəl] *unüberwindbar* – [32] **carbon-adjustment tax** CO_2-*Steuer* – [33] **to comply with** (*fml.*) to act according to an order, set of rules, or request

115 The good news is that the majority of the Americans are not with Trump. Most Americans still believe in Enlightenment values, accept the reality of global warming and are willing to take action. But, as far as Trump is concerned, it should already be clear that reasoned debate will not work. It is time for action. 120

The Guardian Weekly, 9 – 15 June 2017, pp. 1 ff.

COMPREHENSION

2. In a **second reading**, subdivide the article into thematic units and find a suitable headline for each unit/paragraph using your own words.

3. Read Donald Trump's tweets and present his view of global warming and the reasons behind it.

> **Donald J. Trump** ✔
> @realDonaldTrump
>
> This very expensive GLOBAL WARMING bullshit has got to stop. Our planet is freezing, record low temps, and our GW scientists are stuck in ice
> 2:39 AM - Jan 2, 2014
>
> ♡ 5,500 ♡ 10.3K people are talking about this

> **Donald J. Trump** ✔
> @realDonaldTrump
>
> We can't destroy the competitiveness of our factories in order to prepare for nonexistent global warming. China is thrilled with us!
> 6:50 PM - Nov 5, 2012
>
> ♡ 249 ♡ 878 people are talking about this

> **Donald J. Trump** ✔
> @realDonaldTrump
>
> We can't destroy the competitiveness of our factories in order to prepare for nonexistent global warming. China is thrilled with us!
> 6:50 PM - Nov 5, 2012
>
> ♡ 249 ♡ 878 people are talking about this

> **Donald J. Trump** ✔
> @realDonaldTrump
>
> It's really cold outside, they are calling it a major freeze, weeks ahead of normal. Man, we could use a big fat dose of global warming!
> 3:30 PM - Oct 19, 2015 · Manhattan, NY
>
> ♡ 10.2K ♡ 9,220 people are talking about this

> **Donald J. Trump** ✔
> @realDonaldTrump
>
> Snowing in Texas and Louisiana, record setting freezing temperatures throughout the country and beyond. Global warming is an expensive hoax!
> 8:27 AM - Jan 29, 2014
>
> ♡ 847 ♡ 1,075 people are talking about this

4. Describe the cartoon and find quotes in Joseph Stiglitz' text that match its message.
→ Focus on Skills, Analysis of Visuals, p. 409

I'M PULLING OUT OF THE PARIS AGREEMENT

©Ann Telnaes.

ANALYSIS

5. Analyse Joseph Stiglitz' text and explain how he succeeds in conveying his message to the reader. Examine
   a) the line of argument*
   b) the choice of words*
   c) the references and allusions to history, philosophy and politics
   d) the rhetorical devices*.
   → Focus on Skills, Analysis of a Non-Fictional Text, p. 405
   → Focus on Facts, Basic Types of Non-Fictional Texts, p. 396

6. The German left-wing political magazine *Der Spiegel* covered Donald Trump's election campaign and has been increasingly critical of Trump's attitude and political/diplomatic lapses since he took office in January 2017.

   Divide the class into four group, each group working with one of the magazine covers on p. 239.

    Step 1: Describes the covers in detail, using a dictionary for help if necessary. Pay attention to the pictorial and textual elements.
   → Focus on Skills, Analysis of Visuals, p. 409

   Step 2: Explain which events in particular the covers refer to and prepare a short presentation in class.

    Tip: Do research on the Internet and support your findings with facts and background information.

   Step 3: Present and explain your results in class.

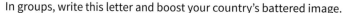

ACTIVITIES

7. Joseph Stiglitz' article, which was published in the renowned British newspaper *The Guardian*, has alarmed several Democratic and Republican American politicians who are concerned about their nation's international reputation and image. A group of you have decided to write an "open letter to the world" in response to Stiglitz' allegations in which you defend your nation and its qualities.

   In groups, write this letter and boost your country's battered image.

8. The German and international reaction to the *Spiegel* magazine covers varied; whereas some readers praised the magazine for its clear position, others considered the front covers tasteless and destructive, claiming that the responsibility of the media is to remain objective.

   Discuss the *Spiegel* covers in class and give reasons for your view on the matter.
   → Focus on Language, Conversation and Discussion, p. 413
   → Focus on Facts, The Press, p. 398

1

DER SPIEGEL

Nr. 17 / 22.4.2017
Deutschland €4,90

TODESSPIEL
Donald Trump und Kim Jong Un riskieren den Atomkrieg

Taliban in Deutschland
Erst Dschihadisten, jetzt Asylbewerber

René Prêtre, Kinderherzchirurg
„Und dann schlägt es wieder – ein tolles Gefühl"

H.-L. Kröber, Justizgutachter
„Ich kriege alles live – Unglück, Liebe, Rache"

2

DER SPIEGEL

Nr. 23 / 3.6.2017
Deutschland €4,90

YOU'RE FIRED!

Die Verlorenen
Junge Intensivtäter aus Nordafrika

Glaube 2017
Wie sich jeder seinen eigenen Gott baut

Evolution
Was Entensex über den Menschen aussagt

3

DER SPIEGEL

Nr. 6 / 4.2.2017
Deutschland €4,90

AMERICA FIRST

SPIEGEL-Gespräch
Martin Schulz: „Es geht in Deutschland nicht gerecht zu"

Kapitalanlage
Autos, Aktien, Anleihen – was tun in heiklen Zeiten?

Schule
Die unverstandenen Problemkinder

4

DER SPIEGEL

Nr. 34 / 19.8.2017
Deutschland €4,90

Das wahre Gesicht des Donald Trump

Hauptstadtflughafen BER
Made in Germany – die Geschichte eines deutschen Versagens

Rügen statt Rimini
Sommer 2017: Der Bau- und Touristenboom an der Ostsee

The Political System of the United States

The U.S. system of government (checks and balances)

The United States Constitution demands a **separation of power.** Each branch of government exercises power over each of the other branches. This prevents any one branch from becoming too powerful.

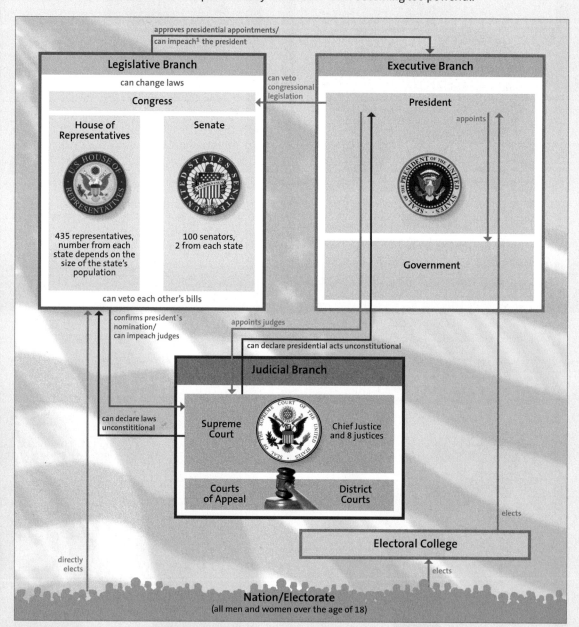

approves presidential appointments/
can impeach[1] the president

Legislative Branch

can change laws

can veto
congressional
legislation

Executive Branch

Congress

President

appoints

House of Representatives

Senate

435 representatives, number from each state depends on the size of the state's population

100 senators, 2 from each state

Government

can veto each other's bills

confirms president's nomination/
can impeach judges

appoints judges

can declare presidential acts unconstitutional

Judicial Branch

can declare laws unconstititional

Supreme Court

Chief Justice and 8 justices

Courts of Appeal

District Courts

elects

Electoral College

directly elects

elects

Nation/Electorate
(all men and women over the age of 18)

The United States has a **first-past-the-post voting system** in which the highest polling candidate is given all the votes and elected. Most states require citizens who wish to vote to be **officially registered**. Every **legal citizen over the age of 18**, regardless of ethnicity or gender, **has the right to vote**. Voting is carried out by **free and secret ballot**[2], in which the voters cast a **ballot (paper)** in a **ballot box** or via (electronic) **voting machines** in **polling places**, or via mail ballots.

[1] **to impeach a president** (US) *ein Amtsenthebungsverfahren* – [2] **ballot** *Wahl, Abstimmung*

Political parties

In 1787, America's founders expected constitutional provisions such as the separation of power, checks and balances, federalism and indirect election of the president by an electoral college[1] would deter[2] the formation of parties. However, **in 1800 the US became the first nation to develop organized political parties** which had executive[3] power. Since the 1860s, the Republican and Democratic parties have dominated American politics. In a 2006 Gallup Poll, ca. 59 percent of Americans identified themselves as either Republicans or Democrats. Those people claiming to be independent normally have partisan[4] leanings[5].

Democratic Party	Republican Party
• evolved from the party of Thomas Jefferson, formed before 1800 • is considered to be more liberal • believes that government has an obligation to provide social and economic programs • favours a higher taxation of the rich • has a stronger obligation to environmental engagement	• was established in the 1850s by Abraham Lincoln and others who opposed slavery • is considered to be more conservative • tends to believe that social and economic programs are too costly to taxpayers • encourages private enterprise • believes that a strong private sector makes citizens less dependent on government

The election process

- the US Constitution stipulates[6] that **a presidential election is to be held once every four years**
- in February of the election year, the parties nominate candidates in so-called state primaries[7] and caucuses (*US, Gremium, Ausschuss*)
- at national party conventions, usually held in the summer, **state delegates vote for the party's presidential candidate**
- on election day (usually the first Tuesday following the first Monday in November) every citizen has an opportunity to vote in **a process of indirect popular election known as the electoral college**, in which the number of electors is based on the population of the state
- these electors assemble following election day, cast their ballots and officially select the next president
- the Constitution mandates[8] that **Senators be elected directly by the voters of their state** once every six years
- the **members of the House of Representatives are also elected directly by the voters** of their state every two years

The inauguration[9] of the president

- the president-elect and the vice president-elect **take the oath of office** and are inaugurated on 20 January
- over the years, the inauguration has been expanded to a day-long event, including the oath-taking[10] ceremony, parades, speeches and balls
- traditionally, the sworn-in president delivers a speech, the so-called **inaugural address**, in which he inspires hope for the future and outlines fundamental plans and objectives[11]

"I ... do solemnly swear that I will faithfully execute the office of President of the United States, and will to the best of my ability, preserve, protect, and defend the Constitution of the United States."

[1] **Electoral College** a group of people who come together to elect the President and Vice-President, based on the votes of people in each state – [2] **to deter sb.** [dɪ'tɜːr] *abschrecken* – [3] **executive** [ɪg'zekjʊtɪv] the part of a government that is responsible for making certain that laws and decisions are put into action – [4] **partisan** strongly supporting a person, principle, political party – [5] **leaning** *Tendenz, Neigung* – [6] **to stipulate** (*fml.*) to state clearly and firmly that something must be done, or how it must be done; *schriftlich vereinbaren* – [7] **(state) primary** *Vorwahlen* – [8] **to mandate** to order sb. to do sth. – [9] **inauguration** [ɪˌnɔːgjʊ'reɪʃən] the ceremony in which sb. is put into an official position – [10] **oath-taking** *den Amtseid ablegen* – [11] **objective** *(politisches) Ziel*

US history		
to abolish sth. [əˈbɒlɪʃ] **abolition of sth.** [ˈæbəˈlɪʃn]	to officially end a law, a system	*etwas abschaffen; Abschaffung*
to become independent of sb./sth.	to be one's own master	*von jdm./etw. unabhängig werden*
independence	freedom from political control by the government of another country	*Unabhängigkeit*
civil rights movement	citizens who fight for the rights that each person has in a society, whatever their race, sex or religion	*Bürgerrechtsbewegung*
discrimination	the practice of treating a person or group less fairly than others	*Diskriminierung*
to escape persecution	to get away from persecution	*Verfolgung entgehen; fliehen*
to found sth.	to start sth., e. g. an organization, a company, etc.	*etwas gründen*
Founding Fathers	sb. who begins sth., e. g. a new way of thinking (here: Thomas Jefferson, Benjamin Franklin, George Washington, etc.)	*Gründungsväter*
the Frontier [ˈfrʌntɪə(r)]	the border between settled/civilized and unsettled/uncivilized country	*das Grenzland*
to gain independence	to become independent	*Unabhängigkeit erlangen*
interventionism	the policy of intervening in the affairs of another sovereign state	*Interventionismus*
isolationism	the policy of nonparticipation in international economic and political relations	*Isolation, Isolationismus*
native	a word used by white people to refer to the people who lived in America, etc. before Europeans arrived	*Ureinwohner*
pilgrim	a religious person who travels to a holy place	*Pilger*
plantation	a large piece of land where crops are grown	*Plantage*
prejudice [ˈpredʒudɪs]	an unreasonable dislike of people who are different	*Vorurteil*
to be prejudiced	having an unreasonable dislike of sb. or sth., mostly because of foreignness	*voreingenommen sein, Vorurteile haben*
protest movement	a large group of people who come together to publicly express disapproval or opposition to sth.	*Protestbewegung*
purchase [ˈpɜːtʃəs]	sth. you buy	*Ankauf*
Puritan [ˈpjʊərɪtən]	a member of a Protestant religious sect in the 16th and 17th centuries, who wanted to make religion simpler	*Puritaner(in)*
racial segregation	when people of different races are kept apart so that they live, work or study separately	*Rassentrennung*
to rebel [rɪˈbel] **rebellion** [rɪˈbeljən]	to oppose or fight against people in authority or against an idea or a situation which you do not agree with; an organized attempt to change the government or a leader of a country, using violence	*rebellieren; Rebellion, Aufstand*
subject (*fml.*)	here: citizen	*Staatsbürger*
trading post	a place where people can buy and exchange goods far away from town, esp. in the past	*Handelsstützpunkt*
politics/constitution		
administration	the government of a country	*Regierung, Verwaltung*
amendment	a change to a law that is still being discussed	*Zusatz (zur Verfassung)*
to amend [əˈmend] **a bill**	to make changes to a (draft) law	*eine Gesetzesvorlage/ein Gesetz ändern*
appointment	the act of choosing sb. for a position or job	*Ernennung*
article	paragraph (of a law)	*Paragraf, Artikel*

civil servant	sb. employed in the civil service	*Beamter*
Constitution	a set of basic laws and principles that a country or organization is governed by	*Verfassung*
to declare sth. unconstitutional	to say officially that sth. is not allowed by the constitution	*etwas für verfassungswidrig erklären*
domestic policy	the internal policy of a country without involving other countries	*Innenpolitik*
to ensure (a right)	to make certain that sth. will happen properly; to assure	*zusichern*
foreign policy	involving or dealing with other countries	*Außenpolitik*
to govern	to rule	*regieren*
grass roots (democracy)	the ordinary people rather than the rulers	*Basis, „Fußvolk"*
Head of State	the main representative of a country, e. g. a king	*Staatsoberhaupt*
to interfere with sth.	to prevent sth. from happening the way that it was planned	*sich in etwas einmischen*
policy	a set of ideas of what to do in certain situations that has been agreed on by a government or a party	*eine bestimmte Politik*
politician [ˈpɒləˈtɪʃn]	someone who works in politics, especially an elected member of the government	*Politiker*
political [pəˈlɪtɪkl]	relating to governmental actions or people	*politisch*
to be (politically) impartial	not supporting one person or group more than another	*unparteiisch sein*
to ratify a treaty	to make a treaty official by signing it	*einen Vertrag unterzeichnen*
reunification	to join the parts of sth. together again, especially a country that was divided	*Wiedervereinigung*
beliefs/values		
achievement	sth. that you succeed in doing by your own efforts	*Errungenschaft*
authority [ɔːˈθɒrəti]	the power you have because of your official position	*Autorität, Amtsgewalt*
cultural patterns/habits	cultural ideas/behaviour	*kulturelle Gewohnheiten*
divine providence	what is thought to be God's intervention in the world	*göttliche Vorsehung*
to be equal; equality [iˈkwɒləti]	to have the same rights and opportunities as everyone else, no matter what your sex, race, age, religion, etc.	*gleichgestellt sein; Gleichheit, Gleichberechtigung*
God's chosen people	in 1630, the founding Puritans believed they were the chosen people of God and had the duty to build an ideal Christian community in the new World	*Gottes auserwähltes Volk*
heterogeneous society [ˈhetərəˈdʒiːniəs]	a very diverse society	*verschiedenartige, breit gefächerte Gesellschaft*
to identify with sb./sth.; identification [aɪˌdentɪfɪˈkeɪʃn]	to feel sympathy for sb./sth. or be able to share their feelings; a strong feeling of sympathy and similarity with someone	*sich mit jdm./etw. identifizieren; Identifikation*
inalienable/unalienable rights [ɪnˈeɪliənəbl]	rights that cannot be taken from you	*unveräußerliche Rechte*
individuality [ˌɪndɪˌvɪdʒuˈæləti]	the qualities that make sb. or sth. different from other people or things	*Individualität*
Manifest Destiny [ˈmænɪfest ˈdestəni]	the belief that the US people had the right and the duty to take land in North America from other people, because this was God's plan	*offensichtliche Bestimmung (amerik. Doktrin des 19. Jahrhunderts; göttlicher Auftrag zur Expansion)*
Melting Pot	the idea of a place where people's different races, cultures, etc. blend together into one nation	*Schmelztiegel (der Kulturen)*
national anthem	the official song of a nation	*Nationalhymne*
national pride	being proud of having a particular nationality	*Nationalstolz*
to offer an opportunity to sb.	to give sb. a chance to do sth.	*eine Gelegenheit bieten*

patriotism [ˈpeɪtriətɪzəm]	when you love your country and are proud of it; national pride	*Patriotismus*
(to be) patriotic	having or expressing a great love of your country	*patriotisch (sein)*
prosperity	wealth	*Reichtum, Wohlstand*
Pursuit of Happiness [pəˈsjuːt]	the act of trying to find happiness	*Streben nach Glück, existenzieller Sicherheit, Zufriedenheit*
rags-to-riches	the idea of becoming very rich after starting life very poor	*vom Tellerwäscher zum Millionär*
religious tolerance [rɪˈlɪdʒəs ˈtɒlərəns]	not discriminating against people from different religions	*religiöse Toleranz*
self-improvement	the process of trying to become a better person	*(selbstständige) Weiterbildung*
thrift	the habit of saving money and spending it carefully	*Wirtschaftlichkeit, Sparsamkeit*
unlimited possibilities	endless/limitless opportunities and possibilities	*unbegrenzte Möglichkeiten*

immigration/minorities

alien	a person who is not a citizen of the country in which they live and work	*Fremde/r*
to assimilate; assimilation	to become a part of a country/community	*anpassen/Anpassung*
border control	measures taken to prevent illegal immigrants from entering a country; immigration control	*Grenzkontrolle*
citizen	a person who has the legal right to belong to a particular country	*Staatsbürger*
descendant	sb. who is related to a person that lived a long time ago	*Nachkomme*
to emigrate (from); emigration	to leave one's own country in order to live in another	*auswandern; Auswanderung*
ethnic; ethnicity	connected with a nation, race or people that shares certain cultural traditions	*ethnisch; Ethnizität, Volkszugehörigkeit*
illegal alien	an illegal immigrant	*illegaler Einwanderer*
Hispanic	a person whose first language is Spanish, esp. one who comes from a Latin American country	*Lateinamerikaner(in), Südamerikaner(in)*
to immigrate (to) [ˈɪmɪɡreɪt]	to come into a country in order to live there	*immigrieren, einwandern*
immigration control	the place where the passports and other documents of people coming into the country are checked	*Einwanderungskontrolle*
(cultural) interaction	the act of communicating with sb. (from a different culture)	*(kulturelle) Interaktion*
multi-ethnic	involving or including different ethnicities	*Vielvölker-*
naturalization	to become a citizen of a particular country	*Einbürgerung*
to be processed through sth.	to be moved forward from one checkpoint to the next	*durchgereicht werden, weitergeschickt werden*
to take an oath of allegiance	a formal promise to be loyal to a country	*den Treueeid schwören*

economy

to go bankrupt; bankruptcy	to become officially unable to pay your debts; to go bust; the state of being unable to pay your debts	*Pleite gehen; Pleite, Bankrott*
capitalism [ˈkæpɪtəlɪzəm]	an economic and political system in which businesses belong mostly to private owners, not to the government	*Kapitalismus*
capitalist [ˈkæpɪtəlɪst]	sb. who owns or controls a lot of money and lends it to businesses, banks, etc. to produce more wealth	*Kapitalist*
commerce	trade	*Handel*
to drop; drop	to fall to a lower level or amount; reduction	*fallen, einbrechen; Absturz, Abfall*
financial recession	a difficult time when there is less business activity, trade, etc. in a country	*finanzielle Rezession, Flaute*

hire and fire policy	to employ and dismiss people in quick succession	*Einstellen und Feuern von Beschäftigten*
homeowner(s)	people who own their home	*Hauseigentümer*
to be low-income	to be below an acceptable or usual level of income	*geringverdienend sein*
ownership society	a society in which personal responsibility, economic liberty, and the possession of property are very important	*von G. W. Bush vertretenes Gesellschaftsmodell, in dem die Bürger für sich und ihr Wohlergehen zuständig sind*
real estate [ˈriːəl ɪˈsteɪt] (*US*)	property in the form of land and houses	*Grundbesitz*
to regenerate [rɪˈdʒenəreɪt]	to make sth. develop and grow strong again	*erneuern, umgestalten*
to subsidize [ˈsʌbsɪdaɪz]	if a government subsidizes a company, activity, etc., it pays parts of its costs	*subventionieren*
subsidy [ˈsʌbsədi]	money that is paid by a government or organization to make prices lower and reduce the cost of producing goods	*Subvention*
to tax sb.	to pay an amount of money to the government according to your income, property, etc.	*jdn./etwas besteuern*
tax system	the system of charging taxes	*Steuersystem*
upward mobility	the act of moving up through the social classes and becoming richer	*sozialer Aufstieg*
to be wealthy; wealth [welθ]	to have a lot of property, money, etc.; a large amount of money, etc. that sb. owns	*wohlhabend sein; Wohlstand*
crises/war/poverty		
to accomplish a mission	to succeed in doing sth.	*eine Mission erfüllen*
combat	fighting, esp. during a war	*Kampf, Gefecht*
civil war	a war in which opposing groups of people from the same country fight each other to gain political control	*Bürgerkrieg*
crisis (crises) [ˈkraɪsɪs]	situation(s) in which problems must be dealt with quickly	*Krise (Krisen)*
to declare war on sb.	to start a war against someone	*jdm. den Krieg erklären*
the (Great) Depression	the world economic crisis during the 1930s	*Weltwirtschaftskrise*
to fall into poverty	to become poor	*verarmen, in Armut stürzen*
to invade; invasion of a country	to enter a country using military force in order to control it	*eindringen, überfallen; Überfall, Einmarsch in ein Land*
occupant	member of the occupying force	*Besatzer*
to occupy [ˈɒkjupaɪ] **occupation of** [ˌɒkjuˈpeɪʃn]	to enter a place in a large group and keep control of it, especially by military force	*belagern, besetzen; Besatzung*
pre-military training	training that people get before joining the army	*militärische Vorbereitung, Training*
to recruit sb. [rɪˈkruːt]	to hire sb.	*jdn. rekrutieren/einstellen*
retaliation	an action against sb. who has done sth. bad to you	*Vergeltung*
social benefits	money provided by the government to people who are not able to work	*Sozialhilfe*
social ranking	related to the social classes people belong to	*soziale Rangordnung*
tense (*adj.*)**; tension**	feeling worried, uncomfortable and unable to relax; the feeling that exists when people or countries do not trust each other and may suddenly attack each other	*(an)gespannt; Spannung*
welfare (state)	a system in which the government provides money, medical care, etc. for people who are unemployed or not able to work	*Wohlfahrtsstaat*
to withdraw; withdrawal	to stop taking part in an activity; to move away an army from the area where they were fighting	*sich zurückziehen; Rückzug*

Globalisation: Making the World Go Round

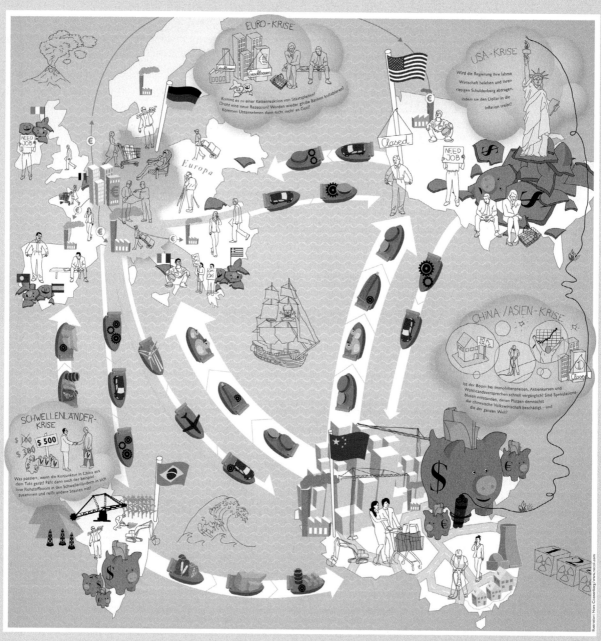

A Dangerous World – Modern Triangular Trade

Tips on vocab »

chain reaction ■ state bankruptcy ■ real estate prices (*Immobilienpreise*) ■ share prices (*Aktienkurse*) ■ speculative bubbles ■ national economy ■ economic activity ■ domino effect ■ machine parts ■ grain(s) ■ crude oil ■ pharmaceuticals [ˌfɑːməˈsuːtɪkəls] ■ plastics/toys ■ chemical products

Rana Foroohar

Globalization in Reverse

From the pages of

TIME

Globalization is often de-fined as the free move-ment of goods, people and money across bor-
5 ders. Lately, all of those have come under threat[1] – and not just because of sanc-tions limiting travel and the flow of money among Rus-sia, the U.S. and Europe. Over the past two years, glob-al trade growth has been lower than global GDP[2]
10 growth. It's the first time that has happened since World War II, and it marks a turning point in the glob-al economy, with sweeping[3] implications for countries, companies and consumers.

There are many reasons global trade is growing more
15 slowly than it has in the past. Europe is still struggling to end its debt crisis, and emerging markets are ex-panding more slowly than they were. But one of the biggest factors is that the American economy is going through a profound shift: the U.S. is no longer the glob-
20 al consumer of last resort[4]. [...] After nearly five years of recovery, the U.S. trade deficit isn't growing but shrinking. [...] Part of the reason the deficit is shrinking is that the U.S. shale-oil[5] and gas boom means Ameri-cans are buying less foreign fossil fuel, and the nation's manufacturing sector is growing. But part of it is that
25 wages haven't come up since the crisis, and consumer spending is still sluggish[6]. In order for the U.S. and the world economy to keep growing, somebody has to shell out[7] for the electronics, cars and other goods we used to buy more of.
30 Unfortunately, no one is doing that. [...]

With global economic integration seemingly in reverse, at the least for the moment, many economists and trade experts are beginning to talk about a new era of deglo-balization, during which countries turn inward. Some
35 of the implications are worrisome. Complaints to the World Trade Organization about protectionism, intel-lectual-property theft and new trade barriers are rising. Trade talks themselves are no longer global but regional and local, threatening to create a destructive so-called
40 spaghetti bowl of competing[8] economic alliances.

TIME, 7 April 2014, p. 14

TIME and the TIME logo are registered trademarks of Time Inc. used under license.

START-UP ACTIVITIES

1. In groups, take a look at the graphic *Modern Triangular Trade* and get an overview of its various elements:
   - Mediate the comments and questions using the vocab box.
   - What are the manifold tasks and challenges the countries worldwide are confronted with?
   - Describe the flow and exchange of products.
   → Focus on Skills, Analysis of Statistical Data, p. 408

2. Compare "modern triangular trade" to its historic counterpart, the "transatlantic triangular trade" of the 18th century. What striking similarities and differences can you detect? What changes have taken place over the last 250 years?
   → Focus on Facts, The British Empire, p. 119

3. In a group, collect photos and further material concerning the topic "the world going global" and design collages that reflect your understanding and opinion of globalisation.

4. Summarize Rana Foroohar's view of globalization and the reasons given for its slow-down.

5. What outlook does Foroohar give on the "new era of deglobalization"?

---

[1] **threat** [θret] *Bedrohung* – [2] **GDP** [ˌdʒiːdiːˈpiː] (*abbr.*) gross domestic product; the total value of goods and services produced by a country in a year – [3] **sweeping** affecting many things or people – [4] **of last resort** *als letzter Ausweg* – [5] **shale-oil** *Schieferöl* – [6] **sluggish** slow; *schleppend* – [7] **to shell sth. out** (*phr. v., infml.*) to pay or give money for sth., usually unwillingly; *für jdn./etw. Geld abdrücken* – [8] **to compete** to try to be more successful than sb./sth. else

Migration: Effects on the World of Work

The Abuse of Migrants – And Still They Come

AWARENESS

According to a 2013 OECD[1] study, there are about 232 million international migrants living in the world today trying to find a better life.

In groups, first collect information about possible reasons why people migrate to other countries, then sort your findings in a mind map and discuss your results in class.

COMPREHENSION

1. **Before reading:**
   The statements below are taken from the 2013 OECD study.

   - During the period 2000–2010, the global migrant stock[2] grew twice as fast than during the previous decade.
   - While the proportion of international migrants continues to rise in the North, it remains stable in the South.
   - Women comprise about 48% of all international migrants.
   - In 2013, only 7% of all international migrants were refugees seeking asylum[3].
   - 34.9 million of the international migrants are below the age of 20.
   - 37 million of the international migrants are aged 60 and above.
   - Ca. 27.3 million of the international migrants are highly educated (tertiary education[4]).
   - Ca. 30% of the international migrants have limited education (less than secondary education).

Step 1: In a Think! Pair! Share! activity, choose two of the statements above and reflect on and discuss
- possible reasons for the trends mentioned,
- the impact of the depicted situation on
   a) the migrants themselves,
   b) the countries the migrants are leaving (sending countries),
   c) the countries the migrants are immigrating to (receiving countries).

Step 2: Take a look at the map on p. 249 and collect information on peak migration trends. Make a ranking of the countries with the highest and lowest numbers of migrants.

Step 3: Speculate on and exchange ideas about the information and data you have collected in steps 1 and 2.
- Why do you think that some countries have a comparatively high percentage of migrants (e. g. Qatar, Kuwait, United Arab Emirates, etc.)?
- Which of the countries shown in the map might be particularly attractive for the different migrant groups mentioned in steps 1 and 2?

[1] **OECD** (*abbr.*) Organization for Economic Co-Operation and Development; an international organization whose members are countries with advanced economies and whose aim is to encourage economic growth around the world – [2] **migrant stock** the total amount of migrant people – [3] **to seek asylum** [əˈsaɪləm] *Asyl suchen* – [4] **tertiary education** relating to education in colleges and universities

Balancing the interests of migrant workers and the countries they live in

What government would tolerate its citizens' passports being confiscated[1], their earnings being withheld[2] and their deaths being covered up? Nepal's, it seems. In September reports of the abuse of Nepalese migrants working on stadiums for the 2022 Football World Cup in Qatar, and the deaths of at least 44 of them, appeared in the Guardian, a British newspaper. The Nepalese government's first response was to recall its ambassador to Qatar: the Guardian had quoted her describing the Gulf state as an "open jail". Shortly afterwards, Nepalese and Qatari officials held a joint[3] press conference in Doha at which they insisted Nepalese workers were "safe and fully respected". Reports to the contrary were false and driven by "inappropriate targets and agendas".

According to Martin Ruhs of Oxford University, the Nepalese government's apparent lack of concern can be explained by looking at the interests of those involved. For all the mistreatment, Nepalese workers earn far more in Qatar than they could at home. Remittances[4] make up a quarter of Nepalese GDP[5]. If the Nepalese government were to insist that rules protecting migrant workers in Qatar should be enforced, Qatari employers might look for workers elsewhere.

Mr Ruhs has drawn up an index of migrant rights (see chart): he finds that countries with more rights for migrant workers tend to be less keen on[6] admitting new ones. In the Gulf states and Singapore, where migrants have few rights on paper, the foreign workforce is huge: 94% of workers in Qatar were born abroad. Sweden and Norway, where migrants can use public services, claim welfare benefits and bring in dependents[7], admit relatively few purely economic migrants.

This trade-off[8] is visible even within the European Union, where the recent accession[9] of 12 relatively poor eastern European countries has sparked[10] a debate about migrants' rights to welfare. In January David Cameron, Britain's prime minister, clashed with his Oxford contemporary[11], Radek Sikorski, Poland's foreign minister. Mr Cameron wants to be able to exclude recently arrived European immigrants from welfare and public housing[12]. "If Britain gets our taxpayers, shouldn't it also pay their benefits?" Mr Sikorski responded.

In Europe the debate is multilateral[13]; Mr Cameron intends to promote his point of view as part of a package to reform the EU's single labour market[14]. Elsewhere the movement of people is increasingly regulated by bilateral agreements and diplomacy. Since a diaspora[15] can help poor countries develop, sending states must try to protect the rights of migrant workers without making them such a burden as to be unwelcome, points out David McKenzie of the World Bank. Receiving countries weigh their national interests, real or perceived[16], against international obligations[17].

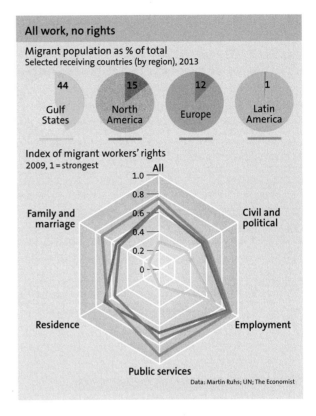

All work, no rights

Migrant population as % of total
Selected receiving countries (by region), 2013

| 44 | 15 | 12 | 1 |
| Gulf States | North America | Europe | Latin America |

Index of migrant workers' rights
2009, 1 = strongest

Data: Martin Ruhs; UN; The Economist

---

[1] **to confiscate sth.** *etw. einziehen, beschlagnahmen* – [2] **to withhold sth.** to refuse to give sth. to sb.; *etw. zurückhalten* – [3] **joint** belonging to or shared between two or more people – [4] **remittance** [rɪˈmɪtəns] *(fml.) Heimatüberweisung* – [5] **GDP** [ˌdʒiːdiːˈpiː] *(abbr.)* gross domestic product; the total value of goods and services produced by a country in one year – [6] **to be keen on sth.** to be very interested or wanting to do sth. very much – [7] **dependent** sb. who depends on your financial support, such as a child or family member who does not work –
[8] **trade-off** a situation in which you accept sth. bad in order to have sth. good – [9] **accession** *Aufstieg* – [10] **to spark** *etw. entzünden* –
[11] **contemporary** *Zeitgenosse* – [12] **public housing** *sozialer Wohnungsbau* – [13] **multilateral** involving more than two groups or countries –
[14] **single labour market** *einheitlicher Arbeitsmarkt* – [15] **diaspora** [daɪˈæspərə] *(fml.)* the spreading of people from one original country to other countries – [16] **perceived** *vermeintlich* – [17] **obligation** sth. that you must do; *Verpflichtung*

The calculations vary from country to country. Some sending countries, such as the Philippines, come down on the side of stronger rights: Filipinos must be offered a high wage to be allowed to leave for a job, and their government sends envoys[18] and inspectors to the main receiving countries. Others, like Nepal, are lax. Amnesty International, an NGO, is almost as critical of its government's tolerance of dodgy[19] recruitment agencies and exploitative brokers[20] as it is of Qatari employers.

A UN convention on migrant workers' rights which came into force in 2003 has been ratified[21] by only 47 countries, most of which are net senders of migrants. It is largely unenforced. A weaker treaty covering just the basics might do more good, argues Mr Ruhs, since the rich countries most migrants move to might sign it, and help to crack down on the worst abuses in places such as Qatar.

The Economist, 19 April 2014, p. 52

COMPREHENSION

2. Give an outline of the situation of Nepalese migrants in Qatar and the Nepalese and Qatari governments' response to the allegations (*Vorwürfe, Beschuldigungen*).

3. Present the correlation between migrants' rights and the admittance policy in countries like the Gulf states, Sweden, Norway and the European Union.

4. In what way do the sending countries take care of the migrants?

ANALYSIS

5. Analyse the author's stance on the matter and examine
  - his/her line of argument* as well as the structure of the article,
  - his/her examples and citations.
  → Focus on Skills, Analysis of a Non-Fictional Text, p. 405

 6. In groups, analyse the graphic on p. 251 and explain the different migrant workers' rights in the respective regions.
What do the comparatively low index numbers reveal about the receiving countries' migration and work policies?
  → Focus on Skills, Analysis of Statistical Data, p. 408

 7. Compare the migrant workers' rights and their violations mentioned in the text to the *Universal Declaration of Human Rights* that was proclaimed by the United Nations (→ FoD, p. 304). Which further violations can you detect and which further rights should migrant workers be guaranteed, according to this document?

8. The concluding paragraph (ll. 66 – 73) of the article refers to a UN convention on migrant workers' rights and Mr Ruhs' suggestion to work out a "weaker treaty" that only covers the basic migrant workers' rights, assuming that this would "crack down the worst abuses".
 Act out a pyramid discussion in which you discuss your view on the controversial matter.

---

[18] **envoy** [ˈenvɔɪ] sb. who is sent from one government or organization to another – [19] **dodgy** (*infml.*) dishonest – [20] **broker** *Zwischenhändler* – [21] **to ratify sth.** (*fml.*) to make an agreement official

ACTIVITIES

9. Do a project on world migration using the links provided on the webcode.
Prepare a presentation in which you provide your class with

- the most relevant background information on the history and development of migration,
- relevant facts and data,
- maps and illustrations.

Tip: Your presentation should be no longer than 5–10 minutes and you should make a handout
(1–2 pages) that contains the most important information.

→ Focus on Skills, Presentations, p. 419
→ Fokus on Skills, Writing a Handout, p. 425

Webcode
SNG-40235-024

Countries with Peak Migration Numbers

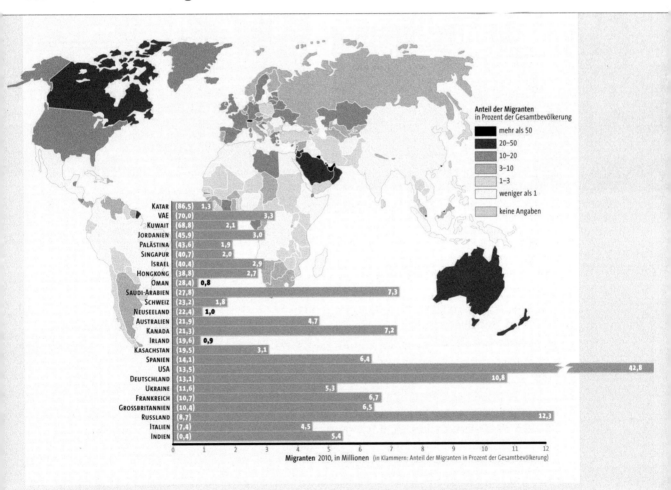

Die Länder mit den meisten Migranten

Quellen: »Trends in Total Migrant Stock: The 2008 Revision«, United Nations Department of Economic and Social Affairs, Population Division, http://esa.un.org/migration, Angaben für 2010.

©2012 Le Monde diplomatique, Berlin

Robert Booth, Pete Pattison

Modern-Day Slavery. Qatar World Cup: Migrants Wait a Year to Be Paid for Building Offices

AWARENESS

In a round robin activity, give short statements about what you associate with the terms
- modern-day slavery,
- labour camp.

Migrant workers from India in Doha, Qatar. The mistreatment of migrant workers, including the late or non-payment of wages, has attracted severe criticism

A worker formerly employed on a project to fit out offices in the Al Bidda Tower who now lives and works illegally after the company that employed him collapsed and failed to pay him for a year

COMPREHENSION

Webcode
SNG-40235-025 @   **Before reading:**

1. Describe the two photographs above: What do they reveal about the working and living conditions of migrant workers in Qatar?

Info ⟫⟫

> The **state of Qatar** is a sovereign Arab country with a population of about 2 million people. It is the world's richest country with a per capita income of ca. $98,814 (2013) (cf. Germany: $44,000) and its wealth is based on its natural gas reserves which are the third largest in the world.
> In 2022, Qatar will be the first Arab country to host the FIFA world cup.
> In 2013, British journalists Robert Booth and Pete Pattison made a documentary for *The Guardian*, accusing Qatar of exploiting its 1.4 million migrant workers.

Webcode
SNG-40235-025 @ 2. Together with a partner, watch the two video clips provided on the webcode and take notes on the aspects listed below.

Tip: Be prepared to watch the video clips at least two times; do not focus on each detail but try to get a general understanding of the information given.

Here are the points you should **focus and take notes on**:

- the FIFA preparations at Aspire Academy and the Aspire Zone Foundation
- the living and working conditions of migrant workers in Qatar
- Qatar's labour system and its rules
- the position of the Qatari government
- the Qatari construction industry
- desert labour camps and accommodations
- recruitment and contracting practices
  - Lee Trading Company   – Katara Projects Company
  - Capital International Manpower   – IBEX Technical Trading and Contracting
- the "sudden death syndrome" and the death of Rishi Kandal in May 2014
- the construction of the Al Wakrah stadium and opportunities to reform the exploitative Qatari migrant worker system.

The article below is one in a series of Robert Booth and Pete Pattison's critical investigative articles about the appalling living and working conditions of migrant workers in Qatar.

1 Migrant workers who built luxury offices used by Qatar's 2022 Football World Cup organisers have told the Guardian they have not been paid for more than a year and are now working illegally from cockroach-infested[1] lodgings.

Officials in Qatar's Supreme Committee for Delivery and Legacy[2] have been using offices on the 38th and 39th floors of Doha's landmark al-Bidda skyscraper – known as the Tower of Football – which were fitted out by men from Nepal, Sri Lanka and India who say they have not been paid for up to 13 months' work.

The project, a Guardian investigation shows, was directly commissioned by the Qatar government and the workers' plight[3] is set to raise fresh doubts over the autocratic[4] emirate's commitment to labour rights as construction starts this year [2014] on five new stadiums for the World Cup.

The offices, which cost £2.5m to fit[5], feature[6] expensive etched glass[7], handmade Italian furniture, and even a heated executive[8] toilet, project sources said. Yet some of the workers have not been paid, despite complaining to the Qatari authorities months ago and being owed[9] wages as modest as £6 a day.

By the end of this year, several hundred thousand extra migrant workers from some of the world's poorest countries are scheduled to have travelled to Qatar to build World Cup facilities and infrastructure. The acceleration[10] in the building programme comes amid international concern over a rising death toll[11] among migrant workers and the use of forced labour.

"We don't know how much they are spending on the World Cup, but we just need our salary," said one worker who had lost a year's pay on the project. "We were working, but not getting the salary. The government, the company: just provide the money."

The migrants are squeezed seven to a room, sleeping on thin, dirty mattresses on the floor and on bunk beds[12], in breach[13] of Qatar's own labour standards. They live in constant fear of imprisonment because they have been left without paperwork after the contractor on the project, Lee Trading and Contracting, collapsed. They say they are now being exploited on wages as low as 50p an hour.

Their case was raised with Qatar's prime minister by Amnesty International last November, but the workers have said 13 of them remain stranded in Qatar. Despite having done nothing wrong, five have even been arrested and imprisoned by Qatari police because they did not have ID papers. Legal claims[14] lodged against[15] the former employer at the labour court in November have proved fruitless. They are so poor they can no longer afford the taxi to court to pursue their cases, they say.

---

[1] **cockroach-infested** *mit Kakerlaken verseucht* – [2] **Supreme Committee for Delivery and Legacy** [ˈlegəsi] *das oberste Planungs- und Veranstaltungskomitee* – [3] **plight** *Notlage, Zwangslage* – [4] **autocratic** *related to a regime with unlimited power that demands obedience from its people* – [5] **to fit sth.** *etw. einbauen* – [6] **to feature sth.** *to include sth. as an important part* – [7] **etched glass** *Glas mit Gravuren* – [8] **executive** [ɪgˈzekjʊtɪv] *here: expensive; for the use of sb. who is considered important* – [9] **to owe sth. to sb.** *jdm. etw. schulden* – [10] **acceleration** *Beschleunigung* – [11] **death toll** *the number of people who die in an accident, a war, a disaster, etc.* – [12] **bunk bed** *Etagenbett* – [13] **to be in breach of sth.** (*fml.*) *to be breaking a particular law or rule* – [14] **legal claim** *Rechtsanspruch* – [15] **to lodge a claim against sb.** *to make an official complaint about sb./sth.*

A 35-year-old Nepalese worker and father of three who said he too had lost a year's pay: "If I had money to buy a ticket, I would go home."

2 Qatar's World Cup organising committee confirmed that it had been granted use of temporary offices on the floors fitted out by the unpaid workers. It said it was "heavily dismayed[16] to learn of the behaviour of Lee Trading with regard to the timely[17] payment of its workers". The committee stressed it did not commission[18] the firm. "We strongly disapprove and will continue to press for a speedy and fair conclusion to all cases," it said.

Jim Murphy, the shadow[19] international development secretary, said the revelation[20] added to the pressure on the World Cup organising committee. "They work out of this building, but so far they can't even deliver justice for the men who toiled[21] at their own HQ," he said.

Sharan Burrow, secretary general of the International Trade Union Confederation, said the workers' treatment was criminal. "It is an appalling abuse of fundamental rights, yet there is no concern from the Qatar government unless they are found out," she said. "In any other country you could prosecute this behaviour."

Contracts show the project was commissioned by Katara Projects, a Qatar government organisation under the auspices[22] of the office of the then heir apparent[23], Sheikh Tamim bin Hamad al-Thani, who is now the emir[24]. He also heads[25] the supreme committee, the World Cup organising body. The committee is spending at least £4bn building new stadiums for the tournament[26], which has become mired[27] in allegations[28] of bribery[29], while there is disbelief at the prospect of playing the tournament in Qatar's 50C summer heat.

Katara said it terminated[30] its agreement with Lee Trading when it discovered the mistreatment of workers and non-payment of wages, and made efforts to repatriate those affected or find them new jobs. It said several workers had been compensated after court settlements[31].

"If there are employees who were not repatriated, did not find employment or did not receive compensation, we would be happy to engage in any effort with the ministry of labour and ministry of interior to rectify[32] the situation," a spokesman said.

3 The problems at the Tower of Football workers are not isolated, despite Qatar's pledges to monitor salary payments and abolish the kafala sponsorship system, which stops migrant workers from changing job or leaving Qatar without their employer's consent. In 2012 and 2013, 70 labourers from India, Nepal and Sri Lanka died from falls or strikes[33] by objects, 144 died in traffic accidents and 56 killed themselves, the government's own figures show. Dozens more young migrant workers die mysteriously in their sleep from suspected heart attacks every summer.

The Guardian discovered more projects where salaries had not been paid. They included a desert camp of 65 workers who had not been paid for several months, were sleeping eight to a room, and were living with dirty drinking water, filthy, unplumbed[34] toilets and no showers.

Another group said they were being paid only sporadically, that there was sometimes no water in their housing and no electricity to power air conditioning.

This month, the Qatar Foundation, a state body, published a report examining trafficking[35], debt bondage[36] and forced labour among migrant workers. It identified practices that contravene[37] International Labour Organisation conventions on forced labour and UN anti-trafficking protocols, "widespread" non-payment of wages and bribery and extortion[38] among recruitment agents and employers.

From January to May this year 87 Nepalese workers died in Qatar, a death rate two-and-a-half times higher than that of British expats, new figures from the Nepal government reveal.

"We know there is much more to do," said Abdullah al-Khulaifi, Qatar's minister of labour and social affairs in a statement detailing progress on labour law reforms. "But we are making definite progress and are determined to build momentum[39]."

www.theguardian.com/global-development/2014/jul/28/qatar-world-cup-migrants-not-paid-building-office, 28 July 2014 [08.11.2014]

---

[16] **dismayed** unhappy and disappointed – [17] **timely** *rechtzeitig, zeitlich angemessen* – [18] **to commission sth.** to formally choose sb. to do a particular task – [19] **shadow secretary** used in the title of important politicians in the main opposition party; *Schattensekretär* – [20] **revelation** *Enthüllung* – [21] **to toil** to work hard – [22] **under the auspices of sb./sth.** [ˈɔːspɪsɪz] (*fml.*) with the protection and support of sb./sth., esp. an organization – [23] **heir** [eə] **apparent** *Thronanwärter, gesetzlicher Erbe* – [24] **emir** [emˈɪə] a ruler of particular Muslim countries in the Middle East – [25] **to head sth.** to be in charge of a group or organization – [26] **tournament** *Turnier, Meisterschaft* – [27] **to be mired in sth.** [maɪəd] to be involved in a difficult situation, especially for a long period of time – [28] **allegation** *Vorwurf, Beschuldigung* – [29] **bribery** *Bestechung* – [30] **to terminate** to end or stop sth. – [31] **court settlement** *gerichtlicher Vergleich* – [32] **to rectify** to correct sth. or make sth. right – [33] **strike** here: a sudden and powerful hit – [34] **unplumbed** *ohne Kanalanschluss* – [35] **trafficking** *Menschenhandel* – [36] **debt bondage** *Schuldknechtschaft* – [37] **to contravene** (*fml.*) to break a rule or law – [38] **extortion** *Erpressung* – [39] **to build momentum** *in Schwung kommen*

3. In a **first reading**, **scan the text** and get a general understanding of what is said.

4. Divide the class into groups of three students, each student working with one section of the article.

Step 1: In a **second reading**, extract the most relevant information given in your section of the text.

Step 2: Clarify unknown words and expressions using a dictionary.

Step 3: Summarize your section of the text in about 100 – 150 words and be sure to
- leave out irrelevant details,
- turn quotations into indirect speech,
- use predominantly the simple present tense.
→ Focus on Skills, Writing a Summary, p. 429

Step 4: In your groups, read the summaries of the respective sections to each other and clarify questions if necessary. Make sure that each student takes notes on the relevant aspects.

5. Explain Qatar's labour system and the *kafala* sponsorship system by referring to evidence given in the article. How are migrant workers lured (*ködern, locken*) into signing contracts and trapped in appalling and life-threatening working and living conditions?
→ Focus on Skills, Analysis of a Non-Fictional Text, p. 405

6. Explain how the author juxtaposes the "two worlds" that live side by side in Qatar: the world of luxury and the world of poverty.

luxury	poverty
• ll. 1 f. luxury offices	• ll. 4 f. cockroach-infested lodgings
• ll. …	• ll. …

7. Examine the style of the article and give evidence from the text that reveals its investigative character. Pay particular attention to
- the choice of words and language register,
- the use of rhetorical devices,
- the author's line of argument*.
→ Focus on Skills, Analysis of a Non-Fictional Text, p. 405
→ Focus on Facts, Basic Types of Non-Fictional Texts, p. 396

8. A group of migrant workers, supported by civil rights activists, have finally decided to file a lawsuit (*einen Prozess anstrengen*) at a Qatari court.

Choose one of the following persons/groups. Write a statement that clarifies and emphasizes your position:
a) a prosecutor (*Ankläger*) accusing the recruitment agencies of enslaving and abusing migrant workers
b) a prosecutor accusing the Qatari government of supporting human trafficking, debt bondage and forced labour among migrant workers
c) a Qatari counsel for the defence (of the recruitment agencies and the government)
d) representatives of the Qatari and international FIFA committee
e) various immigrant workers laying out their situation

f) the British investigative journalists Robert Booth and Pete Pattison giving evidence to the court based on their research and investigations

g) representatives of civil and human rights organizations (e. g. Amnesty International, Human Rights Watch, etc.) who give evidence of the appalling violation of basic human and civil rights

 In a role play, act out the trial and present the respective statements in class. Finally, the class should consider the evidence and find a verdict.

9. After the trial, which has gained international attention, journalists comment on the court's decision. Choose a newspaper or magazine (e. g. *The Qatari Times*, *The Guardian*, *The Indian Times* or a publication for the FIFA World Cup Committee) and write an article that represents the respective point of view.
→ Focus on Skills, Writing a Newspaper Article, p. 427

GRAMMAR / LANGUAGE

10. Imagine you are a migrant worker who has been lured to work in Qatar; you are reflecting on your situation. Use **if-clauses (conditional sentences) of various types** to express what you/the recruitment agency/the Qatari government should have done differently.

Examples:
- If I had been more suspicious when they charged the recruitment fee, I could have avoided … (type III)
- If I were able to escape from … I would have to leave behind … (type II)

11. Turn the passages of direct speech in the article into **indirect speech**. Be sure to
- avoid the overuse of the verb "say" and find more appropriate introductory verbs and formulations (e.g. to explain, to utter, to mention, to criticize, etc.),
- backshift the tenses where necessary.

Example: One of the workers stated that he/they didn't know how much the Qatari government were spending on … but the workers just needed their salary …

Integration: A Working Solution

AWARENESS

At the end of 2016, 65.5 million people were so-called "forced displacements", i. e. refugees trying to escape war, poverty, etc. In 2015, Germany took in 1.1 million migrants, thus ranking second worldwide in the number of migrants taken in. On average, there were 8,789 applicants for asylum per 1 million inhabitants in Germany in 2016. Despite an initial wave of welcome and support for the refugees, there has been a highly controversial discussion about the challenges of taking in and integrating so many people.

 In a first discussion, share *your* views on the matter.

The best way to settle newcomers is to find them jobs

Yehya is one of the lucky ones. A refugee from the northern Syrian city of Aleppo, he reached the Nether-
5 lands in June 2015, before the rush of arrivals swamped[1] the asylum system. He obtained[2] protection in just two months, entitling[3] him to begin integration classes at Implacement, an Amsterdam-based firm that offers refugees three-month courses on language, computer literacy and a basic introduction to Dutch life, taking in 10

---

[1] **to swamp** *überfordern* – [2] **to obtain** (*fml.*) to get sth. esp. by asking for it – [3] **to entitle sb.** to give sb. the right to do or have sth.

everything from taxes to transsexuals ("Muslims find that a bit strange," admits an administrator).

Classes like these began in the early 1980s, springing from[4] a Dutch integration policy written by Rinus Penninx, an academic who feared that the guest workers the Netherlands had been importing, largely from Turkey and Morocco, and their descendants were in danger of becoming an underclass. Initially, economic and social integration was encouraged, but culture, religion and customs were to be left out as part of a laissez-faire approach that later, in the Netherlands and elsewhere, became known as multiculturalism.

In time that changed as some Dutch voters grew anxious about the cultural distance between some groups of migrants and mainstream society. In 2004 the debate sharpened after a Dutch-Moroccan Islamist murdered Theo van Gogh, a controversial film-maker. Integration became, and remains, contested[5] political territory. The government shifted the burden of integration to the migrants themselves, which Mr Penninx frowns on[6]. Today the "Integration in the Netherlands" website baldly[7] states: "You have three years to integrate ... You must pass the integration exam within this period of time." [...]

Many European governments face a dilemma: better conditions for asylum-seekers should help their integration, but many also attract more of them. Under the strict Dutch approach, asylum-seekers may not receive anything more than basic state assistance until their claim has been processed[8]. [...]

Integration is one of the three "durable solutions" the UNHCR [United Nations High Commissioner for Refugees] seeks for refugees. In the poor world, most governments fear unsettling[9] their own citizens by allowing refugees to flood labour markets. That is less of a concern in the developed world; indeed, there is evidence that over time refugees may spur[10] low-skilled natives to move into more productive employment. But the record of rich countries in integrating immigrants into the workforce is mixed. America does well; its flexible labour market creates large numbers of low-skilled jobs, and officials aim to get resettled refugees into work quickly. Last year [2015] the Migration Policy Institute, a think-tank, found that in the United States, between 2009 and 2011 male refugees were more likely to be employed than their locally born counterparts; female refugees fared[11] as well as American women.

In Europe the results are patchier[12]. Some of the more visible signs of failure to integrate earlier immigrants – from the *banlieues*[13] that ring French cities to the divided towns of northern England – make it harder for governments to take in new ones. The country to watch is Germany, which took in 1.1m asylum-seekers last year [2015]. Some will be refused protection, and others will return home voluntarily. But Germany still faces the biggest integration challenge in Europe; failure will discredit Angela Merkel, the chancellor, and hamper[14] her attempts to organize a pan-European resettlement scheme for Syrians. The Cologne assaults[15] stoked[16] concerns about cultural clashes. But the challenge of finding employment for hundreds of thousands of people may prove tougher.

"What is integration? It's a job, and speaking German," says Achim Dercks of the Association of German Chambers of Commerce and Industry (DIHR). Recognising the power of work to integrate newcomers, in 2014 Germany cut the waiting period before asylum-seekers can look for a job to three months. By EU law most countries must open their labour markets to asylum-seekers after nine months, though several do not. All refugees are entitled to work once their claim has been approved.

Access to the labour market is of little use if migrants cannot speak the language. That mattered less for the Turkish and Moroccan guest workers who manned[17] Dutch and German assembly lines in the 1960s and 1970s. But today even basic jobs require linguistic fluency, if only to understand health and safety rules, so most governments lay on language classes for newcomers. That delays entry into the labour market.

A bigger problem is that refugees have tended to flock[18] to countries with little need for low- or unskilled labour. Half of those who have arrived in Sweden in the past two years have nine years or less of schooling, says Susanne Spector, a labour-market economist at the Confederation of Swedish Enterprise, but 95% of jobs

---

[4] **to spring from sth.** (*phr. v.*) to come from or result from sth. – [5] **contested** *umkämpft* – [6] **to frown on sb./sth.** (*phr. v.*) to disapprove of sb./sth.; *etw./jdn. missbilligen* – [7] **baldly** in plain or basic language – [8] **to process sth.** to deal with documents in an official way – [9] **to unsettle sb.** to worry or scare sb. – [10] **to spur** to encourage an activity or development – [11] **to fare** (*old use*) to succeed – [12] **patchy** only existing or happening in some parts – [13] **banlieue** (*French*) the suburb of a large city – [14] **to hamper** to prevent sb. from doing sth. easily – [15] **Cologne assaults** during the 2015/2016 New Year's Eve celebrations, there were mass sexual assaults, 24 alleged rapes, and numerous thefts in Germany, mainly in the Cologne city centre – [16] **to stoke** to encourage bad ideas or feelings in a lot of people – [17] **to man** to operate a machine or vehicle – [18] **to flock** to to move or come together in large numbers

require more than that, and the few basic jobs available attract an average of three applicants each. Germany's Federal Employment Agency reckons[19] that only 10% of the recent arrivals will be ready to work after one year, 50% after five years and 70% after 15. (Mr Dercks is more optimistic.)

That leaves a lot of migrants drawing unemployment benefit; and long-term welfare dependency, particularly of non-citizens, drains[20] treasuries[21] and fosters[22] resentment[23]. [...]

A recent IMF[24] report urges countries to make labour markets more flexible to speed up the integration of refugees. Germany's Hartz labour and welfare reforms, introduced between 2003 and 2005 by the then chancellor, Gerhard Schröder, made it more attractive to take the sort of low-skilled work that may suit many refugees, but plenty more can be done to loosen up[25] what remains a tightly regulated labour market. From this summer a new "3+2" rule will protect refugees on three-year vocational courses[26] from deportation for two years after completing their training, removing a disincentive[27] to recruiting them. Germany may not be crying out for low-skilled labour, but its tradition of vocational training can provide a bridge into work for some. The country could also do a better job of recognising the qualifications of skilled refuges, such as doctors. [...]

Last year's influx of refugees included many children, and educating them will be crucial for long-term-integration. Countries must balance their specific needs – especially language learning, which calls for segregated teaching – against the social value of teaching them in the same classrooms as everyone else. Germany has recruited new teachers and set up one-year "welcome classes" for newcomers with a focus on language teaching.

Housing presents another challenge. In most countries asylum-seekers are placed in reception centres[28] until their cases are heard (unless they can find their own accommodation). Once accepted, they are usually free to live where they like. But cities that are popular with refuges, such as Berlin, may not offer the best work opportunities or be well-placed to provide welfare support. To avoid overconcentration, the German government is considering obliging[29] refugees to stay put for their first two years.

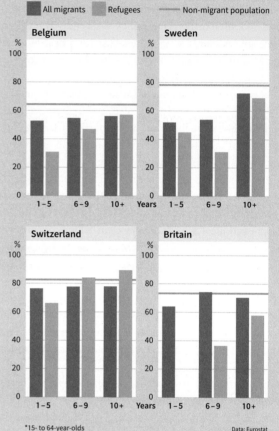

Employment rate* by duration of residence 2014

■ All migrants ■ Refugees — Non-migrant population

Belgium / Sweden / Switzerland / Britain

*15- to 64-year-olds   Data: Eurostat

Canada has tried an alternative to the usual state-led integration model. Since 1978 it has allowed voluntary groups, such as churches or diaspora organisations, to sponsor refugees privately, supporting them financially for a year and introducing them to life in their new home. One-third of the 25,000 Syrian refugees Canada has recently taken in were resettled this way. Privately sponsored refugees tend to integrate more quickly; one study found that after a year 76% had jobs, compared with 45% of those backed by the state. The British government is now considering a scheme along Canadian lines.

But in the poor countries where most refugees live, integration poses an entirely different set of problems. In long-established refugee camps NGOs usually provide services like health care and education, sometimes to a

---

[19] **to reckon** (*infml.*) to think or believe – [20] **to drain sth**. to reduce sth. – [21] **treasury** ['treʒəri] *Staatskasse* – [22] **to foster** to encourage the development or growth of ideas or feelings – [23] **resentment** *Abneigung* – [24] **IMF** (*abbr.*) International Monetary Fund; a part of the United Nations that encourages international trade and gives financial help to poor countries – [25] **to loosen up** to relax; *auflockern* – [26] **vocational course** *berufsbildender Kurs* – [27] **disincentive** sth. that makes people not want to do sth. – [28] **reception centre** *Auffanglager* – [29] **to oblige** [əˈblaɪdʒ] (*fml.*) to force sb. to do sth.

higher standard than is available to the country's ordinary residents, but governments rarely allow the refugees to work. Labour-market restrictions have forced most of the working-age Syrian refugees in Turkey, Lebanon and Jordan into black-market jobs, with the attendant[30] exploitation. Little wonder that so many aspire to a better life in the West, either braving dangerous journeys to get there or accepting a long wait for a state-backed resettlement.

The Economist, 28 May – 3 June 2016, pp. 4 ff.; Special Report Migration

COMPREHENSION

1. **While reading** the article **the first time**, subdivide it into thematic units and find a suitable headline for each of them.

2. Read the article **a second time**, now focusing on details. Find out more about
   a) the problems the (European) countries and the refugees have to cope with
   b) the various attempts to solve the problems and integrate refugees in different countries.
   Collect information and complete the grid below.

integration classes	guest workers	multiculturalism	Islamophobia	the poor world
• three-month courses on language …	• …	• …	• cultural distance • …	• …

America/USA	Europe	Germany	the power of work	schooling
• …	• France: … • England: …	• …	• …	• …

children	housing	Canada's model	work in poor counties
• …	• …	• voluntary groups … • …	• …

ANALYSIS

3. Analyse the statistical data on p. 258 and explain the employment rates of a) all migrants and b) refugees in comparison to the non-migrant population in the respective country.
   → Focus on Skills, Analysis of Statistical Data, p. 408

4. Examine the information given in the map, the line graph and the bar charts (p. 260) and get an overview of
   • the number of registered refugees worldwide,
   • historical population movements due to conflict or war,
   • the development of refugee numbers worldwide since 1951.
   → Focus on Skills, Analysis of Statistical Data, p. 408

5. Examine the author's stance on the matter revealed by his/her specific choice of words in connection with the depicted problems and possible solutions.
   Examples:
   • ll. 5 f.   the rush of arrivals swamped the asylum system → negative connotation; masses of migrants overtax the system
   • ll. 20 ff. laissez-faire approach … known as multiculturalism → countries were too lenient and didn't really take care of the situation
   → Focus on Skills, Analysis of a Non-Fictional Text, p. 405

[30] **attendant** coming with a stated thing or resulting from it; *begleitend*

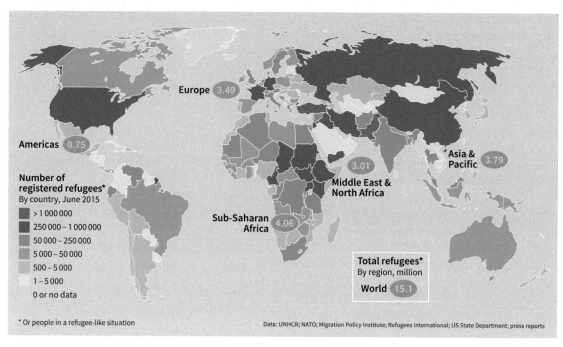

Number of registered refugees*
By country, June 2015

Europe 3.49
Americas 0.75
Asia & Pacific 3.79
Middle East & North Africa 3.01
Sub-Saharan Africa 4.06

> 1 000 000
250 000 – 1 000 000
50 000 – 250 000
5 000 – 50 000
500 – 5 000
1 – 5 000
0 or no data

Total refugees*
By region, million
World 15.1

* Or people in a refugee-like situation

Data: UNHCR; NATO; Migration Policy Institute; Refugees International; US State Department; press reports

On the warpath

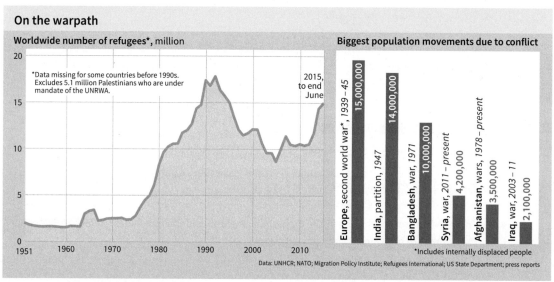

Worldwide number of refugees*, million

*Data missing for some countries before 1990s. Excludes 5.1 million Palestinians who are under mandate of the UNRWA.

2015, to end June

Biggest population movements due to conflict

Europe, second world war*, 1939 – 45 — 15,000,000
India, partition, 1947 — 14,000,000
Bangladesh, war, 1971 — 10,000,000
Syria, war, 2011 – present — 4,200,000
Afghanistan, wars, 1978 – present — 3,500,000
Iraq, war, 2003 – 11 — 2,100,000

*Includes internally displaced people

Data: UNHCR; NATO; Migration Policy Institute; Refugees International; US State Department; press reports

ACTIVITIES

 Webcode SNG-40235-026

6. Do research on the situation of migrants and refugees worldwide using the links provided on the webcode. Work in groups and prepare presentations in class. Flesh out your presentations with photos, maps, statistical data and snippets from newspapers/magazines that show how serious the situation is.

→ Focus on Skills, Presentations, p. 419

7. The article mentions that German Chancellor Angela Merkel wants to organize a pan-European resettlement scheme for Syrians, who are currently the largest group of international refugees. Do you consider this to be a promising strategy or should the refugees themselves decide where they want to live/be resettled? Discuss in class.

→ Focus on Language, Conversation and Discussion, p. 413

Taking Responsibility: Trade and Consumption

Joseph Stiglitz

Why Globalization Fails

AWARENESS

Joseph Stiglitz (*1943) is an American economist and professor at Columbia University in New York City. In 2001, he was awarded the Nobel Memorial Prize in Economic Sciences. His work focuses on global trade, corporate gover-nance and income distribution. He is known for his critical view of the free-market economy and the management of globalization.

Reactivate your knowledge of the relevant components, risks and opportunities of globalization and read the Focus on Facts page *Progress & Responsibility in a Global World* (p. 267).
In groups, make a ranking of the various aspects you think might be beneficial or dangerous to society.

COMPREHENSION

 1. Step 1: In a shared listening activity, team up with a partner and be prepared to listen to the audio text at least twice.

 Step 2: In a **first listening**, get a general understanding of the various aspects Stiglitz mentions about globalization and jot down some notes on what you consider to be relevant information.

Step 3: Exchange your notes with your partner and briefly summarize your notes to each other.

Step 4: Listen to Stiglitz' remarks and observations **a second time**, now paying attention to details and taking notes on the aspects listed below:

- globalization in the 1990s
- changed perceptions of globalization
- reasons for people's antipathy towards globalization
- the management of globalization in
  a) the advanced industrialized world,
  b) developing countries
- (possible benefits) of globalization
- how to manage globalization correctly
- further aspects of globalization
- environmental issues

Step 5: Compare and exchange your notes with your partner, making additions or corrections if necessary.
→ Focus on Skills, Listening Comprehension, p. 394

> ## Tips on vocab »
>
> **to generate sth.** *etw. hervorbringen* ▪ **psychiatry** [saɪˈkaɪətri] relating to mental or emotional disorders ▪ **to be better off** to have more money; to be happier or more satisfied ▪ **to make sb. worse off** to make sb. poorer or be in a worse situation than before ▪ **gains** *Erträge, Gewinne* ▪ **to proceed** to continue as planned ▪ **subsidy** *Subvention* ▪ **to reciprocate** (*fml.*) to behave in the same way as sb. else ▪ **to constitute** to form or make sth. ▪ **to live up to sth.** (*phr. v.*) *den Erwartungen gerecht werden* ▪ **for instance** for example ▪ **capital flow** *Kapitalbewegung, Kapitalstrom* ▪ **foreign direct investment (FDI)** money that is invested in companies, property or other assets by people or organizations from other countries ▪ **recipient** *Empfänger* ▪ **to give sth. short shrift** to be treated without sympathy and with little attention ▪ **to put sth. in jeopardy** [ˈdʒepədi] to put sth. at risk

Webcode
SNG-40235-027 @ **Tip:** In order to get a deeper understanding and better impression of Joseph Stiglitz, you can also watch the video clip provided on the webcode.

ANALYSIS

 2. Listen to Stiglitz' remarks **a third time**. Against the background of your notes taken in task no. 1, together with a partner, compile a mind map that illustrates the various components of globalization as depicted by Stiglitz.

Tip: Draw your mind map on posters or wallpaper, using different colours and pictures to visualize the interdependencies, effects and connections.

Example:

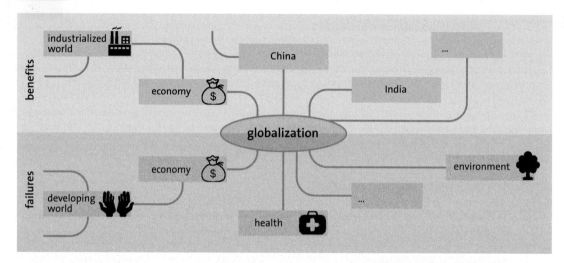

3. Examine and explain Stiglitz' statement that globalization "has put in jeopardy […] values that have enormous consequences". Which values (and their loss) might he be referring to?

4. Describe and analyse the cartoon. To what extent can it be related to Joseph Stiglitz' observations on the failure of globalization?
→ Focus on Skills, Analysis of Visuals, p. 409

Credit: Jeff Danziger, NY Times Syndicate

ACTIVITIES

 5. In class, discuss Joseph Stiglitz' rather negative view of globalization – is he being overly critical?
State whether or not you share his view.
→ Focus on Language, Conversation and Discussion, p. 413

Tips on vocab »

to lean against sth. ■ sneakers ■ to have a grim facial expression ■ to have one's hands in one's pockets ■ to sweat ■ sewing machine ■ piles of (Nike) shoe cartons ■ old-fashioned equipment

GRAMMAR / LANGUAGE

 6. Together with a partner, turn Joseph Stiglitz' statements and explanations into **indirect speech**. Be careful to use appropriate introductory verbs and be sure to backshift **tenses** if necessary.

Example: Stiglitz introduced himself, explaining that he <u>had been involved</u> in the global debates for … He added that in the 1990s, there <u>had been</u> enormous support for …

Info 》》》》

Historical roots of globalization

- Early "world economies" like **Phoenicia** (1200 – 800 B. C.), the **Roman Empire** (510 B. C. – 500 A. D.), the **Silk Road** (1st century) and the **British East India Company** (founded in 1608) establish an international network of trading routes and commercial outposts.
- **Inventions and discoveries** of the late **Middle Ages** and **Renaissance** enable people **in Europe** to sail and **travel longer distances** and become less dependent on weather conditions (e. g. 13th cent.: magnetic compass, mechanical clock, spectacles/lenses, scales for weighing; 16th/17th cent.: pocket watch, thermometer, telescope).
  → International trading and exchange of goods is fostered.
- The **discovery of new continents** and their subsequent conquest in the 16th and 17th centuries gives European countries access to natural resources and labour.
- The **Industrial Revolution**, starting with the invention of James Watt's steam engine, enables the industrialized mass production of goods which is based on the constant input of resources, e. g. from overseas colonies.
- In the **19th century colonialism and imperialism** is at its peak, leading to the growth of Western economic power and dominance, but also dramatic and long-lasting social and economic problems in the colonized countries which linger to this day.

The Emporium[1] Strikes Back

AWARENESS   》》》》》》》》》》》》》

Describe the photo below and discuss its message. Do you think that demonstrations like this can make people aware of "the forces of consumerism" and make them reflect on their consumption habits?

The Blind Ones, photo by Nuno Guimaraes, 2013. Demonstration by students of the University of Sao Paulo, Brazil, in front of a shopping mall to make people aware of the forces of consumerism

Tips on vocab 》》》》

to carry (bunches of) brown paper bags ■ to be blindfolded ■ to be covered with brown paint ■ anonymous ■ wheelchair ■ pavement/sidewalk ■ passers-by ■ to have a blank/dull facial expression

[1] **emporium** (*old-fashioned*) a large shop selling a large range of goods

Retailers in the rich world are suffering as people buy more things online. But they are finding ways to adapt

"The staff at Jessops would like to thank you for shopping with Amazon." With that parting shot[2] plastered to the front door of one of its shops, a company that had been selling cameras in Britain for 78 years shut down in January. The bitter note sums up the mood of many who work on high streets[3] and in shopping centres (malls) across Europe and America. As sales migrate to Amazon and other online vendors[4], shop after shop is closing down, chain after chain is cutting back. Borders, a chain of American bookshops, is gone. So is Comet, a British white-goods[5] and electronics retailer[6]. Virgin Megastores[7] have vanished from France, Tower Records[8] from America. In just two weeks in June and July, five retail chains with a total turnover of £600m ($900m) failed in Britain.

Watching the destruction, it is tempting to conclude that shops are to shopping what typewriters are to writing: an old technology doomed[9] by a better successor[10]. Seattle-based Amazon, nearing its 19th birth-

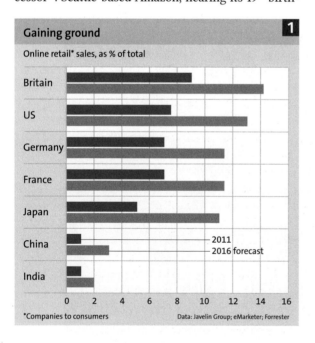

Gaining ground 1

Online retail* sales, as % of total

- Britain
- US
- Germany
- France
- Japan
- China
- India

2011
2016 forecast

0 2 4 6 8 10 12 14 16

*Companies to consumers

Data: Javelin Group; eMarketer; Forrester

day, has lower costs than the vast majority of bricks-and-mortar[11] retailers. However, many shops, of whatever remarkable hypersize, a company builds in the attempt to offer vast[12] choice at low prices, the internet is vaster and cheaper. Prosperous Londoners and New Yorkers ask themselves when was the last time they went shopping; their shopping comes to them. "Retail guys are going to go out of business and e-commerce will become the place everyone buys," pronounces Marc Andreessen, a celebrity venture capitalist. "You are not going to have a choice."

Online commerce has grown at different rates in different countries, but everywhere it is gaining fast (see chart 1). In Britain, Germany and France 90% of the rather modest growth in retail sales expected between now and 2016 will be online, predicts AXA Real Estate, a property-management company.

Old dog, meet new tricks

This would hurt less if shoppers were spending more; smaller slices are more acceptable when they come from bigger pies. But in many rich countries, especially in Europe, consumers are still smarting[13] from the bursting of the credit bubble and high unemployment. American consumers are perkier[14], but seem to be clinging to the bargain-hunting[15] habits of the recession. Services have been consuming a bigger share of their wallets[16] for decades, leaving less to spend on things (see chart 2). Ageing populations could shrink the pie further. Old people shop less.

When shoppers both know what they want and are willing to wait for it they will go online. And retail's simple moneymaking ways of yesteryear – find a catchy concept, fuel growth by opening new shops and attracting more shoppers to existing ones, use your growing size to squeeze suppliers for better margins – have run out of steam. But that does not mean that there are no new options for bricks and mortar.

Shopping is about entertainment as well as acquisition[17]. It allows people to build desires as well as fulfil them – if it did not, no one would ever window-shop[18]. It encom-

---

[2] **parting shot** a remark that you make when you are leaving, so that it has a stronger effect – [3] **high street** a street where the most important shops and businesses in a town are – [4] **vendor** sb. who is selling sth. – [5] **white-goods** large electrical goods for the house, such as cookers and washing machines – [6] **retailer** a person, shop or business that sells goods to the public – [7] **Virgin Records** a record label founded in 1972 – [8] **Tower Records** a US retail music chain (1950–2006) – [9] **doomed** certain to fail, die or be destroyed – [10] **successor** *Nachfolger* – [11] **bricks-and-mortar** businesses with buildings that customers go to (as opposed to online retailers) – [12] **vast** extremely large in amount – [13] **to smart from sth.** to feel upset because of failure or criticism; *von etw. schmerzen* – [14] **perky** happy and full of energy – [15] **bargain-hunting** *Schnäppchenjagd* – [16] **wallet** *Portemonnaie* – [17] **acquisition** the process of getting sth. – [18] **to window-shop** to spend time looking at the goods for sale in shop windows without intending to buy them

passes[19] exploration[20] and frivolity[21], not just necessity. It can be immersive[22], too. While computer screens can bewitch the eye, a good shop has four more senses to ensorcell[23]. No one makes the point better than Apple; in terms of sales per unit area its showrooms-slash-playrooms best[24] all other American retailers.

And shops make money. Bricks-and-mortar retail may be losing ground to online shopping, but it remains more profitable. The physical world is also increasingly capable of taking the fight to its online competitors. Last year online sales of shop-based American retailers grew by 29%; those of online-only merchants grew by just 21%. Apart from Amazon – which has long spurned[25] profits in favour of growth – most pure-play online retailers are losing market share, says Sucharita Mulpuru of Forrester Research. The bricks-and-mortar retrenchment[26] will be painful, but the survivors may make shopping a less formulaic, more satisfying and possibly even more profitable experience, both offline and on.

Many brands still think shops are the best way to attract customers. Inditex of Spain, owner of the ubiquitous[27] Zara fashion brand, opened 482 stores in 2012, bringing its total to 6,009 in 86 countries. Primark, a fast-growing vendor of nearly disposable[28] clothing, sells nothing on its website, relying on its 242 shops for almost all its sales. The same can hold at the luxury end, too – few will buy a $10,000 necklace online, or entrust it to the post. Space on the snazziest[29] streets in London, Paris and New York is in such demand that luxury retailers pay millions in "key money" to secure it, says Mark Burlton of Cushman & Wakefield, a property company.

Offline-only, though, is a shrinking category

[...] The future shopscape[30] will be emptier, but more attractive. Shoppers can expect new rewards for simply showing up. Shopkick, a mobile-phone app, gives American shoppers points that earn them goodies like iTunes songs just for stepping across the threshold of a participating store. Inspired by Apple, shops promise "experience" and hope that sales will follow. Germany's Kochhaus claims to be the first food store organ-

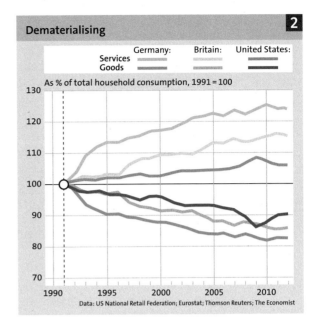

Dematerialising 2

Germany: Britain: United States:
Services
Goods

As % of total household consumption, 1991 = 100

Data: US National Retail Federation; Eurostat; Thomson Reuters; The Economist

ised around recipes rather than grocery categories. The ingredients are strewn[31] across tables, not stacked on shelves. Some shops will opt[32] to sell nothing at all on the premises[33]. Desigual, a Spanish fashion merchant, has shops in Barcelona and Paris that carry only samples[34]. Shoppers are helped to assemble them into outfits that they then buy online.

Shopping centres are reallocating[35] space from the classic form of retailing to leisure and entertainment. [...]

And new hybrids are emerging. Yihaodian, a Chinese company owned by Walmart, has used an app to let phone users visit 1,000 "virtual stores" accessible only at specific sites – many of which, rather cheekily[36], were on the doorsteps of rival retailers. Tesco's Korean subsidiary[37], Homeplus, puts up images of products on posters in the subway; commuters can scan them to get the products delivered. Tangible[38] and virtual retailing may meld[39] in all sorts of unaccustomed ways. Even Amazon has flirted with the idea of opening physical stores. Consumers have reason to cheer the survival of the sexiest.

The Economist, 13 July 2013, pp. 20 ff.

---

[19] **to encompass** (fml.) to include different types of things – [20] **exploration** Erforschung, Erkundung – [21] **frivolity** [frɪˈvɒləti] Frivolität, Leichtsinnigkeit – [22] **immersive** eindringend – [23] **to ensorcell** [ɪnˈsɔːsəl] verhexen, verzaubern – [24] **to best** (fml.) to defeat sb. in a fight or competition; jdn. übertreffen – [25] **to spurn** (fml.) zurückweisen – [26] **retrenchment** Einschränkung, Einsparung – [27] **ubiquitous** [juːˈbɪkwɪtəs] (fml.) seeming to be everywhere – [28] **disposable** Wegwerf- – [29] **snazzy** (infml.) modern and stylish in a way that attracts attention – [30] **shopscape** Verkaufsraum – [31] **to strew** (strewed, strewn) to spread things untidily over a surface – [32] **to opt** here: to choose – [33] **premises** Geschäftsräume – [34] **sample** Muster, Probe – [35] **to reallocate** etw. umverteilen – [36] **cheeky** frech – [37] **subsidiary** [səbˈsɪdiəri] Filiale – [38] **tangible** able to be shown, touched or experienced – [39] **to meld** sich vermischen

COMPREHENSION

1. Give an outline of the damage that online or e-commerce is doing to retailers.

2. Present the shopping habits of European and American consumers.

3. State why "bricks-and-mortar" retail shops are still attractive to consumers.

4. Describe the new strategies and shopping "hybrids" that have been created to motivate people to shop and consume.

ANALYSIS

5. Examine bar chart no. 1 and relate the presented trends and forecast to the new retail strategies depicted in the article.
   → Focus on Skills, Analysis of Statistical Data, p. 408

6. Analyse line graph no. 2 and explain what the peaks and lows reveal about shopping trends in the respective countries.

7. Explain the statement that "[w]hile computer screens can bewitch the eye, a good shop has four more senses to ensorcell" (ll. 64 ff.).
   What further senses – in addition to vision – do "physical stores" appeal to and in what way?
   Give examples.

ACTIVITIES

8. Team up with three other students and collect ideas about the "perfect shop" or shopping environment. Design a "shop", virtual or physical, that meets your desires and needs but is also profitable, competitive (*wettbewerbsfähig*) and environmentally friendly. Draw sketches on posters/wallpaper, then display them in class and discuss and evaluate your various ideas.

9. Annie Leonard is an American proponent (*Befürworter*) of sustainability and a critic of excessive consumerism. In 2008, she created the animated documentary *The Story of Stuff* in which she narrates the lifecycle of material goods and the impact of the materials economy.

Step 1: Watch the video provided on the webcode and get an overview of the "materials economy".

Step 2: Get information about and take notes on the "golden arrow of consumption".

Step 3: Encouraged by the enormous success of *The Story of Stuff*, Annie Leonard and her team have produced further animated films to make people aware of environmental, economic and political grievances (*Missstände*).

Divide your class into six groups, with each group working with one of Lennox' further films.
- The Story of Bottled Water
- The Story of Electronics
- The Story of Cosmetics
- The Story of Broke
- The Story of Change
- The Science of Persuasion

Use the links provided on the webcode and prepare presentations on the various "stories".
Additionally, you should provide your class with a 1–2 page handout that focuses on the most relevant information presented in each film.
→ Focus on Skills, Presentations, p. 419
→ Focus on Skills, Writing a Handout, p. 425

Webcode
SNG-40235-028 @

Progress & Responsibility in a Global World

The three historical periods of globalization

- **exploration (until 1500)**
  - founding and forming of villages, cities and infrastructure
- **colonization (1500 – 1900)**
  - development of writing and printing technologies (e. g. the Gutenberg printing press)
  - the Industrial Revolution (1750 – 1830)
  - advances in communications (e.g. telephone, telegraph)
- **internationalization (1900 – present)**
  - international trade and organizations (e. g. WTO (World Trade Organization), IMF (International Monetary Fund), World Bank, United Nations)
  - technology and global media (e. g. satellite, computers, Internet, WWW)
  - information revolution (e. g. personalization of communications → social networks, etc.)

Components of globalization

environment
- ecology
- global warming
- deforestation
- pollution
- efficient use vs. plunder of resources

culture/society
- education
- language
- shift of norms & values
- Westernization
- tourism
- change of lifestyles

economy
- production
- work
- trade
- markets
- consumption

technology
- scientific & technological advancement
- modernization
- information
- health care

population
- decline (rich countries) vs. expansion (poor countries)
- migration
- overpopulation
- outsourcing
- diseases (e. g. AIDS, HIV)
- ageing

media
- communication
- information
- surveillance

politics
- UN agencies
- NGOs
- NATO

Risks and opportunities

risks	opportunities	future tasks & requirements
<ul><li>rising competition</li><li>increasing (inter-)dependencies</li><li>control by multinationals</li><li>uncontrolled money flow</li><li>growing inequalities</li><li>widening social gaps</li><li>environmental degradation</li><li>degradation of social standards</li><li>widening power imbalances</li><li>concentration of multinational companies</li></ul>	<ul><li>diffusion of new ideas, technologies, products, services, lifestyles</li><li>new potential markets and customers</li><li>increase of communication</li><li>increasing coherence of politics in economy, society and employment due to international standards</li><li>global information network and exchange</li><li>cooperation through partnerships</li></ul>	<ul><li>thinking globally → locally <u>and</u> globally</li><li>being prepared to venture into the unknown</li><li>developing intercultural competencies</li><li>being prepared for crosscultural encounters</li><li>being future-oriented → sustainability</li><li>developing production and service skills</li><li>developing flexibility</li><li>getting access to information</li></ul>

World Trade

World Economic Forum

The **World Economic Forum** (WEF), founded in 1971, is a Swiss non-profit foundation that meets annually in Davos, and **brings together international business and political leaders, intellectuals and journalists to discuss pressing global issues**.

5 Besides its economic focus, the annual meeting has become a neutral platform for political leaders to resolve political differences. In 2008, Microsoft founder Bill Gates gave a keynote speech on "creative capitalism", which combines generating profits and solving the world's inequities by using market forces to address the needs of the poor worldwide. The participants are considered a global elite – a think tank of internationally-oriented experts, including a group of "Young Global Leaders" consisting of under-forty-year-old leaders from all around the 10 world and representing a wide range of disciplines and sectors.

WEF has also **launched several global initiatives**, e. g. the **Global Health Initiative**, the **Global Education Initiative** and the **Partnering Against Corruption Initiative**.

However, there is heavy criticism as well: WEF, along with the G8 and the World Trade Organisation, are viewed as a "mix of pomp and platitude" by anti-globalisation activists and many NGOs.

Further economic forums

- **The Group of Eight (G8):** France, Germany, Italy, Japan, the United Kingdom, the United States, Canada and Russia

This group has occasionally been expanded, e. g.:

- **Outreach Five (O5):** plus Brazil, China, India, Mexico and South Africa
- **Group of Twenty (G20):** the 20 major economies of Africa, North America, South America, East Asia, South Asia, Southeast Asia, Western Asia, Eurasia, Europe and Oceania; the group meets semi-annually, and the last meeting took place in Seoul in November 2010.

Global players – and the consequences

- **multinational companies** (or mega corporations) play an important role in the international economy: they often have powerful influence on local economies, international relations and even politics (→ lobbying)
- **many multinational companies are criticized** due to lax environmental standards, bad labour standards (e. g. sweatshops in developing countries, control of tariffs → unfair wages), marginalization of local businesses/markets
- many multinationals hold **patents** (e. g. Siemens, Adidas) in order to prevent the rise of competitors
- examples of **influential multinational corporations** are: ExxonMobil, Wal-Mart, McDonald's, General Electric, Boeing, Microsoft and British Petrol
- the United Nations declares **2005 the International Year of Microcredit**; microloans are designed to spur entrepreneurship in developing countries and gain acceptance in the mainstream finance industry as a source of future growth

Marius Münstermann, Christian Werner

The Mica[1] Children

AWARENESS

Glittery and metallic fashion items are currently very hip. Even traditional Birkenstock sandals have gotten a metallic makeover. Carry out a survey in your class about the latest "glitter fashion".

- Who of your classmates is wearing glittery shirts, jeans, shoes/sandals, make-up, jewellery or sequined (*mit Pailletten besetzt*) clothes and accessories?
- Who of your classmates/your classmates' parents drives a car with metallic paint?
- What do you/they like about it?
- Do you know where the glittery pigment/material comes from and how it is produced?

They work in India's mines to supply the cosmetics and car paint industries. And sometimes they die.

Badku Marandi was six years old the first time he
5 crept[2] into the tunnels that had been dug deep into the hard earth. During the dry months before the monsoon season begins, there is only one source of income for the poor here in the state of Jharkhand in India's impoverished northeast. It's why they leave their vil-
10 lages, day after day, to try to try their luck in the forested hills.

Some, though, only find death.

Fine particles make the hill sparkle in the sun. The ground here is full of mica – shimmering minerals. The
15 deeper you dig, the bigger the mica fragments[3] become. But with every meter and every strike of the hammer, the danger of being buried alive underground also increases for people like Badku. Even today, Badku still doesn't have any idea what the minerals he and all the
20 others extract day after day are used for.

Chapter 1: In the Tunnel

From lipstick by L'Oréal to automobile paint for BMW and Volkswagen – many large companies and their suppliers purchase[4] mica from Jharkhand and Bihar for
25 use in their products. According to one Indian export database, during the first three months of this year alone, over 1,300 tons of mica were shipped to Germany through Kolkata's[5] port. The reporters of this story interviewed more than a dozen companies that purchase
30 mica from India about their supply chain. They all had the same statement:

Parents and their children working and collecting mica. The families are driven into the situation by poverty.

They are aware of child labor in the mica mines and they are working to improve the situation.

In the mica belt of Jharkhand and Bihar, entire villages sustain[6] themselves by mining the minerals, which 35 they extract from the earth in forests. The Netherlands-based Centre for Research on Multinational Corporations (SOMO) estimates that about 80 percent of the region's mica originates from these kinds of unofficial mines, although mine isn't quite the right term – they 40 are more like pits[7].

Some are as small as rabbit holes, some large enough that they look like they were dug out by excavators[8]. Some can be seen from the edge of the road, but most are hidden deep in the forest. Underage[9] girls sit in the 45 mines with women and older men who are too fragile

---

[1] **mica** ['maɪkə] *Glimmererde* – [2] **to creep** (crept, crept) *kriechen* – [3] **fragment** a small piece or a part, esp. when broken off of sth. larger –
[4] **to purchase** to buy sth. – [5] **Kolkata** Kalkutta; the capital of West Bengal – [6] **to sustain** to keep alive – [7] **pit** *Grube* – [8] **excavator** *Bagger* –
[9] **underage** younger than the lowest age at which a particular activity is legally allowed

for hard work underground. They crumble[10] the mica and sort out the pieces. When they don't find any more mica, they move on.

50 They leave behind hollows[11] that look like moon craters.

But if the workers come upon a promising mica vein[12], they dig deeper. The men dig tunnels into the ground using hammers and crowbars[13] and do not support

55 them with the help of beams[14]. We climb into one of the mines with a 360-degree camera as Badku explains why the work inside is so dangerous.

Abrasions[15] and broken bones are part of daily life in the mica mines. The workers are afraid of scorpions

60 that hide under the rocks – and then there's the quartz dust that they stir up and breathe in. In the evenings, they return home with a rattling cough[16]. Many of the workers contract asthma and black lung disease, which makes them more susceptible[17] to tuberculosis and can-

65 cer. Many families subsequently go into debt to pay for medication and hospitalizations.

To settle those debts, they must mine more mica.

This includes the children. Until they are strong enough to hammer for hours themselves, the boys haul[18] the

70 mica to the surface in baskets.

The nongovernmental organization Bachpan Bachao Andolan (BBA), whose founder Kailash Satyarthi received the Nobel Peace Prize for his fight against child labor in 2014, has been monitoring the mica-mining

75 situation for years. Each month, BBA documents between 10 and 20 deaths in collapsed mica tunnels.

A BBA informant, who doesn't want to be identified by name, says the mica business is sheathed[19] in a "culture of silence." He recalls how, in the case of one woman

80 who died in a mica tunnel, the doctor helped cover it up by describing the cause on her death certificate as a "fall from the roof of a two-story house."

"But in the villages, there are no homes with more than one story," the informant says.

85 He suspects the doctor wanted to avoid questions from the police – this being an illegal business that nobody wants to be associated with. The people here accept that the work is dangerous. What, after all, are the alternatives? Badku was seven years old when a mine he

90 was working in collapsed.

Indian law prohibits anyone under the age of 14 from working – and certainly not in dangerous jobs like mining. That's why the authorities want to crack down on the illegal mica trade. The plan is for the Ministry of Mines to issue new licenses that will only be granted to 95 mine operators who adhere to[20] environmental and labor standards and do not use child labor.

Those who continue illegally extracting mica are to be identified and punished.

Every now and then, police confiscate[21] trucks carrying 100 mica as they drive from the villages to the city. The new licenses were originally supposed to be given out at the beginning of this year, but not a single one has been issued so far. Instead the authorities have announced they want to more aggressively pursue the illegal mica 105 market, making the gray zone that has existed so far even darker.

Out of fear of the police, people are now digging their holes even deeper inside the forest.

To search for mica scraps[22], they climb into tunnels that 110 have, in some cases, been abandoned[23] decades ago. Accidents are reported even less frequently, because people are afraid of being punished by the law. The mica trade continues – and it has become even more nebulous and dangerous. 115

Chapter 2: The Dealers

The dealers' stores are located in a side alley in the market of Jhumri Telaiya, one of the most important mica trading centers in the region. But where does the mica come from that the dealers sell, and who are they 120 selling it to?

We are quickly surrounded by 20, then 30 men.

Child labor? It doesn't exist here, they all claim.

Look around, only old men are working in the stores. Using large scissors[24], they cleave[25] the chunks of mica, 125 layer by layer. The dealers speak with one another, make themselves seem important. Only one is willing to speak in front of the camera. Sandeep Jain takes us aside and sits down in his store. The interview becomes uneasy; the atmosphere is tense. The other dealers 130 stand at our backs in a semi-circle. They whisper and interrupt their colleague when he says something they don't like.

---

[10] **to crumble** to break into small pieces – [11] **hollow** a hole or empty space in sth. – [12] **vein** Ader – [13] **crowbar** ['krəʊbɑːr] Brechstange – [14] **beam** Balken, Träger – [15] **abrasion** Abschürfung, Schürfwunde – [16] **rattling cough** rasselnder Husten – [17] **susceptible** easily harmed by sth. – [18] **to haul** to pull sth. heavy slowly and with difficulty – [19] **to sheathe** [ʃiːð] (lit.) to cover up sth. – [20] **to adhere to** (phr. v.; fml.) to continue to obey a rule – [21] **to confiscate** beschlagnahmen – [22] **scrap** Rest – [23] **to abandon** to leave a place, thing or person, usually forever – [24] **scissors** Schere – [25] **to cleave** (cleft, cleft) to separate or divide

Many of the mine workers are Adivasi, members of India's indigenous[26] ethnic group. They are a segment of
135 society who are often excluded in their own country.
Others are Dalits[27], the so-called "untouchables," trapped
at the lowest level of the Hindu caste system.

Both groups are among the poorest of the poor and very
140 few of them own the land on which they work, meaning
they often also have to pay for a lease or mining rights.
But how else are they supposed to make a living? "The
mica belongs to us," the people here say. They live from
it. It feeds them and allows them to send their kids to
145 school. At least if they don't have to work in the mines.
And the laws?

Chapter 3: The Corporations

Is there a solution? The only company that currently
claims[28] to be buying mica exclusively from legal mines
150 is German chemicals giant Merck, one of the largest
importers of Indian mica. Internal documents shown to
SPIEGEL by Merck claim to prove this.

The problem, though, is that even the Indian authorities themselves say there are no legal mica mines in the
155 region.

Officials at Merck say that because they had little confidence in the Indian authorities, they took their own
initiative a decade ago to find responsible suppliers
who adhere to worker safety standards and don't em-
160 ploy children in their mines.

Together with other corporations – among them, apparel[29] companies H&M and Chanel and consumer
electronics-maker Philips – Merck followed up that
step at the start of this year by establishing the Respon-
165 sible Mica Initiative. Their shared goal: To end child
labor in the mica mines by 2022. After that, the businesses are pledging[30] to purchase mica exclusively from
legal sources. But is it really possible to monitor the
suppliers?
170 Just take the example of Chinese paint pigment manufacturer Kuncai, the region's largest mica buyer aside
from Merck. Kuncai claims to buy mica from mines that
Merck says supply the German chemicals company exclusively. Indeed, our reporting uncovered many such
inconsistencies[31] that are unresolvable given the com- 175
plex and opaque[32] nature of the mica trade.

Merck uses a tracking system to ensure that suppliers
don't include any mica from illegal mines. Under the
system, mine operators use a logbook to record and
keep track of a mine's daily output. They then pay tax- 180
es to the government for this amount. Merck argues
that "if mica from uncontrolled sources is included, the
mine owners must also pay license fees for those
amounts of mica. This doesn't make any economic
sense, because then the mica would be more expensive 185
for the mine owner than that which is extracted from
his own mine." But many dealers admitted in the course
of our reporting that they also pay duties to the government for mica that has been extracted illegally.

What matters to most here is that the business be able 190
to continue, unhindered.

This is also true of the village of Kanichihar, where Badku lives, in the heart of the mica belt. Day after day, the
men keep going into the mines during the long dry season when the rice fields wither[33]. After Badku's acci- 195
dent, he was supposed to return to the tunnels and keep
hammering, like almost all the others here. But Badku
refused. Back into a mine that had buried him alive?
He said "no." And he had a bit of luck.

SPIEGEL ONLINE, http://www.spiegel.de/international/tomorrow/
a-1152334.html [02.07.2017]

---

[26] **indigenous** [ɪnˈdɪdʒɪnəs] *eingeboren* – [27] **Dalit** a member of the lowest caste – [28] **to claim** *etw. vorgeben, behaupten* – [29] **apparel**
[əˈpærəl] *clothes, textiles* – [30] **to pledge** to make a serious or formal promise – [31] **inconsistency** [ˌɪnkənˈsɪstənsi] *Widersprüchlichkeit* –
[32] **opaque** [əʊˈpeɪk] (*fml.*) difficult to understand, not clear – [33] **to wither** [ˈwɪðər] *ausdörren, verkümmern*

COMPREHENSION

 1. Before you read the magazine article, divide the class into 3 – 6 groups, with 1 – 2 groups each focusing on a different chapter of the text.
However, <u>all</u> groups should read the introductory part (ll. 1 – 20).

Introduction:
- Badhu Marandi
- the mica hills in Jharkhand

Chapter 1: In the Tunnel
- the companies that purchase mica
- child labour
- the condition of the mines
- the impact on people's health
- the "culture of silence"
- tackling illegal mining

Chapter 2: The Dealers
- the dealers' behaviour
- interviewing Sandeep Jain
- the Adivasi
- victims of the caste system
- making a living

Chapter 3: The Corporations
- the Merck company's business policy
- the Responsible Mica Initiative
- Badhu's accident

In a next step, the groups remix (see diagram) and exchange their results.

ANALYSIS

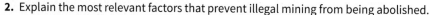

2. Explain the most relevant factors that prevent illegal mining from being abolished.
→ Focus on Skills, Analysis of a Non-Fictional Text, p. 405

3. Categorize the article by identifying and explaining the characteristic features that create the specific style of the text.
→ Focus on Facts, Basic Types of Non-Fictional Texts, p. 396

4. Examine the infographic (p. 273), which is an extract from the Jharkhand State Report of March 2017, published by the Jharkhand Department of Industry and Ministry of Mines.
- How does the government present the mining business?
- What does the government not mention or refer to?
- How does the infographic differ from the text?
→ Focus on Skills, Analysis of Visuals, p. 409

Jharkhand – The Mining Base of India

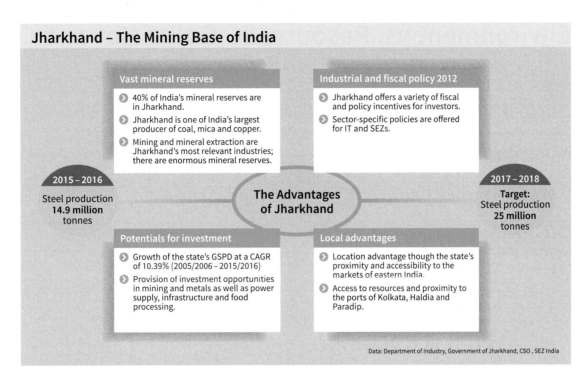

Vast mineral reserves

- 40% of India's mineral reserves are in Jharkhand.
- Jharkhand is one of India's largest producer of coal, mica and copper.
- Mining and mineral extraction are Jharkhand's most relevant industries; there are enormous mineral reserves.

Industrial and fiscal policy 2012

- Jharkhand offers a variety of fiscal and policy incentives for investors.
- Sector-specific policies are offered for IT and SEZs.

2015 – 2016
Steel production
14.9 million tonnes

The Advantages of Jharkhand

2017 – 2018
Target:
Steel production
25 million tonnes

Potentials for investment

- Growth of the state's GSPD at a CAGR of 10.39% (2005/2006 – 2015/2016)
- Provision of investment opportunities in mining and metals as well as power supply, infrastructure and food processing.

Local advantages

- Location advantage though the state's proximity and accessibility to the markets of eastern India.
- Access to resources and proximity to the ports of Kolkata, Haldia and Paradip.

Data: Department of Industry, Government of Jharkhand, CSO , SEZ India

ACTIVITIES

Webcode
SNG-40235-029 **5. Step 1:** Do further research on the mica mining business in India using the links provided on the webcode.

Step 2: After you have investigated the entanglements and legal loopholes of the business, put some of the people involved in the Hot Seat, e. g.:
a) representatives from international companies such as Merck, L'Oréal, BMW, Volkswagen, etc.
b) an Indian politician
c) local mica traders.

Prepare role cards and try to identify with your respective role.

 6. In groups, rewrite (parts of) the magazine article and turn it into:
a) a human interest story
b) the front cover of a tabloid
c) an online article published by a human rights organization
d) an online statement published by a company trying to improve its battered image after it bought mica from mines using child labour.
→ Focus on Facts, The Press, p. 398

 Display and discuss your articles in class.
→ Focus on Language, Conversation and Discusion, p. 413

Environment vs. Resources – Going Hot and Cold

Roger Howard

Is the U.S. Fracking Boom a Bubble?

AWARENESS

In a 4-corners activity, reflect on and discuss your views concerning energy consumption and how to deal with the shortage of resources. Here are some keywords to start with:

- fossil energy
- energy reserves
- hybrid cars
- reducing consumption
- energy efficiency
- insulation of houses
- energy-saving measures
- conventional energy sources (e. g. coal, oil, gas)
- renewable energy (e. g. solar energy, wind power, biogas)

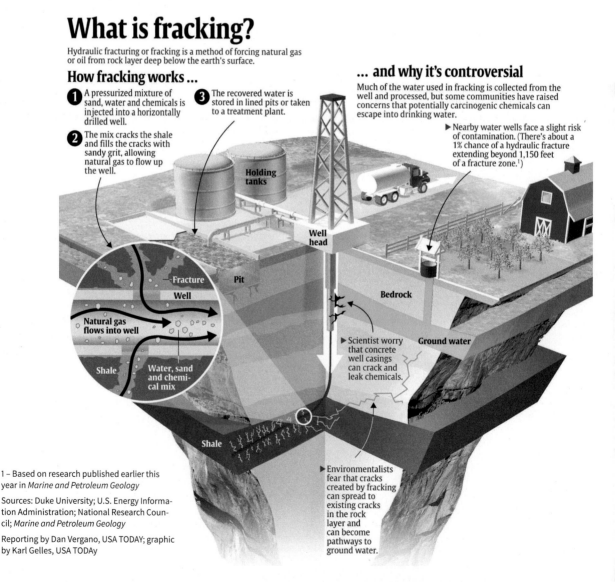

What is fracking?

Hydraulic fracturing or fracking is a method of forcing natural gas or oil from rock layer deep below the earth's surface.

How fracking works ...

1 A pressurized mixture of sand, water and chemicals is injected into a horizontally drilled well.

2 The mix cracks the shale and fills the cracks with sandy grit, allowing natural gas to flow up the well.

3 The recovered water is stored in lined pits or taken to a treatment plant.

... and why it's controversial

Much of the water used in fracking is collected from the well and processed, but some communities have raised concerns that potentially carcinogenic chemicals can escape into drinking water.

▶ Nearby water wells face a slight risk of contamination. (There's about a 1% chance of a hydraulic fracture extending beyond 1,150 feet of a fracture zone.[1])

Holding tanks

Well head

Fracture

Well

Pit

Bedrock

Natural gas flows into well

Shale

Water, sand and chemical mix

▶ Scientist worry that concrete well casings can crack and leak chemicals.

Ground water

Shale

▶ Environmentalists fear that cracks created by fracking can spread to existing cracks in the rock layer and can become pathways to ground water.

1 – Based on research published earlier this year in *Marine and Petroleum Geology*

Sources: Duke University; U.S. Energy Information Administration; National Research Council; *Marine and Petroleum Geology*

Reporting by Dan Vergano, USA TODAY; graphic by Karl Gelles, USA TODAy

1. **Before reading:** By definition, **hydraulic fracturing** [haɪˈdrɒlɪk ˈfræktʃərɪŋ], commonly known as **fracking**, is the creation of fractures in rock formations in the earth using a pressurized mixture of water, sand and chemicals, for the purpose of releasing and extracting natural gas.

Together with a partner, describe the visual on the previous page and prepare a short presentation in which you lay out the process of fracking to your class. Use everyday English as much as possible.
Additionally, prepare a short handout for your listeners that illustrates the complex matter, e. g. by using a visual and giving the most relevant information.
→ Focus on Skills, Writing a Handout, p. 425

Tip: In order to get a better understanding of the complex scientific matter, first clarify important technical terms and transform them into everyday English. Work together with a partner and use a dictionary for help.

1 America's oil boom, one of the most spectacular the world has witnessed, continues at breakneck[1] speed. Last week the Bank of America released figures showing that the US has now become the world's leading oil pro-
5 ducer, overtaking both Saudi Arabia and Russia. Ways of extracting "tight[2]" oil and gas from shale rock[3] and other "unconventional" sources have revolutionized energy production and allowed the US to produce 11 million barrels of oil every day (mbd) in the first half of this year.
10 Yet some experts are asking searching questions about America's shale revolution. Since 2009, when America's domestic production of oil and gas started to accelerate sharply, respected analysts like Arthur Berman, a Texas-based geologist and energy consultant,
15 and David Hughes, a Canadian geoscientist, have claimed that the shale revolution is just a bubble. Now they are reiterating[4] their warnings that this shale bubble could burst with devastating[5] impact, forcing the US to rely, once again, on the Middle East while se-
20 verely denting[6] the drive for greener fuels.

2 Through their sceptical eyes, it is the longevity[7] of the American shale bonanza[8] that is open to question. The International Energy Agency, an independent watchdog[9] based in Paris, ventures[10] some bold[11] predic-
25 tions, claiming that American oil output will continue to climb over the next few years, reaching a high in 2019 and then stabilizing in the 2020s. The US will then remain the world's leading oil producer, continue the IEA

experts, until the early 2030s when other countries will overtake it. But its critics point out that such claims are 30 not really predictions at all but mere[12] conjecture[13].
It is true that the story of American shale neatly illustrates how hard it is to predict the future of energy in particular. As recently as 2008, America's dependency on foreign sources of oil was a very hot political topic 35 in Washington. Our "addiction to oil," as President George W. Bush said in his 2006 State of the Union address, meant relying upon "unstable parts of the world". Nobody foresaw how quickly and dramatically America's energy fortunes[14] would be transformed by the 40 shale revolution.
Sceptics point out that the future of America's shale industry is equally hard to predict – or rather to guess. The US undoubtedly has huge shale reserves but it is impossible to be sure about their size. For example, in 45 2011 the Department of Energy published its findings about one of America's Monterey Shale deposits in California – and claimed it harboured[15] 15 billion barrels of recoverable[16] oil reserves. But just a few weeks ago, the department released a radically revised figure, 50 massively slashing[17] its earlier forecast. Now Monterey was said to hold something closer to 600 million. Some experts think that even this much more modest estimate hugely inflates[18] the true figure.

3 More important than the sheer size of resources, 55 however, is their commercial recoverability[19]. The en-

---

[1] **breakneck** *halsbrecherisch* – [2] **tight** held or fixed in position firmly; difficult to move or undo – [3] **shale rock** *Schiefergestein* –
[4] **to reiterate** [riˈɪtəreɪt] *(fml.)* to say sth. again, once or several times – [5] **devastating** causing a lot of damage or destruction –
[6] **to dent** here: to slow or reduce sth. – [7] **longevity** [lɒnˈdʒevəti] *(fml.) Langlebigkeit* – [8] **bonanza** *Goldgrube* – [9] **watchdog** *Überwachungs-organisation* – [10] **to venture** *(fml.)* to risk saying sth. that might be criticized – [11] **bold** confident; not afraid to say what you feel or to take risks – [12] **mere** *bloß, lediglich* – [13] **conjecture** *Mutmaßung* – [14] **fortune** here: a large amount of money – [15] **to harbour** to contain –
[16] **recoverable** *förderwürdig* – [17] **to slash** to reduce sth. drastically – [18] **in inflate** to make sth. larger or more important – [19] **recoverability** *Ausbeutefaktor*

ergy industry, not just shale in particular, is ultimately all about economics – at what point upfront[20] costs can be recouped[21], profits reaped[22] and risks rewarded.

60 The shale revolution was born in 2008, when American oil production was a very modest 600,000 b/d. It was at this time that the technologies it depends upon became more affordable, and that the global price of oil was high enough to support the very high infra-
65 structure and drilling costs involved. Fracking – the process of hydraulically fracturing shale rock to release oil and gas – is prohibitively[23] expensive, and operators reply upon clear commercial margins[24] to make it viable[25].

70 At the moment, the global price of oil lies close to the breakeven[26] cost that many American companies require[27]. But some industry experts argue that if the price does fall below $90 a barrel – it is currently just over $100 – then the impact will be huge.

75 "Much of the American shale industry could find itself in real trouble and shut down relatively quickly," argues Professor Jonathan Stern of the Oxford Institute of Energy Studies. Even at the $100 figure some producers are reported to be struggling financially.

80 The oil price could fall fast and perhaps far in all manner of circumstances[28]. A Washington-Tehran rapprochement[29] will bring, at some point, voluminous quantities of Iranian crude[30] onto the global market; the Iraqi government might not only placate[31] the country but also
85 coax[32] foreign companies with more generous terms; or a downturn in China would dampen[33] demand.

4 Even in their best-case scenario – of a high and climbing oil price – America's shale producers will be pushed to maintain, or even imitate, the astonishing
90 level of output of recent years.

This is because a shale well[34] has a very limited lifespan, of around seven or eight years on average. Its output plummets[35] drastically after the first three years and then deteriorates[36] steadily thereafter. By contrast
95 a conventional oil field has a longevity that a shale well simply does not possess, producing crude at a

level that wanes[37] slowly over years or decades: Saudi's massive Ghawar field, for example, began production in 1951 and is still pumping out around 5 million barrels every day.
100
The IEA itself points out that the US shale industry will need to bring 2,500 wells into service every year to sustain[38] the output – of one million barrels every day – from just one of its main reserves, located in North Dakota. Some of these wells may also require more 105 investment than their predecessors: "a rising percentage of supplies require a higher breakeven price," as the IEA has said in a separate report, "may be in sight."

Critics like Berman and Hughes conclude that the US needs to hedge its bets[39] and ensure that it can cope 110 when, as they claim it will, the shale phenomenon retreats and disappoints. If this happens, then America could continue to be afflicted[40], as before, by burgeoning[41] domestic demand for both oil and gas. Tens, perhaps hundreds, of thousands of jobs would be lost and 115 the economy would be highly vulnerable to price spikes[42]. The US would, once again, become dependent on foreign suppliers, particularly the Middle Eastern exporters that offer long term, plentiful sources.

5 Such sceptics point to another adverse[43] consequence. 120 Because the US is currently relying too much on shale, they argue, it is failing to address the fundamentals that underwrite the energy market – supply and demand.

Washington should be finding ways of sponsoring fuel efficiency in the United States – for example by 125 subsidizing[44] the use of less gluttonous[45] cars: in 2013, the American public consumed only 6% less gasoline than in 2007, when domestic intake[46] hit an all-time high.

Equally, they say that more emphasis needs to be placed 130 upon developing a generation of greener, cleaner fuels – solar power and fuel cell technology for example – than both oil and natural gas. In their eyes, one danger of the shale revolution is that it makes this seem less of a priority – on economic as well as environmental 135 grounds – than it should be. Shale, in other words, is

---

[20] **upfront** *im Voraus* – [21] **to recoup** [rɪˈkuːp] *ausgleichen* – [22] **to reap profit** *Gewinn erzielen, abschöpfen* – [23] **prohibitive** [prəˈhɪbɪtɪv] *unerschwinglich* – [24] **margin** *Gewinnmarge* – [25] **viable** [ˈvaɪəbl] *realisierbar* – [26] **breakeven** *Rentabilitätsgrenze* – [27] **to require** *to need* – [28] **in all manner of circumstances** *unter allen möglichen Umständen* – [29] **rapprochement** [ræˈprʊʃmõ] *(fml.) Wiederannäherung* – [30] **crude (oil)** *Rohöl* – [31] **to placate** *jdn. besänftigen* – [32] **to coax** *schmeicheln* – [33] **to dampen** *to reduce* – [34] **shale well** *Quellen im Schiefergestein* – [35] **to plummet** *to suddenly fall* – [36] **to deteriorate** *to become worse* – [37] **to wane** *to become less* – [38] **to sustain** *etw. aufrechterhalten* – [39] **to hedge one's bets** *(idm.) sich nach allen Seiten absichern* – [40] **afflicted** *betrübt, geplagt* – [41] **to burgeon** [ˈbɜːdʒən] *(lit.) to develop and grow quickly* – [42] **spike** *a sudden large increase* – [43] **adverse** *nachteilig* – [44] **to subsidize** *subventionieren* – [45] **gluttonous** [ˈglʌtənəs] *gefräßig* – [46] **domestic intake** *heimischer Verbrauch*

making American complacent[47] about the need to find alternative fuels that can sustain the future, delaying the moment when they could be introduced.

Only time will tell if they are right and the shale revolution will end up in disaster. 140

www.newsweek.com/2014/07/18/how-long-will-americas-shale-gas-boom-last-260823.html, 18 July 2014 [03.10.2014]

COMPREHENSION

2. As the text contains a number of technical terms and elaborated vocabulary, it has already been subdivided into five thematic sections to help your reading and understanding.

Step 1: In a **paired reading activity**, team up with a partner and help each other do the respective tasks.

Step 2: Read the section individually first, trying to get a general understanding. Note down the most relevant information as well as questions that you have.

Step 3: Now, team up with your partner and summarize each section of the text to each other. Clarify your questions and make corrections and/or additions to your notes.

3. While reading, concentrate and take notes on these aspects:

1
- the position of the U. S. amid the world's oil-producing nations
- questions raised by scientists and energy consultants
- possible impacts of the energy bubble

2
- predictions of America's (future) oil output
- the history of America's shale industry
- the incalculability of America's shale industry and possible reserves

3
- the (im-)balance of cost and production
- the correlation between oil production and fracking
- consequences of falling oil prices

4
- the lifespan of a shale well
- the lifespan of a conventional oil field
- means of sustaining the output of shale gas in the U. S.
- consequences of declining shale gas production and rising cost

5
- possible solutions to avoiding dependency
- the importance of renewable energies
- consequences of and lessons from the shale revolution

ANALYSIS

4. Step 1: Together with a partner, take a closer look at the visual on p. 274 and explain the possible risks of fracking depicted there.

Step 2: Taking into consideration the information given in the visual as well as the magazine article, juxtapose the possible benefits and risks of fracking. Copy the grid and complete it.

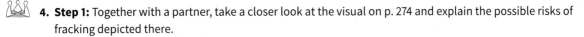

benefits/advantages	risks/disadvantages
• independence from politically unstable oil producers	• contamination of drinking water
• …	• potentially carcinogenic chemicals

[47] **complacent** [kəmˈpleisənt] *selbstgefällig*

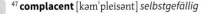

5. Examine the author's line of argument* and state whether or not he is in favour of fracking. Give evidence from the text to support your findings.

→ Focus on Skills, Analysis of a Non-Fictional Text, p. 405

6. Identify the particular type of text by showing and explaining specific characteristics and features (e. g. neutral vs. biased information, topical order, means of persuasion, etc.).

→ Focus on Facts, Basic Types of Non-Fictional Texts, p. 396

Reinhard Kowalewsky, Thomas Reisener

Exxon verspricht harmloses Fracking

AWARENESS

Germany has been extremely critical about "hydraulic fracturing" or "fracking".
In a Round Robin activity, state and share your views on fracking and its potential opportunities and dangers.

Der US-Konzern setzt auf ein neues Chemie-Gemisch. NRW verlängert die Frist für die Abbaurechte[1] von Exxon.

Energiemultis wie Exxon und die deutsche BASF-Tochter Wintershall haben in NRW 20 Claims abgesteckt[2], wie die potenziellen Abbaugebiete[3] für Gas, Gold und Öl im Fachjargon heißen. Ihr Problem: NRW hat 2011 faktisch sogar Probebohrungen[4] verboten. Denn das Gas ist in tiefen Gesteinsschichten eingeschlossen[5] und müsste mit der umstrittenen Fracking-Technologie gefördert werden, bei der ein Chemie-Cocktail tief unter der Erdoberfläche das Gestein aufsprengt. Das gefährdet das Grundwasser. [...]

Der Claim, den Exxon sich nun für weitere drei Jahre hat sichern lassen, heißt „NRW-Nord" und reicht vom nördlichen Münsterland bis Unna und von der niederländischen bis zur niedersächsischen[6] Landesgrenze – es ist einer der größten in NRW. „Damit hat Exxon sich das Zugriffsrecht[7] für Probebohrungen und eine eventuelle Förderung gesichert, falls es irgendwann doch eine gesetzliche Grundlage für Fracking-Genehmigungen geben sollte", sagt [Andreas] Nörten [vom zuständigen Bergamt[8] bei der Bezirksregierung[9] Arnsberg]. [...]

Der Präsident des Bundesverbandes Groß- und Außenhandel, Anton Börner, sagt: „Die USA profitieren vom Boom mit Schiefergas. Wenn Europa ähnliche Vorkommen nutzen würde, könnte uns das unabhängiger von Gasimporten machen." Vor dem Hintergrund des Ukraine-Konfliktes mit Russland ein aktueller Hinweis: Deutschland bezieht 40 Prozent seines Gases aus Russland.

Wohl auch vor diesem Hintergrund startete Exxon gestern eine Imagekampagne. In Zeitungsanzeigen warb Exxon-Chef Gernot Kalkoffen: „Wir möchten in Deutschland für Schiefergas mit höchsten Umweltstandards, modernster Technologie und unter Beteiligung der kritischen Öffentlichkeit neue Maßstäbe setzen[10] – mit Fracking, aber giftfrei."

Auf Nachfrage erklärte ein Exxon-Sprecher, man habe einen neuen Cocktail erfunden, der neben Wasser und Sand mit nur noch zwei Chemikalien auskomme [...]. Beide machten zusammen nur noch 0,2 Prozent des neuen Gemisches aus. Ob das Fracking dann wirklich gefahrenlos wird, wurde von Fachleuten gestern kontrovers eingeschätzt[11].

Rheinische Post, 26 September 2014, p. B1

---

[1] mining/drilling rights – [2] to stake a claim – [3] mining areas – [4] test drilling – [5] embedded/encased – [6] Lower Saxony – [7] access right/authorization – [8] local mining authority – [9] District Council – [10] to set standards – [11] to assess sth.

COMPREHENSION

1. Your American pen pal does not understand why the German government refuses to approve the energy companies' requests to allow fracking in Germany.

Mediate the relevant passages of the German newspaper article and inform your friend about
- the reasons and explanations of the North Rhine-Westphalian government for not approving the energy companies' requests,
- the argumentation of Anton Börger, the president of the association of wholesale and retail trade,
- ExxonMobil's attempts to improve fracking and make it less dangerous.
→ Focus on Skills, Mediation, p. 412

ANALYSIS

2. Mediate and examine ExxonMobil's advertisement which was published in various German newspapers and magazines.
- Explain ExxonMobil's line of argument*: Which aspects do they emphasize in favour of fracking?
- Which linguistic and rhetorical devices* are used to address German consumers and win their confidence?
- How does ExxonMobil allude (*auf etw. anspielen*) to Germany's decision to focus on renewable energies?
→ Focus on Skills, Mediation, p. 412
→ Focus on Skills, Analysis of a Non-Fictional Text, p. 405

ACTIVITIES

3. Write a letter to ExxonMobil Europe's CEO, Gernot Kalkoffen, in which you respond to his "open letter" and his invitation to "critically accompany" ExxonMobil's efforts and begin a dialogue with the company.
→ Focus on Skills, Writing a Formal Letter, p. 424
→ Focus on Language, Connectives and Adverbs, p. 432

4. Step 1: Reactivate your knowledge about the process of fracking and read Roger Howard's article (pp. 274 ff.).

Step 2: Extract arguments for and against fracking from both texts and complete the grid below:

against fracking	in favour of fracking
● use of poisonous, potentially carcinogenic additives ● possibility of groundwater contamination ● …	● only two non-poisonous/non-toxic additives ● additives are biodegradable ● …

Step 3: Based on your findings from steps 1 and 2, discuss whether the concerns expressed there are being met by ExxonMobil Europe and the invention of the "non-poisonous" fracking method.
→ Focus on Language, Conversation and Discussion, p. 413

ExxonMobil Central Europe Holding
Caffamacherreihe 5
20355 Hamburg

ExxonMobil

29. September 2014

Lassen Sie uns über Fracking reden.

Sehr geehrte Damen und Herren,

Deutschland hat sich für die Energiewende[1] entschieden. Dafür braucht unser Land verlässlich[2] und ausreichend Erdgas. Die gute Nachricht ist: Deutschland hat noch für viele Jahrzehnte eigenes Erdgas – insbesondere das heimische Schiefergas.

Wir von ExxonMobil wollen die Energiewende unterstützen und scheuen dabei keine unkonventionellen Wege. Wir möchten in Deutschland für Schiefergas mit höchsten Umweltstandards, modernster Technologie und unter Beteiligung der kritischen Öffentlichkeit neue Maßstäbe setzen – mit Fracking, aber giftfrei.

Es ist uns gelungen, eine Kernforderung[3] aus Öffentlichkeit und Politik zu erfüllen: Es werden nur noch zwei ungiftige und zudem biologisch leicht abbaubare[4] Zusätze zum Einsatz kommen. Schiefergas hat darüber hinaus weitere Vorteile: Der Flächenbedarf[5] ist gering, was gerade in einem dichtbesiedelten Land von zentraler Bedeutung ist. Und schließlich wird kein salziges Wasser aus dem Untergrund mitgefördert, das entsorgt[6] werden muss.

Wir laden Sie ein, uns dabei kritisch zu begleiten. Sprechen Sie uns gerne an.

Gernot Kalkoffen
Vorstandsvorsitzender

Telefon: 0511-641 641 0
E-Mail: dialog.fracking@exxonmobil.com
www.erdgassuche-in-deutschland.de

---

[1] shift to renewable energy – [2] reliable – [3] key demand – [4] biodegradable [ˈbaɪəʊdɪˈɡreɪdəbl] – [5] land requirements – [6] to dispose of sth.

Paul Torday

Salmon Fishing¹ in the Yemen

AWARENESS ▶▶▶▶▶▶

In 2012, a group of 20 penguins was brought to Dubai's indoor skiing mall *Ski Dubai*, a 22,500-square-metre ski resort. A mall in the city of Riyadh in Saudi Arabia plans to open an indoor "snow village". Center Parcs, a UK-based company that runs holiday villages in several European countries, offers so-called "Subtropical Swimming Paradises" that are open all year round.

 Against this background, act out a panel discussion and discuss
  a) the general use and function of these facilities,
  b) whether or not governments should restrict the building of these facilities because of their huge environmental impact.

The following three texts are excerpts from the 2007 novel *Salmon Fishing in the Yemen* which was adapted for a 2011 feature film. One of the novel's protagonists, fisheries expert Dr Alfred Jones, is recruited to realize a sheikh's² vision of introducing the sport of fly fishing to the Yemen desert. The British Prime Minister's press secretary uses this project to help improve political relations between Britain and the Islamic world and suggests the idea of salmon fishing in the Yemen to the PM's office.

1   Article in the International Herald Tribune, 16 August
Yemeni Sheikh Plans New Ecosystem for Wadis³

Sana'a, Yemen Republic

Sheikh Muhammad ibn Zaidi, a key figure in Yemeni political circles, has long been noted for his pro-Western views in a country whose relationship with Western states has sometimes been troubled. On Sunday he urged⁴ President Saleh to lend his backing⁵ to a revolutionary eco-project that has received some support in UK government circles.

Sheikh Muhammad is planning to spend millions of pounds sterling with the British government to introduce wild Scottish salmon into a wadi in the Western Yemen. In stark⁶ contrast to US policy, which currently involves further military build-ups⁷ in Saudi Arabia and Iraq, the UK now appears to be shifting its political ground. Although British government officials deny any formal relationship with Sheikh Muhammad, nevertheless the UK government agency, the National Centre for Fisheries Excellence, has taken a leading role in this environmentally challenging project. British policy in the region now appears to be looking for ways to take cultural and sporting images⁸, likely in an effort to soften the impact of recent military actions in Southern Iraq.

The funding will be provided by Sheikh Muhammad, UK government officials today distanced themselves from the project, claiming it was a private-sector initiative. However, it is likely that such a major scheme involving some of the world's most prestigious fisheries scientists could not proceed⁹ without sanction from Prime Minister Jay Vent's office. Some observers speculate that Sheikh Muhammad's initiative may not be universally welcome in his own province. The area is home to several radical Wahhabi *madrasas*, religious training schools, and it is understood that salmon fishing is regarded as an unacceptable activity by some Wahhabi imams¹⁰. Water is also a scarce resource in the Yemen, and its diversion¹¹ into the wadis to support a run¹² of salmon will not be universally popular in a country where the availability of water is often a matter of life and death.   (pp. 86f.)

---

¹ **salmon fishing** ['sæmən] *Lachs fischen* – ² **sheikh** [ʃeɪk] an Arab ruler – ³ **wadi** ['wɒdi] a valley that has a river that is usually dry except when it has rained – ⁴ **to urge sb.** *jdn. drängen* – ⁵ **backing** support – ⁶ **stark** here: obvious – ⁷ **build-up** a period of preparation before sth. happens – ⁸ **to take … images** here: to publicly present oneself in a certain way – ⁹ **to proceed** to continue as planned – ¹⁰ **imam** [ɪ'mɑːm] a leader in the Islamic – religion – ¹¹ **diversion** [daɪ'vɜːʃən] *Zuleitung, Verteilung* – ¹² **run** here: an area of ground of limited size for keeping animals

2

Article in The Times, 17 August

British Fisheries Scientists in Major Row[13]

Concerns were raised yesterday in Parliament that a key Government agency, the National Centre for Fisheries Excellence (NCFE), is going outside[14] its mandate. Set up a decade ago to support the work of the Environment Agency in monitoring and improving the health of rivers in England and Wales, NCFE is now said to have diverted[15] over 90 per cent of its resources into a project to introduce Atlantic salmon into the Yemen.

The Department for Environment, Food and Rural Affairs (DEFRA) confirmed that the funding for the Yemen salmon project is not coming from the UK taxpayer but has been met entirely from private-sector sources. However, questions are being asked as to whether this is an appropriate use of a key government department at a time when so many environmental and other challenges face rivers in England and Wales as a result of global warming and the risks from agricultural and industrial pollution to our rivers. A spokesman for the RSPB confirmed that, if the Yemen salmon project went ahead, the society would seek to have English cormorants[16] exported to the Yemen, to ensure that the natural checks and balances on any salmon river were maintained.   (pp. 87 f.)

3 Transcript of Interview with the Prime Minister, the RT. Hon.[17] Jay Vent MP[18], on BBC1 – *The Politics Show*

ANDREW MARR [*in vision, facing camera*]: Today we're going to consider the question of salmon fishing, which makes a refreshing change. More specifically, we are going to talk to Prime Minister Jay Vent about salmon fishing in the Yemen. Earlier this week I spoke to the prime minister about this at Number 10 Downing Street.

Studio link to 10 Downing Street. Shot of the prime minister and Andrew Marr seated in armchairs opposite each other, a table with a bowl of roses between them.

AM: Prime Minister, isn't the very[19] thought of salmon fishing in the Yemen an idea from way out on the lunatic fringe[20]?

Jay Vent: You know, Andy, sometimes someone comes up with an idea that is improbable[21], but truly, truly heroic. I think that's what we've got here, with my old friend Sheikh Muhammad. He has a vision.

AM: A lot of people, perhaps not knowing enough about it, would describe it as more of a hallucination than a vision.

JV [*turns to camera*]: Yes, Andy, maybe to some people it does sound a little crazy, but let's not be afraid of thinking outside the box[22]. My government has never stepped away from challenging new ideas, as you know.

You know, Andy, if you'd been a reporter when the first ship was built from iron rather than from wood …

AM [*faces camera*]: Sometimes it feels like I have been doing this job rather a long time, Prime Minister.

JV: Ha ha, Andy. I think you get my point, though. My point is, it probably sounded a little crazy when someone said, "I'm going to build my next ship out of iron and not out of wood." It probably sounded a little crazy when someone said, "I'm going to lay this cable across the Atlantic and send telephone messages along it." People laughed, Andy. But now the world has been changed for the better and all because those people had that heroic, extra bit of vision.

AM: Yes, Prime Minister, that's very interesting, but those were great inventions that changed the lives of millions of people. Salmon fishing in the desert sounds more of a minority sport. Isn't a great deal of money going to be spent for no particular good reason? Why is your government supporting such an apparently bizarre project?

JV: Andy, I don't think that's the question you should be asking.

AM: [*inaudible[23]*]

---

[13] **row** [raʊ] a noisy argument or fight – [14] **to go outside** überschreiten – [15] **to divert** [daɪ:vɜːt] here: to use sth. for a different purpose – [16] **cormorant** [ˈkɔːmərənt] a large black bird with a long neck that lives near the sea or other areas of water – [17] **RT. Hon.** (*abbr.*) Right Honourable; a title given to important British officials – [18] **MP** (*abbr.*) Member of Parliament – [19] **very** here: exact, particular – [20] **on the lunatic fringe** (*infml.*) am Rande des Schwachsinns – [21] **improbable** not likely to happen or to be true – [22] **outside the box** to think imaginatively using new ideas instead of traditional or expected ideas – [23] **inaudible** unable to be heard

JV: I think the question you should be asking is, what can we do to improve the lives of those troubled people who live in the Middle East –

50 AM [*interrupts*]: Well, perhaps, Prime Minister, but that was not the question that I just asked. The question I …

JV [*interrupts*]: … and, you know, Andy, isn't it just a little bit special that we're sitting here talking about 55 changing a Middle Eastern country, and the lives of its people, so much for the better [*camera on prime minister*] without talking about sending out British troops and helicopters and fighter aircraft. Yes, we've done that in the past, because they've asked us to, some of 60 them, and so we've had to. But now it is different. This time, we're going to send out fish.

AM: So, is exporting live salmon to the Yemen now official government policy?

JV: No, no, Andy. Not everything I do or say is official 65 government policy. You chaps[24] in the media attribute all sorts of powers to me, but life isn't really like that. Official government policy is ultimately the business of Parliament. No, I'm merely sharing with you my personal view that the Yemen salmon project is rather a 70 special project that I feel deserves some sympathy and encouragement. That's not the same thing as official government support, Andy.

AM: And why do you personally support this project, Prime Minister? What is it that especially appeals to 75 you about salmon fishing in the Yemen when there are so many other humanitarian crises that demand your attention?

JV: Andy, you're right that there is an endless list of problems out there that need dealing with. And no government has devoted so much of its time to global issues 80 of the kind that you mention than mine has. But what's so special about salmon fishing in the Yemen? Isn't this project a different way forward? Isn't it a form of intervention[25] that is so much kinder and gentler and somehow … more transforming? Water in the desert? Isn't 85 that a powerful symbol of …

AM: [*inaudible*]

JV: … of a different sort of progress? Yemeni tribesmen waiting for the evening rise by the side of a wadi with fishing rods[26] in their hands. Isn't that an image we'd 90 rather have in our mind's eye than a tank[27] at a crossroads somewhere in Fallujah[28]? Salmon smokeries[29] on the edge of the wadis. The introduction of a gentle, tolerant sport that unites us and our Arab brethren[30] in a new and deep way. A path away from confrontation. 95 All this is going to be achieved with the help of UK scientists. And that's another thing: we're a world leader in this fisheries science business. Thanks to the policy of this government. If we can manage to introduce salmon fishing into the Yemen, where else can we do 100 it? Sudan? Palestine? Who knows what new export opportunities this will open up, and not just for the scientists, but for our world-class manufacturers of fishing tackle[31], fishing wear and salmon flies.
So, you see, Andy, maybe it's a little crazy, as you say. 105 And maybe, just maybe, it might work.

AM [*turns to camera, prime minister out of shot*]: Thank you, Prime Minister.

from *Salmon Fishing in the Yemen* by Paul Torday. Weidenfeld & Nicolson, London 2007, pp. 104 ff.

COMPREHENSION

1. Read the fictitious newspaper snippets (**texts 1 and 2**) and take notes on the respective views regarding Sheikh Muhammad's project of introducing salmon fishing in a Yemeni wadi.

International Herald Tribune	The Times
● Sheikh's Muhammad's pro-Western views …	● … major row …
● a revolutionary eco-project …	● NCFE … outside its mandate …
● some support in the UK …	● concerns … in Parliament …
● …	● …

---

[24] **chap** (*infml.*) a man – [25] **intervention** *Eingreifen, Einmischung* – [26] **fishing rod** *Angelrute* – [27] **tank** *Panzer* – [28] **Fallujah** [fɛlˈluːdʒɐ] a city in Iraq, ca. 70 miles west of Baghdad – [29] **salmon smokery** *Lachsräucherei* – [30] **brethren** [ˈbreðrən] (*old-fashioned*) used as a form of address to members of an organization or religious group: brothers – [31] **to tackle** here: equipment

2. Detect the environmental, economic and political aspects that are mentioned in the newspaper articles. Copy the grid into your notebook and complete it. Use different colours for assumed positive (green) and negative (red) effects of the project.

environmental	political	economic
• revolutionary eco-project • diversion of resources • challenging • …	• pro-Western views • Yemen: troubled relationship with West … • in contrast to the U. S. … • …	• spending millions of pounds sterling … • cost … • …

3. Both texts give some clues to the further plot of the novel. In groups, speculate about
  • Sheikh Muhammad's possible reasons for the introduction of salmon fishing,
  • possible political and financial interests of the UK government for realizing this project,
  • the reaction of the British media and population to the project,
  • the reaction of environmentalists and/or animal rights activists.

4. In a paired reading activity, read the **third text**, another excerpt from the novel, and take notes on the following aspects:
  • Prime Minister Jay Vent's justification for supporting the project
  • the PM's references to seemingly crazy ideas in history
  • the PM's personal involvement in the project
  • the PM's ideas of military de-escalation with the Arab world
  • the economic benefits for the UK
  • the journalist's introduction of the subject

ANALYSIS

5. Examine the rhetorical and linguistic devices* that are employed in the newspaper articles (**texts 1 and 2**) and explain how they serve to
  a) give balanced information,
  b) take a conciliatory (*beschwichtigend*) approach on the delicate matter.

Examples:
  • ll. 6 f.: a <u>revolutionary</u> eco-project that has received <u>some</u> support …
    → positive emotive words to describe the project
    → toning down political support on the UK's side
  • ll. 13 f.: the UK <u>appears to be</u> shifting …
    → careful and indistinct formulation …
  → Focus on Skills, Analysis of a Non-Fictional Text, p. 405

6. Take a closer look at **text no. 3**:
  a) Examine the satirical tools that are used by the author and explain who or what is being ridiculed in the "TV interview".
  b) What is the function of the technical directions?
  c) Analyse the PM's line of argument* and his rhetorical strategy to outmanoeuvre the journalist's critical questions.
  d) Identify "typical" and well-tried political phrases and formulations in the PM's statements.

ACTIVITIES

7. Together with a partner, write an interview with Sheikh Muhammad. You are Andrew Marr and are asked to interview the sheikh for BBC1.
   Then, read/act out your interview in class.
   → Focus on Skills, Continuation of a Fictional Text, p. 420

8. Clearly, neither of the dialogue partners truly says what they are thinking (about each other/the project) in the TV interview (text 3).
   Together with a partner, imagine the characters' thoughts and write interior monologues that reflect their real thoughts. Your monologues can be funny, sarcastic, serious, concerned, etc.
   Assign the parts to the students in your class and read/act out the monologues.
   → Focus on Skills, Continuation of a Fictional Text, p. 420

Webcode
SNG-40235-030 @

9. With a partner, watch the trailer of the film version provided on the webcode to get an impression of the film adaptation. Discuss in class whether the film version matches how you imagined the characters and plot.

Communication or Confusion? – English Around the World

Communication … Hearing What Isn't Said …

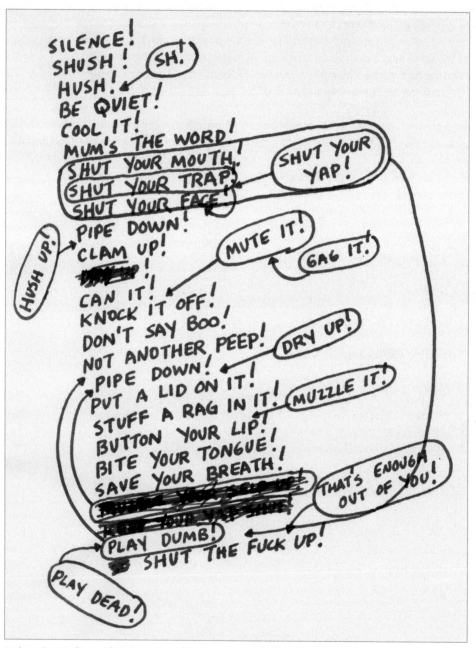

Mel Bochner, *Silence!*, ink on paper, 2008 (copyright: the artist)

Tips on vocab »»»

scribbling (*das Gekritzel*) ▪ capitalization, capital letters (*Großschreibung, Großbuchstaben*) ▪ exclamation marks ▪ synonymous language ▪ (to) paraphrase ▪ slang expressions ▪ informal English ▪ a list of words and phrases

Of course, English is a powerful language, a colonizer's language and a gift to a writer. English has destroyed and sucked up[1] the language of other cultures – its cruelty and vitality.

Louise Erdrich[1]

The price a world language must be prepared to pay is submission[2] to many different kinds of use.

Chinua Achebe

The two words "information" and "communication" are often used interchangeably, but they signify quite different things. Information is giving out; communication is getting through.

Sydney J. Harris

The more elaborate our means of communication, the less we communicate.

Joseph Priestley

Societies have always been shaped more by the nature of the media by which men communicate than by the content of the communication.

Marshall McLuhan

A man's character may be learned from the adjectives which he habitually[3] uses in conversation.

Mark Twain

We gave you a perfectly good language and you f***ed it up.

Stephen Fry about American English

Fainali, xen, aafte sam 2o iers ov orxogrefkl riform, wi wud hev a lojikl, Ingliy-spiking werld.

Mark Twain

If you have an important point to make, don't try to be subtle[4] or clever. Use a pile driver[5]. Hit the point once. Then come back and hit again. Then hit a third time – a tremendous[6] whack[7].

Winston Churchill

There is only one rule for being a good talker – learn to listen.

Christopher Morley

[1] THE ROUND HOUSE by Louise Erdrich. Copyright © 2012, Louise Erdrich, used by permission of The Wylie Agency (UK) Limited

ACTIVITIES

1. In his drawing *Silence!*, a so-called "Thesaurus[8] Painting", American artist Mel Bochner uses different figures of speech to express and describe a single idea or feeling.
   a) In groups, first discuss what idea or message *Silence!* wants to convey.
   b) Choose three or four expressions you like best and turn them into so-called pictograms. Be careful to illustrate <u>exactly</u> your chosen expression and look up its specific meaning in a dictionary if necessary. Display your pictograms in class and discuss whether or not they really match Mel Bochner's expressions.

2. In a pyramid discussion, choose one of the statements above that you agree with the most and give a short comment on it on a sheet of paper. Reflect on and discuss to what extent you agree with the statement and whether or not it matches your understanding of "communication" and the function of language.
   → Focus on Language, Conversation and Discussion, p. 413

3. Discuss the headline above: Is communication really about "hearing what isn't said"?

[1] **to suck sth. up** to absorb sth. – [2] **submission** here: *Duldung* – [3] **habitually** *gewohnheitsmäßig* – [4] **subtle** [ˈsʌtəl] not loud or noticeable – [5] **pile driver** *die Handramme* – [6] **tremendous** very great – [7] **whack** the action of hitting sb./sth. noisily; *Schlag* – [8] **thesaurus** [θɪˈsɔːrəs] (*fml.*) a type of dictionary in which words with similar meanings are arranged in groups; *Synonymwörterbuch*

Peter Lavelle

CrossTalk: English vs. Globish

 AWARENESS

You have been learning English for a number of years now. Looking back at your "biography" as an ESL[1] student, would you say that all the effort you put into learning and studying English vocabulary and grammar has been worth the effort so far?

In a round robin activity, state what you like or dislike about English as a foreign language and whether you are satisfied with your language acquisition so far.

 COMPREHENSION

1. **Before listening:**

   In groups, take a look at the FoF page *English Around the World* (p. 295) and the reasons listed there for the popularity and success of the English language worldwide.
   - Discuss whether or not you identify with the explanations given there.
   - Make a ranking: What do you consider to be the most/least important reasons?
   - Evaluate your own stage and level of language learning and proficiency in English:
     Do you feel well-equipped with regard to the ranking you have just made?
     If not – which further language skills do you need to learn?

   Tips on vocab »»»

   > **emeritus** [ɪˈmerɪtəs] no longer having a position, esp. in a college or university, but keeping the title of the position; *emeritiert* ■ **scholar** [ˈskɒlər] a person who studies a subject in great detail, esp. at a university ■ **for partly** *teilweise* ■ **derivative** [dɪˈrɪvɪtɪv] here: *Ableitung (von einem Wort)* ■ **to comprise** (*fml.*) to have as parts or members; *aus etw. bestehen* ■ **Gibberish** [ˈdʒɪbərɪʃ] spoken or written words that have no meaning ■ **to negotiate meaning** *darum ringen, die Bedeutung eines Begriffes zu erfassen* ■ **a quick fix** (*infml., disapproving*) sth. that seems to be a fast and easy solution to a problem but is in fact not very good ■ **guidance** [ˈgaɪdəns] *Anleitung, Beratung* ■ **to deploy** to use sth., esp. in an effective way; *etw. anwenden* ■ **to go in line with sb./sth.** to agree with sb./sth. ■ **to close a deal** *ein Geschäft abschließen* ■ **to be at ease with sb./sth.** to feel comfortable and relaxed ■ **to equip sb.** to give sb. the skills to do a particular thing; *jdn. mit etw. ausstatten* ■ **assumption** *Annahme, Vermutung* ■ **it's a different ballgame** (*infml.*) *es ist anders gelagert*

2. In 2004, Jean-Paul Nerrière, a former French IBM executive, published the book *Don't Speak English, Parlez Globish*, in which he introduces the international auxiliary language "Globish". He promotes Globish as a reduced set of English patterns with a vocabulary of about 1,500 words, which is based on a subset of English grammar. Globish is intended to serve as common ground that non-native speakers of English use to communicate in order to do international business.

   The recordings you are going to listen to are two excerpts from a video conference in which RTS[2] News Channel host Peter Lavelle talks to Jean-Paul Nerrière as well as two experts on the matter, Robert Phillipson and David Graddol.

    Step 1: In a paired listening activity, team up with a partner and **listen** to the audio text **individually first** and try to get a **general understanding**.

---

[1] **ESL** (*abbr.*) English as a second language – [2] **RTS** (*abbr.*) Royal Television Society, Britain's leading forum for television and related media

Tip: Be prepared to listen to the text at least two times. Jean-Paul Nerrière has a very strong French accent and is difficult to understand at times. In order to get a better impression of the participants you can also watch the video conference using the link provided on the webcode.

Step 2: Take notes on the basic aspects you have understood as well as on questions you have concerning vocabulary or the content of the statements.

Step 3: After a first listening, tell each other what you have understood and try to clarify questions and vocabulary.

Step 4: Now listen to the text individually again and **take notes on the aspects** and questions listed below.

Step 5: Afterwards, compare your notes with your partner and make additions and corrections if necessary.
→ Focus on Skills, Listening Comprehension, p. 394

Take notes on these aspects and questions:

- Who is taking part in the video conference and what is each participant's function and position?
- How does Jean-Paul Nerrière define Globish and what – according to him – is its foremost advantage and purpose?
- What makes Globish a form of "McDonaldization"?
- What concerns does Robert Phillipson express with regard to the wide range of purposes that "real English" has in the "real world"?
- What – according to Peter Lavelle – justifies the "McDonaldization" of English?
- How are native and non-native speakers of English involved when it comes to using and dealing with Globish?

- What are the "two kinds of English" – according to Nerrière?
- What makes Globish particularly important and useful with regard to international business?
- What position should native speakers of English take when communicating with non-native speakers?
- What are Peter Lavelle's concerns about using Globish when doing business and making contracts?
- How does Phillipson view the position of English as a "world language/lingua franca"?
- What does he consider to be wrong about some Danish companies' explanation of failures in business?
- What is Phillipson's conclusion concerning the purpose and use of Globish in complex negotiations?

If necessary, listen to the text again and complete your notes.

3. Summarize both parts of the CrossTalk interview in about 150 – 200 words each.
   → Focus on Skills, Writing a Summary, p. 429

   Tip: Be careful to use **indirect speech** when reporting what the participants said and to **backshift tenses** if necessary.

ANALYSIS

4. Using your notes from task 2,
   a) compare the advantages and disadvantages of Globish,
   b) explain whether Jean-Paul Nerrière's line of argument* is convincing.
   → Focus on Skills, Analysis of a Non-Fictional Text, p. 405

advantages	disadvantages
• limited/efficient list of vocabulary • everybody can participate • …	• McDonaldization (= limitation, reduction) of meaning • lack of differentiation • …

5. Explain Robert Phillipson's statement that Globish is "a bit like McDonaldization, […] a packaged version …" and a "quick fix", and that to in order to be able to "negotiate meaning" and to be "culturally sensitive", people need "real English".

6. Listen to Jean-Paul Nerrière speak again. Does his use of Globish help him to bring his message across to the audience or is there more to communicating in English successfully than just using a simplified version of English? Explain.

7. Take a close look at the example of Globish given below and compare the Standard English formulations to the simplified Globish version. a) Illustrate the differences. b) Discuss whether the Globish version is really easier to comprehend and a convincing alternative.

Standard English with non-Globish vocabulary highlighted	Globish
Globish is a subset of English words and grammar first codified by Jean-Paul Nerrière as documented by the Globish Foundation, and may include extension vocabularies.	Globish uses some English words and ways first defined by Jean Paul Nerrière (documented by the Globish Foundation), and may include extra sets of words.
Globish includes recommended behaviors for use in global communication.	Globish includes useful movements for global communication.
As a subset of English, Globish does not involve any invented words or grammars.	As a part of English, Globish does not involve any invented words or word use.
Globish has a core of only 1,500 words (1,500 is a recognized number for basic, general communication);	Globish starts with only 1,500 words (1,500 is a recognized number for easy, general communication);
the vocabulary is declared (people can use Globish words with confidence and add others by agreement, defining them in Globish);	there is a list of words (people can use any Globish words and add others by agreement, defining them in Globish);
typical behaviors are identified so everyone knows 'how' to communicate (e.g. watching a listener to see if they are following the conversation);	good ways of acting are identified so everyone knows 'how' to communicate (by watching a listener to see if they are following the communication);
Globish assumes the communicator is responsible for understanding (not the person receiving the communication);	Globish makes the speaker responsible for understanding (not the person receiving the communication);
Globish assumes the person receiving the communication will indicate any problems they are having (they are not responsible for their lack of understanding);	Globish says the person receiving the communication must indicate any problems they are having (they are not responsible for their lack of understanding);
Globish does not include exotic tenses and grammar (so it is easier to understand, learn and use);	Globish does not include strange, difficult English (so it is easier to understand, learn and use);
Globish does not include cultural references, idioms, etc. (so understanding is more broadly available);	Globish does not include local ideas, images, (so understanding is more broadly available);
Globish uses active voice, simple-tenses, shorter sentences (so it can be translated easily into other languages);	Globish uses easy speech, simple-tenses, shorter sentences (so it can be changed easily into other languages);

Standard English with non-Globish vocabulary highlighted	Globish
• Globish assumes many accents and even spellings (Australian spelling is not the same as Thai spelling);	• Globish allows for many ways of speaking and spelling (Australian spelling is not the same as Thai spelling);
• having learned Globish, a person can grow their communication to speak and write English, if required;	• a person who knows Globish can learn to speak and write full English, if required;
• with technology, teachers who are non-native speakers of English can teach others to communicate in Globish;	• with computers, teachers who are not native speakers of English can teach others to communicate in Globish;
• with technology, people can learn Globish for themselves, by themselves;	• with computers, people can learn Globish without a teacher;
• people with difficulties with respect to unfettered English communication can use Globish to communicate (inclusive of people with intellectual disabilities, etc.) [...].	• people with difficulties with respect to full English communication can use Globish to communicate (including people with learning problems) [...].

http://globishfoundation.org/about-globish/57-globish-example-1.html [15.01.2015]

ACTIVITIES

8. Globish is a modern simplified version of English. You are learning English the traditional way, and sometimes English grammar can be complicated. What would you rather not learn? What do you think can be left out? Make suggestions, write them on a transparency and present them in class.

Paul Roberts

Set Us Free from Standard English ☒

AWARENESS

What view of the English language (and British culture) do these statements reveal? Discuss in class.

> Even if you do learn to speak correct English, whom are you going to speak it to?
> *Clarence Darrow (1857–1938), American lawyer*
>
> When the English language gets in my way, I walk over it.
> *Billy Sunday (1862–1935), American athlete*
>
> To cultivate an English accent is already a departure away from what you are.
> *Sir Sean Connery (*1930), Scottish actor*

Language is a token[1] of identity as well as a means of communication. It follows that language is part of a complex system allowing speakers to show they belong to a group from which they may exclude others. In this respect, English speakers are similar to speakers of any other language. [...]

---

[1] **token** here: expression

The so-called native speakers of Standard English are those people who have somehow espoused[2] to a particular set of conventions that loosely have to do with the way English has been codified and prescribed in dictionaries, grammar books and guides to good speaking and writing. This group of people includes a large number of those who, having espoused the conventions, nevertheless do not consider themselves to be excellent users of those conventions.

For many of these so-called native speakers the English language is a unique entity[3] that exists outside or beyond its users. Rather than considering themselves owners of English, users often think of themselves as guardians of something precious: they wince[4] when they hear or read uses of English that they consider to be substandard, and they worry, in their letters to newspapers, that the language is becoming degraded. The degradation may be perceived to come from non-native speakers, but much more prevalent[5] is the notion[6] that it is native users of English themselves who are bringing about the decline. Indeed, a fairly commonly held notion claims that "foreigners", or non-native speakers, can, and do, use English better than the native speakers.

Turning things round the other way, I have met native speakers teaching English who have been upbraided[7] by their non-native-speaker employers for accepting their students' idiomatic, non-standard usages and not correcting their English according to standard English conventions.

Those who do feel they have rights and privileges, who have a sense of ownership of the English language and who can make pronouncements[8] about what is or is not acceptable, as well as those to whom these attributes are accorded[9] by others, do not necessarily belong to a speech community whose members learned English in infancy. Native speakers of non-standard varieties of English, in other words, the majority of native speakers of English, have never had any real authority over Standard English and have never "owned" it. The actual proprietors[10] may, after all, simply be those who have learned thoroughly how to use a Standard English to enjoy the sense of empowerment[11] that comes with it.

www.guardian.co.uk/education/2002/jan/24/tefl.wordsandlanguage, 24 January 2002 [04.02.2011]

COMPREHENSION

1. Explain the author's definition of a native speaker of Standard English.

2. What or whom do native speakers of English blame for the degradation of the English language?

3. Point out the author's view of "native" and "non-native speakers" of English and their "authority over Standard English".

ANALYSIS

4. Examine the rhetorical devices* and explain how they create the humorous and ironic tone of the article.

Example: l. 7, l. 16: so-called native speakers → choice of words → calls into question the authority of native speakers
→ Focus on Skills, Analysis of a Non-Fictional Text, p. 405

5. The article is a prime example of Standard English and the use of an elaborated code. Find examples from the text that support this view.

Example: l. 9: conventions → rules, habits

---

[2] **to espouse** [ɪˈspaʊz] (*fml.*) to give your support to a belief, policy, etc. – [3] **entity** (*fml.*) sth. that exists separately from other things and has its own identity – [4] **to wince** [wɪns] *zusammenzucken* – [5] **prevalent** common, widespread – [6] **notion** an idea, a belief or an understanding of sth. – [7] **to upbraid** (*fml.*) *jdn. zurechtweisen* – [8] **pronouncement** (*fml.*) an official announcement; *Verkündigung* – [9] **to accord sth. to sb.** (*fml.*) to give sb./sth. authority, status or a particular type of treatment – [10] **proprietor** [prəˈpraɪətə(r)] (*fml.*) the owner – [11] **empowerment** [ɪmˈpaʊəmənt] *Ermächtigung*

Varieties of English Around the World

AWARENESS

Before listening:

In groups, take a look at the table below:

a) What do you know about these people and their professional and/or personal background?

b) Speculate about the topic of their speech/interview/statement.

c) Judging from their geographical and professional background, what do you expect each person's performance and use of English to be like?

1

Leonardo DiCaprio
Speech at the 2014 UN Climate Change Summit

2

Prince William
On Baby George and Fatherhood

3

Australian Prime Minister Julia Gillard
Speech at U.S. Congress

 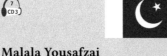 

4

Malala Yousafzai
Nobel Peace Prize Speech

5

Bishop Desmond Tutu
On Post-Apartheid South Africa

6

Usain Bolt
About Training Sessions

Tips on vocab

1 **undeniable** *unleugbar, unstrittig* ■ **drought** *Dürre* ■ **methane plumes** *Methangasschwaden* ■ **unprecedented** *beispiellos* ■ **to vilify** *(fml.)* *jdn. verunglimpfen, verschmähen* ■ **large-scale** large in size ■ **to put a price tag on sth.** to say how much sth. costs ■ **scrutiny** *genaue Untersuchung/Überprüfung* ■ **partisan** belonging to or supporting a political party

2 **dauntingness** the feeling of being frightened or worried about your ability to achieve sth. ■ **heir** *Thronfolger* ■ **to curse sb.** *jdn. verfluchen* ■ **nerve-racking** *nervenzerreißend* ■ **fuss** unnecessary excitement, worry or activity ■ **to stall** *abwürgen*

3 **ultimate sacrifice** here: to die for sth. ■ **grief** *Gram* ■ **ally** *Verbündeter* ■ **resolve** strong determination ■ **safe haven** *Schutzbereich* ■ **prosperity** the state of being successful and having a lot of money ■ **corrosive** here: harmful and causing bad feelings ■ **aimlessness** *Ziellosigkeit*

4 **Nobel laureate** *Nobelpreisträger*

5 **to prevail** *(fml.)* to get control or influence ■ **presto** when sth. appears or happens so quickly and easily that it seems to be magic ■ **ANC** *(abbr.)* African National Congress; social democratic political party ■ **retribution** *Vergeltung, Strafe* ■ **nurse a grudge** *gegen jdn. einen Groll hegen*

6 **track and field** *Leichtathletik*

COMPREHENSION

1. While listening:

Step 1: Listen to the recordings **a first time**.
- Try to get the gist of what is said.
- Identify the topic and the general situation.
- Describe the overall tone and say whether the situation is more formal or informal.

Step 2: In a **second listening**, pay attention to the differences in the varieties of English concerning:
- pronunciation • choice of words • sentence structure • accent • rhythm • speed

→ Focus on Skills, Listening Comprehension, p. 394

ANALYSIS

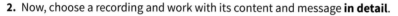

2. Now, choose a recording and work with its content and message **in detail**.

Webcode
SNG-40235-032 @   **Tip:** You can also watch the people speak using the links provided on the webcode.

Listen to the recordings once more, **paying attention to details** and taking notes on:

- DiCaprio's motivation for giving the speech
- his observations of the effects of climate change
- the addressees of his speech
- DiCaprio's demands
- his appeal to take action

- Prince William's emotions as a father
- how Prince William views his obligations and duties as a member of the Royal Family
- Prince William's tightrope walk between personal independence and serving "the system"

- the partnership and bonds between Australia and the U. S.
- shared sorrows and concerns
- shared goals and objectives

- Malala's feelings about being awarded the Nobel Peace Prize
- the importance of the prize to herself and in a wider context
- her introduction of her co-awardee Kailash Satyarthi
- Malala's appeal to the people

- the impact of segregation in South Africa
- gaining freedom and democracy
- the positive impact of forgiving

- Usain Bolt's motivation to become an Olympic champion
- how he deals with pressure
- Bolt's view of winning and losing

→ Focus on Skills, Analysis of a Non-Fictional Text, p. 405
→ Focus on Skills, Analysis of a Political Speech, p. 407

English Around the World

English-speaking countries

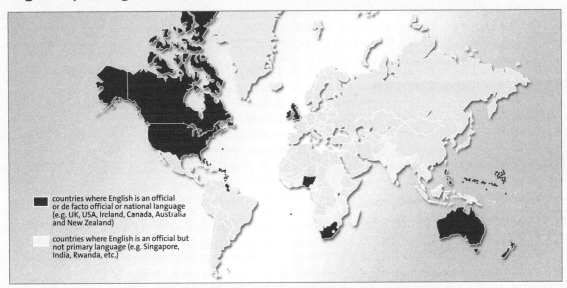

countries where English is an official or de facto official or national language (e.g. UK, USA, Ireland, Canada, Australia and New Zealand)

countries where English is an official but not primary language (e.g. Singapore, India, Rwanda, etc.)

In addition, an increasing number of nations recognize the importance of English as an international language and e.g. teach English as a foreign language (e.g. China, Japan, Russia, Israel, etc.).

Why English?

Reasons for the spread and popularity of English:

- **Historical reasons:** as a result of British or American imperialism a country's main institutions may carry out their proceedings in English (e.g. parliament, educational system, the civil service, courts, the media, etc.)
- **Political reasons:** in a country where many different languages are spoken (e.g. India, Africa) English can serve as a means of communication between different ethnic groups and provide a neutral means of communication
- **Economic reasons:** English is the predominant language used to carry out international trade and business and to participate in global economic markets
- **Practical reasons:** English is the language of international communication (e.g. tourism, international traffic control, emergency services, academic conferences, etc.)
- **Intellectual reasons:** most scientific, technological and academic information is encoded in English and stored in English-based electronic retrieval systems
- **Entertainment reasons:** English is the main language of pop music, satellite broadcasting, home computers, advertising, etc.

History of the English language

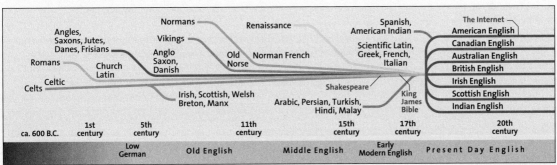

Focus on Facts

Democracy Going Global: Peace, Stability and Human Rights

What's Gone Wrong with Democracy ☒

 Together with a partner, describe the "cycle or roundabout of democracy" as depicted in the cartoon below. Explain the main factors that determine the building and decline of democracy as presented in the cartoon. Finally, discuss whether you think there is some truth in the cartoon or it exaggerates and/or oversimplifies the complicated process of democracy.

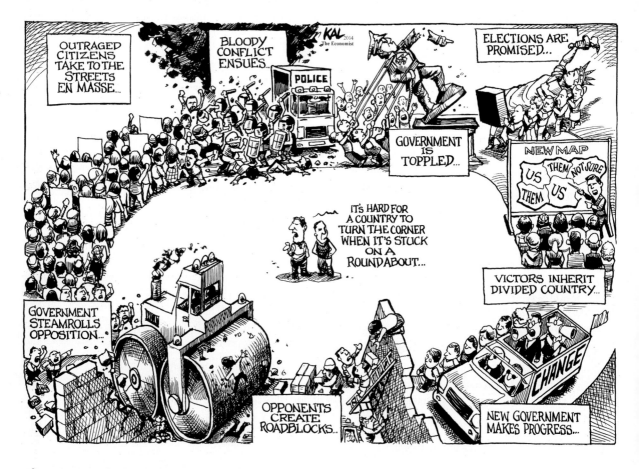

Tips on vocab

to take to somewhere (*phr. v.*) to go somewhere, usually because you are in a difficult or dangerous situation ■ **to ensue** [ɪnˈsjuː] *auf etw. folgen* ■ **to topple** to force a leader or government out of power ■ **to inherit** here: *etw. übernehmen* ■ **to turn the corner** (*idm.*) if a situation turns the corner, it starts to improve after a difficult period; *über den Berg kommen* ■ **roundabout** *Kreisverkehr* ■ **to steamroll sb.** to defeat sb. by using a great amount of force, pressure or influence ■ **steamroller** *Dampfwalze*

1 **Democracy was the most successful political idea of the 20th century. Why has it run into trouble, and what can be done to revive it?**

Democracy is going through a difficult time. Where autocrats[1] have been driven out of office, their opponents have mostly failed to create viable[2] democratic regimes. Even in established democracies, flaws[3] in the system have become worryingly visible and disillusion with politics is rife[4]. Yet just a few years ago democracy looked as though it would dominate the world.

In the second half of the 20th century, democracies had taken root[5] in the most difficult circumstances possible – in Germany, which had been traumatised by Nazism, in India, which had the world's largest population of poor people, and, in the 1990s, in South Africa, which had been disfigured[6] by apartheid. Decolonisation created a host[7] of new democracies in Africa and Asia, and autocratic regimes gave way to democracy in Greece (1974), Spain (1975), Argentina (1983), Brazil (1985) and Chile (1989). The collapse of the Soviet Union created many fledgling[8] democracies in central Europe. By 2000 Freedom House, an American think-tank, classified 120 countries, or 63% of the world total, as democracies.

Representatives of more than 100 countries gathered at the World Forum on Democracy in Warsaw that year to proclaim that "the will of the people" was "the basis of the authority of government". A report issued by America's State Department declared that having seen off "failed experiments" with authoritarian and totalitarian forms of government, "it seems that now, at long last, democracy is triumphant."

Such hubris[9] was surely understandable after such a run of successes. But stand farther back and the triumph of democracy looks rather less inevitable[10].

2 After the fall of Athens, where it was first developed, the political model had lain dormant[11] until the Enlightenment[12] more than 2,000 years later. In the 18th century only the American revolution produced a sustainable democracy. During the 19th century monarchists fought a prolonged[13] rearguard[14] action against democratic forces. In the first half of the 20th century nascent[15] democracies collapsed in Germany, Spain and Italy. By 1941 there were only 11 democracies left, and Franklin Roosevelt worried that it might not be possible to shield[16] "the great flame of democracy from the blackout of barbarism".

The progress seen in the late 20th century has stalled in the 21st. Even though around 40% of the world's population, more people than ever before, live in countries that will hold free and fair elections this year, democracy's global advance has come to a halt, and may even have gone into reverse[17]. Freedom House reckons[18] that 2013 was the eighth consecutive[19] year in which global freedom declined, and that its forward march peaked around the beginning of the century. Between 1980 and 2000 the cause of democracy experienced only a few setbacks, but since 2000 there have been many. And democracy's problems run deeper than mere numbers suggest. Many nominal[20] democracies have slid towards autocracy[21], maintaining the outward appearance of democracy through elections, but without the rights and institutions that are equally important aspects of a functioning democratic system.

Faith in democracy flares up[22] in moments of triumph, such as the overthrow of unpopular regimes in Cairo or Kiev, only to sputter out[23] once again. Outside the West, democracy often advances only to collapse. And within the West, democracy has too often become associated with debt and dysfunction at home and overreach[24] abroad. Democracy has always had its critics, but now old doubts are being treated with renewed respect as the weaknesses of democracy in its Western strongholds[25], and the fragility[26] of its influence elsewhere, have become increasingly apparent. Why has democracy lost its forward momentum?

3 **The return of history**

The two main reasons are the financial crisis of 2007 – 08 and the rise of China. The damage the crisis did was psychological as well as financial. It revealed fundamental weaknesses in the West's political systems, un-

---

[1] **autocrat** *Alleinherrscher* – [2] **viable** ['vaɪəbl] *existenzfähig* – [3] **flaw** a fault, mistake or weakness – [4] **rife** *weitverbreitet* – [5] **to take root** to become established – [6] **disfigured** *entstellt* – [7] **host of sth.** a large number of sth. – [8] **fledgling** sth. that is young, new – [9] **hubris** ['hjuːbrɪs] *(fml.) Hochmut* – [10] **inevitable** [ɪ'nevɪtəbl] *unausweichlich* – [11] **to lie dormant** *ruhend, inaktiv sein* – [12] **Enlightenment** cultural and intellectual movement of the 17th/18th century; *Zeitalter der Aufklärung* – [13] **prolonged** continuing for a long time – [14] **rearguard** [rɪəgɑːd] *Rückzugsgefecht* – [15] **nascent** ['næsənt] *(fml.) aufkeimend* – [16] **to shield** to protect sb./sth. – [17] **reverse** in the opposite way – [18] **to reckon** *(infml.)* to think or believe – [19] **consecutive** [kən'sekjʊtɪv] *aufeinanderfolgend* – [20] **nominal** *(nur) dem Namen nach* – [21] **autocracy** [ɔː'tɒkrəsi] *Alleinherrschaft* – [22] **to flare up** *aufflammen, auflodern* – [23] **to sputter out** to slowly stop to exist – [24] **overreach** *Übervorteilung* – [25] **stronghold** *Bollwerk* – [26] **fragility** [frə'dʒɪlɪti] *Zerbrechlichkeit*

dermining[27] the self-confidence that had been one of their great assets[28]. Governments had steadily extended entitlements[29] over decades, allowing dangerous lev-
85 els of debt to develop, and politicians came to believe that they had abolished boom-bust cycles and tamed risk. Many people became disillusioned with the workings of their political systems – particularly when governments bailed out[30] bankers with taxpayers' money
90 and then stood by impotently as financiers continued to pay themselves huge bonuses. The crisis turned the Washington consensus into a term of reproach[31] across the emerging world.

Meanwhile, the Chinese Communist Party has broken
95 the democratic world's monopoly on economic progress. Larry Summers, of Harvard University, observes that when America was growing fastest, it doubled living standards roughly every 30 years. China has been doubling living standards roughly every decade for the
100 past 30 years. The Chinese elite argues that their model – tight control by the Communist Party, coupled with a relentless[32] effort to recruit talented people into its upper ranks – is more efficient than democracy and less susceptible[33] to gridlock[34]. The political leadership
105 changes every decade or so, and there is a constant supply of fresh talent as party cadres[35] are promoted based on their ability to hit targets.

China's critics rightly condemn the government for controlling public opinion in all sorts of ways, from im-
110 prisoning dissidents[36] to censoring internet discussions. Yet the regime's obsession with control paradoxically means it pays close attention to public opinion. At the same time China's leaders have been able to tackle some of the big problems of state-building that
115 can take decades to deal with in a democracy. [...]

Many Chinese are prepared to put up with their system if it delivers growth. The 2013 Pew Survey of Global Attitudes showed that 85% of Chinese were "very satisfied" with their country's direction, compared with 31%
120 of Americans. Some Chinese intellectuals have become positively boastful[37]. [...]

4 Although democracy may be a "universal aspiration[38]", as Mr Bush[39] and Tony Blair[40] insisted, it is a culturally rooted practice. Western countries almost all extended the right to vote long after the establishment 125 of sophisticated political systems, with powerful civil services and entrenched[41] constitutional rights, in societies that cherished[42] the notions[43] of individual rights and independent judiciaries[44].

Yet in recent years the very institutions that are meant 130 to provide models for new democracies have come to seem outdated and dysfunctional in established ones. The United States has become a byword[45] for gridlock, so obsessed with partisan[46] point-scoring[47] that it has come to the verge[48] of defaulting[49] on its debts twice in 135 the past two years. Its democracy is also corrupted by gerrymandering[50], the practice of drawing constituency[51] boundaries to entrench the power of incumbents[52]. This encourages extremism, because politicians have to appeal only to the party faithful, and in effect disen- 140 franchises[53] large numbers of voters. And money talks louder than ever in American politics. Thousands of lobbyists (more than 20 for every member of Congress) add to the length and complexity of legislation, the better to smuggle in special privileges. All this creates the 145 impression that American democracy is for sale and that the rich have more power than the poor, even as lobbyists and donors insist that political expenditure[54] is an exercise in free speech. The result is that America's image – and by extension that of democracy itself 150 – has taken a terrible battering[55].

Nor is the EU a paragon[56] of democracy. The decision to introduce the euro in 1999 was taken largely by technocrats; only two countries, Denmark and Sweden, held referendums on the matter (both said no). Efforts to 155 win popular approval for the Lisbon Treaty, which consolidated[57] power in Brussels, were abandoned[58] when people started voting the wrong way. During the darkest days of the euro crisis the euro-elite forced Italy and Greece to replace democratically elected leaders with 160 technocrats. The European Parliament, an unsuccessful

---

[27] **to undermine** to make sb. less confident or weaker gradually – [28] **asset** *Vorzug* – [29] **entitlement** *Bezugsrecht* – [30] **to bail sb. out** *jdm. aus der Klemme helfen* – [31] **reproach** *Vorwurf* – [32] **relentless** *unerbittlich* – [33] **susceptible** [səˈseptɪbl] easily harmed or affected – [34] **gridlock** *Stillstand* – [35] **cadre** *Kader* – [36] **dissident** sb. who publicly disagrees with and criticizes their government – [37] **boastful** *prahlerisch* – [38] **aspiration** *Bestreben* – [39] **Mr Bush** George W. Bush, 43rd U. S. President (2001–2009) – [40] **Tony Blair** British Labour politician; Prime Minister (1997–2007) – [41] **entrenched** *fest verwurzelt* – [42] **to cherish** to love, protect and care for sb./sth. – [43] **notion** a belief or idea – [44] **judiciary** [dʒuːˈdɪʃəri] *die Judikative* – [45] **to be a byword for sth.** *gleichbedeutend sein mit etw.* – [46] **partisan** *parteiisch* – [47] **point-scoring** showing that you are better than sb. – [48] **verge** edge, border – [49] **to default** *zahlungsunfähig werden* – [50] **gerrymandering** *(Wahl-)Manipulation* – [51] **constituency** [kənˈstɪtjuənsi] *Wahlbezirk* – [52] **incumbent** *Amtsinhaber* – [53] **to disenfranchise sb.** [ˌdɪsɪnˈfræntʃaɪz] *entrechten* – [54] **expenditure** [ɪkˈspendɪtʃər] *Aufwand* – [55] **to take a battering** *eine Niederlage einstecken* – [56] **paragon** role model – [57] **consolidated** *vereinigt, gestärkt* – [58] **to abandon** to leave a place, person or thing

attempt to fix Europe's democratic deficit, is both ignored and despised[59]. The EU has become a breeding ground for populist parties, such as Geert Wilders's Party for Freedom in the Netherlands and Marine Le Pen's National Front in France, which claim to defend ordinary people against an arrogant and incompetent elite. Greece's Golden Dawn[60] is testing how far democracies can tolerate Nazi-style parties. A project designed to tame the beast of European populism is instead poking[61] it back into life. [...]

5 From below come equally powerful challenges: from would-be breakaway nations, such as the Catalans and the Scots, from Indian states, from American city mayors. All are trying to reclaim power from national governments. There are also a host of what Moisés Naím, of the Carnegie Endowment[62] for International Peace, calls "micro-powers", such as NGOs[63] and lobbyists, which are disrupting[64] traditional politics and making life harder for democratic and autocratic leaders alike. The internet makes it easier to organise and agitate[65]; in a world where people can participate in reality-TV votes every week, or support a petition with the click of a mouse, the machinery and institutions of parliamentary democracy, where elections happen only every few years, look increasingly anachronistic[66]. [...]

The biggest challenge to democracy, however, comes neither from above nor below but from within – from the voters themselves. Plato's great worry about democracy, that citizens would "live from day to day, indulging[67] the pleasure of the moment", has proved prescient[68]. Democratic governments got into the habit of running big structural deficits as a matter of course, borrowing to give voters what they wanted in the short term, while neglecting[69] long-term investment. France and Italy have not balanced their budgets for more than 30 years. The financial crisis starkly exposed the unsustainability[70] of such debt-financed democracy. [...]

6 Adjusting to hard times will be made even more difficult by a growing cynicism towards politics. Party membership is declining across the developed world:

only 1% of Britons are now members of political parties compared with 20% in 1950. Voter turnout[71] is falling, too: a study of 49 democracies found that it had declined by 10 percentage points between 1980–84 and 2007–13. A survey of seven European countries in 2012 found that more than half of voters "had no trust in government" whatsoever. A YouGov opinion poll of British voters in the same year found that 62% of those polled agreed that "politicians tell lies all the time". [...] Democracy's problems in its heartland help explain its setbacks elsewhere. Democracy did well in the 20th century in part because of American hegemony[72]: other countries naturally wanted to emulate[73] the world's leading power. But as China's influence has grown, America and Europe have lost their appeal as role models and their appetite for spreading democracy. The Obama administration now seems paralysed by the fear that democracy will produce rogue[74] regimes or empower jihadists[75]. And why should developing countries regard democracy as the ideal form of government when the American government cannot even pass a budget, let alone plan for the future? Why should autocrats listen to lectures on democracy from Europe, when the euro-elite sacks[76] elected leaders who get in the way of fiscal[77] orthodoxy[78]? [...]

7 Getting democracy right [...]
The combination of globalisation and the digital revolution has made some of democracy's most cherished institutions look outdated. Established democracies need to update their own political systems both to address the problems they face at home, and to revitalise democracy's image abroad. Some countries have already embarked upon[79] this process. America's Senate has made it harder for senators to filibuster[80] appointments. A few states have introduced open primaries and handed redistricting to independent boundary commissions. Other obvious changes would improve matters. Reform of party financing, so that the names of all donors are made public, might reduce the influence of special interests. The European Parliament could require its MPs to present receipts[81] with their expenses[82]. Italy's parlia-

[59] **to despise sb./sth.** *jdn./etw. verachten* – [60] **Golden Dawn** far-right Greek political party – [61] **to poke sth.** to push – [62] **endowment** [ɪnˈdaʊmənt] *Stiftung* – [63] **NGO** *(abbr.)* non-governmental organization – [64] **to disrupt sth.** *stören* – [65] **to agitate** *aufrühren* – [66] **anachronistic** *unzeitgemäß* – [67] **to indulge** *etw. nachgeben* – [68] **prescient** [ˈpresiənt] *(fml.)* *vorherwissend* – [69] **to neglect sb./sth.** *jdn./etw. vernachlässigen* – [70] **unsustainability** *Nicht-Nachhaltigkeit* – [71] **voter turnout** the number of people that actually vote; *Wahlbeteiligung* – [72] **hegemony** [hɪˈɡeməni] *Vormachtstellung* – [73] **to emulate** imitate – [74] **rogue** [rəʊɡ] *Schurke* – [75] **jihadist** [dʒɪˈhɑːdɪst] a Muslim who is fighting for Islam, esp. a radical – [76] **to sack sb.** *(infml.)* to fire sb. – [77] **fiscal** in connection with government money – [78] **orthodoxy** [ˈɔːθədɒksi] *Rechtgläubigkeit* – [79] **to embark upon sth.** *(phr. v., fml.)* to start sth. new or important – [80] **to filibuster sb./sth.** *hinauszögern* – [81] **receipt** [rɪˈsiːt] *Rechnung, Quittung* – [82] **expenses** *Ausgaben*

ment has far too many members who are paid too much, and two equally powerful chambers, which makes it difficult to get anything done.

But reformers need to be much more ambitious. The best way to constrain[83] the power of special interests is to limit the number of goodies[84] that the state can hand out. [...] The key to a healthier democracy, in short, is a narrower[85] state – an idea that dates back to the American revolution. "In framing a government which is to be administered by men over men", Madison[86] argued, "the great difficulty lies in this: you must first enable the government to control the governed; and in the next place oblige[87] it to control itself". The notion of limited government was also integral[88] to the relaunch[89] of democracy after the second world war. The United Nations Charter (1945) and the Universal Declaration of Human Rights (1948) established rights and norms that countries could not breach[90], even if majorities wanted to do so.

These checks and balances were motivated by fear of tyranny[91]. But today, particularly in the West, the big dangers to democracy are harder to spot. One is the growing size of the state. The relentless expansion of government is reducing liberty and handing ever more power to special interests. [...]

Tocqueville[92] argued that local democracy frequently represented democracy at its best: "Town-meetings are to liberty what primary schools are to science; they bring it within the people's reach, they teach men how to use and enjoy it." City mayors regularly get twice the approval ratings of national politicians. Modern technology can implement[93] a modern version of Tocqueville's town-hall meetings to promote civic involvement and innovation. An online hyper-democracy[94] where everything is put to an endless series of public votes would play to the hand of special-interest groups. But technocracy and direct democracy can keep each other in check: independent budget commissions can assess the cost and feasibility[95] of local ballot[96] initiatives, for example.

[...]

John Adams, America's second president, once pronounced that "democracy never lasts long. It soon wastes, exhausts[97] and murders itself. There never was a democracy yet that did not commit suicide." He was clearly wrong. Democracy was the great victor of the ideological clashes of the 20th century. But if democracy is to remain as successful in the 21st century as it was in the 20th, it must be both assiduously[98] nurtured[99] when it is young – and carefully maintained[100] when it is mature.

www.economist.com/news/essays/21596796-democracy-was-most-successful-political-idea-20th-century-why-has-it-run-trouble-and-what-can-be-do, 1 March 2014 [21.09.2014]

COMPREHENSION

1. Divide the class into six groups, each group working with one section of the text (no. 2 – 6) and <u>all</u> groups reading and working with the first part of the article.

Each group should take notes on the most relevant information and data given in the respective section and illustrate its findings on large sheets of paper to be displayed on the blackboard afterwards.

Be prepared to present your findings to the class and point out your results.

These aspects should be considered:

1 **Introduction/overview:**
- disillusions and frustrations about democracy
- democracy in the 20th century
- the triumph of democracy

---

[83] **to constrain** to control and limit sth. – [84] **goody** (*infml.*) a pleasant thing – [85] **narrow** limited to a small area of interest, activity or thought – [86] **James Madison** (1751 – 1836) one of America's founding fathers – [87] **to oblige sb. to do sth.** [ə'blaɪdʒ] to force sb. to do sth. – [88] **integral** necessary and important as part of a whole – [89] **relaunch** restart – [90] **to breach** to break a law or agreement – [91] **tyranny** ['tɪrəni] – [92] **Alexis de Tocqueville** (1805 – 1859) French philosopher, historian – [93] **implement** ['ɪmplɪment] to start using a plan or system – [94] **hyper-** ['haɪpər] more than normal; too much – [95] **feasibility** [ˌfiːzə'bɪlɪti] *Durchführbarkeit* – [96] **ballot** *Abstimmung, Wahl* – [97] **to exhaust** to use all of sth. so that there is none left – [98] **assiduous** [ə'sɪdjuəs] (*fml.*) *gewissenhaft, eifrig* – [99] **to nurture** (*fml.*) to help sth. to develop and be successful – [100] **to maintain** to keep sth. in good condition

2 **Historical overview:**
- democracy in the course of history
- ups and downs in the development of democracy
- democracy in the 21st century
- problems and setbacks
- loss of influence

3 **The financial crisis/China:**
- the impact of the 2007/2008 financial crisis on democracy
- China's economic success
- benefits of China's autocratic political system
- how the Chinese view their government

4 **The West:**
- universal benefits of democracy
- American democracy: faults in the system and their impact
- problems and democratic deficits within the European Union
- Europe's right-wing parties

5 **Various challenges:**
- regionalism
- "micro-powers"
- the Internet and its impact
- the voter and the "pleasure of the moment"

6 **The image of political parties/loss of role models:**
- declining party membership
- loss of trust in parties/politicians
- problems in democracy's heartlands, America and Europe

7 **Getting democracy right:**
- how to cope with globalisation and the digital revolution
- politicians and parties
- a narrower state and means of control
- historical examples of limited government
- Tocqueville's idea about grassroots democracy
- Tocqueville's ideas and modern technology
- how to maintain democracy successfully

ANALYSIS

2. Based on your previous findings compile a "problem – solution" diagram that visualizes the most relevant problems and solutions presented in the article.

problem	solution
● debt/economic problems	→ stability, healthy economy
● bailing out bankers	→ responsible bankers; no wasting of taxes
● lack of talented people	→ …
● failing civil services	→ …
● gridlock	
● corruption	
● …	

3. Explain the reasons that drive voters as well as politicians to political extremism.

4. What – according to the article – is the impact of the media and the Internet on voters' behaviour and attitudes?

5. In groups, study the *Universal Declaration of Human Rights* (→ FoD, p. 304) and do research on the *United Nations Charter* using the links provided on the webcode.

Webcode SNG-40235-033 @

Which "rights and norms that countries could not breach" (l. 261) are given there?
   a) Explain why these rights and norms are indispensable (*unverzichtbar*).
   b) But "if majorities wanted to do so" – would this still be democratic?
   → Focus on Documents, The Universal Declaration of Human Rights, p. 304

ACTIVITIES

6. Despite the fact mentioned in the text that many voters are losing interest in politics, there have been a number of new political parties in recent years, e. g. *Die Piraten, Alternative für Deutschland (AfD)* in Germany and the *Respect Party* in Britain.

   Now you are given the opportunity to create a new party that expresses your political ideas and meets the needs of your country. In groups,
   a) have a brainstorming session to collect ideas and
   b) set up a party programme that reflects your political goals and attracts potential voters.
   Present your different programmes in class and discuss their ideas and political goals.

7. In groups, launch a campaign in which you promote your party.
   Design posters, brochures, flyers, adverts, etc. that demonstrate your party's goals and attract potential voters.

The United Nations

The **United Nations Organization** (UNO, UN) was **founded in 1945 to replace the League of Nations** in order **to stop wars** between countries and as **a platform for international dialogue**. It contains multiple subsidiary organizations with diverse functions to carry out the UN's missions. Today, about 192 nations belong to the UN. When nations become a member of the UN, they agree to accept the obligations of **the UN Charter**, which states the **four basic purposes of the UN**:

- to maintain **international peace and security**
- to develop **friendly relations among nations**
- to be a centre for **harmonizing the actions of nations**
- to cooperate in **solving international problems** and promoting **respect for human rights**

The organization of the United Nations

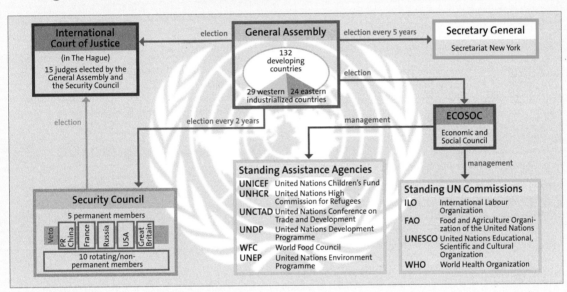

Global issues on the UN Agenda

- Africa
- Ageing
- Agriculture
- AIDS
- Atomic Energy
- Children
- Climate Change
- Culture
- Decolonization
- Demining
- Development Corporation
- Persons with Disabilities
- Disarmament
- Drugs and Crime
- Education
- Elections
- Energy
- Environment

- Family
- Food
- Governance
- Health
- Human Rights
- Human Settlements
- Humanitarian and Disaster Relief Assistance
- Indigenous People
- Information Communications Technology
- Intellectual Property
- International Finance
- Iraq
- Labour
- International Law
- Oceans and the Law of the Sea
- Least Developed Countries

- The Millenium UN General Assembly – The Goals
- Questions of Palestine
- Peace and Security
- Population
- Refugees
- Science and Technology
- Social Development
- Outer Space
- Statistics
- Sustainable Development
- Terrorism
- Trade and Development
- Volunteerism
- Water
- Women
- Youth

www.un.org/issues

Focus on Facts

The Universal Declaration of Human Rights

On **10 December 1948 the General Assembly of the United Nations** adopted and proclaimed the Universal Declaration of Human Rights. Although it is not a legally binding document it outlines a distinct understanding and view of human rights.

Article 1. All human beings are born free and equal in dignity and rights. They are endowed[1] with reason and conscience and should act towards one another in a spirit of brotherhood.

Article 2. Everyone is entitled to all the rights and freedoms set forth in this Declaration, without distinction of any kind, such as race, colour, sex, language, religion, political or other opinion, national or social origin, property, birth or other status. [...]

Article 3. Everyone has the right to life, liberty and security of person.

Article 4. No one shall be held in slavery or servitude; slavery and the slave trade shall be prohibited in all their forms.

Article 5. No one shall be subjected to torture or to cruel, inhuman or degrading treatment or punishment.

Article 6. Everyone has the right to recognition everywhere as a person before the law.

Article 7. All are equal before the law and are entitled without any discrimination to equal protection of the law. All are entitled to equal protection against any discrimination in violation of this Declaration and against any incitement[2] to such discrimination.

Article 8. Everyone has the right to an effective remedy[3] by the competent national tribunals for acts violating the fundamental rights granted him by the constitution or by law.

Article 9. No one shall be subjected to arbitrary[4] arrest, detention[5] or exile. [...]

Article 12. No one shall be subjected to arbitrary interference with his privacy, family, home or correspondence, nor to attacks upon his honor and reputation. Everyone has the right to the protection of the law against such interference or attacks. [...]

Article 16. (1) Men and women of full age, without any limitation due to race, nationality or religion, have the right to marry and to found a family. They are entitled to equal rights as to marriage, during marriage and at its dissolution. (2) Marriage shall be entered into only with the free and full consent of the intending spouses[6]. [...]

Article 17. (1) Everyone has the right to own property alone as well as in association with others. (2) No one shall be arbitrarily deprived[7] of his property. [...]

Article 19. Everyone has the right to freedom of opinion and expression; this right includes freedom to hold opinions without interference and to seek, receive and impart information and ideas through any media and regardless of frontiers. [...]

Article 26. (1) Everyone has the right to education. Education shall be free, at least in the elementary and fundamental stages. Elementary education shall be compulsory[8]. Technical and professional education shall be made generally available and higher education shall be equally accessible to all on the basis of merit[9]. [...]

Article 28. Everyone is entitled to a social and international order in which the rights and freedoms set forth in this Declaration can be fully realized.

www.un.org/en/documents/udhr/index.shtml#atop [03.12.2012]

[1] **to endow sb. with. sth.** [ɪnˈdaʊ] *jdn. mit etw. ausstatten* – [2] **incitement** *Anstiftung* – [3] **remedy** a successful way of curing an illness or dealing with a problem or difficulty – [4] **arbitrary** *willkürlich* – [5] **detention** *Haft, Internierung* – [6] **spouse** wife, husband – [7] **to deprive sb. of sth.** *jdm. etw. aberkennen* – [8] **compulsory** that has to done; *verpflichtend* – [9] **merit** (*fml.*) the quality of being good and deserving praise

The Plague of Global Terrorism

AWARENESS

Terrorism is not a new threat – there have been terrorist attacks and plots for centuries all over the world. One example is the Gunpowder Plot of 1605, when English Catholics attempted – and failed – to blow up the House of Lords during the State Opening ceremony and assassinate King James I of England and VI of Scotland. The night before the State Opening, one of the conspirators, Guy Fawkes, was discovered guarding 36 barrels of gunpowder and was arrested. At the trial, Guy Fawkes was sentenced to be hanged, drawn and quartered.

However, the 20th and 21st centuries have shown new shocking dimensions of terrorism worldwide.

In a placemat activity, share and discuss your knowledge of and thoughts about terrorism in general and certain terrorist acts in particular.

COMPREHENSION

Before reading:

 Step 1: In groups, describe the cartoon below in detail, paying attention to these aspects:
- the depiction of the IS fighter
- how he sees the world
- the IS fighter's vision of Europe, European culture and Europe's religious orientation
- the overall atmosphere of the cartoon
- → Focus on Skills, Analysis of Visuals, p. 409

 Step 2: Discuss the message of the cartoon.
- What is the cartoonist's view of the IS?
- What image of the IS in general does the cartoon convey?

Konkrete Vorstellung

Tips on vocab

the right side: a disguised (*vermummt*) man ■ a thin slit for the eyes ■ to wear an ammunition belt ■ the world is flat (like a disc) ■ a grid (*Raster*)

the left side: a thought bubble ■ a woman wearing a black niqab (= a dress covering the entire body, with a thin slit for the eyes) ■ allusion: Europa, a figure from Greek mythology, sitting on a bull – depicting the continent → personification ■ the bull: a grim facial expression ■ the half-moon as a symbol for Islam

The appalling attacks in Paris on November 13th [2015] are a brutal reminder of the danger of terrorism to the West, mainly from jihadist[1] groups such as Islamic State (IS). Yet terrorism is a threat everywhere. The day before the atrocities[2] in Paris, two bomb blasts killed 37 people in Beirut. On November 17th [2015] a suicide bomber blew up a market in northern Nigeria, leaving at least 36 people dead. Last year 32,700 people were killed in attacks worldwide, nearly twice as many as in 2013. And this year the toll[3] may turn out to be even higher.

Most of the deaths last year (and every year) are in the Middle East and Africa – not the West. Iraq, Nigeria, Syria, Pakistan and Afghanistan together account for three-quarters of the global total. Western countries suffered under 3% of all deaths in the past 15 years. Boko Haram, a jihadist group that operates mainly in northern Nigeria and Cameroon (and recently pledged[4] affiliation[5] to Islamic State), was responsible for over 6,600 deaths according to the Institute for Economics and Peace (which excludes military targets). That is more than any other group in the world – even IS. Nigeria has also been plagued by a new outfit in the south, the Fulani militants, which did not even exist until 2013. The increased bloodiness of both groups contributed to a quadrupling[6] of deaths to 7,500 in 2014, the largest rise ever seen in one country. If deaths caused by war were counted, IS is far more deadly than any other organisation, even using the most conservative estimates.

The Paris attacks and the downing[7] of a Russian airliner in Egypt killed more than 100 people each. Such lethal[8] attacks are rare but are increasing. Last year, there were 26 compared with a handful in 2013. Most were carried out by IS, and most occurred in Iraq. And terrorism is spreading. 67 countries saw at least one death last year compared with 59 the year before. The number of plots by jihadist groups against Western countries has leaped[9], in particular since September 2014 when an IS spokesman called for its followers to attack those Western countries involved in military efforts in Syria and Iraq. Most plots[10] have failed, though a growing number have been successful. But the terrorists only need to carry out one big plot to succeed.

http://www.economist.com/blogs/graphicdetail/2015/11/daily-chart-12, 18 November 2015 [17.07.2016]

COMPREHENSION

1. Find evidence in the text that matches the following statements:
    a) Terrorism cannot be reduced to local conspiracies.
    b) The number of victims of terrorist attacks has risen dramatically.
    c) Africa has suffered most from terrorist attacks.
    d) The IS has become the most dangerous terrorist organization globally.
    e) Terrorism is spreading significantly worldwide.
    f) The number of terrorist attacks against the West is extremely low.
    g) In general, terrorist attacks have been rather unsuccessful.

ANALYSIS

2. Find passages in the article that match the information and figures presented in the statistics on the following page.

    Team up with a partner and explain the correlations to each other.
    → Focus on Skills, Analysis of Statistical Data, p. 408
    → Focus on Skills, Analysis of a Non-Fictional Text, p. 405

[1] **jihadist** [dʒəˈhædist] a Muslim who is fighting for Islam, esp. a radical, who believes in using violence to achieve religious and political aims – [2] **atrocity** an extremely cruel, violent or shocking act – [3] **toll** suffering, deaths or damage – [4] **to pledge** to make a serious or formal promise to make or do sth. – [5] **affiliation** a connection with a political party, religion or organization – [6] **to quadruple** to become four times as big – [7] **downing** *Abschuss* – [8] **lethal** [ˈliːθəl] able to cause or causing death – [9] **to leap** (leapt, leapt) to increase or grow very quickly – [10] **plot** conspiracy

1

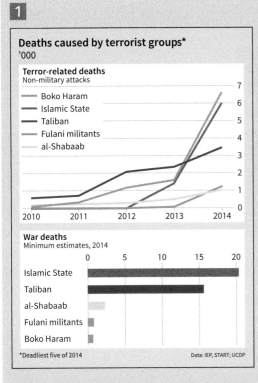

Deaths caused by terrorist groups*
'000

Terror-related deaths
Non-military attacks

— Boko Haram
— Islamic State
— Taliban
— Fulani militants
— al-Shabaab

War deaths
Minimum estimates, 2014

Islamic State
Taliban
al-Shabaab
Fulani militants
Boko Haram

*Deadliest five of 2014   Data: IEP, START; UCDP

2

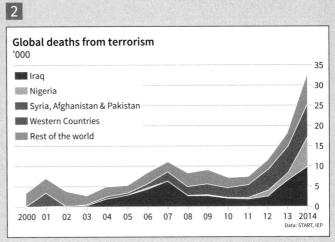

Global deaths from terrorism
'000

■ Iraq
▨ Nigeria
■ Syria, Afghanistan & Pakistan
■ Western Countries
▨ Rest of the world

Data: START, IEP

3

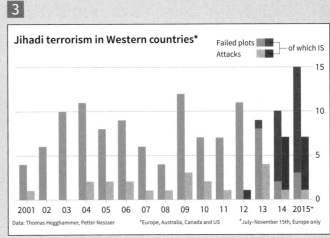

Jihadi terrorism in Western countries*

Failed plots ▨ ┐
Attacks ▨ ┘ of which IS

Data: Thomas Hegghammer, Petter Nessser   *Europe, Australia, Canada and US   +July–November 15th, Europe only

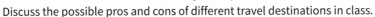

ACTIVITIES

3. Your class is planning the graduation/end-of-school trip, which has led to a very controversial discussion. In light of terrorist attacks in recent years (e. g. in England, France and Sweden), you want to choose a safe – but also affordable – destination for your trip.

Discuss the possible pros and cons of different travel destinations in class.

→ Focus on Language, Conversation and Discussion, p. 413

trade		
(economic) supremacy [suːˈpreməsi]	the position in which a country/an economy is more powerful or advanced than others	*Übermacht, Überlegenheit*
industrialized country	a country that has a lot of factories, etc.	*Industrieland*
Industrial Revolution	the period in the 18th and 19th centuries in Europe and the US when machines began to be used to do work, and industry grew rapidly	*Industrielle Revolution*
secure markets	safe markets	*sichere Märkte*
slavery/slave trade	the system of having slaves/the buying and selling of slaves, especially Africans who were taken to America	*Sklaverei/Sklavenhandel*
taxation	the system of charging taxes	*Besteuerung*
transatlantic trade	trade/business involving countries on both sides of the Atlantic	*transatlantischer Handel*
transportation network	a system of roads/channels/railroads to transport goods	*Transport-Netzwerk*
triangular [traɪˈæŋgjələ] **trade**	trade involving three continents: Europe, Africa and America	*atlantischer Dreieckshandel*
consumerism and consumption		
acquisition of sth.	the act of buying sth.	*Anschaffung, Erwerb*
availability [əˌveɪləˈbɪlɪti]	the fact that sb. is free to be contacted; the fact that sth. is there to be bought	*Verfügbarkeit*
consumer	someone who buys and uses products and services	*Konsument*
customer	someone who buys goods or services from a shop, company, etc.	*Kunde*
discount shopping	to go shopping at a store that sells goods cheaply	*Kauf von preisreduzierter Ware*
distribution of sth.	the act of giving or delivering sth. to a number of people	*Verteilung*
efficiency [ɪˈfɪʃənsi]	the quality of doing sth. well without wasting money or time	*Effizienz, Effektivität*
industrialized mass production	when products are made in large numbers by industrial machines so they can be sold cheaply	*industrielle Massenproduktion*
to instil a desire	to put the idea in sb.'s mind that they desire sth.	*in jdm. eine Begierde wecken*
Internet retailer	Internet shop	*Internet-Versandhandel*
to line the shelves	to offer sth. for sale in large amounts	*den Absatz steigern*
mounting consumer debt	strongly rising consumer debt	*steigende Konsumentenverschuldung*
online shopping portal	a website where you can buy things	*Plattform für Online-Einkäufe*
purchasing power	the amount of money a person or group has available to spend	*Kaufkraft*
shipping	the delivery of goods	*Lieferung, Zustellung*
range of products	selection of products	*Produktauswahl, Produktpalette*
retailer/retail store	a person or store that sells goods	*Händler, Einzelhändler*
trade unions and labour policy		
company board	a group of elected or appointed members who supervise the activities of a company	*Aufsichtsrat*
company pension plan	an arrangement between a company and its employees (or a union representing the employees) to provide money (a retirement pension) for the employees' retirement	*betriebliche Altersvorsorge*
to dismiss	to officially remove sb. from their job	*jdn. entlassen*

employment legislation	laws that govern the employer-employee relations and rights of employees; labour legislation	*Arbeitsrecht*
freelancing	working independently (for different companies)	*freiberuflich arbeiten*
(to work) flexitime	system in which employees work a particular number of hours each week/month but can choose when they start and finish work	*flexible Arbeitszeiten*
(to work) full-time	for all the hours of a week/month which people normally work	*Vollzeit-*
labour contract	contract between employee and employer	*Arbeitsvertrag*
labour market	the number of people who are available for work in relation to the number of jobs available	*Arbeitsmarkt*
to lay off (laid off, laid off)	to stop employing sb.	*entlassen*
(to work) overtime	working more hours than you have to according to your contract	*Überstunden, Mehrarbeit*
(to work) part-time	working for part of the day/week	*Teilzeit-, in Teilzeit*
paternity/maternity leave	time that a father/mother is allowed to spend away from work when they have a baby	*Erziehungsurlaub*
personnel [ˌpɜːsənˈel]	the people working in a firm, etc.; staff	*Personal*
salary	wage, pay; money that you receive for doing your job	*(Jahres-/Monats-)Gehalt*
to (go on) strike	to refuse to work in order to protest against sth.	*streiken*
unemployment benefit	money paid by the government to sb. who is unemployed	*Arbeitslosengeld*
(trade) union	organization of workers to protect their interests	*Gewerkschaft*
wages (*pl.*)	pay, salary; money that you receive for doing your job	*Lohn, Löhne*
works council	a group representing the employees of a company whose members are elected to negotiate working conditions, etc. with the company's management	*Betriebsrat*
globalisation		
capital market	financial market	*Finanzmarkt, Kapitalmarkt*
cultural imperialism	the imposing of a foreign culture on sb.	*kultureller Imperialismus*
domestic demand	amount of money spent on goods and services by the people, companies and government within a particular country	*inländische Nachfrage*
domestic labour market	the number of workers and available jobs within a particular country	*inländischer Arbeitsmarkt*
entrepreneurship [ˌɒntrəprəˈnɜːʃɪp]	running one's own business	*Unternehmertum*
expatriate	a person living (and working) in a country that is not their own	*jd., der sein Heimatland verlässt, um Arbeit zu finden*
to generate capital	to yield/produce money	*Kapital erwirtschaften*
global labour market	global workforce	*globaler Arbeitsmarkt*
infrastructure	the basic systems and services, such as transport or power supplies, that a country or organization uses in order to work effectively	*Infrastruktur*
interdependency	a situation in which people or things depend on each other	*Korrelation, gegenseitige Abhängigkeit*
to internationalize	to make sth. become international	*etw. internationalisieren*
labour standards	the working conditions	*Arbeitsgesetzgebung*
liberalization of sth.	the act of making sth. less strict	*Liberalisierung von etw.*
logistics	the practical organization of sth.	*Logistik*

microcredit	a very small amount of money lent to a person or group, esp. to make it possible for poor people to start a business	*Kleinstkredit, Mikrokredit*
migrant worker	sb. who moves to a richer country in order to work there	*Wanderarbeiter, Gastarbeiter*
multinationals	large companies that operate in several countries	*multinationale Konzerne*
output	amount of sth. that a company produces	*Produktion, Leistung*
outsourcing of work	the act of arranging for sb. outside the company to do work for that company	*Ausgliederung/Auslagerung von Arbeit*
to promote international trade	to do sth. in order to increase international trade	*internationalen Handel fördern*
protectionism	when a government tries to help industries in its own country by taxing or restricting goods	*Protektionismus, Schutzpolitik*
to raise living standards	to improve the level of comfort and increase the amount of money that people have	*Lebensstandards erhöhen*
repatriate	a person who has lived and worked abroad and returns to his or her homeland	*jd., der in sein Heimatland zurückkehrt*
trade negotiation	discussion in order to reach an agreement on trade	*Wirtschaftsverhandlung(en)*
unskilled worker	someone who works in a job that requires little or no training	*Hilfskraft, ungelernter Arbeiter*
ecology and energy		
agriculture	the practice of farming	*Landwirtschaft*
carbon emission	carbon dioxide that planes, cars, factories, etc. produce, which is harmful to the environment	*Kohlenstoffausstoß*
climate change	a permanent change in weather conditions	*Klimawandel*
crops	plants that are grown by farmers and used as food	*Getreide*
deforestation	the cutting or burning down of all the trees in an area	*Waldrodung*
exploitation	when sb. treats sb. else unfairly – esp. to make money from their work	*Ausbeutung*
fracking	a technique used to force oil and natural gas from rock by pumping pressurized fluid into the ground and creating new channels in the rock which makes oil, etc. more easily available	*Fracking*
fragility of sth.	the quality of being easily broken or damaged	*Zerbrechlichkeit*
fossil fuel	fuel such as coal and oil, which were formed underground from plant and animal remains millions of years ago	*fossiler Brennstoff*
greenhouse effect	the gradual warming of the air surrounding the earth as a result of heat being trapped by pollution	*Treibhauseffekt*
to have an impact on sth.	to influence sth.	*etw. beeinflussen*
heatwave	a period of unusually hot weather	*Hitzewelle*
the incineration of trash	the act of burning trash in a facility	*Müllverbrennung*
to pose a threat for/to sb.	to create a threat, problem, etc. that has to be dealt with	*für jdn. eine Bedrohung darstellen*
renewable energies	types of energy such as wind or solar power that can be replaced as quickly as they are used	*erneuerbare Energien*
sustainability [səˌsteɪnəˈbɪlɪti]	able to continue for a long time without causing damage to the environment	*Nachhaltigkeit*
techniques of cultivation	techniques of using land for growing plants or crops	*Anbautechniken*
waste disposal	getting rid of garbage	*Müllentsorgung*
water supply	the water that is provided and treated for a particular area	*Wasserversorgung*

language		
accent [ˈæksənt]	manner of pronunciation characteristic of a region	*Akzent*
acronym	a word formed from the first letters of the words that make up the name of sth., e. g. UN (United Nations)	*Akronym, Kurzwort*
antonym	a word that is opposite in meaning to another word	*Gegensatzwort*
bilingual [baˈlɪŋgwəl]	a person with a command of two languages	*zweisprachig*
colloquial; colloquialism	used in conversation but not in formal speech or writing; an informal expression or word	*umgangssprachlich; um-gangssprachlicher Ausdruck*
communication	activity of exchanging information or meaning	*Kommunikation, Austausch*
communicative competence	a person's awareness of the rules governing the appro-priate use of language in social situations	*kommunikative Fähigkeit/ Kompetenz*
communication strategies	strategies of expressing meaning (e. g. in a second language) without knowing the exact words for it	*kommunikative Strategien*
dialect	variety of language common among a group of speak-ers, usually defined by region	*Dialekt, lokale/regionale Sprachvariante*
ESL [ˌiːesˈel]	English as a Second Language	*Englisch als Zweitsprache*
four-letter words	swear/curse words	*Schimpfwort, Kraftausdruck*
Globish (Global English)	a simplified form of international English	*internationales Englisch*
idiom	combination of words in common use; an expression that cannot be translated word for word	*Redensart*
lingua franca	a medium of communication used by people who speak different first languages	*Verkehrssprache, Lingua franca*
literary freedom	personal variation of language as used by writers, poets, etc.	*dichterische Freiheit*
loanword/borrowing	a word from another language used in its original form	*Lehnwort*
mother tongue	the language that you first learn to speak as a child	*Muttersprache*
multilingual	a person with a command of several languages	*mehrsprachig*
native speaker	a speaker of a certain language as a first language	*Muttersprachler*
Netspeak	language used to communicate on the Internet	*Netzjargon*
non-Standard English	informal or slang vocabulary, grammar or pronuncia-tion	*umgangssprachliches Englisch*
paraphrase	an alternate way of saying sth.	*Umschreibung*
phrase	a group of words that together have a particular meaning	*Wendung*
primary language	the language you learned first, or the one you use most often	*Primärsprache*
pronunciation	the way in which a word is spoken	*Aussprache*
Queen's English (*outdated*)	the standard accent of British English; sometimes also called Oxford English	*Standardenglisch, britisches Englisch*
register	language used in a particular social environment	*Sprachebene*
secondary language	a person's second language or one that is used less often	*Zweitsprache*
slang	informal, non-standard vocabulary	*Umgangssprache*
sociolect	variety of language common among the members of a specific social group	*Soziolekt, Gruppensprache*
synonym	a word that has the same meaning as another word	*sinnverwandtes Wort*
syntax	sentence structure	*Satzbau*
technical term	a word for a particular subject that is difficult to under-stand if you do not know about that subject	*Fachbegriff*
variety [vəˈraɪəti]	diversity, plurality; manner, kind, type	*Varietät; Vielfalt; Art*

Science (Fiction) & Technology – Towards a Better World?!

Saadiyat Island's Zayed National Museum near Abu Dhabi designed by Norman Foster

The British Museum has come under fire over plans to loan hundreds of culturally significant artefacts, including some of its much-prized "highlights", to an organisation in Abu Dhabi which has been accused of abusing the rights of
5 workers.

Curators[1] at the museum have drawn up a list of around 500 objects, a selection of which could be loaned to the Zayed National Museum in the United Arab Emirates for up to five years.

10 It will receive a significant fee for the loan, which it needs to offset[2] the impact of Government cuts.

Last night human rights groups said the Zayed, which was designed by British architect Norman Foster and is due to open next year, is being built using a system of
15 "modern slavery" and urged the British Museum to rethink its loan.

The Zayed is one of a number of cultural destinations currently being built on Saadiyat Island, an idyllic stretch of sand dunes near Abu Dhabi. Tens of thousands of migrant workers have been recruited to help with the giant con- 20 struction project, but it is claimed that many have been housed in slums or deported for complaining about low wages.

The list of treasures shortlisted for loan by the British Museum includes valuable Assyrian reliefs, Sasanian gold belt 25 fittings[3], Greek and Roman jewels and Ming dynasty porcelain.

It initially planned to send only objects in storage[4], but according to The Art Newspaper the list has now been upgraded to include some of the museum's 5,000 "highlights". 30 [...]

"The museums and other developments on Saadiyat Island are all being built on the back of a system of modern slavery," said Sharan Burrow, general secretary of the International Trade Union Confederation. 35

https://www.independent.co.uk/news/uk/home-news/british-museum-criticised-for-loaning-artefacts-to-abu-dhabi-organisation-accused-of-abusing-rights-10293090.html 18 October 2018 [18.08.2018]

[1] **curator** a person in charge of a museum, library, etc. – [2] **to offset sth.** *ausgleichen* – [3] **fitting** *das Teil* – [4] **in storage** the act of keepings things somewhere until they are needed

H. G. Wells

The Time Machine

The utopian novel *The Time Machine* was first published in 1895, and tells the story of an English scientist, the Time Traveller, who invents a machine which enables him to travel to the past or future. However, the scientist decides to travel to the year 802,701 A. D. where he finds himself in a paradise-like world in which he encounters the childlike Eloi race, who live in the upper world, and the Morlocks, ape-like creatures who live underground.

"I must confess that my satisfaction with my first theories of an automatic civilization and a decadent humanity did not long endure. Yet I could think of no other. Let me put my difficulties. The several big palaces I had explored were mere living places, great dining-halls and sleeping apartments. I could find no machinery, no appliances[1] of any kind. Yet these people were clothed in pleasant fabrics[2] that must at times need renewal, and their sandals, though undecorated, were fairly complex specimens[3] of metalwork. Somehow such things must be made. And the little people displayed no vestige[4] of a creative tendency. There were no shops, no workshops, no signs of importations among them. They spent all their time in playing gently, in bathing in the river, in making love in a half-playful fashion, in eating fruit and sleeping. I could not see how things were kept going". [...]

"The great triumph of Humanity I had dreamed of took a different shape in my mind. It had been no such triumph of moral education and general co-operation as I had imagined. Instead, I saw a real aristocracy[5], armed with a perfect science and working to a logical conclusion the industrial system of today. [...] But even on this supposition[6] the balanced civilization that was at last attained[7] must have long since passed its zenith[8], and was now far fallen into decay[9]. The too-perfect security of the Upper-worlders had led them to a slow movement of degeneration, to a general dwindling[10] in size, strength, and intelligence. That I could see clearly enough already. What had happened to the Undergrounders I did not yet suspect; but from what I had seen of the Morlocks – that, by the by[11], was the name by which these creatures were called – I could imagine that the modification of the human type was even far more profound[12] than among the "Eloi", that beautiful race that I already knew". [...]

"So, as I see it, the Upper-world man had drifted towards the feeble[13] prettiness, and the Under-world to mere mechanical industry. But that perfect state had lacked one thing even for mechanical perfection – absolute permanency. Apparently as time went on, the feeding of the Under-world, however it was effected, had become disjointed[14]. Mother Necessity, who had been staved off[15] for a few thousand years, came back again, and she began slow. The Underworld being in contact with machinery, which, however perfect, still needs some little thought outside habit, had probably retained[16] perforce[17] rather more initiative, if less of every other human character, than the Upper. And when other meat failed them, they turned to what old habit had hitherto[18] forbidden. So I say I saw it in my last view of the world of Eight Hundred and two Thousand Seven Hundred and One".

from *The Time Machine* by H. G. Wells. Airmont Publishing Company, New York 1964, pp. 59 ff.

START-UP ACTIVITIES

1. Listen to Pharrell Williams' song *Happy*, and, in a Round Robin activity, say which emotions the song evokes in you and what being "happy" means to you.

2. The word "utopia" is derived from the Greek: "ou" (= not), "topos" (= place) and "eu" (= good). Against this background, describe the place. What do "outopia" and "eutopia" look like?

3. What do the photo and online article imply about utopias and "modern highlights"? In order to get a deeper understanding of the Saadiyat Island project, get further information on the webcode.

Webcode
SNG-40235-034 @

4. Together with a partner, read the excerpt from the novel *The Time Machine*. Which utopian elements can you detect – and where does the excerpt hint at a dystopian society (cf. info box, p. 336)?

---

[1] **appliances** [əˈplaɪənsəz] device, gadget, machine – [2] **fabrics** here: *Kleidungsstücke* – [3] **specimen** a typical example of sth. – [4] **vestige** [ˈvestɪdʒ] (*fml.*) *Spur, Überrest* – [5] **aristocracy** [ˌærɪˈstɒkrəsi] *Adel* – [6] **supposition** *Vermutung* – [7] **to attain** (*fml.*) to succeed in getting sth. – [8] **zenith** [ˈzenɪθ] the most successful point or time – [9] **decay** *Verfall* – [10] **to dwindle** [ˈdwɪndl] to become smaller in size – [11] **by the by** *übrigens* – [12] **profound** *tiefgründig* – [13] **feeble** weak and without energy, strength or power – [14] **disjointed** *unzusammenhängend* – [15] **to stave sb./sth. off** (*phr. v.*) *jdn./etw. abwehren* – [16] **to retain** (*fml.*) to continue to have sth. – [17] **perforce** (*old-fashioned, fml.*) *zwangsläufig* – [18] **hitherto** (*fml.*) *bisher*

Opportunities and Risks: Genetic Engeneering and Robots

Low-Cost Fertility Treatment – Maybe Babies

AWARENESS

Look at the graphic and the information on the development of the world's population below. Against this backdrop, discuss whether or not the ongoing hype of infertility treatments and the artificial fertilization of millions of women is reasonable and should be "low-cost" as the headline suggests.

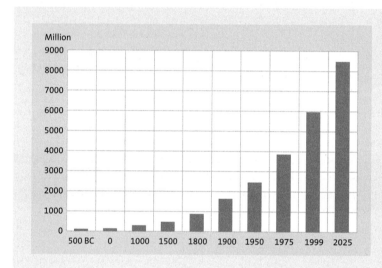

At present the world's population is growing quickly, though this has not always been the case.

- Until the 1800s the world's population grew slowly for thousands of years.
- In 1820 the world's population reached one billion.
- In the early 1970s, the world's population reached three billion.
- In 1999, less than 30 years later, the population doubled to six billion.
- The global rate of population growth is now one billion every 15 years.

www.bbc.co.uk/schools/gcsebitesize/geography/population/population_change_structure_rev1.shtml [01.12.2014]

In vitro fertilisation[1], once seen as miraculous[2], is now mainstream in rich countries. Soon it may be cheap enough to help infertile people in poor places, too.

5 "In France," says Fabrice Houdart, as he dandles[3] his baby, "we are like a circus attraction." The Frenchman lives in Washington, DC, with his American boyfriend and their two children, who were conceived[4] using eggs from a Californian donor and born by a surrogate[5] in Pennsyl-10 vania. Families built with such a variety of help are still rare enough to raise eyebrows. But across the rich world "test-tube[6] babies" no longer draw a second glance[7]. Since the first, Louise Brown, was born in 1978, 5.5 m more have followed, half of them in the past six years.
15 Back then, doctors had to hope that the single egg they retrieved[8] would be fertilised when mixed with sperm,

and that the resulting embryo would be a winner. Success rates were just a few percent. Now, with stronger drugs to stimulate ovulation[9] and better laboratory techniques to manipulate and store embryos, more 20 than a quarter of IVF attempts result in a baby.

For the infertile couples it helps, IVF is close to a miracle. But for many more, the cost is prohibitive[10]. Public health programmes in some rich countries, including Australia, Japan and several European ones, cover[11] IVF 25 for some who need it, but rarely all. Britain's National Health Service, for example, does not manage to pay for the three tries its guidelines recommend for all who would benefit. In America, where IVF is rarely covered by insurance and an attempt costs around $15,000, at 30 most a quarter of those for whom IVF is clinically indicated are actually treated.

---

[1] **in vitro fertilisation (IVF)** *künstliche Befruchtung* – [2] **miraculous** like a miracle; completely unexpected and very lucky – [3] **to dandle** (*old-fashioned*) *jdn. wiegen, schaukeln* – [4] **to conceive** here: to create – [5] **surrogate** *Leihmutter* – [6] **test tube** *Reagenzglas* – [7] **glance** a quick short look – [8] **to retrieve** to get sth. – [9] **ovulation** *Eisprung* – [10] **prohibitive** [prəˈhɪbɪtɪv] *unerschwinglich* – [11] **to cover sth.** here: to pay for sth.

The unmet[12] need in developing countries is higher still. That is partly because people have less money, but also because infertility is more common. Genital mutilation[13], unsafe abortion and poorly attended[14] births cause infections that leave women with blocked[15] Fallopian tubes[16], making normal conception impossible. Sexually transmitted diseases scar[17] both men's and women's reproductive systems. The World Health Organisation estimates that around 50 m couples worldwide have been trying to conceive for at least five years without success. Almost none of those in developing countries can hope to get treatment.

The grief of infertility is sharper in poor countries, too. In Africa and much of Asia it carries a stigma[18], nearly all borne[19] by women. Male-factor infertility is rarely acknowledged except when a man has failed to father children with several women. A "barren[20]" wife is often ostracised[21], beaten or abandoned, or infected with HIV/AIDS as a result of her husband straying[22] in the hope of a child. She is at higher risk of being murdered or committing suicide.

Better health care would mean fewer people in developing countries becoming infertile in the first place. Now fertility doctors are trying to make IVF cheap enough to help many more of those who will still need it. Some are simplifying diagnosis, skipping some tests that are currently standard, but still doing enough to tell, for most patients, which treatment would be best. Others are cutting spending on equipment. Last year Belgian researchers tested a shoebox-sized IVF laboratory built from cheap glass tubes[23] that uses baking soda and citric acid[24] to create the carbon dioxide needed for fertilisation to occur. Pregnancy rates matched those from a standard laboratory and set-up costs are 85–90 % lower. With fewer tests and less monitoring, running costs are slashed[25], too. Though of no use when the man's sperm is sub-par[26] and thus needs to be injected into the egg under a pricey[27] microscope, it should be sufficient[28] for about 70 % of infertile couples, says Willem Ombelet of the Genk Institute for Fertility Technology, who led the first trial.

The Low-Cost IVF Foundation, a non-profit based in Switzerland, is working with Zambia's health ministry to set up an IVF programme later this year. Costs will be shaved[29] wherever possible, with the biggest saving coming from using clomiphene citrate[30], an oral drug that provides a modest boost to ovulation and costs just $12 per IVF attempt, instead of the standard injectable drugs, which cost thousands.

Cut-price approaches will not be suitable for all couples, and success rates per IVF cycle may be lower. But if the savings are big enough, more infertile couples will be able to try at least once and the cost per baby will plummet[31]. The Foundation's long-term aim is to show IVF can be included in a developing country's public health-care system for as little as $300 per attempt, plus staffing[32] costs. Gauging[33] how achievable that figure is will only be possible once such treatment is up and running[34], says Ian Cooke, an emeritus professor at Sheffield University in England and one of its founders. If the programme in Zambia gets anywhere close to it, clinics in rich countries could start slashing prices, too.

www.economist.com/news/international/21607881-vitro-fertilisation-once-seen-miraculous-now-mainstream-rich-countries-soon, 19 July 2014 [22.01.2015]

COMPREHENSION

1. Outline the development and advances IVF has undergone since the 1970s.

2. Present the reasons for infertility in developing countries and the threats this poses, particularly for women.

3. Specify the medical and scientific research and development that is being done to make IVF affordable for people and health care systems in both developing and rich countries.

---

[12] **unmet** *unerfüllt* – [13] **genital mutilation** *Genitalverstümmelung* – [14] **to attend** here: to provide help or service to sb. – [15] **blocked** *verstopft* – [16] **Fallopian tube** *Eileiter* – [17] **to scar** here: to damage/hurt – [18] **stigma** *Schandmal* – [19] **to bear (bore, borne)** (*fml.*) to take responsibility for sth. – [20] **barren** unfertile; *unfruchtbar* – [21] **to ostracise** [ˈɒstrəsaɪz] *jdn. ächten* – [22] **to stray** (*infml.*) *fremdgehen* – [23] **tube** *Röhrchen* – [24] **citric acid** *Zitronensäure* – [25] **to slash** (*infml.*) to very much reduce sth. – [26] **sub-par** below average; *unterdurchschnittlich* – [27] **pricey** (*infml.*) expensive – [28] **sufficient** [səˈfɪʃənt] *ausreichend* – [29] **to shave** (*infml.*) to reduce – [30] **clomiphene citrate** *Clomifenzitrat; Wirkstoff zur Auslösung eines Eisprungs* – [31] **to plummet** to fall very quickly and suddenly – [32] **staffing** personnel – [33] **to gauge** [geɪdʒ] to make a judgement about sth., especially people's feelings or attitudes – [34] **up and running** *in Gang*

Info

> **IVF – In vitro fertilization** is a process in which an egg (ovum) is fertilized by sperm outside the body (in vitro: *lat.*: in glass). In a first step, the woman's ovulatory process (*Eisprung*) is monitored and stimulated. Then, eggs (ova) are removed from the woman's ovaries (*Eierstöcke*) and are fertilized by sperm in a fluid medium in a laboratory. The fertilized egg is cultured for 2 – 6 days in a growth medium and then implanted in the same woman's or a surrogate woman's uterus.

ANALYSIS

4. Examine the author's line of argument* and state what it reveals about his/her stance on low-cost fertility treatment.
   → Focus on Skills, Analysis of a Non-Fictional Text, p. 405

5. Categorize the type of article by referring to specific structural, stylistic or rhetorical devices in the text.
   → Focus on Facts, Basic Types of Non-Fictional Texts, p. 396

ACTIVITIES

6. Critically discuss the implications made in the English magazine article that low-cost fertility treatments in developing countries help women to avoid being "ostracized, beaten or abandoned, or infected with HIV/AIDS … murdered or [committing suicide]" (ll. 50 ff.).
   Is in vitro fertilization the key to solving these problems or should there be different kinds of solutions to the social problems?

7. In vitro fertilization and the donation of eggs and embryos is a particularly sensitive topic – emotionally, ethically and legally.
   Act out a panel discussion in which you exchange views on the controversial matter and juxtapose possible pros and cons.
   Prepare role cards and collect arguments on the different positions, which may include:
   - infertile American/European couples that are longing for a baby
   - Health Service representatives who complain about the immense cost of fertility treatments
   - women from developing countries who demand help in their desperate situation
   - demographers who refer to the unprecedented growth of the world's population
   - a representative from a church

8. Imagine you just found out you were donated as an embryo. Write a letter to your (biological or adopted) parents in which you express your feelings.

GRAMMAR / LANGUAGE

9. Collect the most relevant technical terms and phrases used in the text and formulate equivalent everyday English explanations. Use a dictionary and/or the Focus on vocab pages for help.

   Examples:
   - in vitro fertilization
     → the fertilization of an egg from a woman outside her body
   - surrogate
     → a woman who gives birth to a baby for another woman who is unable to have babies herself

10. Think about possible ethical, economic, emotional or legal concerns or benefits of IVF or the donation of embryos. Make if-clauses (type I, II, III) that reflect on possible risks, (dis-)advantages or benefits.

Examples:
- If I had known that it would take that many attempts at such high costs, I would not have … (type III)
- If the costs are covered by the public health services, women from poorer countries will be able to … (type I)

Brigitte Osterath

Apple and Facebook's "Social Freezing" May Be Problematic

AWARENESS

 Take a look at the cartoon below and, together with a partner,
  a) describe the cartoon in detail using the vocab box
  b) explain the symbolism and message of the cartoon.
   → Focus on Skills, Analysis of Visuals, p. 409

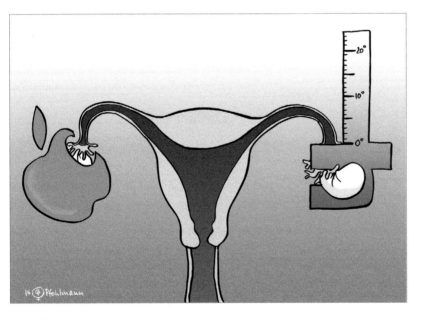

Tips on vocab »»
uterus ['juːtərəs] ▪
ovaries (*Eierstöcke*) ▪
company logo ▪ tubal
ligation (*Eileiterunter-
brechung*) ▪ to clamp
sth. (*etw. einklemmen*) ▪
upside down ▪ clinical
thermometer

COMPREHENSION »»»»»»

1. Before reading:
 Together with a partner, reflect on the term "social egg freezing". What are the social effects of freezing female employees' eggs for pregnancy later in life?

Step 1: Collect ideas about possible benefits and disadvantages for
a) the employees,
b) the companies.

Step 2: Arrange your findings in a grid.

	advantage/benefit	disadvantage/risk
employees	• …	• the eggs may not be able to be used/implanted at a later time • …
company	• employee does not go on maternity leave • …	• …

It sounds like a generous, socially-minded offer from Apple and Facebook to pay for female employees to have eggs frozen for pregnancy later in life. But it's not without its complications.

5 It is an unusual perk[1] – and probably not a completely altruistic[2] one. According to an NBC[3] News report, the US company Facebook covers[4] egg-freezing for non-medical reasons. A spokesperson confirmed the company had launched[5] the scheme in January. The IT
10 company Apple has also announced a similar benefit for its employees from next January. According to NBC news, it is part of the companies' plans to increase the number of female employees. It is said they want to give their employees the opportunity to concentrate on
15 their careers first and to have children later in life.

Save it for later
The method of freezing eggs – "oocyte cryopreservation[6]" as it is known medically – was originally developed for cancer patients needing chemotherapy or
20 radiotherapy. These life-saving procedures destroy oocytes and can – with a lot of bad luck – make a woman infertile. Egg freezing offers a chance to preserve viable[7] eggs so that women can have children at a later date.
The method can also be useful for women who avoid
25 having children because they feel they haven't found the right partner yet. Or for those who want to have a career first. And that is what is called "social egg freezing." If you decide to have eggs frozen, you are given hormone injections which stimulate the ovaries[8] to mature[9] mul-
30 tiple eggs. Other medication triggers[10] ovulation[11]. Then, through a small procedure, the eggs are removed using an ultrasound guided needle through the vagina.

The eggs are immediately frozen using cryoprotect-ants[12] – substances that inhibit[13] the formation of ice crystals inside the cells, and this keeps them viable. 35 Later, whenever you decide you want to get pregnant, the eggs are thawed[14] and fertilized using in vitro ferti-lization (IVF).

Success rate unknown
But there is no guarantee that the eggs will survive years 40 of freezing, and unsuccessful fertilization is also common.
Katrin van der Ven, a senior physician at the department of obstetrics[15] and gynecology[16] at University Hospital Bonn, says the success rate of an fertilization 45 depends on the age of the woman when the egg was removed. "The younger the better," she says.
Women who have their eggs frozen before the age of 30 have the best chances of getting pregnant later on.
Doctors use a relatively new freezing method called 50 vitrification. "Studies have shown that eggs frozen with that method show the same fertilization rates as fresh oocytes," van der Ven says. But she stresses there are no long-term studies on the method yet as it is relatively young. "We can only say that it is a promising method. 55 We don't know what the long-term chances are."

No guarantee
An in vitro fertilization (IVF) does not offer a 100 per-cent chance of pregnancy. According to the German IVF index, 93 percent of all fertilizations in 2012 were 60 successful, so that an embryo could be transferred into the woman's womb[17]. Fifteen percent of all resulting pregnancies, though, ended in a miscarriage[18]. The age of the father also plays a role.

---

[1] **perk** something you receive as well as your wages for doing a particular job – [2] **altruistic** uneigennützig – [3] **NBC** (abbr.) National Broadcasting Company; an American broadcast, television and radio network – [4] **to cover sth.** here: to pay for sth. – [5] **to launch** to start – [6] **oocyte cryopreservation** [ˈəʊəsaɪt ˈkraɪəʊ ˌprezəˈveɪʃn] egg freezing – [7] **viable** [ˈvaɪəbl] here: able to develop into a living being – [8] **ovary** Eierstock – [9] **to mature** reifen – [10] **to trigger** to cause sth. to start – [11] **ovulation** Eisprung – [12] **cryoprotectants** a substance used to protect biological tissue from freezing – [13] **to inhibit** to slow a process – [14] **to thaw** auftauen – [15] **obstetrics** the area of medicine that deals with pregnancy and the birth of babies – [16] **gynecology** [ˌgaɪnəˈkɒlədʒi] Gynäkologie – [17] **womb** [wuːm] Mutterleib, Gebär-mutter – [18] **miscarriage** Fehlgeburt

Sperm from younger men have higher chances of fertilizing eggs.

"We also know that certain genetic diseases occur more often if the father is older," van der Ven says.

So freezing eggs may not be enough – as the woman's partner, the child's father, also ages.

"A good alternative"

Katrin van der Ven has two children and says she struggled to balance her career and her family lives for many years. Freezing eggs "is not the ideal solution," she says, but "for a person who is concerned, it is indeed a good alternative." In fact, she says, women who want to have children and success in their jobs "may have no other choice these days."

It may become a necessity

Politicians from the conservative German Christian Democratic party have described the scheme at Facebook and Apple as "an indecent[19] proposal[20]." Ethicist[21] Joachim Boldt, a deputy head of the institute for ethics and history in medicine at the University of Freiburg, warns there may be certain expectations linked with any such offer.

"If a company pays for this procedure and an employee wants to have children in her 20s anyway, the question might arise: 'Why is she not deferring[22] her desire to start a family until later?'" he says.

"We have to watch out"

Boldt says the main question is why it is being left to individuals to solve this issue, which should be solved by society as a whole. "The fact that women can't combine a career and motherhood is a problem in our society," he says, but adds that Scandinavian countries have found a solution.

Scandinavian countries manage to balance their professional ambitions and family lives with childcare centers and part-time work, Boldt says.

"Part-time work is widely accepted in Scandinavian countries, whereas in Germany it is often seen as a lack of commitment to your job."

"Social egg freezing is not wrong as such," says Boldt, "but we have to be careful."

www.dw.de/apple-and-facebooks-social-freezing-may-be-problematic/a-17999578, 16 October 2014 [27.11.2014]

COMPREHENSION

2. Point out Apple and Facebook's motivation to sponsor egg freezing.

3. Describe the method of freezing eggs.

4. Outline possible risks in connection with
- the freezing itself,
- in vitro fertilization,
- the age of the future parents.

5. What might be a better alternative to egg freezing – according to Joachim Boldt?

ANALYSIS

6. Analyse the author's stance on the matter by examining and explaining these aspects:
- the line of argument*
- the use of positive and negative emotive words
- the juxtaposition of the benefits and risks of social egg freezing
→ Focus on Skills, Analysis of a Non-Fictional Text, p. 405

7. How does the author underline his/her credibility and reliability?
Give evidence from the text.

[19] **indecent** *unanständig* – [20] **proposal** *Vorschlag, Angebot* – [21] **ethicist** *Ethiker* – [22] **to defer sth.** to delay sth. until a later time; *etw. verschieben*

8. Explain the criticism of egg freezing expressed by German conservative politicians and Joachim Boldt. What makes Apple and Facebook's offer "indecent" and might create "certain expectations" (ll. 82 ff.)?

 9. **Step 1:** Describe and mediate the German cartoon.

 Step 2: Explain how it relates to the criticism of social egg freezing depicted in the online article.
→ Focus on Skills, Analysis of Visuals, p. 409

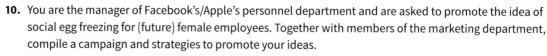

Tips on vocab »»»

to have/attend a meeting ■ to look concerned ■ to be stunned ■ to be dumbfound/puzzled (*sprachlos, verdutzt sein*) ■ to have one's hands in one's lap ■ testicles (*Hoden*) ■ to protect one's genitals ■ to have one's hands folded ■ to be bald (*glatzköpfig sein*)

ACTIVITIES »»»»»»

10. You are the manager of Facebook's/Apple's personnel department and are asked to promote the idea of social egg freezing for (future) female employees. Together with members of the marketing department, compile a campaign and strategies to promote your ideas.

 In groups, create adverts/commerials that are convincing and appealing to employees.

 Tip: Do further research on the Internet and flesh out your adverts/commercials with visuals, employee testimonials (*Erfahrungsberichte*) and/or statistical data.

 11. Against the backdrop of the public discussion on social egg freezing, a growing number of female employees are demanding to discuss the issue with experts and decision-making bodies.

 Form groups and collect information on the controversial topic, then act out a public hearing in which you discuss the various views and opinions.
Participants can be:
- female employees
- employers
- gynaecologists
- politicians
- priests
- works committee members (*Betriebsräte*)
→ Focus on Language, Conversation and Discussion, p. 413

Richard Gray

Pigs Could Grow Human Organs in Stem Cell Breakthrough

AWARENESS

Donating or receiving organs is a highly controversial topic. Thus, scientists are trying to find new ways to meet the constant demand for organs for people who are seriously ill and cannot survive without e. g. a liver or kidney[1] transplant.

Genetically, pigs have a 90 % similarity with humans and therefore could be used as organ donors. Do you think that implanting organs from animals, e. g. pigs or chimpanzees, could be a solution to the problem? Discuss.

Human organs could be grown inside pigs for use in transplant operations following research using stem cells.

Scientists have found they can create chimeric[2] animals that have organs belonging to another species[3] by injecting stem cells into the embryo of another species.

The researchers injected stem cells from rats into the embryos of mice that had been genetically altered[4] so they could not produce their own organs, creating mice that had rat organs.

The researchers say the technique could allow pigs to grow human organs from patients' stem cells for use as transplants.

By using a patient's own stem cells it could help to reduce the risk of the transplanted organ being rejected while also providing a plentiful[5] supply[6] of donor organs.

Current organ shortages mean that patients must endure[7] long waiting lists for transplants.

Professor Hiromitsu Nakauchi, director of the centre for stem cell biology and regenerative medicine at the University of Tokyo in Japan and who led the research, said: "Our ultimate goal is to generate human organs from induced pluripotent[8] stem cells.

The technique, called blastocyst[9] complementation[10], provides us with a novel[11] approach for organ supply. We have successfully tried it between mice and rats. We are now rather confident in generating functional human organs using this approach."

Professor Nakauchi, who presented the study at the annual conference of the European Society of Human Genetics, used a type of adult stem cell known as induced[12] pluripotent stem cells, which can be taken from a sample of tissue[13] such as the skin and encouraged to grow into any type of cell found in the body.

Together with his colleagues, he injected these cells taken from rats into the embryos, or blastocysts as they can be called, of mice that were unable to grow their own pancreas[14], the organ that produces important hormones including insulin.

[1] **kidney** *Niere* – [2] **chimeric** [kaɪˈmerɪk] (*fml.*) relating to Chimera (Greek mythology), a fire-breathing female monster with a lion's head, a goat's body and a serpent's tail – [3] **species** [ˈspiːʃiːz] *Spezies, Art* – [4] **to alter** to change – [5] **plentiful** *im Überfluss vorhanden* – [6] **supply** *Angebot, Vorrat* – [7] **to endure** [ɪnˈdjʊə(r)] *etw. aushalten* – [8] **pluripotent** *vielfältig einsetzbar* – [9] **blastocyst** *Keimblase der Säugetiere* – [10] **complementation** (*genetics*) occurrence of a wild-type phenotype when two closely related, interacting mutant genes are expressed in the same cell – [11] **novel** new – [12] **to induce** *erzeugen* – [13] **tissue** *Gewebe* – [14] **pancreas** *Bauchspeicheldrüse*

When the mice matured[15] to adulthood, they showed no signs of diabetes and had developed a pancreas that was almost entirely formed from the injected rat stem cells. The scientists claim the rat stem cells grew in the niche[16]
45 left by the absent mouse pancreas and so almost any organ could be produced in this way.

If replicated[17] using human stem cells, the technique could produce a way of treating diabetic patients by providing a way of replacing their pancreas.

50 The project has echoes of the bestselling book and film *Never Let Me Go* where clones are used to provide organ donations for the wealthy. In reality researchers are not allowed to create human embryos that lack the ability to grow organs and so they hope to do the same
55 using pigs.

Professor Nakauchi said they hoped to further test the technique by growing other organs and were also seeking permission[18] to use human stem cells.

They have, however, already managed to produce pigs
60 that were able to generate human blood by injecting blood stem cells from humans into pig foetuses[19].

He said: "For ethical reasons we cannot make an organ deficient[20] human embryo and use it for blastocyst complementation.

65 "So to make use of this system to generate human organs, we must use this technique using blastocysts of livestock[21] animals such as pigs instead. Blastocyst complementation across species had never been tested before, but we have now shown that it can work."

70 Professor Chris Mason, chair[22] of regenerative medicine at University College London, said: "There is no doubt that curing diabetes is challenging, but this could be a potential way forward albeit[23] a very long shot[24] requiring sustained[25] resources and major finance for
75 its testing and development. For something like a kidney transplant where it is not urgent[26], it would be highly attractive to be able to take cells from a patient, grow them in this way and deliver a personalised kidney. There is a long way to go before it could result in
80 use-able transplants, but it is an exciting vision."

www.telegraph.co.uk/science/science-news/8584443/Pigs-could-grow-human-organs-in-stem-cell-breakthrough.html, 19 June 2011 [21.09.2012]

Readers' comments

1 This is science going to the extreme. There are limits. Leave animals alone!!! both testing and creating chimeric animals. How much more selfish-minded can humans be? No conscious I guess. I hope it fails and never works. There is a time to just accept life as is and when it's time to die you die. We can't live forever and mother earth is speaking loud and clear on how people have messed up this world with their GREAT ideas! So many have caused more problems than solved them … this is so unethical … too many mad scientists out there willing to do whatever it takes not to think of the pain they cause. Just my opinions.
Anonymous

2 So … why not put the blastocyst in the person who needs the transplant and let it grow there?
Hook it up after it is grown or … what would happen if healthy adult stem cells were applied to the diseased organ? I have a problem with making a Chimera and I do not think we should mix the species.
Jane Fulmer

4 That was my original thought – okay, great you can grow it in a pig, but how about we just grow it in the person who needs it, ESPECIALLY if the plan is to use their own stem cells anyway.
Anonymous

3 How about this as a growth industry? Pay people to grow EXTRA organs in them to use as transplant farms.
Anonymous

www.telegraph.co.uk/science/science-news/8584443/Pigs-could-grow-human-organs-in-stem-cell-breakthrough.html, 19 June 2011 [21.09.2012]

[15] **to mature** *heranreifen* – [16] **niche** [niːʃ] *Nische* – [17] **to replicate** to reproduce – [18] **to seek** (sought/sought) **permission** (*fml.*) *um Erlaubnis/Genehmigung bitten* – [19] **foetus** [ˈfiːtəs] – [20] **deficient** *fehlerhaft, mangelhaft* – [21] **livestock** *Vieh* – [22] **chair** *Vorsitzende(r)* – [23] **albeit** *obgleich* – [24] **long shot** an attempt or a guess that is not likely to be successful but is worth trying – [25] **sustained** *nachhaltig, andauernd* – [26] **urgent** *dringend*

COMPREHENSION

1. Describe the new regenerative technique "blastocyst complementation".

2. Define the specific qualities of "pluripotent stem cells" as reported in the article.

3. Point out the current situation researchers face when dealing with human stem cells.

4. State the potential of growing stem cells in livestock and the advantages for patients.

ANALYSIS

5. Examine what type of text this is and explain how the controversial topic is presented.
   → Focus on Facts, Basic Types of Non-Fictional Texts, p. 396

6. Analyse the language register* and particularly the use of technical terms and explain their function and effect.
   → Focus on Skills, Analysis of a Non-Fictional Text, p. 405

7. Compare the comments made by different readers and relate their views to the statements made in the article.

8. Describe the graffito by famous British artist and political activist Banksy. What allusions concerning the status and rights of animals are made here?
   → Focus on Skills, Analysis of Visuals, p. 409

Banksy graffito of a zebra with a bar code painted on a wall in Dorset, England

ACTIVITIES

9. In a Placemat activity, reflect on whether animals in general or pigs in particular should be used to grow human organs in the future.

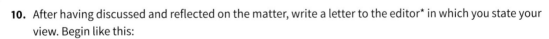

10. After having discussed and reflected on the matter, write a letter to the editor* in which you state your view. Begin like this:

   Example: Dear Mr. Gray, In response to your interesting and informative article … I would like to state my opinion on the controversial matter …
   → Focus on Skills, Writing a Letter to the Editor, p. 431

GRAMMAR / LANGUAGE

11. Try to explain the following technical expressions using everyday English. If necessary, use your dictionary for help.
    - chimeric animals
    - stem cell
    - genetically altered
    - personalized organ
    - transplant
    - donor organ
    - regenerative medicine
    - organ deficient human embryo

Genetic Engineering

Genetic engineering (or genetic modification) is the **human manipulation of an organism's genetic material** to create **a genetically modified organism** that does not exist under natural conditions. During this process, new genetic material (DNA) is inserted into the host genome (= the entirety of an organism's hereditary information). First the **genetic material of interest is isolated and copied**, thereby generating a construct that contains all the necessary genetic elements, which is then **inserted into a host organism** in a second step. Thus, **genetic engineering changes the genetic design or genetic blueprint** (*Kopie*) of an organism and **forms new combinations** of heritable (= *erblich*) genetic material. Although **stem cell research** and **cloning** are not considered to be genetic engineering by definition, they are closely connected to it because they can be used together. In **medicine** genetic engineering is used e. g. for **the mass production of insulin, human growth hormones, follitism (for treating infertility) and vaccines** (*Impfstoff*). Researchers are also working to genetically engineer humans and e. g. **replace defective genes with functional ones** and thus **cure genetic disorders and diseases** like Parkinson's disease, cancer, diabetes, heart diseases and arthritis. Despite all the (possible) benefits there are also **ethical concerns and criticism** that this technology is not only used for treatment but for enhancement, modification or alteration of a human being's character, behaviour, appearance, intelligence or adaptability.

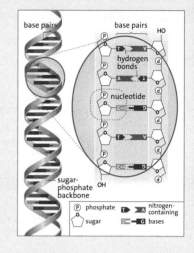

Historical development

year	major scientific discovery or achievement
1856 – 1863	Austrian monk and scientist **Gregor Johann Mendel** (1822 – 1884) shows that the inheritance of certain traits follows particular laws (the **"Laws of Inheritance"**); he is considered to be the "father of modern genetics"
1953	American zoologist **James Watson** and British physicist **Francis Crick discover the double helix**, the chemical structure of DNA which makes up genes
1972	American biochemist **Paul Berg creates the first recombinant** (= altered, modified) **DNA**
1974	German biologist **Rudolf Jaenisch creates a transgenic mouse** by inserting foreign DNA into its embryo
1976	Genetic Engineering Technology Inc. (Genentech Inc.), **the first biotechnology company, is founded in California** by US businessman Robert A. Swanson and biochemist Dr. Herbert Boyer
1978	Genentech Inc. **produces genetically engineered human insulin**
1980	the **US Supreme Court rules that genetically altered life can be patented**
1986	first field trials in the **USA and France: genetically engineered tobacco plants** are resistant to herbicides
1992	**China commercializes virus-resistant tobacco plants**
1994	the **first genetically-modified tomato**, designed to have a longer shell life, is released
June 2000	President Clinton announces **the completion of the first draft of the human genome**
Feb 2001	first analyses of the public and private genome projects are published; the big discovery: **Humans have about 30,000 to 40,000 genes, hardly more than a common weed or worm**
April 2003	the **human genome is declared a finished product**; the announcement coincides with the 50th anniversary of the discovery of the double helix
2008	Craig Venter announces first synthetic organism controlled by a **completely synthetic chromosome**
1996 – 2011	increasing **commercialization of biotech crops** at a growth rate of 8 % (1.7 mio hectares in 1996 – 160 mio hectares in 2011; corn, soybean, cotton)
2013	production of a **synthetic yeast** (*Hefe*) **cell with 16 artificial chromosomes**; creation of **genetically-engineered mice with artificial human chromosomes** in every cell of their bodies
2018	Chinese researcher creates **genetically edited babies**, making them resistent to possible future infection with HIV

Monsanto Dominates the Global Seed Market

AWARENESS

> **Genetic engineering**, **genetic modification (GM)** and **gene splicing** are terms for the process of manipulating genes; it is the direct alteration of specific genetic codes (inclusion, removal, etc.) in order to achieve a desired result.
>
> **Biotechnology** refers to any technical application that uses biological systems, living organisms, or derivatives thereof, to make or modify products or processes for specific use. It also uses micro-organisms, such as bacteria, to perform specific industrial or manufacturing processes.

In groups, study the two definitions above:
What differences and similarities can you detect between the described genetic and biotechnological processes? What feelings do these definitions evoke? Give reasons for your assessment.

COMPREHENSION

 1. In a **first listening**, try to get **a general understanding** of
   a) Monsanto's company policy,
   b) Troy Roush's problems with Monsanto.

2. Then, **while listening** to the recording **a second time**, take notes on the following aspects:

- Monsanto's objectives for the future
- the impact of agricultural technology
- Monsanto's role in biotechnology
- Monsanto's justification of its business tactics and company policy

- Troy Roush's problems with Monsanto
- how Monsanto dictates the rules of farming
- how Roush views his situation as a farmer today
- attorney Adam Levitt's assessment of Monsanto's and the farmers' positions
- the future of farming

→ Focus on Skills, Listening Comprehension, p. 394

Webcode
SNG-40235-035 @ **Tip:** In order to get a deeper understanding of the situation, you can also watch the video on Monsanto and Troy Roush provided on the webcode.

If necessary, listen to the recording **a third time** and complete your notes.

Tips on vocab

yield an amount of sth. positive, such as food or profit, that is produced or supplied ■ **bushel** a unit of measurement equal to ca. 35.2 litres in the U.S. ■ **fierce** strong, powerful and frightening ■ **stakeholder** *Interessengruppe* ■ **breach** an act of breaking a law or agreement ■ **to purchase** to buy sth. ■ **to allege** to state sth. as a fact but without giving proof ■ **to sue sb.** to take legal action against a person or organization; *jdn. gerichtlich verfolgen* ■ **legal bill** *Gerichtskosten* ■ **to mount** to increase ■ **to divulge** to make sth. secret known ■ **suit** *Prozess, Klage* ■ **bottom line** *Reingewinn* ■ **pawn** *Schachfigur* ■ **extended arm** *verlängerter Arm*

ANALYSIS

3. As depicted in the recording, the American biotech corporation Monsanto holds many patents on seeds and crops in the U.S., making it almost impossible for farmers to grow non-modified plants. Farmers like Troy Roush are trying to find ways out of the system that companies like Monsanto impose on them.
   Mediate relevant passages of the German magazine article below and write an English blog entry for the international Internet forum "No Patents on Seeds".
   Explain how farmers in Europe are fighting against corporations like Monsanto and trying to prevent patents on plants, animals and seeds.
   → Focus on Skills, Mediation, p. 412

4. Over time, Europeans, especially Germans, have become particularly critical towards GM food. Environmentalists and scientists have tried to save and re-establish old crops, e. g. certain cultivars (= *Sorten*) of historical potatoes that were planted in the past.

@ Do research on these "old-fashioned" crops (e. g. *Bamberger Hörnchen, La Ratte, Rosa Tannenzapfen, Sieglinde, Blauer Schwede, Ackersegen*, etc.), some of which date back to the early eighteenth century. What advantages do they have over modern GM seeds?

5. Monsanto is a U. S.-based multinational agricultural biotechnology corporation and the world's leading producer of GM seed. It provides the technology for 90 % of the world's GM seeds and holds many patents. One of its leading products, the so-called "Terminator" seed, is sterile, which means it does not flower or grow fruit after the initial planting.

@ Do research on the Monsanto corporation and prepare a short presentation in which you outline the company's philosophy and fields of research.

→ Focus on Skills, Presentations, p. 419

Philip Bethge: Der Brokkoli gehört uns allen

Dürfen Pflanzen und Tiere patentiert werden? In Europa ist das stark eingeschränkt[1]. Patente würden nicht erteilt für „Pflanzensorten[2] oder Tierrassen" sowie „im Wesentlichen biologische" Züchtungsverfahren[3], heißt es im Europäischen Patentabkommen. Doch das Europäische Patentamt (EPA) scheint die Regeln nicht ernst zu nehmen. Etwa 2 400 Patente auf Pflanzen und 1 400 Patente auf Tiere seien schon erteilt worden, kritisiert die Initiative No Patents on Seeds im Vorfeld[4] einer Anhörung[5] vor der Großen Beschwerdekammer[6] des EPA. Aktuell will sich die Firma Plant Bioscience konventionell gezüchteten Brokkoli als Erfindung schützen lassen, das israelische Landwirtschaftsministerium[7] Tomaten. Und es ist zu befürchten[8], dass die Patente am Ende bestätigt werden. Möglich ist dies, weil die Industrie Übung darin hat, auf geschickte Weise rechtliche Schlupflöcher[9] auszunutzen. Eine bestimmte Apfelsorte mit erhöhtem Vitamingehalt beispielsweise lässt sich in Europa nicht patentieren. Wenn indes in der Patentschrift[10] allgemein von vitaminangereicherten Pflanzen die Rede ist (also nicht von einer einzigen Sorte), lassen die EPA-Beamten oftmals mit sich reden.

Die Patentierung hänge „in vielen Fällen" davon ab, „wie geschickt die Ansprüche formuliert werden", gibt die Technische Beschwerdekammer im EPA offen zu. Ein Armutszeugnis[11].

Dabei ist es brisant, wenn Lebewesen geistiges Eigentum von Firmen werden. Der Zugang zur genetischen Vielfalt muss öffentlich bleiben. Sonst können unabhängige Forscher und Züchter nicht mehr uneingeschränkt nach neuen Sorten fahnden[12], um die Nahrungsmittelversorgung für eine wachsende Weltbevölkerung sicherzustellen. Sonst geraten Bauern in Abhängigkeiten, die sie sich gerade in Entwicklungsländern nicht leisten können. Natürlich müssen Saatgutfirmen Geld verdienen können mit ihren Innovationen. Doch Patente sind dafür der falsche Weg – vor allem, wenn sie mithilfe juristischer Wortklauberei[13] zustande kommen.

Die Patentierung von Leben ist eine ethische Grundsatzfrage, die nicht in Hinterzimmern des EPA entschieden werden darf. Nur in einer offenen gesellschaftlichen Diskussion kann geklärt werden, wem die genetische Vielfalt gehört.

DER SPIEGEL, 44/2014, 27 November 2014, p. 127

[1] limited – [2] cultivar – [3] breeding techniques – [4] the forefront of – [5] hearing – [6] Board of Appeal – [7] ministry of agriculture – [8] to fear – [9] legal loophole – [10] patent specification – [11] a demonstration of the poor state of sth. – [12] to pursue sth. – [13] quibbling

Stephen Baxter

Into the Future

In a Think! Pair! Share! activity, describe the cartoons below and specify the different kinds of jobs and services the drones do.

a) Then, discuss whether you think this technology is positive and useful or threatening and unnecessary.

b) Finally, collect ideas about further (useful) services and jobs that could be done by drones.

Robots are increasingly doing jobs a human once did, but is it a path to utopia?

Henry Ford first started selling his famous black-only Model T Fords to the American public 100 years ago. Actually the cars had been in production since 1908, and it had been in 1909 that Ford told his management team "Any customer can have a car painted any colour that he wants so long as it is black" – but it was in 1914 that the black-only policy was finally implemented[1]. And by 1918, half of all the cars in the US were Ford's black Model Ts. Ford's success derived from[2] his innovations, most notably[3] assembly line production to replace individual hand-crafting[4] of the vehicles. All the Model Ts were exactly the same as each other, as symbolized by the "black-only" policy, which created cheapness and reliability.

This represented a huge transformation in the nature of work. New technologies had always destroyed old jobs, but created new ones. Craftsmen in the old horse-based economy could transfer their skills to the new industries – they could build the chassis[5] of a car, rather than the chassis of a horse-drawn trap[6].

But Ford's assembly lines were different, with the manufacture of a vehicle broken down into a series of simpler tasks, each performed by a single less skilled worker, over and over again.

At least, however, assembly-line jobs were still jobs. What of the future? Today we are going through another vast transformation of the workplace. What's striking for economists [...] is that in the US, for example, in the wake[7] of the 2008 banking crisis, the economy has never generated[8] fewer new jobs in any recovery since the records began. The reason is technological advance. Robots are making assembly-line workers unnecessary. High-tech corporations like Google and Facebook are becoming massive economic entities[9], but as much of what they create and distribute is pure data, they are not mass employers the way the old manufacturing industries were.

This trend is surely going to accelerate[10]. The military use of drone aircraft is demonstrating the growing capability of robots to do jobs once monopolized by humans. We can imagine robots replacing people in such services as waste disposal and parking lots; in shops automated tellers are already replacing human assistants. Thanks to driverless cars, as being developed by Google and others, jobs for drivers of all sorts will vanish[11].

We should not be too parochial[12] about this. Workers in some poorer nations, still laboring in primitive conditions, would not be impressed by our complaints about competition with robots and too much leisure[13] time. But given sufficient economic growth we may be seeing a challenge for all of us. Are we heading for a future in which the only meaningful jobs for humans will be at high intellectual levels – the designers of software that will control the new legions of robots?

Perhaps, but there are more positive visions. The elimination of drudgery[14] and danger, from housework to mining, must be a benefit. There will surely always be a role for people in fields like medical care and the raising of the very young. And perhaps we should celebrate the return of leisure. People could work at more personal and rewarding jobs: running micro-breweries[15], for example. Maybe we will see the final reversal of the trend pioneered by Henry Ford, of reducing human craftsmen to the role of robots.

The human race has only been working at its present levels of intensity since the invention of farming some ten thousand years ago. Perhaps, with the help of robots, we will be able to rediscover the rich cultural life enjoyed by our less pressured ancestors.

BBC Focus, Science and Technology, February 2014, p. 31

COMPREHENSION

1. Give evidence from the text that proves the following statements:
   - The automated production of goods was/is a blessing for the consumer but a curse for the workers.
   - The impact of technological advancement was more beneficial in the past than it is today.

[1]**to implement** to start using a plan or system – [2]**to derive from** (*phr. v.*) to come from sth. – [3]**notable** important and deserving attention – [4]**hand-crafting** a skilled activity in which sth. is made in a traditional way with the hands; *Handarbeit, Handwerk* – [5]**chassis** [ˈʃæsi] the frame of a vehicle, including the wheels and the engine; *Fahrgestell* – [6]**trap** a light carriage with two wheels pulled by a horse, used esp. in the past – [7]**in the wake of sth.** (*idm.*) *als Folge von* – [8]**to generate** to create sth. – [9]**entity** [ˈentɪti] (*fml.*) *Gebilde, Einheit* – [10]**to accelerate** to start to go faster – [11]**to vanish** to disappear, esp. in a sudden, surprising way – [12]**parochial** [pəˈrəʊkiəl] *engstirnig* – [13]**leisure** [ˈleʒə(r)] *Freizeit* – [14]**drudgery** hard boring work – [15]**micro-brewery** *Hausbrauerei*

2. Juxtapose the assumed positive and negative effects of robotized production and services as depicted in the last part of the text (ll. 57 – 71).

assumed benefits/advantages	assumed risks/disadvantages
• relief/support for workers in primitive working conditions • …	• the only meaningful jobs are at high intellectual levels • …

ANALYSIS

3. Explain Henry Ford's "black-only" policy: What was his production and marketing policy?

4. Examine and analyse the stylistic devices and show how they emphasize the author's stance on robots. Pay particular attention to
- the use of rhetorical questions,
- the thematic structure of the text,
- the use of irony,
- the use of contrast/antithesis,
- the use of grammatical tenses.
→ Focus on Skills, Analysis of a Non-Fictional Text, p. 405

ACTIVITIES

5. Discuss the author's introductory question (ll. 1 f.) in a pyramid discussion.
Are robots and automated production the way to utopia?
→ Focus on Language, Conversation and Discussion, p. 413

6. In groups, work out a future scenario in which the following have become reality:
- "designers of software … will control the new legions of robots" … **or**
- the reduction of "human craftsmen to the role of robots" … **or**
- the rediscovery of a "rich cultural life" …

Tip: Your scenarios can be utopian or dystopian; they can be written as dialogue, diary entries, a travel log, etc.
Choose a literary genre of your liking and flesh it out with the corresponding stylistic devices.

Finally, read out/act out your scenarios in class and evaluate their content and style.

GRAMMAR / LANGUAGE

7. You work in a PR (Public Relations) team of a company that produces drones and various kinds of robots.
In groups, think about campaigns to promote your products to companies and/or private households. Pay attention to
- present the benefits and advantages of your company's robots,
- dispel people's fear of being replaced by robots at their workplace.
Use a dictionary and look up **adjectives and adverbials** that emphasize the robots' qualities.

8. Tess, the robot shown on the following page, was one of the major attractions of the 2014 *CeBit*, the world's largest international industry trade fair focusing on office automation, information technology and telecommunication.

In class, first mediate the information given beside the photo. Second, discuss whether you consider a "female" robot stripper or table dancer to be an appropriate advertising gag to attract customers' attention and evoke their interest in robotics.

10.03.2014 – Wie eine Stripperin

Tess trägt hohe Schuhe, nimmt die Beine leicht auseinander, bewegt sich lasziv und umtanzt die Stange wie eine Stripperin in einem Bordell. Das macht den Roboter mit seinem 12-Volt-Motor zu einer Attraktion auf der CeBit in Hannover. Tess lässt sich von einem Android-Smartphone aus steuern. Die Firma Tobit Software in Ahaus modifizierte Tess und sagt: „Wir wollten ihn ein bisschen interessanter machen." Preis: 39 500 Dollar.

DER SPIEGEL, Chronik 2014, 4 December 2014, p. 51

Matt Haig

Echo Boy

>>>>>> **AWARENESS** >>>>>>

Robots and digital machinery have become irreplaceable tools in everyday life. Usually, they function perfectly and reliably. But what happens if something goes wrong and important control modules fail?
In groups, think about possible scenarios that might happen when digital technology like satellites, computers, etc. malfunction. What might the consequences be?

The protagonists and alternating narrators of the science fiction novel *Echo Boy* are 15-year-old Audrey and a so-called Echo (= Enhanced Computerised Humanoid Organism): a physically perfect but emotionless android named Daniel. One day Audrey's parents are murdered by an apparently malfunctioning Echo called Alissa, who works as a domestic robot.

The thing with Echos is that you weren't meant to notice them, they weren't meant to get in the way. Think of those ads of holovision[1] that Sempura and Castle[2] do. *Enhance[3] your life, without even noticing ... Meet Darwin, the friend you don't have to think about ... Here's Lloyd, Sempura's latest Echo. He'll cook, he'll clean, but he'll rarely be seen.* That is how they were designed. To be there when we needed them, but never to distract[4] us in any way. But Alissa was sometimes there when we didn't need her.

For instance, the first Friday she was here – before she'd even started tutoring me or anything – Dad was making a spicy black bean stew (he loved Brazilian food). It was probably bad for his leg to be standing so

---

[1] **holovision** a special type of image made with a laser in which the objects shown look solid, as if they are real, rather than flat –
[2] **Sempura and Castle** fictitious broadcasting companies – [3] **to enhance** to improve the quality of sth. – [4] **to distract** jdn. ablenken

long, as he had to prop[5] his walking stick next to the oven, but he'd been feeling quite good and wanted to cook something. Alissa had stood next to him as the scent[6] of fried garlic filled the air, saying, "I can cook this. I am here to help. You do not need to do any cooking. Sit down and relax with your family. You are injured. You are not physically capable. Your time is precious."

My dad had looked at her crossly[7]. That was the only way he was ever to look at an Echo. "Just get out of the kitchen, OK?" I was there. I can picture Dad with his beard, in jeans and house socks and a tatty[8] sweater, looking frustrated. "I know my time is precious, but I actually like cooking. And I'm not a bloody invalid. OK? You are a machine. Machines obey instructions. When you stop obeying instructions you stop being a machine, and then humanity is in trouble."

Dad continued his rant[9] the next day in an h-log[10] that went viral[11] and was picked up by *Castle Watch* and a few other places. People loved it when he criticized Echos – well, tech-sceptics and anti-AI protestors did. They loved the fact that the brother of Alex Castle himself was against everything that Castle Industries stood for. "Bet their family Christmases are uncomfortable," one person commented on the h-log, which wasn't true, as we had never spent Christmas with my uncle.

Dad did speak to Uncle from time to time. H-calls[12] that he made in his office. "We are grown-ups," he said, in a way I almost believed. "And the thing about grown-ups is, they can have different opinions, even strongly different opinions, and get along in a civilized way. Though if it was up to your uncle, civilization would soon be overrun by robots."

And obviously, an Echo wasn't an average robot. Apart from the E on the back of the left hand and the origin mark on the shoulder, an Echo is almost identical to a human, in terms of looks. Meant to be, anyway.

To be honest, I never really got it.

Echos were too perfect. Their skin did not look like our skin. There were never any lines or spots or blemishes[13] on an Echo's skin. And Dad always said that the day we get too sentimental about a glorified robot is the day we forget who we are. The day we stop being human. […]

As I drew level with the doorway, I saw everything. All at once. A whole shock-load of images I have no way of forgetting.

My parents, dead, killed in the most brutal and old-fashioned way imaginable.

With a knife.

A knife she must have taken from the kitchen.

Dad's blood leaking into Mum's self-clean suit, the blood disappearing into the fabric, but not being fully absorbed. It was too much even for the carpet to absorb and clean away like it usually did when Dad spilled a coffee or red tea.

My parents' blood.

It seemed impossible – and I suppose, when I think about it now, it was the idea that my parents were just physical. When someone is alive, the last thing you think is that they are just a biological organism made of blood and bone and other matter. They are people – wise, quiet, serious, humorous, sometimes annoying, sometimes grumpy, tired, loving people. And death – especially this horrible kind of death – took all that away, and said it was a lie, and that my parents were nothing more than the sum of their parts.

And, of course, *she* was there.

Alissa. With her blonde hair and too-perfect smile. Standing there, with the blood-soaked[14] knife.

"I was waiting for you to come," she said. "I was waiting for you to come, I was waiting for you to come …"

She kept saying it, like a broken machine, which I suppose she was.

from *Echo Boy* by Matt Haig. The Bodley Head, London 2014, pp. 24 ff.

COMPREHENSION

1. Describe how Echos are supposed to function and what they are capable of doing.

2. Why does the narrator's father not like Echos?

[5] **to prop** *abstützen* – [6] **scent** a pleasant smell – [7] **cross** annoyed or angry – [8] **tatty** *schäbig* – [9] **rant** a long, angry and confused speech; *Schimpftirade* – [10] **h-log** a holographic recording of a person talking about sth. (like a holovision vlog) – [11] **viral** ['vaɪərəl] used to describe something that quickly becomes very popular or well known by being published on the Internet or sent from person to person by email, phone, etc. – [12] **h-call** a way of communicating that uses sound and a holographic image of the speaker – [13] **blemish** *Schönheitsfehler, Makel* – [14] **soaked** here: covered

3. Present the incident that took place in the family's kitchen – what actually went wrong?

ANALYSIS

4. Analyse the mode of presentation* and explain its function and effect.
→ Focus on Skills, Analysis of a Fictional Text, p. 402

5. Examine the use of direct and indirect characterization* and illustrate how Alissa and the narrator's father are depicted in the excerpt.
→ Focus on Skills, Characterization of a Figure in Literature, p. 411

 6. Interpret the narrator's attempt to comprehend her parents' death (ll. 61 ff.) and her remark that they "were just physical" and "nothing more than the sum of their parts" (ll. 72 ff.).
How does this relate to the novel's topic – the Echos, "Enhanced Computerised Humanoid Organisms"?

ACTIVITIES

 7. Put yourself in the narrator's or Alissa's position: Why were the parents killed and what might happen next? In a group, collect ideas concerning the further plot of the novel and continue the story.

Tip: Be careful to take up the narrative style of the excerpt as well as the narrator's way of reflecting and re-marking on people's character and behaviour.
→ Focus on Skills, Continuation of a Fictional Text, p. 420

GRAMMAR / LANGUAGE

8. Transform the following terms and phrases into everyday English.
If necessary, use a dictionary for help.

• robotics	• personal computers	• humanoid organism	• animate/inanimate beings
• android(s)	• artificial intelligence	• technological evolution	

9. After the horrifying death of her parents, Audrey writes a blog entry in which she reproaches the companies *Sempura* and *Castle* for the malfunctioning of the Echos in general and Alissa in particular.
Write that blog entry, using **conditional sentences** and explain what went wrong.

Examples:
- If you hadn't programmed Alissa to intrude into people's lives, she would not have …
- This would have never happened, if …

Visions of the Future: Utopia & Dystopia

P. D. James

The Children of Men

AWARENESS

Look at the book cover and speculate on the possible plot of the novel.

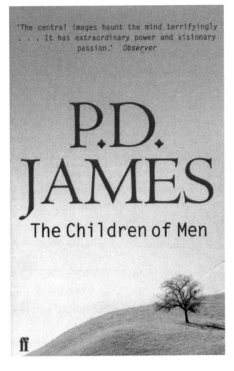

'The central images haunt the mind terrifyingly . . . It has extraordinary power and visionary passion.' *Observer*

P.D. JAMES

The Children of Men

ff

Friday – 1 January 2021

Early this morning, 1 January 2021, three minutes after midnight, the last human being to be
5 born on earth was killed in a pub brawl[1] in a suburb of Buenos Aires, aged twenty-five years two months and twelve days. If the first reports are to be believed,
10 Joseph Ricardo died as he had lived. The distinction[2], if one can call it that, of being the last human whose birth was officially recorded, unrelated as it was to
15 any personal virtue or talent, had always been difficult for him to handle. And now he is dead. The news was given to us here in Britain on the nine o'clock pro-
20 gramme of the State Radio Service and I heard it fortuitously[3]. I had settled down to begin this diary of the last half of my life when I noticed the time and thought I might as well catch the headlines to the
25 nine o'clock bulletin. Ricardo's death was the last item mentioned, and then only briefly, a couple of sentences delivered without emphasis in the newscaster's carefully non-committal[4] voice. But it seemed to me, hearing it, that it was a small additional justification for beginning
30 the diary today; the first day of a new year and my fiftieth birthday. As a child I had always liked that distinction, despite the inconvenience[5] of having it follow Christmas too quickly so that one present – it never seemed notably superior to the one I
35 would in any case have received – had to do for both celebrations. As I began writing, the three events, the New Year, my fiftieth birthday, Ricardo's death, hard-
40 ly justify sullying[6] the first pages of this new loose-leaf notebook. But I shall continue, one small additional defense against personal accidie[7]. If there is
45 nothing to record, I shall record the nothingness and then if, and when, I reach old age – as most of us can expect to – we have become experts of prolonging[8]
50 life – I shall open one of my tins of hoarded matches[9] and light my small personal bonfire of vanities[10]. I have no intention of leaving the diary as a record of one man's last years.
55 Even in my most egoistical moods I am not as self-deceiving[11] as that. What possible interest can there be in the journal of Theodore Faron, Doctor of Philosophy, Fellow of Merton College in the University of Oxford, historian of the Victorian age, divorced, childless, soli-
60 tary, whose only claim to notice is that he is the cousin to Xan Lyppiatt, the dictator and Warden of England. No additional personal record is, in any case, necessary. All over the world nation states are preparing to

---

[1] **brawl** a noisy quarrel or fight – [2] **distinction** *Besonderheit* – [3] **fortuitously** [fɔːˈtjuːɪtəsli] (*fml.*) happening by chance (*zufällig*) –
[4] **non-committal** *unverfänglich* – [5] **inconvenience** [ˌɪnkənˈviːniəns] *Unannehmlichkeit* – [6] **to sully** *besudeln* – [7] **accidie** [ˈæksɪdi] *Trägheit* –
[8] **to prolong sth.** to lengthen – [9] **tin of hoarded matches** *in einer Dose gehortete Streichhölzer* – [10] **bonfire of vanities** reference to the burning of objects that are considered to be occasions of sin; this dates back to festivals in Italy in the 15th century – [11] **self-deceiving** *selbstbetrügerisch*

65 store their testimony for the posterity[12] which we can still occasionally convince ourselves may follow us, those creatures from another planet who may land on this green wilderness and ask what kind of sentient[13] life once inhabited it. We are storing our books and manu-
70 scripts, the great paintings, the musical scores and instruments, the artefacts[14]. The world's greatest libraries will in forty years' time at most be darkened and sealed. The buildings, those that are still standing, will speak for themselves. The soft stone of Oxford is likely to survive
75 more than a couple of centuries. Already the University is arguing whether it is worth refacing the crumbling[15] Sheldonian. But I like to think of those mythical creatures landing in St Peter's Square[16] and entering the great Basilica, silent and echoing under the centuries of
80 dust. Will they realize that this once was the greatest of man's temples to one of his many gods? Will they be curious about his nature, this deity[17] who was worshipped with such pomp and splendor[18], intrigued[19] by the mystery of his symbol, at once so simple, the two
85 crossed sticks, ubiquitous[20] in nature, yet laden with gold, gloriously jeweled and adorned[21]? Or will their values and their thought processes be so alien to ours that nothing of awe[22] or wonder will be able to touch them? But despite the discovery – in 1997 was it? – of a planet
90 which the astronomers[23] told us could support life, few of us really believe that they will come. [...]
I can clearly remember the confident words of one biologist spoken when it had finally become apparent that nowhere in the whole world was there a pregnant wom-
95 an: 'It may take us some time to discover the cause of this apparent universal infertility[24].' We have had twenty-five years and we no longer even expect to succeed. Like a lecherous[25] stud[26] suddenly stricken with impotence, we are humiliated at the very heart of our faith in
100 ourselves. For all our knowledge, our intelligence, our power, we can no longer do what the animals do without thought. No wonder we both worship and resent[27] them.

The year 1995 became known as Year Omega and the term is now universal. The great public debate in the late 1990s was whether the country which discovered a 105 cure for the universal infertility would share this with the world and on what terms. It was accepted that this was a global disaster and that it must be met by the response of a united world. We still, in the late 1990s, spoke of Omega in terms of a disease, a malfunction[28] 110 which would in time be diagnosed and then corrected, as man had found a cure for tuberculosis, diphtheria[29], polio and even in the end, although too late, for AIDS. As the years passed and the united efforts under the aegis[30] of the United Nations came to nothing, this re- 115 solve of complete openness fell apart. Research became secret, nations' efforts a cause of fascinated, suspicious attention. The European Community acted in concert, pouring in research facilities and manpower. The European Centre for Human Fertility outside Paris was 120 among the most prestigious in the world. This in turn cooperated, at least overtly[31], with the United States whose efforts were if anything greater. But there was no inter-race co-operation; the prize was too great. The terms on which the secret might be shared were a cause 125 of passionate speculation and debate. It was accepted that the cure, once found, would have to be shared; this was scientific knowledge which no race ought to, or could, keep to itself indefinitely. But across continents, national and racial boundaries, we watched each other 130 suspiciously, obsessively, feeding on rumour and speculation. The old craft of spying returned. Old agents crawled out of comfortable retirement in Weybridge and Cheltenham[32] and passed on their trade craft. [...]
The spying still goes on but it is twenty-five years now 135 since a human being was born and in our hearts few of us believe that the cry of a new-born child will ever be heard again on our planet. Our interest in sex is waning[33]. Romantic and idealized love has taken over from crude carnal[34] satisfaction despite the efforts of the 140

---

[12] **posterity** [pɒˈsterəti] (*fml.*) all the people in the future who will be alive when you are dead – [13] **sentient** [ˈsentiənt] (*fml.*) able to be experienced through the senses – [14] **artefact** an object such as a tool or weapon that was made in the past and is historically important – [15] **to crumble** *bröckeln, zerfallen* – [16] **St Peter's Square** a big square located in front of St Peter's basilica in Vatican City, Rome – [17] **deity** [ˈdeɪəti, ˈdiːəti] a god or goddess – [18] **splendor** impressive beauty, esp. of a large building – [19] **intrigued** [ɪnˈtriːgd] very interested in sth. because it seems strange or mysterious – [20] **ubiquitous** [juːˈbɪkwɪtəs] (*fml.*) found everywhere – [21] **to adorn sb./sth.** (*fml.*) to decorate – [22] **awe** [ɔː] *Ehrfurcht* – [23] **astronomer** [əˈstrɒnəmə(r)] a scientist who studies the stars and planets – [24] **infertility** when sb. is unable to have a baby – [25] **lecherous** [ˈletʃərəs] *lüstern* – [26] **stud** [stʌd] (*infml.*) *Sexprotz* – [27] **to resent sb./sth.** to feel angry or upset about sb./sth., esp. because you think it is not fair – [28] **malfunction** a fault in the way a machine or a part of sb.'s body works – [29] **diphtheria** [dɪfˈθɪəriə] a serious infectious throat disease that makes breathing difficult – [30] **under the aegis** [ˈiːdʒɪs] with the protection or support of a person or organization – [31] **overt** *offenkundig* – [32] **Weybridge and Cheltenham** towns in south-east England with expensive housing – [33] **to wane** to become gradually less strong or important – [34] **carnal** (*fml.*) relating to sex or sb.'s body

Warden of England, through the national porn shops, to stimulate our flagging[35] appetites. But we have our sensual substitutes; they are available to all on the National Health Service. Our ageing bodies are pummeled[36], stretched, stroked[37], caressed[38], anointed[39], scented[40]. We are manicured and pedicured, measured and weighed. Lady Margaret Hall has become the massage centre for Oxford and here every Tuesday afternoon I lie on the couch and look out over the still-tended[41] gardens, enjoying my state-provided, carefully measured hour of sensual pampering[42]. And how assiduously[43], with what obsessive concern, do we intend to retain[44] the illusion, if not of youth, of vigorous[45] middle age. Golf is now the national game. If there had been no Omega, the conservationists would protest at the acres of countryside, some of it our most beautiful, which have been distorted[46] and rearranged to provide ever more challenging courses. All are free; this is part of the Warden's promised pleasure. Some have become exclusive, keeping unwelcome members out, not by prohibition, which is illegal, but by those subtle, discriminating signals which in Britain even the least sensitive are trained from childhood to interpret. We need our snobberies, equality is a political theory not a practical policy, even in Xan's egalitarian[47] Britain. [...]

We should have been warned in the early 1990s. As early as 1991 a European Community Report showed a slump in the number of children born in Europe – 8.2 million in 1990, with particular drops in the Roman Catholic countries. We thought that we knew the reasons, that the fall was deliberate, a result of more liberal attitudes to birth control and abortion, a postponement[48] of pregnancy by professional women pursuing their careers, the wish of families for a higher standard of living. And the fall in population was complicated by the spread of AIDS, particularly in Africa. Some European countries began to pursue a vigorous campaign to encourage the birth of children, but most of us thought the fall was desirable, even necessary. We were polluting the planet with our numbers; if we were breeding less it was to be welcomed. Most of the concern was less about a falling population than about the wish of nations to maintain their own people, their own culture, their own race, to breed sufficient[49] young to maintain their economic structures. But as I remember it, no one suggested that the fertility of the human race was dramatically changing. When Omega came it came with dramatic suddenness and was received with incredulity[50]. Overnight, it seemed, the human race had lost its power to breed. The discovery in July 1994 that even the frozen sperm stored for experiment and artificial insemination[51] had lost its potency was a peculiar horror casting over Omega the pall[52] of superstitious[53] awe, of witch-craft, of divine[54] intervention. The old gods reappeared, terrible in their power.

The world didn't give up hope until the generation born in 1995 reached sexual maturity[55]. But when the testing was complete and not one of them could produce fertile sperm, we knew that this was indeed the end of *Homo sapiens*.

from *The Children of Men* by P. D. James. Faber and Faber, London 1992, pp. 3 ff.

COMPREHENSION

1. State all the autobiographical data mentioned by the narrator*, Theodore Faron.

2. Point out the events which led to the end of mankind's ability to procreate. Draw a timeline.

3. Describe how the world is preparing for the moment that human life will cease to exist.

---

[35] **flagging** becoming tired or losing strength – [36] **to pummel** ['pʌml] to beat – [37] **to stroke** to move your hand gently over sb. – [38] **to caress** [ka'res] to stroke sb. – [39] **to anoint** einölen, salben – [40] **to scent** [sent] to put perfume on sb. – [41] **to tend sb./sth.** to look after sb. – [42] **to pamper sb.** jdn. verhätscheln – [43] **assiduous** [ə'sɪdjuəs] (fml.) very careful – [44] **to retain sth.** (fml.) to keep sth. – [45] **vigorous** ['vɪgərəs] having a lot of energy and strength – [46] **to distort sth.** [dɪ'stɔːt] verfälschen – [47] **egalitarian** [i,gælɪ'teəriən] gleichmacherisch – [48] **postponement** the act of pushing back the time or date of a planned event – [49] **sufficient** [sə'fɪʃnt] (fml.) enough – [50] **incredulity** ['ɪnkrə'djuːləti] feeling of disbelief – [51] **artificial insemination** künstliche Befruchtung – [52] **pall** [pɔː] (lit.) Dunstglocke – [53] **superstitious** [,suːpə'stɪʃəs] (often derog.) abergläubisch – [54] **divine** [dɪ'vaɪn] coming from or relating to God or a god – [55] **maturity** the state of being fully grown or developed

ANALYSIS

4. Examine the narrator's metaphorical language and show how it creates the specific tone of the text.

5. Analyse the narrator's particular point of view* and explain what effect it has on the reader.

6. Illustrate how this excerpt not only depicts the narrator's memories but also serves as a means of criticizing politics.
   → Focus on Skills, Analysis of a Fictional Text, p. 402

7. Specify and explain elements of dystopian literature found in the excerpt (cf. info box below).

Info »»

> **Dystopia** derives from the Greek words "dus" (bad, abnormal, painful, disordered) and "topos" (= place); this refers to **a fictional society** that has degraded into **a repressive and authoritarian state**, often giving its inhabitants false promises of a utopian world. Dystopias in literature are often **used to warn people** of totalitarian forms of government that will deprive them of individual freedoms and put them under total control of the state or the military.
> Sometimes dystopias deal with the extinction of mankind, the degeneration of society, war or natural disasters. Often the protagonist questions society or suspects that something is terribly wrong, but doesn't have the words to express his/her concerns.
> Further topics of dystopian novels include the manipulation of people through brainwashing or drugs, the artificial creation of beings, torture, etc.
> Dystopian societies often follow a caste-like organization, with the higher, educated classes controlling the lower class which often lacks education and suffers from poverty.
> Famous dystopias are *Nineteen Eighty-Four* (George Orwell), *Brave New World* (Aldous Huxley), *Fahrenheit 451* (Ray Bradbury) and *The Handmaid's Tale* (Margaret Atwood).

8. In groups, study the Focus on Documents page *Thomas Morus: Utopia* (p. 337).
   a) Explain how the different cities and societal groups are organized.
   b) Take a close look at l. 16: What do you think the social position of the "bondmen" in this "utopian" world is? Can a society which has slaves be called a utopia – or is the description of Thomas Morus' *Utopia* just window dressing (*Augenwischerei*)?

Thomas Morus: Utopia

The fictional narrative *Utopia* by Thomas More (*Latin*: Morus), published in 1516, depicts an island society and its religious, social and political customs. According to the spelling of the time, the third-person singular "s" was spelled "th" and some verbs which are irregular in modern English, e. g. build, were regular (built → builded).

The island of Utopia containeth in breadth in the middle part of it (for there it is the broadest) 200 miles. Which breadth continueth through the most part of the land. Saving that by little and little it cometh in and waxeth narrower towards both the ends. Which fetching about a circuit or compass of 500 miles, do fashion the whole island like to the new moon. [...] The forefronts or frontiers of the two corners, what with fords[1]
5 and shelves and what with rocks, be very jeopardous and dangerous. In the middle distance between them both standeth up above the water a great rock, which therefore is nothing perilous because it is in sight. Upon the top of this rock is a fair and a strong tower builded, which they hold with a garrison and men. Other rocks there by lying hid under the water, which therefore be dangerous. The channels be know only to themselves. And therefore it seldom chanceth that any stranger unless be he guided by an Utopian, can
10 come into this haven. [...]
There be in the island fifty-four large and fair cities, or shire[2] towns, agreeing all together in one tongue, in like manners, institutions, and laws. They all be set and situate alike, and in all points fashioned alike, as far forth as the place or plot suffereth. [...]
They have in the country, in all parts of the shire, houses or farms builded, well appointed and furnished
15 with all sorts of instruments and tools belonging to husbandry[3]. These houses be inhabited of the citizens which come thither[4] to dwell[5] by course. No household or farm has fewer than forty persons, men and women, besides two bondmen[6] which be all under the rule and order of the good man and the good wife of the house, being both very sage, discreet, and
20 ancient persons. [...]
These husbandmen[7] plough[8] and till the ground, and bryde up cattle, and provide and make ready wood, which they carry to the city either by land or by water as they may most conveniently.
25 They bring up a great multitude of pullen[9], and that by a marvellous policy. For the hens do not sit upon the eggs, but by keeping them in a certain equal heat they bring life into them and hatch them. The chickens, as soon as they be come out of the shell, follow
30 men and women instead of the hens. [...]
They sow corn only for bread, for their drink is either wine made of grapes or else of apples or pears, or else it is clear water. And many times mead made of honey or liquorice sodden in water, for thereof they have
35 great store. And though they know certainly (for they know it perfectly indeed) how much victuals[10] the city with the whole country or shire round about it doth spend, yet they sow much more corn and breed up much more cattle than serveth for their own use,
40 parting the overplus among their borderers.

www.gutenberg.org/files/2130/2130-h/2130-h.htm [23.01.2015]

Woodcut of the 1516 book edition of the novel

Focus on Documents

[1] **ford** a shallow place in a river where it is possible to walk across, *Furt* – [2] **shire** (*old use*) a county – [3] **husbandry** (*old use*) farming – [4] **thither** (*old use*) to or towards that place – [5] **to dwell** to live – [6] **bondman** (*old use*) slave – [7] **husbandman** (*old use*) the man of the house – [8] **to plough** [plaʊ] *pflügen* – [9] **pullen** (*old use*) chicken – [10] **victuals** (*old use*) food and drink

Cormac McCarthy, Joe Penhall
The Road

AWARENESS

In groups, look at the film still below from the 2010 film adaptation of Cormac McCarthy's Pulitzer Prize-winning dystopian novel *The Road*.
Describe the atmosphere conveyed in the film still and speculate about the plot of the novel. What might the function of "The Road" be and where might it lead to?

Tips on vocab 》》》

rows of power poles ■ cables/lines ■ deserted landscape ■ a demolished car blocking the way ■ apocalyptic ■ smoldering fires (*Schwelbrände*) ■ debris (*Schutt*) ■ shapes/silhouettes of human figures

COMPREHENSION

1. **Before listening:**
   As you already know, Cormac McCarthy's novel is a dystopia that takes place in a post-apocalyptic (*Endzeit*) world.

   Step 1: Reactivate your knowledge of the literary genres "utopia" and "dystopia" and their characteristic features (cf. pp. 313, 336).

   Step 2: The title of the novel does not reveal much about its plot or literary genre – it could be about a utopia or dystopia.

     Divide the class into two groups, with each of the groups dealing with one of these genres.
   Anticipate and develop a storyline of either a dystopian or a utopian world – both entitled "The Road".
   Employ the respective characteristic features and create imaginary characters. Sketch out a rough plot and compile storylines on posters or wall hangings.
   Finally, display your storylines in class and compare "The Roads" and how they lead to disaster or happiness.
   → Focus on Facts, Screenplays and Storyboards, p. 397

2. The audio text presents the introductory sections of Cormac McCarthy's novel.

Tips on vocab »»

> **onset** the beginning of sth. unpleasant begins ▪ **glaucoma** *grüner Star* ▪ **tarpaulin** *Plane* ▪ **cave** *Höhle –*
> **flowstone** *Tropfstein* ▪ **pilgrim** *Pilger* ▪ **granitic** *Granitstein* ▪ **flue** *Schacht, Kamin* ▪ **to toll** to ring slowly and
> repeatedly ▪ **to cease** to stop ▪ **to swing (swung swung)** *schaukeln, schwingen* ▪ **scent** smell ▪ **to crouch**
> *hocken* ▪ **translucent** *durchscheinend* ▪ **to cast up** *hervorscheinen* ▪ **bowels** *Eingeweide* ▪ **dull** *matt, stumpf*
> ▪ **to lurch** *taumeln* ▪ **to lope** *beschwingt gehen* ▪ **to squat** *kauern* ▪ **barren** *kahl, leer* ▪ **knapsack** *Rucksack* ▪
> **to clamp** *klemmen* ▪ **serpentine** *Schlangenlinie* ▪ **reed** *Schilfrohr* ▪ **blacktop** *Teerdecke* ▪ **to shuffle** *schlurfen*

Step 1: Listen to the recording **a first time** and try to get a **general understanding** of the situation and atmosphere that is revealed.

Step 2: Exchange your first listening impressions with a partner and outline to each other what these sections are about. Do not go into detail but focus on the gist.

Step 3: While listening a **second time**, take notes on these tasks and questions:
- Describe the overall atmosphere of the setting.
- What is revealed about the man and child's living conditions?
- What strange encounter does the man have in his dream?
- What information is given about the country and the environment?
- What are the protagonists' belongings?
- Where are the man and child headed (*auf dem Weg sein nach*)?

Step 4: Exchange and compare your findings and notes with your partner again and make additions and corrections to your notes if necessary.
→ Focus on Skills, Listening Comprehension, p. 394

3. In a paired reading activity, read the excerpt taken from the screenplay of the film.
- Sketch out the situation depicted there, focusing on the w-questions.
- Write a summary of the excerpt in about 150 words.
→ Focus on Skills, Writing a Summary, p. 429

ANALYSIS »»»»»»»»

4. In groups, listen to/read the excerpts once more and compare them.
a) Specify the similarities and differences between
- the action,
- the setting,
- the characters.

b) Explain how the screenplay creates the ghostly atmosphere depicted in the novel.
→ Focus on Skills, Analysis of a Fictional Text, p. 402
→ Focus on Skills, Analysis of a Screenplay, p. 404

5. Step 1: Analyse the narrative perspective* of the excerpt from the screenplay (p. 341) and explain how it underlines the depressing atmosphere.

Step 2: Examine the technical directions given in the screenplay (p. 341) and explain how they take up and implement the narrative perspective of the novel.

6. Interpret the symbolism of the man's dream described in the first section of the novel. Pay particular attention to colours and the adjectives/adverbs employed in this part.

7. The different settings described in the screenplay imply a great deal of symbolism as well. In a first step, interpret their meaning. Second, relate them to the symbolism employed in the novel. Which correlations do you see?

8. Both texts create a lot of mystery and suspense. Give examples from the excerpts and explain their effect and function.

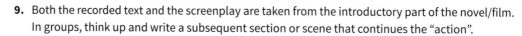

ACTIVITIES

9. Both the recorded text and the screenplay are taken from the introductory part of the novel/film. In groups, think up and write a subsequent section or scene that continues the "action".

   Tip: Use the (hidden) hints/clues given in either text (e. g. "watch the road behind him", cannibalism, etc.) and take up the narrative style of the respective text.
   → Focus on Skills, Continuation of a Fictional Text, p. 420

10. Choose one of the film stills and write
    a) an interior monologue* of one of the characters shown or
    b) a dialogue* between the two characters.
    Read/act out your monologues/dialogues in class and discuss whether/to what extent they pick up on the situation depicted in the two excerpts.

Post-apocalyptic bonding …
Viggo Mortensen and Kodi
Smit-McPhee in *The Road*

EXT. LAKE – DAY

They trudge[1] past a vast[2] lake filled with dead trees
…

MAN. (V.O.[3])

5 I think it's October but I can't be sure. I haven't kept a calendar for 5 years.

EXT. MOUNTAINSIDE – DAY

They truck[4] along with the trolley through the fog, the ghostly shapes of dead trees on either side and
10 the shapes of barren[5] mountains in the background …

MAN. (V.O.)

Each day is more gray than the one before. Each night is darker – beyond darkness. The world gets
15 colder week by week as the planet slowly dies. No animals have survived. All the crops are long gone.

EXT. EDGE WOODS – DAY

A tree falls behind them with a Whump and they jump …

20 MAN. (V.O.)

Someday all the trees in the world will have fallen.

EXT. GAS STATION – DAY

The MAN forages[6] for petrol, checking the nozzle[7] of the pumps[8], rummaging[9] through empty oil cans, he
25 upends[10] a bin to get at the empty oil bottles.

The BOY picks up a phone on a wall and listens to the dead earpiece[11].

MAN. (V.O.)

The roads are peopled by refugees towing[12] carts and road gangs carrying weapons, looking for fuel and 30 food.

EXT. LONG ROAD – DAY

They head down through a long straight road towards a dark, forbidding looking tunnel – a turnpike[13].

MAN. (V.O.)   35

There has been cannibalism. Cannibalism is the great fear.

EXT. CITY – DAY

They emerge before a view of a deserted city-state …

EXT. MALL – DAY   40

They forage in a deserted mall …
There are skeletons and human bones here and there.

MAN. (V.O.)

Mostly I worry about food. Always food. Food and our shoes.   45

C.U.[14] – the BOY examines the head of a moose[15] mounted on a wall in a SEARS[16] hunting store.

MAN. (V.O.) (CONT'D)

Sometimes I tell the boy old stories of courage and justice – difficult as they are to remember.   50
All I know is the child is my warrant and if he is not in the word of God, God never spoke.

www.pages.drexel.edu/~ina22/splaylib/Screenplay-Road,%20The.pdf
[27.11.2014] by Joe Penhall based on *The Road* by Cormac McCarthy

---

[1] **to trudge** *sich schleppen* – [2] **vast** extremely big – [3] **V.O.** (*abbr.*) voice over – [4] **to truck** *etw. transportieren* – [5] **barren** *öde, kahl* – [6] **to forage** ['fɒrɪdʒ] to go from place to place searching for food – [7] **nozzle** *Zapfventil* – [8] **pump** *Benzinpumpe* – [9] **to rummage** *durchstöbern* – [10] **to upend** *etw. hochkant stellen* – [11] **earpiece** *Hörer* – [12] **to tow** [təʊ] *etw. abschleppen* – [13] **turnpike** a main road that you usually have to pay to use – [14] **C.U.** (*abbr.*) close-up – [15] **moose** *Elch* – [16] **Sears** a chain of American department stores

genetic engineering		
biotechnology [baɪəʊtek'nɒlədʒi]	the use of living things such as cells or bacteria to make drugs, destroy waste, etc.	*Biotechnologie*
cloning	the act of producing an identical plant or animal artificially from the cells of another plant or animal	*Klonen*
controversial	causing a lot of public discussion and disagreement	*kontrovers, umstritten*
DNA [ˌdiːenˈeɪ]	the chemical in all living things that carries genetic information	*DNA, Desoxyribonukleinsäure*
DNA fingerprinting	the process of examining the pattern of someone's genes; genetic fingerprinting	*einen genetischen Finger-abdruck erstellen*
embryonic stem cell	a basic type of cell in the body of an embryo which can develop into cells with particular functions	*Embryonenstammzellen*
ethical concern	a concern that is connected with beliefs and principles about what is right and wrong	*ethische Bedenken*
fertile ['fɜːtaɪl]; **fertility** [fə'tɪlɪti]	able to produce babies, new plants, young animals; the ability of a human being, soil, or an animal to produce babies, etc.	*fruchtbar; Fruchtbarkeit*
gene [dʒiːn]	a unit inside a cell which controls a particular quality in a living thing	*Gen*
genetics [dʒə'netɪks]	the study of how the qualities of living things are passed on in their genes	*Genetik*
genetic disorder	a disease that is passed from the genes of the parents to those of the child before the child is born	*genetischer Defekt*
genetic engineering	the science of changing the information in a living being's genes	*Gentechnik*
genome ['dʒɪːnəʊm]	the complete set of genes in a cell or living thing	*das Genom, der Chromo-somensatz*
GM food	genetically modified food	*gentechnisch veränderte Lebensmittel*
to implant sth. into	to put an organ, group of cells or device into the body in a medical operation	*etw. implantieren*
in vitro fertilization (IVF) [ˌaɪviːef]	the process by which eggs are fertilized outside of the body (in vitro = in a glass; i. e., in a test tube)	*künstliche Befruchtung außer-halb des Körpers*
laboratory [lə'bɒrətri]	a room or building used for scientific research, experi-ments or testing	*Labor*
to manipulate [mə'nɪpjuleɪt]	to control or influence sb./sth., often in a dishonest way	*manipulieren*
to modify sth. genetically	to change the genetic code of sth.	*den genetischen Code von etw. verändern*
reproductive technology	technology connected with reproducing babies, young animals, plants, etc.	*Reproduktionstechnologie*
social egg freezing	technology to extract, freeze and store a woman's egg cells for later fertilization and implantation when she is ready to have a child	*das Einfrieren unbefruchteter Eizellen ohne medizinischen Grund*
science and technology		
artificial intelligence	the study of how to make computers copy intelligent human behaviour	*künstliche Intelligenz*
assembly line production	a system of making things in which the product moves past a line of workers who each make or check one part	*Fließbandproduktion*
to develop sth.	to think of or produce a new product; to design	*entwickeln*
drone	a vehicle, e. g. an aircraft or missile, that does not have a pilot but is remote-controlled	*unbemanntes (Luft-)Fahrzeug*
enhanced [ɪn'hɑːnst]	improved, better	*erweitert, verbessert*

findings	results	*Ergebnisse*
to invent sth.; invention	to make, design or think of a new type of thing; a useful machine, tool, instrument, etc. that has been invented	*etw. erfinden; Erfindung*
manufacturing	the business of producing goods in large numbers	*Herstellung*
microelectronics [ˌmaɪkrəʊˌɪlekˈtrɒnɪks]	the science and technology involved in the making and using of very small electronic parts	*Mikroelektronik*
progress; progressive	the process of improving or developing, or of getting closer to finishing or achieving sth.; in favour of new or modern ideas, methods and change	*Fortschritt; fortschrittlich*
research; researcher	the careful study of a subject; sb. who studies a subject in detail in order to discover new information	*Forschung, Recherche; Forscher*
robot	a machine that can perform a complicated series of tasks automatically	*Roboter*
robotics	the science of operating and designing robots	*Robotertechnik*
scientist [ˈsaɪəntɪst]	an expert who studies or works in the sciences	*Wissenschaftler*
to verify	to determine whether sth. is correct, to confirm	*überprüfen, bestätigen*
utopia/dystopia		
allegory [ˈæləgəri]; **allegorical** [ˌæləˈgɒrɪkəl]	a story, painting, etc. in which the events and characters represent ideas or teach a moral lesson; a fictional text which has both a literal and figurative meaning	*Gleichnis, Allegorie; sinnbildlich*
anti-utopia	a futuristic world in which individual freedom is severely limited	*Anti-Utopie*
apocalyptic literature	literature which deals with the end of the world	*apokalyptische Literatur, Endzeit-Literatur*
authoritarian state [ˌɔːθɒrɪˈteəriən]	a state in which people are forced to obey authority and rules, even when these are wrong and unfair	*autoritärer Staat*
to be doomed	to be certain to fail or suffer	*dem Untergang geweiht sein*
dystopia; dystopian [dɪsˈtəʊpiən]	a failed or fallen society; related to an imaginary state or place in which everything is extremely bad or unpleasant	*Dystopie; dystopisch*
to envision	to imagine	*sich ausmalen, sich vorstellen*
fictitious [fɪkˈtɪʃəs]	invented by a writer	*fiktiv*
futuristic	extremely modern and unusual in appearance, as if belonging to a future time	*futuristisch*
imaginary [ɪˈmædʒɪnəri]	existing only in your mind or imagination	*erfunden, eingebildet*
nightmare; nightmarish	a dream that is very frightening or unpleasant; frightening, horrific	*Albtraum; albtraumhaft, beklemmend*
snooper state (*infml.*)	a state that tries to find out private things about people	*Schnüffelstaat*
totalitarian state [təʊˌtælˈteəriən steɪt]	a state in which there is only one political party that has complete power and control over the people	*totalitärer Staat*
surveillance [sɜːˈveɪləns]	the act of carefully watching a person or a place because they may be connected with crime	*Überwachung*
utopia [juːˈtəʊpiə]; **utopian**	an imaginary place or state in which everything is perfect	*Utopie; utopisch*
visionary [ˈvɪʒənəri]	with the ability to imagine how a country, society, etc. will develop in the future	*visionär*

Modern Media – Social, Smart and Spying?!

Walk the walk, don't talk the talk, Washington D.C.

START-UP ACTIVITIES

1. In groups, reflect on the title of this unit: What are "modern media"? What are the positive and negative sides of modern media? What opportunities and pitfalls (*Fallstricke*) are connected with them? Compile mind maps that include the various aspects and discuss them in class.

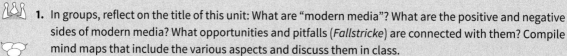

2. Look at the photo above showing a divided sidewalk for distracted pedestrians in Washington D.C. Do you think this a good idea? What are your experiences with phoning and walking – or other people who are distracted while texting or phoning?

3. Listen to and/or watch the Associated Press news coverage on "Distracted Walking" using the link on the webcode.

- Why has this topic become a serious issue?

- Discuss: Do you think that creating "e-lanes" or "distracted walking bills" are effective ways of handling the problem?

Webcode
SNG-40235-036

4. Read Michael Grunwald's article and compare the advantages and disadvantages of "Big Data".

5. In a pyramid discussion, discuss whether "Big Data" "optimize" or "overtax" (*überfordern*) most people. Have we lost "serendipity", and do people live in "online cocoons"?

Michael Grunwald

The Second Age of Reason[1]:
Information Overload Will Improve Our Lives

From the pages of

TIME

The Roman philosopher Seneca worried about information overload nearly 2,000 years before it was cool. [5] "What is the point of having countless books and libraries whose titles the owner could scarcely[2] read through in a whole lifetime?" he wondered. [...]

Today, the smartphone in your pocket gives you easy access to billions of times as much information as was held in all the li-[10] braries on earth since Seneca's day. You can find out in real time what's happening with Ukraine, your high school friends or the price of soybean futures[3]. You're a swipe[4] away from knowing the best way to get somewhere, the best temperature to grill burgers or the best deal on a new laptop. [...]

[15] We're living in a golden age of answers. And it's awesome. At any moment, any schlub[5] can call upon the accumulated[6] wisdom of humankind to settle a bar bet[7], translate any document into any language or, as the schlub writing this article once did, diagnose a woozy[8] Boston terrier with a severe case of ate-the-[20] dog-sitter's-marijuana in time to get its stomach pumped. We can now monitor our home electricity use when we're not home, access our personal genetic codes to learn our risk factors, check who's given how much money to our politicians and figure out when it's likely to stop raining. Of course, infor-[25] mation is not knowledge or wisdom, and data can mislead. [...] Privacy can also be a problem in a digital world where everything you've clicked, liked, posted and favorited online can potentially be used to sell things to you, evaluate you, embarrass[9] or oppress you. Your digital footprints tend to be permanent, [30] unless you leave them on Snapchat, and your friends are not the only ones who know that you just checked in somewhere on Facebook. These days, your iPhone, E-ZPass, even your digital thermostat can also provide information to others that you might prefer to keep to yourself.

[35] But revolutions always create collateral[10] damage. Wikipedia killed the encyclopedia. Apps killed maps. [...] Things do get lost in this ocean of info. We no longer bother to remember stuff we can easily look up. GPS killed the fun of bumbling around in a new city. We spend too much time reconnecting on Facebook with that kid we barely knew in summer camp and [40] not enough time connecting with real friends in real life. [...]

It's fundamentally convenient[11] that we no longer need to carry maps, compasses, calendars, address books, calculators or watches now that our phones perform their functions through the magic of ones and zeros. Photo albums, music collections [45] and video libraries – as well as newspapers, magazines and books – no longer need to occupy physical space either.

Now everything we do – every online purchase[12], e-prescription[13] and tweet – adds to the digital tsunami known as Big Data. That can sound ominous[14], but big data is producing bet-[50] ter information, not just more information, about our economy, our health and everything else, because we have better tools for slicing and dicing[15] data, for searching, sifting[16] and sorting through the barrage[17] of keystrokes[18]. [...]

A friend recently showed me how his Internet-optimized dat-[55] ing apps have fine-tuned his social life, sending him multiple prospects[19] a day that he can accept or reject with a swipe. I couldn't stop marveling[20] at how efficient it seemed, so much better than small talk with strangers at bars and awkward[21] parties, until it occurred to me that no dating app would have [60] paired me with my wife. We met at an awkward party. I had never dated anyone like her; she had never dated anyone like me. No algorithm could have predicted our great optimization. If there's a cost to the age of answers, it's probably our loss of serendipity[22]. We've honed[23] our daily news feeds to send us [65] stuff that already interests us, so we're less likely to stumble upon a quirky[24] story on page B-13. We gravitate[25] toward online cocoons of like-minded people who don't challenge our assumptions. Optimizing isn't always optimal.

But for the most part, answers are good to know. You just have [70] to ask the right questions.

TIME, September 8 – 15, 2014, pp. 33 ff.

---

[1] **Age of Reason** Zeitalter der Aufklärung (ca. 1650 – 1800) – [2] **scarcely** not at all reasonable or likely – [3] **futures** Terminhandel, Terminbörse – [4] **swipe** Wischen – [5] **schlub** (US, infml.) sb. who is stupid and not attractive – [6] **to accumulate** anhäufen – [7] **bet** Wette – [8] **woozy** (infml.) wirr – [9] **to embarrass sb.** jdn. blamieren – [10] **collateral** here: additional, as a side-effect – [11] **convenient** suitable or comfortable – [12] **purchase** the act of buying sth. – [13] **e-prescription** Online-Rezept (Arzt) – [14] **ominous** beunruhigend – [15] **to slice and dice data** here: etw. portionieren – [16] **to sift** here: to examine – [17] **barrage of sth.** a great number of sth. – [18] **keystroke** Tastendruck – [19] **prospect** a person who is likely to be successful in a competition – [20] **to marvel at sb./sth.** to show great surprise or admiration – [21] **awkward** uncomfortable, difficult to deal with – [22] **serendipity** [ˌserənˈdɪpɪti] (fml.) glücklicher Zufall – [23] **to hone** to improve the quality of sth. – [24] **quirky** schrullig – [25] **to gravitate to/toward sb./sth.** (phr. v.) to be attracted by sb./sth.

The Media: Influencing Public Opinion and Personal Life

Cecilia Kang

1 Podcasts Are Back – And Making Money

AWARENESS

Act out a pyramid discussion in which you discuss your use of online services for downloading music, videos or games to your smartphone, iPod or computer.
How much are you willing to pay for such services? Use the vocab box below and/or a dictionary for help.

> **Tips on vocab**
>
> to access the Web/Internet ▪ to go online ▪ to access/connect to a server ▪ to browse/surf/search the Internet ▪ to accept/block/delete cookies ▪ to visit/check a website/sb.'s blog ▪ to download/upload music/software/a podcast ▪ to post a comment/message on a website/a web forum ▪ to stream video/audio/music over the Internet ▪ to join/participate in an online/Internet forum/group ▪ to monitor Internet traffic

They were too clunky[1] to download. The topics were sometimes a little too obscure. And they didn't really make any money.

Podcasts, the short-form audio files that entered the mainstream with the original Apple iPod, have been around for more than a decade. But while Apple this year discontinued the classic version of its iconic[2] device, the podcast is resurgent[3], drawing hard-core fans who want to listen to other people talk about, well, pretty much everything.

An average of 1.5 million listeners a month download "99 % Invisible," a program produced on a shoestring on the theme of design. [...]

And, importantly, podcasts are finally profitable.

"It's sort of a renaissance. Podcasts are in vogue," said Todd Cochrane, chief executive of RawVoice, a podcast data research firm.

Maybe it's the intimacy of hearing soothing[4] voices piped into your ears through a pair of headphones – or maybe it's just how much time people need to kill listening to something. Americans spend more than three hours a day commuting, working out and doing household chores[5] that can be accompanied by audio entertainment, according to census data studied by Matt Lieber, a former public radio producer who co-founded the podcast company with Blumberg[6].

Smartphones and Bluetooth-enabled cars have made it easier than ever for listeners – who are still mostly men – to load up their favorite programs. And instead of the old way of downloading them from iTunes onto a computer and syncing[7] with an iPod, listeners can grab shows straight from the Internet onto their smartphones. Last year, Apple said subscriptions of podcasts through iTunes reached 1 billion. RawVoice, which tracks 20,000 shows, said the number of unique monthly podcast listeners has tripled to 75 million from 25 million five years ago.

And the connection that people can feel toward their favorite podcasts is exactly the sort of relationship that many media companies are trying to build with their users. At a time when people can easily skip TV ads, messages from sponsors on podcasts have a way of sinking in, especially when they're read by the hosts of the show themselves, analysts say. As a result, this second wave of podcasts – unlike the first go-round – is promising to make more money.

"Five years ago, podcasting was very much a hobbyist's activity and many people weren't making them to make

---

[1] **clunky** large and awkward – [2] **iconic** very famous or popular – [3] **resurgent** (*fml.*) *wiederauflebend* – [4] **soothing** making you feel calm –
[5] **household chores** [tʃɔː(r)s] *häusliche Aufgaben/Pflichten* – [6] **Alex Blumberg** an American producer for public radio and television –
[7] **to sync sth.** (*infml.*) to synchronize sth.

money," said Tom Webster, a vice president of strategy at polling firm Edison Research. "But audience sizes have grown consistently, and each listener is listening to more shows as part of their weekly habit. That's brought major producers to embrace podcasting."

When Roman Mars began his quirky public radio show on the topic of design, he never expected it to amount to much.

The show "99% Invisible" was small in every way. Each episode ran for just 4 minutes 30 seconds, short enough to wedge between segments of big shows like NPR's "Morning Edition." It was esoteric, with back stories on the way the periodic table and parking meters were designed. Mars had a tiny budget of $5,000 and wrote, narrated and produced the show from the bedroom of his Oakland, Calif., home.

The show was warmly received when it started airing four years ago on San Francisco's KALW[8]. But off the airwaves – in the world of podcasts – the show was a blockbuster. It is now consistently in the 20 most-downloaded podcasts on iTunes.

Mars quit his old public radio job and now works full time on "99% Invisible," funded entirely by the show's fans and a handful of sponsors. The show is still broadcast on a few public radio stations, but that "distribution means less and less over time," Mars said in a recent phone interview from Dublin, where he was putting on a live show for European fans. "They have a great reach and I'm a huge fan of NPR[9], but right now, if I'm able to reach my audience directly through podcasts, the writing is on the wall."

Despite some early enthusiasm, podcasts faded in popularity in the early 2000s, partly because of the many steps required to download them and play them in a vehicle. The introduction of the iPhone in 2007 changed that, making podcasts as convenient to access as a Netflix[10] show. It's easier to play them in cars, too, as automakers build wireless media functions into more and more models. And faster WiFi and mobile data speeds have made podcasts a snap[11] to stream.

Radio is still far more popular and lucrative than the fledgling[12] world of podcasts. The industry has withstood the disruption that the Internet wrought[13] on newspapers and TV, partly thanks to an enormous audience of commuters trapped in cars. But podcast enthusiasts believe preferences are beginning to change. "This is where radio syndication was 30 years ago, and this is just the beginning," said industry veteran Norm Pattiz, chief executive of celebrity podcast channel PodcastOne. "What Netflix did for video is what podcasts are doing for radio today."

Podcasters also like the personal connection they have with fans who listen through ear buds or headphones, which can make shows feel more intimate than other forms of media.

Mars said he keeps that in mind and mikes[14] himself more closely than he used to. This allows him to use a quieter voice, which he calls a "head voice," in the hopes of more closely connecting with listeners.

"My connection to the audience is something I completely cherish[15] and is part of that medium that is really unique," he said.

The flexibility of podcasts appeals to radio industry veterans whose shows have been dictated by rigid time blocks and long-held industry rules. Mars's shows are now 20 minutes in length, allowing for deeper reporting and developed story lines. "Longform," a podcast that interviews authors and magazine writers, runs much longer – too long to get picked up by any radio stations.

Even with the rise of six-second Vine[16] videos and viral[17] listicles[18] on the Web, Mars believes there is a strong appetite for long-form audio storytelling. It's what keeps listeners committed for 20 minutes to stories about, for instance, Ikea hackers – people who mix and match Ikea furniture as a hobby.

Fans are so devoted that they have helped to raise nearly $600,000 in the past three years – money that has allowed Mars to hire three reporters and producers.

The money for podcasts is coming from not just fans but advertisers, too.

www.washingtonpost.com/business/technology/podcasts-are-back-and-making-money/2014/09/25/54abc628-39c9-11e4-9c9f-ebb47272e40e_story.html, 25 September 2014 [27.12.2014]

---

[8] **KALW** a public radio station in the San Francisco Bay area – [9] **NPR** (abbr.) National Public Radio; an American public radio station network – [10] **Netflix** an American provider of on-demand Internet streaming media – [11] **snap** (US, infml.) sth. that can be done without any difficulty – [12] **fledgling** new and without experience – [13] **wrought** (used only in the past tense, fml.) caused sth. to happen/change – [14] **to mike** (infml.) to attach a microphone to sb./sth. – [15] **to cherish** wertschätzen – [16] **Vine** (abbr.) video network; a video sharing service launched by Twitter – [17] **viral** ['vaɪərəl] used to describe sth. that quickly becomes very popular or well-known by being published on the Internet or sent from person to person by email, phone, etc. – [18] **listicle** a newspaper, magazine or online article that is in the form of a list

2 Musik liegt in der Luft

Jahrelang litt die Musikindustrie unter großen Umsatzeinbrüchen durch illegales Kopieren, auch der Verkauf von Klingeltönen konnte den Abwärtstrend nicht bremsen. Die Nutzer haben gerade die legalen Musikdown-loads akzeptiert – schon kommt der nächste Umbruch auf sie zu: In Zukunft werden wir nicht einmal mehr eine digitale Kopie der Musik besitzen – wir empfangen nur noch Lied für Lied als Datenstrom aus dem Netz.

Der Markt der Zukunft

Beim Streaming* wird die Musik nicht gespeichert. Der Hörer empfängt sie über eine Onlineverbindung. Er zahlt eine Monatsgebühr oder hört kostenlos, aber mit Werbeeinblendungen.

7.–13. Mai 2012 · 31 Mio. Streams
24.–30. Dez. 2012 · 99 Mio. Streams
23.–29. Dez. 2013 · 175 Mio. Streams

2012   2013

Mai 2012   Januar 2013

* Zahl der Streams (ein Stream = ein Song) in Deutschland

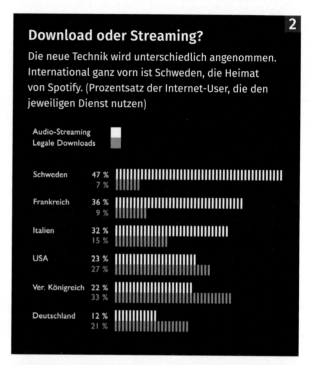

Download oder Streaming?

Die neue Technik wird unterschiedlich angenommen. International ganz vorn ist Schweden, die Heimat von Spotify. (Prozentsatz der Internet-User, die den jeweiligen Dienst nutzen)

Audio-Streaming
Legale Downloads

	Streaming	Downloads
Schweden	47 %	7 %
Frankreich	36 %	9 %
Italien	32 %	15 %
USA	23 %	27 %
Ver. Königreich	22 %	33 %
Deutschland	12 %	21 %

Wovon Interpreten Leben

Eine Umfrage in den USA unter 5000 Musikern ergab: Im Durchschnitt beziehen sie nur 6 % ihrer Einnahmen aus dem Verkauf der Musik. Bei den Topverdienern ist der Anteil höher.

2 Merchandising
22 Unterricht
6 Einkommen aus Musikverkäufen
19 Gehalt als Orchester- oder Bandmitglied
6 Tantiemen als Komponist und Textdichter
28 Gagen aus Livekonzerten
7 Sonstiges
10 Einkommen als Studiomusiker

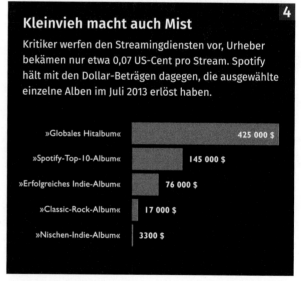

Kleinvieh macht auch Mist

Kritiker werfen den Streamingdiensten vor, Urheber bekämen nur etwa 0,07 US-Cent pro Stream. Spotify hält mit den Dollar-Beträgen dagegen, die ausgewählte einzelne Alben im Juli 2013 erlöst haben.

»Globales Hitalbum«	425 000 $
»Spotify-Top-10-Album«	145 000 $
»Erfolgreiches Indie-Album«	76 000 $
»Classic-Rock-Album«	17 000 $
»Nischen-Indie-Album«	3300 $

Die Zeit, 23 October 2014, p. 41

Tips on vocab ⋙

1 a monthly fee ▪ commercials/ads **2** to accept/embrace sth. **3** artist/performer ▪ musician ▪ on average ▪ a share of sth. ▪ share of the profits ▪ composer ▪ ongwriter **4** to accuse sb. of sth. ▪ to counter ▪ to generate proceeds (*Einkünfte, Erträge*)

3 Kilian Trotier: Fürs Kindle – Wie Amazon systematisch die Kultur entwertet[1]

Kinder lieben Geschenke. Vor allem zu Weihnachten. Das weiß auch Amazon. Und weil Amazon sich gerne als gütiger Geschenkweihnachtsmann ausgibt, hat es neues Angebot im Gepäck, das zunächst einmal die
5 amerikanischen Kinderherzen – und damit natürlich nicht minder auch die der Eltern – höherschlagen[2] lassen soll. Wenn sie sich für das Amazon-Tablet Kindle Fire entscheiden, werden sie mit einem prall gefüllten Sack an sogenanntem Content belohnt: mit Tausenden
10 von E-Books, Filmen, Computerspielen, TV-Serien und Apps, ausgewählt für Kinder zwischen drei und acht Jahren. Das kulturelle Winterwunderland mit Disney-Filmen, Bob dem Baumeister und der *Sesamstraße* öffnet seine Tore[3] auf dem Kindle Fire, sobald die Eltern
15 die App Kindle FreeTime Unlimited installieren und dafür einen lächerlich[4] kleinen Obolus[5] bezahlen: Eine monatliche Flatrate kostet für ein Kind 4,99 Dollar, ein Familien-Abo gibt's für 9,99 Dollar.

Das Erstaunliche[6] an dem Angebot ist nicht, dass
20 Amazon Kinder für sich entdeckt. Dass die Kleinsten[7] möglichst früh und möglichst positiv mit den eigenen Produkten in Berührung kommen, ist für jedes Unternehmen entscheidend[8]. Was den neuen Vorstoß[9] so frappierend[10] macht, ist etwas anderes: Amazon weitet
25 seine Billiglogik[11] auf die Inhalte aus. Waren es bislang nur die Geräte, die sie für Spottpreise[12] verkauften, werden jetzt auch Bücher, Filme und Spiele verramscht[13].

Amazon bleibt sich damit zwar treu[14]: In den USA, wo es keine Buchpreisbindung[15] gibt, drückt der Konzern die Preise brutal und verkauft Bestseller fürs Kindle für
30 bis zu vier Dollar billiger, als es Buchläden tun können. Allerdings kostet das einzelne Buch dann meist immer noch 9,99 Dollar. Was mit der Flatrate passiert, ist nun eine völlige Erosion der Preise und eine Implosion dessen, was uns Bücher, Filme, Lieder wert sind.
35

Amazon rückt bedrohlich nahe an die Gratis[16]-Downloads im Netz und übernimmt die Verkaufstaktik[17] von Firmen wie Spotify: Beim Internet-Streaming-Dienst kann jeder Kunde für 9,99 Euro im Monat auf all seinen Geräten aus Millionen von Liedern auswählen. Die In-
40 terpreten bekommen weniger als einen Cent, wenn einer ihrer Songs angehört wird.

Marxisten könnten jetzt sagen: So schlimm ist das doch gar nicht, endlich wird die schon immer verlogene[18] Markt-Kunst-Bindung aufgelöst[19]. Aber die perfi-
45 de[20] Amazon-Logik läuft auf etwas anderes heraus, auf die völlige Entwertung[21] des Kulturprodukts. Denn sie heißt, zugespitzt formuliert: Scheiß auf[22] die Bücher, Filme und Spiele. Wir benutzen sie nur, um die Leute in unseren Verwertungskreislauf[23] reinzuzie-
50 hen. Die wirklichen Gewinne[24] machen wir dann mit Kühlschränken und Waschmaschinen.

Die Zeit, 13 December 2012, p. 49

---

1. Form four groups with each group working on a different task.

1   **Step 1:** Read the English newspaper article and collect information about
   a) reasons why podcasts have become popular and successful (again),
   b) the development of podcasting,
   c) Roman Mars's show *99 % Invisible* and its success story,
   d) the advantages of the radio.

Step 2: Now the groups remix, with each group consisting of at least one member from the other groups. In this new group, each member informs the group about the results of the initial group.

2   **2.** In your initial groups, get an overview of the statistical data as well as the introductory text (p. 348).

---

[1] to devalue sth. – [2] to make one's heart skip a beat – [3] gate – [4] ridiculous(ly) – [5] small fee – [6] astounding/astonishing – [7] the little ones – [8] crucial/essential – [9] approach – [10] striking – [11] five-and-dime strategy (*infml.*) – [12] knockdown price – [13] to sell sth. at a loss – [14] to remain true to one's principles – [15] fixed book prices – [16] free – [17] sales strategy – [18] false/dishonest – [19] to dissolve sth. – [20] perfidious – [21] devaluation – [22] to hell with (*sl.*) – [23] utilization cycle – [24] profits

Step 1: Each of the four groups chooses one of the diagrams and mediates the information given into English. Focus on these aspects:

- the development from (illegal) downloads to streaming
- how streaming works
- how downloading and streaming are received by consumers
- musicians' different sources of income
- the success of certain albums

Use the vocab box below the info graphic and/or your dictionary for help.
→ Focus on Skills, Mediation, p. 412
→ Focus on Skills, Analysis of Statistical Data, p. 408

Step 2: Next, the groups remix again and exchange their findings.

ANALYSIS

3. Compare and analyse the statistical data about the music industry.
- How does the music business generate its revenue – and how much of it is left to the actual musician/creator?
- What role does the consumer play in this scenario?
→ Focus on Skills, Analysis of Statistical Data, p. 408

4. Within a year of its launch in January 2013, Amazon AutoRip delivered more than two billion digital music tracks to customers.

   a) Against this backdrop, mediate the German newspaper article into English, explaining Amazon's strategy of luring customers to buy electronic devices in connection with the download of products.
   b) Explain the author's criticism expressed in the headline: Why/How does Amazon "systematically devalue culture"?
→ Focus on Skills, Analysis of a Non-Fictional Text, p. 405

ACTIVITIES

5. Imagine you are a musician who feels cheated out of your share of the profits as well as your authorship and copyright of the music and lyrics.

Prepare a short speech, which you plan to upload on YouTube, in which you reveal and explain your situation and arguments. Deliver your speech in class and discuss the views taken and arguments given.
→ Focus on Skills, Writing a Speech Script, p. 428
→ Focus on Skills, Giving a Speech, p. 418
→ Focus on Language, Conversation and Discussion, p. 413

6. Divide your class into two groups and perform a public hearing on the matter.
Participating interest groups can be:
- musicians
- streaming servers like Amazon, Spotify, etc.
- music agents
- Internet users/customers

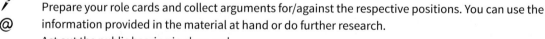

Prepare your role cards and collect arguments for/against the respective positions. You can use the information provided in the material at hand or do further research.
Act out the public hearing in class and
   a) exchange your views on the controversial matter,
   b) try to find a compromise/reach an agreement that offers a win-win situation for all participants.

The Media

In the domain of communication, **media** are tools used to store or transmit information and/or data. The term **mass media** or **public media** is used to describe the sum of mass distributors of news and entertain-
5 ment. These media include **print media**, **electronic media**, and **digital media**. Gutenberg, who perfected the printing press with movable types in 1454, is considered the inventor of "print media". Today, modern communication media facilitate so-called **"many-to-**
10 **many communication"** (e.g. via e-mail or Internet forums), whereas more traditional media typically represent **"one-to-many communication"** (e.g. TV, radio, cinema). Generally, the purpose of mass media is to promote businesses and their products by providing entertainment, information and socially-relevant services.

Tools of media and types of communication

digital media
- Internet (websites)
- e-mail
- mobile phone
- blogs (web logs)
- vlogs (video logs)
- RSS feeds
- podcasts
- QR code
- video games
- social networking
→ digital distribution

print media
- books
- newspapers
- magazines
- catalogues
→ from the late 15th century
→ physical distribution

broadcast/electronic media
- radio (ca. 1910)
- recorded music (late 19th century)
- film/cinema (ca. 1900)
- TV (ca. 1950)
- discs (1908s), tapes (1920s)
- e-book (1990s)
- podcasts
- e-publishing
→ electronic distribution

public communication
- TV
- newspapers/magazines
- social networking
→ many-to-many communication

personal communication
- telephony
- mail (post)
- mobile phones
→ person-to-person communication

Impact and influence of the media

advantages/positive effects	risks/dangers/negative effects
<ul><li>effective and quick exchange of information</li><li>possibility of being interconnected supports people in authoritarian states, e.g. the Arab Spring of 2011 – "democratization" process</li><li>giving public access to hidden/withheld information</li><li>(almost) unlimited access to information even in remote places, e.g. developing countries</li><li>exchange of cultural and social values</li><li>achievement of social control (e.g. public polls, citizen journalism)</li><li>platforms for individual presentations and contributions</li></ul>	<ul><li>influencing politics and public opinion</li><li>spying and surveillance (e.g. domestic wiretapping; *Telefonüberwachung*), datamining, etc.</li><li>publishing secret information (e.g. WikiLeaks)</li><li>influencing children and teenagers (e.g. exposure to violence, role models, advertising, etc.)</li><li>creation of an illusionary world (e.g. through soap operas – escapism)</li><li>imbalance of information (e.g. developed vs. developing world)</li></ul>

Richard Gray

The Challenge of Fake News

AWARENESS

Together with a partner, choose one of the statements below and discuss the implications made concerning the reliability and truth of information.

"Even when a correction reached a lot of people and a rumour reached a lot of people, they were usually not the same people. The problem is, corrections do not spread very well."   *Paul Resnick, University of Michigan*

"We shouldn't think of social media as just peer-to-peer communication – it is also the most powerful advertising platform there has ever been."   *Will Moy, Director of Full Fact*

"There is a large proportion of the population living in what we would regard as an alternative reality."   *Stephan Lewandowsky, University of Bristol*

"We got a lot of feedback that people did not want to be told what was true or not."   *Ben Fletcher, IBM Watson Research*

"Clickbait[1] is king, so newsrooms will uncritically print some of the worst stuff out there, which lends legitimacy to bullshit."   *Brooke Binkowski, Editor at the debunking website Snopes*

"Nowadays it's not important if a story's real [...]. The only thing that really matters is whether people click on it."   *Neetzan Zimmerman, senior director at the DC publication The Hill*

Who was the first black president of America? It's a fairly simple question with a straightforward answer. Or so you would think. But plug[2] the query[3] into a search engine and the facts get a little fuzzy[4].

[5] When I checked Google, the first result – given special prominence[5] in a box at the top of the page – informed me that the first black president was a man called John Hanson in 1781. Apparently, the US has had seven black presidents, including Thomas Jefferson and Dwight Ei-[10] senhower. Other search engines do little better. The top results on Yahoo and Bing pointed me to articles about Hanson as well.

Welcome to the world of "alternative facts." It is a bewildering maze[6] of claim[7] and counterclaim, where [15] hoaxes[8] spread with frightening speed on social media

and spark[9] angry backlashes[10] from people who take what they read at face value[11]. Controversial, fringe[12] views about US presidents can be thrown centre stage by the power of search engines. It is an environment where the mainstream media is accused of peddling[13] [20] "fake news" by the most powerful man in the world. Voters are seemingly misled by the very politicians they elected and even scientific research – long considered a reliable basis for decisions – is dismissed as having little value. [...] [25]

BBC Future Now asked a panel of experts about the grand challenges we face in the 21st century – and many named the breakdown of trusted sources of information as one of the most pressing problems today. In some ways, it's a challenge that trumps all others. [30]

---

[1] **clickbait** (*infml.*) articles, photographs, etc. on the Internet that are intended to attract attention and encourage people to click on links to particular websites – [2] **to plug** (*infml.*) here: to type, to enter – [3] **query** [ˈkwɪəri] question – [4] **fuzzy** (*infml.*) not clear – [5] **prominence** the state of being easily seen or well known – [6] **maze** Labyrinth – [7] **claim** Behauptung – [8] **hoax** a plan to deceive sb. or a trick – [9] **to spark** to cause the start of sth., esp. an argument or fight – [10] **backlash** heftige Gegenreaktion – [11] **to read/take sth. at face value** to believe that sth. is what it appears to be, without questioning it – [12] **fringe** (*disapproving*) considered to be very extreme and crazy – [13] **to peddle sth.** *mit etw. hausieren gehen*

Without a common starting point – a set of facts that people with otherwise different viewpoints can agree on – it will be hard to address any of the problems that the world now faces.

35 The example at the start of this article may seem a minor, frothy[14] controversy, but there is something greater at stake here. Leading researchers, tech companies and fact-checkers we contacted say the threat posed by the spread of misinformation should not be underestimated.

40 Take another example. In the run-up to the US presidential elections last year [2016], a made-up story spread on social media claiming a paedophile[15] ring involving high-profile members of the Democratic Party was operating out of the basement of a pizza restaurant in 45 Washington DC. In early December a man walked into the restaurant – which does not have a basement – and fired an assault rifle. Remarkably, no one was hurt.

Some warn that "fake news" threatens the democratic process itself. "On page one of any political science 50 textbook it will say that democracy relies on people being informed about the issues so they can have a debate and make a decision," says Stephan Lewandowsky, a cognitive scientist at the University of Bristol in the UK, who studies the persistence[16] and spread of misin-55 formation. "Having a large number of people in a society who are misinformed and have their own set of facts is absolutely devastating[17] and extremely difficult to cope with." [...]

We need a new way to decide what is trustworthy. "I 60 think it is going to be not figuring out what to believe but who to believe," says Paul Resnick, professor of information at the University of Michigan. "It is going to come down to the reputations of the sources of the information. They don't have to be the ones we had in the 65 past."

We're seeing that shift already. The UK's Daily Mail newspaper has been a trusted source of news for many people for decades. But last month editors of Wikipedia voted to stop using the Daily Mail as a source for infor-70 mation on the basis that it was "generally unreliable."

Yet Wikipedia itself – which can be edited by anyone but uses teams of volunteer editors to weed out[18] inaccuracies – is far from perfect. Inaccurate information is a regular feature on the website and requires careful checking for anyone wanting to use it. [...]   75

"The major new challenge in reporting news is the new shape of truth," says Kevin Kelly, a technology author and co-founder of Wired magazine. "Truth is no longer dictated by authorities, but is networked by peers. For every fact there is a counterfact. All those counterfacts 80 and facts look identical online, which is confusing to most people."

For those behind the made-up stories, the ability to share them widely on social media means a slice[19] of the advertising revenue[20] that comes from clicks as 85 people follow the links to their webpages. It was found that many of the stories were coming from a small town in Macedonia where young people were using it as a get-rich scheme, paying Facebook to promote their posts and reaping the rewards[21] of the huge number of 90 visits to their websites.

"The difference that social media has made is the scale and the ability to find others who share your world view," says Will Moy, director of Full Fact, an independent fact-checking organisation based in the UK. "In the 95 past it was harder for relatively fringe opinions to get their views reinforced. If we were chatting around the kitchen table or in the pub, often there would be a debate."

But such debates are happening less and less. Informa-100 tion spreads around the world in seconds, with the potential to reach billions of people. But it can also be dismissed[22] with a flick of the finger[23]. What we choose to engage with is self-reinforcing[24] and we get shown more of the same. It results in an exaggerated "echo 105 chamber" effect.

"What is noticeable about the two recent referendums in the UK – Scottish independence and EU membership – is that people seem to be clubbing together with people they agreed with and all making one another an-110 grier," says Moy. "The debate becomes more partisan[25], more angry and people are quicker to assume they are being lied to but less quick to assume people they agree with are lying. That is a dangerous tendency."

http://www.bbc.com/future/story/20170301-lies-propaganda-and-fake-news-a-grand-challenge-of-our-age , 1 March 2017 [25.03.2017]

---

[14]**frothy** not serious – [15]**paedophile** [ˈpiːdəfaɪl] sb. who is sexually interested in children – [16]**persistence** *Beharrlichkeit* – [17]**devastating** causing a lot of damage or destruction – [18]**to weed sb./sth. out** (*phr. v.*) to get rid of unwanted things or people from a group – [19]**slice** a part of sth., such as an amount of money – [20]**revenue** *Ertrag, Einnahme* – [21]**to reap the rewards** to get sth. good as a result of your own actions – [22]**to dismiss** *etw. verwerfen, abtun* – [23]**a flick of the finger** *Fingerschnipp* – [24]**self-reinforcing** to make oneself stronger – [25]**partisan** *parteiisch, voreingenommen*

COMPREHENSION

1. Together with a partner, get an overview of the information the article provides and
   a) subdivide the text into thematic units
   b) assign the following headings to these thematic units.
   Be careful: The headings below do not follow the topical order of the text.

   a) Major shifts in truthfulness   b) Threatening democracy itself
   c) Black American presidents   d) The danger of misinformation
   e) The power of social media   f) Alternative facts and fake news
   g) Today's most pressing problems   h) The echo chamber effect

2. Point out why search engines have such enormous influence and power.

3. Outline the reasons why "fake news" and the "breakdown of trusted sources of information" are a devastating threat to democracy.

4. Define the "new shape of truth" (ll. 76 f.).

5. Give examples of how social media change/influence people's world view.

ANALYSIS

6. Explain the author's observations depicted in the last paragraph. What makes people become more angry and suspicious of being lied to?

7. Divide the class into 3 – 6 groups, with 1 – 2 groups each working with <u>one</u> of the cartoons on p. 355.

   Step 1: Describe your cartoon in detail, referring to textual and pictorial elements.

   Tip: Use a dictionary and look up words and phrases for a precise description.

   Step 2: Explain the symbolic meaning of the various elements of the cartoon as well as allusions to politicians, cultural events, scandals, etc.

   Step 3: Each group presents its respective cartoon to the class.

   → Focus on Skills, Presentations, p. 419
   → Focus on Skills, Analysis of Visuals, p. 409

8. Based on the results of the previous task, choose one of the cartoons and relate its message to the BBC article.

ACTIVITIES

9. The author describes that a panel of experts stated that "[w]ithout a common starting point – a set of facts that people with otherwise different viewpoints can agree on – it will be hard to address any of the problems that the world now faces" (ll. 31 ff.).
   How can you make sure that a source is trustworthy and real versus fake news? How, in general, do you know who to believe?

   Exchange your ideas in class. Try to find strategies for dealing with misinformation online and identifying reliable, trustworthy sources.

The Digital Revolution: Digits and Big Data

Lev Grossman

The Man Who Wired[1] the World – Mark Zuckerberg's Crusade[2] to Put Every Single Human Being Online

AWARENESS

Look at the map below depicting the number of people worldwide with no access to the Internet.
a) What might be the reasons for the lack of Internet access?
b) Imagine these countries' citizens had access to the Internet. What might be the possible consequences – would it be a blessing or a burden?
Discuss in class.

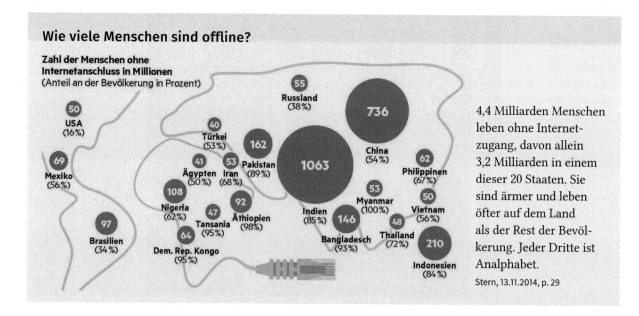

Wie viele Menschen sind offline?

Zahl der Menschen ohne Internetanschluss in Millionen
(Anteil an der Bevölkerung in Prozent)

50 USA (16%)
69 Mexiko (56%)
97 Brasilien (34%)
55 Russland (38%)
40 Türkei (53%)
162
41 Ägypten (50%)
53 Iran (68%)
Pakistan (89%)
1063
736
China (54%)
62 Philippinen (67%)
108 Nigeria (62%)
47 Tansania (95%)
92 Äthiopien (98%)
64 Dem. Rep. Kongo (95%)
Indien (85%)
146
53 Myanmar (100%)
Bangladesch (93%)
48 Thailand (72%)
50 Vietnam (56%)
210 Indonesien (84%)

4,4 Milliarden Menschen leben ohne Internetzugang, davon allein 3,2 Milliarden in einem dieser 20 Staaten. Sie sind ärmer und leben öfter auf dem Land als der Rest der Bevölkerung. Jeder Dritte ist Analphabet.

Stern, 13.11.2014, p. 29

From the pages of

TIME

The story of Facebook's first decade was one of relentless[3], rapacious[4] growth, from a dorm-room[5] side project to a ⁵ global service with 8,000 employees and 1.35 billion users, on whose unprotesting backs Zuckerberg has built an advertising engine that generated $7.87 billion last year, a billion and a half of it profit. Lately, Zuck-¹⁰ erberg has been thinking about what the story of Fa-cebook's second decade should be and what most be-comes[6] the leader of a social entity[7] that, if it were a country, would be the second most populous in the world, only slightly smaller than China. [...] Fulfilling the actual mission, connecting the entire ¹⁵ world, wouldn't actually literally be possible unless everybody in the world were on the Internet. So Zuck-erberg has decided to make sure everybody is. [...] Last year, Zuckerberg formed a coalition of technology companies that includes Ericsson[8], Qualcomm[9], Nokia[10] ²⁰

[1] **to wire sb./sth.** *jdn./etw. verkabeln* – [2] **crusade** *Kreuzzug* – [3] **relentless** continuing in an extreme way – [4] **rapacious** [rəˈpeɪʃəs] (*fml.*) *raubgierig* – [5] **dorm-room** *Schlafsaal* – [6] **to become sb.** (*fml.*) to be suitable for sb. – [7] **entity** an organization or business that has its own separate legal and financial existence – [8] **Ericsson** Swedish multinational provider of communications technology and services – [9] **Qualcomm** an American global company that designs and markets wireless telecommunication products and services – [10] **Nokia** a Finnish multinational communications and information technology company

and Samsung[11]. The name of this group is Internet.org, and it describes itself as "a global partnership between technology leaders, nonprofits, local communities and experts who are working together to bring the Internet to the two-thirds of the world's population that doesn't have it." […]

Using maps and data from Ericsson and NASA – including a fascinating data set called the Gridded[12] Population of the World, which maps the geographical distribution of the human species – plus information mined[13] from Facebook's colossal user base, the Internet.org team at Facebook figured out that most of their work was already done. Most humans, or about 85% of them, already have Internet access, at least in the minimal sense that they live within range of a cell tower with at least a 2G data network. They're just not using it.

Facebook has a plan for the other 15%, a blue-sky wi-fi-in-the-Sahara-type scheme involving drones and satellites and lasers, which we'll get to later, but that's a long-term project. The subset[14] of that 85% of people who could be online but aren't: they're the low-hanging fruit. […]

Internet 911[15]

Not to keep you in suspense, but Facebook figured out the answer to how to get all humanity online. It's an app. Here's the idea. First, you look at a particular geographical region that's underserved, Internet-wise, and figure out what content might be compelling[16] enough to lure its inhabitants online. Then you gather that content up, make sure it's in the right language and wrap it up in a slick[17] app. Then you go to the local cell-phone providers and convince as many of them as possible that they should offer the content in your app for free, with no data charges. There you go: anybody who has a data-capable phone has Internet access – or at least access to a curated[18], walled[19] sliver[20] of the Internet – for free. […]

But the hard part is persuading the cell-phone companies to offer the content for free. The idea is that they should make the app available as a loss leader[21], and once customers see it (inside Facebook they talk about people being "exposed to data"), they'll want more and be willing to pay for it. In other words, data is addictive, so you make the first taste free. […]

Colonialism 2.0

There's another way to look at what Facebook is doing here, which is that however much the company spins[22] it as altruistic[23], this campaign is really an act of self-serving techno-colonialism. Facebook's membership is already almost half the size of the Internet, Facebook, like soylent green[24], is made of people, and it always needs more of them. Over the long term, if Facebook is going to keep growing, it's going to have to make sure it's got a bigger Internet to grow in.

Hence[25] Internet.org. And if that Internet is seeded[26] by people who initially have limited options online, of which Facebook (and no other social network) is one, all the better. Facebook started up a similar program in 2011 called Facebook Zero, targeted at developing markets, which made a streamlined mobile version of Facebook available for free, with no data charges. At the time this was not considered altruism; it was just good, aggressive marketing (it's actually illegal in Chile because it violates Chilean Net-neutrality laws). Facebook Zero bears a strong family resemblance[27] to Internet.org.

There's something distasteful about the whole business: a global campaign by a bunch of Silicon Valley jillionaires[28] to convert literally everybody into data consumers, to make sure no eyeballs anywhere go unexposed[29] to their ads. Everybody must be integrated into the vast cultural homogeneity[30] that is the Internet. It's like a zombie plague: World War Z(uckerberg). After all, it's not as though anybody asked two-thirds of humanity whether they wanted to be put online. It makes one want to say, there are still people here on God's green earth who can conduct[31] their own social lives without being marketed to. Can't we for God's sake leave them alone? […]

---

[11] **Samsung** a South Korean multinational conglomerate company – [12] **gridded** *vernetzt* – [13] **to mine** to extract from a source; *herausziehen* – [14] **subset** *Teilmenge* – [15] **911** phone number used in the US to call the emergency services; anyone can call this number, even without a phone plan – [16] **compelling** here: strong, convincing – [17] **slick** attractive to look at, but not very meaningful – [18] **curated** *gepflegt* – [19] **walled** surrounded by a wall, i. e. limited – [20] **sliver** (*fml.*) a very small, thin piece of sth. – [21] **loss leader** *Lockangebot* – [22] **to spin sth.** to present information or a situation in a particular way, especially one that makes you or your ideas seem good; *etw. drehen, wenden* – [23] **altruistic** *selbstlos* – [24] **soylent green** reference to a 1973 American dystopian science fiction film in which mankind survives on a food called Soylent Green, said to be made of high-energy plankton (but really made of people) – [25] **hence** therefore – [26] **to seed** to provide money to start a new company/business as an investment – [27] **resemblance** *Ähnlichkeit* – [28] **jillionaire** sb. who is indefinitely rich – [29] **unexposed** *nicht ausgesetzt sein* – [30] **homogeneity** [ˌhɒmədʒəˈneɪɪti] *Gleichartigkeit* – [31] **to conduct sth.** to do sth.

The other way of looking at Internet.org is the way Internet.org wants to be looked at: it's spreading Internet access because the Internet makes people's lives better. It improves the economy and enhances[32] education and
105 leads to better health outcomes. In February, Deloitte[33] published a study – admittedly commissioned by Facebook – that found that in India alone, extending Internet access from its current level, 15%, to a level comparable with that of more developed countries, say 75%,
110 would create 65 million jobs, cut cases of extreme poverty by 28% and reduce infant mortality by 85,000 deaths per year. Bottom line, this isn't about money; it's about creating wealth and saving lives. [...]

Universal Internet access has, like Facebook, some of the feel of manifest destiny. The tipping point[34] is al-
115 ready past[35], digital threads[36] are woven too deeply into human life. We can't go back, only forward. [...]

TIME, 15 December 2014, pp. 34 ff.

TIME and the TIME logo are registered trademarks of Time Inc. used under license.

COMPREHENSION

1. In a **first reading**, try to get **a general understanding** of Mark Zuckerberg's plan and its possible impact.

2. **While reading** the text a second time, complete the statements below using evidence from the article:
   a) Internet.org is about …
   b) Facebook is a social entity which …
   c) Offering Internet access for free means …
   d) Facebook is techno-colonialism because …
   e) Facebook's objective is to …

3. Summarize the article in about 200 – 250 words, juxtaposing the positive and negative aspects of "wiring the world" as depicted in the text.
   → Focus on Skills, Writing a Summary, p. 429

   Tip: Before writing the summary, copy the grid and complete it:

positive aspects	negative aspects
● enhancing education …	● luring people into (useless) consumption …
● …	● …

ANALYSIS

4. Examine the author's stance on the matter and categorize the article by explaining the effect and function of
   ● the author's choice of words*,
   ● his use of rhetorical devices*,
   ● his line of argument*.
   → Focus on Facts, Basic Types of Non-Fictional Texts, p. 396
   → Focus on Skills, Analysis of a Non-Fictional Text, p. 405

5. Compare your results from the awareness task and the data in the map (p. 356) with the information given in the article about Facebook's "mission".
   What might be interesting and unique about the people and countries that have not been "wired" so far?
   → Focus on Skills, Analysis of Statistical Data, p. 408

---

[32] **to enhance sth.** to improve the quality of sth. – [33] **Deloitte** one of the largest professional services companies – [34] **tipping point** a time during a process when an important decision has to be made – [35] **past** gone by in time – [36] **thread** Faden

6. In groups, discuss Lev Grossman's allegations (*Unterstellungen, Behauptungen*) that
   a) Facebook "spins" its true objectives,
   b) Facebook's "campaign is really an act of self-serving techno-colonialism" (ll. 71 f.).
   → Focus on Language, Conversation and Discussion, p. 413

7. Imagine you are a citizen of one of the countries presented in the map and do not have access to the Internet.
You have heard about the Internet.org initiative, and now you want to respond to the article.
First, choose a country, then write a letter to the editor* in which you either
   a) approve of Facebook's plan and the steps taken by Internet.org **or**
   b) disapprove of the project and express concern about its possible negative impact.
   → Focus on Skills, Writing a Letter to the Editor, p. 431

Afterwards, read out your letters in class and discuss the hopes and concerns expressed by the citizens.
   → Focus on Language, Conversation and Discussion, p. 413

Dave Eggers
The Circle

Dave Egger's 2013 novel follows the career of recent college graduate Mae Holland at the Internet company the Circle, beginning with her first day of work. Starting out in customer services, Mae quickly climbs the company ladder by unreservedly (*vorbehaltslos*) accepting and internalizing the company's mottos "secrets are lies", "sharing is caring" and "privacy is theft".
One of the company's technological inventions, called "SeeChange", are light, portable cameras which provide real-time videos all day long and are worn, for example, by politicians wishing to be "transparent" to the public, i. e. showing that they are honest and reliable.
In groups, speculate about the above-mentioned mottos and their implications, especially with regard to the company's main focus and field of work, the Internet.

My God, Mae thought. It's heaven.
The campus was vast and rambling, wild with Pacific color, and yet the smallest detail had been carefully considered, shaped by the most eloquent[1] hands. [...]
5 Mae was making her way through all of this, walking from the parking lot to the main hall, trying to look as if she belonged. The walkway wound[2] around lemon and orange trees and its quiet red cobblestones were replaced, occasionally, by tiles[3] with imploring messages of inspiration. "Dream," one said, the word laser-cut 10 into the red stone. "Participate," said another. There were dozens: "Find Community." "Innovate." "Imagine." She just missed stepping on the hand of a young man in a grey jumpsuit[4]; he was installing a new stone that said "Breathe." [...] 15
Ty Gospodinov, the Circle's boy-wonder visionary, was wearing nondescript[5] glasses and an enormous hoodie[6], staring leftward and smiling; he seemed to be enjoying

---

[1] **eloquent** able to express a feeling – [2] **to wind** (wound, wound) *sich winden, schlängeln* – [3] **tile** *Fliese, Kachel* – [4] **jumpsuit** *Overall* –
[5] **nondescript** very ordinary – [6] **hoodie** *Kapuze*

some moment, alone, tuned[7] into some distant frequen-
cy. People said he was borderline Asperger's[8], and the
picture seemed intent[9] on underscoring[10] the point.
With his black unkempt[11] hair, his unlined face, he
looked no more than twenty-five. [...]

Ty had devised the initial system, the Unified Operating System, which combined everything online that
had heretofore[12] been separate and sloppy[13] – users' social media profiles, their payment systems, their various passwords, their email accounts, user names, preferences, every last tool and manifestation of their
interests. The old way – a new transaction, a new system, for every site, for every purchase[14] – it was like
getting into a different car to run any one kind of errand[15]. "You shouldn't have to have eighty-seven different cars," he'd said, later, after his system had overtaken
the web and the world.

Instead, he put all of it, all of every user's needs and
tools, into one pot and invented TruYou – one account,
one identity, one password, one payment system, per
person. There were no more passwords, no multiple
identities. Your devices knew who you were, and your
one identity – the *TruYou*, unbendable[16] and unmaska-
ble – was the person paying, signing up, responding,
viewing and reviewing, seeing and being seen. You had
to use your real name, and this was tied to your credit
cards, your bank, and thus paying for anything was
simple. One button for the rest of your life online.

To use any of the Circle's tools, and they were the best
tools, the most dominant and ubiquitous[17] and free,
you had to do so as yourself, as your actual self, as
your TruYou. The era of false identities, identity theft,
multiple user names, complicated passwords and payment systems was over. Anytime you wanted to see
anything, use anything, comment on anything or buy
anything, it was one button, one account, everything
tied together and trackable and simple, all of it opera-
ble via mobile and laptop, tablet or retinal[18]. Once you
had a single account, it carried you through every corner of the web, every portal, every pay site, everything
you wanted to do.

TruYou changed the internet, in toto[19], within a year.
Though some sites were resistant at first, and free-in-
ternet advocates shouted about the right to be anonymous online, the TruYou wave was tidal[20] and crushed
all meaningful opposition. It started with the commerce sites. Why would any non-porn site want anonymous users when they could know exactly who had
come through the door? Overnight, all comment boards
became civil, all posters held accountable. The trolls[21],
who had more or less overtaken the internet, were driv-
en back into the darkness.

And those who wanted or needed to track the movements of consumers online had found their Valhalla[22]:
the actual buying habits of actual people were now
eminently mappable and measurable, and the marketing to those actual people could be done with surgical[23]
precision. Most TruYou users, most internet users who
simply wanted simplicity, efficiency, a clean and
streamlined experience, were thrilled with the results.
No longer did they have to memorize twelve identities
and passwords; no longer did they have to tolerate the
madness and rage of the anonymous hordes; no longer
did they have to put up with buckshot[24] marketing that
guessed, at best, within a mile of their desires. Now the
messages they did get were focused and accurate and,
most of the time, even welcome.

[...] Mae knew that she never wanted to work – never
wanted to be – anywhere else. Her hometown, and the
rest of California, the rest of America, seemed like some
chaotic mess in the developing world. Outside the walls
of the Circle, all was noise and struggle, failure and
filth[25]. But here, all had been perfected. The best people
had made the best systems and the best systems had
reaped[26] funds, unlimited funds, that made possible this,
the best place to work. And it was natural that it was so,
Mae thought. Who else but utopians could make utopia?

from *The Circle* by Dave Eggers. Alfred Knopf, New York 2013, pp. 1 ff.

---

[7] **to tune in to sth.** *sich auf etw. einstellen* – [8] **Asperger syndrome** an autism spectrum disorder characterized by difficulties with social interaction and nonverbal communication – [9] **intent** having an intention to do sth. – [10] **to underscore** to emphasize – [11] **unkempt** *ungekämmt* – [12] **heretofore** (*fml.*) before this point in time – [13] **sloppy** lacking care – [14] **purchase** sth. that you buy – [15] **errand** *Besorgung* – [16] **unbendable** *unbeugsam* – [17] **ubiquitous** [juːˈbɪkwɪtəs] (*fml.*) *allgegenwärtig* – [18] **retinal** virtual retinal display: a technology whereby an image is projected directly into the eyes – [19] **in toto** (*lat., fml.*) as a total or whole – [20] **tidal** [ˈtaɪdəl] *wie eine Flut* – [21] **troll** (*infml.*) a person who posts/sends things on the Internet deliberately to make other people angry – [22] **Valhalla** (*in ancient Scandinavian stories*) a palace in which some chosen men who had died in battle went to live with the god Odin forever; heaven, paradise – [23] **surgical** *chirurgisch* – [24] **buckshot** *Schrotmunition* – [25] **filth** thick unpleasant dirt – [26] **to reap** to make big profit

COMPREHENSION

1. Read the introductory part (ll. 1–15) and the last part (ll. 86–95) of the text:
   - What is Mae's impression of the Circle?
   - What differences does she perceive between the Circle and "the rest of America"?

2. Now, read the main part of the excerpt (ll. 16–85) and describe how people used the Internet *before* and *after* the installation of the "unified operating system" TruYou.

before TruYou	after TruYou
various passwords	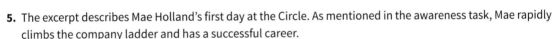 combining and connecting everything online
different …	…
…	…

ANALYSIS

3. Compare the concept of *TruYou* to Michael Grunwald's description of "The Second Age of Reason" and people's "Internet-optimizing" (p. 345). What similarities and disparities can you find?

4. Most parts of the excerpt could serve as a script for a commercial or advertising campaign promoting the Circle, its inventions and objectives.
   Find evidence from the text that supports this thesis, paying particular attention to stylistic, structural and rhetorical devices.
   → Focus on Skills, Analysis of a Fictional Text, p. 402

ACTIVITIES

5. The excerpt describes Mae Holland's first day at the Circle. As mentioned in the awareness task, Mae rapidly climbs the company ladder and has a successful career.
   In a group, use the clues given in the introduction and the excerpt and add a further (part of a) chapter. Think about other characters, inventions or a specific incident on the Circle campus. Imagine how the story might go on. Your texts can be utopian or dystopian.

   Finally, read/act out your texts in class and evaluate your continuations of the novel.
   → Focus on Skills, Continuation of a Fictional Text, p. 420

6. Do a project and watch the 2012 American drama film *Disconnect* which illustrates the negative sides of modern communication technologies such as social networking, cyber-bullying and identity theft.
   Prepare a presentation on the film's plot and related topics for your class.
   → Focus on Skills, Presentations, p. 419

Webcode SNG-40235-037 @ **Tip:** As a first step, watch the trailer of the film provided on the webcode.

7. Against the backdrop of global terrorism and terrorist threats, governments worldwide, in addition to companies and organizations, are also interested in collecting information about citizens.
   Do research on the Internet and collect information on these aspects:
   - the storage of
     – location data,   – call detail records,   – telephony,   – Internet traffic and transaction data,
   - traffic analysis and surveillance,
   - data retention/data preservation (*Vorratsdatenspeicherung*).

   Prepare short presentations on the respective topics and exchange your findings in class.

Andreas Gruhn

Daten sind das Öl des 21. Jahrhunderts

AWARENESS

In a Think! Pair! Share! activity, reflect on and discuss the headline of this text.
What makes "Big Data" as important as or even more important than oil in the 21st century?

Ein Gespenst geht um in der digitalen Welt, und sein Name birgt Verheißung[1] und Verdammnis[2] zugleich. Big Data heißt es, und es macht möglich, wovon die Menschheit ziemlich lange geträumt hat: Der Blick in
5 die Zukunft auf Grundlage der Analyse riesiger Datenmengen erlaubt die Optimierung der Welt, wie sie ein Unternehmen gerne hätte. Vereinfacht gesagt: Big Data macht das Wetter nicht besser, aber es sorgt dafür, dass die Menschen immer optimal ausgestattet sind für das
10 Wetter in den nächsten Stunden. Und das ist vielen unheimlich wie ein Gespenst.

Aber: Was ist so schlimm daran, wenn ein Navigationsgerät[3] genau weiß, wo wie viele Autos auf welcher Strecke zu meinem Ziel unterwegs sind und wie schnell
15 sie fahren? Warum soll die Verbreitung[4] einer Erkältung[5] nicht über die Häufung[6] von Foreneinträgen[7] im Netz zum Thema Halsschmerzen[8] vorhergesagt werden? Wo liegt das Problem, wenn der Supermarkt weiß, dass in einem Stadtteil viele Menschen im Internet
20 nach Tipps zum Grillen suchen – und dann eben mehr Fleisch als sonst in der Kühltruhe bereit liegt? Bisher mussten das Marktforschungsunternehmen[9] aufwendig herausfinden, künftig reicht ein einziger Datenanalyst. Denn die Informationen hat die Masse ja bereit-
25 willig zur Verfügung gestellt. Vor allem bei Gesundheit, Sicherheit und Verkehr sorgt eine kleine gelieferte Datenmenge des Einzelnen für eine Verbesserung für die Allgemeinheit.

Big Data ist aber Fluch und Segen zugleich. Ein hoch-
30 rangiger Google-Vertreter bekannte[10] neulich, es werde für Nutzer künftig immer schwerer, Angebote zu erhalten, die nicht auf sie zugeschnitten[11] sind. Und Big-Data-Experte und Buchautor Viktor Mayer-Schönberger warnt: „Wir werden als Menschen immer vorhersehba-
35 rer[12]. Anhand der Daten lässt sich ablesen, wie wir denken und wie wir in der Zukunft handeln werden."

Für den Konsumenten wirken sich analysierte Daten so aus, als würde er mit Scheuklappen[13] durch ein Kaufhaus rennen. Zielgerichtet wird er aufmerksam
40 gemacht auf das, was er gerade braucht und das, was ihn interessiert. Auf der anderen Seite sieht er kaum mehr das, was abseits seines Regals auf ihn wartet, wonach er bisher einfach nicht gesucht hat. Die ureigenste[14] Eigenschaft der Internetnutzung wandert aus
45 der digitalen Welt in die Wirklichkeit: Der Mensch findet nichts mehr, er sucht nur noch. Das veranlasst einige Experten dazu, das Ende des Zufalls[15] über die Menschheit hereinbrechen[16] zu sehen. Die düsterste Vision: Algorithmen bestimmen die Lebenswelt des
50 Konsumenten und entscheiden, was er erlebt und konsumiert und was nicht. Die Welt wird eine Suchmaschine, und Daten sind ihr Öl. Das Öl des 21. Jahrhunderts.

Der Unterschied ist: Die Daten sprudeln[17] unendlich[18], ihre Quellen sind unerschöpflich[19], aber sie liegen an
55 allen Ecken und Enden des Internets. Nur wer sie geschickt zu verknüpfen versteht, der kann Zusammenhänge erkennen und nutzen, um sich einen Wettbewerbsvorteil zu verschaffen: Man ist der erste, der ein Produkt anbietet, das übermorgen gebraucht
60 wird. Man produziert keine Überschüsse mehr, die schon morgen kein Mensch mehr haben will – und minimiert so finanzielle Einbußen[20]. Für Geschäftsführungen sind aus der Datenanalyse gewonnene Erkenntnisse eine riesige Entscheidungshilfe. „Der
65 breite Einsatz von Big Data ist eine Frage der Wettbewerbsfähigkeit[21] der deutschen Wirtschaft", sagt Dieter Kempf, Präsident des IT-Branchenverbands Bitkom.

Digitale Wertschöpfung[22] heißt das – und steht in
70 Deutschland erst am Anfang. Rund zehn Prozent aller Unternehmen in Deutschland setzen bisher Big-Data-

---

[1] promise – [2] perdition – [3] GPS device – [4] spread of sth. – [5] cold – [6] accumulation – [7] entries on forums – [8] a sore throat – [9] market research company – [10] to admit sth. – [11] to tailor sth. to sb./sth. – [12] predictable – [13] blinkers – [14] innate – [15] coincidence – [16] to befall sb. – [17] to gush – [18] endlessly – [19] inexhaustibe – [20] losses – [21] competitiveness – [22] creation of value/added value

Lösungen ein, berichtet Bitkom. Doch ihr Anteil wird weiter steigen: Fast 31 Prozent haben konkrete Pläne,
75 dies künftig zu tun. Die Umsatz[23]-Vorhersagen[24] für den Markt überbieten sich im Jahresrhythmus. Nach einer Bitkom-Erhebung, die zur Computermesse Cebit im März veröffentlicht wurde, wird sich der Umsatz für Big-Data-Lösungen von 6,2 Milliarden Euro in diesem Jahr bis 2016 mehr als verdoppelt haben.

80 Dafür, dass es nicht noch schneller geht, haben die Unternehmen eine ganz einfache Erklärung: Es gibt nur zu wenig Spezialisten.

Rheinische Post, 10 August 2014, p. B3

COMPREHENSION

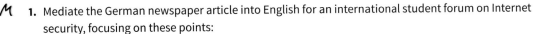

M **1.** Mediate the German newspaper article into English for an international student forum on Internet security, focusing on these points:
- Big Data and the optimization of people's lives
- the practical use of Big Data
- risks and threats of Big Data for consumers
- how to use Big Data efficiently and productively
- plans of German companies to use Big Data
→ Focus on Skills, Mediation, p. 412

ANALYSIS

M **2.** Additionally, mediate the bar chart on the following page and explain the expected potentials and business revenues (*Erträge*) in connection with Big Data.
→ Focus on Skills, Mediation, p. 412
→ Focus on Skills, Analysis of Statistical Data, p. 408

Step 1: Contrast the assumed advantages and benefits of collecting and using people's data to possible risks. Copy the grid below and complete it.

benefits	risks
• coordinating traffic and preventing traffic jams • preventing food shortages or waste of food • …	• manipulation of consumers' shopping habits • limitation of … • …

Step 2: Discuss in class:
a) Does the analysis and use of people's data really lead to the "optimization of the world"? (compare also: "the loss of serendipity", Students' Book, p. 345, ll. 64 ff.).
b) Do the assumed benefits of Big Data justify the risks and disadvantages?
→ Focus on Language, Conversation and Discussion, p. 413

3. Relate the list of examples and alleged advantages to the excerpt from Dave Egger's novel *The Circle* (pp. 359 f.) in which the benefits of *TruYou* are presented.
To what extent do the two "visions" match?
→ Focus on Skills, Analysis of a Non-Fictional Text, p. 405
→ Focus on Skills, Analysis of a Fictional Text, p. 402

[23] sales/turnover – [24] prediction/forecast

ACTIVITIES

4. Divide the class into groups and work creatively with the information you collected on Big Data and their possible (ab-)use.

Imagine scenarios in which, for example, consumers want to go shopping in a mall or supermarket for fun or relaxation but are constantly guided or lured into certain shops or to certain products based on the analysis of their personal data.

Write a short scene or story in which you include dialogues*, interior monologues*, etc.
Your texts can be funny, ironic or scary and threatening. Additionally, you can use props and details to flesh out the action.

Finally, read and/or act out your texts in class and discuss the different views taken.

GRAMMAR / LANGUAGE

5. Together with a partner, compile a flyer in which you promote the collection of "Big Data" and the potential value this adds to people's lives.

Use **future tenses** (will-future, going-to future) and **conditional sentences** to depict the advantages of "Big Data" for people's future lives.

Examples:
- Customers will not have to waste their precious time looking for bargains and special offers because …
- If retailers are able to predict customers' wishes and needs, they will …

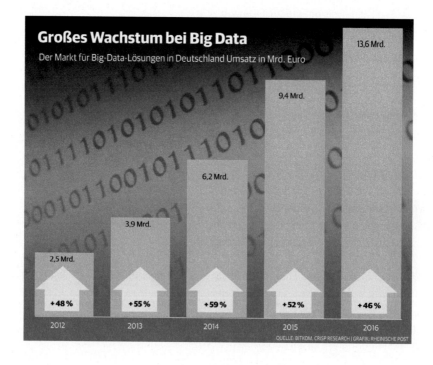

Spying Everywhere on Everyone? – (Social) Media and Networks

Alexandra Suich

Little Brother

COMPREHENSION

1. **Before reading:**
   Divide the class into groups, with 1–2 groups working with <u>one</u> of the three diagrams.
   Then take a look at the charts below and identify
   - the importance of different media with regard to advertising spending in the US,
   - the Internet-advertising spending on certain media globally,
   - users' time spent daily on different media.
   → Focus on Skills, Analysis of Statistical Data, p. 408

Each group should prepare a short presentation of their findings to the class and explain the most relevant data and trends.
   → Focus on Skills, Presentations, p. 419

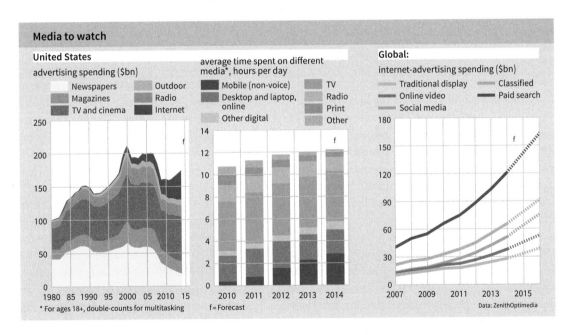

Media to watch

[...] The world wide web turned 25 in March [2014], and the first banner ad[1] on it ran 20 years ago, but until a few years ago advertising on the internet did not add up to much. That has changed. Last year online adver-
5 tising made up about a quarter of the $500 billion global advertising business, and it is rising fast. Some of the 21st century's most powerful companies, including Google, emerged[2] on the back of[3] it. Companies that used to flourish in pre-digital advertising have strug-
10 gled to keep up. "Media used to be based on scarce[4] dis-

---

[1] **banner ad** an advertisement that appears across the top of a page on the Internet or in the newspaper – [2] **to emerge** to appear –
[3] **on the back of sth.** soon after an earlier success, as the result of it – [4] **scarce** *mangelnd*

tribution[5]," says Dave Morgan, an internet veteran and the boss of Simulmedia, a television-advertising company. By contrast, online advertising space is unlimited and prices are low, so making money is not as easy as it was in the offline world, even for digital natives such as Yahoo.

All the same, new entrants[6] continue to join the fray[7], enticed[8] by the big opportunities they see as well as by the falling cost of starting digital-media businesses. According to eMarketer, a research firm, Americans spend over 12 hours a day consuming media (sometimes concurrently[9]), and digital media account for around half of that total.

Digital advertising is being buoyed[10] by three important trends. The first is the rise of mobile devices, such as smartphones and tablets, which began when Apple introduced the iPhone in 2007. Now more than 1.7 billion people (around 20 % of the world's population) use smartphones.

Mobile devices, which are intimately connected to their owners, have changed the way in which people travel the internet. Users now prefer apps (self-contained programmes on smartphones) to websites' home pages, and in America they are spending less time on desktop computers. "It took 150 years for the newspaper industry to contract[11]," says Meredith Kopit Levien, head of advertising for the *New York Times*. "The desktop industry will contract because of mobile in a tenth of that time." [...]

The Economist, 13 September 2014, Special Report Advertising and Technology, pp. 3 ff.

The World Wild Web

"Have you ever clicked your mouse right here?" asked the first banner advertisement in 1994. "You will," it confidently predicted. These days advertisers are feeling less certain of themselves. They are still trying to come to grips[1] with the radical changes technology has brought to the way advertising is consumed, sold and personalized[2].

If technology can help advertising become more relevant, clever and innovative, that is worth celebrating. Firms such as Facebook, which gives each consumer a different landing page[3] with updates about their friends, and Google, which tailors[4] search results to what the system knows about the user, have shown that personalised content can have great appeal. The same idea might work for advertising.

But advertisers and data firms have to be careful. When consumers sign up for services like Facebook and Google, they have a fair idea that information about them might be used in all kinds of ways, though few of them are aware of how much tracking goes on. Yet when online data are gathered by third parties, making it possible to target ads across the web, it is often done without consumers' consent[5] or knowledge and with few, if any, checks and balances.

Brand[6] owners are trying to harness[7] technology to help them understand their customers better without making them feel they are being spied on. The boundaries are shifting all the time. In "Minority Report", a science-fiction film with Tom Cruise made in 2002, screens recognise people's eyes and show ads tailored to particular individuals. That no longer seems all that outlandish[8]. Conversely[9], web users have adjusted their online behaviour in response to revelations[10] about government spying made by Edward Snowden, who used to work for America's National Security Administration and subsequently[11] leaked[12] large quantities of documents. According to one study, people are now less likely to search for sensitive information online. [...]

A study by BCG[13] suggests it is a myth that youngsters are more comfortable than older people with sensitive data about them being collected online. The privacy of personal data remains a big concern for around 75 % of consumers in most countries. American and European

---

[5] **distribution** [ˌdɪstrɪ'bjuːʃən] *Verteilung* – [6] **entrant** *Teilnehmer* – [7] **fray** *Schlachtgewühl* – [8] **to entice** [ɪn'taɪs] *jdn. locken* – [9] **concurrent** happening or existing at the same time – [10] **to buoy** [bɔɪ] to support – [11] **to contract** to become generally smaller

[1] **to come to grips** *mit etw. zurechtkommen* – [2] **to personalize** to make sth. suitable for the needs of a particular person – [3] **landing page** a web page that customers are taken to when they click on a link or online advertisement – [4] **to tailor** *etw. auf jdn. zuschneiden* – [5] **consent** permission or agreement – [6] **brand** *Marke* – [7] **to harness** to control sth., usually to use its power – [8] **outlandish** strange and unusual – [9] **conversely** *umgekehrt* – [10] **revelation** *Enthüllung* – [11] **subsequent** *nachfolgend* – [12] **to leak** here: to allow secret information to become generally known – [13] **BCG** (*abbr.*) The Boston Consulting Group; a global management consulting company

consumers share similar views about online privacy – although their respective regulators[14] do not.

Gathering and sharing data will become ever more complex as more digital devices collect information about users and more media connect to the internet. Consumers already trust their mobile devices with written communications, credit-card details, personal apps and more, and will continue to use them for ever more online purchases[15]. The coming internet of things, which will connect objects ranging from fridges to shoes to the web, will complicate things even more because it will generate[16] vast additional quantities of personal information. [...]

That makes it all the more important to set up a system of rules for online data collection and advertising. Christopher Soghoian, a privacy activist, suggests that consumers could start a "fair data" movement, in the vein[17] of "fair trade" campaigns. They could support firms with transparent and ethical policies on data-sharing, privacy and security, in the same way that they might choose to give their business to firms that were considerate to their employees and to the environment. Verizon[18], a wireless company, recently launched a programme offering subscribers[19] discounts and other deals if they agree to share information, such as browsing activity and location, and accept that it will be used for targeted advertising.

In future there might be two options for targeted advertising, says Clement Tsang, an online-advertising executive in China, just as there is now talk of creating a two-tier[20] internet, with a free slower version and a paid-for faster one. Consumers could continue to get free services from Facebook, Google and others on the understanding that their personal data will be collected and used; or they could pay a monthly fee to ensure the site did not track them. [...]

The Economist, September 13 – 19, 2014, Special Report Advertising and Technology, p. 16

COMPREHENSION

2. In September 2014, the British magazine *The Economist* published an extensive special report on how advertising is used in the new media and technologies.

Step 1: Read the texts **a first time** and try to get a general understanding.

Step 2: While reading the articles **a second time**, find passages in the texts that refer to these issues:
- the consumption of media in the US
- new media and devices and user habits
- spying and surveillance of users
- the two-tier Internet
- the conversion of pre-digital advertising into digital formats
- tailoring and personalizing of advertising
- privacy and fair data

ANALYSIS

3. Examine the authors' choice of words* in connection with
 a) the advertising business and its objectives and strategies,
 b) the consumers and their concerns and rights.
 Explain what this reveals about his/her stance on the matter.

 Examples:
 - text 1, ll. 6 ff.: Some of the ... <u>most powerful</u> companies <u>emerged on the back</u> of ...
   → superlatives; exploitation of others ...
 - text 1, ll. 13 ff.: ... online advertising space is unlimited ... prices are low ...
   → endless possibilities; consumers can get swamped (*überhäuft werden mit etw.*) ...
 - → Focus on Skills, Analysis of a Non-Fictional Text, p. 405

[14] **regulator** *Regulierungsbehörde* – [15] **purchase** sth. that you buy – [16] **to generate** to produce sth. – [17] **vein** a particular style or manner – [18] **Verizon** [vərˈaɪzən] an American broadband and telecommunications company – [19] **subscriber** *Abonnent* – [20] **tier** [tɪər] one of several layers or levels

4. Throughout the article, the author tries to encourage readers and give them the impression that
   a) advertising companies are not as powerful and influential as they might appear
   b) Internet users are not just ignorant victims that fall prey to companies' tricks.
   Detect examples in the text that support this.

   Examples:
   - text 1, ll. 8 ff.: … companies that used to flourish … have struggled … → …
   - text 2, ll. 4 f.: … they are still trying to come to grips … → …

ACTIVITIES

5. In the concluding paragraph ot text 2 the author refers to the "two-tier internet" (l. 75) for which consumers "could pay a monthly fee to ensure the site did not track them" (ll. 79 f.).

Discuss this suggestion made by a Chinese online-advertising executive.
Should consumers pay companies like Google and Facebook in order to not be spied on?
→ Focus on Language, Conversation and Discussion, p. 413

6. The author of text 2 states that "it is a myth that youngsters are more comfortable than older people with sensitive data …" (ll. 40 ff.).

Being a youngster yourself, write a letter to the editor in response to the concerns and suggestions expressed in the article.
→ Focus on Skills, Writing a Letter to the Editor, p. 431

@   **7.** Do research on the Internet and collect cartoons on
   - Internet security,
   - the NSA spying scandal,
   - governments spying on their citizens,
   - violations of citizens' privacy worldwide.

Display the cartoons in class and compare the different views taken on the matter by international cartoonists.

8. Study article 12 of the *Universal Declaration of Human Rights* (→ FoD, p. 304) and explain its implications with regard to
   a) governments spying on citizens and
   b) companies collecting data from customers.

means of communication		
to access sth.; (to have) access to sth. [ˈækses]	to find information, esp. using a computer; to have a computer, a car, etc. that you can use	*auf etw. zugreifen; Zugang (zu etw. haben)*
blog; blogger	web log, a web page containing information or opinions from a particular person or about a particular subject, to which new information is added regularly; sb. who writes a blog	*Blog (das, der); Blogger*
to broadcast (broadcast, broadcast)	to send out radio or television programmes	*ausstrahlen, senden*
cell phone	mobile phone	*Handy*
to communicate with sb.	to exchange information, news, ideas, etc. with sb.	*kommunizieren*
to connect; connected (to)	to join two or more things together; to be joined to a large system or network	*verbinden; verbunden (mit)*
cyberbullying [ˈsaɪbəˌbʊliɪŋ]	the activity of sending Internet or text messages to insult or threaten sb.	*Cybermobbing*
to design a website	to create or develop a website	*eine Internetseite erstellen*
digital traffic	the number of people who have clicked or used a website	*Zahl der Besucher einer Website; Datenverkehr*
to distribute sth. via the Internet	to share things, e. g. news, among a group of people (using the Internet), esp. in a planned way	*etw. (über das Internet) ver-breiten*
podcast	a digital medium consisting of a series of audio files users can download or stream to a mobile device	*Podcast (der)*
to post sth. online	to put sth. on a website	*im Internet veröffentlichen*
on the net	on the Internet	*im Internet*
(online) privacy [ˈprɪvəsi, *BE*; ˈpraɪvəsi, *US*]	the state of being free from the attention of others (when using the Internet)	*Privatsphäre im Internet*
to reply (replied, replied); reply	to answer; an answer	*antworten; Antwort*
to revolutionize sth.	to completely change the way that sth. is done	*umwälzen, revolutionieren*
search engine	a computer programme that searches the Internet for information	*Suchmaschine*
search term	a term/word which you enter in a search engine	*Suchbegriff*
to share	to let sb. have/use sth. that belongs to you; to tell others about your ideas, opinions, etc.	*etw. teilen; mitteilen*
smart phone	a mobile phone with an operating system	*Smartphone*
social networking (service)	a platform people can use to share their ideas and opinions and to stay in contact	*soziales Netzwerk(en); soziales Vernetztsein*
source of information	the place where sb. finds information	*Informationsquelle*
to subscribe	to pay money regularly to become a member of an organization, or to use a service regularly	*sich bei etw. anmelden; etw. abonnieren*
to text (message)	to send someone a written message on a mobile device	*SMS schreiben*
wireless communication	a system of sending and receiving signals that does not use wires	*drahtlose Kommunikation*
electronic and digital media		
(targeted) advertising	the activity of telling the public about a product or service in order to persuade them to buy it (aiming at a particular group of potential customers)	*(gezielte) Werbung*
app(lication)	a software designed to perform operations on computers or mobile devices	*Anwendungssoftware*
audio file	a file on a computer in which sound data are stored	*Audiodatei*
to collect data	to gather information	*Daten sammeln*

compatibility [kəmˌpætəˈbɪlɪti]	the ability of computers and programmes to be used together	*Verträglichkeit, Kompatibilität*
computer-literate (*adj.*)	able to use a computer	*sich mit Computern auskennen; wissen, wie man einen Computer bedient*
data [ˈdeɪtə, ˈdɑːtə]	facts or information, esp. when examined and used to find out things or to make decisions	*Daten*
data preservation	the activity of storing data for later use or analysis	*Vorratsdatenspeicherung*
data protection	the act of guaranteeing that personally identifiable information is safe from being exposed	*Datenschutz*
data theft	the act of stealing data	*Datendiebstahl*
GPS	global positioning system	*Globales Positionsbestimmungssystem*
interactive media systems	media systems which allow information to be passed continuously and in both directions between the system/computer and the person using it	*interaktive Medien*
to invade sb.'s privacy	to affect sb.'s privacy in an unpleasant or annoying way	*in jds. Privatsphäre eindringen*
to spy	to secretly collect information	*spionieren, ausspähen*
to track	to search for sb. by following the marks they leave behind them	*jdn. verfolgen*
to transfer data	to move information from one place to another	*Daten übertragen*
virtual	made, done, seen on the Internet or on a computer, rather than in the real world; artificial	*virtuell, nicht real, künstlich*
virus [ˈvaɪrəs]	instructions hidden in a computer programme, designed to cause faults or destroy data	*Computervirus*
online journalism		
24/7 news cycle (*infml.*)	when news stories are investigated and reported all day and all night long, at a very fast pace	*Nachrichten rund um die Uhr*
breaking news	a special report on an important topic, usually interrupting the regular programme	*Eilmeldung*
to comment on sth.	to express an opinion about sb. or sth.	*etw. kommentieren*
infographic	visual representation of data or information in the form of charts, maps, etc.	*Infografik*
news agency	an organization that collects news stories and supplies them to newspapers, radio stations, etc.	*Presseagentur*
newsfeed	a way of providing online readers with constantly updated news	*Nachrichteneinspeisung*
newsworthy	important or interesting enough to be reported	*berichtenswert*
paywall	a system asking readers to pay for content that is available online, e. g. on the website of a newspaper	*Bezahlschranke*
press coverage	when a subject or event is reported in the media	*Berichterstattung*
to quote; quotation	to repeat exactly what someone else has said or written; a sentence or phrase from a book, speech, etc. which you repeat e. g. in a piece of writing	*zitieren; Zitat*
short attention span	the period of time during which you continue to be interested in sth. is not very long	*kurze Aufmerksamkeitsspanne*
sound bite	a very short part of a speech or statement, esp. one made by a politician, that is broadcast on a news programme	*kurzes, prägnantes Zitat*
responsibility of the media/post-truth realities		
allegation	a statement, made without giving proof, that sb. has done something wrong or illegal	*Beschuldigung, Unterstellung*

alternative facts	a phrase used by U.S. Counselor to the President Kelly-anne Conway during a Meet the Press interview on 22 January 2017, in which she defended then White House Press Secretary Sean Spicer's (false) statement about the attendance numbers at Donald Trump's presidential inauguration ceremony	*alternative Fakten (→ Lügen)*
assertion	sth. a person claims to be true	*Behauptung*
biased ['baɪəst]	showing an unreasonable like or dislike for a person based on personal opinions	*voreingenommen*
to bombard sb. with sth.	to attack sb. with a lot of questions, criticisms, etc. or by giving them too much information	*jdn. mit etw. bombardieren*
bot	robot, automatic computer program	*Bot; selbstständig arbeitendes Computerprogramm*
cyberwar	warfare using computer hacking and the Internet	*virtuelle Kriegsführung*
to expose sb. to sth.	to make it likely that someone will experience something harmful or unpleasant	*jdn. etw. aussetzen*
fake news	false stories that appear to be news, spread on the Internet or using other media, usually created to influence political views or as a joke	*Falschnachricht*
gutter press	newspapers that pay more attention to shocking stories about crime and sex than to serious matters	*Boulevardpresse*
hate mail	unpleasant or cruel letters from someone who dislikes you	*Hassmail*
hate-mongering	creating hatred	*Hass predigen*
to incite sth.	to encourage sb. to do or feel sth. unpleasant or violent	*zu etw. aufhetzen*
manipulation; to be manipulated	controlling sb. or sth. to your own advantage, often unfairly or dishonestly	*Manipulation; Beeinflussung*
to misinform sb.	to tell sb. information that is not correct	*jdn. fehlinformieren*
post-truth (politics)	a political culture in which debate is framed largely by appeals to emotion disconnected from the details of policy	*postfaktisch*
to play on sb.'s emotions	to manipulate sb.'s emotions to achieve a certain effect	*mit jds. Gefühlen spielen*
the public's right to know sth.	relating to laws or policies that make certain government or company data and records available to any individual who wants or needs to know their contents; the freedom of the press to inform the public about this	*das Recht der Öffentlichkeit auf Information über etw.*
to scapegoat sb.	to blame a person for everything bad, though it is not their fault	*jdn. zum Sündenbock abstempeln*
to screen out	to prevent sth. from passing through; to filter out	*etw. ausfiltern*
shit storm	in German, the term is used as a loanword and refers more specifically to a sudden, massive outburst of negative criticism on social media	*Shitstorm*
smear/hate campaign	a planned attempt to harm the reputation of a person or company by telling lies about them	*Hetzkampagne*
source of information	sb. or sth. that supplies information	*Informationsquelle*
subversive	trying to destroy or damage sth., especially an established political system	*subversiv; umstürzlerisch*
target group	the particular group of people that an advertisement is intended to reach	*Zielgruppe*
twitterstorm	a sudden large increase in the number of tweets (= messages) about a particular subject on Twitter	*ein Twittersturm*

Find more vocabulary on Focus on Facts, The Press (p. 398) and Focus on Facts, The Media (p. 351).

Focus on Vocab

Shakespeare: Such Stuff As Dreams Are Made On ...

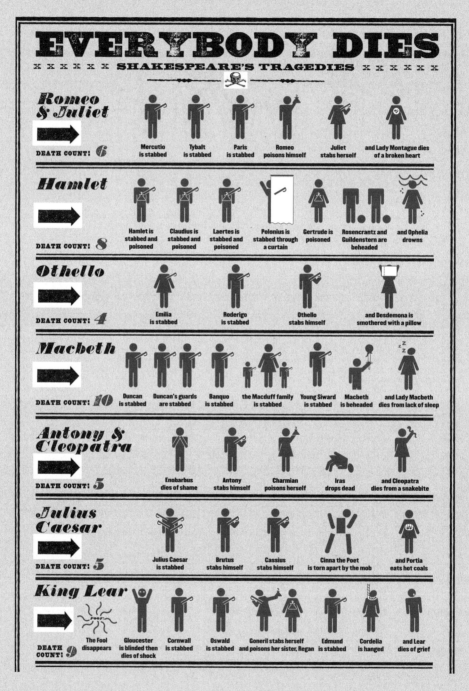

EVERYBODY DIES

x x x x x **SHAKESPEARE'S TRAGEDIES** x x x x x

Romeo & Juliet

DEATH COUNT: **6**

| Mercutio is stabbed | Tybalt is stabbed | Paris is stabbed | Romeo poisons himself | Juliet stabs herself | and Lady Montague dies of a broken heart |

Hamlet

DEATH COUNT: **8**

| Hamlet is stabbed and poisoned | Claudius is stabbed and poisoned | Laertes is stabbed and poisoned | Polonius is stabbed through a curtain | Gertrude is poisoned | Rosencrantz and Guildenstern are beheaded | and Ophelia drowns |

Othello

DEATH COUNT: **4**

| Emilia is stabbed | Roderigo is stabbed | Othello stabs himself | and Desdemona is smothered with a pillow |

Macbeth

DEATH COUNT: **10**

| Duncan is stabbed | Duncan's guards are stabbed | Banquo is stabbed | the Macduff family is stabbed | Young Siward is stabbed | Macbeth is beheaded | and Lady Macbeth dies from lack of sleep |

Antony & Cleopatra

DEATH COUNT: **5**

| Enobarbus dies of shame | Antony stabs himself | Charmian poisons herself | Iras drops dead | and Cleopatra dies from a snakebite |

Julius Caesar

DEATH COUNT: **5**

| Julius Caesar is stabbed | Brutus stabs himself | Cassius stabs himself | Cinna the Poet is torn apart by the mob | and Portia eats hot coals |

King Lear

DEATH COUNT: **9**

| The Fool disappears | Gloucester is blinded then dies of shock | Cornwall is stabbed | Oswald is stabbed | Goneril stabs herself and poisons her sister, Regan | Edmund is stabbed | Cordelia is hanged | and Lear dies of grief |

Tips on vocab »»»

pictogram ■ **to stab sb.** *jdn. erstechen* ■ **dagger** *Dolch* ■ **to drown** *ertrinken* ■ **to smother sb.** *jdn. ersticken* ■ **shame** here: *Schande* ■ **to drop dead** *tot umfallen* ■ **grief** *Gram, Kummer*

START-UP ACTIVITIES

1. When William Shakespeare "turned 450" in April 2014, he was celebrated all over the world. Despite his age, Shakespeare himself as well as his work are still an icon in popular culture. In a round robin activity,
   a) give short statements on what you know about Shakespeare and his work,
   b) speculate about possible reasons for his undiminished popularity.

2. Divide the class into seven groups and assign each group one of the tragedies in the pictogram.
   - In a first step, try to identify the clues given in the respective graphic and speculate about
     a) the characters and b) the plot of the tragedy.
   - Usually, each of Shakespeare's plays focuses on a specific topic (→ FoF, p. 379) in connection with certain leitmotifs.

   In your groups, do research on your chosen tragedy and get an overview of
   a) the constellation of the main characters, b) the plot and c) the topic and relevant leitmotifs.

   - Prepare short presentations using your research results and the visual in the Students' Book.
   - Additionally, you can compile handouts which provide the most relevant information.
   → Focus on Skills, Presentations, p. 419
   → Focus on Skills, Writing a Handout, p. 425

3. Take a look at the cartoon above. Against the background of your results from task no. 2, discuss the lady's complaint: Are Shakespeare's plays a lineup of "sex and violence"?

4. Thomas Platter, a Swiss tourist, described his impressions of amusements and spectacles which he witnessed in London in 1599 in his diary.
   Listen to Thomas Platter's description of Elizabethan London and take notes on these aspects:
   - playhouses and theatres
   - ale-houses and beer gardens

5. Speculate on what made London a magnet for tourists and people of all kinds.
   Discuss in class.

Shakespeare: The World that Made Him

James Shapiro

Shakespeare's Professional World

During his career, William Shakespeare worked as a professional playwright, a professional actor and was also a share-holder[1] of a theatre company, which required business skills. What is your understanding of being "professional" – and which characteristics and qualifications should a "professional" author or playwright and actor have? Discuss in class.

For two decades, from 1594 until he stopped writing and acting around 1613, Shakespeare was one of eight or so shareholders in the Chamberlain's Men (renamed the King's Men after the accession[2] of James I in 1603).
5 The company was made up of veteran actors, most of whom had already worked with each other in compa-nies that had broken up and reformed in the early 1590s – including Strange's Men and Pembroke's Men (the vulnerable actors, always viewed with suspicion[3] by
10 London's city fathers, needed the official patronage and protection of noblemen). […]
Shakespeare and his fellow sharers spent their morn-ings rehearsing[4] and their afternoons performing alongside hired men and boys who were needed to fill
15 out the cast of approximately[5] fifteen. Except for a break during Lent[6] and the occasional closing of the theatres due to scandal or plague[7], performances went on all year round. As Elizabethan audiences expected a different play every day, actors had to master a score
20 of[8] new roles every year – as well as recall old favour-ites needed to flesh out the repertory. Shakespeare had the added pressure of providing his company with, on average, two new plays a year, though he tended to write plays in inspired bunches[9]. Other new plays were
25 acquired from a score of freelance dramatists who were paid on average £6 a play (at a time when a schoolmas-ter might earn £20 a year). What little free time Shake-speare had at the start and end of his working day must have been devoted to reading and writing. We know
30 that Shakespeare was still acting alongside his fellow sharers as late as 1603 […] and there is little evidence that he took time off to write. The unrelenting[10] sched-ule of rehearsing, performing, reading and writing was a punishing[11] one and may explain why Shakespeare stopped writing plays at the age of forty-nine – at the 35 height of his powers – and probably gave up full-time acting sometime before that. […]
For the duration of Shakespeare's career the Chamber-lain's/King's Men was a remarkably[12] profitable and stable company. […] 40
While some of the success of the Chamberlain's Men can be attributed to luck, timing, organization and sta-bility, much of it was a function of a raw talent[13]. No other company was nearly as successful. The Cham-berlain's/King's Men were blessed with the best play- 45 wright in the land, the best clowns, the most dramatic male leads[14] and the greatest depth. Though their names are lost to us, their boy actors, who played wom-en's parts for whom Shakespeare wrote such demand-ing roles as Juliet, Beatrice, Rosalind, Lady Macbeth 50 and Cleopatra – must have been exceptionally talented. […]
All plays had to be submitted to the Revels[15] Office for approval[16]. Once Shakespeare had finished writing and revising a play he would turn it over to a professional 55 scribe to prepare a clean copy to be vetted[17] by the au-thorities (the Master of the Revels was responsible for ensuring that staged plays contained nothing seditious[18] or otherwise offensive; censorship of printed works was under the supervision of the Archbishop of Canter- 60 bury and the Bishop of London). After the text of the play was authorized, it remained in the possession of the company and may have served as the playhouse promptbook[19]. A scribe would copy out on strips of pa-

---

[1] **shareholder** Teilhaber – [2] **accession** Thronbesteigung – [3] **suspicion** Argwohn – [4] **to rehearse** [rɪ'hɜːs] proben – [5] **approximately** circa –
[6] **Lent** Fastenzeit – [7] **plague** [pleɪg] Pest – [8] **a score of** many – [9] **in bunches** in Schüben – [10] **unrelenting** unaufhörlich – [11] **punishing** here:
kräftezehrend – [12] **remarkable** beachtlich – [13] **raw talent** Naturtalent – [14] **leads** [liːds] actors playing main parts in plays – [15] **Master of
the Revels** ['revlz] oberster Zensor/Aufsichtsbehörde – [16] **approval** Zustimmung, Erlaubnis – [17] **to vet** durchsehen – [18] **seditious** [sɪ'dɪʃes]
(fml.) aufwieglerisch – [19] **promptbook** Textbuch für den Souffleur

per the lines for each actor, which were then pasted together on a separate scroll[20] or roll (which is why we speak of actors learning their roles, from the French *role*). [...]

Over the course of his career Shakespeare performed many times at royal residences – including Richmond, Wilton, Hampton Court and especially Whitehall. These visits not only put him in the orbit of the court, with its gossip, faction[21] and intrigue[22], but also brought him into contact with some of the great collections of art in the realm[23]. Shakespeare was inspired both by what he read and by what he saw and heard, and much of what he experienced at court – from an ornate tapestry[24] of the 'murder' of Julius Cesar to sermons by leading preachers like Lancelot Andrews – had an impact on his work.

from *Searching for Shakespeare* by Tarnya Cooper. Yale University Press, New Haven 2006, pp. 23 ff.

COMPREHENSION

1. Give an outline of Shakespeare's multitasking career as a writer and actor.

2. Point out the economic pressure a theatre company faced and state what made Shakespeare's company exceptionally successful.

3. Describe the production process of a play/a printed work in Shakespeare's time.

ANALYSIS

4. What was Shakespeare's source of inspiration?

5. Explain the different tasks Shakespeare had to perform and manage simultaneously:
- rehearsing
- reading
- performing
- writing

Which personal and professional qualifications do these tasks require?

ACTIVITIES

6. Like in Shakespeare's times, today there is a lot of competition and playhouses are expected to stage new productions regularly in order to attract visitors.
Compare Shakespeare's professional world to the situation of an actor or playwright today. What similarities and differences regarding the work of theatres, actors and playwrights can you think of? Discuss in class.

@ **7.** Do research and find out about the theatrical productions and activities in your local theatres. Which attractions are they offering?
Bring printouts or brochures of their repertoires and playing schedules to class and compare them. Make rankings of plays that you would like to see and give reasons for your choice.

Webcode SNG-40235-038 @ **8.** Use the link on the webcode and do research on various Shakespeare productions by different international Shakespeare companies. What do the photos of the stage performances convey about the respective production companies' cultural backgrounds?

---

[20] **scroll** *Papierrolle* – [21] **faction** opposition, disagreement – [22] **intrigue** [ɪnˈtriːg] – [23] **realm** [relm] kingdom; *Reich* – [24] **ornate tapestry** *Wandteppich mit Ornamenten*

John Russell Brown

Onstage and Backstage (The Art of "Bewitching[1]" an Audience)

AWARENESS

Look at the visual on p. 378 and get an overview of the onstage and backstage facilities and features of a theatre during Shakespeare's time. Use your dictionaries and, in groups, describe the picture. Speculate and try to find out which modern theatre equipment and facilities that we use today did not exist back then.

Everyone is able to imagine a world of his own. You can sit at home in a room that is real, among familiar surroundings, and yet forget all this reality. In your own mind you may be on top of a mountain or in a crowd at
5 a railway station. You can be reliving an adventure or a long, difficult job you once tried to do. You can imagine yourself in a country you have never visited, talking to people you have never met. And this imaginary world can seem more real to you than the fact of your sitting
10 at home, as seen by someone who does not know what is happening inside your head.

Television can also transport us to another reality, as we lose ourselves in the picture on the screen. And so can a play in performance in a theatre today. [...]
15 Painted scenery, and steps, doorways, windows, furniture and fittings[2], together with subtle[3] lighting-effects, recorded sound, the appropriate clothes and, occasionally, real bricks or sand or motor cars, all signal unmistakably where the characters are meant to be.
20 [...]

In contrast, Shakespeare's theatre depended much more on the audience's imaginary reality. In the Globe you would not sit in the dark, and nothing separated you from the platform on which the play was in action:
25 the actors could even speak to you, face to face. In that sense theatre was more real, but only in that sense. No one tried to create another world on the stage, a living picture complete in every detail. Only one element of a play was real – the actors. They were the centre of at-
30 tention. What they said and what they did provided the small seed from which a full and exciting imaginative experience came to life in the minds of the spectators. [...] The audience created the setting of a play with their own imagination. [...]
35 In Shakespeare's theatre plays were put on the stage, even new plays with large casts, in hours rather than days. That is why the term "production" was unknown.

[...] Shakespeare's [stagecraft] used very simple materials that were easy to manipulate. It was possible to achieve marvelous and eloquent effects, and Shake- 40 speare took the characters of his plays to mountain-tops, forests, battlefields, dungeons[4], palaces and hovels[5]. But only in the minds of the audience did these marvels find their fulfillment. [...]
How did so little do so much? How did a play "bewitch" 45 the audience?
The key word is "action". Everything came from the *actors*. Most obviously, Shakespeare's plays and those of his contemporaries have many, many words: an Elizabethan text has two, three or four times as many as the 50 average modern play. The actors' first task was to speak clearly and with "lively and spirited action". By making the words "real" for each character, the actors brought them to life on stage and in the minds of every listener. So an extraordinary world could be imagined. In the 55 history play, *King Henry the Fifth*, Shakespeare gave an actor words with which to paint a picture when nothing at all was happening on stage:
Let us …
On our imaginary forces work … 60
Think, when we talk of horses, that you see them
Printing their proud hoofs in the receiving earth;
For 'tis your thoughts that now must deck our kings.
[...]
The shape of the Globe Theatre and its stage encour- 65 aged very active performances. The actors had to keep on the move, for only at the very back of the stage could they face all part of the audience that surrounded them from three sides. Everywhere else on stage, including its focal centre[6], they had to turn this way and 70 that to be seen by all spectators, and they had to be very sure that their impersonations and actions were so physically complete that they would express what was necessary to the play from all points of view. [...]

---

[1] **to bewitch** *verhexen, verzaubern* – [2] **fitting** *Ausstattung* – [3] **subtle** [sʌtl] *raffiniert* – [4] **dungeon** *Verließ, Kerker* – [5] **hovel** *Elendswohnung* –
[6] **focal centre** *Blickpunkt* – [7] **trap-door** *Klapptür, Bodenklappe*

75 Some very simple tricks were also managed. The stage had at least one trap-door[7], which could indicate a grave or the entrance to a dungeon or to hell. In *The Tragedy of Hamlet*, the dead body of Ophelia, whom the prince had loved, is "buried" in the hole left by the 80 removal of the trap-door, and her brother leaps[8] into this "grave" in a passion of grief[9] at her loss. The simple trap-door would be accepted as a grave especially since a grave-digger has just prepared it in full view of the audience, digging earth out of the hole with a spade and tossing[10] old bones and skulls that he says 85 have come from earlier burials[11]. This is a good example of the way in which words and a few simple actions, together with stage-properties, were used by Shakespeare to "locate" the scenes in his plays and "move" the characters from one situation to another. 90

from *Shakespeare and His Theatre* by John Russell Brown. Penguin Books, London 1982, pp. 37 ff.

COMPREHENSION

1. Describe the possibilities of taking people/viewers to another reality as depicted in the text.

2. Point out why in Shakespeare's time the actors and the imagination of the audience were the most important factors for achieving great effects.

3. Specify how "words" were used to inspire the audience's imagination and "bewitch" them.

4. State how the (round) shape of the Globe theatre and simple "tricks" were used to facilitate (*ermöglichen*) interaction between the audience and actors and take the audience to imaginary places.

ANALYSIS

5. Explain Shakespeare's trick to make the actors "paint" a picture with words when nothing at all was going on on stage. Illustrate the tasks given to actors to "speak clearly and with 'lively and spirited action'" (ll. 51 f.).

6. Examine the challenge for Globe actors to perform "in the middle" of the audience who were not separated from the stage and did not sit in the dark.
   What possible advantages and/or disadvantages does this way of performing have?

ACTIVITIES

7. In groups, develop ideas for short scenes that you perform "without words", i. e. as a pantomime. Choose everyday situations and as few props as possible for your play. Here are some ideas:
   - You and your friends/family are in a restaurant and are served a meal that you have been waiting for for a long time. Now,
     a) it turns out to be cold and/or
     b) it is over-salted and tastes awful.
     You talk to the waiter about it and demand to speak to his boss ...
   - You and your classmates are given back an English test which turned out to be a disaster and your teacher is very angry. You try to "justify" your bad results by telling him that
     a) you didn't have enough time to study for it
     b) the tasks were much too difficult
     c) ...

   Finally, perform your "silent plays" in class and discuss their themes and the quality of the performances.

---

[8] **to leap** (lept, lept) to jump – [9] **grief** *Gram, Kummer* – [10] **to toss** to throw around – [11] **burial** *Beerdigung*

A longitudinal cut through the stage and backstage facilities

Shakespeare's Stage

Through the 1580s and 1590s London's Lord Mayors tried to **have plays banned** because **they were thought to be profane and ungodly**. Moreover, plays took apprentices and workmen away from their jobs, since they were performed in daylight each afternoon. As a consequence, the theatre companies began to move outside the city walls, and in **1594**, two new theatres were founded:

Reconstruction of the Globe in London, Southwark

- the **Lord Chamberlain's Men** played at the **Theatre**, the company which Shakespeare joined as an actor and wrote plays for
- the **Lord Admiral's Company** played at the **Rose** and performed Christopher Marlowe's[1] plays.

In **1599**, the **Globe** was built on the south bank of the Thames, **in the suburb of Southwark**, which at that time was full of wayfarers'[2] inns for the many travellers who crossed London Bridge to get into or out of the city. During Shakespeare's time there were **ten open-air amphitheatres in London** with thousands of people going to see new plays every day. Until the **Globe** was destroyed in a fire in 1613, it was **the most successful and prosperous theatre** of the time.

Shakespeare's Globe, also called the **wooden O**, could hold around three thousand people. There was **no "theatre etiquette"** – people did not have to sit still or stand quietly; often theatres were drunken, rowdy places. Some **ticket prices** of the time (a typical wage in 1594 was eight old pence a day):

- one penny: standing in the yard around the stage (→ for the "groundlings")
- twopence: a wooden seat in a covered gallery
- another penny: a cushion[3] for the seats
- sixpence: a seat in the "Lords' Gallery" – seats placed on either side of the balcony at the back of the stage

On the outside an Elizabethan playhouse had plain, white-plastered walls, but inside it was a blaze of colour. The first **Globe was described as "the glory of the Banke"**. The Globe had **a rectangular[4] stage**, projecting halfway into the yard. Above the stage was **a balcony** for musicians and actors. Its decorated ceiling was called the *Heavens*. Beneath the stage lay *Hell* out of which ghosts and devils would emerge through a trap door.

The **demand for new plays was huge** and playwrights likely wrote several new plays every year. Of the thousands of plays which were written during that time, only **230 are still in existence – 39 are Shakespeare's plays** that have survived the last four centuries.

Some **topics and leitmotifs of Shakespeare's plays**:

- **Sex & crime vs. honour & virtue** (e. g. *Romeo and Juliet, Much Ado About Nothing, A Midsummer Night's Dream*)
- **Distant worlds vs. local colour** (e. g. *The Tempest, Much Ado About Nothing*)
- **Women's rights vs. patriarchal[5] structures** (*The Taming of the Shrew, Much Ado About Nothing*)
- **Racism** (e. g. *The Merchant of Venice, Othello*)
- **Language and social class** (verse vs. prose → e. g. *Romeo and Juliet* (Nurse), *Macbeth* (Porter), *A Midsummer Night's Dream* (craftsmen))
- **Crime (ocular proof[6])** (e. g. *Hamlet, Othello, Macbeth, Julius Cesar, Richard III*)
- **Sanity/madness … order/disorder** (e. g. *King Lear, Hamlet, Macbeth*)
- **Social class → climbing the social ladder** (e. g. *Coriolanus, Romeo and Juliet, Much Ado About Nothing*)

---

[1] **Christopher Marlowe** (1564–1593) English playwright, poet and translator who influenced Shakespeare – [2] **wayfarer** (*old use*) Wanderer, Reisender – [3] **cushion** ['kʊʃən] pillow – [4] **rectangular** rechteckig – [5] **patriarchal** [ˌpeɪtri'ɑːkəl] ruled or controlled by men – [6] **ocular proof** sth. that can be seen with the eye

Drama and Theatre

Drama

A **drama or play** is written to be performed by **actors** in a theatre, in a film, on television or on the radio. Traditionally, a play is composed of **acts** (units that reflect main stages in the development of the action), which are further subdivided into **scenes** (= sequences of continuous, uninterrupted action). Modern plays may just present a sequence of scenes. More reduced forms are **one-act plays**. One of the basic elements of drama is a
5 **conflict between opposing characters (= protagonist/antagonist)**, or contrasting ideas, attitudes and interests. Conflict creates tension and **dramatic action**, which unfolds in **dialogues** and/or **monologues**. Good dialogues or monologues must capture the personalities, social positions, attitudes, thoughts and emotions of the characters. **Stage directions** given by the **author/playwright** help the director and the actors perform the play on stage. Such directions may be rather short and leave room for individual interpretation, while others are
10 very detailed and indicate the precise design and arrangement of the **setting** (= time and place), **scenery, props** (= properties, i. e. furniture, decoration, etc.), the characters' appearances, movements, gestures, ways of speaking, or the **sound and lighting** to be used.

Drama is the generic[1] term for the genre. The most important subclasses are:

- the **traditional tragedy**, which develops dramatic action like this:

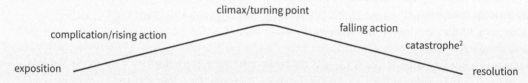

- the **traditional comedy**, which develops dramatic action like this:

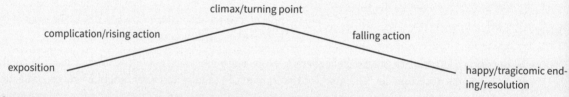

Theatre

Here are some of the important elements of a theatrical stage:

Note: Explanations of the respective technical terms can be found in the Literary Terms section, pp. 433 ff.

[1] **generic** shared by, including or typical of a whole group of things; not specific – [2] **catastophe** [kəˈtæstrəfi]

Modern Adaptations – Dreams and Demons[1] …

Death, Devils … Dissolution[2]

AWARENESS >>>>>>>>

Richard III, one of Shakespeare's earlier historical plays, depicts the dramatic rise and short reign of Richard III of England, a member of the House of York.

In the play, he is an anti-hero – an ugly, physically deformed hunchback whose character is evil, sly and villainous. After having his older brother Clarence imprisoned in the Tower of London, Richard begins to woo Lady Anne, a member of the rival House of Lancaster, though he murdered her husband, Edward, and father-in-law, King Henry VI. They are married and later crowned queen and king.

Look at the photos of American actor Kevin Spacey and English actress Annabel Scholey, who played the roles of Richard III and Lady Anne in a 2011 performance in London's Old Vic Theatre. What do their body language, facial expressions and props reveal about the characters and their relationship?

1 **Richard III (Duke of Gloucester) enters and sees Lady Anne and**
the corpse of King Henry VI

GENTLEMAN   My lord, stand back, and let the coffin
    pass.

RICHARD III (DUKE of GLOUCESTER)
Unmanner'd dog! stand thou, when I command:
5 Advance thy halberd[3] higher than my breast,
Or, by Saint Paul, I'll strike thee to my foot,
And spurn upon[4] thee, beggar, for thy boldness[5].

LADY ANNE   What, do you tremble? are you all
    afraid?
10 Alas, I blame you not; for you are mortal,
And mortal eyes cannot endure the devil.
Avaunt[6], thou dreadful[7] minister[8] of hell!
Thou hadst but power over his mortal body,
His soul thou canst not have; therefore be gone.

15 RICHARD III   Sweet saint, for charity[9], be not so
    curst[10].

LADY ANNE   Foul devil, for God's sake, hence[11], and
    trouble us not;
For thou hast made the happy earth thy hell,
20 Fill'd it with cursing cries and deep exclaims.

If thou delight to view thy heinous[12] deeds,
Behold this pattern of thy butcheries[13].
O, gentlemen, see, see! dead Henry's wounds
Open their congeal'd[14] mouths and bleed afresh!
25 Blush, Blush, thou lump[15] of foul deformity;
For 'tis thy presence that exhales this blood
From cold and empty veins, where no blood dwells[16];
Thy deed, inhuman and unnatural,
Provokes this deluge[17] most unnatural.
30 O God, which this blood madest, revenge his death!
O earth, which this blood drink'st revenge his death!
Either heaven with lightning[18] strike[19] the murderer
    dead,
Or earth, gape[20] open wide and eat him quick,
35 As thou dost swallow up this good king's blood
Which his hell-govern'd arm hath butchered!

RICHARD III   Lady, you know no rules of charity,
Which renders good for bad, blessings for curses.

LADY ANNE   Villain[21], thou know'st no law of God
40   nor man:
No beast so fierce[22] but knows some touch of pity.

---

[1] **demon** [ˈdiːmən] an evil spirit – [2] **dissolution** *Auflösung* – [3] **halbert** *Spießdolch, Hellebarde* – [4] **to spurn upon sb.** *jdn. verächtlich zurück-weisen* – [5] **boldness** here: *Dreistigkeit* – [6] **avaunt** [əˈvɔːnt] (*exclamation*) go away – [7] **dreadful** [ˈdredfəl] very bad, shocking, sad – [8] **minister** *Gesandter* – [9] **charity** here: kindness – [10] **curst** (*old use*) unhappy, annoying – [11] **hence** (to go) away from here – [12] **heinous** [ˈheɪnəs] (*fml.*) very bad and shocking – [13] **butchery** [ˈbʊtʃəri] cruel killing – [14] **congealed** [kənˈdʒiːld] *erstarrt* – [15] **lump** *Klumpen* – [16] **to dwell** here: circulate – [17] **deluge** [ˈdeljuːdʒ] here: a large amount of blood – [18] **lightning** *Blitzschlag* – [19] **to strike** to hit – [20] **to gape** to be or become wide open – [21] **villain** [ˈvɪlən] a criminal – [22] **fierce** strong, powerful, violent

RICHARD III   But I know none, and therefore am no beast.

LADY ANNE   O wonderful, when devils tell the truth!

45 RICHARD III   More wonderful, when angels are so angry.
Vouchsafe[23], divine perfection of a woman,
Of these supposed evils, to give me leave[24],
By circumstance, but to acquit[25] myself.

50 LADY ANNE   Vouchsafe, defused[26] infection of a man,
For these known evils, but to give me leave,
By circumstance, to curse[27] thy cursed self.

RICHARD III   Fairer than tongue[28] can name thee, let me have some patient leisure to excuse myself.

55 LADY ANNE   Fouler than heart can think thee, thou canst make no excuse current, but to hang thyself. [...]

RICHARD III   Say that I slew[29] them not?

LADY ANNE   Why, then they are not dead:
But dead they are, and devilish slave, by thee.

60 RICHARD III   I did not kill your husband. [...]

LADY ANNE   He is in heaven, where thou shalt never come. [...]

LADY ANNE   Thou art the cause, and most accursed[30] effect.

65 RICHARD III   Your beauty was the cause of that effect;
Your beauty: which did haunt[31] me in my sleep
To undertake the death of all the world,
So I might live one hour in your sweet bosom.

70 LADY ANNE   If I thought that, I tell thee, homicide,
These nails should rend[32] that beauty from my cheeks.

RICHARD III   These eyes could never endure sweet beauty's wreck;
You should not blemish[33] it, if I stood by:
75 As all the world is cheered[34] by the sun,
So I by that; it is my day, my life.

LADY ANNE   Black night o'ershade thy day, and death thy life!

RICHARD III   Curse not thyself, fair creature thou
80 art both.

LADY ANNE   I would I were, to be revenged on thee.

RICHARD III   It is a quarrel most unnatural,
To be revenged on him that loveth you.

LADY ANNE   It is a quarrel just and reasonable,
85 To be revenged on him that slew my husband.

RICHARD III   He that bereft[35] thee, lady, of thy husband, did it to help thee to a better husband.

LADY ANNE   His better doth not breathe upon the earth.

90 RICHARD III   He lives that loves thee better than he could.

LADY ANNE   Name him.

RICHARD III   Plantagenet[36].

LADY ANNE   Why, that was he.

95 RICHARD III   The selfsame[37] name, but one of better nature[38].

LADY ANNE   Where is he?

RICHARD III   Here.

[She spitteth at him]

100 Why dost thou spit at me?

---

[23] **vouchsafe sth. to sb.** [ˌvaʊtʃˈseɪf] (*fml.*) to give sth. to sb. in a gracious or condescending manner; *die Güte haben, etw. zu tun* – [24] **leave** (*fml.*) here: permission or agreement – [25] **to acquit sb.** (*fml.*) to decide and state officially in court that sb. is not guilty of a crime – [26] **defused** shapeless – [27] **to curse** *verfluchen* – [28] **tongue** here: language – [29] **to slay** (slew slain) (*old use*) to kill in a violent way – [30] **accursed** *verflucht* – [31] **to haunt** *jdn. (im Traum) verfolgen* – [32] **to rend** (*old use*) to tear sth. apart violently – [33] **to blemish sth.** [ˈblemɪʃ] to spoil sth. – [34] **to cheer sth. (up)** (*phr. v.*) to make a place look brighter – [35] **to be bereft of sth.** *ohne etw. sein* – [36] **Plantagenet** a family originally from France whose members held the English throne until 1485 – [37] **selfsame** exactly the same – [38] **nature** here: character

LADY ANNE   Would it were[39] mortal poison, for thy sake!

RICHARD III   Never came poison from so sweet a place.

105 LADY ANNE   Never hung poison on a fouler toad[40]. Out of my sight! thou dost infect my eyes.

RICHARD III   Thine eyes, sweet lady, have infected mine.

LADY ANNE   Would they were basilisks[41], to strike
110   thee dead[42]!

1592

William Shakespeare, *Richard III*, I, 2

2 Macbeth, King of Scotland

SEYTON   The queen, my lord, is dead.

MACBETH   She should have died hereafter;
There would have been a time for such a word.
To-morrow, and to-morrow, and to-morrow,
5 Creeps in this petty[43] pace[44] from day to day
To the last syllable[45] of recorded time,
And all our yesterdays have lighted[46] fools
The way to dusty death. Out, out, brief candle!
Life's but a walking shadow, a poor player
10 That struts[47] and frets[48] his hour upon the stage
And then is heard no more: it is a tale
Told by an idiot, full of sound[49] and fury[50],
Signifying[51] nothing.   *1606*

William Shakespeare, *Macbeth*, V, 5

3 Prospero's Epilogue

Our revels[52] now are ended. These our actors,
As I foretold you, were all spirits, and
Are melted[53] into air, into thin air:
And like the baseless[54] fabric[55] of this vision,
5 The cloud-capp'd tow'rs, the gorgeous[56] palaces,
The solemn temples, the great globe itself,
Yea, all which it enherit[57], shall dissolve,
And, like this insubstantial pageant[58] faded,
Leave not a rack[59] behind. We are such stuff
10 As dreams are made on; and our little life
Is rounded with a sleep.   *1611*

William Shakespeare, *The Tempest*, IV, 1

Info 》》》

Much of Shakespeare's work is written in **verse**, which means that it has **a particular rhythm**. In Shakespeare's poetry, as a general rule, kings and queens speak in verse and ordinary people speak in prose. When Shakespeare writes in verse, he sometimes uses **blank verse (= verse that doesn't rhyme)** and sometimes **rhyming verse**.

The most commonly used rhythm in Shakespeare's plays is **iambic pentameter** which corresponds to the natural rhythm of the language spoken aloud.

Poetry with a steady, regular rhythm is known as **metrical poetry**, which is an alternation between strong and weak syllables and thus has a **heartbeat-like rhythm**.

Iambic pentameter is a line of poetry that consists of ten syllables (= five metrical feet). It has become very popular on stage because it is easy to say in one breath and therefore sounds natural. Moreover, the steady recurring rhythm is easy to memorize. Here is an example:

syllables	1st		2nd	3rd	4th	5th		6th		7th		8th	9th		10th
feet		1			2			3			4			5	
stress	x		\	x	\	x		\		x		\	x		\
sound	de-		**DUM**	de-	**DUM**	de-		**DUM**		de-		**DUM**	de-		**DUM**
		Shall	I		com · pare	thee		to		a		sum · mer's			day?

[39] **would it were** I wish it were – [40] **toad** *Kröte* – [41] **basilisk** *Kroneidechse* – [42] **to strike sb. dead** *jdn. erschlagen* – [43] **petty** ['peti] small, unimportant – [44] **pace** the speed at which sb./sth. moves – [45] **syllable** ['sɪləbl] *Silbe* – [46] **to light** here: to show the way – [47] **to strut** *stolzieren* – [48] **to fret** to be nervous or worried – [49] **sound** noise – [50] **fury** extreme anger – [51] **to signify** (*fml.*) to mean – [52] **revel** ['revəl] (*lit.*) noisy celebration – [53] **to melt** *schmelzen*, here: *sich auflösen* – [54] **baseless** here: unreal – [55] **fabric** here: substance – [56] **gorgeous** ['gɔːdʒəs] very beautiful or pleasant – [57] **to enherit** (*old use*) to inherit, *etw. übernehmen* – [58] **pageant** ['pædʒənt] a colourful and impressive show – [59] **rack** here: ruin

William Shakespeare: Sonnet 73

That time of year thou mayst in me behold,
When yellow leaves, or none, or few do hang
Upon those boughs[1] which shake against the cold
Bare ruined choirs[2], where late the sweet birds sang.
5 In me thou seest the twilight of such day,
As after sunset fadeth in the west,
Which by and by black night doth take away,
Death's second self that seals up all in rest.
In me thou seest the glowing of such fire,
10 That on the ashes of his youth doth lie,
As the death-bed, whereon it must expire[3],
Consumed with that which it was nourished[4] by.
    This thou perceiv'st[5], which makes thy love more
                      strong,
    To love that well, which thou must leave ere long.

1599

Wolf Biermann: 73

An mir magst du sie anschaun, diese Jahreszeit
Da gelbe Blätter taumeln – paar noch krалln sich bang
An das Gezweig. Die Kälte reißt das letzte Kleid
Vom kahlen Chorgestühl, wo süß manch Vöglein sang

5 Das Zwielicht solchen Tags, an mir schau es dir an
Wenn in das Schwarz der Nacht der Sonnenwagen karrt
Dann kommt der Doppelgänger, der vom Knochenmann
Krallt sich das Licht und hält es fest, bis es erstarrt

Durchschau das Flackern solcher Flammen, deren Glut
10 Auf ihrer eignen Jugend Asche stirbt! grad das
Siehst du an mir. Auf seinem Sterbebette ruht
Das Feuer, selbst gefressen nun von seinem Fraß

    Na siehste – all dies stachelt ja dein Lieben noch
    Du liebtest mich, grad weil ich schon nach Sterben roch

2005

from *Das ist die feinste Liebeskunst. 40 Shakespeare Sonette.* Kiepenheuer & Witsch, 2. Auflage, Köln 2005, p. 51

COMPREHENSION

 1. Divide the class into three groups, with each group dealing with one of the excerpts from Shakespeare's plays (texts 1, 2, 3).

@ **Step 1:** In your groups, do further research on the respective play and collect information about
- the plot,
- the major topics and leitmotifs*,
- the protagonists and significant characters.

Step 2: Now read the excerpt from the play and find words and phrases from the text that relate to the headline and sub-headline of this thematic unit (e. g. dreams, demons, death, devils, etc.) and complete the grid below.

 Step 3: Next, the groups remix, with each group consisting of at least one member from all the other groups. In this new group, each member informs the others about the results of the initial group.

Richard III	Macbeth	Prospero
● the corpse of King Henry VI	● the queen … is dead …	● revels … ended …
● …	● …	● …

---

[1] **bough** [baʊ] (*lit.*) large branch of a tree – [2] **choir** [kwaɪə(r)] *Chorgestühl* – [3] **to expire** (*lit.*) to die – [4] **to nourish** *etw. nähren, pflegen* –
[5] **to perceive** *etw. wahrnehmen*

2. After having gained a general overview of the excerpts, choose <u>one</u> of the following materials for further analysis and take notes on the questions and tasks below.

 1 **Richard III**

- Listen to the audio version of the excerpt and characterize the actors' ways of speaking.

 Tips on vocab >>>

> to hesitate ▪ to hiss ▪ to quaver (*mit zittriger Stimme sprechen*) ▪ to accentuate/stress sth. ▪ to shout ▪ to yell ▪ to scream ▪ to shriek ▪ to bellow (to shout in a deep voice) ▪ to blurt out (*etw. ausstoßen, mit etw. herausplatzen*) ▪ to snap (*jdn. anblaffen*) ▪ to bark at sb. (*jdn. anherrschen*) ▪ deep dark voice ▪ high-pitched voice ▪ speech pauses

- Examine the use of language in the dialogue between Richard III and Lady Anne. Pay particular attention to the use of
  – irony*/sarcasm*,
  – metaphors*,
  – insults,
  – hyperbole*,
  – conditional sentences,
  – rhetorical questions*.

  How do the respective devices underline
  a) Richard's character,
  b) the poisoned relationship between the characters?
  → Focus on Skills, Analysis of a Fictional Text, p. 402

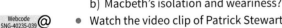 **2** **Macbeth, King of Scotland**

- Listen to the recording of Macbeth's monologue and describe the gloomy and desperate picture Macbeth paints of the situation.
- Analyse and interpret the function and effect of the stylistic devices employed in the monologue. How do they emphasize
  a) Macbeth's unstable state of mind after having committed and commissioned so many murders,
  b) Macbeth's isolation and weariness?
- Watch the video clip of Patrick Stewart's rendition of Macbeth's famous monologue provided on the webcode.

Webcode SNG-40235-039 @

  a) How do the recording and Stewart's performance differ?
  b) Which vocal and speaking devices does Stewart employ to express Macbeth's character and the desperate situation?

 3 **Prospero's Epilogue**

- Listen to the audio version of Prospero's monologue and examine how the speaker conveys the melancholy and dreamlike atmosphere.
- Specify the leitmotif of the monologue and explain how the imagery (= the use of descriptive and emotive words and phrases) serves to illustrate and emphasize it.

- *The Tempest*, the play this excerpt is taken from, is one of Shakespeare's last works. Find examples in Prospero's monologue that relate to this circumstance.

3. Sonnet 73

Step 1: Together with a partner, listen to the recording of the sonnet and

a) specify and explain the use of imagery,

b) explain how the leitmotifs of death and transitoriness are conveyed,

c) characterize the speaker's mood.

Step 2: Describe and explain the structure of the sonnet.

Step 3: What in particular is the advice the speaker gives the addressee of the sonnet?

Step 4: Compare the German version of *Sonnet 73* to the original. Pay particular attention to

- its use of imagery,
- its mood and atmosphere,
- its language register.

Info »»

A sonnet is a poem of fourteen lines which follows a strict rhyme pattern. It is usually divided into two parts: the octave (= the first 8 lines) and the **sestet** (= the last 6 lines). The octave and the sestet are separated by a break in thought: a general statement made in the octave is illustrated or amplified (*verstärken*) in the sestet.

The Shakespearean Sonnet has a much simpler rhyme pattern. It consists of three stanzas with four lines each (= quatrain) and an ending of two lines (= couplet) – which is 14 lines in all.

```
a b a b  ⎫
c d c d  ⎬  3 quatrains
e f e f  ⎭
gg  ⟶  a couplet with a conclusive thought
```

ACTIVITIES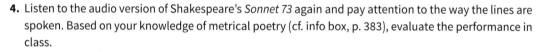

 4. Listen to the audio version of Shakespeare's *Sonnet 73* again and pay attention to the way the lines are spoken. Based on your knowledge of metrical poetry (cf. info box, p. 383), evaluate the performance in class.

 5. The sonnet depicts an "I" speaking to an imaginary "you"/"thou" or "thee".
Together with a partner, turn the sonnet into a dialogue, imagining what "you" might answer.
Then perform your dialogues in class.

 6. In groups, work creatively with the excerpt from *Richard III* and prepare a short performance. You can add further characters, e. g. the ghost of Lady Anne's murdered husband Edward or the off-stage voice of Richard's imprisoned brother Clarence.

 In order to get more "verbal ammunition" for the characters to insult and offend each other, you can use the Insult Generator provided on the webcode.

 Act out your scene in class and have fun "insulting" each other!

7. Many of Shakespeare's plays are so-called "historical plays" and deal with kings, queens or aristocrats who lived centuries ago. Are these topics and leitmotifs still relevant for modern/contemporary audiences?

 Use the link provided on the webcode and watch American actor Kevin Spacey explain how *Richard III* "speaks to audiences today".

Then discuss in class whether or not you agree with Kevin Spacey's opinion.
→ Focus on Language, Conversation and Discussion, p. 413

Kenneth Branagh
Explosionen im Gehirn

AWARENESS

Irish actor Kenneth Branagh and German actor Ulrich Matthes are both renowned for their excellent performances of complex characters and dramatic works. On occasion of Shakespeare's 450th birthday in 2014, they were interviewed about their personal and professional experiences with Shakespeare's literary work.

Speculate about and discuss the headlines of the two newspaper articles: Why might dealing with Shakespeare cause "explosions in the brain" and lead to "inevitable failure"?

Die Inszenierungen[1], die ich im Alter von 13 und den frühen Zwanzigern sah, waren Explosionen in meinem Hirn. Als ich 16 Jahre alt war, sah ich *King Lear*, ich erinnere mich, wie ich das Programmheft[2] öffnete und mir ein versehrtes[3] Gesicht entgegenblickte, mit diesem Zitat: *„Wir Neugeborenen weinen, zu betreten die große Narrenbühne ..."* Da war so etwas Trauriges, es fühlte sich wahr an. Keine Ahnung, warum ein 16-Jähriger darauf anspringen sollte. Obwohl ich das Wort *fool* mochte – *fool*, der Narr: Da ist eine Sanftheit[4], eine Weisheit. *Fool* hat auch etwas Humorvolles, und zugleich etwas Episches, Großes. Ich erkannte, dass ich jemandem begegnet war, der große Dinge wusste.

König Lear beginnt mit dieser häuslichen Auseinandersetzung[5], wie sie an jedem Frühstückstisch losbrechen kann, einer fragt: „Wer will noch Kaffee?", und jemand sagt: „nicht jetzt!", und schon geht es los. Wir streiten noch immer über dieselben Dinge wie die Leute im Jahr 1590 oder 1599. Und dann, im selben Stück, ist da dieser Mann auf der Heide[6], nackt, im Regen, es war eine sehr theatralische Aufführung mit wirklichem Regen, ein sehr starkes Bild[7]. Ich sah in einem einzigen Stück die Kleinheit[8] der Menschen – und zugleich die Tapferkeit. Und Torheit[9] – was wollte er erreichen, im Regen, nackt gegen die Elemente anbrüllend[10]? Es war überwältigend. [...]

Shakespeare hält der Natur den Spiegel vor. Es liegt in der Natur des Menschen, überraschend zu sein, widersprüchlich, oft enttäuschend. Shakespeares Charaktere und Stücke erlauben uns, das zu erkennen – und wie viel Traurigkeit in der Welt ist. Wir sehen Shakespeare und verstehen, dass wir nicht alleine sind mit unseren Enttäuschungen. Bei ihm findet sich alles, was den Menschen ausmacht. Er ist, auf umfassende[11] Weise, wir. [...]

Ich war 19 Jahre alt, als ich Hamlet zum ersten Mal spielte. Wer Hamlet spielt, muss sich grundlegenden Fragen stellen – ob man an Gott glaubt oder was nach dem Tod passiert oder wie Gefühle den Eltern gegenüber sein sollten oder sind. Es geht um prinzipielle moralische Erwägungen[12] – glaubt man an Rache? Hat man Humor? Ist Humor essenziell? Welche Tabus gibt es, ist es erlaubt, im Angesicht des Todes[13] zu lachen? [...]

Shakespeare zu spielen ist eine Herausforderung, die keine Grenzen kennt. [...] Wenn es gut geht, dann hat man alle seine Fähigkeiten, alle Gefühle, Gedanken, seinen Witz[14], alles hineingelegt, jede Farbe, Emotion, Leidenschaft, deren man irgendwie fähig ist, und diese Vorstellung endet mit dem Gefühl, dass die Luft mit Poesie erfüllt[15] ist – und doch bleibt ein Geheimnis.

Die Zeit, 10 April 2014, p. 47

Ulrich Matthes: „Man kann nur scheitern"

Das Beglückende[16] daran, Shakespeare zu spielen, ist dies: Man kann ohnehin nur scheitern. Er ist einfach zu groß. Andere Autoren – Tschechow, Kleist, Büchner – sind auch groß, man hat aber die Hoffnung, ihnen nahekommen zu können. Die kann man bei Shakespeare gleich vergessen. Daher können Proben[17] und vielleicht auch die Aufführungen – im Bewusstsein des Scheiterns geborgen[18] – frei, offen und eher fragend[19] als antwortend[20] sein.

Die Zeit, 10 April 2014, p. 47

---

[1] (theatrical) production – [2] programme – [3] hurt/injured – [4] gentleness – [5] domestic quarrel – [6] moor – [7] strong/powerful/intense image – [8] smallness – [9] foolishness – [10] to bawl/roar at sb./sth. – [11] general – [12] consideration – [13] at death's door – [14] wit – [15] to permeate – [16] delightful – [17] rehearsal – [18] secure – [19] questioning – [20] clarifying

COMPREHENSION

1. Over time, there has been an ongoing discussion about whether or not Shakespeare should be read and taught to ESL[1] students – or what should be done/changed in order to make Shakespeare's complex works more accessible to young audiences/readers.

   M Mediate the two texts for an online forum of international ESL students, focusing particularly on these aspects:
   - King Lear: between foolishness and wisdom
   - how people and events from the 1590s are related to the present
   - sadness and loneliness
   - the complexity of Hamlet
   - the challenge of performing Shakespeare
   - Shakespeare: more questions than answers
   → Focus on Skills, Mediation, p. 412

ANALYSIS

2. Examine and analyse the views taken here:
   What does the situation of 16-year-old teenagers have to do with
   - foolishness,
   - sadness,
   - vulnerability,
   - domestic quarrels,
   - loneliness,
   - humour,
   - death,
   - failure?
   → Focus on Skills, Analysis of a Non-Fictional Text, p. 405

3. Study the Focus on Facts page *Shakespeare's Stage* in your Students' Book (p. 379), focusing on the examples given on topics and leitmotifs of Shakespeare's plays (ll. 33 ff.).
   a) How relevant are these topics in contemporary, everyday life?
   b) What relevance do these topics have for adolescents worldwide today?

ACTIVITIES

Webcode
SNG-40235-040 @

4. Do further research on the influence of Shakespeare's work on young people using the links provided on the webcode.
   Collect information and prepare short presentations on "Hip Hop Shakespeare" and "Akala Shakespeare" in class.
   → Focus on Skills, Presentations, p. 419

[1] **ESL** English as Second Language

Marc Norman, Tom Stoppard

Shakespeare's Weekly Confession ...

The 1998 British-American romantic comedy-drama film *Shakespeare in Love* is set in 1593 Elizabethan London, when William Shakespeare was at the zenith of his creativity. In one of the introductory scenes, he seeks the help and advice of Dr. Moth, "apothecary[1], alchemist, astrologer[2], seer, interpreter of dreams, and priest of psyche[3]", because he is suffering from writer's block.

INT. DR. MOTH'S HOUSE. DAY

A stuffed alligator hangs from the ceiling, pills, potions[4], amulets and charms[5], star charts and mystic paraphernalia[6] festoon[7] the place. Testimonials and framed degrees[8]
5 *hang on the walls.*
Will lying on a couch, on his back. His eyes are closed. Dr. Moth sits by the couch, listening to Will and occasionally making a note on a pad he holds on his knee. What we have here is nothing less than the false dawn[9] of anal-
10 *ysis. The session is being timed by an hour-glass.*

WILL   Words, words, words ... once, I had the gift ... I could make love out of words as a potter makes cups out of clay ... love that overthrows empires, love that binds two hearts together, come hellfire and brim-
15 stone[10] ... for sixpence a line, I could cause a riot in a nunnery[11] ... but now ...

DR. MOTH   And yet you tell me you lie with[12] women?

Will seems unwilling to respond. Dr. Moth refers to his notes.

20 DR. MOTH (*Cont'd*)   Black Sue, Fat Phoebe, Rosaline, Burbage's Seamstress; Aphrodite, who does it behind the dog and ...

WILL (*interrupting*)   Aye, now and again, but what of it? I have lost my gift.

25 DR. MOTH   I am here to help you. Tell me in your own words.

WILL   I have lost my gift. (*Not finding this easy*). It's as if my quill[13] is broken. As if the organ of my imagination

has dried up. As if the proud tower of my genius has collapsed.   30

DR. MOTH   Interesting.

WILL   Nothing comes.

DR. MOTH   Most interesting.

WILL (*interrupting*)   It is like trying to pick a lock with a wet herring[14].   35

DR. MOTH (*shrewdly[15]*)   Tell me, are you lately humbled[16] in the act of love?

Will turns to him. How did he know that?

DR. MOTH (*Cont'd*)   How long has it been?

WILL   A goodly length in times past, but lately –   40

DR. MOTH   No. no. You have a wife, children ...

---

¹**apothecary** [əˈpɒθəkəri] – ²**astrologer** [əˈstrɒlədʒə(r)] – ³**psyche** [ˈsaɪki] – ⁴**potion** *Zaubertrank* – ⁵**charm** *Glücksbringer* – ⁶**paraphernalia** [ˌpærəfəˈneɪliə] *equipment* – ⁷**to festoon** *(mit Girlanden) schmücken* – ⁸**degree** *Abschluss, Titel* – ⁹**false dawn** *falsches Morgenrot* – ¹⁰**hellfire and brimstone** *torments suffered by sinners in hell* – ¹¹**nunnery** *Kloster für Nonnen* – ¹²**to lie with sb.** *here: to have sex with sb.* – ¹³**quill** *Federkiel; allusion to the male sexual organ* – ¹⁴**wet herring** *here: allusion to Will's lack of erection* – ¹⁵**shrewd** *scharfsinning* – ¹⁶**humbled** *gedemütigt*

The sand runs through the hourglass.
LATER
Not much sand left.

45 WILL   I was a lad of eighteen. Anne Hathaway was a woman, half as old again.

DR. MOTH   A woman of property?

WILL (*shrugs*[17])   She had a cottage. One day, she was three months gone with child, so …

50 DR. MOTH   And your relations[18]?

WILL   On my mother's side the Ardens …

DR. MOTH   No, your marriage bed.

WILL   Four years and a hundred miles away in Stratford. A cold bed, too, since the twins were born. Ban-
55 ishment[19] was a blessing.

DR. MOTH   So now you are free to love …

WILL   – yet cannot love nor write it.

Dr. Moth reaches for a glass snake bracelet[20].

DR. MOTH   Here is a bangle[21] found in Psyche's temple on Olympus – cheap at four pence. Write your 60 name on a paper and feed it in the snake.

Will looks at the snake bangle in wonder.

WILL   Will it restore my gift?

DR. MOTH   The woman who wears the snake will dream of you, and your gift will return. Words will flow 65 like a river. I will see you in a week.

He holds out his hand. Will drops a sovereign[22] into it, and takes the bracelet.

from *Shakespeare in Love. A Screenplay* by Marc Norman and Tom Stoppard. Reclam Verlag, Stuttgart 2000, pp. 13 ff.

COMPREHENSION

1. In a **first reading**, **scan** the text and try to understand the **gist**.

2. After a **second reading**, summarize Shakespeare's "psychoanalytic session" in about 150 words.
   → Focus on Skills, Writing a Summary, p. 429

3. Describe the film still on p. 389: How does it render Shakespeare's emotions?
   → Focus on Skills, Analysis of Visuals, p. 409

ANALYSIS

4. At first glance, Shakespeare seems to be suffering from writer's block and is desperate to regain his creativity. However, after taking a closer look at the dialogue it becomes obvious that the true reason for his despair is his lacking sexual performance, i. e. he is impotent.

   Together with a partner, read the excerpt again and detect ambiguous (= *doppeldeutig*) lines that refer to Shakespeare's true problem.
   → Focus on Skills, Analysis of a Screenplay, p. 404

5. The use of ambiguity and playing with the hidden meaning of certain words, e. g. when pronounced in a certain way (e. g. hour → whore), was very common in Shakespeare's time.

   Read John Donne's poem *The Flea*, provided on the webcode, and find out about the true meaning of "exchanging liquids" via a flea bite.
   → Focus on Skills, Analysis of Poetry and Lyrics, p. 406

---

[17] **to shrug** *mit den Schultern zucken* – [18] **relations** *Verwandtschaft, Beziehungen*; also: sexual relations/intercourse – [19] **banishment** to send sb. away – [20] **bracelet** *Armband* – [21] **bangle** *Armreif* – [22] **sovereign** an old British gold coin worth one Pound Sterling

ACTIVITIES

6. In a group, listen to the description given by Thomas Platter again (cf. Students' Book, p. 373).
Now discuss: Why was it important for poets and playwrights to write not only about historical and philo-sophical topics, but also to include "sex and crime" and crude humour and wit into their plays and poetry?
→ Focus on Facts, Shakespeare's Stage, p. 379
→ Focus on Language, Shakespeare's Language, p. 392

7. Watch the scene from the film *Shakespeare in Love* and
   a) get an impression of Elizabethan London,
   b) pay attention to the facial expressions and gestures that underline the sexual allusions made in the dialogue.
   → Focus on Skills, Analysis of a Film Scene, p. 403

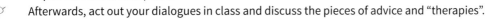

GRAMMAR / LANGUAGE

8. After the "psychoanalytic session" Dr. Moth discusses Shakespeare's "case" with another "priest of psyche".
Together with a partner, write a dialogue in which
   a) Dr. Moth reports to his colleague what Shakespeare told him, using **indirect speech** and **backshifting the tenses** where necessary,
   b) both Dr. Moth and his colleague talk shop (*fachsimpeln*) about further "therapies" that might help patients like Shakespeare.
Afterwards, act out your dialogues in class and discuss the pieces of advice and "therapies".

Shakespeare's Language

Shakespeare's plays/scripts were written to be performed, not read. At Shakespeare's time, stage machinery, lighting, sound effects and sets were far from what we find in modern theatres.

Accordingly, most of **Shakespeare's "scene painting"** was done in
5 words; **dramatic effects** were evoked in the audience's imagination **through language** and the **extensive use of stylistic devices**, e. g. metaphors, repetition, irony, word play (puns), rhetoric, enumeration and insults.

Imagery

Imagery is the use of **emotionally charged words** which evoke **vivid mental pictures** in the reader's or viewer's imagination. Images play a key role in Shakespeare's plays and are often taken from nature, e. g.:

- *Will the great Neptune's ocean wash this blood clean from my hand?* (*Macbeth*, II, 2)
- *I have begun to plant thee, and will labour to make thee full of growing.* (King Duncan in *Macbeth*, I, 4)

Verse vs. prose

In Elizabethan England, theatre audiences expected most plays to be about kings, queens and aristocrats. Thus, the characters used heightened language and often verse: **nobles** would speak in **verse** and **lower-status characters** would use **prose**. Shakespeare's characters' use of prose or verse is often a reflection of their personal
5 and moral integrity, e. g. an aristocratic but villainous (*schurkisch*) or mad character uses prose whereas a lower-status character who is benevolent (*gütig, wohlwollend*) and morally upright speaks in verse.

Most of Shakespeare's verse is written in **iambic** [aɪˈæmbɪk] pentameter
(→ info box, p. 383) which imitates the rhythm of the human heartbeat, e. g.

x \ x \ x \ x \ x \
O blessed, blessed night! I am afeared,
Being in night, this is but a dream,
Too flattering-sweet to be substantial. (Romeo in *Romeo and Juliet*, II, 1)

New words

In Shakespeare's time, poets and playwrights used language to create dramatic effects. They invented **new words** (neologisms) and **adapted or reshaped old words** to give them a new meaning.
5 Shakespeare made up nonsense words (e. g. hurly burly → chaos), added **prefixes** to existing words (e. g. bemask, disburden, unsex, endanger) and created **compound/hyphenated words** (e. g. sea-change, sight-outrunning, pinch-spotted) to achieve a certain effect. Additionally, Shakespeare loved to have characters **insult** each other on stage and invented insults or **swear words**, e. g.

- *Thou clay-brained guts* • *Thou knotty-patted fool* • *Thou whore-son obscene greasy tallow-catch*
10 - *Horse-back-breaker! Huge hill of flesh!* • *You stock-fish!*
- *Roasted Manningtree Ox with the pudding in his belly* (Falstaff and Prince Hal in *King Henry IV*, Part I)

You, thou, thee, thine, thy

In Elizabethan England, different **personal/possessive pronouns** were used, depending on the **social status** and relationship between the speakers. Here are some examples of possible implications:

- thou [ðaʊ] → used a) to express closeness or contempt, b) to indicate friendship to an equal or superiority
5   over sb. socially inferior, c) by lower classes talking to each other, d) by superiors talking to inferiors, e) for special intimacy, f) by a character talking to sb. absent
- you   → more formal; suggesting respect for a superior or courtesy to a social equal

Sometimes, characters switch from "you" to "thou" or vice versa to express a change in attitude towards one another.   thee → you   thine → yours   thy → your

Competences, Skills & Methods

Note: An overview of **all** Focus on pages in thematic and alphabetical order can be found in the front cover of the Students' Book.

Listening Comprehension

Language learning is dependent on good listening. Therefore, it is important to **learn to adjust one's listening to various situations** in order to be able to interact well in spoken communication. These situations can be listening to a song, an interview, (watching and)
5 listening to a film, or listening to somebody in a conversation. Usually, you already have a lot of background knowledge, e. g. about the topic, the person, and of course, you already know a lot of the vocabulary used in the spoken text you are supposed to listen to. Before you start **taking notes**, make use of the following strategies
10 that can help you to understand texts more easily.

"HIS MASTER'S VOICE"

Strategies that can help to understand

a) Listening for the main idea
- Try to understand the gist of the text by paying attention to key nouns, people's names, official place names, etc.
- Try to find answers to the W-questions (who? what? where? when? why?).

b) Predicting
This technique helps you to mentally prepare yourself for the text.
- Try to imagine what the text will be about by judging from the title/headline.
- Try to make predictions about the further text after the first sentence or the first part of the text.

c) Drawing inferences – intelligent guessing
- Make use of German words that are very similar to English words (e. g. mouse – *Maus*, mile – *Meile*, house – *Haus*, etc.). However, watch out for false friends (e. g. become ≠ *bekommen*, chef ≠ *Chef*, etc.).
- Make use of other foreign languages that you know and link them to anglicized words (e. g. French *la qualité* – quality, *la circonstance* – circumstance, etc.).
- Listen for internationally-used English words (e. g. *crew*, *team*, *display*, *design*, etc.) and relate them to the possible contents of the text.
- Connect (parts of) words that you already know to words in the text that sound similar (e. g. to teach – *teacher*, to grow – *growth*, etc.).
- Double-check your guessed meaning of the word by relating it to the context.

d) The given-new strategy
- Pay attention to certain keywords employed in the text that emphasize an additional aspect given in a sentence (e. g. *The weather was warm, **but** rainy.*). Further keywords or phrases are: **before**, **after**, **although**, **such as**, **another**, **as you know**, **to sum up**, **conclusion**, etc.

Strategies that can help to process and memorize the information

Note-taking – mind mapping – summarizing
- Use your notes taken while or after listening to order and (re-)arrange your understanding of the text.
- Relate your findings to other contexts.
- Draw a mind map of your notes and try to find further useful details from the text.
- Write a summary using your notes and try to explain the text you listened to in your own words.
→ Focus on Skills, Writing a Summary, p. 429

Focus on Skills

Basic Types of Fictional Texts

1. narrative texts	**a) Novels** • are an extended and complex work of fiction written in prose. • contain a variety of characters, action and a greater complication of plot. • present a sustained exploration of the milieu, the characters, their motives. • can vary greatly in form, style and content; one less complex form is the novella (e. g. John Steinbeck, *Of Mice and Men* or *Cannery Row*). • have certain subclasses, e. g. the social novel (e. g. Harriet Beecher-Stowe, *Uncle Tom's Cabin*), the coming-of-age story (e. g. Mark Twain, *Tom Sawyer and Huckleberry Finn*; Paul Auster, *Moon Palace*). **b) Short stories** • are written in prose and are shorter and less complex than a novel. • are mostly confined to one setting, a limited number of characters and events. • often employ an open plot with an abrupt opening and ending. • do not put focus on the development of a character but on a significant incident or decisive moment that reveals strengths and weaknesses of characters, mostly presented as a snapshot of life. • are told from the point of view of a narrator who is created by the author. • place maximum significance on the few things mentioned, which are aimed at producing a certain effect in the reader's mind. • emerged in the USA in the 19th century in response to the development of the newspapers, which required shorter forms of text; Edgar Allan Poe (1809 – 1849) is often regarded as the originator of the short story; other famous writers of short stories include Ernest Hemingway, Annie Proulx, and T. C. Boyle. **c) Fables** • are a short text in which animals represent human types (→ the beast fable). • are a form of allegory exemplifying an abstract moral thesis or principle of human behaviour. • are didactic and are intended to teach the reader a moral lesson. • Two famous writers of fables are James Thurber and George Orwell.
2. dramatic texts	**a) Dramas/plays** • are any work designed for performance in a theatre. • require actors/actresses who take on the roles of different characters, performing the actions and speaking the dialogue or monologue. • usually contain stage directions included by the playwright, telling the actors how and where to move on stage as well as giving information about how to arrange the stage, what props, sound effects or lighting to use. → Focus on Facts, Drama and Theatre, p. 380 **b) Screenplays/scripts** • are a written work, especially for a film or a television programme. • consist of numbered scenes which show action and dialogue descriptions. • have numbered slug lines telling the reader that the story has changed in location and time (e. g. INT. WAREHOUSE – NIGHT; EXT. STREET – DAY) → Focus on Facts, Screenplays and Storyboards, p. 397
3. poetry/ lyrics	**a) Poetry** • is a type of literature that is not prose, in which ideas, experiences and feelings are expressed in compact, imaginative and often musical language. • may be arranged in lines and may contain patterns of rhyme/rhythm. • often contains figures of speech and imagery to appeal to the readers' and listeners' emotions and imagination. **b) Lyrics** • are a set of words that accompany music, either spoken or sung. → Focus on Skills, Analysis of Poetry and Lyrics, p. 406

Focus on Facts

Note: Explanations of the respective technical terms can be found in the Literary Terms section, pp. 433 ff.

Basic Types of Non-Fictional Texts

The 4 basic types of non-fictional texts

1. **Descriptive texts:** the author wants to inform in a relatively balanced and neutral way (e. g. description of a landscape, a place, a person, an object …)

2. **Narrative texts:** the author wants to inform the reader about a development or a sequence of events; the report (objectively or subjectively) gives answers to the questions *who? what? where? when? why?* and *how?* and often presents further details. Reports* are often made livelier by fictional elements, e. g. a detailed description of people or the way people are affected by an event, etc. (e. g. travel report, report on the development of a situation …)

3. **Expository texts:** complicated and difficult facts are presented and explained in a matter-of-fact way; the structure/pattern of such texts is called **topical order** (= a sequence of points follows a statement of the topic at the beginning of the text) (e. g. explanatory notes, scientific reports, factual texts, descriptions of historical events …)

4. **Argumentative texts:** the author tries to influence the reader directly; this text type tends to be more critical and appellative, using persuasive arguments (e. g. commentary, criticism, review*, essay*, sermon*, pamphlet, political speech* …); these texts usually deal with controversial topics; reasons are given for and/or against the matter and are arranged in a well-planned order

Forms of argumentative texts

structure	type 1	type 2	type 3
introduction	Presenting a topic and giving opinions on the problem	Presenting a topic and giving opinions on the problem	Presenting a topic and giving opinions on the problem
↓	**arguments** ↓	**arguments** ↓	**arguments** ↓
main part	supporting facts	counter-arguments and refutation to stress the author's position	argument → counter-argument argument → counter-argument argument → counter-argument, etc. [mainly used in disputes and debates]
↓	↓	↓	↓
conclusion	conclusion	conclusion	conclusion

A non-fictional text* that puts forth a personal view has a **unity of thought**, and usually follows a clear **structure** (line of thought*, train of thought*, line of argument*).

Here are some of the most common **compositional patterns for structuring texts**:

listing structure:	**method:** Enumerating, numbering of facts, ideas, arguments **effect:** Clarity and coherence through parallel arrangement
progressive structure:	**method:** Using a clearly-defined starting point; developing on a cause-to-effect or problem-solution arrangement **effect:** Clarity through unity and logical coherence
antithetical structure:	**method:** Contrasting and juxtaposing of facts, ideas and arguments **effect:** Clarity and emphasis through comparison and contrast

Screenplays and Storyboards

The process of making a film is very complex and requires a number of preparatory arrangements such as **scriptwriting**, **shooting**, **editing** and finally **distributing the film** to the audience. Usually, it involves a large number of general staff and specialists and can take up to several years to complete. Here are two of the most relevant preparatory steps.

Screenplay

- A screenplay or script is a written work for a film or television programme. It can be an original work or an adaptation from an existing work like a novel, short story, etc.
- A screenplay focusses on **describing** the literal, **visual aspects of the story**, rather than the internal thoughts of its characters.
- The major components are **action** and **dialogue**. The description of the "action" is always written in the present tense.
- One page of a screenplay usually equates to one minute of screen time.

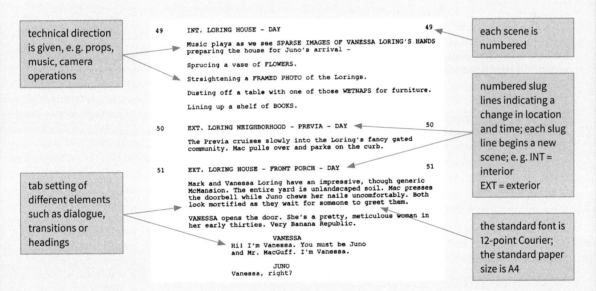

technical direction is given, e. g. props, music, camera operations

each scene is numbered

numbered slug lines indicating a change in location and time; each slug line begins a new scene; e. g. INT = interior EXT = exterior

tab setting of different elements such as dialogue, transitions or headings

the standard font is 12-point Courier; the standard paper size is A4

Storyboard

- Storyboards are **graphic organizers** that display images in sequence in order to pre-visualize a film as it is to be seen through the camera lens.
- Before the shooting of the film begins, each storyboard maps out the **director's vision of where the camera will be placed** for action sequences in a film.
- A storyboard helps the director to find potential problems or brainstorm further ideas.
- Technical details are described either in picture form or additional text; often, there are arrows or instructions that indicate movement.

The Press

An overview of different newspaper and magazine formats

newspapers	characteristics	tips on vocab
British quality newspapers/broadsheets*: *The Times, The Guardian, The Daily Telegraph, The Sunday Telegraph, The Financial Times, The Independent, The Observer, etc.* **Scottish quality newspapers/broadsheets*:** *The Scotsman, The Herald, etc.* **American quality newspapers/broadsheets*:** *The New York Times, International Herald Tribune, The Wall Street Journal, The Chicago Tribune, The Washington Post, The Los Angeles Times, USA Today, etc.*	• usually in larger formats and typically with more pages • headlines on the front page are smaller in size and more informative and factual • proportionally more text than photos and in smaller print • more informative/credible coverage • articles are in-depth, present facts, dates/numbers/statistics; are more balanced • use of quotations from credible people • language is more objective/precise/elaborate/formal • information is based on serious research; analysis; hard news • objectivity through a variety of perspectives and credible sources • offer critical comments on issues	▪ to publish a newspaper edition/copy ▪ accuracy ▪ informative (-ness) ▪ visual material ▪ thought-provoking ▪ ironic/satirical ▪ column ▪ to cover a subject/topic ▪ editorial ▪ to generate sth. ▪ source of information ▪ to be in/to hit the headlines ▪ headline-grabbing ▪ sophisticated ▪ special feature ▪ current affairs ▪ to focus on sth.
(British tabloids/"popular newspapers"/"supermarket tabloids": *The Sun, Daily Star, Daily Mirror, Daily Express, The Daily Mail, etc.* **American tabloids/"popular newspapers"/"supermarket tabloids":** *Chicago Sun-Times, New York Post, World Weekly, Examiner, Newsday, Globe, etc.*	• smaller formats and fewer pages • use of banner headlines in bold type • more sensationalist and play on people's emotions • often one-sided and exaggerated reporting • no sharp line between fact and fiction, fact and opinion • use of subjective, often informal language to appeal to the readership's emotions • often lack of reliable sources of information • doubtful/dubious/debatable sources of information • focus on 'less serious' content, e. g. crime stories, celebrities, etc.	▪ to skim a newspaper ▪ entertaining ▪ biased ▪ prejudiced ▪ gossip ▪ attention-grabbing ▪ to hound sb. ▪ to invade sb.'s privacy ▪ exaggeration/to exaggerate ▪ superficial/superficiality ▪ inaccuracy ▪ (political) leanings
British magazines/periodicals*: *Cosmopolitan, The Economist, Look, New Scientist, New Statesman* **American magazines/periodicals*:** *TIME, Esquire, Cosmopolitan, Reader's Digest, Newsweek, Forbes, O – The Oprah Magazine, Vanity Fair, People, The New Yorker, Harper's Magazine*	• periodical publications • published (bi-)weekly, monthly, etc. • printed in colour on glossy paper • financed by advertising • two broad categories: consumer magazines and business magazines • often contain cartoons/reviews • sometimes essays or preprints of books by famous journalists/authors	▪ to incorporate ▪ supplements ▪ subscription/to subscribe ▪ circulation ▪ editor ▪ publisher ▪ compilation of a front page

Further important components of newspapers and magazines

- **advice column/agony aunt*:** a part of a newspaper or magazine in which a person (not necessarily an expert) gives advice to readers about their personal problems
- **human interest story*:** a feature story that presents people and their problems in an emotional way that attracts interest and evokes sympathy in the reader; often criticized as "soft", sensationalistic news or manipulative news
- **letter to the editor*:** a letter sent to a publication about issues of concern to its readers; usually appears in the same specific place (e. g. at the beginning of a newspaper or magazine); comments on or is related to a current or previous edition; can be critical or praising
  → Focus on Skills, Writing a Letter to the Editor, p. 431

Understanding Complex Texts

A text can be "complex" for different reasons:

- It is a **historical document** or a **historical play** (e. g. Shakespeare) that contains words with a different spelling and meaning than in contemporary English (e. g. "thee", "thou" → Elizabethan English).
- A **legal text** which is written in formal English and contains many technical terms (e. g. The Declaration of Independence, the Civil Rights Act, the Bill of Rights, etc.).
- The text is **very long** and does not have obvious paragraphs or sections (e. g. the scene of a play, etc.).
- The text has a **scientific topic**, is written in formal English, employs technical terms/academic language.
- The (literary) text contains a lot of **implicit meaning** (e. g. figurative language, symbols, allusions, etc.), lapses in time (*Zeitsprünge*), multiple points of view, etc.
- The text **requires a lot of life experience** from the reader (e. g. cultural, historical, literal background knowledge, etc.) and expects the reader to "read between the lines" to understand the underlying references.

Step 1: Before reading

- Read the headline of the text and try to **anticipate what the text will be about**. Take notes and/or make a mind map of the topic, the plot or possible arguments the text might deal with.
- If the text is about a scientific or historical topic, you can **do some research in advance** in order to get a first overview of the matter.
- If the text is fictional, e. g. a play or novel, try to **get information on the respective topic** of the text and/or the author/playwright first.

Step 2: While reading

- Be prepared to **read the text at least twice**:
  - in a **first reading**, try to get a **general understanding** (w-questions)
  - in a **second reading**, focus on **details in connection with the assignments** you are given.
- **Annotate the text** and **use different colours** for different aspects (e. g. blue – contents/plot; red – characters/stylistic devices; orange – structure/line of thought; green – allusions or references; etc.)
- **Highlight** or **underline** relevant information, e. g.
  - names of people/places
  - main ideas/arguments
  - special vocabulary/technical terms
  - unknown vocabulary
  - statistical data/numbers
  - references/allusions

  Tip: Do not underline whole sentences but focus on essential keywords or arguments, etc.
- **Make notes in the margin.** For example:
  - Divide the text into paragraphs/thematic units.
  - Write a summarizing headline or sentence of each paragraph/thematic unit.
  - Write your own definitions or explanations of difficult terms
  - Translate ideas into your own words (paraphrasing); use a dictionary if necessary.
  - Ask questions about aspects you do not understand or you are critical about.
  - Distinguish between information/facts given and personal remarks or evaluations made in the text.
  - Comment on ideas/arguments of the author or thoughts/dialogues of characters in a play/novel.
  - Identify the message of the text and the author's intention.

Tip: Make sure that you have **understood the assignments correctly** and focus on the aspects you are required to examine, to explain or to comment on or evaluate. (→ Standardized Terminology for Tasks, pp. 11 ff.)

Step 3: After reading

- **Sort and structure your notes** (e. g. by numbering them) and make sure that you do not distort (*verfälschen*) the information given in the text.
- **Use your pre-reading** research on the matter and cross-check the information given in the text. You can use it for your evaluation or analysis as well.

Focus on Skills

Camera Operations

Camera perspectives/camera positions

over-the-shoulder shot: taken with the camera behind a person, looking over his or her shoulder; usually used in dialogue scenes

reverse-angle shot: shot opposite to that in the preceding scene, showing the dialogue partner

overhead shot (bird's eye view): makes an object less prominent or gives orientation

Camera movements

static shot: camera does not move; aims at evoking a calm, quiet, peaceful state

to pan left/right (*horizontal schwenken*): used for orientation or to follow a person

to tilt up/down (*vertikal schwenken*): used to indicate height or to follow a person/an object (e. g. leaf, water, snowflake, etc.)

to zoom in/away from sth./sb.: zooming in can focus on important details; zooming out can establish the context of the whole situation

tracking shot: camera is on a vehicle (= "dolly") moving on the ground, following a moving character or object, or is moved freely (**hand-held camera or steady cam**); used to indicate the steady movement through the setting

crane shot: camera moves flexibly in all directions on a crane; camera might also pan or tilt

Field size/camera distance

long shot (*Totale*): people/objects shown from a distance; usually to introduce a new setting (see establishing shot)

full shot: shot of the whole body/object and not much else; to emphasize action and the constellation of characters

medium shot: upper body/part of an object; usually to show one or two characters in action

 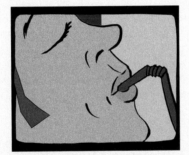 

close-up (*Nahaufnahme*): head, face and shoulders of a person are shown; focus is on the expression of the face (*Mimik*) e. g. to show emotions

extreme close-up (*Detailaufnahme*): detailed shot of parts of the face/the object; often used to create suspense

point-of-view shot: a shot seen through a character's eyes; e. g. an establishing shot at the start of a scene

Camera angle

high-angle shot (bird's eye view, shot from above): used to make people seem smaller, weak, helpless, humiliated, less important

low-angle shot (worm's eye view, shot from below): used to make people seem bigger, stronger, superior, self-confident, powerful, threatening

eye-level shot (straight-on angle): relatively neutral and restrained

Analysis of a Fictional Text

The 3 basic types of fictional texts

a) **Narrative texts** (e.g. novel, short story, fable)
b) **Dramatic texts** (e.g. drama/play, screenplay/script)
c) **Poetry/lyrics** (e.g. poem, song, etc.)

Step 1: Analysis of the general meaning

- Identify and specify the type of text as well as the theme/topic/subject of the given text.
- Answer the W-questions: who, what, where, when, why?
- Write a summary of the given text of about 150 – 200 words at the most.
- Identify the narrator and specify what point of view is being used to tell the story.
- Develop a first (general) evaluation of the meaning and message of the text.

Step 2: Analysis of basic elements

a) **Identify the structural and narrative/stylistic devices** and show **what effect and function** they have. The following grid contains some terminology and tips for your analysis. The most relevant vocabulary can be found in the Literary Terms section.

narrator, narrative situation, point of view, mode of presentation	first-person narrator, witness/observer narrator, third-person narrator, objective/reliable narrator, subjective/unreliable narrator, limited point of view, unlimited/omniscient point of view, panoramic presentation, scenic presentation, relation of acting time and narrating time
structure	• (How) is the text structured? • What time span does the narration cover? • What is the relation between acting time and narrating time ? • Which conflict is the story based on? • How does the action develop – or stagnate? • Are there any leitmotifs?
characters	flat/round characters, protagonist vs. antagonist, minor character(s), hero(ine), anti-hero, outward appearance, behaviour, relationship to other characters, direct or indirect characterization
setting **(= time and place)**	scenery, mental climate, basic mood, social environment, atmosphere • Does the scenery/setting itself imply any symbolism? (e.g. thunderstorm = danger, large city = liveliness, anonymity, etc.) • What is the effect on the audience? • What intention might the author/playwright have had?
language/style	level of speech, manner of speaking, style, syntax, choice of words, inner monologue, chain of associations, stream of consciousness, register

b) **Never forget to quote** from the text to demonstrate the correctness and accuracy of your work.

Step 3: Comment on and evaluation of the text

- Classify and evaluate the text and its message.
- Relate the given text to other texts of the same epoch/time and compare it with other texts by the same author that you have dealt with. Pay attention to striking similarities and differences.
- Critically comment on the text and finish with a concluding sentence.

Note: Explanations of the respective technical terms can be found in the Literary Terms section, pp. 433 ff.

Analysis of a Film Scene

General tips on viewing and analysing a film

- Watch the film scene at least two times.
- Work systematically and concentrate on the devices employed in the scene in a certain order.
- Take notes while or immediately after each viewing of the film scene.
- Whenever you identify and specify a certain narrative technique and/or cinematic device used in a film scene, explain and illustrate its function and effect on the viewer.
- In order to explain the use and function of cinematic devices precisely and correctly, make use of technical terms.
  → Literary Terms section, pp. 433 ff., and Focus on Facts, Camera Operations, pp. 400 f.
- When viewing and analysing a film scene, it is not possible to explain and demonstrate every single detail; therefore, you should focus on the most striking and relevant devices employed in the scene.

Step 1: Focus on narrative techniques

guiding elements	function
• **setting**: What is the time and place of the action? What is the atmosphere like?	→ orientation for the viewer → general exposition
• **plot:** What happens and why?	→ drawing the viewers into the action, evoking and raising interest
• **suspense**: Which questions are raised and remain unanswered?	→ evoking the viewers' curiosity and keeping them interested
• **appearance of characters**: What do(es) the character(s) look like?	→ evoking interest, sympathy, antipathy, etc.
• **body language**: What is/are the character(s)' movements, gestures, postures, facial expressions?	→ revealing character traits, quirks, etc.
• **language/communication**: What choice of words and tone do(es) the character(s) use? How do they interact?	→ exposition of the intellectual background, demonstration of the characters' relationship(s)

Step 2: Focus on cinematic devices

cinematic device	function
• **camera operations**: Which field sizes, camera angles, camera positions, camera movements, etc. are employed?	→ transferring narration into film/images/pictures
• **visual symbols**: Which visual symbols (e. g. cross, blood, tombstone, eagle) are employed?	→ visual leitmotifs serve as links and help to express/ to intensify a deeper contextual meaning
• **film music/sound**: What kind of music/what (background) sounds are employed?	→ to show/emphasize a mood, to create suspense, to foreshadow, etc.
• **(special) effects**: What further effects (e. g. slow motion, voice-over narration) are employed?	→ to intensify the action, to reveal thoughts, to suggest speed, etc.

Step 3: Explanation of the function of the scene (in the context of the film)

- Place the scene in the context of the film.
- Explain and give examples of how the scene
  a) moves the action forward and creates suspense,
  b) presents an unexpected turning-point in the action,
  c) reveals a new character trait of the protagonist,
  d) introduces (a) new character(s),
  e) defines (a) relationship(s) between characters.

Analysis of a Screenplay

A screenplay or film script is a written work for a film or TV programme. Basically, a film script depicts the **movement, actions, expressions and dialogues of characters** and gives **technical directions and instructions**, e. g. concerning the camera operations. The "action" is always written in the present tense. Here are further characteristic features of film scripts that you should consider in your analysis.

"Whatta you mean 'minor script changes?' It's supposed to be a western."

Format and style

- A screenplay **focuses on what is audible and visible** on screen.
- Screenplays have a **specific layout and codified[1] notations[2]** of technical or dramatic elements, e. g. scene transitions[3], changes in the narrative perspective, sound effects, emphasis on dramatically relevant objects, emphasis on characters speaking from outside a scene. These notations are always **written in capital letters**.
- **Different scene elements** are visualized by **tab settings[4]**, e. g. dialogue, scene headings, transitions or parentheticals[5].
- The **beginning** of a scene is usually marked with "FADE IN:", the **ending** with "FADE TO BLACK."

Slug lines[6]

One of the **most relevant and unique features** of screenplays are slug lines; they are always written in **capital letters** and are usually divided into three parts.
Part 1 ... determines the **general setting** of a scene, e. g. inside (interior = INT.) or outside (exterior = EXT.).
Part 2 ... determines the **location** of the scene, e. g. SUSAN'S APARTMENT – KITCHEN, JIMMY'S CAR, etc.
Part 3 ... determines the **time** of the scene, e. g. DAY, NIGHT, DAWN, LATE NIGHT, etc.
If a character starts inside and then walks outside during a scene, a new slug line is needed which begins with CONTINUOUS[7].

Examples:
- INT. ALICE'S HOME – BATHROOM – NIGHT
- EXT. PARK – DAY/MORNING

Further characteristics:
- each slug line begins a new scene
- slug lines are numbered consecutively[8]
- any change of time or location requires a new slug line
- slug lines are on their own lines, flush with the left margin[9] and are completely typed in capital letters.

Common abbreviations used in scripts

ELS	extreme long shot	2-S or 3-S	two-shot or three shot	VO	voice-over
MLS	medium long shot	INT	interior	OSV	offscreen voice
LS	long shot	EXT	exterior	DIS	dissolve[10]
MS	medium shot	BG	background	MIC	microphone
MCU	medium close-up	POV	point of view shot	VTR	videotape
CU	close-up	ZI or ZO	zoom in or zoom out	ANNCR	announcer
ECU	extreme close-up	SOT or SOF	sound on tape or sound on film	SUPER	superimposition[11]
OS	over-the-shoulder-shot	SFX or F/X	special effects (sound or visual)	Q	cue[12]

→ Focus on Facts, Screenplays and Storyboards, p. 397

[1] **to codify** festschreiben – [2] **notation** Bezeichnung – [3] **transition** Übergang – [4] **tab setting** Tabellator – [5] **parenthetical** Einschub – [6] **slug line** a line of abbreviated text; master scene heading – [7] **continuous** andauernd – [8] **consecutive** fortlaufend – [9] **flush with left margin** linksbündig – [10] **to dissolve** sich auflösen, verschwinden – [11] **superimposition** Einblendung, Überlagerung – [12] **cue** Stichwort, Regiesignal

Analysis of a Non-Fictional Text

Step 1: Analysis of structure and content

- Identify and specify the theme/topic/subject* of the given text.
- Identify the characteristics of the heading* (e. g. provocative, ironic, funny, etc.).
- Divide the text into parts and relate these parts to the heading and the whole text.
- Write a summary of 150 words at most.
- Determine the message of the text. Predict the basic characteristics of the text (type).
- Clarify the line of argument, the train of thought* (general structure of the text).

Step 2: Analysis of stylistic devices/use of language

a) **Identify the stylistic devices** and show what effect and function they have.
   The following grid contains some vocabulary for your analysis. The most relevant vocabulary is marked with
   * and can be found in the Literary Terms section (pp. 433 ff.).

register (= *Sprachebene*)	slang, colloquial, everyday English, written language, (in)formal, poetic, sophisticated, familiar, technical terms, scientific, religious, metaphorical
choice of words	denotations*, connotations*, keywords, figurative*/literal meaning of words, emphatic/negative function of words, euphemisms*, synonyms*, abstractions
style	plain, sober, natural, matter-of-fact, clear, precise, concise, vigorous, fluent, passionate, elegant, artificial, stilted, wordy, colourless, cliché-ridden, snappy, lengthy, clumsy, spontaneous, trite, expressing doubt/certainty
tone	humorous, playful, colloquial, conciliatory, depressive, serious, solemn, ironic, satirical, sarcastic, warm-hearted, aggressive, whining, reproachful
rhetorical devices	alliteration*, anaphora*, allusion*, reference*, antithesis*, ellipsis, hyperbole*, irony*, metaphor*, paradox*, personification*, simile*, symbol*, understatement, exaggeration*, parallelism*, employment of leitmotifs*, repetitions*, juxtapositions, (rhetorical) questions*, quotations, enumerations, appeals, comparisons, digressions from the main topic, grammatical tenses, illustrations, superlatives, personal pronouns/grammatical persons (we – they, I – you, our – their, us – them)

b) **Do not forget to include quotes** to demonstrate the correctness and accuracy of your work. This is how to do it:
   - When **referring** to an important part of the text without quoting the words, give the page(s) and/or line(s): e. g. *Obama tells the audience about his jogging with foreign students (ll. 10 – 15).*
   - You can **integrate the quotation** into your sentence: e. g. *Obama is determined to establish "an environment of lifelong learning" (l. 74), which means that …*
   - You can **use a full quotation**: e. g. *Obama starts with the most important point: "First, to help every child begin school healthy and ready to learn." (l. 10).*
   - Note the abbreviations:
     - one page or line: p. 17 / l. 12
     - more pages or lines: pp. 10 – 14 / ll. 25 – 30
     - the following page(s), line(s): f. / ff. (e. g. pp. 12 f. or pp. 10 ff.)
   - **Omissions** of any kind are indicated by square brackets and three dots: […]. Remarks or **changes from the original text** are indicated by square brackets: *He* [Obama] *says …*

Step 3: Evaluation of the text

- State whether (or not) the text is well-structured/convincing/effective/appropriate …
- Discuss whether/to what extent the text/author is able to address the reader(ship).
- Critically comment on the text, and refer to similar texts that you have dealt with.
- Finish with a concluding sentence.

Analysis of Poetry and Lyrics

Poetry (from the Greek "poiesis" = making, creating) is a type of literature in which **ideas, experiences and feelings are expressed** in compact, imaginative, and often musical language. Poets arrange words in ways designed to touch readers' senses, emotions and minds. Lyrics are a set of words that accompany music, either by
5 speaking or singing. The word *lyric* derives from the Greek word "lyrikos" (= a song sung by the lyre). Most poems and lyrics are written in lines that may contain patterns of rhyme and rhythm to help convey their meaning. They often use **figures of speech and imagery to appeal to the readers' and listeners' emotions and imagination**. The poet or songwriter usually invents a speaker from whose point of view the feelings, ideas, experiences, etc. are expressed. Poems and songs may be
10 divided into stanzas (groups of lines) or sections and can greatly vary in structure, theme and atmosphere.

general meaning/ content	● What situation/topic is presented? ● What is the theme; are there any (striking) leitmotifs? ● What is the author's/singer's intention; what is the message of the poem/song? ● What kind of register of English has been chosen (poetic, colloquial, archaic, slang, etc.)? ● What is the melody like (harmonious, rhythmical, tuneful, staccato, etc.)?
formal analysis: a) structural devices	● Examine – the structure of the poem/song (stanzas, lines, (lack of) punctuation, refrain(s), break(s), enjambements, chorus, etc.), – the use of repetitions and/or enumerations/parallelisms, – the use of contrast(s)/antithesis, – the use of an illustration (= an example to make an idea clear), – the rhyme scheme (e. g. pair rhyme aa bb cc; cross rhyme abab; enclosed rhyme abba), – the use of free verse.
b) sense devices	– (How) are objects and ideas/thoughts brought together? – What type(s) of sentence(s) is/are used (hypotactical/paratactical sentences, questions, commands, etc.)? – Are there allusions/references to a certain topic (e. g. nature, city, love, etc.)? – Check on the use of simile (a direct comparison: "like, as"), metaphor (an implied comparison without a connective word: "an ocean of tears"), personifications (something non-human is given human characteristics: "the frosty cliffs were asleep"), or symbols (an object that also stands for some abstract idea: a red rose → symbol of love, beauty). – the use of grammatical tenses – the speaker's point of view – the use of hyperbole/exaggeration
c) sound devices	● Examine – the use of alliteration/anaphora, – the use of rhymes and/or assonances (= imperfect rhymes), – the use of a particular rhythm, beat, – the use of onomatopoeia (= words that imitate a sound: buzz, cuckoo, etc.), – the instrumentation, beat, vocal/instrumental type of music, vocals, etc. → **Show how these devices support, stress/emphasize the meaning/content of the poem/song (→ function/effect).** → **Show how style and content are connected.** → **Show how sound and lyrics match and support each other.**
d) final comment and evaluation	Try to classify the given poem/song (refer to other poems/songs by the same author or authors of the same background). Evaluate the poem/song (Is the poem/song convincing? Has the author/singer succeeded in conveying his/her message? etc.). What do you consider to be the final message of the poem/song? What do you consider to be the effect on the reader/listener?

Note: Explanations of the respective technical terms can be found in the Literary Terms section, pp. 433 ff.

Analysis of a Political Speech

General aspects of political rhetoric

The purpose of most political speeches is persuasion rather than information. There is always a (hidden, underlying) message involved, often related to certain attitudes and values of the speaker. A political statement intends to affect the listeners by making use of diverse structural and rhetorical devices. In order to understand and evaluate a political speech, one should consider the following aspects:

first (general) impression:	• topic, subject matter, general tone, issues and purpose of the speech
contents and structure:	• salient and striking topics, important aspects • organization of the text, arrangement of parts (e. g. introduction, main part or body, conclusion) • train of thought, composition, line of argument
circumstances of the speech/ political context:	• time and place/medium (e. g. TV, radio, face-to-face, Internet) • position of the speaker (president, leader of a political party, leader of a protest movement, etc.) • audience (mass audience, a limited group of people) • occasion (election campaign, protest demonstration, political debate, informal gathering) • genre and type (presidential address to the nation, sermon, speech at a demonstration, campus speech, testimony)
formal and stylistic devices: **a) language**	• keywords and phrases • word groups/clusters related to a certain topic • different registers for different addressees (e. g. sophisticated language to address wealthy and/or educated people, use of dialect, etc.) • choice of words (colloquialisms, slang expressions, poetic expressions)
b) grammar	• sentence structure/syntax (use of main/sub-clauses) • use of grammatical tenses (indirect references to history, future, etc.)
c) rhetoric	• use of rhetorical questions • use of contrast and oppositions (positive/negative, familiar/alien, near/distant, etc.) • use of key symbols, slogans, stereotypes • abstractions and generalizations • use of grammatical persons (I, us, we – you, they: patterns of identification and solidarity or vice versa) • metaphors, personifications • allusions and references to history (American Dream, important political/historical issues, good/bad times, tradition, future, etc.); quotations • repetitions (alliterations, anaphora); parallelisms • comparisons, numbers, factual information • irony, exaggerations, simplifications • imperatives, emotionally-loaded words • concentration on essential points vs. wordy elaboration • insertions
d) manner of speaking/voice	• volume, tempo, stress, intonation, abrupt changes, pauses, rhythm
evaluation:	→ Comment on the personal integrity of the speaker, the general political circumstances, the impact on the listeners. → Compare the speech/speaker to other political speeches/speakers. Was he/she convincing?

Note: Explanations of the respective technical terms can be found in the Literary Terms section, pp. 433 ff.

Focus on Skills

Analysis of Statistical Data

different types

	1992	2001	2020
USA	230 mn	260 mn	300 mn
China	800 mn	1,000 mn	1,300 mn
India	600 mn	800 mn	1,100 mn

A table gives raw data as the basis for analysis and consists of a grid with numbers arranged in lines and columns. Typically, it aims to present data in an ordered way, thus making the information easy to understand.

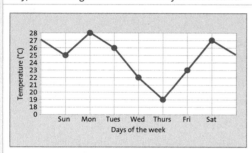

A (line) graph presents one or more lines in a system of coordinates/axes – a horizontal and a vertical axis. It shows the development of figures/variables over a period of time (trends, tendencies).

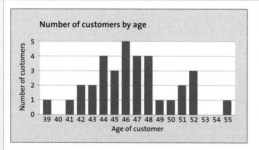

A bar chart shows differences between various things. It presents boxes/bars of different heights in a system of coordinates. The bars can be arranged horizontally or vertically.

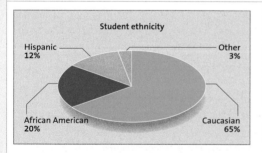

A pie chart shows percentages of a whole. It consists of a circle/pie divided into different sections/segments.

general aspects

- How reliable/trustworthy is the source?
- Are the numbers up-to-date?
- Consider why a chart/graph/table has been chosen as the means of visual representation.
- Are the figures absolute numbers or percentage figures – and what is the function of this presentation?
- What do the numbers/data suggest?
- Turn the percentage figures/data into words and compare them.
- Relate the data to the given context.

useful terms and phrases

■ to reach a peak/a low point/an all-time high/low of … ■ to remain constant/stable ■ to go through a period of growth ■ to increase/rise/grow/go up ■ to decrease/fall/drop/go down ■ a fall/decline/drop/decrease ■ an increase/a rise/growth ■ to grow … by 10 %/at a certain rate ■ a rise of 8 %/in temperature/to €25 ■ steep/strong/rapid … growth ■ a gradual/steady/continual … fall ■ a slight/barely noticeable … rise

useful terms and phrases

■ in comparison with/compared with ■ in contrast to ■ to achieve an average/below-average/above-average figure ■ to be at the top/bottom of the ranking ■ to rank first/second … last ■ the highest/lowest figure/score ■ no/little/a big difference between A and B (… with regards to … last year …) ■ the figures are identical/similar to … ■ the vast majority of/only a minority … ■ to experience a sudden rise/drop ■ after a brief recovery …

useful terms and phrases

■ the pie chart is divided into … ■ segments/sections ■ each segment represents … ■ the share of 5 % of the total amount is about 2 million euro … ■ the biggest/the smallest section ■ the whole circle represents/stands for … ■ the chart reveals the share of … ■ percentage-wise ■ a marginal percentage of … ■ an infinitely small amount of …

Analysis of Visuals

Visuals or images can be all kinds of graphical material, e. g. photos, film stills, adverts, paintings, etc.

Analysis of cartoons

A **cartoon** is a **comic or satirical drawing** in a newspaper, a magazine or on the Internet that aims at humorously criticizing current, and especially political, events. It usually consists of a drawing (**pictorial part**) and speech balloons and a comment or a caption (= a short title), which is most frequently placed underneath (**textual part**). However, all the elements are not necessarily used in each cartoon.

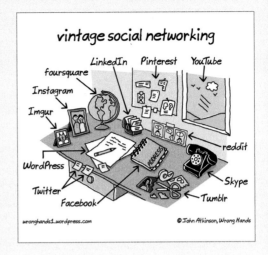

Step 1: Author and source
- What is the title or caption of the cartoon?
- Which artist drew the cartoon (if known)?
- Where was the cartoon published (newspaper, magazine, Internet, etc.)?

Step 2: Descriptive level
- Describe the people, objects and the setting in the cartoon in detail. What action is taking place?
  Tip: Structure your description: What do you see e. g. in the foreground, centre, background, etc.?
- Which visual elements are employed, e. g. colours (black-white contrast), which visual metaphors?
- Which (political, historical, social) events or issues may have inspired the cartoon?

Step 3: Symbolic/figurative level
Cartoonists (often) employ pictures and words to express their personal opinions.
- What tools are used to convey a certain message?
- What do the symbols used stand for?
- Which person/group does the cartoon focus on?

irony	The recognition of the difference between reality and appearance. In **verbal irony**, there is a contrast between what is said and what is actually meant. **Situational irony** refers to a situation in which the opposite of what you expect to happen actually does happen.
parody	In literature, a text that imitates and slightly changes another well-known text in order to ridicule it, comment on it or trivialize it.
caricature	In literature, for example a character whose traits have been exaggerated to create a comic effect.
sarcasm	A bitter or aggressive remark used to express mockery or disapproval; often this is a statement which conveys the opposite of its literal meaning. In contrast to irony, which is gentle and more subtle, sarcasm is bitter and usually openly expressed.
pun	An expression involving a play on words, in which one word has two different meanings, so that a sentence can be understood in two different ways.
allusion/reference	An allusion or reference to for example a well-known (historical) person or event, politics, popular culture, the arts or a statement from a famous work of literature.
stereotype/ labeling	A word or phrase that describes a person in a way that is too general and often not true (*jdn. abstempeln*); cf. cliché
hyperbole	A figure of speech that contains an exaggeration.
symbol	An element of imagery in which a concrete object stands not only for itself but for some abstract idea or larger concept as well (e. g. rose → love).
visual/pictorial metaphor	The representation of a person, thing or idea by a visual image, e. g. Uncle Sam for the United States, an elephant for India, an orange for sunshine, etc.
black humour	Humorous effects resulting rather from grotesque, morbid or macabre situations. Black humour aims to shock and disorient readers, making them laugh in the face of anxiety, suffering or death.

Step 4: Meaning and evaluation
- What is the message of the cartoon?
- Do you think the cartoon is effective in conveying its message? Is the pictorial presentation convincing?

Analysis of photos

To help you analyse visuals or images, here are some steps for you to follow:

Step 1: Production
- When and where was the image taken?
- Who created the image (e. g. a professional photographer, a private person, an advertising agency, etc.)?
- Was the picture arranged or was it a snapshot?
- Is the picture presented in the original version or has it e.g. been photoshopped or blue-pencilled?

Step 2: Image
- **Describe the visual elements of the image and how they are arranged.**
  - What is being shown? (e. g. surroundings, people, facial expressions, gestures, posture, clothing, accessories, etc.)
  - What are the main visual components and how are they arranged?
    Tip: In order to get a better overview of the various elements, their arrangement and relationship to each other, make a rough draft before you start to describe them.
  - Where is the viewer's eye drawn to the picture – and why? (eye-catching/visually-dominant elements)
  - What use is made of colour?
- **Explain the function and effect of visual elements and symbols.**
  - What medium is the image taken from (e. g. film, advert, photo campaign, Internet, etc.)?
  - Is the image contradictory?
  - What visual symbols are employed – and what is their function and effect?
  - State whether they imply a deeper, symbolic meaning.
  - Point out whether they appeal to the viewer/the target audience/the addressee(s).

Step 3: Addressing the audience
- **Identify and explain the message of the photo/picture.**
  - Who does the image address?
  - Is there a particular target group (e. g. a snapshot of a demonstration, etc.)?
  - What relationship is created between the image and the viewer?
  - Is more than one interpretation possible?
  - How might different viewers interpret the image and its message?
  - What emotions does the image appeal to?
  - Is there a strategy behind the image? If so, which one?
  - Are there any political/cultural/social implications?
  - Are there any historical/political/religious references?
- **State whether the visual/image/picture is effective and convincing in its message.**

visual elements:
- dancing children → motion/vitality
- a street scene → everyday life
- b/w photo → focus on contrast

visual metaphor: black and white child playing together → overcoming racism

surroundings: street in New York City

snapshot: a glimpse of reality

use of contrast: black and white

function: emotional appeal to the viewer and (indirect) political message

Helen Levitt. New York, 1940s

Characterization of a Figure in Literature

Fictional characters can be presented in a number of ways. In general, a character in a fictional text is developed through action, description, language and ways of speaking.

Types of characters

relevance within the text and characteristics	
• **protagonist** (the main character around whom most of the work revolves)	• **major characters** (main characters who dominate the story)
• **antagonist** (the person who the protagonist is against; often the villain)	• **minor characters** (less important persons who support the main character(s) by letting them interact or reveal their personalities, etc.)
• **the modern hero** (the average man/woman)	• **dynamic character** (changing and developing, with different traits)
• **the anti-hero** (often dishonest, graceless or inept person who struggles in life; the loser)	• **static characters** (unchanging, often stereotypical)
• **the tragic hero** (e. g. *Macbeth*; person who ends tragically as a result of personal flaws)	• **round character** (three-dimensional, with different and changing facets to the personality)
• **romantic hero** (a character with a strong will and personality who goes against established norms; often this figure experiences melancholy, isolation and unfulfilled and unhappy love)	• **flat character** (one-dimensional, viewed only from one side, often stereotypical)
• **the Hemingway hero** (a character who has been at war, drinks too much, the loner, "cowboy")	

Types of characterization in literature

- In a **direct characterization of a character** the narrator or one of the other characters **tells** the readers/audience what the character's personality is like.
- In an **indirect characterization** the writer **shows/presents** the character talking and acting, which reveals the character's personality. Indirect characterization can be achieved through:
  a) **Speech** (What does the character say, how does he/she communicate and interact with others?)
  b) **Thoughts** (What is revealed through the person's private thoughts, e. g. in a monologue, soliloquy, a diary entry, etc.?)
  c) **Effect on others/on the character** (How does the person react/respond to others? Does he/she have any relationships? How do others react to the person?)
  d) **Actions** (What does the person do, how does he/she behave?)
  e) **Looks** (appearance, body language, gestures, facial expression, etc.)

How to write a literary characterization

Step 1: Collect the facts and clues given in the text and move from the outward features and characteristics to the inward nature of the character:

- **personal data** (name, age, sex, nationality)
- **attitudes/views** (thoughts, dreams, emotions)
- **relationships** (social background, family, friends)
- **outward appearance** (body, face, clothes, etc.)
- **behaviour** (toward other characters, actions)

Step 2: Draw your conclusions about the person's character and relate your findings to the text by referring to specific lines. Use the simple present for your characterization.

Step 3: Follow the "introduction – main part – conclusion" pattern in your characterization. Write an introductory sentence that answers the w-questions.

→ Focus on Language, Literary Terms, pp. 433 ff.

Mediation

Mediating a text means translating a written or recorded text from one language into another (e. g. German → English, English → German). In general, the person who is mediating must **consider the addressee(s), the meaning of the text/message, as well as cultural and situational aspects**.

When you are in a foreign country, you are constantly confronted with information/facts that you have to read or listen to: road signs, brochures, maps, (radio) announcements, advertisements, commercials, films, flight/train schedules, websites, letters, instructions, prescriptions, people talking to you, etc.

In a written examination you must consider the following aspects when asked to mediate a text:

How to mediate a text in a written examination

- **Select the most relevant information** from the text you are asked to mediate. Leave out less important details.
- **Focus** on the information **your communication partner** needs to know or what is important for the **topic**.
- Give an **analogous rendition** (*sinngemäße Wiedergabe*) of the text, not a literal translation.
- **Consider** the **addressee** (e. g. his/her cultural background).
- Take **situational aspects** into account (e. g. private, professional, etc.).
- Give **additional information** and explanations if necessary (e. g. on geography, culture, politics, etc.).
- **Consider** the **type of text you are required to write** (*Zieltextformat*) (e. g. a blog, a formal/informal letter, etc.).
- **Use compensation strategies** (i. e. paraphrasing, synonyms, etc.)

Criteria for evaluation

- Has the **purpose and intention** of the text been conveyed?
- Has the **addressee** been considered appropriately?
- Have the **assignments and standardized formulations** (*Operatoren*) been taken into consideration?
- Have the **characteristics of the type of text** (*Zieltextformat*) been considered?
- Is the **formulation self-directed** (*eigenständig*) and independent?
- Do the **style and choice of words** match the intention of the text?
- Does the **construction of sentences** vary (e. g. use of linking words and connectives)?
- Is the text **grammatically correct** (grammar, spelling, punctuation, word order)?

10 tips to help mediate a written or recorded text

1. Do not translate the text word for word.
2. Listen to/watch out for keywords and the most relevant/useful/appropriate information.
3. Leave out minor details and irrelevant information (→ summarizing).
4. Try to understand the gist of the text and put it into your own words (but do not change the facts!).
5. Sometimes there are words that cannot be translated into German/English because they imply cultural differences (e. g. homecoming, gap year, cheerleading or *Schützenfest*, *Abigag*, etc.). In such cases, give examples to illustrate the situation, or add information on the cultural background if necessary.
6. Do not interpret or evaluate the text, just mediate it.
7. Express difficult passages more simply; technical terms should be replaced by everyday language.
8. Make use of paraphrases (e. g. a cheerleader is a girl who …).
9. If you do not know a word, use a synonym (= word or expression that has the same or nearly the same meaning as another in the same language).
10. If you cannot think of the right word, try simply using the opposite.

→ Proverbs can reveal a great deal of cultural background. Try to find the equivalent proverb rather than trying to translate literally (e. g. *vom Regen in die Traufe* → out of the frying pan and into the fire).

→ Beware of false friends, i. e. English words that sound or look like German ones but **differ** in meaning (e. g. become, actual, sensible, etc.).

Conversation and Discussion

opening a conversation

You should always start a discussion with some kind of introductory phrase:

- I saw an interesting programme on TV last night …/
  I read a fascinating article in the newspaper yesterday about …/What do you think about …?
- Have you ever thought about …/What would it be like if …?
- I was really surprised to find out that …
- Did you know that …?
- Do you mind if I join you?
- Excuse me, …
- (I'm) sorry (to trouble you), but …
- Have you got time to …?

expressing your opinion/giving an opinion

- In my view, …
- In my opinion, …
- As I see it, …
- To my mind, …
- If you ask me, …
- I am sure/certain that …
- I think/believe/feel that …
- It seems to me that …
- There should be …/ought to be …
- I would like to …/I wouldn't like to …
- It would be a good idea to … (because …)

making suggestions/recommendations

- If I were you, I would …
- The best thing would be to …
- You'd better …
- Why don't you …?
- How about …?
- Have you tried/thought of … (+ gerund)?
- You should/could …

including your conversation partner

Sometimes in a discussion, you may find that you are monopolizing the conversation, and you would like to know what your partner thinks:

- So what do you think, … (+ name)?
- How do you feel about that?
- What is your view on this (matter)?
- What is your opinion about/of/on …?

interrupting your conversation partner

Sometimes it is the other way round. Your partner is monopolizing the discussion and you want to have your say:

- Can I jump in here?
- Can I just make a point?
- Perhaps I can interrupt you there.
- I'd like to get in on that if I may.
- Do you mind if I say something on that point?
- Wait a minute …
- (I'm) sorry to interrupt, but …
- Sorry, may I interrupt you for a second …
- Sorry, but did you say …?
- Can I just say/add that …
- Yes/You're right/I agree, but …
- I hope you don't mind, but …

changing the subject

These expressions help you to bring in further aspects:

- (Oh) by the way, …
- Before I forget,…
- I just thought of something …
- There's something else I wanted to ask you/say …
- Oh, now I know what I wanted to say/ask you …
- I know this has got nothing to do with what we are talking about, but …
- Could I just say … (before I forget …)
- Let's also consider …
- While I think of it, …

holding the floor

Sometimes you notice that someone is trying to interrupt you, but you haven't finished what you want to say, so you try to carry on:

- If I might just say this.
- Do you mind if I just finish what I was saying?
- I'd just like to finish making this point and then it's over to you.
- Let me just add one more thing.
- This is my final point.
- Would you please let me finish (this sentence/thought)?

returning to the original subject

Sometimes people stray from the main issue of a debate and it is necessary to get back to the topic:

- As I was saying, …
- (Now) what was I saying/what were we talking about?
- To get back to what we were talking about, …
- Let's get back to …
- (Yes, well) anyway, …
- Let's get back to the point …
- But we digress…
- Where were we before we got onto this topic?

Focus on Language

defending yourself

If someone attacks you in a discussion, you can say:
- That's not what I said/meant at all. I was merely pointing out that …
- You've got that all wrong. What I said was …
- You're putting words in my mouth.
- You are distorting what I actually said.

expressing surprise

- I don't believe it/that!
- That's strange/funny …
- Are you (being) serious?
- Are you pulling my leg?
- Really?
- You can't mean that seriously!/You can't be serious!
- I doubt it/that/whether …
- Are you kidding me?

ending a discussion/a conversation

When you feel that you have effectively finished your discussion, that the conversation is not getting anywhere or that you have exhausted the topic, you can finish off.
- We'll just have to agree to disagree on that point.
- Further discussion is pointless, so let's end there.
- We've heard some interesting points/some new ideas, so let's stop there and go away and think about them.
- I can understand you better now, even though I don't completely agree with you.
- Well, anyway …
- Would you excuse me now, please?
- Sorry, but I've got to go now.
- I'd love to stay and discuss this further, but …
- It's been a very interesting discussion. However …
- Perhaps we can continue this another time.
- Look after yourself.
- Take care.

using fillers

- Well …
- Actually …
- You know/see …
- Let's see …
- I/you mean …
- Now let me think/see …
- In fact, …
- I wonder …
- The thing is …
- I see what you mean.
- Right then.
- Let's say …

expressing complete agreement

- You're absolutely right.
- I completely agree with you on that point.
- Precisely/Exactly.
- So do I./Me too. (agreement with a positive statement)
- Nor do I./Me neither. (agreement with a negative statement)
- That's what I think, too.

expressing partial agreement

- You're right up to a point.
- That might be the case/true.
- You could be right.
- You've got a point.
- Maybe that's true.
- That's true enough.

partial disagreement

- Do you really think so?
- Are you sure?
- That's an exaggeration.
- That's not necessarily the case/true.
- It's not as simple as that.
- I wouldn't quite say that.
- I can't imagine that.
- I find that hard to believe.

complete disagreement

Careful with this one! You do not want to make enemies, do you? Try not to be abrupt or too direct.
- That is definitely not the case.
- I'm 100 % certain of that. (disagreement with a previous negative statement)
- That's not true at all.
- You're quite wrong there.
- I totally disagree with you.

Job Interview

"Well, I guess a master's degree is a master's degree, even if it *is* in skateboarding."

How to prepare yourself for the interview

- **Research** the company where you will have the interview, e. g.
  - the company's history and background (founder, etc.),
  - make sure to use the company's correct name,
  - the company's range of products and/or services.
- **Think of possible questions** you might be asked and **prepare suitable answers**.
- **Rehearse a job interview** with a friend and have them ask you questions (some that you have prepared *and* some surprise questions).
- **Evaluate** the "mock interview" with your friend:
  - Which answers turned out well and which ones need to be improved?
  - What impression did your friend have of you (body language, nervousness, friendliness, etc.)?
- Think of **questions that you want to ask** the interviewer. Your questions should reveal that you already know something about the company and its management and structure (cf. Tips on vocab below).
- **Dress** nicely, neatly and **appropriately**.
- **Arrive early** so that you have time to collect your thoughts and appear calm and relaxed.

Tips on vocab ⟫

the company's corporate culture/identity ∎ challenges/innovations for the future ∎ plans for future expansion ∎ approach taken towards managing employees ∎ management philosophy

What to do during the interview

- **Smile and maintain eye contact** with your interviewer. **Be positive** and try to convey that you are enthusiastic and energetic.
- If the interviewer tries to lighten the interview with some **small talk, be prepared to chat** with him/her.
- **Speak clearly and slowly.** Do not rush through your answers and give yourself time to think before you answer. You do not want to convey the impression of being thoughtless or superficial.
- Do not hesitate **to ask the interviewer to repeat** or explain his/her question.
- **Do not simply answer questions with "yes", "no" or "I don't know".** The interview is your chance to express your thoughts and convince the interviewer that you are the best choice for the job.
  But: be careful not to talk too much – **keep your answers clear and concise**.
- If there is still time (or the interviewer asks you to do so) **you can ask the questions** that you prepared.
- **Thank your interviewer** at the end.

Tips on vocab ⟫

I didn't have any difficulty finding you. The map your secretary sent me was very helpful. ∎ As you can see from my CV … ∎ … perhaps you would like me to tell you something about my experience in … ∎ Is there anything specific you would like to know about me? ∎ Could you tell me more about …? ∎ Thank you very much for seeing me. ∎ Thank you for your time.

After the interview

- After a short time (ca. 2 weeks), **send a follow-up mail/letter** thanking your interviewer.
- **Express your interest** in the company again.
- Ask politely **when you can expect a reply**/a decision.

Tips on vocab ⟫

How shall we proceed? ∎ When can I expect to hear from you? ∎ When will a decision be made? ∎ When are you likely to make a decision? ∎ I had an interview for the position of a … three weeks ago and would like to enquire whether a decision has been taken yet.

Focus on Skills

Oral Examinations

Oral exams are a lot like job interviews, so you can prepare for these in the same way that job applicants prepare – predict likely questions and practice the answers. In general, an oral exam is an opportunity for you to **demonstrate your knowledge, your presentation and speaking skills as well as your ability to communicate**. Examinations can be formal or informal, but in either case you must listen carefully to the questions and answer them directly.

The **formal exam** usually consists of a set of prepared questions and the evaluation criteria usually follow a right/wrong format. In contrast, **informal exam questions** are more open, answers are usually longer and evaluated based on problem-solving, analysis, method as well as communication and presentation skills.

Preparing for the exam

- **Collect all the material** that is likely to be covered in the exam and **try to predict essay-type questions** (i. e. questions that require a more complex answer and include a wider range of aspects. If you work with a textbook, you can use the table of contents to find possible topics.
- **Write down possible questions** on an index card. Then practice answering each possible question out loud.
- Make **a list of vocabulary terms and phrases** in connection with the possible questions.
- Then select three index cards at random (*stichprobenartig*). Pretend to be the tester and ask a question that **connects the three aspects together**. This helps you to make connections between the different topics.
- If you are a **visual learner**, you may want to draw images to boost your memory.
- **Turn off electronic equipment.**

During the exam

- Some oral exams begin with a presentation by the student. For an introduction, **give some indication of what the topic or problem is about** and why it is important.
- Give the examiner **your full attention** and look interested. Maintain **good posture** and **eye contact**.
- **Listen carefully** to the questions and make sure that you **understand exactly** what is being asked. If a short answer is requested, keep it short – if more detail is desired, give a longer response.
- Give yourself a moment to **think before you answer**. If you do not know the answer right away, feel free to take time to think. If you are able to use a blank sheet of paper and a pencil, take notes and/or draw the images you created as memory boosters.
- If you do not understand the question, **ask the examiner to reformulate, rephrase or repeat** it.
- If you cannot answer a question, **state directly that you do not know the answer** and go on.
- **Do not simply answer with "yes" or "no"**; demonstrate your knowledge by explaining aspects and backing up your answers with two or three key points or examples.
- If you are asked to describe, analyse and discuss a picture or cartoon, use the **present tense** or **present progressive** for your description. Describe the picture/cartoon **systematically** (e. g. from the foreground to the background, from right to left, etc.).
- If you need a moment to decide what to say, you can stall with formulations like "If I remember correctly", "That reminds me of …" or "If that is the case …", etc.
- If you are being evaluated together with a partner or in a group, **remember to interact with your partner(s)** and respond to his/her/their remarks. (→ FoL, Conversation and Discussion, p. 413)

Follow-up

- Reflect on your performance (e. g. where you did well or poorly).
- Note how you could do better next time.
- Speak with the examiner if you have questions on the material and/or your performance. Ask if there is anything that you should have answered that would have improved your performance.

Telephoning

Telephone conversations, especially business conversations, usually follow a certain pattern or scheme and are often made to request information or to ask for clarification.

Common pattern of business telephone conversations

- someone answers the phone and asks if she/he can help
- the caller makes a request – either to be connected to someone or for information
- the caller is connected, given information or told that the requested person is not in the office at the moment
- if the person is not in the office, the caller is asked to leave a message
- the caller leaves a message or asks other questions
- the phone call ends

Tips to slow down native speakers on the phone

Usually, one of the biggest problems is that native speakers, especially business people, tend to speak very quickly on the phone. However, it is important that both sides understand each other. Therefore you should try to slow the speaker down:

- Immediately ask the speaker **to speak slowly**.
- When taking note of a name, date or other important information, **repeat** each piece of **information** as the person speaks.
- **Do *not* say you have understood if you have not.**
  Ask the person to repeat until you have understood.
- If all else fails and the person does not slow down, **begin speaking in your own language to signal that there is a lack of communication.**
  Usually, the person will understand that communicating in a different language, especially on the phone, is difficult. However, be careful not to offend the speaker and **be polite and friendly**.

Important phrases for telephone calls and voice mails

Telephone call

Introducing yourself
- *Hello, this is Susan/my name is Susan …*
- *Excuse me, who is this?*
- *Can I ask who is calling, please?*

Asking who is on the phone
- *Could I speak to …?*
- *Can I/May I speak to …? (more formal)*
- *Is Susan in? (informal idiom)*
- *Can I have extension 255?*

Connecting someone
- *I'll put you through (= connect you).*
- *Can you hold the line?*
- *Can you hold on a moment?*

How to reply when someone is not available
- *I'm afraid … is not available at the moment.*
- *The line is busy. (the extension is being used)*
- *Mr Johnson isn't in …*
- *Mr Johnson is out at the moment.*

Taking a message
- *Could/Can/May I take a message?*
- *Could/Can/May I tell him/her who is calling?*
- *Would you like to leave a message?*

Leaving a message/voice mail

Introduction
- *Hello, this is Susan.*
- *Hello, my name is Susan Smith. (more formal)*

Stating the time of day/the reason for calling
- *It's eight in the morning. I'm calling/phoning to find out if …/to ask whether …/to see if …/to let you know that …/to tell you that …*

Making a request
- *Could you call/phone/ring me back?*
- *Would you mind calling me back?*
- *Could you tell … to call me back?*

Leaving your telephone number
- *My number is …*
- *You can reach me at …*
- *Call me at …*

Finishing the call
- *Thanks a lot, bye.*
- *I'll talk to you later, bye.*

Focus on Skills

Giving a Speech

Why giving a speech is good for you

- You learn to **speak effectively** in **different situations** and to audiences of **different backgrounds** and **levels of knowledge** and improve your **general speaking abilities**.
- The ability to speak well enough to **interest, influence or persuade people** is a major asset for your future life.
- You **gain self-confidence** by learning to overcome and manage nervousness and excitement.
- You learn **different techniques** of **using and varying your voice** and tone of speaking.
- You learn to control your **body language** and to **choose the right words** in the respective situation.
- You learn to **listen to people** in order to speak more effectively to them.

Non-verbal communication

The **major tools** you will use as you speak are **your voice and your body language**. Here are some aspects that help you to check yourself and be better prepared for a speech:

Voice:

- Is my voice (too) loud or (too) soft?
- Do I speak (too) slowly or (too) quickly?
- Is my voice monotonous?
- Do I articulate clearly or do I mutter?
- Will my accent be a problem for my audience?
- Do I run out of air and gasp when I speak?

→ Try to **speak naturally and clearly**, and check (ask your audience) whether you can be heard.
→ **Do not shout**, because this is hard on the voice and uncomfortable for the listener.
→ Go in advance to the **room** in which you will be speaking and **familiarize yourself with its layout**.
→ Try to **vary your speech** by raising and lowering your voice, stressing and emphasizing keywords.
→ **Mark up your script or notes** using a highlighter on the points you want to stress.
→ **Make pauses in your talk** and give the audience and yourself time to think and reflect (e. g. use visual aids and ask if there are any questions).

Body language:

- Do I rush into the room or walk in confidently and determined (*entschlossen, bestimmt*)?
- Do I look down, hunch my shoulders and shuffle my feet (lacking confidence)?
- Do I look at the audience and smile at them before starting to speak (eye contact)?
- Do I look comfortable and businesslike?
- Do I look (too) casual or nervous?
- Do I use my hands and arms to indicate or reinforce a detail of my speech?

→ **Smile at the audience** to make them feel welcome and to **establish a good relationship**.
→ **Tell yourself that it will be a good, friendly and supportive audience** to calm yourself down.
→ **Show a cheerful**, enthusiastic **and positive state of mind**.
→ **Make eye contact** with the audience; it gives the audience the impression that you are trustworthy and honest.
→ **Put your script at the right distance** for **reading and look** up at the audience occasionally.
→ Do **not fold your arms in front of you** or put your hands in your pockets.
→ **Open your hands to show an outgoing and friendly nature** – a clenched fist indicates aggression.
→ Do not move backwards and forwards all the time while talking – you will make the audience nervous and distract them.
→ **At the end** of your speech, **leave the audience with a smile** and do not flop back in your chair with a look of exhaustion or irritation. Do not forget: The last impression will stay in the audience's mind!

For further information: → Focus on Skills, Presentations, p. 419

Presentations

Five good reasons for giving a presentation

- Presentations get a discussion going.
- Presentations offer a variety of perspectives.
- Presentations provide good practice for oral examinations.
- Presentations are a good opportunity for students who can present themselves better verbally than by using written means.
- The ability to give presentations is a skill required in many occupations.

Just do the presentation, Williams, and let the numbers speak for themselves.

Preparing a presentation

- Have a clear focus – decide on the **key messages/information** that you want to get across.
- Be selective – identify the most relevant points.
  Avoid overloading the audience with everything that you know.
- Make use of the **postcard technique**:
  a) Break your presentation into sections.
  b) Give each section a heading.
  c) Write one heading and a few easily-read prompt words on each postcard.
  d) Number the postcards in the order that you want to present these points.
  → These postcards structure your talk and give you confidence.
- **Prepare audio-visual aids**, e. g. transparencies/an overhead projector, a PowerPoint, a CD and CD player, a large poster, etc. Don't overdo it, however – your talk should take centre stage and not your technical equipment.
- **Do not simply read out** what is on your transparencies or posters, etc. – paraphrase and explain them.
- **Practise your presentation** several times, going slowly and timing yourself. If your presentation is too long, edit it down. Talk slightly more slowly than in normal speech. Use a clock to time yourself.
- Provide a visual aid/handout for each person.

Giving a presentation

- Greet the audience, introduce yourself and smile at them – this creates a friendly and more relaxed atmosphere.
- Wait until everybody is quiet before you start speaking.
- Tell your audience whether you would prefer questions during the presentation or at the end.
- **Speak more slowly and loudly than usual.**
- Look up and **make eye contact** with at least two people in your audience.
- Don't apologize for anything you have not done or you feel could be better – act as though you are confident and well-prepared. This way you will win your audience's attention and confidence.
- At the beginning, briefly outline your topic by summing up what you are going to say and in which order.
- Go though your cards – pause and take a breath after each point.
- If you use difficult words or technical terms, write them on the board or on a flipchart and explain them to your audience.
- At the end, briefly sum up what you have said.
- End your presentation with a pithy (= *prägnant*) last line.
- Thank the audience for paying attention and ask them if there are any questions they want to ask.

→ Focus on Skills, Giving a Speech, p. 418

Focus on Skills

Continuation of a Fictional Text

Types of fictional texts you might be required to continue are
- **narrative texts** (novel, short story),
- **dramatized texts** (drama, play, one-act play),
- **film scripts** (screenplays).

Possible assignments

The assignment to continue a fictional text will usually be part of the task of working creatively with the text subsequent to the comprehension and analysis of a text. Accordingly, this task requires you to use your previous results and continue, complement or pad the text at hand with further details. You could be asked to:

- **rewrite** a scene/dialogue **from a different narrative perspective**, e. g. by choosing another character or by creating and adding a new character
- **rewrite** a scene/dialogue and **change the ending**, e. g. by turning the happy ending into a tragic ending or vice versa
- **elaborate on unspoken thoughts** of a character, e. g. by writing an interior monologue or a diary entry
- **continue a scene** from a play/screenplay or **a chapter** from a novel
- **change the genre of the text**, e. g. by turning a rather descriptive part in a novel into a scene in a screenplay or into dialogue with two or more characters interacting
- **change time and place** of the text and continue the scene/dialogue, etc. after a lapse of time, e. g. after 20 or more years when one of the characters has grown up, has aged and is looking back at his/her life, etc.

Your composition

Step 1: Be aware of the characteristic features of the literary genre and the type of text you are required to work with creatively. Here are some examples:

narrative texts		dramatized texts		film script
novel	**short story**	**classical drama**	**modern play**	**screenplay**
<ul><li>narrator/narrative perspective</li><li>character(s)</li><li>panoramic/scenic presentation</li><li>main/sub-plot stream of consciousness</li><li>interior monologue</li><li>development of action/plot</li><li>disruptions/lapses in time/foreshadowing/flashback, etc.</li><li>spoken/everyday English, informal English</li></ul>	<ul><li>immediate beginning</li><li>open ending</li><li>exceptional incident in everyday life</li><li>spoken English</li></ul>	<ul><li>protagonist/antagonist/hero</li><li>dialogue/monologue/soliloquy</li><li>stage directions</li><li>acts/scenes</li><li>spoken English</li><li>development of a conflict</li><li>often linear development</li><li>happy/tragic ending/resolution</li></ul>	<ul><li>everyday character(s)</li><li>internal conflict</li><li>current topics, e. g. society, politics, crisis, war, etc.</li><li>stage directions</li><li>disruptions/lapses in time</li><li>spoken English</li></ul>	<ul><li>slug lines</li><li>dialogue/monologue</li><li>action</li><li>focus on visual aspects</li><li>technical directions (props, music, camera operations)</li><li>spoken English</li></ul>

Step 2: Employ the above-mentioned **formal characteristics of the respective genre** in your text.

Step 3: The **stage directions** require you to briefly characterize the speaker's intentions, emotions or behaviour. In order to avoid overusing verbs like "think", "say" or "give", use a dictionary to find alternative formulations, e. g. to reflect, to boast, to complain, to whine, to mutter, to whisper, to shout, to consider, to offer, etc.

Step 4: Pay attention to **making the characters interact** and not just delivering monologues. They can: use feedback phrases or questions (Oh, really?; You don't say!); interrupt each other (Are you sure?; Are you suggesting that …?); etc.

Writing a Comment and a Review

Comment

A written comment expresses your personal opinion on a certain topic or issue. It is a common means used in print media in order to present one's opinion to the readership in a more or less critical way.

Take some notes first, and structure your thoughts systematically before starting to write.

1. Introduction
- Make some introductory remarks in which you raise a question, refer to a current problem, etc.
- The introduction should clarify your topic/concern.

2. Main part – arguments
- State, demonstrate and describe the positive and negative effects of a topic/situation.
- Support your view of the situation by giving examples. You can, for example, refer to or quote famous people or experts on this matter, or relate your view to other comparable issues.
- Emphasize the argument by referring to further/future consequences.

3. Conclusion
- Conclude your comment by giving your personal view of the situation/problem.
- Strategically, it is smart to relate your final remarks to your introduction in order to finally "wrap up" the topic and make your point.

→ Focus on Language, Conversation and Discussion, p. 413

Review of a fiction book or film

Step 1: Plot*/characters*/theme*
- Briefly summarize the plot of the book/film (approx. 150 words). ("Who/where/when/what/why"-questions should be answered.)
- Include the type of film (e.g. feature film*, western)/book (e.g. historical novel), title, author/director, publishing/release year, edition, special features.
- Briefly describe the main characters* and how they are related.
- Briefly outline the basic theme(s) and leitmotif(s)*.
- Describe the overall atmosphere.

Step 2: Narrative/cinematic aspects
- Point out striking narrative qualities (e.g. point of view*, metaphorical language, structure of the plot*).
- Refer to any striking cinematic devices that create/reinforce the atmosphere of the film.
- Mention which actors were chosen for the respective roles.
- Explain what the book's/film's message and the author's/director's intention may be.

Step 3: Evaluation
- Say what you like or dislike about: the plot, structure, directing, camera work, sound, special effects, casting and performance of the actors.
- Explain whether the book/film has successfully conveyed any/its core message.
- Comment on the actors: Have they successfully personified and typified the characters?
- Consider and quantify shortcomings/weaknesses and strengths of the book/film.
- If the film is a literary adaptation: How well has the story been adapted? – Is there anything missing (in comparison to the novel or in comparison to other books/films by the same author/director)?

Step 4: Conclusion
- Is the film worth viewing?/Is the book worth reading?
- Would you recommend the book/film? – What was your favourite part of the book/film?

Writing an Analysis

Writing a text analysis usually follows a standardized pattern, regardless of what kind of text or material you are required to analyse, e. g. a fictional or non-fictional text, a political speech, an excerpt from a play or a cartoon.

General aspects

Before writing:

- **Read the assignment carefully** and make sure that you have understood what exactly you are required to do. Pay particular attention to the **standardized terminology** (*Operatoren*) which tell you what to focus on. (→ Standardized Terminology for Tasks, pp. 11 ff.)
- Pay attention to **additional keywords** given in the assignment, e. g. which (stylistic) aspects of the text or which features of a character you are expected to analyse in particular.
- Read the text as often as necessary to **understand it thoroughly**. Underline and/or highlight the parts that are significant and important with regard to the assignment. Note down your observations and make notes in the margin of the text. Use your dictionary to crosscheck that you have understood expressions and formulations in the text correctly.
- Find the **main issue or message** that the text addresses and the **writer's position** in this regard.

While writing:

- Check for **features/references to lines to support your findings**, e. g. arguments, line of argument, choice of words, facts and numbers given, quotes from further experts, etc.
- Prepare a **draft outline** (*Entwurf, Konzeption*) of the text you want to write. Do not write every single sentence line-by-line but take notes on
  a) how you want to structure your composition, b) which textual references and quotes you want to use and c) what background knowledge you want to use and refer to.
- Pay attention to details: do not cover everything but focus on the most relevant/striking aspects.
- **Avoid wordy and generalized explanations** and repetitions but be **specific and precise**.
- Do not include your personal opinion or beliefs on the matter but be **factual and neutral**.

After writing:

- **Proofread** your analysis and crosscheck that you have not forgotten anything from your draft outline. Check for grammatical correctness, punctuation, spelling and that your composition is written in the **present tense**.

Your composition

Introduction

- Formulate a **connecting sentence at the beginning** in which you refer to a relevant aspect from your comprehension. Briefly state that the writer for example uses a specific line of argument to underline his ideas.
  Example: *As I have pointed out in the first part of my composition, the writer XY aims at persuading the reader of his critical view of the USA. In order to emphasize his position he uses several persuasive techniques which will be explained in the following.*
- Give a **concise** (*kurzgefasst*) **outline of the structure** of the text, referring to the writer's train of thought and/ or line of argument and the general message of the text.
- **Do not repeat** the introductory part from your first assignment (w-questions).

Main part

- Use the **three-step method** for your analysis:

Step 1: Quote from the text	Step 2: Use the correct technical term	Step 3: Explain the function
(ll. 10 f.) "… some citizens, many people, the whole world …"	→ climax, parallelism	→ emphasis on numbers and amounts involved

- Do not just follow the chronological order of the text but also **focus on relevant aspects, stylistic devices, characters**.
- Be careful to **quote correctly**. (→ Focus on Facts, Basic Types of Non-Fictional Texts, p. 396)

Conclusion
- End your text by **referring to your introduction** and formulating a **concluding sentence** in which you for example refer to the message or the type of the text (again).
- **Do not evaluate** the text. Stay factual and concise.

A newspaper commentary/an editorial

In contrast to a newspaper report, **a commentary or an editorial presents the newspaper's opinion on an issue**. Editorial writers build on an argument and try to influence the reader's opinion, **criticize** a certain issue or try to **clarify a complicated or controversial** matter. Sometimes they ask people to take action. In a nutshell, editorials are **opinionated news stories** which are **personalized** and which **evaluate** issues or events.

Structure

"Sleaze, please."

- **headline**
- **introduction, body, paragraphs, conclusion**
- **an objective explanation of the issue**
- **opinions from the opposing viewpoint**
- **opinions of the writer**
- **alternative solutions to the problem or issue being criticized**
- **a solid and concise conclusion**

How to write a newspaper commentary/an editorial

Step 1: Choose a significant topic that would interest readers.

Step 2: Do research and collect information, facts, statistical data, interview people, etc.

Step 3: In an introduction, state your opinion briefly, e. g. *Have you ever thought about … ? Taking into account that … Looking at the latest results of … one should … I think that …*

Step 4: Explain the topic/issue objectively and explain why this topic is important, e. g. *Looking at the facts/ numbers we do have to realize that … therefore it is our responsibility to …*

Step 5: Give the opposing viewpoint first with its quotations and facts, e. g. *On the contrary one might think that … the numbers suggest that … on the surface the situation appears to be …*

Step 6: Refute the opposing viewpoint and develop your case:
- present at least three arguments
- the strongest argument should come last
- back up your arguments by facts, e. g. statistics, quotations, expert information, etc.
- if you comment on a text, refer to the text with quotes to substantiate your arguments

Step 7: Repeat key phrases to reinforce an idea, e. g. *Let us get back to … Let us take a closer look at … This situation requires a clear judgment … We have no option but to …*

Step 8: Employ rhetorical devices to make your article more convincing (e. g. comparison, antithesis, metaphorical expressions, etc.).

Step 9: Give a (realistic) solution to the problem and encourage constructive criticism and pro-active reaction.

Step 10: Sum up the information and recapture important points and solutions. Refer back to your introductory remarks and statement. Your conclusion should have some punch, e. g. *If we do not take action against dangerous and poisonous food, who will?*

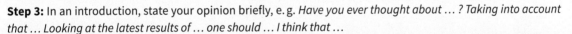

Focus on Skills

Writing a Formal Letter

Business letter/letter of complaint – layout

reference initials

inside address, including street, ZIP code, country

salutation
- *Dear Sir or Madam* → used if name is unknown
- *Miss* → unmarried woman (old use)
- *Mrs* → married woman
- *Ms* → unclear if the woman is married or not
- *Mr* → man
- no comma at the end of the salutation

complimentary close
- *Yours sincerely* → most common use
- *Yours faithfully* → formal, only used if the name of the addressee is unknown
- *(Best) Regards, Best wishes* → friendly
- signature, name, position of the signatory

letterhead with postcode, telephone and fax numbers and e-mail

date

attention line

subject line (optional)
- after salutation in the UK
- before salutation in the USA
- in bold type
- capitalized

body of the letter
- begin with a capital letter
- paragraphs are separated by a free line

enclosure (*Anlagen*)
- Enc (singular), e. g. *order form*
- Encs (plural), e. g. *cheque, folder*

Tel: +49(0)221 123456
Fax: +49(0)221 1234567
tobymueller@web.de

Gartenweg 20
54327 Köln
Germany

15 May 2016

Your ref: TBS/1234

Digital World Inc.
8607 Main Street
Cornerstone, NJ 23657
USA

Attention: Ms Goldwell, Customer Services

Dear Ms Goldwell

**My Order No. CF-23405 – Smartphone "Stay Connected",
black, dated 4 March 2016**

The above-mentioned smartphone was delivered to me today and on opening the package I found that
- the touchscreen is badly scratched
- the GPS navigation does not work properly
- applications cannot be downloaded
- the headset is missing

Obviously the smartphone was poorly packed and roughly handled in transit and something must have gone wrong in production and while packaging the phone.

Needless to say, I cannot use the phone and thus would like to return it at your expense.

I am looking forward to hearing what you have to say about the matter and would welcome an immediate replacement of the damaged article.

Yours sincerely

Tobias Müller
Tobias Müller

Enc.: Copy of the packaging slip and invoice

Basic types of business letters

- **Enquiry:** a request for or question about information about sth. (*Anfrage*)
- **Offer:** a voluntary but conditional promise given by a buyer or seller to another for acceptance (*Angebot*)
- **Order:** a request to make or supply goods (*Bestellung*)
- **Reminder:** a request for an overdue payment that should have been paid by an earlier date (*Mahnung*)
- **Letter of complaint:** a request to deal with and solve a problem, e. g. delay in delivery, unsatisfactory or defective goods, wrong goods, etc. (*Beschwerdebrief, Reklamation*)

Writing a Handout

A handout is a useful tool that serves as a memory aid (= *Gedächtnisstütze*) for the listeners of a presentation and helps them to follow the presenter's line of argument or train of thought.

It should provide a short overview of the presentation, the most relevant facts, keywords and data, and may include some interesting or provocative statements for the audience to consider.

Structure

1. **Heading**
   - name of school/college/university
   - subject/course
   - name of teacher/lecturer/professor
   - name of student

2. **Main part/body**
   a) title/topic of the presentation
   b) introduction of the topic, e. g. main ideas, the central theme (= *roter Faden*)
   c) depiction of the most relevant aspects in keywords; structuring elements such as bullet points, subheadings, etc.
   d) conclusion and results of the project/coursework/presentation

3. **List of references/indication of sources**
   - bibliographical references (e. g. books, essays, etc.)
   - references of Internet websites, links, etc.
   → Focus on Skills, Research, p. 442

Example

Karl Kraus Gymnasium
Subject: English
Teacher: Mr/Ms …
Student: Katharina Müller   10 May 2016

The British Empire

Outline/overview:

1. Introduction/definition   4. The Impact on India
2. Historical background   5. Gandhi
3. The Raj   6. Conclusion

1. Introduction/definition
   – British expansion …
   – …

2. Historical background
   – Queen Elizabeth I …
   – …

3. …

List of references

Bibliographical references:
Darwin, John, Unfinished Empire: *The Global Expansion of Britain*, Penguin, London 2013, pp. xy

Internet:
www.bbc.co.uk/history/british/modern/endofempire_overview_01.shtml [03.04.2015]

Writing an Interview

In a written examination you might be required to **write an interview as a creative writing task** in addition to the comprehension and the analysis tasks. Your written interview text should be written in such a way that it can serve as a script or draft (*Vorlage*) for an interview you are asked to conduct. In general, an interview is a conversation between two (or more) people, (an) **interviewer(s)** and an **interviewee**, where (usually pre-formulated) questions are asked by the interviewer(s) to obtain information, facts or statements on a certain topic. In journalism, interviews are used to collect information, or present views and assessments to viewers or listeners. Interviews are also important in qualitative research, e.g. when interviewing an expert in some field.

Types of interviews

- **informal, conversational interview**
  No pre-formulated questions are asked; the interviewer stays as open and adaptable to the interviewee's nature, response and priorities as possible.
- **general interview**
  The focus is on collecting more general information from the interviewee; the interviewer pre-formulates questions but stays open to the interviewee's focus and priorities on a certain matter.
- **standardized, open-ended interview**
  The same, standardized and pre-formulated questions are asked to different interviewees. This method allows for rather fast interviews that can be easily analysed and compared.
- **closed, fixed response interview**
  All interviewees are asked the same pre-formulated questions and are asked to choose questions from the same set of alternatives.

The interviewer

Although the general aim of an interview is to elicit (*hervorlocken*) information from an interviewee by strategically and skilfully posing questions, the interviewer should follow certain rules. He/She should be **neutral**, **unemotional** and **unbiased**.

Technique and structure

- **introduction of the topic**; the reason for the interview/the occasion; introduction of the **interviewee(s)**, their background, position and reason for being interviewed on the matter, e.g. *Good evening … today our topic is … I would like to welcome our special guest … who is an expert in …*
- asking a **well-structured** sequence of (pre-formulated) questions
- **listening and reacting** to the interviewee(s) in order to achieve more focus and attention to detail
- asking **follow-up questions** throughout the interview to
  a) enable the interviewee to elaborate on certain topics and to gain more comprehensive information
  b) to clarify complicated or confusing aspects, e.g. *What do you mean by saying …? Could you elaborate on … and give us some more details on …?*
- asking **precise and respectful questions** in order not to offend the interviewee or make him/her become defensive or unwilling to share
- making the interviewee(s) feel comfortable and respected by **avoiding interrupting** him/them whenever possible
- **ending the interview** by
  a) summarizing the result of the discussion or the views taken by the participants
  b) thanking the participants, e.g. *I am sorry to say that our time is up. Thank you, … it has been most comprehensive … informative … It has been a pleasure to have you with us.*
- using **spoken English** (not formal, but avoiding colloquial English or slang)

Writing a Newspaper Article

In general, newspaper reports aim **at informing their readership** about events that have happened in their local area, or about national and international news. Newspaper reports usually **provide answers** to questions (who, what, where, when, why, how). They should be **easy to read, objective and present reliable, unbiased facts and information** and should be written in a snappy and concise style. However, the style of an article and the language register (formal, informal) depends on the type of newspaper the article is published in, e.g. a quality paper, a popular paper, etc. (→ Focus on Facts, The Press, p. 398).

Types of newspaper articles

- **local news** (focussing on the neighbourhood/the region)
- **national news** (focussing on one's country)
- **international news** (world news)
- **a feature article** ("soft news", e.g. about a celebrity; a person who does volunteer work in the community; a movie review, etc.; it is **not** considered a news story)
- **editorial** (an article that contains the writer's, publisher's or editor's opinion on an issue)
- **a column** (an article written by the same person on a regular basis, about for example subjects of interest to him/her, current events or community happenings; it is not considered a news story)

General structure/layout

- **headline** (catching the reader's attention)
- **sub-headlines** (structuring the article)
- **columns/paragraphs** (structuring the article; all paragraphs relate to the main idea/topic)
- **pictures, photos, graphics, visuals,** etc. (illustration, proof)
- **first paragraph** (introduces the main point of the story (who?); introduces the main idea (what?))
- **following paragraphs** (provide answers to the other questions (where, when, why, how); develop the main idea)
- **paragraphs** (short, punchy, not too long)
- **information** (clear, concise, factual)
- **language** (precise, clear sentence structure, explanation of technical terms)
- **grammatical tense** (usually past tense – when an event has already taken place)
- **references** to a) what people said (quotations/direct speech; reported speech),
  b) sources, further/former articles on the topic, etc.

How to write a newspaper report

Step 1: Select your target group (e.g. students, readers in a small town, a neighbourhood, etc.).

Step 2: Find a subject of interest (e.g. the expenses of schoolbooks or field trips; the quality of clothes, etc.).

Step 3: Do research on the matter (e.g. interviewing people, Internet research, etc.).

Step 4: List your potential sources. They shoud be reliable and credible (e.g. authority, expert, celebrity, hero, witness, ordinary people, etc.).

Step 5: Write your lead-in (the introductory paragraph).

Step 6: Write the rest of your article and
- structure it into paragraphs of 4 – 5 lines,   – develop a clear train of thought and line of argument,
- employ references to prove the reliability of your information.

Step 7: Find a suitable title for your report. It should be vivid and catchy and announce the topic in a short and concise way. Try to evoke your reader's interest by asking a question (*Why is ethical fashion so expensive?*) or using an exclamation mark (*No Boring Lessons Any Longer!*).

Note: The information given in a newspaper article should be true, objective and original.

Writing a Speech Script

In your written examination, you might be asked to write a speech in response to a text you analysed or on an issue related to the text at hand. A good speech always has a clear and distinct structure and follows clear-cut lines of argumentation and trains of thought.

Structure

Introduction

In order to **win your audience's attention** and **attract their interest** you can start by
- saying sth. thought-provoking,
- citing an interesting quotation or
- saying sth. controversial,
- telling a joke.

After having gained their attention, you should **introduce yourself** and **the subject** you are going to talk about. Additionally, you can make a positive remark/pay a compliment to the place where you are speaking, the audience, etc. – this will help you to bond with your audience.

Tips on vocab ⟫⟫

Good evening, ladies and gentlemen. ▪ Dear friends … ▪ I feel deeply honoured to speak to such an illustrious audience. ▪ Let me thank you for inviting me to this impressive meeting. ▪ It is a great pleasure to be here and to talk to you. ▪ As … said, it is never too late to take action. ▪ Wouldn't it be wonderful if we managed to … ▪ Let me assure you …

Main part/body of the speech

This is the longest part of your speech and should therefore have a clear structure, following a topical order, a line of argumentation or a train of thought.
- Start with a **thought-provoking** and **important thought** or argument.
- Decide on which pattern you want to choose for the **body of your speech**:
  a) **progressive structure** (developing on a cause-to-effect or problem-solution arrangement)
    → effect: clarity, unity and logical coherence
  b) **antithetical structure** (contrasting and juxtaposing of facts, ideas, arguments)
    → effect: clarity and emphasis through comparison and contrast
- **Support your arguments** with
  a) information (e. g. statistical data, facts),
  b) examples,
  c) quotations (e. g. of experts, political authorities, etc.),
  d) references to similar situations.
- **Work in some rhetorical devices**, e. g. alliterations, repetitions of relevant phrases/words/numbers, contrast, comparison, climax, rhetorical questions.
- **Use linkers and connectives** to vary the beginning of your sentences and to connect your thoughts and arguments.

Conclusion

This part of your speech is very important because it gives you the opportunity to end with a punch and/or an appeal that will stay in your audience's mind.
- Give a **concise summary of the most relevant points** of your speech.
- Finish with a **punchy remark, a call for action** or sth. personal to **reinforce your line of argument**.
- Relate your finishing remarks to the beginning of your speech in order to **round off your speech**.

Tips on vocab ⟫⟫

Let me quote … again, … ▪ (to put it) in a nutshell … ▪ to put it bluntly … ▪ Let us be honest, shouldn't we … ▪ Now that you have realized the importance of … ▪ I put my trust in you to … ▪ I have absolutely no doubt that you will make the right decision. ▪ Let us roll up our sleeves and get to work.

→ Focus on Skills, Giving a Speech, p. 418   → Focus on Skills, Presentations, p. 419
→ Focus on Skills, Analysis of a Political Speech, p. 407

Writing a Summary

A **summary or an abstract** (*Zusammenfassung, Inhaltsangabe*) is common in all forms of writing and is aimed at **highlighting the major points** of a piece of writing and outlining the most important facts. Furthermore, it helps you to obtain a better **orientation and understanding of the structure and contents of a text** which you need for additional analysis and evaluation.

General aspects

A summary ...

- gives the **most relevant facts** and the overall meaning of a text,
- must not contain your own thoughts and opinions,
- begins with an **introductory sentence**,
- is about 150–200 words long, depending on the length of the text that is to be summed up,
- **must not contain direct speech or quotations**,
- should be **factual**,
- leaves out irrelevant details,
- should usually be written in the **present tense**,
- should present the events in **chronological order** (→ no suspense),
- closes with a sentence that **sums up the main message of the text and its intention**,
- prepares the analysis part of your composition – it must not analyse the text but **strictly focuses on depicting** (*wiedergeben*) **the text** in your own words.

Your composition

Before writing:

- **Underline** the most relevant aspects and facts given in the text.
- **Divide the text into paragraphs**/thematic units and **find a suitable headline** for each paragraph.
- Make sure that you understand everything – if necessary, **crosscheck the meaning of words** or expressions in your dictionary.
- Do not underline every detail but focus on the **most important information/striking keywords.**

While writing:

- **Use the present tense** for your text.
- Write an **introductory sentence** which answers the **w-questions** and informs about the **source** of the text: author, title of the text, type of text, topic, place and year of publication, information about whether the text is an excerpt or was abbreviated.
- Do not copy the words and expressions used in the text but **use your own words and/or try to find synonyms to paraphrase** the main aspects. Use your dictionary to find alternative formulations.
- **Do not quote** from the text and **do not use direct speech** (!).
- **Do not refer to any specific lines** in the text.
- **Use formulations** to state what the text/author writes about or wants to express.
  Example: *The author makes remarks on …; The author expresses his/her concerns about …*
- Be careful to not just follow the chronology of the text, but **restructure it and focus on key aspects/focal points** (*Schwerpunkte*).
- **Do not use short forms**.
- **Use standard English** for your summary even though the text you are to summarize may be written in informal English or in verse, etc.

After writing:

- **Proofread your text** and check for grammatical correctness, punctuation and spelling. Make sure that you have used the **present tense**.

Writing a CV and a Letter of Application

Tel: +49 (0)221 123456

Gartenweg 20
54327 Köln
Germany

your own address in the top right-hand corner

15 May 2016

date of writing

reference number or keywords related to the position

Your ref: TBS/1234

Roots & Shoots
The Jane Goodall Institute
1595 Spring Hill Road
Vienna, VA 22182
USA

address in full, as on envelope

Dear Madam or Sir,

Use "Madam or Sir" if you do not know the name of the person.

I am writing to apply for an internship at your institute.
Please find enclosed a copy of my CV.

introductory paragraph; reason for your letter; start with a capital letter

Since graduating from St. Thomas Grammar School, I have gained experience in working with various environmental groups as well as in a zoo. I have also had the opportunity of working in an animal shelter and have experienced the importance of giving more to these animals than just medical treatment.

body of letter; your qualifications; reason(s) why you want the job

I would welcome the opportunity to work in one of your camps and look forward to your response.

Yours faithfully

T. Müller

**If you started with "Dear Madam or Sir," end with "Yours faithfully".
If you know the surname, e. g. "Dear Ms. Brown," end with "Yours sincerely".**

Tobias Müller

Enc. CV

Sign your name and print it in full afterwards.

Curriculum Vitae

Name	Tobias Müller
Address	Gartenweg 20
	54327 Köln (Cologne)
Telephone No.	+49(0)221 123456
Mobile	+49(0)1723456789
Email	tobymueller@web.de
Nationality	German
Date/place of birth	25 July 1999, Cologne
Profile	a highly motivated and creative Graduate from a Grammar School with experience in animal care
Education	
2009 – 2017	Grammar School (A-Level)
2005 – 2009	Elementary School
Employment/	practical work as animal caretaker/ keeper in a zoo and at an animal shelter
Interests	judo, tennis, music

- only refer to your most relevant qualifications or skills
- if possible, you can include references (= people that can be contacted in order to give a judgment of your qualifications, experience, character, etc.)
- enclose photocopies of relevant certificates
- begin with the most recent employment/qualification and work backwards

Tips on vocab »»»

I noted with interest … ■ I am writing in response to … ■ With reference to your advertisement in … ■ As you can see from my CV, … ■ I am currently studying at … ■ Having gained a degree in …, ■ This position interests me because … ■ I would be grateful for the opportunity to … ■ I have extensive experience in … ■ I am available for an interview … ■ If you consider my qualifications to be suitable …

Writing a Letter to the Editor

A letter to the editor is a **formal letter** that has **different functions**:

A reader …

… **responds to an article** in a newspaper/magazine/on the Internet he/she has read and **states his/her opinion on the matter**.

… **expresses his/her criticism or support** of a stance taken by the publication.

… responds to **another reader's letter** to the editor.

… **comments on a current issue** or a problem of public interest.

… **remarks on materials** that have appeared in a (previous) publication.

… **corrects** a perceived **error or misinterpretation**.

Tips for writing

- **Read the publication thoroughly** and underline/highlight key phrases and the most relevant parts.
- Pay attention to the **focus and the standardized terminology** used in **your assignment**, e.g. *Write a letter to the editor and <u>assess</u> the <u>author's view</u> of <u>immigration to Great Britain</u>.*
- **Name the article** you are responding to in the first sentence of the body of your letter or in a subject line.
- Include your **name, address and e-mail address (phone number)** at the top of your letter to give the editor the opportunity to verify your identity.
- Since your letter may be edited, **get to the point and be concise** (*knapp und präzise*) and focused. Do not write a lengthy argument.
- Limit your letter to **two or three paragraphs**:
  a) **Introduce** the subject matter and briefly state your opinion/objection (*Einwand*).
  b) Include a few sentences (**arguments, examples**) to support your view.
  c) End with a **concluding remark** and a clever, punchy (*ausdrucksstark*) line.
  Keep in mind that a letter to the editor is a formal letter. Use **Standard English** and write in **a matter-of-fact style**, using clearly structured arguments. Avoid informal and insulting (*beleidigend*) or offensive language and do not be overly emotional.
  Start your letter like this:
  Dear Editor/Sir/Madam,
  I am writing in response to the article …
- **If you do not want your name published**, state so clearly, e.g. in the last paragraph.
  Example: *Please note, I do not want my (full) name published with this letter.*
- **Proofread** your letter to check for poor grammar and spelling errors.
- **Submit** your letter by e-mail (if possible) to enable the editor to cut and paste your letter.

Tips on vocab ⟫⟫⟫

> to have a good/positive opinion about sb./sth. ▪ to (strongly) (dis-)agree with sb. about sth. ▪ to approve of sb./sth. (*billigen*) ▪ to advise sb. to do sth. (*raten, beraten*) ▪ to acknowledge that … (*anerkennen*) ▪ to show one's solidarity with … ▪ to argue in support of sb./sth. (*sich aussprechen für …*) ▪ to take a negative view of sb./sth. ▪ to refute sb.'s arguments (*entkräften, widerlegen*) ▪ to express criticism of … ▪ to call sth. into question ▪ to express doubts about sb./sth. (*jdn./etw. anzweifeln*) ▪ to protest against ▪ to have reservations about (*Vorbehalte haben*) ▪ to disassociate oneself from sb./sth. (*sich distanzieren von*) ▪ to make remarks on ▪ to make observations about ▪ to maintain/claim that … (*behaupten*)

→ Focus on Skills, Writing a Comment and a Review, p. 421
→ Focus on Skills, Writing a Formal Letter, p. 424

Focus on Skills

Connectives and Adverbs

In order to improve your style and speak and write more fluently, you should employ connectives and adverbs. **Try to vary the beginnings of your sentences** and use sub-clauses to express your opinion and thoughts in a more diversified way.

listing/order first, second, third; firstly, secondly, thirdly; for one thing … (and) for another (thing); to begin with; to start with; initially/in the first place; then; finally; to conclude[1]; last but not least	**adding/reinforcing[11]** also; as well; too; furthermore; moreover; then; in addition to; above all; what is more; again; equally; generally speaking
comparison/similarity[2] equally; likewise; similarly; in the same way; compared to …; both; but while the first …; although; though	**summary/conclusion/consequence** then; all in all; to sum up; in conclusion; accordingly; as a result; briefly; consequently; generally speaking; hence; it follows that; taking everything into account; thus; therefore
exemplification[3] namely; for example (e.g.); for instance; that is (i.e.); that is to say	**reformulation** or rather; to put it another way; in other words
alternative alternatively; on the other hand	**contrast** on the contrary; in contrast; by contrast; on the one hand … on the other hand; compared to; although; likewise
concession[4] besides; however; nevertheless; still; though; in spite of that; on the other hand; despite this; admittedly[5]	**reason and purpose** as; because of; consequently; for this/that reason; hence; in order to; on account of; since; so; that explains why; this is why; therefore
emphasis[6] as a matter of fact; at any rate; clearly; evidently[7]; ideally; undoubtedly[8]	**condition** as long as; even if; if; in any case; on the condition that; provided that; unless
your own opinion from my point of view; in my opinion; in my view; the way I see it; to my mind; to my way of thinking	**an opposite point of view** alternatively; but; despite/in spite of (the fact); except for; however; in contrast to; instead of; nonetheless; on the contrary
reference[9] to something/someone according to; as for; the former; the latter; with reference to; referring to; with regard to; concerning	**assumption[12]** assuming that; given that; presumably; probably; granted that; allegedly[13]; seemingly; on the face of it; supposedly[14]
toning down[10] arguments a little (worrying); almost; fairly; hardly; more or less; somewhat; on second thought; at first sight	**emphasizing arguments** actually; absolutely; (not …) at all; badly (needed); completely; extremely; entirely; indeed; not in the least; perfectly; really; seriously; thoroughly; totally; utterly[15]; very

[1] **to conclude sth. from sth.** *schlussfolgern* – [2] **similarity** the state of being like sth./sb. but not exactly the same – [3] **exemplification** illustration, giving an example – [4] **concession** *Zugeständnis* – [5] **admittedly** accepting that sth. is true – [6] **to put emphasis on sth.** to stress sth. – [7] **evidently** clearly, obviously – [8] **undoubtedly** *zweifellos* – [9] **reference** sth. that you connect or relate to sth. else – [10] **to tone down sth.** to express an opinion in a less extreme or offensive way – [11] **to reinforce sth.** to make a feeling/an idea stronger – [12] **assumption** *Annahme, Vermutung* – [13] **allegedly** *angeblich* – [14] **supposedly** *angeblich, vermutlich* – [15] **utterly** totally, very much

Literary Terms

This glossary of literary terms is designed to help you understand the meaning of terms used in connection with literature or the analysis of literary texts.

Important terms marked with the asterisk symbol (*) throughout the Students' Book can be found here in thematic order.

Fiction/fictional texts

a) narrative texts (e. g. novel, short story, fable)

- **structure and plot**

allegory [ˈæləgəri]	a text that may be understood on a superficial or factual level and a deeper, more philosophical level; the characters are often personifications of abstract ideas (e. g. evil, love, etc.)
climax	the moment when the conflict is most intense
conflict	a struggle between different forces which produces suspense
dénouement [ˌdeɪˈnuːmɑ̃ː] (resolution)	the final outcome, when the conflict is resolved
epigram	a short, witty statement which may be written in prose or verse
exposition	the very beginning of a fictional text which introduces the main character(s), the theme, the setting and the atmosphere
falling action	a reduction of suspense
flashback	an episode/event which interrupts the chronological order of a text and goes back in time to show what happened earlier
foreshadowing	hinting at later events
internal conflict	a struggle between two opposing views/values which takes place in a character's mind
(leit)motif [ˈlaɪtməʊtiːf]	a theme/expression/object which recurs throughout the text and which refers to a certain person, situation or atmosphere
open ending	the conflict remains unresolved → the reader is left to reflect on possible resolutions
plot	the author's selection and structure of action as a set of events connected by cause and effect that are meant to create suspense
rising action	an increase in suspense
setting	place and time of a story/play
surprise ending	a sudden and unexpected turn of fortune/action
suspense	a feeling of tension/expectation
tension	the emotional strain caused by a conflict

- **narration**

acting time	the time from the beginning to the end of an episode in a text, this is usually longer than the narrating time because the writer can describe the passing of years in just a sentence; *erzählte Zeit*
interior monologue	a technique used within the stream of consciousness; a special kind of scenic presentation, often not in chronological order
mode of presentation – panoramic presentation – scenic presentation	the way the writer narrates events; *Darstellungsart* – the narrator tells the story as a condensed series of events, summarizing in a few sentences what happens over a longer period of time – the narrator shows an event in detail as it occurs, using dialogue, depicting thoughts and emotions, describing a scene, etc.

Focus on Language

narrating time (= reading time)	the time it takes to relate an episode in a text (= reading time); it depends on the mode of presentation; *Erzählzeit*
narrator – omniscient [ɒmˈnɪsiənt] narrator – third-person narrator – first-person narrator – witness/observer narrator – objective/reliable – subjective/unreliable	person who tells the story (*not* the author!) – a narrator who seems to know everything – a narrator who stands outside the story and describes events in the third person – a narrator who is a character in a story; this is a limited point of view – a narrator who is a character in a story (protagonist or minor character) – a narrator who the reader can trust – a narrator who the reader is critical of
point of view/viewpoint – unlimited point of view – limited point of view	the perspective from which the characters, topics and events are presented (*not* the author!) – the reader can examine the action/characters from various angles – e. g. a first-person narrator who only has limited insight into the action/characters
stream of consciousness [ˈkɒnʃəsnəs]	the presentation of experience through the mind of one character in a text

b) drama (any work meant to be performed on stage or as a film)

act	the major division of a drama; an act consists of scenes
comedy	a drama which deals with a (light) topic in a more amusing way; it always has a happy ending
comic relief	a comic episode in a serious drama which aims at relieving tension by amusing the audience
dialogue	two or more people speaking to each other in a text
monologue	an extended speech by one character in a text; it might address other characters or the audience
one-act play	a short drama consisting of only one act
play	any dramatic work intended to be presented on stage, in film or on TV
scene	a subdivision in a drama
setting	the place and/or time in which an action takes place
short play	a short drama which takes about 30 minutes to perform
soliloquy [səˈlɪləkwi]	a speech delivered by a character alone on stage (used to reveal the character's thoughts, feelings or motives to the audience)
stage directions	a playwright's notes about how the drama is to be performed
tragedy	a drama in which the protagonist undergoes a series of misfortunes until he or she finally falls; the hero(ine) has to experience a reversal of fortune, i. e. from happiness to misery

• characters

antagonist	the opponent of the protagonist
anti-hero(ine)	a protagonist who does not have the qualities of a typical hero, and is either more like an ordinary person or is morally bad and does not fit into society
characterization – direct characterization – indirect characterization	the way of presenting a character in a text – the narrator or another character describes the character; alternatively, the character may describe him- or herself – the reader/audience learns about the character through action and dialogue
flat character	a minor character who does not develop in the course of the action
hero(ine) [ˈhɪərəʊ; ˈherɜʊɪn]	the principal male or female character in a drama; he/she is usually in conflict with another character, fate and/or society
minor character	a character of less importance for the course of the action

protagonist (= main character)	the main character in a drama/play
round character	a character who develops in the course of action and therefore has the ability to change

c) poetry (literature that has a certain pattern, such as rhyme, rhythm, sentence structure)

anapaest ['ænəpiːst]	metrical foot of three syllables (unstressed – unstressed – stressed): e. g. *underneath –* – '–
concrete poem	a type of poem in which the words form a shape or picture
connotation	additional meaning of a word beyond its dictionary definition, for example, due to the associations that are formed through personal experience
dactyl ['dæktɪl]	metrical foot of three syllables (stressed – unstressed – unstressed): e. g. *merrily* '– – –
denotation	the actual definition of a word (its dictionary definition)
end rhyme	a rhyme at the end of two lines
enjambement [ɪn'dʒæmbmənt] (= run-on line)	a sentence which runs from one line to another without a pause/break
foot	a group of stressed and unstressed syllables within a line of poetry which forms a metrical unit
free verse	a poem written without a particular rhyme scheme or regular metre
iamb ['aɪæm(b)]	metrical foot of two syllables (unstressed – stressed) e. g. *become* – '–
imagery ['ɪmɪdʒəri]	term for the use of images created by words that are used to appeal to the reader's imagination → often metaphors and/or similes
line	a structural unit in a poem; it is usually classified by a certain number of feet
metre	the regular rhythmic patterns of a poem/the arrangement of words according to stressed and unstressed syllables
poem	a composition which contains a structured line sequence and a special arrangement of words, a special rhythm, the use of imagery
rhyme	using words that repeat syllable sounds
rhyme scheme [skiːm] – rhyming couplets – alternate rhyme – embracing rhyme	the arrangement of rhymes in a poem – two consecutive lines with the same rhyme: aa bb – lines with the rhyme scheme: ab ab – lines with the rhyme scheme: abba
rhythm	the arrangement of stressed or unstressed syllables in writing
sonnet ['sɒnɪt] – quatrain – couplet	poem consisting of 14 lines, usually written in iambic pentameter; e. g. the Shakespearean sonnet consists of three quatrains and a couplet with the rhyme scheme abab cdcd efef gg – a stanza of four lines (e. g. in a sonnet) – two successive rhyming lines (e. g. at the end of a sonnet)
speaker	the fictional person who is imagined as saying the text of a poem (*not* identical with the poet!)
stanza	a major division in a poem consisting of several lines
trochee ['trəʊkiː]	metrical foot of two syllables (stressed – unstressed) e. g. *happen* '– –
verse	a stanza in a poem or song; poetry written in metre

Focus on Language

d) lyrics/songs (in addition to the aspects mentioned under *poetry*, also consider these devices)

genre of music	a particular type or style of music, e. g. Jazz, Rap, Funk, Heavy Metal, Protest Song, etc.
instrumentation	selection and combination of the musical instruments that are used in a song, e. g. electronic instruments, percussion, violin, etc.
onomatopoeia [ˌɒnəˌmætəˈpiːə]	words that imitate a sound associated with the thing being named, e. g. buzz, cuckoo, hum, etc.
registers of English	the words, style and grammar used, e. g. poetic, formal, slang, non-standard, in order to express a certain message or set of values
rhythm, beat	the regular pattern of long and short notes in music
vocals	the part of a piece of music that is sung, for example, by a lead singer, a choir, etc.

Non-fiction/non-fictional texts

text type

argumentation	an argumentative text deals with ideas and/or controversy; it expresses a clear opinion and gives reasons/arguments to support it
description	a descriptive text aims at describing things/developments, etc.
exposition	in an expository text, the writer explains a rather complex problem in a precise and objective way
instruction	an instructive text gives advice about a particular matter; it typically includes commands and recommendations

text form

comment	a kind of argumentation in which the writer/speaker gives his or her opinion on a certain topic
editorial	a comment, usually written by the chief editor, that gives his or her opinion on a certain topic of common interest
essay (= literary appreciation)	a text in which the writer expresses his or her personal views on a certain topic; it usually follows a certain compositional pattern, i. e. the use of unity and balance (= statement – development – conclusion)
feature story	a report written to arouse human interest, typically by concentrating on an individual case that many readers can identify with
interview	a dialogue in which someone, usually a journalist, asks another person questions on a topic of common interest; may appear in a newspaper, on TV, etc.
leader/leading article	the most important or prominent news story in a magazine/newspaper
letter to the editor	a letter written by a reader to the editor of a magazine/newspaper in order to express a personal opinion on some topic (→ comment)
news story	a report based on facts and background information that deals with a topical event that the public is interested in
report	a text that aims at answering the "five w's": who?, what?, when?, where? and why?, which can be checked and verified by the reader
review	a short critical evaluation of a work of art (literature, film, etc.)
scientific report	a text written for scientific purposes, usually containing many technical terms (→ report)
sermon	a religious discourse delivered as part of a church service
speech – political speech – laudatory [ˈlɔːdətəri] speech	a formal talk or an address delivered to an audience – an address delivered for a political purpose, e. g. the inaugural address of a president or a crisis speech – a speech delivered in order to express praise, e. g. when sb. is awarded a prize

Focus on Language

- **structural devices**

column ['kɒləm]	*Textspalte*; mostly used in newspapers and magazines
conclusion	the main idea is often re-stated here or the main aspects of the text may be recapped (*kurz zusammenfassen*) in summary
heading/headline	a caption that is written above a text to arouse the reader's interest
introduction	lead-in to the topic, often by referring to the "five w's" in order to attract the reader's interest and lure him or her into the story
line of argument(ation)	the way different reasons are gradually developed and structured to convince a reader of a particular point of view (→ train of thought)
main part	the part of the text in which the writer demonstrates a topic/explains his or her intention/discusses a topic or problem, etc.
paragraph	a division of a text dealing with a particular idea that begins on a new line
passage	a short extract from a text that may consist of several paragraphs
subheading	a caption that subdivides a text into logical sections
theme/topic/subject	a central idea in a text which binds all of its elements together
train of thought	the way a series of ideas is gradually developed and structured

- **rhetorical/stylistic devices**

alliteration	the repetition of a sound, usually a consonant, at the beginning of neighbouring words
allusion	indirect reference to a famous event, person or piece of literature
anaphora [ə'næfərə]	successive sentences starting with the same word
antithesis [æn'tɪθəsɪs]	contrast; opposing words, phrases, views, characters, etc.
choice of words	the decision to use a particular word based on such aspects as style, register, connotation, etc.
euphemism ['juːfəmɪzəm]	using polite expressions for sth. unpleasant
exaggeration/hyperbole [haɪ'pɜːbəli]	making sth./sb. sound better, more exciting, dangerous, etc. than in reality
image	a word intended to appeal to the reader's imagination and to bring a new perception to an object (→ figurative language, e. g. metaphors, similes)
irony	saying the opposite of what you mean
(leit)motif	a theme, expression or object which recurs throughout a text and which refers to a certain person, situation or atmosphere
manner of speaking	a style that is typical of a particular person, e. g. politician or worker, etc.
metaphor ['metəfə(r)]	poetic comparison without using *like* or *as* (e. g. an ocean of love)
paradox	seeming impossible at first glance but recognized as true on second thought
parallelism	repeating similar or identical words/phrases in neighbouring lines/sentences/paragraphs
personification	presenting ideas/objects/animals as persons (e. g. a smiling moon)
pun	a play on words
reference	a connection to sth. else (→ allusion)
register/level of speech	the words, style and grammar used, e. g. formal/informal English, colloquialisms, slang, non-standard English, etc.; such aspects are typically adjusted according to the addressees
repetition	deliberately using a word/phrase more than once
rhetorical question	question to which the answer is obvious or to which no answer is possible/expected
simile ['sɪməli]	comparison using *like* or *as*

symbol	sth. concrete (object, character, event) standing for sth. abstract (cross – Christianity; horseshoe – luck)
syntax ['sɪntæks] – hypotactical structure – paratactical structure	arrangement of words in a phrase/sentence/text – rather complicated and long sentences, involving sub-clauses – a rather simple sentence structure, mostly consisting of main clauses, sometimes connected with the conjunctions *and, or*
tone	the manner or mood, e. g. macabre, optimistic, etc.

The media

agony aunt/uncle	a person who writes for a newspaper or magazine giving advice in reply to people's letters about their personal problems
feature story/human interest	a story or part of a story in a newspaper that people find interesting because it describes the feelings, experiences, etc. of the people involved
front page – cover story – special feature – leading article/editorial	the first page of a newspaper where the most important news is printed – the main story in a magazine that goes with the picture shown on the front cover – a special article or report on sb./sth. (*Sonderbeitrag*) – an important article in a newspaper that expresses the editor's opinion about a news item or a particular issue
headline	the title of a newspaper article printed in large letters, especially at the top of the front page
Internet – blog – chatroom – website – web forum	an international computer network connecting other networks and computers – a personal record that sb. puts on their website giving an account of their activities and their opinions, and discussing other sites on the Internet, events, etc. – a site on the Internet where people can communicate with each other in real time – a set of interconnected webpages, generally located on the same server, and prepared and maintained by a person, group or organization – a site on the Internet where people can exchange opinions and ideas on a particular issue
letter to the editor	a (mostly critical) letter written by the reader of a newspaper/magazine in response to an article or a story
masthead ['mɑːsthed]	– the name of the newspaper at the top of the front page – the part of a newspaper or a news website which gives details about the people who work on it or other information about it
television/radio – broadcasting company/ corporation – channel – programme – commercial (break) – documentary [ˌdɒkjuˈmentri] – factual report – feature film – live coverage – soap (opera)	– a company whose business is to make and transmit radio and TV programmes – a television station (*Programm*) – sth. that you watch on TV or listen to on the radio (*Sendung*) – an advertisement on the radio or on television – a film, radio or television programme giving facts about something – a report based on facts (*Tatsachenbericht*) – *Spielfilm* – sth. broadcast/sent while the event is actually happening, not pre-recorded (*Direktübertragung*) – a story about the life and problems of a group of fictional people that is broadcast every day or several times a week on TV or radio
the press – quality newspapers/ broadsheets – tabloids/popular newspapers – magazines/periodicals	– usually larger formats that have in-depth articles and present facts that are based on serious research – usually smaller formats that are more sensationalist – periodical publications financed by advertising; printed in colour on quality paper

Films/movies

documentary (film)	a film, television or radio programme that gives detailed factual information about a particular subject
docusoap	a supposedly unscripted television programme that shows what happens in the daily life of real people (= reality TV)
feature film	a full-length film that has a story, which is acted out by professional actors, and is usually shown in a cinema (*Spielfilm*)
screenplay/script – shooting script	the words that are written down for actors to say in a film, and the instructions that tell them what they should do – a script with additional information/details given by the director (e. g. drafts, technical details, arrows to indicate how to move the camera, etc.)
slug lines	numbered lines between the dialogue lines that indicate a change in location and time (e. g. INT, EXT); each slug line begins a new scene
storyboard	a graphic organizer that displays images in sequence (like a picture story) in order to help the film crew to know where the cameras are to be positioned or where/how a character has to stand/move, etc.

Vocabulary and Phrases for Text Analysis

When you are asked to analyse and interpret a text, you should express yourself precisely and appropriately. Therefore, it is important to use a specific terminology that employs **technical terms** (e. g. stylistic devices) and a variety of formulations that make your text more fluent and less repetitive.

The following words and phrases are related to the most relevant aspects.

introduction	the author
<ul><li>The text deals with/is about …</li><li>The theme of the text is …</li><li>The text is composed of/consists of …</li><li>Three/two … different parts can be distinguished …</li><li>The first part runs from line … to line …</li><li>At the beginning of the text, …</li><li>The author begins by saying …</li><li>At the end of the text,/Finally,/Lastly, …</li><li>The first part forms the introduction …</li><li>The main/central/principal idea is …</li><li>In the conclusion, the author states that …</li><li>In the final part, the author …</li></ul>	<ul><li>The author thinks/says/believes that …</li><li>According to the author, …/In his/her view …</li><li>The author illustrates his/her point of view with …</li><li>The author makes a comment on …</li><li>The author is convinced that …</li><li>The author's judgments are (un)realistic/not objective/ unfounded/well-founded …</li><li>The reader can sympathize with the author's view on …</li><li>The author expresses doubts/questions …</li><li>The author makes remarks on …</li><li>The intention/aim/objective of the author is …</li><li>The author portrays believable characters.</li><li>The author gives a detailed/vague description of …</li></ul>
the text/plot/story	**the characters**
<ul><li>The story is told from the perspective of …</li><li>The plot is set in …</li><li>The text is written in an ironic tone.</li><li>The text contains comical elements.</li><li>The setting of the action is unreal/imaginary.</li><li>The action becomes more/less intense …</li><li>The situation seems quite absurd…</li><li>Suspense is created because/by …</li><li>The ending of the story is believable …</li></ul>	<ul><li>The main/principal character in the story is …</li><li>The author characterizes him/her as …</li><li>He has many positive traits …</li><li>His behaviour is marked by …</li><li>Another essential quality is …</li><li>She shows her superiority by saying that …</li><li>He is characterized as …</li><li>The protagonist lacks …</li><li>As far as his outward appearance is concerned, …</li><li>She plays an important/a secondary role …</li></ul>
the structure	**the action**
<ul><li>The exposition gives information about …</li><li>The first scene introduces …</li><li>The starting point for the action is …</li><li>The conflict reaches its climax in …</li><li>The turning point is indicated by …</li><li>The crisis is in scene …</li><li>In the last scene, …</li><li>This play/story has a happy/tragic ending.</li></ul>	<ul><li>The action takes place in …</li><li>The action develops in … stages …</li><li>The action progresses fast …</li><li>The scene contains a flashback.</li><li>The action is interrupted by …</li><li>This is one of the central scenes …</li><li>The development of the action is slowed down by …</li></ul>

Note: Explanations of the respective technical terms can be found in the Literary Terms section, pp. 433 ff.

purpose (of texts)	vocabulary
• The author wants to arouse the reader's interest. • The text appeals to … • He/She tries to manipulate … • He/She wants the reader to become aware of … • The text addresses young/poor/… people … • It is the author's objective to create a feeling of … • The author attempts to influence the reader by … • The advert suggests to the reader that …	• The vocabulary contains many colloquial expressions/technical terms … • This word/term expresses fear … • This word has a negative meaning/negative associations … • This phrase suggests … • These phrases are examples of spoken language. • The choice of words gives the text its romantic/technical/… character. • These expressions are typical of …
criticizing the author	**further useful expressions**
• I (dis-)agree with the author on … • I do not understand why he/she … • I consider it to be wrong/difficult to … • This … cannot be taken seriously … • I would like to comment on … • It must be pointed out that … • This statement contradicts his/her view of … • There is a contradiction in … • It goes without saying that … • It is essential that … • This raises the question as to why he/she … • What really matters is … • This problem has nothing to do with … • This is of no importance/significance for … • As far as … is concerned, … • From this point of view, … • Generally speaking, … • As a matter of fact, … • In theory, …, but in reality, …	• To give an explanation for … • The author pretends to know … • The author describes the characteristics of … • The article is based on … • The author makes an allusion to … • This sentence reveals the true character of … • He/She appeals to emotions rather than … • He/She quotes some experts as an example of … • The article relates … to … • The text conveys the impression that … • The writer establishes a relationship between … • The author's theses are … • He supports his thesis with … • Her outlook on life is … • He/She takes a positive/negative view of … • The author generalizes about … • This is a great simplification of …

→ When you analyse or interpret a text, you should use **Standard English**.

→ You should generally use the **present tense** when you describe, explain or analyse specific aspects of the text.

→ Be careful not to imitate the tone or the language of the text – when you write about a text written in colloquial English, you should still use Standard English in order to appear **impersonal and objective**.

→ Try to **vary the beginnings of your sentences** by employing different connectives.

→ Even when you express your personal opinion about a text/the author, etc., your choice of words should be appropriate and respectful. It can be helpful *not* to begin sentences with "I …" or "I think …" but to **focus on the text, the author**, etc. (e. g. *The article gives the impression that …, The author seems to intend to …*). This appears much more impersonal and academic.

→ **Do not overdo it by being too formal** or stilted – your text should reflect your view and stance on the matter.

→ Be careful **not to use short forms** (e. g. don't, doesn't, there's, haven't, you're, etc.) in the tasks that are related to the **comprehension, analysis and comment/evaluation** of texts. They should only be used in creative writing tasks, e. g. in an informal conversation, diary entry, or interior monologue, when you are asked to express your thoughts in a rather informal way. However, when you write e. g. a letter to the editor, you should use formal English.

Note: Explanations of the respective technical terms can be found in the Literary Terms section, pp. 433 ff.

Focus on Language

Research

Before you start your research, you should check these aspects:

1. Read the assignment carefully – make sure that you understand what *exactly* your research task is.

2. Start a file in which you collect all your findings and research results.

3. Formulate research questions and aims.

4. Collect keywords and topics that can be used for your research.

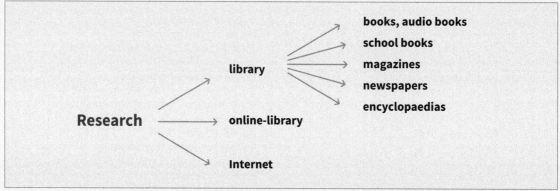

Indicators to check the quality/validity/reliability of the websites used

- The website has an author.
- The website has an impressum/copyright.
- The author is an expert in the respective subject matter/the author is recommended by other experts.
- The website is published by or related to a well-known organization, university, public institution, etc.
- The information provided on the website is relevant and up-to-date.
- The intention of the website is obvious; there is no hidden advertising or links to commercial websites (→ integrity, respectability).
- If there is any advertising, it is clearly distinguishable from the factual content of the website.
- The text is written in Standard English (few or no orthographic mistakes, colloquialisms, etc.).
- The author refers to his/her sources.
- There is more than *one* opinion.
- The views/opinions of others are respected.
- Statistical data and/or visuals are related to the text and are relevant (not just decorative elements).
- There are further links to other trustworthy websites/suggested reading.
- The website is designed appropriately for teenagers/children (in terms of contents, colours, graphics, animation etc.); it displays appropriate and functional pictures, videos, audio samples, etc.
- The website has a clear structure.
- The content of the website and the information given can be double-checked on other websites; there are references/links to other authors and/or other websites.
- The target group and the purpose of the website (e. g. commercial, educational, etc.) can be clearly identified.

Citing sources

In order to demonstrate the quality and credibility of your work, you need to name the sources that you have used. There are different citation styles. Here are some examples of how to cite different sources correctly:

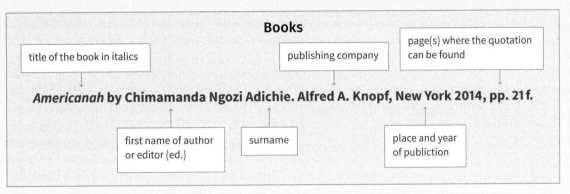

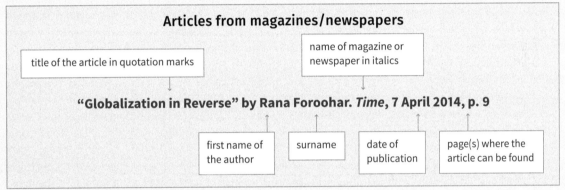

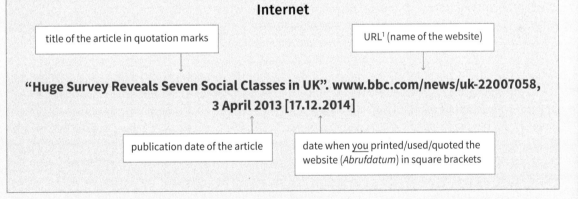

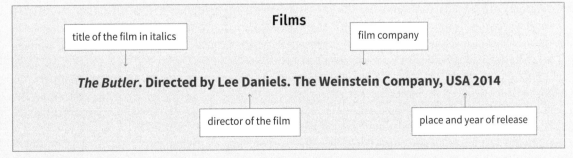

[1] **URL** (*abbr.*) uniform/universal resource locator (the address of a World Wide Web page)

Acknowledgements

Images

|action press, Hamburg: Collection Christophel (The Road, Regie John Hillcoat, Dimension Films/2929 Productions/Nick Wechsler Productions/Chockstone Pictures, USA 2009) 338; SOUTH WEST NEWS SERVICE LTD / Courtesy of Pest Control Office - Banksy 323. |akg-images GmbH, Berlin: 102, 337; Lessing, Erich 102. |alamy images, Abingdon/Oxfordshire: Alex, Aaron 185; Barritt, Peter 120; Boethling, Joerg 135; Dagnall, Ian 183; Granger Historical Picture Archive 176; Green, Leigh 223; grzegorz knec 241, 241, 268; Lebrecht Music and Arts Photo Library 103; Pearson, David 293; Pictorial Press Ltd 103; PRISMA ARCHIVO 182; Prisma by Dukas Presseagentur GmbH 102; Rosenstock, Stacy Walsh 39; Savage, Nick 55; Science History Images 103, 202; Stocktrek Images, Inc. 103, 182; White, Jonny 87, 87. |Andertoons, Schaumburg: Mark Anderson 25. |Art Explosion, Calabasas, CA: 131, 219, 293, 293, 293, 293, 380, 421, 421, 421; ./. 293, 293. |Barry, Boubacar, New York: boubah360 18. |beck*cartoons, Leipzig: 155. |Berghahn, Matthias, Bielefeld: 397, 431. |Bochner, Mel, New York: Silence! 2008 ink on paper 11 x 8,5 inches 286. |bpk-Bildagentur, Berlin: 27. |Bulls Pressedienst GmbH, Frankfurt am Main: © Mike Peters 373. |Cagle Cartoons, Santa Barbara, CA: 2011 Daryl Cagle, msnbc.com, and PoliticalCartoons.com 172; Copyright 2008 Jeff Parker - All Rights Reserved. 178; © 2010 Bob Englehart - All Rights Reserved 351; © 2014 Keith Knight 193; © John Cole 355; © Paresh Nath 91; © Randy Bish 327; © Rick McKee 355; © Steve Sack 217; © Tim Eagan 231. |Cartagena, Alejandro, Monterrey, Nuevo Leon: 221, 221. |Cartoon Movement, Amsterdam: © Miguel Villalba Sánchez (Elchicotriste) 75. |Cartoonist Group, Seattle: Ann Telnaes Editorial Cartoon used with the permission of Ann Telnaes and the Cartoonist Group. All rights reserved. 237; Clay Bennett Editorial Cartoon used with the permission of Clay Bennett, the Washington Post Writers Group and the Cartoonist Group. All rights reserved. 48. |CartoonStock.com, Bath: 36, 36, 404, 415, 419, 423. |Courtesy of Pest Control Office - Banksy, London: 170. |Danziger, Jeff, New York: 262. |ddp images GmbH, Hamburg: CAMERA PRESS/Norrington, Nigel 381; Capital Pictures (Viggo Mortensen und Kodi Smit-McPhee in: The Road, Regie John Hillcoat, Dimension Films/2929 Productions/Nick Wechsler Productions/Chockstone Pictures, USA 2010) 340; interTOPICS /Evening Standard 78; Senator Film (Viggo Mortensen und Kodi Smit-McPhee in: The Road, Regie John Hillcoat, Dimension Films/2929 Productions/Nick Wechsler Productions/Chockstone Pictures, USA 2010) 340. |Deutsches Museum, München: Archiv, BN38583 103. |DIE ZEIT, Hamburg: Aurel Märki: Grafik "Musik liegt in der Luft"; DIE ZEIT 44/2014 348, 348, 348, 348; Nora Coenenberg: Grafik "Eine gefährliche Welt" in: DIE ZEIT 29/2011 246. |Domke, Franz-Josef, Hannover: 24, 39, 46, 61, 61, 61, 68, 76, 86, 87, 119, 120, 128, 130, 132, 136, 149, 149, 150, 150, 157, 157, 163, 188, 195, 198, 240, 249, 258, 260, 260, 262, 264, 265, 273, 295, 295, 303, 307, 307, 307, 314, 324, 365, 408, 408, 408, 424; Foto: stock.adobe.com/artisticco 380. |Ebert, Nik, Mönchengladbach: 83, 90, 305. |Edelbrock, Iris, Viersen: 50, 50, 93, 176, 392. |Evans, Malcom, Auckland: 159. |ExxonMobil Central Europe Holding GmbH, Hannover: 280. |Faber & Faber Ltd, London: Front cover of 'The Children of Men' by P.D. James, published by Faber & Faber in 2006 (ISBN 9780571228522). Reproduced by permission of Faber & Faber Ltd. 333. |Fishman, Loren, Northfield: Humoresque Cartoons 31. |Focus Photo- u. Presseagentur GmbH, Hamburg: Magnum Photos/erwitt, elliott 213; MagnumPhotos/Bendiksen, Jonas 133, 134. |fotolia.com, New York: jpegwiz 418; kraska 417; niroworld 351; Pixel Embargo 429; ralko 321; sguk 218; wwwebmeister 218. |Froment, Aurélien: 52. |Gentleman, David, London: John Russell Brown: Shakespeare and his theatre. London: Penguin, p. 36, Illustrations copyright: © David Gentleman, 1982 378. |Getty Images, München: AFP/MacDougall, John 330; Bettmann/CORBIS 205, 206, 214; DIBYANGSHU SARKAR/AFP 108; INDRANIL MUKHERJEE/AFP 143; Museum of the City of New York/Phillips, Burt G. 215; VINCENZO PINTO/AFP 160; WireImage/MacMedan, Dan 41; WireImage/Mazur, Kevin 208. |Granlund, Dave, Waconia MN: www.davegranlund.com 197, 327. |Guardian News & Media Limited, London: Paul Scruton/The Guardian, Copyright Guardian News & Media Ltd 2018 34. |HEART AGENCY, London: © Tom Gauld 420. |Imago, Berlin: Xinhua 293. |iStockphoto.com, Calgary: Marongiu, Eugenio 20. |Jennings, Ben, Berkhamsted: 101. |KAL/Kevin Kallaugher, Glyndon, MD: 216; The Economist, Kaltoons.com. 296. |Kassing, Reinhild, Kassel: 26, 26, 400, 400, 400, 400, 400, 400, 400, 400, 400, 401, 401, 401, 401, 401, 401, 401, 401, 401, 407, 422, 442. |Laux, Hans-Dieter, Bonn / Thieme, Günter, Köln: Die USA auf dem Weg in eine multiethnische Gesellschaft: Ergebnisse des Zensus 2010. In: Geographische Rundschau 63 (2), 2011, S. 64 219. |Lemay, Yannick, Quebec: 227. |Lörscher, Sebastian, Berlin: aus: Making Friends in Bangalore. Mit dem Skizzenbuch durch Indien (S. 70) Copyright © 2014 Büchergilde Gutenberg 124. |Marshall, Helen, London: TopFoto.co.uk / Mike O'Keefe Custodian of the Official Royal Image Library of HM The Queen and HRH The Duke of Edinburgh www.royalimages.co.uk 97. |Mester, Gerhard, Wiesbaden: 71, 226. |Metro-Goldwyn-Mayer Studios Inc., Beverly Hills, CA: Cannery Row, Regie David S. Ward, Metro-Goldwyn-Mayer/Chai Productions, USA 1982 189. |Mette, Til, Hamburg: 320. |National Theatre, London: 2013

Texts

Group Limited 2011/2018. **pp. 88 f.:** © 2017 Time Inc. All rights reserved. Excerpted from TIME and published with permission of Time Inc. Reproduction in any manner in any language in whole or in part without written permission is prohibited. **pp. 126 ff.:** Republished with permission of The Economist, from www.economist.com/node/21560263, 11 August 2012; permission conveyed through Copyright Clearance Center, Inc. **p. 130:** © 2012 Time Inc. All rights reserved. Excerpted from TIME and published with permission of Time Inc. Reproduction in any manner in any language in whole or in part without written permission is prohibited. **pp. 141 f.:** © 2013 Time Inc. All rights reserved. Excerpted from TIME and published with permission of Time Inc. Reproduction in any manner in any language in whole or in part without written permission is prohibited. **pp. 145 ff.:** Republished with permission of The Economist, from www.economist.com/news/britain/21595908-rapid-rise-mixed-race-britain-changing-neighbourhoodsand-perplexing, 8 February 2014; permission conveyed through Copyright Clearance Center, Inc. **pp. 160 f.:** Republished with permission of The Economist, from www.economist.com/news/leaders/21589887-unreformed-commonwealth-deserves-die-improved-it-could-be-rather-useful-what-it, 16 November 2013; permission conveyed through Copyright Clearance Center, Inc. **pp. 172 ff.:** Excerpt(s) from AMERICA AND AMERICANS by John Steinbeck, copyright © 1966 by John Steinbeck, renewed © 1984 by Elaine Steinbeck and Thom Steinbeck. Used by permission of Viking Books, an imprint of Penguin Publishing Group, a division of Penguin Random House LLC. All rights reserved. Any third party use of this material, outside of this publication, is prohibited. Interested parties must apply directly to Penguin Random House LLC for permission. **pp. 189 f.:** Excerpt(s) from CANNERY ROW by John Steinbeck, copyright © 1945 by John Steinbeck; copyright renewed © 1973 by Elaine Steinbeck, Thom Steinbeck, and John Steinbeck IV. Used by permission of Viking Books, an imprint of Penguin Publishing Group, a division of Penguin Random House LLC. All rights reserved. **p. 194:** Republished with permission of The Economist, from The Economist, 21 September 2013, p. 41; permission conveyed through Copyright Clearance Center, Inc. **pp. 195 f.:** Republished with permission of The Economist, from The Economist, 1 February 2014, p. 35; permission conveyed through Copyright Clearance Center, Inc. **pp. 198 f.:** Republished with permission of The Economist, from www.economist.com/news/united-states/21582019-poverty-has-moved-suburbs-broke-burbs, 20 July 2013; permission conveyed through Copyright Clearance Center, Inc. **p. 205:** The Heirs to the Estate of Martin Luther King Jr., New York. **pp. 207 ff.:** 4th Estate UK. **p. 220:** By Jimmy Santiago Baca, from IMMIGRANTS IN OUR OWN LAND, copyright © 1979 by Jimmy Santiago Baca. Reprinted by permission of New Directions Publishing Corp. **pp. 228 f.:** © 2016 Time Inc. All rights reserved. Excerpted from TIME and published with permission of Time Inc. Reproduction in any manner in any language in whole or in part without written permission is prohibited. **pp. 231 ff.:** Republished with permission of The Economist, from The Economist, 1 July 2017, p. 9; permission conveyed through Copyright Clearance Center, Inc. **p. 247:** © 2014 Time Inc. All rights reserved. Excerpted from TIME and published with permission of Time Inc. Reproduction in any manner in any language in whole or in part without written permission is prohibited. **pp. 248 ff.:** Republished with permission of The Economist, The Economist, 19 April 2014, p. 52; permission conveyed through Copyright Clearance Center, Inc. **pp. 256 ff.:** Republished with permission of The Economist, from The Economist, 28 May – 3 June 2016, pp. 4 ff.; permission conveyed through Copyright Clearance Center, Inc. **pp. 263 ff.:** Republished with permission of The Economist, from The Economist, 13 July 2013, pp. 20 ff.; permission conveyed through Copyright Clearance Center, Inc. **pp. 296 ff.:** Republished with permission of The Economist, from www.economist.com/news/essays/21596796-democracy-was-most-successful-political-idea-20th-century-why-has-it-run-trouble-and-what-can-be-do, 1 March 2014; permission conveyed through Copyright Clearance Center, Inc. **pp. 314 ff.:** Republished with permission of The Economist, from www.economist.com/news/international/21607881-vitro-fertilisation-once-seen-miraculous-now-mainstream-rich-countries-soon, 19 July 2014; permission conveyed through Copyright Clearance Center, Inc. **pp. 321 f.:** © Telegraph Media Group Limited 2011/2018. **p. 345:** © 2014 Time Inc. All rights reserved. Excerpted from TIME and published with permission of Time Inc. Reproduction in any manner in any language in whole or in part without written permission is prohibited. **pp. 356 ff.:** © 2014 Time Inc. All rights reserved. Excerpted from TIME and published with permission of Time Inc. Reproduction in any manner in any language in whole or in part without written permission is prohibited. **pp. 359 f.:** Excerpt(s) from THE CIRCLE by Dave Eggers, copyright © 2013 by Dave Eggers. Used by permission of Alfred A. Knopf, an imprint of the Knopf Doubleday Publishing Group, a division of Penguin Random House LLC. All rights reserved. **pp. 365 f.:** Republished with permission of The Economist, from The Economist, 13 September 2014, Special report Advertising and technology, pp. 3 f.; permission conveyed through Copyright Clearance Center, Inc. **pp. 366 f.:** Republished with permission of The Economist, from The Economist, 13 September 2014, Special report Advertising and technology, p. 16; permission conveyed through Copyright Clearance Center, Inc.

All other sources can be found below the texts.

Index